Chanter m'estuet

CHANTER M'ESTUET

Songs of the Trouvères

Edited by
Samuel N. Rosenberg
Music edited by
Hans Tischler

INDIANA UNIVERSITY PRESS

Bloomington

This book was brought to publication with the assistance of a grant from the Andrew W. Mellon Foundation.

Manufactured in the United States of America

Library of Congress Cataloging in Publication Data
Main entry under title:

Chanter m'estuet.

    "Includes music with all texts for which music has been preserved."
    Bibliography: p.
    Includes index.
    1. Songs, French. I. Rosenberg, Samuel N., 1936-
II. Tischler, Hans, 1915-
M2.C44   784.3'06   80-8383
ISBN 0-253-14942-8   1 2 3 4 5   85 84 83 82 81

Contents

Chansons de croisade

Sottes chansons

Chansons satiriques

Chansons pieuses

Rondeaux

Varia

ASCRIBED SONGS

Chrétien de Troyes

Blondel de Nesle

Conon de Béthune

Richard Coeur de Lion

Châtelain de Couci

Chanson de croisade

Gace Brulé

Chansons

Jehan Bodel

Pastourelle

Audefroi le Bâtard

Chanson de toile

Richart de Semilli

Pastourelles

Gautier de Dargies

Descort

Thibaut de Blaison

Gontier de Soignies

Guiot de Dijon

Moniot d'Arras

Andrieu Contredit d'Arras

Richart de Fournival

Raoul de Soissons

Etienne de Meaux

Jacques d'Autun

Jacques de Dosti

Mahieu le Juif

Henri III, duc de Brabant

Perrin d'Angicourt

Raoul de Beauvais

Jehan Erart

Gillebert de Berneville

Colin Muset

Jehan Bretel

Adam de la Halle

Thibaut II, comte de Bar

Duchesse de Lorraine

Gamart de Vilers and Jehan Cuvelier

Sainte des Prés and Dame de la Chaussée

Jacques de Cysoing

Guillaume de Béthune

Rutebeuf

Introduction

I. GENERAL. Well over two thousand lyrics for single voice
have survived from the rich production of the twelfth- and
thirteenth-century trouvères of Northern France, preserved
in more than thirty chansonniers and a variety of other manuscripts. Almost half of the texts are unique, while the
rest occur in as many as a dozen or more redactions; although all these poems were meant to be sung, music survives
for only about half of them.

The great majority have been edited at least once since
the eighteenth century, some quite often. Editions have
been prepared according to varying criteria, however, and
for different purposes; the editions take variant manuscript
readings into account to differing extents and satisfy modern critical norms with different degrees of success; musical transcriptions are most often not included, although
most editors have always agreed in principle that music is
an integral part of these medieval lyrics. Edited texts,
moreover, are widely scattered and frequently inaccessible.

Most editions are narrow in scope, limited to one poet,
one lyric genre, one manuscript source, or the like. Even
the classic collections of Karl Bartsch (1870)[1] and Hans
Spanke (1925), substantial as they are, are restricted, in
the first case, to a few compositional and thematic types
and, in the second, to the anonymous works contained in a
small group of related codices; melodies are absent from
Bartsch and only minimally present in Spanke. More recently, several rather broadly ranging anthologies have ap-
peared, notably those of Cremonesi (1955), Toja (1966), and
Bec (1978). As compilations of earlier scholars' critical
texts, however, they reveal on a reduced scale all the editorial disparateness that characterizes the published trouvère corpus as a whole; more crucially, they offer no music,
which distorts the nature of the songs and the intellectual
and esthetic experience of them.

The present volume has a broad scope and addresses itself to a wide public of both specialists and non-special-
ists. It has three principal features. The collection
attempts to be representative of almost all types of Old
French monophonic song from its beginning around 1150 to the
end of the thirteenth century. It offers texts newly edited
from the surviving manuscripts, established according to a
consistent critical practice. And it includes music with
all texts for which music has been preserved.

To achieve representativeness, we selected poems mainly according to the criteria of formal type, subject or

theme, authorship, and chronology, as well as artistic interest. There is thus a wide spectrum of lyric genres,
ranging from those defined chiefly by form--e.g., the *ballette*, *rondeau*, *estampie*, *jeu-parti*--through those defined
as much by content--e.g., the *chansons de toile*, the *pastourelle*, and above all the courtly *chanson* derived from the
Provençal *canso*--to those identified essentially by content
alone--e.g., the *aube* and *reverdie*. The genres belonging to
this third class are the most numerous, comprising such
works as crusade songs, political and historical songs, devotional songs, laments of unhappy wives and other women's
songs, scenes of amorous encounter, debates about love,
celebrations of rustic life, songs of invective, and jongleur songs. The selection includes songs with fixed refrains (*chansons à refrain*) and songs with variable refrains
(*chansons avec des refrains*) as well as refrainless compositions, works of popular inspiration and works of courtly
origin. Lines of demarcation are frequently blurred, and
our identifying labels will reflect that fact.[2]

Many of the Old French songs are anonymous and destined
to remain so; for the others, authorship is a matter of
somewhat variable certainty. To the extent that auctorial
representativeness can be achieved--and that extent is,
after all, not negligible--we considered it a significant
desideratum. Above all, it offers the best assurance of
chronological representativeness within our period of some
one hundred fifty years and so ensures in the present collection fair evidence of evolution within the lyric genre.
Then, despite the frequently discussed formalism and imper-
sonality of Old French lyric poetry, it remains true that
there is very often a clearly individual imprint upon the
work of a given poet; and the nature and measure of that
originality merit no little attention, particularly in the
case of trouvères who, to judge by the prominence of their
compositions in the chansonniers or by historical references, were held in high esteem by their contemporaries.
Finally, some writers of songs are well known in other con-
texts; that separate fame, whether stemming from other literary pursuits or from involvement in public affairs, occa-
sionally guided our choice no less than the inherent interest of their poems. The presentation of ascribed works,
insofar as the periods of artistic activity of the various
trouvères may be identified, will follow a chronological
pattern.

II. THE TEXTS. In editing the texts, we were guided chiefly
by the principle of minimal intervention. This means

especially that, for songs with more than one source, we did
not prepare a composite text but opted instead to present a
single extant version chosen for its overall superiority and
emended only where fairly clear scribal defectiveness or
compositional incoherence made correction necessary.   In
view of what is known or believed to be known about the circumstances of lyric creation and diffusion in the Middle
Ages, about textual instability and the imponderables of
oral and manuscript transmission, it would be vain to attempt, through a combinatory method, to reproduce a song in
its original state.[3] There are, even so, some instances
where manuscript corruption is such, or where deviation from
what must have been the poetic intention is so manifest,
that a kind of composite text, or at least one emended more
than minimally, becomes preferable, emerging as a perhaps
significantly more accurate reflection of trouvère art than
any single surviving version of the poem in question. We
permitted ourselves such editing when we found it urged by
special conditions--sometimes by melodic considerations--and
acceptable to a pragmatic mind. In any case, the critical
apparatus will both make our procedure clear and allow read-
ers to imagine other solutions.

The selection of versions to be presented was determined principally by relative textual integrity, both literary and linguistic. On occasion, we were influenced by
musical facts, though never to the point of rejecting a
clearly superior text; in the few instances of considerable
disparity between quality of text and quality of accompany-
ing melody, we judged it best to pair different manuscripts.
Such couplings will be explicitly marked in the presentation
of the songs. There are two rather common criteria for
selection which we chose not to heed: sameness of manuscript
source for all the works of a given trouvère and concordance
of the scripta of a given text with what may be reasonably
considered to have been the poet's own dialect or, failing
this, with a conventional Central French. In the first instance, the fact is that the stemmatic history of each song
tends more toward uniqueness than toward conformity with the
others, and the superiority of one text in a particular codex is not necessarily matched by that of another in the
same source. In the second instance, it often happens that
the precise dialect of composition does not admit of ready
identification; and it is rather anachronistic and distor-
tive of medieval linguistic realities to prefer one version
of a song to another because it is dialectally less eccen-
tric. Underlying the rejection of both criteria were our
acceptance of the freedom, or unfixedness, of the medieval

song once it had left its author's hands and our belief that
each work has its own history.

III. THE MUSIC. The debate about editing the melodies of
medieval monophonic songs has gone on ever since the beginning of this century. Similarly, when one listens to recit-
als or recordings of such songs, he will discover the most
diverse interpretations, ranging from a completely free
rhythm to rigidly pursued patterns of the so-called rhythmic
modes; the use of instruments differs greatly, both in number and kind of instruments playing and in what they play;
so do tempo, dynamics, and vocal rendition.

The chansonniers that preserve the trouvère repertory,
like all other manuscripts of medieval songs, offer only the
pitches of the melodies, the texts, and in some instances
the rhythm. There are no indications of what instruments
were involved or what they played; no indications of expression, such as tempo, dynamics, or tone production; no hint
at improvisational input; no guide to the poet's approach to
meter. Whereas performers have to wrestle with all these
problems, the music editor has three primary tasks: to establish a good reading of the melodic line; solve the problem of rhythm in a satisfactory way where the manuscripts do
not indicate it; and coordinate the poetic text, established
in collaboration with a philologist, with the tune. He may
or more usually, as in this volume, may not deal with the
other aspects of performance.

Just as the text problem has been often dealt with by
philologists without the aid of musical advice, the editors
of melodies have usually lacked philological aid. Such
onesidedness has been overcome in this volume by a close
cooperation between both disciplines. Thus, indications in
the manuscripts' musical scores, such as bars which indicate
ends of lines or rests, melodic repetitions, and the number
of notes, at times clarify the elision or non-elision of
syllables, elsewhere the number of syllables in a word, the
end of a line, or the omission or erroneous insertion of a
word. Conversely, the poetic text at times proves that a
note is missing or redundant, where a phrase ends or a refrain begins; most importantly, the scansion of the text,
the anacrustic beginnings of lines, masculine and feminine
endings, and rhymes are among the prime determinants of
musical rhythm and phrasing.

Sometimes several poems employ the same melody; elsewhere a single lyric is set to several melodies. Only in a
few such instances will in this volume two tunes be offered
in connection with one poem, chiefly to show how different

such settings may be. Elsewhere the melody presented is
always from the same manuscript as the text unless otherwise
noted. To establish a good reading of a melody it is above
all necessary to consider all of its extant versions.
Scribes' errors, omissions, or more or less extensive variants can then be detected and the preferable version discovered. It seems clear that the several versions of a song
often reflect the influence of improvisation, particularly
with regard to ornamentation.[4] The manuscripts show that
improvised ornaments were rather simple and rarely lengthy,
indicating a generally rather fresh tempo.

Some accidentals are given in the manuscripts, but
others may have to be added. This usually depends on the
tonality, that is, the Church mode that characterizes the
particular tune. Among these modes some are akin to the
modern major, others to the minor; and, interestingly, the
former are about twice as frequent in these songs as the
latter. Many editions have conveyed wrong impressions by
ignoring these indications for accidentals familiar to the
medieval musician and by not providing the accidentals which
the contemporary performer had learned to supply "for beauty's sake" through improvisation, as *musica ficta*, and which
may appear in parallel versions.

The range of all the songs stays within that of the
late medieval gamut established by Guido of Arezzo about
1025/30, namely, one covering G to e^2. In fact, the extreme
pitches, G, d^2, e^2 never occur at all, and even the next few
notes on either end of this range are rarely found. Sixty
percent of the songs have individual ranges of an octave or
a ninth, the upper and lower limits being the twelfth and
the fifth.

The thorniest and most controversial problem in this
repertory is that of rhythm. As has been mentioned, some
manuscripts employ a notation that clearly indicates the
rhythm, a so-called mensural notation. Where the rhythm is
given, it proves to be flexible, its two most important
determinants being the scansion of the poetry and the distribution of ornaments. It may change from one rhythmic
pattern to another when the poetry or tune demands it, sometimes within a single line; but often it follows one of the
basic patterns of contemporary polyphony throughout or
through complete phrases or sections, these patterns being
the six rhythmic modes taught by the theorists of the mid-
thirteenth century. This approach should be expected, since
trouvères such as Adam de la Halle also were active com-
posers of polyphonic music. Indeed, a number of chansonniers also include collections of motets side by side with

trouvère songs. In fact, an important clue to the metric
character of trouvère songs comes from the hundreds of passages from such songs, textual, musical, or both, that are
included in thirteenth-century motets, where their metric-
rhythmic character is certain; and the text scansion of such
passages fits naturally into their musical rhythm. In fact,
a number of complete trouvère songs are incorporated in motets and some even set to new Latin texts in conductus,[5] and
all of them are treated in strict meter. Finally, there are
many dance and dance-related songs, rondeaux and virelais,
in the repertory, which are clearly metric.

    Thus, the musical clues all favor a metric-rhythmic
interpretation of trouvère songs in general, even where the
notation does not indicate relative note values. In itself
this premensural notation cannot be taken as contradicting
the foregoing analysis, since it is the same notation that
was used for the strictly metric motets and conductus of the
period. The fact is that in the late twelfth and early
thirteenth centuries this notation derived from the very
first one to indicate rhythm, one invented by Leonin (active
ca. 1165-85) and perfected by his successor, Perotin (active
ca. 1185-1205), at Notre Dame de Paris--a notation in which
strictly metric rhythm was implied by specified sequences of
ligatures, groups of two, three, or more notes. When the
note groups of this "modal," that is, patterned notation,
which could be used only for melismatic melodies, had to be
broken up to coordinate the single notes with the successive
syllables of conductus or motets, the rhythmic implications
remained, but the notes were not differentiated in shape to
symbolize their relative lengths, until in the middle of the
thirteenth century mensural notation, which employed different note shapes for the various note values, was invented to
deal with this problem.

    Scholars of Old French have held that the versification
of trouvère poetry is based on counting syllables rather
than on stress patterns. This idea is, however, contra-
dicted by the feminine verse endings, which are not counted
by these scholars. If it were a matter of mere counting,
such endings would be unthinkable, for they depend on
stress. If lines of seven syllables and those of seven syllables plus an eighth weak one can correspond to each other,
for example, this can be explained only by assuming stress
is involved; and stress implies meter. Below there will be
also occasion to refer to anacruses. To be sure, the ubiq-
uitous iambs, trochees, and dactyls present in this poetry
cannot even be conceived without agogic, dynamic, or pitch
stresses or combinations of two or all three of these in

languages such as French and English that do not recognize
long and short syllables.[6]

Roger Dragonetti's fundamental work[7] has become a
standard reference with regard to the structure of trouvère
lyrics. This is what he contributes to the present problem
in the key passage in which he analyzes the rhythm and meter
of their poetic texts:

> Dans un vers régulier, le rythme (un des aspects
> formels de sa structure) s'organise suivant un *temps
> rationnel*....
>
> Tout rythme, en effet, dégage une mesure, laquelle
> n'est pas un simple artifice qui lui est surajouté,
> mais coexiste avec lui parce qu'elle est une condition
> essentielle de sa perception ...
>
> ... toute structure rythmique introduit un conflit
> ou une entente entre deux ordres temporels: c'est-à-
> dire entre le temps homogène, tout fait, par conséquent
> prévisible de la mesure, et le rythme, qui est irrédu-
> cible à la divisibilité du temps rationnel, parce que
> c'est une genèse sans précédents.
>
> La structure rythmique d'un vers régulier résulte de
> la rencontre de ces deux ordres, mais le style en dif-
> fère suivant que la carrure métrique renforce ou
> contredit le rythme.
>
> La mesure y assume, par conséquent, une fonction
> constructive, et c'est ce qui ressort très nettement de
> l'analyse des vers courtois où l'action régulatrice des
> schèmes métriques y joue un rôle particulièrement im-
> portant ... (p. 501f.)

An interesting argument, illustrated by a dozen examples, is the transcription by two scholars[8] of the same
songs in different modal versions. A dual possibility of
interpretation hardly invalidates the application of the
rhythmic modes to trouvère songs, of course; indeed, it
nicely illustrates a point worth remembering, namely, that
the medieval musician might easily perform a piece differently at various times, as is borne out repeatedly by the
manuscripts--different in rhythm, in accidentals, in ornamentation, played on an instrument or sung or both, with a
different melody to the same text or with a different text
to the same melody. This point is most clearly documented
by another song cited by Dragonetti, p. 526, which is actually notated by the medieval scribes of two different
manuscripts in two different modes, namely the dactylic
third mode in the *Chansonnier Cangé* (ms. O) and in the up-
beat first mode, iambically, in the *Chansonnier du Roi* (ms
M).[9] And this is a song by Robert de Castel d'Arras who,

according to Dragonetti, was active during the third quarter
of the thirteenth century, that is, during the very time
when the two manuscripts were copied.

Incidentally, this twofold rhythmic interpretation re-
sults in several metric stresses falling on normally unac-
cented syllables, a thing that Dragonetti elsewhere calls
"massacring the verse." Apparently, however, the medieval
poets felt no compunction about giving some naturally weak
syllables metric stress and leaving some normally strong
ones unstressed; indeed, verse and prose scanning do not
necessarily always coincide in any language, whether French,
English, or German, not to speak of Latin from which the
ambivalence of stress derives. This ambivalence stands out
clearly in thirteenth-century motets, all definitely sung in
measured rhythm, needed to coordinate its several voice
parts, and with a strong metric pulse.

In general, considering the possibilities of different
interpretation and of ambivalent stress or floating accent,
it is often difficult to decide which meter was intended.
Even the medieval performer had such difficulties, as has
just been shown. The problem becomes compounded when the
various stanzas of a poem do not exhibit the same stress
pattern. In such instances two approaches are helpful for
finding the best solution: (1) scanning all stanzas and
determining the meter in which the fewest "wrong" stresses
occur; (2) giving primary evidentiary weight to the first
stanza as the one probably most carefully considered, from
which the other stanzas may well deviate here and there.

Once the meter, that is, musically, the barring, has
been established, the rhythm is the next problem. It is a
complex one and must be solved individually for each poem.
A trochee, for example, can be equally well represented by
various rhythms within the three-subbeat units universally
employed at the time, namely │♩.♩.│ , ♪ ♪ , or ♪♪ , and each
of these rhythms may be varied by using several shorter
notes for either of the two note values to ornament them,
for example│♫♫♩♪│, ♫♪ , or ♪♫. Which of these rhythms
may be best applied is a musical question, and it may well
be surmised that medieval performers might apply different
rhythms to a poem at various renderings. Whereas barring,
that is, a basic regularity of stressed and unstressed syllables, seems absolutely necessary for the performance of
metric poetry, the choice of rhythm is secondary. It will
largely depend on the distribution of ornaments in the melody. Here the contemporary motet once more furnishes evidence. Indeed, many ornaments were sung on short, unstressed syllables; and in the multiple versions of many

motets the ornaments freely migrate among strong and weak
beats. Yet with the clue to their rhythm furnished in many
instances by the patterned tenor (*cantus firmus*), the over-
whelming evidence points to the longer note values of the
modal patterns as the carriers of the majority of ornaments.
Since this evidence involves many quotations from trouvère
songs, its application to the contemporary monophonic repertory in general can be readily accepted.

Hitherto, it has been held that the rhythmic interpretation of trouvère songs admits of only two alternatives:
either modal rhythm or free declamation. But a third possibility exists. A quarter of a century ago Heinrich Husmann
demonstrated that at least four trouvère chansons share
their music with polyphonic conductus.[10] These chansons
must therefore be presumed to have been amenable to the same
rhythm as the related conductus, and Husmann showed that in
both some hexasyllabic lines follow the modified modal
rhythm ♩.♪|♪♩♩.| .[11] One of the four songs is by the late
twelfth-century trouvère Blondel de Nesle, and all four seem
to have antedated the related conductus, as their typical
structures are highly unusual for conductus. This observation pushes metric interpretation of trouvère songs back
into the last decades of the twelfth century. There seems
to be evidence, moreover, that polyphonic music of the early
twelfth century, the so-called St. Martial or Aquitanian
repertory, was also sung in measured rhythm.[12] This may
have been a rhythm akin to modal rhythm or perhaps one frequently found in early conductus, namely, one in which all
or most syllables have an equal duration, an approach which
proves applicable to many trouvère songs as well as minne-
lieder. Latest research would extend rhythmic interpretation even further back. In a recent paper it was shown that
a trope of the mid-eleventh century, which thus antedates
William of Aquitaine's earliest songs, is notated and was
sung in what appears to be a 6/8 meter similar to the first
rhythmic mode, expressing the rhythm of an *a–b, a–b, a–b, a*
stanza as follows: *a*♩.♩♪♩.♩♪|, *b*♪♩♪♩♪♩.♩♪|.[13] In the
light of what has been known about Spanish-Moorish poetry of
the tenth to eleventh centuries this is, indeed, quite possible.

To sum up: The basic fact is that courtly poetry does
possess metric structure, and metric structure can be re-
flected in modern notation only by means of bar lines and an
intelligible note-value system. Otherwise the meter, which,
as Dragonetti firmly states, is an essential structural element of this poetry, is lost in a modern edition. The free
rhythm proposed by many scholars in fact mistakes poetry for

prose. With some flexibility and some musical sensitivity, metric-rhythmic transcriptions that parallel and support the meter and versification of the medieval singer-poets can and must be produced, if their songs are to be brought back to life. A single, pervasive modal approach has to be rejected in favor of at least two possible approaches, namely, either modal solutions with frequent so-called "irregularities" and modal mixtures, such as were taught by Franco of Cologne in the mid-thirteenth century, or transcriptions in which all syllables receive equal length except where lengthy melis-mata occur or at verse endings; both types must be barred. The initial meter signature, however, may well change in the course of a song, a procedure often necessary also in mo-tets.

It should be added that the motets of the last decades of the century prove that meter and metric stress then de-clined in poetry, together with regular line length, as an organizing factor. The poetry of these later motets pro-ceeds in free verse, in lines of greatly differing lengths, held together by rhymes only, but rhymes without pattern. Considerations of stress, let alone regular stress, are com-pletely absent from that poetry which, significantly, is contemporary with the demise of both troubadour and trouvère poetry. At this point syllable count seems to have become the paramount structural consideration in poems with regular verse schemes.

It is impossible to justify the rendition of each of the many transcriptions of songs that follow. The discus-sion of each piece would on the average take a page or more. It must be kept in mind that most transcriptions present only one of several possible solutions, but hopefully a vi-able one. In a few instances two versions of a melody or two melodies are given for a poem to show the types of pos-sible variety. The choice between modes 3 (♩. ♫ ♩) and 6 (♪ ♪ ♪) is often particularly difficult to make. As an example of both possibilities two melodies are presented for RS 1574. Most of the songs here rendered in the third mode may be equally well sung in the sixth, though, to be sure, the eighth-note would then be considerably longer than in the third mode.

The melodic forms of the songs are greatly varied. Many exhibit different repetitive forms, others are through-composed; but any section of a tune, whether it is repeti-tively formulated or through-composed, may include partial repetitions of all kinds. Where several melodies accompany a poem, their forms may differ; one, for example, may have an A-A-B structure, while the other is through-composed.

Indeed, the musical forms do not necessarily reflect those of the respective poems.

IV. PRESENTATION OF THE SONGS. The songs are presented in two groups: anonymous compositions, organized by genre, and ascribed compositions, organized by authorship. The trouvères are in an approximate chronological order. *Jeux-partis*, composed by two poets, are arranged according to the writer of the first stanza.

Each song is presented according to the following scheme:

1. Trouvère, if known.
2. Type(s) of poem. For the sake of tradition and universal ease of recognition, the names of the common genres are given in French.
3. Identifying numbers in standard bibliographies, as applicable: Spanke, *G. Raynauds Bibliographie* . . ., abbreviated as RS; Mölk-Wolfzettel, *Répertoire* . . ., abbreviated as MW; and Van den Boogaard, *Rondeaux* . . ., abbreviated as B. (See Works Cited for bibliographical details.) There are as many B numbers as there are refrains in the song. If B lists another song or other songs in which a particular refrain occurs, this is noted in parentheses.
4. Manuscript sources. Manuscripts are identified by their conventional sigla in all cases where these exist. (See Manuscripts Cited for complete data.) The first one cited is the base for the edited text; the others follow in alphabetical order, all upper-case sigla preceding lower-case sigla. With few exceptions, numbers designate folios, and both recto and verso are marked. The notable exceptions are: I, which is followed by section number and number of poem within the section, and K, followed by page numbers.
5. Music. Presence or absence of music in the various manuscripts is indicated here; all other notes on music are provided below.
6. Authorship. The word "attribution" refers specifically to the trouvère identification provided above, which proceeds from a rubric or an index in the manuscript(s). Occasional other indications are self-explanatory.
7. MELODY, if preserved, together with the first stanza of the text. In this edition it was not possible to show all variant readings; therefore, a good version was selected in each instance, and, wherever necessary, emendations from other manuscripts were incorporated, always marked: Square brackets enclose any editorial additions where notes or rests seem to be missing, and parentheses

indicate additions from other versions; elsewhere footnotes
clarify emendations or variant readings. Unless otherwise
noted, the melody presented is from the same manuscript as
the text.

Any accidental that appears in the source on which the
transcription is based is shown in the usual manner, directly before the note it affects (rather than where it may be
actually placed in the manuscript, often several notes
earlier). If such an accidental seems to retain its power
for a subsequent note of the same pitch in the same staff,
the accidental appears in parentheses. If the accidental is
given only in a parallel version, it is placed above the
respective note. And if it is a purely editorial addition,
it appears above the note and in parentheses. Editorial
accidentals try to respond to the tonality (Church-modality)
of the particular phrase or section, which, rather than always the entire song, seem to be the significant tonal units
in these songs. In some songs a *B-flat* appears so consist-
ently in the source that it is here shown as a key signature.

The structure of each tune is clarified by its section-
al arrangement on the page and by letters. Any phrase
covering one text line will be labeled by a lower-case letter, and any segment or section serving two or more lines,
by a capital letter. A low index number after a letter indicates a melodically different phrase of the section sym-
bolized by that letter; an upper index number points to a
variant of the phrase labeled by the letter or letter plus
low index number.

8. TEXT, including the first stanza even when it
has been underlaid to the melody. Square brackets are used
for unrecorded repetitions of refrain material and for editorial conjectures of entire words; they are not used when a
lacuna in the base manuscript has been filled with a reading
taken from another source; such editorial intervention will
be marked explicitly in the Rejected Readings and implicitly
in the Variants. Just as *i*, *j*, *u*, and *v* are corrected as
necessary--and without comment--to conform to modern practice, final *x* is replaced when appropriate by *us*, as in the
substitution of *Deus* for *Dex*. Roman numerals are spelled
out. Instances of enclisis are made clear by the use of an
internal period, as in *je.1*, rather than *jel*, for the contraction of *je le*. In certain texts of Eastern provenance,
where the occurrence of *c* for *s* or *s* for *c* might prove dis-
concerting, spelling is modified in accordance with Central
norms in the case of such words as demonstrative and possessive adjectives and pronouns; such changes are noted in the

Rejected Readings. Refrains are distinguished from stanzas
not only by type-face but usually also by not being explicitly attributed, through the use of quotation marks, to per-
sonages quoted within the stanzas; quotation marks are used
only when the text makes it absolutely certain that the refrain forms part of the speech quoted in the preceding
stanza. Finally, in the use of diacritical marks, we were
guided above all by the recommendations made in Alfred
Foulet and Mary Blakely Speer, *On Editing Old French Texts*
(Lawrence: The Regents Press of Kansas, 1979), pp. 67-73.
The distribution of acute accent and dieresis calls, then,
for no special comment save the following: first, non-Cen-
tral forms ending in diphthongal *ie + t* receive no acute
accent, as in *pitiet* for Central *pitié*; second, internal *ie*,
although unmarked by a *tréma*, is disyllabic in the words
desfiement, *hardiement*, *joliete*, *jolieté*, and *liement*.

   9. Music Notes (=MN). These begin with a list of
manuscripts in which the music is preserved in mensural
notation, that is, those in which the rhythm is more or less
clearly indicated, and manuscripts which contain other melodies for the same poem. There follows an outline of the
musical structure; here lower-case letters signify phrases
serving single text lines; capital letters, larger units;
"rf" a refrain; "vrf" the variable refrains of *chansons avec
des refrains*. In the footnotes that usually follow, reference is made to variant, rejected, and emended readings;
here "ms" always refers to the manuscript from which the
melody comes; others are identified by their sigla.

   10. Rejected Readings (=RR). When any emendation
other than an obvious one is due to an earlier editor or
commentator, credit is given next to the reading rejected.
In the case of a passage marked "missing," the reading in
the edited text is taken from another manuscript unless an
editorial conjecture is specified; the other manuscript(s)
may be identified by consulting the Variants. Hypermetric
and hypometric lines are specified by numbers preceded by +
or -. Abbreviations and ligatures are resolved, but elision
is left unmarked and the letters *i*, *j*, *u*, *v*, and final *x* are
given as they occur in the manuscript; capital letters are
used always and only in verse-initial position, irrespective
of occurrence in the manuscript.

   11. Variants (=V). These are understood as readings that differ, not necessarily from the base manuscript,
but from the critical text. Unlike the rejected readings,
the variants are presented selectively. Orthographic variants, whether reflective of dialectal phonological distinc-
tions (e.g., *le/lou*) or not (e.g., *seignor/seingnor*), are

excluded. All others are presented, viz., those that in any
way affect sense or meter and those that are of morphosyn-
tactic interest, the latter including most notably all instances of variation in case-flexion. Abbreviations, elision, etc., are treated as in the Rejected Readings; see
foregoing paragraph.
          12. Editions (=E). Listed in chronological order,
these include selected early publications, scholarly editions, and selected other editions, especially those intended for an English-speaking public and accompanied by translations.
          13. Dialectal Features (=DF). Dialect is identi-
fied when the scripta is to some extent characteristic of an
area well outside that of Central Old French. There is no
systematic attempt to distinguish between dialectal traits
due to the poet and those due to the copyist. The list of
features divergent from Central Old French is not necessarily exhaustive; the features themselves, usually formulated
only in scriptal terms, may be exemplified either completely
or incompletely.
          14. Notes (=N). The nature and scope of the notes
vary with the requirements of the individual texts as these
requirements could be defined within the space limitations
of the present volume. The notes may consist of glosses,
remarks on editorial procedure, historical information, comments on compositional form, discussion of poetic content,
etc. They do not include a systematic presentation of versification data, for which RS and MW may be consulted.

                              Notes

1   See Works Cited (part II of Bibliography) for bibliographical details of this work and others cited here.
2   For the most thorough recent attempts to establish a
classification of Old French songs, see Zumthor *Es* (1972)
and Bec (1977). Notably absent from our collection are
poetic types which were in all likelihood not linked to
music--e.g., the *fatrasie*--and the Arthurian *lai*, the ms.
sources of which are so numerous and so distinct from those
of the songs presented here that practical consideration
alone sufficed to exclude examples of it.
3   See, on this subject, Istvan Frank, "De l'art d'éditer
les textes lyriques," *Recueil de travaux . . . Clovis Bru-
nel*, Mémoires et Documents, 12 (Paris: Société de l'Ecole
des Chartes, 1955), I, 463-475, reprinted in English translation in Christopher Kleinhenz, ed., *Medieval Manuscripts*

and Textual Criticism, North Carolina Studies in the Romance
Languages and Literature, Symposia, 4 (Chapel Hill: U. of
North Carolina, 1976), 123-138; Armand Machabey, "Comment
déterminer l'authenticité d'une chanson médiévale?" *Mélanges
. . . René Crozet*, ed. P. Gallais and Y.-J. Riou (Poitiers:
Société d'Etudes Médiévales, 1966), II, 915-920; Maurice
Delbouille, "La Philologie médiévale et la critique tex-
tuélle" and Philippe Ménard, "L'Edition des textes lyriques
du moyen âge, réflexions sur la tradition manuscrite de
Guillaume le Vinier," *Actes du 13e Congrès International de
Linguistique et Philologie Romanes, 1971* (Quebec: P.U.
Laval, 1976), I, 57-73 and II, 763-777, resp.; and Chapter
2, "Le Poète et le texte," pp. 64-106, in Zumthor *Es* (1972).
4   Hans-Herbert Räkel, in his *Die musikalische Erschei-
nungsform der Trouvèrepoesie* (Publikationen der Schweize-
rischen musikforschenden Gesellschaft, Serie II, Band 27.
Bern: Paul Haupt, 1977), bases his chief argument on ornamentation, namely that early trouvères improvised within an
oral tradition, leading to considerable divergences in ornamentation and even structural notes, whereas the trouvères
of the mid-thirteenth century established a written repertory, fixing the tunes and often "correcting" them.
5   *Cf.* Heinrich Husmann, "Zur Rhythmik des Trouvère-
gesanges," *Die Musikforschung* 5 (1952), 110-113.
6   The general cultural and historical arguments for this
approach have been aired in Hans Tischler, "Rhythm, Meter,
and Melodic Organization in Medieval Songs," *Studies in
Medieval Culture* 8/9, Western Michigan University 1976, 49-
64, especially pp. 52f.
7   *La Technique poétique . . .*; see Works Cited.
8   Respectively, Jean Beck and Pierre Aubry.
9   See Manuscripts Cited.
10   See note 5.
11   Derived from the second mode: ♩♪♩ ♪♩♪♩ ♪♩♩.
12   *Cf.* Theodore C. Karp's forthcoming book on the music of
St. Martial; also, among others, T.C. Karp, "St. Martial and
Santiago de Compostela; an Analytical Speculation," *Acta
musicologica* 39 (1967), 144-160; Bruno Stäblein, "Modale
Rhythmen im Saint-Martial-Repertoire?" *Festschrift Friedrich
Blume* (Kassel: Bärenreuter-Verlag, 1963), 340-362.
13   *Cf.* John Boe, "Rhythmical Notation in the Beneventan
Gloria Trope *Aureas arces*," *Musica Disciplina* 29 (1975),
5-42.

Bibliography

I. MANUSCRIPTS CITED. Comprehensive enumeration and description of the manuscript sources of Old French lyric poetry may be found in RS (see Works Cited); E. Schwan, *Die altfranzösischen Liederhandschriften, ihre Verhältnis, ihre Entstehung und ihre Bestimmung* (Berlin, 1886); A. Jeanroy, *Bibliographie sommaire des chansonniers français du moyen âge*, Classiques Français du Moyen Age (Paris, 1918); and F. Gennrich, "Die beiden neuesten Bibliographien altfranzösischer und altprovenzalischer Lieder," *Zeitschrift für romanische Philologie* 41 (1921), 289-346.
  The manuscripts listed below are those that served in the preparation of the present volume. (Facsimile, diplomatic, and other editions are cited only when particularly pertinent.) We are deeply grateful to the following libraries for having made photographic copies available: Arras, Bibliothèque Municipale; Berne, Stadtbibliothek; London, British Library; London, Guildhall; Modena, Biblioteca Estense; Oxford, Bodleian Library; Paris, Bibliothèque de l'Arsenal; Paris, Bibliothèque Nationale; Rome, Biblioteca Vaticana; Siena, Bibliotheca Comunale. We offer special thanks to Mr. Hugo Kunoff and, through him, to the Library of Indiana University for having assembled the photographic copies and made them available for our use.

A   Arras, Bibliothèque Municipale, 657.
B   Berne, Stadtbibliothek, 231.
C   Berne, Stadtbibliothek, 389.
F   London, British Library, Egerton 274.
G   London, Lambeth Palace, Misc. Rolls 1435.   Ed.: Wallensköld, A. "Le ms. Londres, Bibliothèque de Lambeth Palace, Misc. Rolls 1435," *Mém. de la Soc. Néo-Philologique de Helsingfors* 6 (1917), 1-40.
H   Modena, Biblioteca Estense, R 4, 4.
I   Oxford, Bodleian Library, Douce 308.
K   Paris, Bibliothèque de l'Arsenal, 5198.
L   Paris, Bibliothèque Nationale, français 765.
M   Paris, Bibliothèque Nationale, français 844.
Mt (Insertion in M.)
N   Paris, Bibliothèque Nationale, français 845.
O   Paris, Bibliothèque Nationale, français 846.
P   Paris, Bibliothèque Nationale, français 847.
Q   Paris, Bibliothèque Nationale, français 1109.
R   Paris, Bibliothèque Nationale, français 1591.
S   Paris, Bibliothèque Nationale, français 12581.
T   Paris, Bibliothèque Nationale, français 12615.

U   Paris, Bibliothèque Nationale, français 20050.
V   Paris, Bibliothèque Nationale, français 24406.
W   Paris, Bibliothèque Nationale, français 25566.
X   Paris, Bibliothèque Nationale, nouv. acq. fr. 1050.
Z   Siena, Bibliotheca Comunale, H. X. 36.
a   Rome, Biblioteca Vaticana, Reg. 1490.
b   Rome, Biblioteca Vaticana, Reg. 1522.
c   Berne,Stadtbibliothek, A. 95. Ed.: Bertoni, G. "Le
    tenzoni del frammento francese di Berna A. 95," *Arch.
    Rom.* 3 (1919), 43-61.
e   (Present location unknown.) Ed.: Wallensköld, A. "Un
    fragment de chansonnier, actuellement introuvable, du
    XIIIe siècle," *Neuphil. Mitteil.* 18 (1917), 2-17.
i   Paris, Bibliothèque Nationale, français 12483.
j   Paris, Bibliothèque Nationale, nouv. acq. fr. 21677.
    Ed.: Bédier, J. "Un feuillet récemment retrouvé d'un
    chansonnier français du XIIIe siècle." *Mélanges de phi-
    lologie romane et d'histoire littéraire offerts à M.
    Maurice Wilmotte.* 2 vols. Paris: Champion, 1910, pp.
    895-922.
za Zagreb, University Library. Facsimile: Roques, M. "Le
    Chansonnier français de Zagreb." *Mélanges de linguis-
    tique et de littérature offerts à M. Alfred Jeanroy.*
    Paris: Droz, 1928, pp. 509-536.
London, British Library, Addison 16559.
London, British Library, Cotton, Caligula A XVIII.
London, Guildhall, *Liber de antiquis legibus.*
Paris, Bibliothèque de l'Arsenal, 3517.
Paris, Bibliothèque Nationale, français 837.
Paris, Bibliothèque Nationale, français 1593.
Paris, Bibliothèque Nationale, français 1635.

II. WORKS CITED. The works listed here are those to which
reference is made (in abbreviated form) through the pages of
the present volume. They do not at all constitute a comprehensive bibliography of the Old French song. For more ample
data, see the bibliographies contained in RS (1955), MW
(1972), and Bec 1 (1977). There are some recent works, per-
taining to particular songs, which are cited only in the
notes to those songs.

     For an index of recorded performances of trouvère
songs, see Larry S. Crist and Roger J. Steiner, "Musica Ver-
bis Concordet: Medieval French Lyric Poems with their Music
(a Discography)," *Mediaevalia* 1:2 (1975), 35-61.

     The following collections are designated in the biblio-
graphical entries in abbreviated form: Classique Français du

Moyen Age = CFMA, Société des Anciens Textes Français = SATF, and Textes Littéraires Français = TLF.

B   Van des Boogaard, Nico H.J. *Rondeaux et refrains du 12e siècle au début du 14e.* Paris: Klincksieck, 1969.
MW   Mölk, Ulrich and Friedrich Wolfzettel. *Repertoire métrique de la poésie lyrique française des origines à 1350.* Munich: Fink, 1972.
RS   Spanke, Hans. *G. Raynauds Bibliographie des altfranzösischen Liedes.* Leiden: Brill, 1955.
Abbott   Abbott, Claude C. *Early Mediaeval French Lyrics.* London: Constable, 1932.
Adnès   Adnès, André. *Adenès, dernier grand trouvère. Recherches historiques et anthroponymiques.* Paris: Picard, 1971.
Archibald   Archibald, J.K. "La Chanson de captivité du roi Richard." *Cah. d'Et. Méd.* "Epopées, légendes et miracles" (1974), 149-158.
Arnaud   Arnaud, Leonard E. "The *Sottes Chansons* in *Ms Douce 308* of the Bodleian Library at Oxford," *Speculum* 19 (1944), 68-88.
Aspin   Aspin, Isabel S.T. *Anglo-Norman Political Songs.* Anglo-Norman Texts, 11. Oxford: Blackwell, 1953.
Aspland   Aspland, C.W. *A Medieval French Reader.* Oxford: Oxford U. Press, 1979.
Banitt   Banitt, Max. "Le vocabulaire de Colin Muset. Rapprochement sémantique avec celui d'un prince-poète, Thibaut de Champagne." *Romance Philology* 20 (1966-67), 151-167.
Bartsch   Bartsch, Karl. *Romances et pastourelles françaises des XIIe et XIIIe siècles. Altfranzösische Romanzen und Pastourellen.* Leipzig, 1870; rpt. Darmstadt: Wissenschaftliche Buchgesellschaft, 1967.
Bartsch "Lieder"   Bartsch, Karl. "Geistliche Umdichtung weltlicher Lieder." *Zeit. für rom. Phil.* 8 (1884), 570-585.
Bartsch-Wiese   Bartsch, Karl. *Chrestomathie de l'ancien française.* 12th ed. rev. by L. Wiese. Leipzig: Vogel, 1920; rpt. New York-London: Hafner, 1969.
Baum   Baum, Richard. "Der Kastellan von Couci." *Zeit. für franz. Spr. und Lit.* 80 (1970), 51-80 and 131-148.
Bec   Bec, Pierre. *La Lyrique française au moyen âge (XIIe et XIIIe siècles). Contribution à une typologie des genres poétiques médiévaux.* Vol. 1: Etudes. Vol. 2: Textes. Paris: Picard, 1977-78.

Bec "Aube"   Bec, Pierre. "L'aube française 'Gaite de la
tor': pièce de ballet ou poème lyrique?" *Cah. de Civ.
Méd.* 16 (1973), 17-33.

Becker   Philipp August Becker. *Zur romanischen Literaturgeschichte.* Munich: Franke, 1967.

Bédier *Col*   Bédier, Joseph. *Les Chansons de Colin Muset.*
CFMA. 2nd ed. Paris: Champion, 1938.

Bédier *Nic*   Bédier, Joseph. *De Nicolao Museto (gallice:
Colin Muset), franco-gallico carminum scriptore.* Diss.
Paris, 1893. Paris: Bouillon, 1893.

Bédier *Wil*   Bédier, Joseph. "Un feuillet récemment re-
trouvé d'un chansonnier français du XIIIe siècle." *Mélanges de philologie romane et d'histoire littéraire offerts à M. Maurice Wilmotte.* 2 vols. Paris: Champion,
1910, pp. 895-922.

Bédier-Aubry   Bédier, Joseph and Pierre Aubry. *Les Chansons de croisade.* Paris: Champion, 1909.

Berger   Berger, Rudolf. *Canchons und Partures des alt-
französischen Trouvere Adan de le Hale le Bochu d'Aras.*
Vol. I: Canchons. Romanische Bibliothek. Halle a. S.:
Niemeyer, 1900.

Boogaard "Wilart"   Van den Boogaard, Nico H.J. "Les Chansons attribuées à Wilart de Corbie." *Neophilologus* 55
(1971), 123-141.

Bossuat *Man*   Bossuat, Robert. *Manuel bibliographique de la
littérature française du moyen âge.* Melun: Argences,
1951. *Supplément (1949-1953).* Paris: Argences, 1955.
Second Supplément (1954-1960). Paris: Argences, 1961.

Brakelmann 1   Brakelmann, Julius. *Les plus anciens chansonniers français.* Paris: Bouillon, 1870-1891.

Brakelmann 2   Brakelmann, Julius. *Les plus anciens chansonniers français: Fortsetzung des 1891 erschienenen
ersten Teiles.* Marburg: Elwert, 1896.

Brakelmann "Pastourelle"   Brakelmann, Julius. "Die Pastourelle in der nord- und süd- französischen Poesie, III."
Jahrb. für rom. und engl. Spr. und Lit. 9 (1868), 307-337.

Brandin   Brandin, Louis. "Die Inedita der altfranzösischen
Liederhandschrift Pb[5] (Bibl. Nat. 846)." *Zeit. für franz.
Spr. und Lit.* 22 (1900), 230-272.

Brittain   Brittain, Fred. *The Mediaeval Latin and Romanic
Lyric.* Cambridge: Cambridge University Press, 1937.

Brown   Brown, Carleton. *English Lyrics of the Thirteenth
Century.* Oxford: n.p., 1932.

Burger   Burger, Michel. *Recherches sur la structure et
l'origine des vers romans.* Geneva: Droz; Paris: Minard,
1957.

Camus   Camus, J. "Notices et extraits des manuscrits français de Modène antérieurs au XVIe siècle." *Rev. des lang. rom.* 35 (1891), 169-262.

Chastel   Chastel, André. *Trésors de la poésie médiévale.* Paris: Le Club Français du Livre, 1959.

Chaytor   Chaytor, Henry John. *The Troubadours and England.* Cambridge: Cambridge University Press, 1923.

Cocito   Cocito, Luciana. "Ancora sulla 'Gaite de la tor'." *Saggi di filologia romanza.* Genoa: Bozzi, 1971, pp. 49-56.

Cohen   Cohen, Gustave. *Anthologie de la littérature française du moyen âge.* Paris: Delagrave, 1946.

Coussemaker   Coussemaker, Edmond de. *Oeuvres complètes du trouvère Adam de la Halle.* Paris: Société des Sciences, des Lettres et des Arts de Lille, 1872.

Cremonesi   Cremonesi, Carla. *Lirica francese del medio evo.* Milan-Varese: Cisalpino, 1955.

Crépet   Crépet, Eugène. *Les Poëtes français.* Vol. I: Du XIIe au XVIe siècle. Paris: Quantin, 1887.

Crescini   Crescini, Vincenzo. "Per le canzoni di Chrétien de Troyes." *Studi letterari e linguistici dedicati a Pio Rajna.* Milan: n.p., 1911, pp. 627-656.

Cullmann   Cullmann, Arthur. *Die Lieder und Romanzen des Audefroi le Bastard.* Halle a. S.: Niemeyer, 1914.

Delpit   Delpit, Jules. *Collection générale des documents français qui se trouvent en Angleterre.* Paris, 1847.

Dembowski   Dembowski, Peter. "Vocabulary of Old French Courtly Lyrics--Difficulties and Hidden Difficulties." *Critical Inquiry* 2 (1975-76), 763-779.

Dinaux   Dinaux, Arthur. *Trouvères, jongleurs et ménestrels du Nord de la France et du Midi de la Belgique.* 4 vols. Paris, 1837; Paris-Valenciennes, 1839; Paris-Valenciennes, 1843; Paris: Téchener; Brussels: Heussner, 1863.

DobHar   Dobson, E.J. and F. Ll. Harrison. *Medieval English Songs.* New York: Cambridge U. Press, 1979.

Dolly-Cormier   Dolly, Martha R. and Raymond J. Cormier. "*Aimer, souvenir, souffrir*: les chansons de Thibaut de Champagne." *Romania* 99 (1978), 311-346.

Dragonetti   Dragonetti, Roger. *La Technique poétique des trouvères dans la chanson courtoise.* Bruges: "De Tempel", 1960.

Dronke   Dronke, Peter. *The Medieval Lyric.* London: Hutchinson, 1968.

Ellis   Ellis, A.J. *On Early English Pronunciation.* Part I. London, 1869.

Elwert   Elwert, W. Theodor. "Die Reimtechnik in der höfischen Lyrik Nordfrankreichs und ihr Verhältnis zum provenzalischen Vorbild." *Aufsätze zur provenzalischen, französischen und neulateinischen Dichtung.* Studien zu den rom. Spr. und Lit., Bd. 4 Wiesbaden: Steiner, 1971, pp. 40-79.

Ertzdorff   Ertzdorff, Xenja von. "Die Dame im Herzen und das Herz bei der Dame. Zur Verwendung des Begriffs 'Herz' in der höfischen Liebeslyrik des 11. und 12. Jahrhunderts." *Zeit. für deut. Phil.* 84 (1965), 6-46.

Faral   Faral, Edmond. "Les Chansons de toile ou chansons d'histoire," *Romania* 69 (1946-47), 433-62.

Faral "Pastourelle"   Faral, Edmond. "La Pastourelle." *Romania* 49 (1923), 204-259.

Faral-Bastin   Faral, Edmond and Julia Bastin. *Oeuvres complètes de Rutebeuf.* 2 vols. 7th ed. Paris: Picard, 1977.

Fath   Fath, Fritz. *Die Lieder des Castellans von Coucy.* Heidelberg: J. Hörning, 1883.

Fiset   Fiset, Franz. "Das altfranzösische Jeu-Parti." *Rom. Forsch.* 29 (1906), 407-544.

Flutre   Flutre, Louis-Fernand. *Table des noms propres avec toutes leurs variantes figurant dans les romans du moyen âge écrits en français ou en provençal.* Poitiers: Centre d'Et. Sup. de Civ. Méd., 1962.

Foerster   Foerster, Wendelin. *Kristian von Troyes Wörterbuch zu seinem sämtlichen Werken.* Halle a. S.: Niemeyer, 1914.

Foulet   Foulet, Lucien. *Petite Syntaxe de l'ancien français.* CFMA. 3rd. ed. Paris: Champion, 1963.

Foulon   Foulon, Charles. *L'Oeuvre de Jehan Bodel.* Trav. de la Fac. des Lettres et Sci. Hum. de Rennes, ser. 1, vol. 2. Paris: Presses Universitaires de France, 1958.

Frank   Frank, István. *Trouvères et Minnesänger.* Vol. I: Recueil de textes. Saarbrücken, 1952. Vol. 2: (see Müller-Blattau).

Frappier   Frappier, Jean. *La Poésie lyrique en France aux XIIe et XIIIe siècles.* Les Cours de Sorbonne. Paris: Centre de Doc. Univ., 1963.

Gennrich *Alt Lied*   Gennrich, Friedrich. *Altfranzösische Lieder.* 2 vols. Tübingen: Niemeyer, 1955-56.

Gennrich *Alt Ron*   Gennrich, Friedrich. *Das altfranzösische Rondeau und Virelai im 12. und 13. Jahrhundert.* (Vol. 3 of *Rondeaux, Virelais und Balladen.*) Summa Musicae Medii Aevi, 10. Langen bei Frankfurt, 1963.

Gennrich *Bib*   Gennrich, Friedrich. "Die beiden neuesten Bibliographien altfranzösischer und altprovenzalisher Lieder," *Zeit. für rom. Phil.* 61 (1921), 289-346.

Gennrich *BibMot*   Gennrich, Friedrich. *Bibliographie der
ältesten französischen und lateinischen Motetten*. Darmstadt, 1958.
Gennrich *BVer*   Gennrich, Friedrich. *Bibliographisches Ver-
zeichnis der französischen Refrains des 12. und 13. Jahrhunderts*. Summa Musicae Medii Aevi, 14. Langen bei Frankfurt, 1964.
Gennrich *Cant*   Gennrich, Friedrich. *Cantilenae Piae, 31
altfranzösische geistliche Lieder*. Musikwiss. Stud.-
Bibl., 24. Langen bei Frankfurt, 1966.
Gennrich *Ex*   Gennrich, Friedrich. *Exempla altfranzösischer
Lyrik. 40 altfranzösische Lieder*. Musikwiss. Stud.-Bibl.,
17. Darmstadt, 1958.
Gennrich "Melodien"   Gennrich, Friedrich. "Internationale
mittelalterliche Melodien." *Zeit. für Musikwiss*. 11
(1928/29), 321-348.
Gennrich *Ron*   Gennrich, Friedrich. *Rondeaux, Virelais und
Balladen aus des Ende des XII., dem XIII. und dem ersten
Drittel des XIV. Jahrhunderts*. Vol. I: Texte. Gesell-
schaft für romanische Literatur, 43. Dresden, 1921. Vol.
II: Materialen, Literaturnachweise, Refrainverzeichnis.
Ges. für rom. Lit., 47. Göttingen, 1927.
Gennrich *Rot*   Gennrich, Friedrich. *Die altfranzösische
Rotrouenge*. Halle a. S.: Niemeyer, 1925.
Gennrich "Simon"   Gennrich, Friedrich. "Simon d'Authie,
ein pikardischer Sänger." *Zeit. für rom. Phil*. 67 (1951),
49-104.
Goldin   Goldin, Frederick. *Lyrics of the Troubadours and
Trouvères: An Anthology and a History*. Garden City, New
York: Anchor Press/Doubleday, 1973.
Groult   Groult, P., V. Emond, and G. Muraille. *Littérature
française du moyen âge*. 2 vols. 3rd ed. rev. Gembloux:
Duculot, 1964-67.
Guy   Guy, Henry. *Essai sur la vie et les oeuvres litté-
raires du trouvère Adan de le Hale*. Paris: Hachette, 1898.
Henry "Chanson"   Henry, Albert. "La Chanson R1298." *Roma-
nia* 75 (1954), 108-115.
Henry *Chrest*   Henry, Albert. *Chrestomathie de la littéra-
ture en ancien français*. 2 vols. in one. Bibliotheca Ro-
manica, 3/4. 4th ed. Berne: Francke, 1967.
Henry *Hen*   Henry, Albert. *L'Oeuvre lyrique d'Henri III duc
de Brabant*. Bruges: "De Tempel", 1948.
Hoepffner   Hoepffner, Ernest. "Les Chansons de Jacques de
Cysoing." *Studi Medievali* 11 (1938), 69-102.
Hoffman   Hoffman, Ruth Cassel. *Aspects théoriques de la
parodie, avec application particulière aux sottes chansons*. Diss. Chicago, 1976.

Hofmann "Anzahl" Hofmann, Konrad. "Eine Anzahl altfranzö-
sischer lyrischer Gedichte aus dem Berner Codex 389."
Sitzungsber. der Kögl. bayer. Akad. der Wiss. Munich,
1867, pp. 486-527.
Hofmann "Pastourellen" Hofmann, Konrad. "Altfranzösische
Pastourellen aus der Berner Handschrift Nr. 389." *Sitz-
ungsber. der Kögl. bayer. Akad. der Wiss.* Munich, 1865.
Huet *Gace* Huet, Gédéon. *Chansons de Gace Brulé.* SATF.
Paris: Firmin-Didot, 1902.
Huet *Gautier* Huet, Gédéon. *Chansons et descorts de Gau-
tier de Dargies.* SATF. Paris: Firmin-Didot, 1912.
Järnström 1 Järnström, Edw. *Recueil de chansons pieuses
du 13e siècle*, I. Sumalaisen Tiedeakatemian Toimituksis
(Annales Academiae Scientarum Fennicae), ser. B, 3. Hel-
sinki, 1910.
Järnström-Långfors 2 Järnström, Edw. and A. Långfors. *Re-
cueil de chansons pieuses du 13e siècle*, II. Suomalaisen
Tiedeakatemian Toimituksia (Annales Academiae Scientarum
Fennicae), ser. B, 20. Helsinki, 1927.
Jeanroy *Lais* Jeanroy, Alfred, Louis Brandin, and Pierre
Aubry. *Lais et descorts français du XIIIe siècle. Texte
et musique.* Mélanges de Musicologie Critique, 3. Paris:
H. Welter, 1901.
Jeanroy "Modène" Jeanroy, Alfred. "Les Chansons fran-
çaises inédites du manuscrit de Modène." *Rev. des lang.
rom.* 39 (1896), 241-268.
Jeanroy *Or* Jeanroy, Alfred. *Les Origines de la poésie
lyrique en France au moyen âge.* Paris: Champion, 1889;
4th ed. 1965.
Jeanroy "Philippe" Jeanroy, Alfred. "Les Chansons de
Philippe de Beaumanoir." *Romania* 26 (1897), 517-536.
Jeanroy-Guy Jeanroy, Alfred and Henri Guy. *Chansons et
dits artésiens du XIIIe siècle.* Bordeaux: Feret et Fils;
Paris: Libraires associés; Montpellier: Coulet; Toulouse:
Privat, 1898.
Jeanroy-Långfors Jeanroy, Alfred and Arthur Långfors.
Chansons satiriques et bachiques du 13e siecle. CFMA.
Paris: Champion, 1921.
Jeanroy-Långfors "Chansons" Jeanroy, Alfred and Arthur
Långfors. "Chansons inédites tirées du manuscrit français
846 de la Bibliothèque nationale." *Archivum Romanicum* 3
(1919), 1-27; 355-356.
Joly Joly, Raymond. "Les Chansons d'histoire." *Roman-
istisches Jahrbuch* 12 (1961), 51-66.
Jubinal Jubinal, Achille. *Oeuvres complètes de Rutebeuf,
trouvère du XIIIe siècle.* 3 vols. 2nd ed. Bibl. Elzevi-
rienne, 85. Paris: Daffis, 1874-1875.

Jubinal *Nouv Rec*   Jubinal, Achille. *Nouveau recueil de contes, dits, fabliaux, et autres pièces inédites des XIIIe, XIVe et XVe siècles, pour faire suite aux collections Legrand d'Aussy, Barbazan et Méon.* Vol. II. Paris: Challamel, 1842.

Karp   Karp, Theodore. "The Trouvère Manuscript Tradition." *Twenty-fifth Anniversary Festschrift (1937-1962)*, ed. Albert Mell. New York: Queens College Press, 1964, pp. 25-52.

Keller   Keller, Adelbert. *Romvart. Beiträge zur Kunde mittelalterlicher Dichtung aus italiänischen Bibliotheken.* Mannheim: Bassermann; Paris, Renouard, 1844.

Kressner   Kressner, Adolf. *Rutebeufs Gedichte, nach den Handschriften der Pariser National-bibliothek.* Wolfenbüttel: Zwissler, 1885.

La Borde *Es*   La Borde, J.-B. de. *Essai sur la musique ancienne et moderne*, Vol. II. Paris: P.-D. Pierres, 1780.

La Borde *Mém*   La Borde, J.-B. de. *Mémoires historiques sur Raoul de Coucy.* 2 vols. Paris: P.-D. Pierres, 1781.

Långfors *Mél*   Långfors, Arthur. "Mélanges de poésie lyrique française" in various volumes of *Romania*. (See individual citations for volume numbers and dates.)

Långfors *Not*   Långfors, Arthur. *Notice du manuscrit français 12483 de la Bibliothèque nationale.* Notices et extraits des manuscrits de la Bibliothèque nationale et autres bibliothèques, 39, 2e partie. Paris: Imprimerie nationale, 1916.

Långfors *Rec*   Långfors, Arthur. *Recueil general des jeux-partis français.* 2 vols. Paris: Champion, 1926.

Långfors *Sot*   Långfors, Arthur. *Deux recueils de sottes chansons.* Annales Academiae Scientarum Fennicae, ser. B, 53. Helsinki, 1945.

Långfors-Solente   Långfors, Arthur and S. Solente. "Une pastourelle nouvellement découverte et son modèle." *Neuphil. Mitteil.* 30 (1929), 215-225.

Langlois   Langlois, Ernest. *Le Roman de la Rose par Guillaume de Lorris et Jean de Meun publié d'après les manuscrits.* 5 vols. SATF. Paris: Firmin-Didot, 1914-1924.

La Ravallière   La Ravallière, Levesque de. *Les Poésies du roy de Navarre.* Paris: H.L. Guerin and J. Guerin, 1742.

Lerond   Lerond, Alain. *Chansons attribuées au Chastelain de Couci.* Paris: Presses Universitaires de France, 1964.

Leroux de Lincy   Leroux de Lincy, Antoine. *Recueil de chants historiques (1ère série).* Paris: Gosselin, 1841.

Levy   Levy, Raphael. "Remarques lexicographiques sur les chansons de Colin Muset." *Romanic Review* 59 (1968), 241-248.

Lindelöf-Wallensköld   Lindelöf, E. and A. Wallensköld.
"Les Chansons de Gautier d'Epinal." *Mém. de la Soc. Néo-Phil. de Helsingfors* 3 (1901), 206-320.
Lubinski   Lubinski, Fritz. "Die Unica der Jeux-partis des
Oxforder Liederhandschrift (Douce 308)." *Rom. Forsch.* 22
(1908), 506-598.
Maillard *Anth*   Maillard, Jean. *Anthologie de chants de
trouvères.* Paris: Zurfluh, 1967.
Maillard *Er*   Maillard, Jean. *Lais et chansons d'Ernoul de
Gastinois.* Musicological Studies and Documents, 15. Amer-
ican Institute of Musicology, 1964.
Maillard *Lai*   Maillard, Jean. *Evolution et esthétique du
lai lyrique des origines à la fin du XIVe siècle.* Diss.
Paris 1963. Paris: Centre de Doc. Univ., 1963.
Marshall   Marshall, J.H. *The Chansons of Adam de la Halle.*
Manchester: Manchester U. Press, 1971.
Mary   Mary, André. *Anthologie poétique française: Moyen
âge.* 2 vols. Paris: Garnier-Flammarion, 1967.
Mätzner   Mätzner, Eduard. *Altfranzösische Lieder berichtigt
und erläutert.* Berlin: Dümmler, 1853; rpt. Bonn: Dümmler,
1969.
Ménard   Ménard, Philippe. *Les Poésies de Guillaume le Vi-
nier.* TLF. Geneva: Droz; Paris: Minard, 1970.
Meyer   Meyer, Paul. *Recueil d'anciens textes bas-latins,
provençaux et français.* Vol II. Paris: Franck, 1877.
Meyer "Mélanges"   Meyer, Paul. "Mélanges." *Romania* 19
(1890), 102-106.
Michel   Michel, Francisque. *Chansons du Châtelain de
Coucy.* Paris: Crapelet, 1830.
Michel *Documents*   Michel, Francisque. *Collections de docu-
ments inédits sur l'histoire de France, Rapports au Mi-
nistre.* Paris, 1839.
Moignet   Moignet, Gérard. *Grammaire de l'ancien français.*
Paris: Klincksieck, 1973.
Monmerqué-Michel   Monmerqué, Nicolas and Fr. Michel.
Théâtre français au moyen âge. Paris: Firmin-Didot, 1939.
Morawski   Morawski, Joseph. *Proverbes français antérieurs
au XVe siècle.* CFMA. Paris: Champion, 1925.
Müller-Blattau   Müller-Blattau, Wendelin. *Trouvères und
Minnesänger.* Vol. 2: Kritische Ausgaben der Weisen. (For
vol. 1, see Frank.) Saarbrücken, 1956.
Muraille   Jodogne, O., A. Henry and F. Vercauteren. "Rap-
ports sur le mémoire: *Les Trouvères lyriques du XIIe
siècle,* par Guy Muraille." Acad. Roy. de Belgique,
Bull. de la Classe des Lettres, 5e sér., 51 (1965), 113-
119.

Newcombe *Jeh*   Newcombe, Terence. *Les Poésies du trouvères Jehan Erart*. TLF. Geneva: Droz; Paris: Minard, 1972.

Newcombe "Raoul"   Newcombe, Terence. "Les Poésies du trouvère Raoul de Beauvais." *Romania* 93 (1972), 317-336.

Newcombe *Songs*   Newcombe, Terence. *The Songs of Jehan Erart, 13th Century Trouvère*. Corpus Mensurabilis Musicae, 67. American Institute of Musicology, 1975.

Newcombe *Thib*   Newcombe, Terence H. *Les Poésies de Thibaut de Blaison*. Geneva: Droz, 1978.

Nicod   Nicod, Lucie. *Les Jeux partis d'Adam de la Halle*. Paris: Champion, 1917.

Nissen   Nissen, Elisabeth. *Les Chansons attribuées à Guiot de Dijon et Jocelin*. Diss. Minnesota, 1928. CFMA. Paris: Champion, 1928.

Noack   Noack, Fritz. *Der Strophenausgang in seinem Verhältnis zum Refrain und Strophengrundstock in der refrainhaltigen altfranzösischen Lyrik*. Marburg: Elwert, 1899.

Oulmont   Oulmont, Charles. *La Poésie française du moyen âge*. Paris: Mercure de France, 1913.

Paris   Paris, Gaston. *Mélanges de littérature française du moyen âge, pub. par M. Roques*. Paris: Champion, 1912.

Paris-Langlois   Paris, Gaston and Ernest Langlois. *Chrestomathie du moyen âge*. Paris: Hachette, 1897.

P. Paris   Paris, Paulin. *Le Romancero françois. Histoire de quelques anciens trouvères, et choix de leurs chansons*. Paris: Téchener, 1833.

Pauphilet   Pauphilet, Albert. *Poètes et romanciers du moyen âge*. Bibl. de la Pléiade. Paris: Gallimard, 1952.

Payen   Payen, Jean-Charles. *Le Motif du repentir dans la littérature française médiévale*. Publ. Romanes et Françaises, 98. Geneva: Droz, 1968.

PetDyg "Charles"   Petersen Dyggve, Holger. "Personnages historiques figurant dans la poésie lyrique française des XIIe et XIIIe siècle. XXV: Charles, comte d'Anjou." *Neuphil. Mitteil.* 50 (1949), 144-174.

PetDyg *Gace*   Petersen Dyggve, Holger. *Gace Brulé, trouvère champenois*. Mém. de la Soc. Néophil. de Helsinki (Helsingfors), 16. Helsinki, 1951.

PetDyg "Garnier"   Petersen Dyggve, Holger. "Personnages historiques figurant dans la poésie lyrique française des XIIe et XIIIe siècles. XXIV: Garnier d'Anches et son destinataire 'le bon marquis'." *Neuphil. Mitteil.* 46 (1945), 123-153.

PetDyg "Moniot"   Petersen Dyggve, Holger. "Moniot d'Arras et Moniot de Paris." *Mém de la Soc. Néo-Phil. de Helsinki* 13 (1938), 1-252.

PetDyg "Onom"   Petersen Dyggve, Holger. "Onomastique des
trouvères." Suomalaisen Tiedeakatemian Toimituksia (Annales Academiae Scientarum Fennicae), ser. B, 30. Helsinki, 1934, pp. 1-254.

PetDyg "Trouvères"   Petersen Dyggve, Holger. "Trouvères et
protecteurs de trouvères dans les cours seigneuriales de
France." *Commentationes Philologicae in honorem Arthur
Långfors*. Suomalaisen Tiedeakatemian Toimituksia (Annales
Academiae Scientiarum Fennicae), ser. B, 50. Helsinki,
1942, pp. 39-247.

Picot   Picot, Guillaume. *La Poésie lyrique au Moyen-âge*.
2 vols. Classiques Larousse. Paris: Larousse, 1963.

Pinguet   Pinguet, A. *Les Chansons et pastourelles de Thibaut de Blaison*. Angers: Soc. des Amis du Livre Angevin,
1930.

Pottier   Pottier, Bernard. *Textes médiévaux français et
romans. Des gloses latines à la fin du XVe siecle*. Paris:
Klincksieck, 1964.

Räkel   Räkel, Hans Herbert. *Die musikalische Erscheinungs-
form der Trouvèrepoesie*. Publ. de la Soc. Suisse de Musicologie, II, 27. Berne-Stuttgart: Haupt, 1977.

Raynaud   Raynaud, Gaston. *Mélanges de philologie romane*.
Paris: Champion, 1913.

Réau   Réau, Louis. *Iconographie de l'art chrétien*. 6 vols.
Paris: Presses Universitaires de France, 1955-59.

Reese   Reese, Gustave. *Music in the Middle Ages*. New
York: Norton, 1940.

Regalado   Regalado, Nancy F. *Poetic Patterns in Rutebeuf:
A Study in Noncourtly Poetic Modes of the Thirteenth Century*. New Haven-London: Yale U. Press, 1970.

Restori   Restori, A. "La Gaite de la tor." *Miscellanea
nuziale Petraglione-Serrano*. Messina, 1904, pp. 4-22.

Richter   Richter, Max. *Die Lieder des altfranzösischen
Lyrikers Jehan de Nuevile*. Diss. Halle a. S. 1904. Halle
a. S.: C.A. Kaemmerer, 1904.

Rivière   Rivière, Jean-Claude. *Pastourelles*. 3 vols. TLF.
Geneva: Droz, 1974, 1975, 1976.

Rivière *Jac*   Rivière, Jean-Claude. *Les Poésies du trouvère
Jacques de Cambrai*. Geneva: Droz, 1978.

Rivière "Remarques"   Rivière, Jean-Claude. "Remarques sur
le vocabulaire des pastourelles anonymes françaises du
XIIe et du XIIIe siècle." *Rev. de Ling. Rom*. 36 (1972),
384-400.

Roquefort   Roquefort-Flaméricourt, B. de *De l'état de la
poésie française dans les 12e et 13e siècles*. Paris:
Fournier, 1815.

Rosenberg   Rosenberg, Samuel N. "Observations on the Chan-
son of Jacques d'Autun (R.350/351)." *Romania* 96 (1975),
552-560.
Saba   Saba, Guido. *Le "chansons de toile" o "chansons
d'histoire"*. Modena: Società Tipografica Modenese, 1955.
Saville   Saville, Jonathan. *The Medieval Erotic Alba*. New
York: Columbia U. Press, 1972.
Scheler 1   Scheler, Aug. *Trouvères belges du XIIe au XIVe
siècle*. Brussels: Closson, 1876.
Scheler 2   Scheler, Aug. *Trouvères belges (nouvelle sé-
rie)*. Louvain: P. et J. Lefever, 1879.
Schiller   Schiller, Gertrud. *Iconography of Christian Art*.
Trans. J. Seligman. 2 vols. Greenwich, Conn: New York
Graphic Soc., 1972.
Schläger   Schläger, Georg. "Uber Musik und Strophenbau der
altfranzösischen Romanzen." *Forschungen zur Romanischen
Philologie. Festgabe für Hermann Suchier*. Halle a. S.:
Niemeyer, 1900, pp. 115-160.
Schläger *Tagelied*   Schläger, Georg. *Studien über das Tage-
lied. Ein Beitrag zur Literaturgeschichte des Mittelal-
ters*. Jena, 1895.
Schmidt   Schmidt, Reinhold. *Die Lieder des Andrieu Contre-
dit d'Arras*. Diss. Halle a. S. 1903. Halle a. S.: C.A.
Kammerer, 1903.
Schöber   Schöber, Susanne. *Die altfranzösische Kreuzzugs-
lyrik des 12. Jahrhunderts*. Diss. der Univ. Salzburg, 7.
Vienna: Verband der Wissenschaftlichen Gesellschaften
Osterreichs, 1976.
Schossig   Schossig, Alfred. *Der Ursprung der altfranzö-
sischen Lyrik*. Halle a. S.: Niemeyer, 1957.
Schultz-Gora   Schultz-Gora, Oskan. "Einige unedierte Jeux-
partis." *Mélanges Chabaneau. Festschrift Camille Chaba-
neau zur Vollendung seines 75. Lebensjahres. 4. März 1906*.
Erlangen: Junge, 1907, pp. 497-516.
Schutz   Schutz, Richard A. *The Unedited Poems of Codex 389
of the Municipal Library of Berne, Switzerland*. Diss.
Indiana 1976.
Schwan   Schwan, Eduard. *Die altfranzösischen Liederhand-
schriften, ihr Verhältnis, ihre Entstehung und ihre
Bestimmung*. Berlin: Weidmann, 1886.
Simon   Simon, Philipp. *Jacques d'Amiens*. Berliner Beit-
räge zur germ. und rom. Phil. Romanische Abteilung, Nr. 3.
Berlin: Vogt, 1895.
Spanke *Bez*   Spanke, Hans. *Beziehungen zwischen romanischer
und mittellateinischer Lyrik mit besonderer Berück-
sichtigung der Metrik und Musik*. Abh. der Gesellshaft der

Wissenschaften zur Göttingen, Phil-Hist. Klasse. Dritte
Folge, 18. Berlin: Weidmann, 1936.
Spanke "Chans"   Spanke, Hans. "Der Chansonnier du Roi."
Rom. Forsch. 57 (1943), 38-104.
Spanke *Lied*   Spanke, Hans. *Eine altfranzösische Lieder-
sammlung.* Halle a. S.: Niemeyer, 1925.
Spaziani *Ant*   Spaziani, Marcello. *Antica lirica francese.*
Modena: Soc. Tipografica Modenese, 1954.
Spaziani *Canz*   Spaziani, Marcello. *Il canzoniere francese
di Siena.* Biblioteca dell'"Archivum Romanicum," 1st ser.,
46. Florence: Olschki, 1957.
Springer   Springer, Hermann. *Das Altfranzösische Klagelied
mit Berücksichtigung der verwandten Litteraturen.* Ber-
liner Beiträge zur germ. und rom. Phil. Romanische
Abteilung, Nr. 2. Berlin: Vogt, 1895.
Steffens *Per*   Steffens, Georg. *Die Lieder des Troveors
Perrin von Angincourt.* Romanische Bibliothek. Halle a.
S.: Niemeyer, 1905.
Steffens "Richart"   Steffens, Georg. "Der kritische Text
der Gedichte von Richart de Semilli." *Beiträge zur rom.
und engl. Philologie. Festgabe für Wendelin Foerster.*
Halle a. S.: Niemeyer, 1902, pp. 331-362.
Streng-Renkonen   Streng-Renkonen, Walter O. *Les Estampies
françaises.* CFMA. Paris: Champion, 1930.
Stengel   Stengel, Edmund. "Der Strophenausgang in den
ältesten französischen Balladen." *Zeit. für franz. Spr.
und Lit.* 18 (1896), 85-114.
Sudre   Sudre, Léopold. *Chrestomathie du moyen âge.* Paris:
Delagrave, 1898.
Tarbé *Blon*   Tarbé, Prosper. *Les Oeuvres de Blondel de
Neele.* Reims: Dubois, 1862.
Tarbé *Chans*   Tarbé, Prosper. *Les Chansonniers de Champagne
aux XIIe et XIIIe siècle.* Reims: Regnier, 1850.
Tarbé *Thib*   Tarbé, Prosper. *Chansons de Thibaut IV, comte
de Champagne et de Brie, roi de Navarre.* Reims: Regnier,
1851.
Tobler-Lommatzsch   Tobler, Adolf and Erhard Lommatzsch.
Altfranzösisches Wörterbuch. Berlin: Weidmann--Wies-
baden: Steiner, 1925--(still publishing).
Toja   Toja, Gianluigi. *Lirica cortese d'oïl, sec. XII-
XIII.* Bologna: Pàtron, 1966.
Tyssens   Tyssens, Madeleine. "An avril au tens pascour."
*Mélanges de philologie romane dédiés à la mémoire de Jean
Boutière.* Ed. Irénée Cluzel and François Pirot. Liège:
Soledi, 1971, pp. 589-603.
Ulrix   Ulrix, Eugène. "Les Chansons inédites de Guillaume
le Vinier d'Arras." *Mélanges de philologie et d'histoire*

littéraires offerts à M. Maurice Wilmotte. 2 vols. Paris:
Champion, 1910, pp. 785-814.
Van dW *Chans*   Van der Werf, Hendrik. *The Chansons of the
Troubadours and Trouvères. A Study of the Melodies and
their Relation to the Poems.* Utrecht: Oosthoek, 1972.
Van dW *Trouv*   Van der Werf, Hendrik. *Trouvères-Melodien I.*
Monumenta Monodica Medii Aevi, II. Kassel-Basel-Tours-
London: Bärenreiter, 1977.
Villemarqué   La Villemarqué, Th. Hersart de. "Rapport sur
une mission littéraire accomplie en Angleterre," *Archives
des missions scientifiques et littéraires,* sér. I, 5,
(1856), 89-116.
Voretzsch   Voretzsch, Karl. *Altfranzösisches Lesebuch.*
Halle a. S.: Niemeyer, 1921. 3rd. ed. Tübingen: Niemeyer,
1966.
Wagner   Wagner, Robert Léon. *Textes d'études (ancien et
moyen français).* TLF. Lille: Giard; Geneva: Droz, 1949.
Waitz   Waitz, Hugo. "Der kritische Text der Gedichte von
Gillebert de Berneville mit Angabe sämtlicher Lesarten
nach den Parisen Handschriften." *Beiträge zur rom. Phil.
Festgabe für Gustav Gröber.* Halle a. S., 1899, pp. 39-118.
Waitz "Nach"   Waitz, Hugo. "Nachtrag zu den in der 'Fest-
gabe für Gustav Gröber' herausgegebenen Liedern von Gille-
bert de Berneville." *Zeit. für rom. Phil.* 24 (1900), 310-
318.
Wallensköld *Conon 1*   Wallensköld, Axel. *Chansons de Conon
de Béthune.* Diss. Helsinki 1891. Helsinki: Imprimerie
Central de Helsingfors, 1891.
Wallensköld *Conon 2*   Wallensköld, Axel. *Les Chansons de
Conon de Béthune.* CFMA. Paris: Champion, 1921.
Wallensköld *Thib*   Wallensköld, Axel. *Les Chansons de
Thibaut de Champagne, roi de Navarre.* SATF. Paris:
Champion, 1925.
Wentzlaff-Eggebert   Wentzlaff-Eggebert, Friedrich-Wilhelm.
Kreuzzugsdichtung des Mittelalters. Berlin: De Gruyter,
1960.
Wiese   Wiese, Leo. *Die Lieder des Blondel de Nesle.*
Gesellschaft für rom. Lit., 5. Dresden, 1904.
Wilkins   Wilkins, Nigel. *The Lyric Works of Adam de la
Hale.* Corpus Mensurabilibis Musicae, 44. [Dallas:] Amer-
ican Institute of Musicology, 1967.
Winkler   Winkler, Emil. *Die Lieder Raouls von Soissons.*
Halle a. S.: Niemeyer, 1914.
Wolf   Wolf, Alois. *Variation und Integration. Beobach-
tungen zu hochmittelalterlichen Tageliedern.* Impulse der
Forschung, 29. Darmstadt: Wissenschaftliche Buchgesell-
schaft, 1979.

Wolff   Wolff, Hans. *Dichtungen von Matthäus dem Juden und Mattäus von Gent.* Diss. Greifswald 1914.

Woledge *Eos*   Woledge, Brian. "Old Provençal and Old French." *Eos: An Enquiry into the Theme of Lovers' Meetings and Partings at Dawn in Poetry.* Ed. Arthur T. Hatto. The Hague: Mouton, 1965, pp. 344-389.

Woledge *Peng*   Woledge, Brian. *The Penguin Book of French Verse.* Vol. I: To the Fifteenth Century. Hammondsworth: Penguin, 1961.

Zai   Zai, Marie-Claire. *Les Chansons courtoises de Chrétien de Troyes.* Publ. Univ. Européennes, 13th ser, 27. Berne: Herbert Lang; Frankfurt: Peter Lang, 1974.

Zarifopol   Zarifopol, P. *Kritischer Text der Lieder Richards de Fournival.* Diss. Halle a. S. 1904. Halle a. S.: Karras, 1904.

Zink *Chans*   Zink, Michel. *Les Chansons de toile.* Paris: Champion, 1978.

Zink *Past*   Zink, Michel. *La Pastourelle. Poésie et folklore au moyen âge.* Paris-Montreal: Bordas, 1972.

Zitzmann   Zitzmann, Rudolf. "Die Lieder des Jacques de Cysoing." *Zeit. für rom. Phil.* 65 (1949), 1-27.

Zumthor *Es*   Zumthor, Paul. *Essai de poétique médiévale.* Paris: Seuil, 1972.

Zumthor *Lang*   Zumthor, Paul. *Langue et techniques poétiques à l'époque romane (XIe-XIIIe siècles).* Paris: Klincksieck, 1963.

Anonymous
Songs

<u>1</u>   I. (Chanson de femme)

RS 1564, MW 417, B 1515
Ms. I 4:6. No music (see note below).

Por coi me bait mes maris?
Laisette!

I   Je ne li de rienz meffis,
      Ne riens ne li ai mesdit
      Fors c'acolleir mon amin   5
            Soulete.
      [Por coi me bait mes maris?
            Laisette!]

II   Et s'il ne mi lait dureir
      Ne bone vie meneir,   10
      Je lou ferai cous clameir
            A certes.
      [Por coi me bait mes maris?
            Laisette!]

III   Or sai bien que je ferai   15
      Et coment m'an vangerai:
      Avec mon amin geirai
            Nüete.
      Por coi me bait mes maris?
            [Laisette!]   20

      MN   The melody is extant only as the tenor of a motet
(No. 16) by Guillaume de Machaut. Form: rf (A) B A rf.
1. Machaut writes c# and adds the following measure after

ll. 2 and 6 , then repeats ll. 1-2 and 5-6,
ending with *d*. Cf. Paris, B.N. fr. 1584, f. 429v; Paris, B.
N. fr. 1586, f. 220v; Paris, B.N. fr. 9221, f. 137v; Paris,
B.N. 22546, f. 117v; Paris, Ms. Vogüé, f. 275v.   2. Machaut
replaces l. 4 by a repetition of l. 3.

RR   I   3 Je ne li ai rienz meffait *(em. sugg. by
Bartsch)*   7 s'il] cil

E   Bartsch, 20-21; Gennrich *Ron* 1, 102-103; 2, 104-
109; Pauphilet, 864-865; Gennrich *Alt Lied* 1, 54-55; Gennrich *Ex*, 35-36; Chastel, 774-775; Toja, 129-131; Mary 1,
298-299; Bec 2, 166-167.

DF   Lorraine, including *ai* for *a*, as in *bait* (1),
laisette (2); *ei* for tonic *e*, as in *acolleir* (5), *dureir*
(9); *amin* (5) for *ami*; *lou* (11) for *le*.

N   This poem occurs among the texts identified in ms.
I as "pastorelles". The poem is found again in a later context: it occurs as the Tenor in Guillaume de Machaut's motet
"Lasse, comment oublieray" and is there accompanied by music. For a textual analysis, see Zumthor *Lang*, pp. 138-139.

II. (Chanson de femme)   2

RS 386, MW 410, B 193
Ms. I 4:13. No music.

       Au cuer les ai, les jolis malz.
          Coment an guariroie?

   I   Kant li vilains vait a marchiet,
        Il n'i vait pais por berguignier,
        Mais por sa feme a esgaitier   5
           Que nuns ne li forvoie.
        Au cuer les ai, les jolis malz.
          Coment en guariroie?

   II   Vilains, car vos traites an lai,
        Car vostre alainne m'ocidrait.   10
        Bien sai c'ancor departirait
           Vostre amor et la moie.
        [Dieus,] j'ai a cuer [les jolis malz.
          Coment en guariroie?]

III   Vilains, cuidiez vos tout avoir,   15
       Et belle dame et grant avoir?
       Vos avereiz lai hairt on col,
       Et mes amins lai joie.
       Dieus, j'ai a cuer [les jolis malz.
       Coment en guariroie?]   20

     RR   III   15 O vilains *(+1)*

     E   Bartsch, 21; Gennrich *Ron* 1, 104; 2, 109; Bec 2,
169-170.

     DF   Lorraine, including *a* (13) for *au*; *ai* for *a*, as
in *pais* (4), adverb *lai* (9), article *lai* (17), *hairt* (17);
nuns (6) for *nus* and *amins* (18) for *amis*; preservation of
final *t*, as in *vait* (3), *marchiet* (3); 3rd-pers. sing. fut.
in *-ait*, as in *ocidrait* (10), *departirait* (11).

     N   6 Understand direct object *la* before indirect *li*.
9 *traites*, 2nd-pers. plur. imp; cf. *faites*, *dites*.   17
avereiz = *avrez*; *on*, like *ou*, is a contracted form of *en le*.

3   III. (Chanson de femme)

RS 59a (= 983), MW 502, B 469
Ms. I 5:91. No music.

     Deduxans suis et joliette, s'amerai.

I   Ier matin me levai droit au point dou jour,
      On vergier mon peire antrai ki iert plains de
                                              [flours;
      Mon amin plus de cent fois i souhaidai.   4
      [Deduxans suis et joliette, s'amerai.]

II   J'amerai mon amin, ke proiét m'an ait;
      Il est biaus et cortois, bien deservit l'ait;
      Mon fin cuer mal greit peire et meire li
                                              [donrai. 8
      [Deduxans suis et joliette, s'amerai.]

III   Chanson, je t'anvoi a toz fins loialz amans,
      Qu'il se gaircent bien des felz mavais
                                              [mesdisans,

Car j'ain tant bien sai ke covrir ne m'an
[porai. 12
[Deduxans suis et joliette, s'amerai.]

RR   III   11 se] ce

E   Stengel, 103; Gennrich *Ron* 1, 185-186; 2, 129; Bec
2, 166.

DF   Lorraine, including *ai* for *a*, as in *gaircent*
(11); *ei* for tonic *e*, as in *peire* (3), *greit* (8); *amin* (4)
for *ami*; preservation of final *t*, as in *proïet* (6), *deservit*
(7), *greit* (8); 3rd-pers. sing. pres. ind. *ait* (6, 7) for *a*.

N   The meter of this poem is highly irregular, most
lines containing twelve syllables, but as many as four containing eleven; the caesura, moreover, is variable, occurring after as few as five syllables and as many as eight. No
underlying pattern is clear enough to warrant correction of
the deviant verses, and no melody exists which could help
validate such emendation. Nor is it by any means certain
that metrical irregularity is not an inherent feature of the
composition. Attempts at regularization are to be found in
Jeanroy *Or* and in Gennrich *Ron*, but they must be regarded as
arbitrary.
    11 *gaircent*, present subjunctive of *garir* 'to pro-
tect'.

IV. (Chanson de rencontre)   <u>4</u>

RS 1184, MW 1859, B 1353 (one other source)
Ms. I 5:16. No music.

Ne mi bateis mie,
Maleüroz maris,
Vos ne m'aveis pas norrie!

I   L'autrier par une anjornee
Chivachoie mon chamin;   5
Novelette mariee
Trovai leis un gal foilli,
Batue de son mari,
Si en ot lou cuer doulant
Et por ceu aloit dixant   10
Cest motet par anradie:
[Ne mi bateis mie,

Maleüroz maris,
Vos ne m'aveis pas norrie!]

II   Elle dist: "Vilains, donee   15
Suix a vous, se poice mi;
Mais par la virge honoree,
Pués ke me destraigniés ci,
Je ferai novel ami,
A cui qui voist anuant;   20
Moi et li irons juant,
Si doublerait la folie."
[Ne mi bateis mie,
Maleüroz maris,
Vos ne m'aveis pas norrie!]   25

III   Li vilains, cui pas n'agree
La ranponne, si li dit:
"Pace avant"; grande pamee
Li donait, pués la saixit
Par la main et se li dit: 30
"Or rancomance ton chant,
Et Deus me dont dolor grant
Se je bien ne te chastie!"
Ne me [bateis mie,
Maleüroz maris,   35
Vos ne m'aveis pas norrie]!

RR   R   1 mies   III   26 cu   33 Ce

E   Stengel, 110; Bartsch, 46; Gennrich *Ron* 1, 116–117; 2, 111.

DF   Lorraine, including *ei* for tonic *e*, as in *bateis* (1), *leis* (7); *c* for *s(s)*, as in *poice* (16), *pace* (28), *ce* (33 RR); *lou* (9) for *le*; *ceu* (10) for *ce*; *se* (30) for *si*; 3rd-pers. sing. pret. in *-ait*, as in *donait* (29); 3rd-pers. sing. fut. in *-ait*, as in *doublerait* (22).

N   5 Note that *chamin* [-î(n)] rhymes with *foilli* and *mari.* 16 *se* = *si*? *ce*? See DF above. 18 *ci* = *si*? See DF above. 20 *qui* = *que*? *cui*? or, less likely, *qu'i*, as in Gennrich *Ron*? *anuant* = *ennuiant.* 26 The ms. reading *cu* is interpreted in Gennrich *Ron* as *c[e]u* (= *ce*). Apart from the slight syntactic awkwardness created by such an emendation, the change fails to take into account the other instances of omission of *i* in vocalic digraphs which are found

in this poem as well as elsewhere in ms. I; cf. 1. 20 *anuant*
and 1. 32 *dont*.

V. (Chanson pieuse, chanson de femme)   5

RS 1646, MW 311, B 1223
Ms. i 253r. Music.

Li debonnaires Dieus m'a mis en sa prison.

I   Vous ne savez que me fist
          Jhesucrist, li miens amis,
          Qu[ant] jacobine me fist
                   Par grant amours.   5
     Li debonnaires [Dieus m'a mis en sa prison].

II   Il m'a si navré d'un dart,
          M[ais que] la plaie n'i pert.
          Ja nul jour n'[en] guariré
                   Se par li non.   10
     Li debonn[aires Dieus m'a mis en sa prison].

III   Dieus, son dart qui m'a navré,
          Comme il est dous et souefz!
          N[uit] et jour mi fait penser
                   Con Dieus [est] douz.   15
     Li debonnaires [Dieus m'a mis en sa prison].

IV   Quant regart par paradis,
          Dont [li] rois est mes amis,
          De larmes [et] de soupirs
                   Mes cuers font to[us].   20
     Li debonnaires [Dieus m'a mis en sa prison].

IV   Se je souvent plouroie
          Et tre[s] bien Dieu amoie,
          Il me donr[oit] sa joie,
              Autrement non.   25
    Li debo[nnaires Dieus m'a mis en sa prison].

V   Quant je pense a Marie,
          Qui fu [de] nete vie,
          J'ai une jalousie
              Que [...] bon.   30
    Li debonn[aires Dieus m'a mis en sa prison].

VI   Prions [a] la pucele,
          Qui fu saint[e et] honneste,
          Qu'en paradis nous [mete]:
              C'est mout biau don.   35
    Li debonn[aires Dieus m'a mis en sa prison].

MN   Form: through-composed + rf.
1. The small notes indicate the rhythm of stanzas 5-7.

RR   With the exception of refrain lines and of l. 32,
brackets indicate conjectures necessitated by mutilation of
the manuscript.
II   7   nauree *(+1)*   VII   32 P. la p. *(-1)*

E   Bartsch "Lieder", 581-582; Jeanroy *Or*, 483-484;
Järnström-Långfors 2, 189-191.

N   This is one of a number of *chanson pieuses* composed in imitation of secular songs.   "Elle a été composée,
. . . ainsi que l'indique le v. 3 (*Quant jacobine me fist*),
pour une confrérie féminine affiliée à l'Ordre de saint
Dominique, auquel appartenait le compilateur du manuscrit i"
(Järnström-Långfors 2, pp. 30-31).   The refrain seems to
have been inspired by the secular *Sa bochete vermoillete m'a
mis an prixon* (B 1641).
    The homophony is crude, and the meter somewhat proble-
matic.   In both Jeanroy *Or* and Järnström-Långfors, it is
noted that the long verses of the last three stanzas contain
six syllables each rather than seven, as in stanzas 1-4.
What remains to be added, however, is that the same "six"-
syllable lines are also the only feminine verses in the
poem.   At least from a textual point of view, it appears,
then, that there is no difference in syllable-count: one
need only regard final *-e* as constituting a seventh syllable.

The conjectured readings provided above in brackets are
largely the same as those found in earlier editions.   For
l. 30, no conjecture has been offered; for l. 32, Jeanroy
offers [Or] *prions la pucele*, while no additional syllable
is suggested in Järnström-Långfors.

VI. (Chanson pieuse, chanson de femme)   <u>6</u>

RS 747, MW 78, B 123 (one other source)
Ms. i 264r-v. Music.

Amis, amis,
Trop me laissie[z en]´ estrange païs.

I   L'ame qui quiert Dieu de [veraie en]tente
      Souvent se plaint [et] forment se demente
      Et [s]on ami, cui venue est trop len[te],   5
      Va regretant que ne li atalente.
            Amis, amis,
      [Trop me laissiez en estrange païs].

II   [T]rop me laissiez [ci] vous longue [m]ent
                                              [querre.
        En [ci]el regnés et en [m]er et en terre;   10
        [E]nclose sui en cest cors qui me serre,
        [D]e ceste char qui souvent me fait guerre.
                [A]mis, amis,
        [Trop me laissiez en estrange païs].   14

III   [D]ieus, donnez moy ce que mes cuers desirre,
        [P]our cui languis, pour cui sui a martire.
        [J]hesucrist est mes amis et mon sire,
        [L]i biaus, li bons, plus que nul ne scet
                                              [dire.
                [A]mis, amis,
        [Trop me laissiez en estrange païs].   20

IV   [M]on createur, quar je sui sa faiture,
        [Q]ui me nourrit et de tout me procure,
        [M]es amis est, quar en moy mist tel cure
        [Que] par amour se joint a ma nature.   25
                [A]mis, amis,
        [Trop me laissiez en estrange païs].

V   [I]l m'apela ains que je l'apelasse,
        [S]i me requist ainz qu'aprez lui alasse.
        [O]r est bien drois qu'en lui querre me lasse
        [S]i que cest mont pour lui trouver   30
                                              [trespasse.
                [A]mis, amis,
        [Trop me laissiez en estrange païs].

VI   [E]t quant j'avray passé ceste bruïne
        [O]u li jour faut et le vespre decline,
        [Ci]lz qui les cuers alume et enlumine   35
        [Se] moustrera; lors avray joie fine.
                [A]mis, amis,
        [Trop me laissiez en estrange païs].

        MN   Form: rf a a B (rf) (ballade).
1. In l. 2, this figure is missing. 2. In l. 1 the next
two notes are missing.

        RR   With the exception of ll. 8, 14, 20, 26, 32, and
38, paired brackets indicate conjectures necessitated by
mutilation of the manuscript.

E   Bartsch "Lieder", 582-584; Jeanroy *Or*, 480-481;
Järnström-Långfors 2, 195-197; Bec 2, 66-67.

N   This is one of a number of *chansons pieuses* composed in imitation of secular songs. In this case, the secular model is most evident in the typically feminine refrain. Cf. RS 1646.
    3 The conjectured reading given here, as in Järnström-
Långfors, differs from that proposed in Jeanroy *Or: de
[toute s'en]tente*.   24 Perhaps meant to be heard behind
the obvious abstract sense of *nature* is the word's concrete
sexual sense.

CHANSONS DE TOILE

<u>7</u>   I

RS 2037, MW 43, B 869
Ms. U 69v-70r. No music.

I   Quant vient en mai que l'on dit as lons jors,
      Que Franc de France repairent de roi cort,
      Reynauz repaire devant el premier front;
      Si s'en passa lez lo meis Arembor,
      Ainz n'en dengna le chief drecier amont.   5
              E Raynaut, amis!

II   Bele Erembors a la fenestre au jor
      Sor ses genolz tient paile de color,
      Voit Frans de France qui repairent de cort
      Et voit Raynaut devant el premier front.   10
      En haut parole, si a dit sa raison:
              E Raynauz, amis!

III   "Amis Raynauz, j'ai ja veü cel jor
      Se passisoiz selon mon pere tor,
      Dolanz fussiez se ne parlasse a vos."   15
      "Ja.l mesfaïstes, fille d'empereor;
      Autrui amastes, si obliastes nos."
              E Raynauz, amis!

IV   "Sire Raynauz, je m'en escondirai;
      A cent puceles sor sainz vos jurerai,   20
      A trente dames que avuec moi menrai,
      C'onques nul home fors vostre cors n'amai.
      Prennez l'emmende et je vos baiserai."
              E Raynauz, amis!

V   Li cuens Raynauz en monta lo degré,   25
      Gros par espaules, greles par lo baudré;
      Blonde ot lo poil, menu recercelé.
      En nule terre n'ot si biau bacheler.
      Voit l' Erembors, si comence a plorer.
              E Raynauz, amis!   30

VI   Li cuens Raynauz est montez en la tor,
      Si s'est assis en un lit point a flors;
      Dejoste lui se siet bele Erembors.
      Lors recomencent lor premieres amors.
              E Raynauz, amis!   35

<u>RR</u>   II   10   Raynaut] R. *here and in all following
occurrences*   12   Raynauz] R. *here and in all following occurrences*   IV   16   Iel   VI   *one verse missing somewhere in this stanza*   34   recomence

<u>E</u>   P. Paris, 49; Leroux de Lincy, 15-18; Bartsch, 3-
4; Meyer, 365; Crépet, 42-45; Bartsch-Wiese, 45-46; Voretzsch, 72-73; Pauphilet, 825-826; Spaziani *Ant*, 23-24;
Cremonesi, 39-40; Saba, 68-69; Woledge *Peng*, 83-84; Toja,
120-122; Henry *Chrest* 1, 228-229; 2, 68; Bec 2, 35-37; Zink
Chans, 93-95; Aspland, 149-151.

<u>DF</u>   Lorraine: *meis* (4) for *mes*; article *lo* (4) for
le.

<u>N</u>   2 *Franc de France*, borrowed from epic poetry, de-
notes the Franks of the limited territory of Carolingian
France in contrast to those from the rest of the empire; it
is no doubt to be understood as connoting special distinction.   2 The phrase *roi cort* appears to be the only example in OF of a preposed genitive complement taking the
form of a non-proper noun and not introduced by a deter-
miner: one would expect *le* (or *la*) *roi cort*; cf. *mon pere
tor* in 1. 14.   Adolf Tobler (*Mélanges de grammaire française*, trans. Kuttner and Sudre [Paris, 1905], pp. 89-90)
suggests that *roi*, designating in a given society a unique
figure, may need no more determination than *Dieu*.   Faral, p.
452, sees the construction as a pseudo-archaism lending some
support to his contention that the *chansons de toile* are not
the early, popular compositions that they have traditionally
been judged to be.   It may be, however, that the grammatical
or stylistic problem of *roi cort* is an illusion.   On the one
hand, it is normal for the contraction of *de* and *le* to appear in ms. U as *del* (like *al* from *a* + *le*); on the other
hand, it is not uncommon to find scribal distraction result-
ing in unfinished words.   The phrase *de roi cort*, then, may
be nothing more than the copyist's error for *del roi cort*.
For more on the dating of the genre in general and RS 2037
in particular, see Maria Simonelli, "Due note rudelliane,"
Cultura Neolatina 25 (1965), 113-127.
   11 *parole = elle parle*.   13 Understand *que* (= *où*)
after *jor*.   16 The unusual expression *le mesfaire* 'to do
wrong, be guilty of a misdeed' is discussed in A. Henry,
"Ancien français *le mesfaire*," *Romania* 75 (1954), 389-390.
27 Etymologically feminine, *blonde* is well attested as a
masc. alternative to *blont*.   34 Cremonesi retains the ms.
reading *recomence* and emends *premieres*, *amors* being either

singular or plural, to the singular *premiere*. The unelided
-e which this change introduces into the verse is not at all
unusual in OF poetry; see, for example, l. 21 *que avuec*.

31-34 It is generally believed that one verse is missing somewhere in this stanza, although an argument might be
advanced--inspired by Paul Zumthor, "La chanson de Bele Aig-
lentine," *Travaux de Linguistique et de Littérature* [Stras-
bourg] 8 (1970), 325-337--that stanzaic length need not be
uniform in the *chansons de toile* and that the present stanza
is complete as it stands. Voretzsch, in his edition of the
text, inserted between l. 31 and l. 32 a conjectural verse
furnished by H. Suchier: *Plorant la vit, dont l'en prist
grant tendror.*

<u>8</u>   II

RS 143, MW 302, B 1830
Ms. U 146r-v. No music.

I   Lou samedi a soir fat la semainne;
       Gaiete et Oriour, serors germainnes,
       Main et main vont bagnier a la fontainne.
            Vante l'ore et la rainme crollet;
            Ki s'antrainment soweif dorment.   5

II   L'anfes Gerairs revient de la cuitainne,
       S'ait chosit Gaiete sor la fontainne;
       Antre ses bras l'ait pris, soueif l'a
                                        [strainte.
            Vante l'ore et la rainme crollet;
            Ki s'antrainment soueif dorment.   10

III   "Qant avras, Orriour, de l'ague prise,
       Reva toi an arriere, bien seis la ville;
       Je remainra Gerairt, ke bien me priset."
            Vante l'ore et la rainme crollet;
            Ki s'antrainment soweif dorment.   15

IV   Or s'an vat Orious, stinte et marrie;
       Des euls s'an vat plorant, de cuer sospire,
       Cant Gaie sa seror n'anmoinnet mie.
            Vante l'ore et la rainme crollet;
            Ki s'antrainment soweif dorment.   20

V   "Laise," fait Oriour, "com mar fui nee!
       J'a laxiét ma serour an la vallee,

L'anfes Gerairs l'anmoine an sa contree."
Vante l'ore et la rainme crollet;
    Ki s'antrainment soweif dorment.   25

VI   L'anfes Gerairs et Gaie s'an sont torneit,
     Lor droit chemin ont pris vers sa citeit;
     Tantost com il i vint, l'ait espouseit.
     Vante l'ore et la rainme crollet;
         Ki [s'antrainment soweif dorment].   30

RR   I   2 germainne   4 li r.   5 santrainmet so-
weit   II   *Stanza occurs after final refrain and is fol-*
lowed by cist dairiens vers doit aleir apres lou premier   7
Gaiete] orior   8 ses] ces   10 santrainme   III   11
aures   15 santrainme   IV   18 gaiete sa suer *(em.*
Bartsch)   19 li r.   20 santrainmet   V   25 santrainmet

E   Leroux de Lincy, XLII; Dinaux 4, 315-316; Bartsch,
8; Crépet, 46-48; Paris-Langlois, 278-280; Bartsch-Wiese,
46; Brittain, 115-116; Pauphilet, 827-828; Cremonesi, 44-45;
Saba, 72-73; Chastel, 400-403; Toja, 126-128; Mary 1, 92-93;
Bec 2, 43-44; Zink *Chans*, 100-101.

DF   Lorraine, including *a* for *au*, as in *a* (1) and *fat*
(1); *ai* for *a*, as in *Gerairs* (6) and *laise* (21); preservation of final *t*, as in *crollet* (4), *chosit* (7), *vat* (16),
laxiét (22), *torneit* (26); pres. ind. *ait* (7) for *a*; *ei* for
tonic *e*, as in *soweif* (5), *torneit* (26), *citeit* (27); 1st-
pers. sing. forms with *-a* for *-ai*, as in *remainra* (13) and
j'a (22); absence of prothesis in *strainte* (8) and *stinte*
(16); article *lou* (1) for *le*.

N   The treatment of the decasyllabic line here is
unusual, in that the caesura occurs at the sixth syllable
instead of the fourth.
4 Here and in the repetitions of the refrain, Bartsch
emends to *li raim crollent*.   7 It is very likely that the
verse should begin with unelided *Se* (= Francien *si*), in
which case the *césure lyrique* would give way to a *césure*
épique, considerably more common in the *chansons de toile*.
Other occurrences of the *césure épique*: ll. 12, 26 (and
prise in l. 8?).   13 'I shall remain Gerart's, with Gerart'.
     For an interesting recent discussion of this poem,
partly in relation to Apollinaire's "Le pont Mirabeau," see
J. Batany, *Français médiéval* (Paris-Montreal: Bordas, 1972),

113-123. See, too, Joly, p. 58; Zink *Chans*, pp. 98-99; Paul
Pieltain, "Une chanson médiévale," *Cahiers d'Analyse Tex-
tuelle* 6 (1964), 23-31; and Alice Planche, "Gaiete, Oriour
et le copiste distrait," *Cahiers de Civilisation Médiévale*
20:1 (1977), 49-52.

<u>9</u>   I I I

RS 594, MW 77, B 18
Ms. U 65v-66r. Stanza I also in Henri d'Andeli, *Le Lai
    d'Aristote*, ed. M. Delbouille (Paris, 1951), p. 81.
    Music in U.

I   En un vergier lez une fontenele
        Dont clere est l'onde et blanche la gravele
        Siet fille a roi, sa main a sa maxele;
        En sospirant, son douz ami rapele:
            Aé, cuens Guis, amis!   5
        La vostre amors me tout solaz et ris.

II   "Cuens Guis, amis, com male destineie!
        Mes pere m'a a un viellart donee
        Qui en cest meis m'a mise et enserree,
        N'en puis eissir a soir n'a matinee."   10
            Aé, cuens Guis, amis!
        La [vostre amors me tout solaz et ris].

III   Li mals mariz en oï la deplainte,
        Entre el vergier, sa corroie a desceinte;
        Tant l'a bati q'ele en fu perse et tainte,   15

Entre ses piez por pou ne l'a estainte.
Aé, cuens Guis, amis!
[La vostre amors me tout solaz et ris].

IV   Li mals mariz, quant il l'ot laidangie,
Il s'en repent, car il ot fait folie,   20
Car il fu ja de son pere maisnie;
Bien seit q'ele est fille a roi, koi qu'il
                                                    [die.
Aé, cuens Guiz, amis!
[La vostre amors me tout solaz et ris].

V   La bele s'est de pameson levee,   25
Deu reclama par veraie penseie:
"Donez moi, sire, que ne soie obliee,
Ke mes amis revengne ainz la vespree."
Aé, cuens Guiz, amis!
[La vostre amors me tout solaz et ris].   30

VI   Et nostre sires l'a molt bien escoutee:
Ez son ami, qui l'a reconfortee;
Assis se sont soz une ante ramee,
La ot d'amors mainte larme ploree.
Aé, cuens Guiz, amis!   35
[La vostre amors me tout solaz et ris].

<u>MN</u>   Form: a a a b rf (ballade?).
1. In 1. 2 ms. repeats this note as though *l'onde* were unelided.

<u>RR</u>   II   9   enserre   V   26 *followed by the appar-*
ently spurious line bels sire douz ia mauez uos formee   27
oblie

<u>E</u>   P. Paris, 37; Bartsch, 13; Gennrich *Rot*, 22-24;
Gennrich *Alt Lied* 1, 36-37; Saba, 60-62; Gennrich *Ex*, 12-13;
Toja, 114-116; Mary 1, 96-97; Bec 2, 41-42; Zink *Chans*, 85-
88.

<u>DF</u>   Lorraine: *ei* for tonic *e* in *destineie* (7), *meis*
(9), and *penseie* (26); *ie* for *iee* in *laidangie* (19) and
maisnie (21).

<u>N</u>   For discussion of *chansons de toile* and of this
text in particular, see Payen, pp. 262-269.

10   IV

RS 1352, MW 61, B 716 (one other source)
Ms. U 66r-v. Music.

I   Bele Doette as fenestres se siet,
       Lit en un livre mais au cuer ne l'en tient;
       De son ami Doon li resovient
       Q'en autres terres est alez tornoier.
                    E or en ai dol!   5

II   Uns escuiers as degrez de la sale
       Est dessenduz, s'est destrossé sa male.
       Bele Doette les degrez en avale,
       Ne cuide pas oïr novele male.
                    E or en ai dol!   10

III   Bele Doette tantost li demanda:
       "Ou est mes sires, que ne vi tel pieç'a?"
       Cil ot tel duel que de pitié plora;
       Bele Doette maintenant se pasma.
                    E [or en ai dol]!   15

IV   Bele Doette s'est en estant drecie;
       Voit l'escuier, vers lui s'est adrecie;
       En son cuer est dolante et correcie
       Por son seignor dont ele ne voit mie.
                    E [or en ai dol]!   20

V   Bele Doette li prist a demander:
       "Ou est mes sires cui je doi tant amer?"
       "En non Deu, dame, ne.l vos quier mais celer:
       Morz est mes sires, ocis fu au joster."
                    E or [en ai dol]!   25

VI   Bele Doette a pris son duel a faire:
      "Tant mar i fustes, cuens Do, frans
                            [debonaire,
      Por vostre amor vestirai je la haire,
      Ne sor mon cors n'avra pelice vaire.
          E or en ai dol!   30

VII   "Por vos ferai une abbaïe tele,
      Qant iert li jors que la feste iert nomeie,
      Se nus i vient qui ait s'amor fauseie,
      Ja del mostier ne savera l'entreie."
          E or en ai dol!   35

VIII Bele [Doette] prist s'abaiie a faire,
      Qui mout est grande et adés sera maire;
      Toz cels et celes vodra dedanz atraire
      Qui por amor sevent peine et mal traire.
          E or en ai dol!   40

MN   Form: A A rf.
1. In l. 4 ms. writes *c'*. 2. The melody below for the second refrain, which follows stanzas 6-8, is conjectural, derived from line 4 + rf; after stanzas 6 and 7 the first
line of the refrain reads: *Por vos devenrai nonne.*

RR   VI   30 *followed by* por uos deuenrai nonne en
leglyse saint poul   VII   35 *followed by* por uos deuenrai
nonne a leglise saint poul   VIII   36 *-3* 40 *followed
by* por uostre amor deuenrai nonne a leglise saint poul

E   P. Paris, 46; Bartsch, 5-6; Gennrich *Rot*, 18-20;
Brittain, 116-117; Cremonesi, 41-42; Saba, 66-67; Gennrich
Ex, 8-9; Groult 1, 167-168; Toja, 118-120; Maillard *Anth*,
74-77; Mary 1, 92-95; Zink *Chans*, 89-92.

DF   Lorraine: *ei* for tonic *e* in *nomeie* (32), *fauseie*
(33), *entreie* (34); *ie* for *iee* in *drecie* (16), *adrecie* (17),
correcie (18).

N   For recent discussion of the age of this song, see
Joly, pp. 61-63. 4 *Q'* (= *que*) is probably better inter-

preted as a nominative relative pronoun than as a completive
conjunction.   7 *s'est = s'ait*, Lorraine for *si a* 'and he
has'.   31 *Que*, correlative of *tele*, is understood.

11   V

RS 1847, MW 74, B 571
Ms. U 64v–65r. Music.

I   Bele Yolanz en ses chambres seoit;
        D'un boen samiz une robe cosoit;
        A son ami tramettre la voloit.
        En sospirant, ceste chançon chantoit:
                Deus, tant est douz li nons d'amors,   5
                Ja n'en cuidai sentir dolors.

II   "Bels douz amis, or vos voil envoier
        Une robe par mout grant amistié.
        Por Deu vos [pri], de moi aiez pitié."
        Ne pot ester; a la terre s'assiet.   10
                Deus, tant est douz li nons d'amors,
                [Ja n'en cuidai sentir dolors].

III   A ces paroles et a ceste raison
        Li siens amis entra en la maison.
        Cele lo vit, si bassa lo menton;   15

Ne pot parler, ne li dist o ne non.
Deus, tant est douz li nons d'amors,
[Ja n'en cuidai sentir dolors].

IV　"Ma douce dame, mis m'avez en obli."
Cele l'entent, se li geta un ris;　　　　　　　20
En sospirant, ses bels braz li tendi;
Tant doucement a acoler l'a pris.
Deus, tant est douz li nons d'amors,
[Ja n'en cuidai sentir dolors].

V　"Bels douz amis, ne vos sai losengier,　　　25
Mais de fin cuer vos aim et senz trechier.
Qant vos plaira, si me porrez baisier;
Entre voz braz me voil aler couchier."
Deus, tant est douz li nons d'amors,
[Ja n'en cuidai sentir dolors].　　　　　30

VI　Li siens amis entre ses braz la prent;
En un biau lit s'asīent seulement.
Bele Yolanz lo baise estroitement;
A tor françois en mi lo lit l'estent.
Deus, tant est douz li nons d'amors,　　　35
Ja n'en cuidai sentir dolors.

<u>MN</u>　Form: a a B rf (ballade).
1. In 1. 2 ms. omits this note.

<u>RR</u>　II　9　*-1*

<u>E</u>　P. Paris, 39; Bartsch, 10; Gennrich *Alt Lied* 1,
37-39; Saba, 62-63; Gennrich *Ex*, 9-10; Toja, 116-118; Zink
Chans, 76-79.

<u>DF</u>　Lorraine: *boen* (2) for *bon*; *se* (·20) for *si*; *lo*
(33, 34) for *le*; perhaps *a* (34) for *au*.

<u>N</u>　8 *Césure lyrique*, rather uncommon in the *chansons
de toile*. Cf. *césure epique* in ll. 13 and 19.　32 *Au tour
françois* is a well-attested term for some riding maneuver
the exact nature of which is unclear; its metaphoric value
here awaits clarification. The grammatically unspecified
subject and the epicene direct object (*l'*) of *estent* lend
further obscurity to the verse.

<u>12</u>   VI

RS 1710, MW 62, B 351
Ms. U 70r-v. No music.

    I   Bele Yolanz en chambre koie
          Sor ses genouz pailes desploie;
          Cost un fil d'or, l'autre de soie.
          Sa male mere la chastoie:
          Chastoi vos en, bele Yolanz.   5

    II   "Bele Yolanz, je vos chastoi;
          Ma fille estes, faire lo doi."
          "Ma dame mere, et vos de coi?"
          "Je vos dirai, par ma foi."
          Chastoi vos en, bele Yolanz.   10

    III   "Mere, de coi me chastoiez?
          Est ceu de coudre ou de taillier
          Ou de filer ou de broissier?
          Ou se c'est de trop somillier?"
          Chastoi vos en, b[ele Yolanz].   15

    IV   "Ne de coudre ne de taillier
          Ne de filer ne de broissier,
          Ne ceu n'est de trop somillier,
          Mais trop parlez au chevalier."
          Chastoi vos en, [bele Yolanz].   20

    V   "Trop parlez au conte Mahi,
          Si en poise vostre mari;
          Dolanz en est, je.l vos affi;
          Ne.l faites mais, je vos en pri."
          Chastoi vos en, [bele Yolanz].   25

    VI   "Se mes mariz l'avoit juré,
          Et il et toz ses parentez,
          Mais que bien li doie peser,
          Ne lairai je oan l'amer."
          Covegne t'en, bele Yolanz.   30

    <u>E</u>   P. Paris, 53; Bartsch, 9; Pauphilet, 826-827; Cre-
monesī, 46-47; Saba, 69-70; Toja, 122-124; Zink *Chans*, 96-
97.

N   3 *Cost* 'she sews' appears in Bartsch and Saba as
co'st (= *c'est*).   31 *Covegne t'en* 'do as you like, or
'much good may it bring you' appears in P. Paris as *Sovegne
t'en* and in B as *Çovegne t'en* 'remember it'. The latter interpretation is apparently based on the well-known confusion
of *s* and *c* in the work of Lorraine scribes, but it seems
poorly motivated in this text, which, unlike various others
in ms. U, is relatively free of Lorraine features.

VII   <u>13</u>

RS 586, MW 306, B 792
Ms. U 145v. No music.

I   An halte tour se siet belle Yzabel;
       Son bial chief blonc mist fuers per un
                                            [crenel;
       De larmes moillent li lais de son mantel.
                    E, amins!
       Por medissans seus fors de mon païs.   5

II   "Laise!" fait elle, "or mi vat malemant.
       Livree seus a une estrainge gent;
       De mes amins nus secors nen atant."
                    E, amins!
       Por medissans seus fors de mon païs.   10

III   "Laise!" fait elle, "com si ait grant dolour!
       On m'apeleivet fille d'anpareor,
       Et on ait fait d'un vilain mon signor."
                    E, amins!
       [Por medissans seus fors de mon païs.]   15

IV   Sa damoselle davant li vient esteir.
       "La moie dame, c'avés ke si ploreis?"
       "C'est a boen droit." "Ne degniez [vos]
                                            [ameir?"
                    E, amins!
       [Por medissans seus fors de mon païs.]   20

V   "Se je savoie un cortois chivelier
       Ke de ses armes fust loeiz et prisiez,
       Je l'ameroie de greit et volentiers."
                    E, amins!
       [Por medissans seus fors de mon païs].   25

VI   "La moie dame, je sai un chivelier
       Ke de ses armes est loeiz et prisiez;
       Amerait vos, cui c'an poist ne cui griet."
            E, amins!
       Por medissans seus fors de mon païs.   30

       RR   II   6 *preceded by supernumerary verse* Elle se
plaint la belle an sospirant   IV   17   si] ci   18 *-1*
V   22   ses] ces   VI   27   ses] ces

       E   P. Paris, 70; Leroux de Lincy, XLVI; Bartsch, 7;
Cremonesi, 43-44; Saba, 71-72; Toja, 124-126; Zink *Chans*,
98-99.

       DF   Lorraine, including *ai* for *a*, as in *lais* (3),
laise (6), *estrainge* (7); *ei* for tonic *e*, as in *esteir* (16),
ploreis (17), *ameir* (18), *loeiz* (22), *greit* (23); *boen* (18)
for *bon*; *amins* (4) for *amis*; nominative relative *ke* (22);
seus (5) for *sui*; pres. ind. *ait* (11) for *a* and fut. *amerait*
(28) for *amera*; impf. ind. in *-e(i)ve-*, as in *apeleivet*
(12).

       N   3 'The laces of her cloak become wet with tears'.

RS 2015, MW 475, B 884
Ms. U 83r-v. Music.

I   Gaite de la tor,
               Gardez entor
          Les murs, se Deus vos voie!
             C'or sont a sejor
               Dame et seignor,   5
          Et larron vont en proie.
          Hu et hu et hu et hu!
               Je l'ai veü
          La jus soz la coudroie.
          Hu et hu et hu et hu!   10
               A bien pres l'ocirroie.

II   D'un douz lai d'amor
               De Blancheflor,
          Compains, vos chanteroie,
             Ne fust la poor   15
               Del traïtor
          Cui je redotteroie.
          Hu et hu [et hu et hu!
               Je l'ai veü
          La jus soz la coudroie.   20
          Hu et hu et hu et hu!
               A bien pres l'ocirroie.]

III   Compainz, en error
            Sui, k'a cest tor
        Volentiers dormiroie.   25
            N'aiez pas paor!
            Voist a loisor
        Qui aler vuet par voie.
    Hu et hu et hu et hu!
            Or soit teü,   30
        Compainz, a ceste voie.
    Hu et hu! Bien ai seü
        Que nos en avrons joie.

IV   Ne sont pas plusor
            Li robeor;   35
        N'i a c'un que je voie,
        Qui gist en la flor
            Soz covertor,
        Cui nomer n'oseroie.
    Hu [et hu et hu et hu!   40
            Or soit teü,
        Compainz, a ceste voie.
    Hu et hu! Bien ai seü
        Que nos en avrons joie.]

V   Cortois ameor   45
            Qui a sejor
        Gisez en chambre coie,
            N'aiez pas freor,
            Que tresq'a jor
        Pöez demener joie.   50
    Hu [et hu et hu et hu!
            Or soit teü,
        Compainz, a ceste voie.
    Hu et hu! Bien ai seü
        Que nos en avrons joie.]   55

VI   Gaite de la tor,
            Vez mon retor
        De la ou vos ooie;
            D'amie et d'amor
            A cestui tor   60
        Ai ceu que plus amoie.
    Hu et hu et hu et hu!
            Pou ai geü
        En la chambre de joie.
    Hu et hu! Trop m'a neü   65
        L'aube qui me guerroie.

> VII   Se salve l'onor
>   Au Criator
>   Estoit, tot tens voudroie
>   Nuit feïst del jor: 70
>   Jamais dolor
>   Ne pesance n'avroie.
>   *Hu et hu et hu et hu!*
>   *Bien ai veü*
>   *De biauté la monjoie.*   75
>   *Hu et hu!   C'est bien seü.*
>   *Gaite, a Deu tote voie.*

<u>MN</u>   Form: A A B.

<u>RR</u>   II   15   poors   III   26   Naient   V   48   pas
paor f.

<u>E</u>   P. Paris, 66; Leroux de Lincy, 139-143; Schläger
Tagelied, 89; Restori, 4-22; Bartsch-Wiese, 167-168; Brittain, 159-161; Cocito, 49-56; Bec "Aube", 17-33; Bec 2, 27-
30; Aspland, 151-154.

<u>N</u>   This song has provoked more interpretative commen-
tary than perhaps any other in Old French, the principal
questions being 1) whether it is essentially a dramatic
work, even meant to be choreographed, or a purely lyric composition, and 2) whose voices are heard in the various stanzas. Since the ms. offers nothing beyond text and music,
speculation has ranged rather broadly. See, among others,
Jeanroy *Or*, p. 79; Restori; Jeanroy's review of the latter
in *Romania* 33 (1904), 615-616; Joseph Bédier, "Les plus an-
ciennes danses françaises," *Revue des Deux Mondes* (janv.-
févr. 1906), 398-424; Woledge *Eos*, pp. 388-389; Becker, pp.
169-173. More recently, Cocito argues that the poem combines a traditional (Provençal) watchman's song and a dawn-
song *strictu sensu*; Bec "Aube" makes use of this notion in a
masterful analysis which affirms the uniquely lyric nature
of the composition. It is Bec's distribution of the stanzas
--as well as his view that the refrains form a lyric entity
independent of the speakers--that we accept as the most persuasive, viz., stanza 1: the lover, stanzas 2-5: the watchman, stanzas 6-7: the lover.
    8 The pronoun *l'*, without antecedent, no doubt desig-
nates the "jaloux," the lady's husband, referred to as *traï-
tor* in l. 16 and explicitly left nameless in l. 39.   13
Blancheflor appears a number of times as the name of the
heroine in medieval romance literature, most notably in

Floire et Blancheflor; see Flutre, p. 30. It is likely that
the name is mentioned here for its generally evocative value
rather than some reason specifically relevant to the context.   23 *error* 'anxiety, apprehension' rather than 'error'.   24 *a cest tor*, understood by Bédier, op. cit., p.
421, as a technical term of the dance and thus considered
evidence for his balletic interpretation of the work, means
no more than 'now, at this point'; similarly, 1. 60 *a cestui
tor*.   61 *ceu = ce*.   69 Understand *que* before *Nuit*.

<u>15</u>   II. (Chanson de femme)

RS 1029, MW 2240, B 892 (one other source)
Ms. I 4:43. No music.

    I   Entre moi et mon amin,
        En un boix k'est leis Betune,
        Alainmes juwant mairdi
        Toute lai nuit a la lune,   4
          Tant k'il ajornait
        Et ke l'alowe chantait
        Ke dit: "Amins, alons an."
        Et il respont doucement: 8
         Il n'est mie jours,
        Saverouze au cors gent;
        Si m'aït Amors,
        L'alowette nos mant.   12

    II   Adont se trait pres de mi,
        Et je ne fu pas anfruine;
        Bien trois fois me baixait il,
        Ausi fix je lui plus d'une,   16
          K'ainz ne m'anoiait.
        Adonc vocexiens nous lai
        Ke celle neut durest sant,
        Mais ke plus n'alest dixant: 20
         Il n'est mie jours,
        [Saverouze au cors gent;
        Si m'aït Amors,
        L'alowette nos mant.]   24

   <u>RR</u>   I   11 Si meut *(em. Bartsch)*   II   13 se] ce
15 Il me b. bien iii fois *(em. Bartsch)*

   <u>E</u>   Bartsch, 27-28; Brittain, 150-151; Woledge *Peng*,
88-89; Woledge *Eos*, 370-371; Bec 2, 25-26.

   DF   Lorraine, including *ai* for *a*, as in *mairdi* (2)
and *lai* (4); *leis* (2) for *les*; *anfruine* (14) for *enfrune*;
amin (1) for *ami*; *neut* (19) for *nuit*; intervocalic *w*, as in
juwant (3); *x* for *s(s)*, as in *vocexiens* (18), *dixant* (20);
confusion of *s* and *c*, as in *vocexiens* (18) and *sant* (19);
3rd-pers. sing. pret. in *-ait*, as in *ajornait* (5), *chantait*
(6); 3rd-pers. sing. impf. subj. in *-est*, as in *durest* (19);
use of relative *ke* (*k'*) for nominative (2, 7).

   N   This poem occurs among the texts identified in ms.
I as "pastorelles". For a commentary, see Próspero Saíz,
*Personae and Poiesis: The Poet and the Poem in Medieval Love
Lyric* (The Hague-Paris: Mouton, 1976); Saville, pp. 148-150;
Wolf, pp. 22-24.   20 *Mais* 'moreover'.

<u>16</u>   I

RS 318, MW 562
Mss. K 314-315, N 150r, X 199r-v. Music in all mss.

I   Volez vous que je vous chant
       Un son d'amors avenant?
            Vilain ne.1 fist mie,
       Ainz le fist un chevalier
       Souz l'onbre d'un olivier   5
            Entre les braz s'amie.

II   Chemisete avoit de lin
       Et blanc peliçon hermin
            Et blīaut de soie,
       Chauces ot de jaglolai   10
       Et sollers de flors de mai,
            Estroitement chauçade.

III   Çainturete avoit de fueille
       Qui verdist quant li tens mueille;
            D'or ert boutonade.   15
       L'aumosniere estoit d'amor;
       Li pendant furent de flor,
            Par amors fu donade.

IV   Si chevauchoit une mule;
       D'argent ert la ferreüre,   20
            La sele ert dorade;

              Seur la crope par derrier
              Avoit planté trois rosiers
                 Por fere li honbrage.

    V   Si s'en vet aval la pree;   25
              Chevaliers l'ont encontree,
                 Biau l'ont saluade:
              "Bele, dont estes vous nee?"
              "De France sui, la löee,
                 Du plus haut parage.   30

    VI   "Li rosignous est mon pere
              Qui chante seur la ramee
                 El plus haut boscage;
              La seraine, ele est ma mere
              Qui chante en la mer salee   35
                 El plus haut rivage."

    VII   "Bele, bon fussiez vous nee,
              Bien estes enparentee
                 Et de haut parage;
              Pleüst a Dieu nostre pere   40
              Que vous me fussiez donee
                 A fame espousade."

    MN   Form: through-composed.

        V   I   3 Ui lains X; ne le N   4 uns cheualiers
X   II   8 dermin X   10 out N, auoit X   11 flor X
III   15 er N   17 furent] erent X   IV   19 Et NX
22 derriers N, deriers X   V   30 dou X   VI   31
rosingnoyr N   34 ma mē N   35 chantee en la m. seraine
X   36 haut *missing N*   VII   37 bien fussies X   40
pere *missing N*   41 donee *missing N*

    E   Bartsch, 23-24; Spanke *Lied*, 26-28, 358-359; Brit-
tain, 155-156; Pauphilet, 863-864; Gennrich *Alt Lied* 1, 49-
51; Gennrich *Ex*, 23-24; Chastel, 404-407; Woledge *Peng*, 119-
121; Maillard *Anth*, 80-81; Mary 1, 292-295; Bec 2, 60-61.

    N   This song of love and spring is one of the most
mysteriously enchanting in Old French. Gaston Paris speaks
of it as "le chef-d'oeuvre de cette poésie printanière,
. . . pleine d'une charmante et bizarre poésie, bien rare
dans notre littérature" (*Mélanges*, p. 555), and such words
have ever since been repeated by other writers.
    Note that the female vision so amply described in

stanzas 2-4 is not identified even by a subject pronoun;
only later is she named, quite simply, *Bele* (28, 37).   The
versification is no less striking than the content itself,
mixing rhyme and assonance, including one case of only approximate homophony (*soie*[9] : *chauçade* [12]), varying the
rhyme scheme, introducing Provençalized participles in *-ade*
into an otherwise purely French text, and changing from
hexasyllabic final lines to pentasyllabic in the last three
stanzas.

For some recent discussion of this song and the genre
to which it belongs, see Tyssens, pp. 589-603; Bec 1, pp.
136-141; and A. Drzewicka, "Fantaisie et originalité dans la
poésie lyrique médiévale: la chanson 'Volez vos que je vos
chant?'," *Kwartalnik Neofilologiczny* 21 (1974), 441-458.

31-36 For an identification of the nightingale and the
serin with ancient Celtic fertility-deities, see Schossig,
esp. p. 139.

17   II

RS 2006, MW 59
Mss. K 410-411, U 152 and 151.   Music in K.

11.Je vi l'o-ri-ou 12. et le ro-si-gnou,
13. si vi le pin-çon 14. et l'es-me-ril-lon,
15. Deus! 16.et tant des au-tres oi-siaus, de quoi je ne sai pas le non,
17. qui sor cel ar-bre s'as-si-strent et com-men-cent lor chan-çon.

I   En avril au tens pascour,
              Que seur l'erbe nest la flor,
              L'alöete au point du jour
              Chante par mult grant baudor.
           Pour la douçour du tens nouvel,   5
           Si me levai par un matin,
           S'oï chanter sor l'arbroisel
            Un oiselet en son latin.
Un petit me sozlevai pour esgarder sa faiture.
Ne soi mot que des oisiaus vi venir a desmesure. 10
               Je vi l'oriou
               Et le rosignou,
               Si vi le pinçon
               Et l'esmerillon,
                  Deus!   15
Et tant des autres oisiaus, de quoi je ne sai pas
                           [le non,
Qui sor cel arbre s'assistrent et commencent lor
                           [chançon.

II   Tuit chanterent a un tor,
              N'i ot autre jougleor.
              Je m'en alai soz la flor   20
              Por oïr joie d'amor.
           Tout belement par un prael
            Li deus d'amors vi chevauchier.
           Je m'en alai a son apel,
            De moi a fet son escuier.   25
Ses chevaus fu de deport, sa sele de signorie,

Ses frains [fu] de son dangier, ses estriers de
                                        [fil de sie.
        Ses hauberz estoit
        D'acoler estroit,
        Ses hiaumes de flors   30
        De pluseurs colors.
                Deus!
Lance avoit de cortoisië, espee de fuel de glai,
S'ot chauces de mignotië, esperons de bec de jai.

MN   Form: A A B B c c¹ D.

    RR   I   5 du] au   11 lorion   12 rosignon   II
18-19 occur as the very last lines of the text · 18   a un
son   19 Onc ni ot a. j. (+1)   26 deporz sa s. de ses
dangiers   27 Ses escuz fu de cartiers de besier et de soz-
rire; fu retained for meter   33 Sa lance est de c. e. de
flor de g.   34 Ses

    V   Order of lines in ms. U: (f. 152r) 1-8, 11-17; (f.
151r) 9-10 plus a third verse of fourteen syllables, 18-34.
Stanza I is followed on f. 152r by an apocryphal version of
ll. 9-17 (see below). The right edge of f. 151 is cut away;
missing readings are given below in brackets.
I   1 aurit a tant   2 Ke nest la fueille et la flor   3
au] a   4 Ch. et loie son signor   6 Si men antra an .j.
jardin   8 Les ozeles an lour l.   9 Un petit me tras
auant ke veoir voi lor f.   10 Ne s. m. ca[nt] de lor gent
vis v. et d., followed by il an i ot plus de .c. toz de
diue[rse] faiture   11 loriour   12 rasignor   15 missing
16 Et t. d. a. ozillons dont je ne s. dire l. n.   17 Ke
desor l. sasisent chacuns chantait sa ch.
II   18 Tut commansent a un son   20 [soz] la tor   21
amors   22 Se regarda p. un p.   23 Lou duc damo[r] viz
ch.   25 escuei[er]   26 Ces; celle   27 Ces; fu missing;
d an gier; cen estrier   28 Ces   30 C[es]   31 De diuers
c.   33 e. ot de   34 mignotise esperon
Second version of ll. 9-17: Un petit me trais arriere ke
corresier nes osoie/ Et ses pris a regardeir la ioe ke il
monoient/ Vi lou roisignor/ Demeneir badour/ Tut sont antor
lui/ Et grant et menour/ Et chantent tut antor lui et de-
moinnent feste grignor/ Ke dune grande luee puet on oir la
tantour

    E   Bartsch, 25-27; Spanke Lied, 241-242, 406-407;
Pauphilet, 837-838; Gennrich Alt Lied 1, 47-49; Woledge
Peng, 117-119; Tyssens, 589-603; Bec 2, 58-59.

N   Both manuscript sources of this text are corrupt
and present problems of considerable weight. For remarkable
progress toward solution, see Tyssens. The text presented
here owes much to her reconstructed version of the song.

For the description of the God of Love in this song and
its relation to allegorical description in narrative, see
the introduction to *Le Fablel dou Dieu d'Amors*, ed. I.C.
Lecompte, *Modern Philology* 8 (1910/11), 63-86. For the
relation of the reverdies to OF pastourelles and Goliardic
poetry, see M. Delbouille, *Les origines de la pastourelle*,
in *Mémoires de l'Académie Royale de Belgique* 20:2 (Brussels,
1926). For an analysis of the poem, see Próspero Saíz, *Personae and Poiesis: The Poet and the Poem in Medieval Love
Lyric* (The Hague-Paris: Mouton, 1976).

9 *sa faiture* , i.e., what the bird was like.   10 *que
des o.* 'how many b.'.

RS 654a (= 731), MW 96:1
Ms. I 2:12. No music.

I   Doucement,
                    Sovant
                    M'esprent
                    Forment
          Amours et dame anvoixie,   5
          Qui volanteit et talent
          M'ait doneit tout mon vivant,
               Ke por li chant
               Jolietemant.
                 Je m'i presant   10
                 De cuer joiant,
                    Bonement,
                    Liement.

                    Avenant
                      Cors gent,   15
                      Riant,
                      Plaixant
          A celle qui me maistrie,
          Qui toz jors vait semonant
          Mon cuer, qui a li se rant   20
                 Antierement
                 Par un dous samblant;
                 Dont an airdant
                 Je voix uzant
                   Mon jovent   25
                   An pansant.

II   Mais esperence m'afi
          Ke j'avrai aligement.
          Por ceu me voix desduxant,
               Car je m'atant   30
               C'onkes facement
               N'alai servant,
               Ne repentant,
                 Recreant
                 Ne faillant   35

          Ne vi mon cuer vers celi
          Ou toute valour apant.

                    Kant je l'ai en remirant,
                       Joie ai si grant
                     Ke tout mon torment   40
                       Voix oubliant.
                     Nuns malz ne sant
                        Tant ne kant.
                      Por ç' ain tant.

III   Se li pri   45
                          De mi
                        Ait mercit,
                      K'a son amin
         Me taigne, si m'averait mout bien meri
                   Et [de] tout gari.   50

                       Et s'a li
                        Failli
                       Ai ansi,
                    Ke de pair li
         N'aie pitiet, bien puis dire ke mar vi   55
                   La biautei de li.

IV   Mais an mon boin espoir m'afi,
                 Qui de confort garni
                    Et anrechit
                   M'ait; s'an graci   60
              Bone Amor, ke j'ai servi.

           Or soit de ma griétei sor li!
             S'il li plait c'an obli
                   Ou amainrit
                  [Jai] soient mi   65
              Mal, de joli cuer l'otri.

        RR   I   24 uoi   II   44 P. ceu ai t. *(+1)*   III
50   *-1*   IV   63 Cil   65 *-1*

        E   Streng-Renkonen, 24-26.

        DF   Lorraine, including *ai* for *a*, as in *airdant* (23),
pair (54), *jai* (65); *ei* for tonic *e*, as in *volanteit* (6),
doneit (7), *biautei* (56); *nuns* (42) for *nus* and *amin* (48)
for *ami*; *facement* (31) for *faussement*; *x* for *s*, as in *anvoixie* (5), *voix* (29); preservation of final *t*, as in *doneit*
(7), *mercit* (47), *pitiet* (55); *ceu* (29) for *ce*; 3rd-pers.
sing. pres. ind. *ait* (7) for *a* (cf. subjunctive *ait* in l.
47); 3rd-pers. sing. fut. in *-ait*, as in *averait* (49).

There are at least two features more typical of Picard than
Lorraine: epenthesized future *averait* (49) for *avra* and *boin*
(57) for *bon*.

N   For the most recent discussion of the estampie as
a genre, see Bec 1, pp. 241-246.   44 The ms. reading shows
one syllable too many. Streng-Renkonen suggests the possibility of emending to *Por c'ai tant*, but the meaning of the
line so emended is unclear.   45 Understand *que* after *pri*.
65-66 One line in Streng-Renkonen: *Soient mi mal, de joli
cuer l'otri*. Hans Spanke, reviewing Streng-Renkonen (*Zeit.
für rom. Phil.* 52 [1932], 637-640), is right to see that the
verse should be divided, but the division that he proposes,
Soient mi mal, de joli/Cuer l'otri, fails to establish the
metric identity with ll. 60-61 that the form of the poem requires.

19   II

RS 301a (= 725), MW 21:4
Ms. I 2:17. No music.

I   Je chans
                        Sovent
                De cuer amerouzement,
                Ke pris suis si doucement
                De cors bien fait, avenant,   5
                    A cui me rant
                    Trestout mon vivant;
                Car kant je l'ai en remirant,
                    An moi s'estant
                Mes cuers et esprant   10
                    An chantant
                    Gaiement.

                        Riant,
                        Plaixant
                Ait lou vis cleir, fremiant,   15
                Jante, jone de jovent,
                Eus por ambleir cuer d'amant,
                    Regairt prenant.
                    Si sutivement
                M'ait saixit par son dous samblant,   20
                    D'or an avant
                    De cuer bonement

Ferai son comant,
An sa merci atandant.

II   Car qui welt ameir,   25
Il se doit aviseir
C'on nou puist nullement faus troveir,
Saiges, cortois, sosfrans, sans mueir,
Sans lui vanteir,
Loialz, sans guileir,   30
Jolis et gais, sans orgoil moustreir
Et gardeir
An pairleir.

Ou l'amour dureir
Ne puet, si andureir   35
Ne vuelt lou dous mestier sans ameir.
Qui ansi se seit amesureir
Ne doit douteir
Joie recovreir;
Car pitiet sert de fran cuer donteir   40
Et d'amant tenceir
Et de sa joie doubleir.

III   Por ceu voil maintenir
Bone amor et tant servir
Que je puisse recuillir   45
Par obeïr
Lou don de merir,
S'Amor sosfrir lo welt, et joïr,
Et pitiez s'i welt consentir,
Ki alegir me puet mon dezir   50
D'un dous confort por moi resjoïr
Et perir
Mon languir.

Ainz puisse je fenir
Ke j'aie cuer de faillir   55
Ne de ma dame guerpir!
Mais son plaisir
Vorrai acomplir;
Et s'il li vuelt de moi sovenir,
Je cut bien a joie venir.   60
Si atandrai son tres dous plaisir,
Car, cant la remir,
J'ai espoir de bien joïr.

IV   Dame, jai n'an partirai
            Et si ne sai   65
          S'an vos troverai
       Mercit, ke tant dezirei ai.
          G'i averai
       Esperance tant con vivrai.
          A mon esmai   70
       Me conforterai,
          S'an dirai
          De cuer vrai:

       "Amours, vos malz plaixans ai,
          Dont voloir n'ai   75
          Ne jai n'averai
       De garir; ains vos servirai
          Tant ke vairai
       Se de vos confort troverai.
       An teil estat mon tens userai,   80
          Car plus bel ne sai
       Andureir les malz ke j'ai."

RR   I   9 cestant   19 Ci   II   26 ce   37 Et
(+1); ce   III   59 cil

E   Streng-Renkonen, 35-38.

DF   Lorraine, including *ai* for *a*, as in *regairt* (18),
saiges (28), *pairleir* (33), *jai* (64); *ei* for tonic *e*, as in
cleir (15), *ameir* (25), *teil* (80), *dezirei* (67); *c-* for *s-*
(see RR); *x* for *s*, as in *plaixant* (14), *saixit* (20); preservation of final *t*, as in *saixit* (20), *pitiet* (40); *w* for *vu*,
as in *welt* (25); *ceu* (43) for *ce*; *lou* (36, 47) and *lo* (48)
for *le*; 3rd-pers. sing. pres. ind. *ait* (15) for *a*.

N   The text is divided into four bipartite stanzas of
variable length and meter. The two halves of each stanza
are identical except for the meter of the last two lines of
each half. Note that there is a four-syllable discrepancy
between l. 71 and its counterpart, l. 80; like Streng-
Renkonen, we have no correction to propose.
       27 *nou = ne le.*   60 *cut = cuit.*   68 *averai = avrai;*
also in l. 76.   78 *vairai = verrai.*

RS 1698a (= 1708), MW 2
Ms. K 376. Music.

I   L'autrier quant je chevauchoie, desouz l'onbre
                                        [d'un prael
        Trouvai gentil pastorele, les euz verz, le
                                        [chief blondel,
                Vestue d'un blïaudel,
        La color fresche et vermeille; de roses fet
                                        [un chapel.   4

II   Je la saluai, la bele; ele me respont
                                        [briément.
        "Bele, avez vous point d'ami qui vous face
                                        [biau senblant?"
                Tantost respont en riant:
        "Nenil voir, chevalier sire, mes g'en aloie
                                        [un querant."   8

III   "Bele, puis qu'ami n'avez, dites se vos
                                        [m'amerez."
        Ele respont conme sage: "Oïl, se vous
                                        [m'espousez.
                Lors ferez voz volentez,
        Et, se querez autre chose, ce seroit
                                        [desloiauté." 12

IV   "Bele, ce lessiez ester; n'avons cure
                                        [d'espouser!
        Ainz demerrons nostre joie tant com la porrons
                                        [mener,

             De besier et d'acoler,   15
    Et je vous ferai fiance que je n'avrai autre
                                             [a per."

V   "Sire, vostre biau senblant va mon cuer si
                                    [destraignant
     Vostres sui, que que nus die, des cestui jour
                                       [en avant."
              N'ala pas trois pas avant;
     Entre ses braz l'a sesie deseur l'erbe
                                       [verdoiant.   20

     MN   Form: A A B.
1. In 1. 2 ms. writes a bar. 2. In 1. 2 ms. writes no
bar.

     RR   III 9 ditez

     E   Brakelmann "Pastourelle", 331-332; Bartsch, 194-
195; Spanke *Lied*, 174-175, 389; Rivière 2, 121-122.

     N   Bartsch and Spanke *Lied* present this song with
long lines divided; the latter adds the observation, p. 389,
that "der metrische Aufbau der Strophe ist unklar und inkon-
sequent;" and so, indeed, it appears when words such as *chevauchoie*, *pastorele*, and *vermeille* all occur in rhyme position and rhyme with nothing. It is much more satisfactory
to regard the poem as containing 15-syllable verses, of the
type studied, for example, in Jeanroy *Or*, pp. 345-349, and
Burger, pp. 63-64; MW identifies them as such, and Rivière
shows the same lineation as here. In reality, the
long verses are composed of two hemistichs of seven syllables each, the first sometimes augmented by an uncounted
-e (*césure épique*).
     18 Understand *que* before *Vostres*.   20 Note that this
final statement, in the third person, represents (perhaps
together with 1. 19) a shift from the first-person narrative
of the beginning of the song. Both Bartsch and Spanke *Lied*,
detecting a scribal mistake here, emend to *mes braz l'ai*.
However, in view of the existence of several other songs of
this genre in which the same shift occurs, e.g., RS 1709 and
RS 1699 (version of ms. U), it is probably better to respect
the ms. reading.

II   <u>21</u>

RS 1984, MW 518
Mss. K 318, N 152r, P 166r-v, X 200v-201r. Music in all
  mss.

I   Enmi la rousee que nest la flor,
        Que la rose est bele au point du jor!
                Par mi cele arbroie
                Cil oisellon s'envoisent   4
                Et mainent grant baudor.
                    Quant j'oi la leur joie,
                Pour riens ne m'i tendroie
                D'amer bien par amors.   8

II   La pastore ert bele et avenant;
        Ele a les euz verz, la bouche riant.
                Benoet soit li mestre
                Qui tele la fist nestre,   12
                Bien est a mon talent.
                    Je m'assis a destre,
                Si li dis: "Damoisele,
                Vostre amor vous demant."   16

III   Ele me respont: "Sire champenois,
        Par vostre folie ne m'avrois des mois,
                Car je sui amie
                Au filz dame Marie,   20
                Robinet le cortois,
                    Qui me chauce et lie
                Et si ne me let mie
                Sanz biau chapiau d'orfrois."   24

IV   Quant vi que proiere ne m'i vaut noient,
      Couchai la a terre tout maintenant,
            Levai li le chainse,
            Si vi la char si blanche,   28
            Tant fui je plus ardant,
            Fis li la folie.
            El ne.1 contredist mie,
            Ainz le vout bonement.   32

V   Quant de la pastore oi fet mon talent,
      Sus mon palefroi montai maintenant,
            Et ele s'escrie:
            "Au filz sainte Marie,   36
            Chevalier, vos conmant;
            Ne m'oubliez mie,
            Car je sui vostre amie,
            Mes revenez souvent."   40

      MN   Form: A A B B.
1. In 1. 2 ms. writes a bar.

      RR   I   1 En mai

      V   I   1 En mai NPX   8 par *missing in X*   II   9
ert] est NP   10 El N; a] out P; vairs X; la *missing in*
N   11 beneet NPX; le NX   13 Quele e. N, Ele e. P
14 a terre P   16 V. a amor P   III   17 Eele P   18
folie] proiere PX   19 Car fui a. N   IV   26 Coucha P
28 Si li ui la X   V   34 maintenant *missing in N*   38
Ne m. uos mie X

      E   La Ravallière 2, 95; Tarbé *Chans*, 23; Bartsch,
184-185; Spanke *Lied*, 32-33, 360; Gennrich *Alt Lied* 2, 8-10;
Toja, 176-178; Rivière 2, 111-113.

      N   The metric structure of the decasyllabic lines is
variable, as is sometimes the case in pastourelles and similar compositions. Thus, 1. 1 shows 5 + e + 4; 11. 2 and 9,
5 (+ e?) + 4; 11. 10 and 17, 5 + 5; 1. 18, 5 + e + 5, and so
forth. For a discussion of the question, with specific reference to this song, see Burger, pp. 44-46. Note that the
poem shows, too, a certain irregularity in rhyming, e.g.,
st. 1, *arbroie:s'envoisent, baudor:amors*; st. 2, *destre:da-
moisele*.
      1 Like Bartsch, Rivière accepts the ms. reading *mai*.
He translates: "'En mai, à la rosée, quand naît la fleur
. . .', *la rousee* étant un complément de temps sans

préposition." 10 *verz* = *vairs*. 11 *Benoet* is disyllabic. 18 *ne . . . des mois*, i.e., never.

III   22

RS 599, MW 46, B (see note below)
Mss. N 146v-147r, K 308, P 160v-161r, X 195r-v. Music in
all mss.

I   Quant voi la flor nouvele
         Paroir en la praele
         Et j'oi la fontenele
         Bruire seur la gravele,   4
     Lors mi tient amors nouvele,
         Dont ja ne garrai.
     Se cist maus ne m'asouage,
         Bien sai que morrai.   8

II   "Je sui sade et brunete
         Et joenne pucelete,
         S'ai color vermeillete,
         Euz verz, bele bouchete;   12
     Si mi point la mamelete
         Que n'i puis durer.
     Resons est que m'entremete
         Des douz maus d'amer.   16

III   "Certes, se je trouvoie
         Qui m'en meïst en voie,
         Volentiers ameroie;
         Ja por nul ne.l leroie.   20
     Car bien ai oï retrere
         Et por voir conter

```
                Que nus n'a parfete joie
                   S'el ne vient d'amer."                    24


        IV      Vers la touse m'avance
                Por oïr s'acointance;
                Je la vi bele et blanche,
                De simple contenance.                        28
                Ne mist pas en oubliance
                   Ce que je li dis.
                Maintenant sanz demorance
                   S'amor li requis.                         32


        V       Pris la par la main nue,
                Mis la sus l'arbe drue;
                Ele s'escrie et jure
                Que de mon geu n'a cure:                      36
                "Ostés vostre lecheüre!
                   Deus la puist honir!
                Car tant m'est asprete et dure
                   Ne la puis souffrir."                      40


        VI    , "Bele, tres douce amie,
                Ne vos esmaiez mie;
                Oncor ne savez mie
                Con ce est bone vie.                          44
                Vo mere n'en morut mie,
                   Ce savez vos bien.
                Non fera, certes, la fille,
                   N'en doutez de rien."                      48


        VII     Quant l'oi despucelee,
                Si s'est en piez levee;
                En haut s'est escrïee:
                "Bien vos sui eschapee.                       52
                Treze anz a que je fui nee,
                   Par mien escïent;
                Onques mes n'oi matinee
                   Que j'amasse tant."                        56
```

MN   Form: A A B B¹.

<u>RR</u>   II   11 Sa 13-14 si mi p. lamelete durer   V
40 la *missing*   VI 48 rient

<u>V</u>   Stanzas: X   I II III IV V VII
    ,   KP I II III IV V
I 8 quen P   II 15 Reson P   III   19 *missing in*

X   20 nus K   21 Car iai touz iorz oi dire   K   22   et
p. v. reconter   X   IV   26 P. auoir K   28 Par la main
lalai prendre K   V   34   seur KPX; dure P   VII   50
Si cest   X   53 q. ie ne f. n.   X   56 Que ie a masse t.
X

E   Bartsch, 191-193; Bartsch-Wiese, 217-218; Spanke
Lied, 14-16, 355-356; Rivière 2, 135-138.

N   On the basis of a metrical and musical analysis,
Spanke *Lied*, pp. 355-356, expects the final two lines of
each stanza to form a refrain and indeed, in view of their
content, identifies as such the last couplets of stanzas 1,
2, and 3. The first of these does in fact occur in two
other ms. sources, and it figures in Gennrich *Ron* as No. 138
and in B as 1662. The others are listed in B as well, as
1624 and 1578, respectively; and Rivière 2, p. 138, agrees
that all three "peuvent être considérés comme des refrains."
MW makes no mention of refrains in this song.
    Note that there are several instances of irregularity
in rhyming: ll. 7, 21, 27 (dialectal explanation?), 33, 34,
47. In view of the frequent appearance of assonance in relatively early songs, of which RS 599 is no doubt one, the
only surprising case is that of l. 7 *asouage*; curiously,
this is also the only irregular rhyme-word whose correctness
is ensured by external sources (see preceding paragraph).
    12 *verz = vairs.*   29-30 This statement would seem
more satisfactory following ll. 31-32.   34 *l'arbe =
l'(h)erbe.*   40 Understand *que* before *Ne.*   43-44 These
lines may be read as a question, as in Rivière.

IV   <u>23</u>

RS 608, MW 1201, B 1920 (stanzas 1-3)
Ms. K 414-415. Music.

I   L'autrier en une praele
      Trouvai pastore chantant;
      Mult fu avenant et bele
      Et cortoise et bien parlant.
         Trestout maintenant   5
      Descendi jus de ma sele
      Et li dis: "Ma damoisele,
         M'amor vous present
         Jolivetement."

II   Ore öez de la dancele   10
      Qu'ele me dist en riant:
      "Je vous conois bien," fet ele,
      "Je vous voi auques souvent
         Par ci chevauchant."
      Lors me dona sa cordele   15
      Et son chapel a pucele,
         Que j'aim loiaument,
         Jolivetement.

III   Onques ne vi pastorele
      De mes euz si tres plesant;   20
      Une coiffe ot a vizelle
      Seur son chief blont reluisant,
         Cors ot bel et gent,
      Blanc piz et dure mamele.
      Pour li ai une estencele   25
         Qui me va poignant
         Jolivetement.

IV   Quant la douce savoree
      M'ot doné si riche don
      Com d'une corde nöee   30
      Dont el lioit son gaignon,
         Je m'en vins adons,
      Mes en li mis ma pensee
      Qui ja mes n'en ert ostee,
         Ainz la servirai   35
         De fin cuer verai.

V   Tel touse soit honoree,
      Enondeu ensi soit mon.
      Onc ne vi si bele nee
      Ne de tant bele façon;   40
         Je croi que preudon
      L'ait norrie et engendree.
      Hé! franche riens honoree,

Je vous servirai
De fin cuer verai.   45

<u>MN</u>   Form: A A B.
1. In l. 1 ms. writes *e.*   2. In l. 4 ms. writes this figure a 2nd lower.

<u>E</u>   Brakelmann "Pastourelle", 334-335; Bartsch, 197-
199; Spanke *Lied*, 245-247, 408; Rivière 2, 130-132.

<u>N</u>   This pastourelle is notable for the extent to
which it aristocratizes the shepherdess and expresses the
suitor's quest in courtly diction. The shift in register is
perhaps most telling in the change from a popular refrain,
Jolivetement, in stanzas 1-3, to its courtly replacement,
. . . *servirai/De fin cuer verai*, in the final stanzas. The
very substitution of one refrain for a quite different one
midway through the song is highly unusual.
15-16 It is a commonplace of pastourelles that the
suitor offers one or more presents to the shepherdess; these
are generally items of adornment and may often be interpreted as erotic symbols. (See Schossig, pp. 196-214.) It is
exceptional to find, as here, the shepherdess taking the
rôle of donor.

V   <u>24</u>

RS 292, MW 10
Mss. K 307-308, N 146r-v, P 160r-v, X 194v-195r. Music in
all mss.

I   Hui main par un ajornant
           Chevauchai ma mule anblant;

Trouvai gentil pastorele et avenant;
Entre ses aigniaus aloit joie menant.   4

II   La pastore mult m'agree,
               Si ne sai dont ele est nee
         Ne de quels parenz ele est enparentee;
         Onques de mes euz ne vi si bele nee.   8

III   "Pastorele, pastorele,
               Vois le tens qui renouvele,
         Que raverdissent vergiers et toutes herbes;
         Biau deduit a en vallet et en pucele."   12

IV   "Chevalier, mult m'en est bel
               Que raverdissent prael,
         Si avront assez a pestre mi aignel;
         Je m'irai soëf dormir souz l'arbroisel."   16

V   "Pastorele, car souffrez
               Que nos dormons lez a lez,
         Si lessiez voz aigniaus pestre aval les prez;
         Vos n'i avrois ja damage ou vous perdez."   20

VI   "Chevalier, par saint Simon,
               N'ai cure de conpaignon;
         Par ci passent Guerinet et Robeçon,
         Qui onques ne me requistrent se bien non."   24

VII   "Pastorele, trop es dure,
               Qui de chevalier n'as cure;
         A cinquante boutons d'or avroiz çainture,
         Si me lessiez prendre proie en vo pasture."   28

VIII   "Chevalier, se Deus vos voie,
               Puis que prendre voulez proie,
         En plus haut lieu la pernez que ne seroie;
         Petit gaaigneriez et g'i perdroie."   32

IX   "Pastorele, trop est sage
               De garder ton pucelage;
         Se toutes tes conpaignetes fussent si,
         Plus en alast de puceles a mari."   36

MN   Form: A b b¹.

RR   V   20 aurais

<u>V</u>   Stanzas VII, VIII, and IX are not included in P.
I   3 gente X   II   5 pastorele X   6 Mes ne NPX; el
NP   8 Onc de P; vi plus bele P   III   10 qui reno N
IV   13 Ch. ce mest mlt bel P   V   18 dormon P; lez a
lez *missing in X*   20 aurez NP   VI   22 Na NP   24
onc ne X   VII   26 Quant de NX   28 en uostre p. N
VIII   29 que dex N   31 le proie que X   32 gaingne-
ries X   IX   33 Pastore X

<u>E</u>   Monmerqué-Michel, 44-45; Tarbé *Chans*, 20; Bartsch,
183-184; Spanke *Lied*, 12-13, 355; Pauphilet, 831-832; Gennrich *Alt Lied* 2, 2-4; Groult 1, 189-190; Toja, 171-174;
Rivière 2, 107-110.

<u>DF</u>   Picard: *aigniaus* (4), *biau* (12) for *aigneaus,
beaus*; *vo* (28) for *vostre*; *pernez* (31) for *prenez*.

<u>N</u>   Lines 3 and 4 of each stanza contain eleven syl-
lables, a type not rare in pastourelles and similar compositions; note that there is a certain mobility in the caesura.
For some discussion of such verses, see Jeanroy *Or*, p.
343ff., and Burger, pp. 54-57.
   11 *herbes*, the only instance of assonance in the poem,
is probably a copyist's error. This reading occurs, however, in all four mss., despite the claim in Bartsch and in
Gennrich *Alt Lied* that ms. X shows *toute herbele*.   20 *ou
vous perdez* 'in which you would lose [anything]'; *perdez* is
in the subjunctive.   32 Spanke *Lied* and Gennrich *Alt Lied*
add initial *Vous* to reach eleven syllables; the same end can
be achieved, without any change in the ms. reading, by in-
terpreting *gaaigneriez* as a 5-syllable form.

                          VI   <u>25</u>

RS 607, MW 856
Stanza I: B 1463 (two other sources), st. II: B 877 (one
      other source), st. III: B 1644 (one other source), st.
      IV: B 34 (two other sources), [st. V: B 1353 (one other
      source), st. VI: B 1112 (three other sources)].
Mss. K 337-338, N 163r-163v, P 186v-187r, T 171v, U 154r
      (=U[1]), U 156v-157v (=U[2]), X 221v-222r. Music in all
      mss. except U[1] and U[2].

1. En   u- ne pra-e- le 2. m'en-trai l'au-trier;
5. Li   ber-giers la be- le 6. vou-loit be- sier,

I   En une praele
                          M'entrai l'autrier,
                    Trouvai pastorele
                          Lez son bergier.
                    Li bergiers la bele   5
                          Vouloit besier,
                    Mes en fesoit ele
                          Mult grant dangier,
                    Car de cuer ne l'amoit mie,
                    Oncor fust ce sa plevie,   10
                          Si avoit ele ami
                          Autre que son mari,
                    Car son mari, je ne sai pour quoi,
                    Het ele tant qu'ele s'escrioit:
                          Ostez moi l'anelet du doit,   15
                          Ne sui pas marïee a droit!

II   "A droit, non!" fet ele
            A son bergier;
            "En pur sa gounele
              Eusse plus chier   20
            Celui qui frestele
              En ce vergier
            Sus la fontenele
              Lez le rochier
        Que avoir la seignorie   25
        D'Anjou ne de Normendie;
         Mes je i ai failli,
         Certes ce poise mi."
        Dist la douce criature
            A haute voiz: 30
       Honiz soit mari qui dure
          Plus d'un mois!

III   "Un mois, suer doucete!"
           Dist li pastors;
           "Ceste chançonete   35
            Mi fet iros;
          Trop estes straingete
            Vers moi toz jors,
          Mult estes durete
            De vos amors;   40
        Mes se tele est vo pensee
        Qu'a moi soiez acordee,
         Donc si haez Garnier
         Qui est en cel vergier."
       Et ele dist que ja por li   45
         Ne.l lera a amer:
     S'amor--sa-de-ra-do-re-li--
         Ne mi lesse durer!

IV   "Durer, Joanete!"
           Dist li jalos;   50
          "Fole ennuieusete,
           Qui amez vos?"
         Dist la bergerete:
           "Biau sire, vos."
          "Tu mens voir, garcete,   55
           Ainz as aillors
       Mis ton cuer et ta pensee;
       Moi n'aimes tu, de riens nee,
        Ainz aimes melz Garnier
         Qui est en cel vergier   60
         Que ne fais mi,

          [Et] maintes gens le me dīent."
               Aimi, aimi!
           Amoretes m'ont traïe!

<u>MN</u>   Form: A A B vrf.
1. For the next three notes in lines 5-6 ms. writes *f, a, b*.
2. The melodies for the ends of stanzas 2-4 are conjectured
by analogy to the end of st. 1. However, ms. T provides a
related refrain for st. 2 with a different melody, and a motet in ms. Montpellier H 196 (Mo), No. 178 (f. 231r-v), includes a refrain related to that of stanza 3 with a different melody; both are given below:

<u>RR</u>   I   2 lez un uergier   7 Mes ele en fesoit   8
M. tres g. d. *(+1)*   II   20 Auroie p. c. *(+1)*   21 Garin
q. f.   22 Lez c. v.   III   34 D. il ialos   37 T. e.
durete   38 De uos amors   39 Ie uous pris a fame   40
Souuiengne uous   41 Et se   43 Dont   46 Ne lera   47
Saderalidore samor   IV   49 D. suer doucete   53 Ce
dist ioanete   58 *missing*   62 *missing*   64 trai

<u>V</u>   Stanza IV is not included in T; except for the
first line and the first word of the following line, stanza
IV is not included in U[1] either.
I   2 Mantra latre ier U[2], troua(i) la(u)trier TU[1], lez
un uergier NPX   3 Vne p. T, Vne bergerete U[1], Troua
bergerete U[2]   5 La bergiers U[1]; bergier NP; la pele P
7 Mes ele en fesoit (faisoit X) NPX, Et el(l)e lan fist
(len faisoit T) TU[1]U[2]   8 Tres g. d. X, M. tres g. d.
NPU[1]U[2]   9 mies U[1]   10 ce] se U[1], ceu U[2], ele P; f.
en sa baillie T   11 Sauoit TU[1]U[2]   13 Car *missing* U[1];
Car s. m. *missing TU[2]*   14 H. e. t. can halt sescrioit (hat
cescrioit U[2]) U[1]U[2]   15 lanelez N; dou d. XTU[1]U[2]   16
seus U[1]U[2]; marie NP
II 18 Sire(s) bergiers U[1]U[2] 19 pure s. U[2]; sa coutele N
20 Auroie p. c. NPX   21 Guerin N, Garin X, Robin P,
celi ke U[1]; frestele *missing X*   22 Lez c. v. NX, Lez loliuier P; cel TU[2], cest U[1]   23 *missing P*; A la f. T,
Leis la fontenelle (fontenete U[2]) U[1]U[2]   24 *missing P*;
Lez le rogier N, Sous cel pumier T, Soz loliuier U[1]U[2]
25 Ke vous ne la s. T, Ke de vos la s. U[1]U[2]   26 Dans
Jehans de N. U[1]   27 Mes or (ore X) iai f. NX, Lasse

mais f. T, Or i ai (ait U^1) f. U^{1}U^2 28 Iai ce T; se
p. U^{1}U^2 31 Honi NX; Mau dehait m. T; maris PU^{1}U^2
III   33 En m. T, Dun m. U^{1}U^2; m. bergerete U^{1}U^2, s.
douce T   34 D. li ialos NX   36 me NU^{1}U^2; fist X   37
Saichies bregerete T; straingete] estrainge U^2, durete
NPX   38 De uos amors NPX, Par mal de vous T   39 Trop
mestes d. T, Ie uos pris a fame (feme X) NPX   40 Por
vos a. TU^{1}U^2, Souuiengne (souueigne X) uos NPX   41 Et
se NPX; Mais se (si U^2) vo(u)s aues (auies U^2) la bee
TU^{1}U^2 42 soiez] fuisies U^1, fuissiez U^2 43 Dont NP,
missing TU^{1}U^2   44 cest v. U^1 45 dit PX; lui XTU^1
46 Ne PXT, Non (nou ?) U^{1}U^2; l. ai a. U^2 47 Saderalidore (Saderalidure N, Vaderalidonde P) samor NPX, Hadela-
reudous diex samors T, Vadalaridon deu samor U^1, Deus va-
delaritonde samor U^2 48 Ne me U^1; durer *final word in T*
IV   49 D. suer doucete NPX; D. Jehennete U^{1}U^2 51
Folle *final word in U^1*; F. u(n?)icelete U^2 52 cuj ameis
v. U^2 53 La bergiere dist U^2, Ce (se P) dist ioanete
(iouante N) NPX   54 Biaz U^2 55 T. m. garselete U^2
58 *missing N*; rien U^2 59 Plus ainmes garnier U^2 60
Qui qui est P; cel rochier N   61 faiz N, fas P; moi
P; Ke tu ne fais moi ne ne toi U^2 62 *missing NPX*; die
U^2 63 Amin amin amin U^2 64 trai NPX; Deus amoretes
mosient U^2

The mss. show the following divergent continuations,
neither of which fully corresponds to the prosodic or musical pattern of the first four stanzas:

Ms. K (and NPX)

Amoretes m'ont traïe!   64

V   "Traï voir," fet ele,   65
     "Vilain chetis!
     Traï estes vous, je
     Le vous plevis;
     Car li miens amis est
     Mult melz apris   70
     De vous et plus biaus
     Et plus jolis,
     Si li ai m'amor donee."
     "Hé, fole desmesuree,
     Pour l'amor de Garnier,   75
     Le conperrez ja chier."
     Et la touse li escrie:
     Ne me batez pas, dolereus mari,
     Vous ne m'avez pas norrie!
     Se vos me batez, je ferai ami, 80
     Si doblera la folie!   80a

Ms. U²

V   Deus, amoretes m'ocïent!   64

         "Occïent, bergiere,   65
            Non font, par foi."
         "Si font, biaz douz sìre,
            Foi ke vos doi;
         Il ont traïsons
            Dites de moi."   70
         "Tu mans, garselete,
            Je ne te croi,
       Ke tu es trop janglerece
       Et trop fole vanteresse."
         Il la vait ferir   75
       Si k'il la fist cheïr.
   Celle a redrecier vit ses dras honis,
   Vint a bergier, si s'escrie:
   Ne me bateis pais, delirous maris,
      Vos ne m'aveis pas norrie!   80

VI   "Norrie, bergiere,
            N'ai je pais toi,
         Mais tu ais ta foit
            Mentit ver moi."
         Garnier ki frestelle   85
            En oït l'efroi,
         Si vint a bergier
            De grant deroi.
       De son frestel leis l'oïe
       Li ait doneit teil congnie   90
            K'il lou fist verseir
            Et en halt s'escrïer.
       Par la main la bele ait prise,
       Ceste chanson vat notant:
         J'an moins par les dois m'amie,   95
         S'an voix plus mignotemant!

Mss. KNPX   V   72 et] est P   76 conparroiz N   79
pas *missing P*; norrie *final word in KX*   80 fera P
Ms. U²   V   64 mosient   65 Occie   69 Il uos traison
(em. Bartsch)   77 v. ces d.   VI   88 Kest de g. d.   92
En halt cest escrieis *(em. Bartsch)*
    Note that the dialectal features of U² are typical of
Lorraine, most notably *a* (ll. 77, 78, 87) for *au*, *ai* (as in
ll. 83, 90) for *a*, *ei* (as in ll. 79, 89) for *e*, and final *t*
(as in ll. 82, 83) for *ø*.

E   Monmerqué-Michel, 46-47; Bartsch, 143-145; Spanke *Lied*, 100-105, 372-373; Rivière 2, 92-98.

N   Association of refrains with the dialogue is re-inforced by the formal device of repeating the last word or phrase of each refrain at the beginning of the following stanza (*coblas capfinidas*).
13-16 The last two lines of the stanza contain nine syllables each, while the refrain is composed of octosyl-lables. This difference is inconsistent with what occurs in the following stanzas: metrical identity of final verses and refrain lines. It is supported by the melody, however. 21 *frestele*: verb derived from *frestel(e)*, a multi-reed musical instrument resembling a panpipe, restricted to pastoral use. 55 For ms. U^2 *garselete*, see Rivière "Remarques", p. 389.

VII   26

RS 580, MW 461, B 1854
Ms. U 58v-59r. Music.

1.La dou-çors del tens no-vel 2.fait chain-gier ire en re-vel
4.Por lo co-man-ce-ment bel 5.dou douz mai, lez un bos-chel
3.et a-cre-stre joi-   e.
6.tot seus che-val-choi-   e.
7.Entre un pre et u-ne voi- e 8.e-spring-goi-ent sor l'her-boi- e
9.pa-sto-res et pa-sto-rel 10.et en lor muse a fre-stel
11.vont chan-tant un do-ren-lot.
12.Vos a-vroiz lo pick-en-pot 13.et j'a-vrai lo do-ren-lot.

I   La douçors del tens novel
    Fait chaingier ire en revel
       Et acrestre joie.
    Por lo comancement bel
    Dou douz mai, lez un boschel   5
       Tot seus chevalchoie.
    Entre un pré et une voie
    Espringoient sor l'herboie
    Pastores et pastorel
    Et en lor muse a frestel   10
    Vont chantant un dorenlot.
     Vos avroiz lo pickenpot
     Et j'avrai lo dorenlot.

II   Por faire le cointerel
    Ot chascuns un vert chapel   15
       Et blanche corroie
    Et ganz couez et coutel
    Et cotte d'un gros burel
       A diverse roie.
    S'ot chescuns lez lui la soie   20
    Et chescune se cointoie
    Por son cointe vilenel.
    Biatris, estroit graislel,
    Va chantant un dorenlot.
     Vos avroiz lo pickenpot   25
     Et j'avrai lo dor[enlot].

III   Entre Guibor et Ansel
    Marchent del pré lo prael,
       Guioz lez Maroie
    Refasoit lo lecherel,   30
    Et font croller le cercel
       Si qu'il en peçoie.
    Cil et cele se desroie,
    Fierent del pié sor l'arboie,
    Chescuns i fait son merel   35
    Et Guis en son chalemel
    Cointoie lo dorenlot.
     Vos avrez lo pikempot
     Et j'avrai lo dor[enlot].

IV   Senz semonse et senz apel,   40
    De mon palefroit morel
       Dessent lez l'arbroie;
    En la dance molt isnel
    Me mis lez un sotterel

Cui forment ennoie,   45
Car de celi l'esloignoie
Qui l'amoit, si s'en gramoie,
Si a dist: "Seignor tousel,
Cil qui fait lo damoisel
Nos tout nostre dorenlot."   50
Vos avrez lo pikenpot
[Et j'avrai lo dorenlot].

V   Dist Perrins: "Sire donzel,
      Querez aillors vostre avel,
          Lassiez autrui proie!"   55
      Kant cil oï son aidel,
      En sa main prist un caillel,
          Vers moi lo paumoie;
      Kant vi la force n'iert moie,
      Sor mon cheval remontoie,   60
      Mais l'un d'aus oing lo musel,
      D'un baston li fis borsel,
      Puis querpi lo dorenlot.
      Vos avroiz lo pikenpot
      [Et j'avrai lo dorenlot].   65

VI   Lors me sui mis a la voie
      Et chascuns d'els me convoie
      De baston ou de chaillel;
      Lor chiens Tancre et Mansael
      M'ont hüé senz dorenlot.   70
      Vos avrez lo pikenpot
      Et j'avrai lo dorenlot.

MN   Form: A A B rf (ballade); the envoy is sung to
ll. 7-11.
l. In l. 5 ms. writes no rest.

RR   I   8   soz   VI   71   pinkenpot

E   Bartsch, 135-137; Bartsch-Wiese, 216-217; Cremonesi, 59-61; Gennrich *Ex*, 22-23; Mary 1, 244-247; Zink *Past*,
136-138; Rivière 2, 77-80.

DF   Lorraine: *chaingier* (2) for *changier*; *lo* (4) for
le.

N   8 Confusion between *herboie* 'grass-covered
ground' and *arbroie* 'stand of trees' (l. 42) no doubt ac-
counts for the ms. reading *soz* as well as for the form

arboie (l. 34), which is clearly a variant of *herboie*.
Note, similarly, l. 20 *chescuns* and l. 21 *chescune*, but l.
67 *chascuns*.   45 *Cui* is the dative object of impersonal
ennoie.   59 Understand *que* after *vi*.   61 *l'un d'aus* is
to be understood as a dative.   69 Bartsch-Wiese, like
Bartsch, emends to *Tancré et Mansel*.

27   VIII

RS 575, MW 1790
Stanza I: B 539 (four other sources), st. II: B 1692 (two
    other sources), st. III: B 1872 (five other sources),
    st. IV: B 281, st. V: B 114 (two other sources), st.
    VI: B 1430 (one other source).
Ms. U 56v-57r.   Music.

         I   En avril au tens novel,
                Que florissent cil vergier,
                En chamoi soz Mirabel
                Chevalchoie seus l'autrier.
                Trovai seant un bergier   5

En un pré lez un boison,
Qui sa bergiere Rechon
Regrate et dit, senz decevoir:
Deus, li cuers me faudra ja,
Tant la desir avoir!   10

II   Quant j'oï le pastorel
       Si durement correcier,
       Sor mon palefroi inel
       Vers lui vois lo droit sentier.
       Bien se sot en piez drecier,   15
       Et je l'ai mis a raison:
       "Bergier, es tu se bien non?"
    Et il m'a dit: "Je vos affi,
  Se la bele n'a de moi merci,
Je ne vivrai gaires longuement ensi."   20

III   "Bergiers, seroit vos il bel,
       Qui vos en poroit aidier?"
       "Oïl, sire. Un gras agnel
       Vos donroie de loier
       Se vos m'en poiez aidier,   25
       Et lo pain de mon giron.
       D'autre part chastel Charlon
    La troverez ou je la vi.
  Et qant la verrez, por Deu dites li
Q'a la [mort] m'a mis, se nen a merci."   30

IV   A cest mot m'en departi,
       Que plus n'i vols demorer.
       D'autre part Richon oï
       Entre ses agnels chanter.
       Ne la vols pas trespasser,   35
       Car meuz me plaist acointier
       De li que de son bergier.
    Lors li ai dit que sospris m'a:
  Blonde, se vos ne m'amez,
Jamais mes cuers joie n'avra.   40

V   "Sire, j'ai lo cuer marri;
       Por ceu ne vos puis amer.
       Chascun jor veons Hanri
       Nostre païs triboler;
       Ne savons quel part torner,   45
       Tant redotons l'aversier.
       D'autre part, amors ne quier

      Fors que les Gauteron que j'ai."
    A mes premieres amors me tenrai.

VI   Maintenant que j'entendi   50
       La pastorele parler
       De Gauteron son ami,
       Dessanz por li acoler,
       Por son gen cors remirer
       Et sa boichette baisier.   55
       Tant l'ai servi senz dangier
     K'ele me dist au departir:
     Or ai bone amor novele a mon plaisir!

    <u>MN</u>   Form: A A B vrf.
1. In l. 1, ms. initially omits the word *novel* and its music
but adds both in left margin. 2. Ms. contains music for
only the first of the six refrains; part of the melody of
refrain 2 comes from a motet in ms. Wolfenbüttel 1206,
f.232v-233 (see also RS 1596, refrain 5); that of refrain 5,
from two different motets in the same manuscript, f.201v-202
and f.243v-244, the latter written a 5th higher than here
given and with some variants; refrain 4 may be sung to ll.
7-8 and refrain 6 to the melody of refrain 5.

    <u>RR</u>   III   30 *-l (em. Bartsch)*

    <u>E</u>   Brakelmann "Pastourelle", 325-326; Bartsch, 134-
135; Brakelmann 2, 82-83; Pinguet, 82-89; Maillard *Er*, 40-
42; Zink *Past*, 133-135; Rivière 2, 74-76; Bec 2, 49-51.

    <u>DF</u>   Lorraine: *chamoi* (3) for *chaumoi*; *lo* (14) for *le*;
ceu (<u>42</u>) for *ce*; *boichette* (55) for *bo(u)chete*.

    <u>N</u>   This poem has been attributed by different commen-
tators to Thibaut de Blaison and to Ernoul de Gastinois; see
Pinguet, p. xiv, and Maillard *Er*, pp. 40-41. There seems,
however, to be no cogent evidence in favor of either attribution. 27 Understand *de* before *chastel*.

<u>28</u>   IX

RS 89, MW 1878, B 474 and 1679
Ms. C 122r. No music.

I L'autrier a doulz mois de mai
  Ke nest la verdure,
 Ke cil oxelet sont gai,
  Plain d'envoixeüre,
 Sor mon cheval l'ambleüre   5
  M'alai chevalchant;
 S'oï pastoure chantant
  De jolit cuer amerous:
  Se j'avoie ameit un jor,
   Je diroie a tous   10
   Bones sont amors.

II Ausi tost com j'entendi
  Ceste chansonnete,
 Tout maintenant descendi
  Per desor l'erbete,   15
 Si resgardai la tousete
  Ke se desduisoit
 Et ceste chanson chantoit
  De jolif cuer amerous:
  Se j'avoie ameit [un jor, 20
   Je diroie a tous
   Bones sont amors].

III Tantost comme j'entendi
  Celle bergerete,
 Maintenant me trais vers li 25
  Soz une espinete;
 Et Robins de sa musete
  Davant li musoit,
 Et elle se rescrioit
  De jolit cuer amerous: 30
  Se j'avoie ameit [un jor,
   Je diroie a tous
   Bones sont amors].

IV Lors m'escriai a haut ton,
  Sens poent d'arestence: 35
 "Li lous enporte un mouton!"
  Et Robins s'avance,
 S'ait deguerpie la dance;
  La blonde laissait,
 Et elle se rescriait   40
  De jolit cuer amerous:
  Se j'avoie ameit [un jor,
   Je diroie a tous
   Bones sont amors].

V   La pastourelle enbraissai,   45
            Ki est blanche et tendre;
        Desor l'erbe la getai,
            Ne s'en pout desfendre.
        Lou jeu d'amors sens atendre
            Li fix per delit,   50
        Et elle a chanteir se prist
            De jolit cuer amerous:
            Se j'avoie ameit trois jors,
            Je di[roie a tous
            Bones sont amors].   55

RR   I   5 Sors   III   26 Sor   IV   38 Sai

E   Hofmann "Pastourelles", 316; Bartsch, 112-113;
Rivière 2, 33-35.

DF   Lorraine, including *a* (1) for *au*; *ai* for *a*, as in
enbraissai (45); *ei* for tonic *e*, as in *ameit* (9), *chanteir*
(51); *poent* (35) for *point*; preservation of final *t*, as in
ameit (9); *x* for *s*, as in *oxelet* (3), *fix* (50); *lou* (49) for
le; 3rd-pers. sing. pres. ind. *ait* (38) for *a*; 3rd-pers.
sing. pret. in -*ait*, as in *laissait* (39), *rescriait* (40).

N   17 *Ke = qui*, as is often the case in ms. C (Lorraine).   38 Rivière, unlike Bartsch, retains the ms. reading *S'ai*, though the context clearly requires *Robins* as subject.

29   X

RS 57, MW 294, B 1222
Ms. I 4:50. No music.

I   Heu main matin jueir alai
        Leis un bouchet ke je bien sai;
        Une pastourelle trovai
            Seant deleiz sai proie.   4
        Kant je la vi, je m'arrestai
        Et je l'oÿ chanteir ensi:
            Les mamelettes me poignent;
            Je ferai novel amin.   8

II   Cant je la vi, vers lei alai,
        Cortoisement l'ai saluai;
        L'un des bras a col li getai

        Et l'autre a la corroie.   12
    Molt doucement li demandai
    Por coi elle chantoit ansi:
        Les mamelettes [me poignent;
        Je ferai novel amin].   16

III   Elle respont: "Jou vos dirai.
        Trois jors ait que Robin n'amai;
        Ce poize moi kant lou laixai.
            Por coi lou celleroie?   20
        Ainz plus biau de lui n'acointai,
        Et por lui chanterai ansi:
            Les mamelettes [me poignent;
            Je ferai novel amin]."   24

IV   "Belle, por moi ansi chanteiz,
        Et de moi vostre amin fereis.
        Biaus jüelz vos vorrai doneir,
            Sainturelle de soie;   28
        Toz jors ferai a vostre grei,
        Mais ke por moi chanteiz ansi:
            Les mamelettes [me poignent;
            Je ferai novel amin]."   32

V   "Certes, sire, jai nou ferai,
        Jai por vos Robin ne lairai;
        Mais monteiz sor vos pallefroi,
            Fuieiz, alleiz vos voie!"   36
        Cant je l'oÿ, boin grei l'an sai,
        Si la laixai chantant ansi:
            Les mamelettes mi poignent;
            Je ferai novel amin.   40

RR   III   19 Se   IV   30 Maikes p.

E   Bartsch, 169-170; Rivière 1, 142-144.

DF   Lorraine, including *ai* for *a*, as in *sai* (4), *jai*
(33); *ei* for tonic *e*, as in *jueir* (1), *leis* (2), *chanteiz*
(25), *grei* (29); *heu* (1) for *hui*; *amin* (8) for *ami*; *boin*
(37) for *bon*; *s* for *c*, as in *sainturelle* (28) and Rejected
Readings; *lei* (9) for *li*; *lou* (19) for *le*; *vos* (35, 36) for
vostre; 3rd-pers. sing. pres. ind. *ait* (18) for *a*. Note
that *ai* and *oi* have the same phonetic value: *pallefroi* (35)
rhymes with *ferai*, *lairai*, etc.

N   17 *Jou* here may be a typically Lorraine form of
je or else a contraction of *je le*; cf. 1. 33 *nou = ne lou*.

<u>30</u>   XI

RS 1363, MW 1453, B 731
Ms. I 4:35. No music.

I   A lai foillie a Donmartin
            A l'entree dou tens novel,
            S'asamblerent par un matin
            Pastorelles et pastorelz.
                Roi ont fait dou plus bel;   5
              Mantel ot de kamelin
                Et cote de burel.
              S'ont lou museour mandei,
                Et Thieris son bordon
                    Ait destoupeit   10
                Ke dixoit: "Bon bon bon bon bon!
          Sa de la rire dural durei lire durei."

II   Lou roi ont mis sor un cussin,
            Si l'acirent an un praiel;
            Puéz si demanderent lou vin.   15
            Grant joie moinnent li donzel:
                Gatier fait lou müel
              Et Jaiket lou pellerin
                Et Gui lou roubardel
              Et Badowin fait l'anfleit,   20
                Et Thieris son bordon
                  Ait destoupeit
                Ki dixoit: "Bon [bon bon bon bon!
          Sa de la rire dural durei lire durei]."

III   Li rois an jurait saint Martin   25
            Et l'airme son peire Robert:
            "Qui comencerait lou hustin,
            On lou geterait ou ruxel."
                Dont i vint Gaterel,
              Li filz lo maistre Xavin,   30
                A son col un gastel,
              Por les conpaignons dineir;
                Et Thieris son bordon
                  Ait destoupeit
                Ke dixoit: "Bon bon bon bon bon!   35
          Sa de la rire dure durei lire durei!"

<u>RR</u>   III   30   xauing

<u>E</u>   Bartsch, 160–161; Rivière 1, 119–121.

<u>DF</u>   Lorraine, including *a* for *au*, as in *Gatier* (17);
ai for *a*, as in *lai* (1), *Jaiket* (18), *airme* (26); *ei* for
tonic *e*, as in *mandei* (8), *destoupeit* (10), *anfleit* (20),
peire (26); *puéz* (15) for *puis*; *c* for *ss*, as in *acirent*
(14); preservation of final *t*, as in *destoupeit* (10), *anfleit* (20); *x* for *s(s)*, as in *ruxel* (28), *Xavin* (30); *lou*
(8) for *le*; 3rd-pers. sing. pres. ind. *ait* (10) for *a*; 3rd-
pers. sing. pret. in -*ait*, as in *jurait* (25); 3rd-pers.
sing. fut in -*ait*, as in *comencerait* (27), *geterait* (28);
relative *ke* (11) used as nominative.

31   I. (Débat)

RS 980, MW 102
Mss. K 340-341, N 164v-165r, P 188r-v-189r, X 222r-v. Music
     in all mss.

I   Au renouvel du tens que la florete
        Nest par ces prez et indete et blanchete,
Trouvai soz une coudrete coillant violete
Dame qui resenbloit feë et sa conpaignete,
              A qui el se dementoit   5
         De deus amis qu'ele avoit
              Au quel ele ert amie:
         Ou au povre qu'est cortois,
         Preuz et larges plus que rois
              Et biaus sanz vilanie,   10
Ou au riche qu'a assez avoir et manandie,
Mes en li n'a ne biauté ne sens ne cortoisie.

II   "Ma douce suer, mon conseil en creez:
        Amez le riche, grant preu i avrez;
Car se vous volez deniers, vous en avrez assez;   15
Ja, de chose que il ait, mes sousfrete n'avrez.
              Il fet bon le riche amer,

Q'il a assez a doner;
   Je seroie s'amie.
Se je lessoie mantel   20
D'escarlate por burel,
   Je feroie folie;
Car li riches veut amer et mener bone vie,
Et li povres veut jöer sanz riens donner s'amie."

III   "Or ai oï ton conseil, bele suer,   25
   Du riche amer; ne.l feroie a nul fuer!
Certes, ja n'iert mon ami par deseure mon cuer.
Dame qui a cuer joli ne.l feroit a nul fuer.
   Dames qui vuelent amer
   De bone amor sanz fausser,   30
    Conment que nus me die,
   Ne doivent riens demander,
   Pour nus qu'en sache parler,
    Fors bone amor jolie.
Toutes fames je les hé, et Jhesus les maudie,   35
Qu'aiment honme pour doner; c'est grant
                [ribauderie.

IV   "E! fine Amor, tant m'avez oublïee
   Que nuit ne jor ne puis avoir duree,
Tant m'a sa tres grant biauté tainte et
              [descoloree; 39
Tant pens a li nuit et jor que toute en sui müee.
   Rosignol, va, si li di
   Les maus que je sent pour li,
    Et si ne m'en plaing mie;
   Di li q'il avra m'amor,
   Car plus bele ne meillor   45
    De moi n'avra il mie;
Di li q'il avra assez puis que je sui s'amie,
Q'il ne lest pas pour deniers a mener boune vie."

  MN   Form:aa bb CC bb (lai?).
1. In l. 8, all mss. write *qui est* (*ert*), and mss. K and N
repeat this note.

  RR   I 8 qui est *(+1)*   11 qui a *(+1)*   II   15
d. assez en auerez   III 26 a. ne   33 qui en *(+1)*   36
Qui aiment *(+1)*   IV 43 plaig

  V I 2 N. en N; inde X 5 ele N 7 Au q.
seroit a. N 8 qui est (ert P) NPX 9 1. conme .i.
(come X) rois PX 10 biau P 11 qui a NPX 12 M.

il na en li b. N   II   14 i aueres P   15 d. assez
(-s) en auerez (aures X) PX 16 Iames de riens q. N; q.
aies m. X; a sousfraite nauerez P   24 sanz] et N   III
26 a. ne NPX; nus N   28 nus N   31 *missing P*   33
missing P; Poir N; qui en NX   35 Toute N; iesu P; maudi P   36 Qui aiment NPX; d. ce est g. ribaudie X   IV
38 et j. N; ni NP   40 lui et nuit X; jors P   44
m'amor *missing X*   45-46 *missing X*   47 di li q'il avra
missing X   48 Et P; boune *missing N*

    E   Jeanroy *Or*, 465-468; Spanke *Lied*, 107-109; 373-
374.

    N   See Jeanroy *Or* for a quite different lineation: 10
10 7 6 7 6 7 7 6 7 7 6 7 6 7 6. This arrangement led him to
see various errors in rhyming which are not really present
and to judge that "notre poète n'était pas scrupuleux". Indeed, Jeanroy was inclined to believe that "la pièce était
incomplète et n'avait que les trois premiers couplets dans
l'original; un interpolateur, la jugeant trop courte, aurait
ajouté le quatrième".
    8 *qu'* = *qui*; similarly, ll. 11, 33, 36.

32   II

RS 1916, MW 1086
Ms. H 218v. No music.

    I   Quant noif remaint et glace funt,
        Qe resclarcisent cil ruissel
        Et cil oisiel grant joie funt
        Por la doçor del tens novel   4
        Et florissent cil arbroisiel
        Et tuit cil pré plain de fluer sunt
        Et fine Amor ce mi semunt
        Que je face un sonet novel...   8

    II   Un main suer mon palefroi munt,
        En mai quant chantent cil oisiel,
        Si ai trové au pié d'un munt,
        Chapel faisant en un prael,   12
        La fille au seignor d'un chastel,
        La tres plus belle riens del munt
        De cors et de vis et de front,
        En blanc chainse et en ver mantel.   16

III   Je la salue. Ele respont
        Et laisse a faire sun chapel:
        "Sire, Deux grant joie vos doint
        De la riens dun plus vos est bel,   20
        Et a çaus doint Deux lor avel
        Qui vers dames leiaus cuers unt,
        Et cil qui bone amor defont
        Soient oni, Deu en apel."   24

IV   "Ma doce dame, je l'otroi,
        Qar maint mal m'unt fait gileor;
        Et sachoiz bien que de lor loi
        Ne sui je mie, [ne] des lor;   28
        Je n'amai unques tricheor.
        Mais faites vostre ami de moi,
        S'avreiz trové en bone foi
        Dedenz fin cuer leial amor."   32

V   "Danz chevalier, parler vos oi,
        Ce m'et avis, de grant folor,
        Qar en tot cet païs ne voi
        Pucele de tant bel ator   36
        Ne dame de si grant valor
        Qui mieuz amee soit de moi.
        Por ce, celi fausser ne doi
        Qui m'aime senz cuer gileor."   40

VI   *Ja de celi que mon cuer a*
            Ne partirai mais a nul jor.

VII   *A mes premieres amors me tendrai,*
            Et quant eles me faudrunt, si morai.   44

RR   I   4 des t.   5 arboisiel   7 a. remisemunt
(em. *PetDyg)*   II   10 chante   IV   25 j. letroi *(em.*
Bartsch)   28 *-1*   VI   42 mai   VII   44 q. eses

E   Bartsch, 47-48; Camus, 239; PetDyg "Moniot", 133-
135.

N   16 *ver = vert.*   20 *dun = dont.*   25 In PetDyg
"Moniot", ms. *je letroi* is corrected to *je le croi.*   34
m'et = m'est.   41 *que* serves here as a nominative.   41-44
These stanzas, which can hardly be regarded as envoys, have
all the appearance of refrains. As such, their occurrence
at the end of an otherwise refrainless composition is highly
unusual. In Bartsch, they are relegated to the Rejected

Readings; in PetDyg "Moniot", on the other hand, they are
incorporated into the text to the point of forming the con-
clusion of the maiden's final speech. The couplets do not
appear among the refrains in Boogaard, although the first is
quite similar to B 167 *Amour m'est el cuer entree,/ja n'en
partirai nul jour* and the opening line of the second is
identical to the single-verse refrain, B 114 *A mes premieres
amors me tenrai.*

33   III

RS 1698, MW 855
Stanza I: B 1396 (three other sources), st. II: B 1348, st.
     III: B 437 (one other source), st. IV: B 961 (two other
     sources).
Mss. K 351-352, N 170v-171r, X 229v-230r. Music in all mss.

IV.58. car il m'a trop fet lan- guir et sous-pi- rer.

V.59. S'aim trop melz un pou de joie a de- me- ner
60. que mil marz d'ar- gent a- voir et puis plo- rer."

I   Quant je chevauchoie
    Tot seus l'autrier,
   Jouer m'en aloie
    Tout un sentier;
   Dejoste une arbroie   5
    Pres d'un vergier,
   Dame simple et coie
    Vi onbroier.
  Mult estoit bele et jolie,
  Cors bien fet, gorge polie.   10
   Quant el me vit venant,
   Si chanta maintenant
   Ceste chançonete:
Nus ne doit lez le bois aler
  Sanz sa conpaignete.   15

II   Vers l'onbre de l'ente
    Ou cele estoit
   Chevauchai ma sente
    A grant esploit.
   Cortoise ert et gente;   20
    Vers li ving droit:
   S'amor m'atalente,
    Car mult valoit.
  Gentement l'ai salüee.
  El respont conme senee: 25
   "Sire, [que] Deus vous saut,
   Mes de vous ne me chaut.
   Traiez vous arrier!"
  N'atouchiez pas a mon chainse,
   Sire chevalier!   30

III   "Dame gente et bele,
    Pour vostre amor
   Li cuers mi sautele
    Et nuit et jor.
   En ceste praele   35
    Sor la verdor

             Merrons no berele
              Tout sanz sejor."
       "Sire, je sui marīee
       Et a un vilain donee,   40
          Mes je ne l'aime pas.
         Or merrons noz solaz
        S'il en devoit crever."
      Dame qui a mal mari,
        S'el fet ami,   45
       N'en fet pas a blasmer.

IV   "Dame renvoisie,
          Pour Dieu, merci!
        Or soiez amie:
          Vez ci ami!   50
        Ne soiez marrie
          Pour vo mari;
        Jamés bone vie
          N'avroiz de li."
      "Je ne pris mon mari mie   55
     Une orde ponme porrie.
       Or soit en sa meson
       Et nos nos deduiron,
Car il m'a trop fet languir et souspirer."
  S'aim trop melz un pou de joie a demener   60
  Que mil marz d'argent avoir et puis plorer.

    <u>MN</u>   Form: A A B vrf.
1. In l. 2, ms. writes no rest. 2. In l. 10, ms. writes a
bar. 3. In l. 12, ms. writes no rest. 4. No music is extant for refrains 2-4; conjectured versions, derived from
refrain 1, are here offered, including a conjectured last
line for stanza 4.

    <u>RR</u>   II   19 A mult g. e. *(+1)*   26 *-1*   III   31
D. bele et gente   34 Et la n. et le j. *(+2)*

    <u>V</u>   I   2 seul N, soul X   II   17 ele N   19 A
mult g̅.e̅. NX   25 Ele X   26 S. d. v. s. NX   27 Mes
missing N   30 Sire *missing N*   III   31 D. bele et gente
NX   33 cues N   34 Et *missing X*; la n. et le j. NX   36
uerdure X   37 nostre N   40 a *missing X*   42 n. degras
X   43 greuer N   IV   47 renuoisee X   54 lui NX
59 fet trop N   60 Et saim trop n. N, Et saim m. X

    <u>E</u>   Bartsch, 50-51; Spanke *Lied*, 132-134, 379-380.

DF   Picard: *-ie* for *-iee* in *renvoisie* (47); *no* (37)
for *nostre* and *vo* (52) for *vostre*.

N   37   *merrons* = *menerons*; also in l. 42.   43   *s'*
'even if'.

IV   <u>34</u>

RS 1713, MW 759
Stanza I: B 617 (one other source), st. II: B 901 (one other
      source), st. III: B 622, st. IV: B 1597 (one other
      source), st. V: B 264.
Ms. I 4:12. No music.

I   L'autre jour me departoie
        De Nivers sospris d'amors;
        En un bruelet leis ma voie
        Trovai dame an un destour.
        Euz ot vairs, la crine bloie,   5
        Frechë avoit la colour,
        Et chantoit et menoit joie
        Tout an despit son signor:
            Doucement me tient amors.

II   Ses amins l'avoit tenue,   10
        Mais d'amors se confortoit.
        Este vos aval la rue
        Son marit qui la queroit,
        Que mout bien l'ait entendue,
        La chanson k'elle dixoit: 15
        "Ez folette, malestrue!
        Je vos taing en mon destroit."
            J'ai a cuer les malz d'amors
                Orendroit.

III   "Li malz d'amors me maistrie.   20
        S'or i venoit mes amins
        A cui je suix otroiie,
        Vos seriez jai mal baillis:
        Il vos feroit vilonie,
        La moie foit vos plevis,   25
        Dans vilains, bairbe florie,
        Car vos estes si wiris."
            Dous amins,
        Por vos mi destraint mes maris.

IV   Ses maris li prist a dire: 30
          "Puéz ke je vos taing ici,
          Jamais jor an sa bailie
          Ne vos tanrait vos amis,
          Et si sereiz mal vestie,
          La moie foi vos plevis.   35
          Vos m'aveiz fait vilonie,
          Si vos an randrai merci!"
          Ki feme ait, a joie ait faillit.

V   "Mes maris n'estes vos mie,
          Mavais vilainz rasouteiz.   40
          Vos me ronchiez les l'oïe
          Cant je dor leis vos costeiz,
          Et si ne me faites mie
          Lou jeu d'amors a mon greit.
          Mais toz les jors de ma vie   45
          Ceste chanson chanterai:
          Bien doit soffrir les dongiers son marit
          Qui amors ait tout a sa volenteit."

RR   I   5 lescrine blowe   8 d. de son *(+1)*   II
11 se] ce   16 malle estrute   17 *followed by* et le debo-
naire disoit   III   22 otroieie

E   Bartsch, 41-42; Långfors-Solente, 215-218.

DF   Lorraine, including *ai* for *a*, as in *jai*(23),
bairbe (26); *ei* for tonic *e*, as in *leis* (3), *sereiz* (34),
greit (44); *puéz* (31) for *puis*; *amins* (10) for *amis*; preservation of final *t*, as in *marit* (13), *foit* (25), *faillit*
(38), *greit* (44); *a* (18) for *au*; *lou* (44) for *le*; 1st-pers.
sing. pres. ind. *taing* (17) for *tien*; 3rd-pers. sing. pres.
ind. *ait* (14) for *a*; 3rd-pers. sing. fut. in -*ait*, as in
tanrait (33).

N   This poem is one of the texts identified in ms. I
as "pastorelles". For an isolated composition (RS 1746a)
derived from this one, see Långfors-Solente.
     27 The meaning of *wiris* is unclear. It is suggested
in Långfors-Solente that the form may be a variant of *uisif/
oisif* or of *wihot* 'cuckold'; to these possibilities might be
added *vuidif*, which shares with the first the meaning
'idle'.

V   35

RS 1371, MW 1797, B 1220
Ms. I 4:23. No music.

I   Je me levai ier main matin
        Un pou devant soloil luxant,
        Si m'an antrai an un jardin,
        Mes mainches aloie lassant,
        Et oï an un preit chantant   5
        Une sade plaisans brunette
        Qui chantoit a voix seriette;
        Grant desdus fut de l'escouteir.
            Les jolis malz d'amorettes
                Ne puis plus celleir.   10

II   Volantiers oï lou regret
        K'elle dixoit an sopirant:
        "Dieus, j'ai perdu mon amïet,
        Lou biau, lou blon, qui m'amoit tant;
        Et je li ou an covenant   15
        Ke je seroie s'amïette,
        Si an fix une foliette
        Dont nuns ne m'an dovroit blasmeir."
            [Les jolis malz d'amorettes
                Ne puis plus celleir.]   20

III   "Et ou est ores li valés
        Qui neut et jour m'aloit dixant:
        'Dame, cuer et cors vos preneiz;
        Reteneiz moi a vostre amant,
        Je vos servirai loialment'?   25
        Et je suis si toute soulette!
        Fait ai tant ke ma sainturette
        Ne puet a son point retorneir."
            [Les jolis malz d'amorettes
                Ne puis plus celleir.]   30

IV   "Or me covient mon sainturet
        Remettre un petitet avant,
        Car li ventres m'est jai grossés
        Et adés me vait angroissant.
        Lors si m'alai apercevant   35
        Ke n'estoie plus pucelette;
        Si dirai ceste chansonette
        De boin cuer, ne puis oblieir:

> *[Les jolis malz d'amorettes*
> *Ne puis plus celleir.]"*   40

    V   Et je qui volantiers l'oï
            Me traix un petitet avant;
            Et la belle tantost me vit,
            Se prist a mueir colour grant.
            Et je li ai dit an riant: 45
            "S'avient a mainte pucelette."
            Et elle fut un pou pailette,
            De honte n'ozait plus chanteir:
              Les jolis malz d'a[morettes
              Ne puis plus celleir].   50

    RR   III   23 v. present *(em. Bartsch)*   IV   31   ma
sainturette *(em. Bartsch)*   36 Ke ie n. p. pucelle *(em.*
Bartsch)   V   44 Ce

    E   Bartsch, 43-44.

    DF   Lorraine, including *ai* for *a*, as in *mainches* (4),
jai ($\overline{33}$), *pailette* (47); *ei* for tonic *e*, as in *preit* (5),
escouteir (8), *preneiz* (23); *u* for *ui*, as in *luxant* (2),
desdus (8); *neut* (22) for *nuit*; *boin* (38) for *bon*; *nuns* (18)
for *nus*; preservation of final *t*, as in *preit* (5); *x* for *s*,
as in *luxant* (2), *dixoit* (12), *fix* (17); *lou* (11, 14) for
le; 1st-pers. sing. pret. *ou* (15), from *avoir*, for *oi*; 3rd-
pers. sing. pret. in *-ait*, as in *ozait* (48).

    N   This poem occurs among the texts identified in
ms. I as "pastorelles".

36   VI

RS 1156, MW 353, B 1126 (one other source)
Mss. C 196r, U 161v-162r. No music.

    I   Quant ce vient en mai ke rose est panie,
          Je l'alai coillir per grant drüerie;
          En pouc d'oure oï une voix serie
          Lonc un vert bouset pres d'une abïete:
          Je sant les douls mals leis ma senturete.   5
          Malois soit de Deu ke me fist nonnete!

    II   "Ki nonne me fist, Jesus lou maldie!
          Je di trop envis vespres ne complies;

J'amaixe trop muels bone compaingnie
Ke fust deduissans et amerousete."   10
Je sant [les douls mals leis ma senturete.
Malois soit de Deu ke me fist nonnete]!

III   Elle s'escriait: "Com seux esbaihie!
        E Deus! ki m'ait mis en ceste abaïe?
        Maix jeu en istrai, per sainte Marie!   15
        N'i vestirai mais souplis ne gonnete."
        Je sant [les douls mals leis ma senturete.
        Malois soit de Deu ke me fist nonnete]!

IV   "Celui manderai a cui seux amie
        K'il me vaigne querre en ceste abaïe;   20
        S'irons a Parix moneir bone vie,
        Car il est jolis et je seux jonete."
        Je sant [les douls mals leis ma senturete.
        Malois soit de Deu ke me fist nonnete]!

V   Quant ses amis ot la parolle oïe,   25
        De joie tressaut, li cuers li fremie;
        A la porte en vient de celle abaïe,
        Si en getait fors sa douce amïete.
        Je sant les dous mals [leis ma senturete.
        Malois soit de Deu ke me fist nonnete]!   30

RR   I   1 ce] se   4 b. pees   II   9 m. moneir
bone uïe   III   13 cescriait   14 Deus ke seans m. m.
16 Ne ni vesterai cotte ne gonelle   V   27 Et uint a la
porte de celle; abaie *missing*   29 mals *followed by* desous

     V   Stanzas: I III V II. Stanza IV not included.
I 1 est florie   4 De dans vn bosket leis vne a.   5 a
ma senturett   6 nonnet   II   7 Ke n. mest fist   8 Je
ne dirai maist v.   9 Car asets aim m.   10 Ki est d.
11-12 *complete*   III   13 com] trop   17 les dous mas
added   V   25 Cant li amans   29-30 *complete*

     E   Bartsch, 28-29; Bartsch-Wiese, 220-221; Cremonesi,
67-68; Bec 2, 20-21.

     DF   Lorraine, including *ei* for tonic *e*, as in *leis*
(5), *moneir* (21); *senturete* (5) for *ceinturete*; *lou* (7) for
le; *jeu* (15) for *je*; *seux* (13) for *sui*; *amaixe* (9) for
amasse; 3rd-pers. sing. pres. ind. *ait* (16) for *a*; 3rd-pers.
sing. pret. in *-ait*, as in *escriait* (13), *getait* (28); relative *ke* used as nominative (6, 10).

<u>37</u>   VII

RS 1370, MW 2297, B 1712
Ms. I 4:10. No music.

    I   L'autrier un lundi matin
           M'an aloie ambaniant,
           S'antrai an un biau jardin,
           Trovai nonette seant.
               Ceste chansonette   5
               Dixoit lai nonette:
               "Longue demoree
           Faites, frans moinnes loialz."
               Se plus suis nonette,
                Ains ke soit li vespres,   10
            Je morrai des jolis malz.

    II   Cant la nonette antendi,
           Que si s'aloit gaimentant,
           Maintenant me dexendi
           Sor l'erbette verdoiant.   15
               Et elle s'escrie:
               "Je morrai d'envie
               Por la demoree
           Ke faites, moinnes lëaulz."
               Se plus suis nonette,   20
                Ains ke soit li vespres,
            Je morrai des jolis malz.

    III   La nonain se gaimentoit;
           Resgardait aval un preit,
           Vit lou moinne qui venoit,   25
           Qui avoit son frot osteit.
               Droit vers lai nonette
               Maintenant s'adresse,
               Si l'ait escolee;
           Et elle s'escrie an haut: 30
                Duez, tant buer fu nee,
                Cant serai amee
            De vos, frans moinnes loialz!

    <u>RR</u>   II   16 cescrie   III   30 cescrie   33 *fol-*
lowed by se plus suis.

    <u>E</u>   Bartsch, 29-30; Meyer, 378; Bec 2, 55-56.

DF   Lorraine, including *ai* for *a*, as in *lai* (6); *ei* for tonic *e* and preservation of final *t*, as in *preit* (24), *osteit* (26); *lou* (25) for *le*; 3rd-pers. sing. pres. ind. *ait* (29) for *a*; 3rd-pers. sing. pret. in *-ait*, as in *resgardait* (24).

N   This composition is included among the texts which ms. I identifies as "pastorelles". It is one of a small group of OF songs expressing the amatory desires of a nun; for another, see RS 1156.

CHANSONS

I. (Chanson de femme)

RS 1937, MW 827, B 1716
Mss. U 47v, C 168v-169r. Music in U.

I L'on dit q'amors est dolce chose,
Mais je n'en conois la dolçor;
Tote joie m'en est enclose,
N'ainz ne senti nul bien d'amor.
Lasse! mes mals ne se repose,
Si m'en deplaing et faz clamor.
Mar est batuz qui plorer n'ose,
N'en plorant dire sa dolor.

5

> Ses duels li part qui s'ose plaindre;
> Plus tost en puet son mal estaindre.   10

II   De ce me plaing qu'il m'a traïe;
     S'en ai trop grant duel acoilli,
     Quant je qui sui leals amie
     Ne truis amor en mon ami.
     Je fui ainçois de lui baisie,   15
     Si lo fis de m'amor saisi;
     Mais tels baise qui n'aime mie:
     Baisier ont maint amant traï.
     [Ses duels li part qui s'ose plaindre;
     Plus tost en puet son mal estaindre.]   20

III Estre cuidai de lui amee
     Quant entre ses braz me tenoit;
     Cum plus iere d'amors grevee,
     A son parler me refaisoit;
     A sa voiz iere si sanee   25
     Cum Piramus quant il moroit:
     Navrez en son flanc de s'espee,
     Au nom Tisbé les iauz ovroit.
     [Ses duels li part qui s'ose plaindre;
     Plus tost en puet son mal estaindre.]   30

<u>MN</u>   Form: A A B rf (ballade).

<u>RR</u>   I   6 deplaig   10 Plust   II   11   qui

<u>V</u>   I   3 j. ait en li e.   4   nuls biens damors
II <u>13</u> loiaul   III   25 Asauoir

<u>E</u>   Schutz, 202-203.

<u>N</u>   It is impossible to determine whether this song
was actually composed by a woman or falls into the small
group of courtly love-songs whose speaker is a woman but
which are known to have been written by men. In his discussion of the "women's" songs of unknown authorship (in which
he quotes st. 2 of RS 1937), Jeanroy concludes that they
must be attributed to male poets: "Si ces chansons étaient
dues à des femmes on y trouverait sans doute un accent plus
tendre, plus ému, plus de discrétion surtout et quelque
ombre de pudeur féminine" (Jeanroy Or, p. 96). This judgment not only betrays, ninety years later, the heavy influence of 19th-century attitudes, but also reveals little
awareness of the formalist esthetic of the courtly chanson.

25-28 Cf. Ovid, *Metamorphoses* IV, 142-146:
 "Pyrame," clamavit, "quis te mihi casus ademit?
 Pyrame, responde! tua te carissima Thisbe
 nominat: exaudi vultusque attolle iacentes!"
 ad nomen Thisbes oculos a morte gravatos
 Pyramus erexit visaque recondidit illa.
In the 12th-century adaptation, this becomes:
   "Piramus, ves ci vostre amie.
   Car l'esgardez, si ert garie."
   Li jovenciaus, la ou moroit,
   Entr'oevre les iex et si voit
   Que ce iere Tisbé s'amie
   Qui l'apeloit toute esmarie.
(*Piramus et Tisbé*, ed. C. de Boer [Paris, 1921], ll. 892-
897). Note that it is to the male figure that the female
speaker in RS 1937 compares herself; note, moreover, that
the song makes no mention of the death which in the story
immediately follows Pyramus' glance at Thisbe.

<u>39</u>   II. (Chanson de femme)

RS 517, MW 801
Ms. C 136r-v. No music.

   I La froidor ne la jalee
      Ne puet mon cors refroidir,
      Si m'ait s'amor eschaufee,
      Dont plaing et plor et sospir;
      Car toute me seux donee   5
        A li servir.
      Muels en deüsse estre amee
       • • • • •
      De celui ke tant desir,
      Ou j'ai mise ma pensee.   10

   II Ne sai consoil de ma vie
      Se d'autrui consoil n'en ai,
      Car cil m'ait en sa baillie
      Cui fui et seux et serai.
      Por tant seux sa douce amie 15
        Ke bien sai
      Ke, por rien ke nuls n'en die,
        N'amerai
      Fors lui, dont seux en esmai.
      Quant li plaist, se m'ocie!   20

III   Amors, per moult grant outraige
       M'ocieis, ne sai por coi;
       Mis m'aveis en mon coraige
       D'ameir lai ou je ne doi.
       De ma folie seux saige   25
           Quant je.l voi.
       De porchaiscier mon damaige
           Ne recroi.
       D'ameir plux autrui ke moi
       Ne li doinst Deus couraige.   30

IV   Ensi, laisse! k'en puis faire,
       Cui Amors justice et prant?
       Ne mon cuer n'en puis retraire,
       Ne d'autrui joie n'atent.
       Trop ont anuit et contraire   35
           Li amant:
       Amors est plux debonaire
           A l'autre gent
       K'a moi, ki les mals en sent,
       Ne nuls biens n'en puis traire.   40

V   Ma chanson isi define,
       Ke joie ait vers moi fineir;
       Car j'ai el cors la rasine
       Ke ne puis desrasineir,
       Ke m'est a cuer enterine,   45
           Sens fauceir.
       Amors m'ont pris en haïne
           Por ameir.
       J'ai beüt del boivre ameir
       K'Isoth but, la roïne.   50

RR   I   2 refroidier 8 *missing*   III   26 j. uo
30 douraige   V 42 finei *(em. Bartsch-Wiese)*

E   Bartsch-Wiese, 222-223; Bec 2, 8-10.

DF   Lorraine, including *ai* for *a*, as in *outraige*
(21), *lai* (24), *porchaiscier* (27), *laisse* (31); *ei* for tonic
e, as in *ocieis* (22), *ameir* (29), *fineir* (42); *c* for *s(s)*
and *s* for *c*, as in *justice* (32), *fauceir* (46), *rasine* (43);
preservation of final *t*, as in *beüt* (49); 3rd-pers. sing.
pres. ind. *ait* (3) for *a*; *seux* (14) for *sui*.

N   There is no certainty that this song was composed
by a woman. See note to RS 1937. 8 It is suggested in

Bartsch-Wiese that *par desir* fill this lacuna.   20 *se* =
adverbial *si*.   45 *ke* = *qui*.

<u>40</u>   III

RS 1981, MW 1320
Mss. U 44r-v, C 248v-249r. No music.

    I   Al renoveler de la flor
        M'estuet chanter en sospirant,
        K'entre mon cuer et fine Amor
        A ma dame vont demandant
        Ice que doit que je ne chant;   5
        S'est bien droiz que je m'i ator,
        Des que il lor vient a talant.

    II   Je sai de voir k'a la meillor
        Del mont ai mis mon pansement.
        Ne li os conter ma dolor,   10
        Ne ja ne.l savra autrement.
        Sachent tuit, por la melz vaillant
        Qui soit el mont sospir et plor;
        Ja ne li dirai altremant.

    III   De li vienent li mal que j'ai   15
        Et sovent en plaing et sospir,
        Ne ja de li ne partirai,
        Ainz en voil bien les mals soffrir.
        S'il vos en dangne sovenir,
        Cant toz jors soffert les avrai,   20
        Molt tost les me porrez merir.

    IV   Dame, molt durement m'esmai
        De ceste amor que tant desir,
        Ne ja de vos ne partirai;
        Ceste amors est senz repentir;   25
        Ensi m'en doigne Deus joïr,
        Com je l'aim de fin cuer verai
        Et amerai jusq'au morir.

    V   Chascuns dit qu'il n'ose nomer
        La rien qui plus lo fait doloir,   30
        Mais je ne la quier ja celer,
        Bien s'en puet on apercevoir,
        K'ele a plus valor et pooir

De totes vaillanz, la nonper.
Celi aim je senz decevoir.   35

VI   Chancenette, fai li savoir,
      Quant ele te fera chanter,
      Que de li ne me puis movoir.

RR   I   4 Et   7 quil *(-1)*   IV   26 ioiir

V   Stanza VI not included in C.
I 1 Uers lou nouel de la f.   6 Cest; acort   7 kil
II   8 ken la   12 Tuit saichent   13 Del mont souant s.
et p.   14 Ne del dire nai herdement   III   16 plor et
17 Ne iai nul ior nen p.   19 Se v.   21 le me   IV   25
amor   26 daigne   27 Quant   28 Et a. sens repentir   V
34 nonpeirs

E   Schutz, 269-270.

N   3-5 'for my heart and true Love have both been
asking my lady what it means that I am not singing (i.e.,
why I am silent)'.

                            IV   41

RS 4, MW 900
Ms. C 222r-v. No music.

      I   S'onkes nulz hons se clamait
            D'Amors, bien m'en doi [je] plaindre,
            Kant [a] la tres belle m'ait
            Doneit mon cuer, ne ains prandre
            A moi congiet n'en dignait;   5
            Maiz de tant vos veul aprandre,
            Pués c'Amors m'i fait entandre.
            Ki vairoit lou cors k'elle ait,
            Sa bouche et sa faice tendre,
            Bien diroit ke cristaulz ait   10
            Vers son vis color de sendre.

      II   Onkes tant ne so deffandre
            Mon cuer ke il n'alaist lai
            Dont la mort m'estuet atandre,
            Car jai joie n'en avrai   15
            Se pitiés ne l'en veult prandre.
            A morir me covanrait,

Si morai quant li plairait;
Et s'elle me voloit randre
Por mon cuer ke tolut m'ait   20
Un baixier sens plux riens prandre,
De ma mort pardon avrait.

III   Ensi seux com li fenis
Ke tous s'airt por li occire,
Car per mes euls seux la mis   25
Dont je port corrous et ire.
Lais! s'en seux si esbaihis
Ke ne l'os a nelui dire;
Ainçois me lairoie frire
Comme lairt ki est remis,   30
Ke deïsse mon martire
A nul home ki soit vis.
Tant com li plairait veul vivre.

IV   E lais! ne puis troveir mire
Des mals dont seux si sopris,   35
Et adés vers moi s'empire
Celle a cui seux fins amins;
S'en ai plux jane ke cire
Lou cors, les menbres, lou vis,
Et ceu me fait aincor pix   40
Quant por mon mal la voi rire.
Nonporcant, tant seux gentils
Quant son tres gent cors remire,
Plux que nuls seux posteïs.

V   A defin de ma chanson,   45
Proi Deu ki boen pooir ait.
Vos requier un gueridon,
Dame, teil com vos plairait.
Pitiés, vai, si l'en semon,
Car se le gueridon n'ait   50
Mes cuers, ke servie l'ait,
Je brairai a tout le mont,
En keil leu k'elle serait,
Celle ke m'ait en prixon:
Hareu! haro! la voi lai!   55

RR   I 2 -1 3 Kan; -1   II   19 celle   22 aurai   III 23 fenise   V   50 li   54 en sa p. (+1)
55 haro ie la (+1)

E   Schutz, 254-256.

    <u>DF</u>   Lorraine, including *ai* for *a*, as in *faice* (9), *jai* ($\overline{15}$), *airt* (24), *esbaihis* (27); *a* for *au*, as in *jane* (38); *ei* for tonic *e*, as in *troveir* (34), *teil* (48); *boen* (46) for *bon*; *amins* (37) for *amis*; *sendre* (11) for *cendre*; *x* for *s*, as in *baixier* (21), *plux* (21); preservation of final *t*, as in *doneit* (4), *congiet* (5), *tolut* (20); *lou* (8) for *le*; *ceu* (40) for *ce*; 3rd-pers. sing. pres. ind. *ait* (3) for *a*; 3rd-pers. sing. fut. in -*ait*, as in *plairait* (18), *avrait* (22), *serait* (53); *seux* (23) for *sui*. Note that *plaindre* (2) rhymes with *prandre* (= *prendre*) (4), etc., and *avrai* (15) with *covanrait* (17), etc. Such rhymes, peculiar to Lorraine, indicate the regional origin of the poem and not merely that of the manuscript.

    <u>N</u>   3-5 'since [Love] gave my heart . . . and never deigned to ask my permission'.   8 *vairoit* = *verroit*.   11 *vers* 'in comparison with'.   24 *li* = *lui*, used here as a reflexive.   52 *ke* occurs here as a nominative, as is frequently the case in this Lorraine manuscript; likewise, l. 54.

V   <u>42</u>

RS 1386, MW 835, B 719
Ms. C 174v-175r. No music.

<table>
<tr><td>I</td><td>Or seux liés del dous termine</td><td></td></tr>
<tr><td></td><td>Ke naist la flor premerainne,</td><td></td></tr>
<tr><td></td><td>Ke croist la flor en l'espine</td><td></td></tr>
<tr><td></td><td>Et l'erbe leis la fontainne;</td><td></td></tr>
<tr><td></td><td>Lors ne puis avoir saixine</td><td>5</td></tr>
<tr><td></td><td>De celi ke m'est lontainne,</td><td></td></tr>
<tr><td></td><td>N'el vergier desous cortine</td><td></td></tr>
<tr><td></td><td>Joie de volenteit plainne.</td><td></td></tr>
<tr><td></td><td>*Et pués ke j'en atent les biens,*</td><td></td></tr>
<tr><td></td><td>*Drois est ke li mals en soit miens.*</td><td>10</td></tr>
<tr><td>II</td><td>El cuer desous la poitrine</td><td></td></tr>
<tr><td></td><td>M'ait navreit k'ensi me moinne,</td><td></td></tr>
<tr><td></td><td>Maix del dairt ist une espine,</td><td></td></tr>
<tr><td></td><td>Se m'ait navreit en teil voinne</td><td></td></tr>
<tr><td></td><td>Dont puet bien estre mescine</td><td>15</td></tr>
<tr><td></td><td>Celle k'est de biauteit plainne,</td><td></td></tr>
<tr><td></td><td>K'elle ait mon cuer et l'orine</td><td></td></tr>
<tr><td></td><td>Des mals ke trais la semainne.</td><td></td></tr>
</table>

Et pués [ke j'en atent les biens,
Drois est ke li mals en soit miens].   20

III   Ma chansonnete define,
         Si sai bien c'Amors la moinne
         A la plux cortoise et fine
         Ke soit en trestout cest regne.
         Mis me seux en sa saixine;   25
         Bien puet aligier ma poene,
         Car je l'ain plux d'amor fine
         Ke Paris ne fist Helenne.
         Et pués ke j'en atent les biens,
         Drois est ke li malz en soit miens.   30

RR   I   7   Kel *(em. Schutz)*

E   Schutz, 211-212.

DF   Lorraine, including *ai* for *a*, as in *dairt* (13);
ei for tonic *e*, as in *leis* (4), *teil* (14); preservation of
final *t*, as in *volenteit* (8) and *navreit* (12); phonological
equivalence of *ainne, oinne, egne, oene, enne; x* for *s*, as
in *saixine* (5), *plux* (27); 3rd-pers. sing. pres. ind. *ait*
(12) for *a*; *seux* (25) for *sui*; nominative use of relative *ke*
(12, 16, 24).

N   12   *k'* 'she who'.

43   VI

RS 724, MW 479
Mss. P 143v-144r, X 212r-v. Music in both mss.

1. A-mors, qui sou-prent 2.quan-qu'a li se prent,
4. en pou d'ore es-prent 5.son e-sper-ne-ment   3. m'a sou-pris;
                                                6. m'a es-pris.

7. S'en-si l'e-ust pri-se 8.et en ses las mi-se 9.ce-le qui m'a pris,
10. tot a ma de-vi-se 11.fust en mon ser-vi-se,

12.s'il li ple-ust 13.qe el e-ust 14.d'a-mors tot le pris.

I

Amors, qui souprent
Quanqu'a li se prent,
　M'a soupris;
En pou d'ore esprent,
Son espernement　　　5
　M'a espris.
S'ensi l'eüst prise
Et en ses las mise
Cele qui m'a pris,
Tot a ma devise　　　10
Fust en mon servise,
　S'il li pleüst
　Qe el eüst
D'amors tot le pris.

II

Son sens, son confort,15
Son tres douz deport
　M'a lachiez;
Les maus que je port
M'ont doné la mort;
　C'est pechiez.　　20
Ma tres douce amie,
Fetes moi aïe
D'estre ralazchiez,
Ou je pert la vie.
Ne m'oublïez mie,　25
　Fins cuers loiaus,
　Mes de mes maus
Vos praigne pitiez!

III

Et quant je regart
Son tres douz regart　30
　Et son vis,
Issi ait Deus part
En m'ame, q'il gart,
　Q'il m'est vis

MN　　Form: A A B.

Que il n'ait tant bele 35
Dame ne pucele
En tot cest païs.
Amez moi, suer bele!
Vostre amor m'apele
　La grant biauté,　　40
　La loiauté
Qu'a Deus en vos mis.

IV

Bele, vos avés
Mon cuer, ce sevez,
　En prison.　　　45
Se vos ne.l gardez,
Certes vos ferés
　Mesprison;
Car il a fiance
Et bone esperance　　50
D'avoir raenson.
Ne fetes nuisance
Mes de la puissance
　Que vos avés,
　Se vos voulez,　　55
D'aidier li ou non.

V

"Biau tres douz amis,
Quant si vos voi pris
　Et laschiez,
A vostre devis　　　60
Serés, je.l plevis,
　Ralaschiez;
Car qui merci crie
Por avoir aïe
Doit estre alegiés.　　65
J'ere vostre amie,
Ne en doutez mie;
　De moi ferés
　Vos volentez,
Tot cert en soiez!"　　70

RR   I   2 Quan que a   5 Son *repeated*   III   42
Que dex a en v. m. *(+1)*   IV   47 Sertes   52 Ne li f. n.
(+1)

V   I   1 sorprent   3 sorpris   II   24-25 *transposed*   III   32 Ensi   35 Quil n. t. b.   IV   52 Ne
li f. n.   V   63 prie   67 Nen d. uos m.

E   Spanke *Lied*, 71-73, 368.

N   39 *m'apele = me rapele.*   52-53 Understand *Ne
fetes mes nuisance de la puissance.*   57-70 The appearance
of the lady's answer, unusual in any case, would be unthinkable in a love-song of the normal type; but both versification and diction have already suggested a certain lightness.

44   VII

RS 1645, MW 662
Ms. K 401-402. Music.

A

1. Au nou-viau tens, tou-te   riens ses-jo- ist:
3. en ces ver-giers vi- o- le- te flo-rist,

2. Cil oi-   sel- lons con-men-cent nou-viaus sons,
4. et par a- mours chan-tent a-manz chan-cons.

B

5. Si ne m'est pas. Tou-te   joi- e me   nuist,

6. quant plus en voi et il mains m'en-be- list,

7. quant pas n'a-tent a a-   voir gue-   ri-son

8. de la be- le, mes so- vent a lar- ron

9. de cuer plore et sou- spi-   re.

I   Au nouviau tens, toute riens s'esjoïst:
     Cil oisellon connmencent nouviaus sons,
     En ces vergiers violete florist,
     Et par amours chantent amanz chançons.
     Si ne m'est pas. Toute joie me nuist;   5
     Quant plus en voi et il mains m'enbelist,
     Quant pas n'atent a avoir guerison
     De la bele, mes sovent a larron
              De cuer plore et souspire.

II   Je cuidai bien avoir, s'estre poïst,   10
     En aucun tens de ma dame pardon,
     Ne qu'a nul jor autre mari ne prist
     Fors moi tot seul, qui [sui] ses liges hon;
     Car si senblant, oncor ne[.l] me desist,
     Me disoient qu'avant touz me vousist   15
     Amer. Por ce ai mis en sa prison
     Moi et mon cuer, et ore a pris baron!
              S'en muir de duel et d'ire.

III Riens ne me plest en cest siecle vivant,
     Puis que je ai a la bele failli,   20
     Qu'ele donoit a moi par son senblant
     Sens et honor, hardement, cuer joli.
     Ore est torné ce derrieres devant,
     Car a touz jorz avrai cuer gemissant,
     Plain de dolor, plorant, tristre et marri,   25
     Ne ja nul jor ne.l metrai en oubli;
              S'en sui en grant martire.

IV   Biau sire Deus, par son faintis senblant
     M'a ma dame confondu et traï;
     Mes ce ont fet li sien, apertement: 30
     Pour son avoir l'ont donee a celui
     Qui ne deüst pas aler regardant.
     Dolenz en sui; mes s'el m'amast autant
     De loial cuer com je fesoie li,
     Maugré aus touz i eüst il failli: 35
              Ja, pour ce, n'en fust pire.

     MN   Form: A A B.

RR   I   10 poïst] deust   12 ne prist] neust   13
-1   14   si] son; ne.l] ne   IV   32 ne] nel   *All emen-*
dations except the last were proposed in Jeanroy "Modène".

E   Jeanroy "Modène", 265-266; Spanke *Lied*, 224-225,
403.

N   As noted in Jeanroy "Modène", p. 243, this is one
of only a tiny group of OF songs which speak, and with
clearly personal reference, of marriage. The others are RS
518 (anon.) and RS 557 (Philippe de Remi); cf., too, RS 351
(Jacques d'Autun). Two elements of the poet's craft merit
particular attention. Note, first, the words rhyming in
-*ire*, only one of which occurs in each stanza, in the final
line, and whose distant echo is reinforced by their semantic
association.   Second, there is a tendency to break the normal rhythmic flow of the 4 + 6 verse: see the treatment of
the caesura in ll. 5, 10, 16, 32 and the instances of enjambment, or relative enjambment, at the end of ll. 7, 8,
15, 16, 33.
        8 *a larron* 'furtively'.   14 *oncor* . . . 'although
she did not tell me so [explicitly]'.   30 Spanke's emendation of *apertement* to *apartenant* is gratuitous.   32 The
ms. reading *nel*, accepted without comment in both Jeanroy
"Modène" and Spanke *Lied*, is unsatisfactory: while *Qui* is
acceptable as a subject (referring, of course, to *celui*), .*1*
(= *le*) is not as a feminine direct object. In our emended
line, *Qui* (= *cui*) serves as the object of *regardant* and the
lady is the subject of *deüst*; thus, 'whom she should not
[even] have been considering'. From the point of view of
sense alone, either choice of subject and object will do:
the man was unworthy of considering her or was unworthy of
being considered by her.   36 'For this reason, i.e., her
indifference, the situation could not be worse'.

45   VIII

RS 1900, MW 858
B 758 (Stanza IV only; one other source)
Mss. P 143r-v, X 211v-212r. Music in both mss.

1. Chan-ter voil un   no- vel   son   2. por mes do- lors ra- le- gier.
3. Cil n'est pas hors de pri- son   4. q'A-mors ont a   ju- sti- sier;

5. ce- le fet grant tra-i- son 6. qui de-çoit a l'a- coin- tier

7. et puis guer-pist le pri- son, 8. quant el l'a mis el sen- tier

9. de li a- mer. 10. Ne me sai de fause a- mor a cui cla- mer.

I   Chanter voil un novel son
      Por mes dolors ralegier.
      Cil n'est pas hors de prison
      Q'Amors ont a justisier;
      Cele fet grant traïson   5
      Qui deçoit a l'acointier
      Et puis guerpist le prison,
      Quant el l'a mis el sentier
        De li amer.
  Ne me sai de fause amor a cui clamer. 10

II   Amors m'ont en lor las mis,
      Qui maint en ont deceü;
      Sanz amie sui amis,
      Bien m'en sui aperceü.
      Juré m'avoit et promis   15
      Amors, li faus mescreü,
      Qu'amez seroie toz dis,
      Mes or ai aperceü
        Sa fause foi.
  Fausement s'est contenue Amors vers moi. 20

III   Amors est bien losengier
      Et atraire et decevoir;
      Vers lui ne vaut riens dangier
      Ne prouece ne valor.
      Cuer trenbler, color changier   25
      Fet Amors sanz percevoir;
      Bien set trere sanz lancier
      Amor ce que veut avoir
        A son pleisir.
  Fouz est qui de faus amor cuide joïr. 30

IV   Amors n'i garde a nul droit;
              L'un fet trenbler et l'autre art,
              L'un a chaut et l'autre a froit;
              Chascun trait d'un divers dart;
              L'un suesfre toz les tormens.   35
              Ce n'est pas loial esgart.
              S'Amors croire me vouloit,
              Ja batroie de ma part
                 Tel jugement.
       Fouz est qui de fause amor suesfre torment.   40

V   Chançon, va t'en a celi
              Por qui je te conmençai.
              Je li mant, et tu li di,
              Que je l'aim de cuer verai;
              Ja ne partise de li   45
              S'el amast de bone foi
                 Son fin amant.
       Deus, a vos conmant celi por qui je chant.

MN   Form: A A B; the envoy is sung to ll. 3-10.
1. In l. 4 ms. writes this note too early and omits the
rest.

RR   I   3 Il   II   13 amis] ami   15 et pleui
III   21 A. soit 24 poueece 27 sanz lauoir   V 41
celui 43 li dis

V   I   2 alegier   II   20 contenu   III   22 Et
traire et d. 23 V. li 28 Amors 30 fausse   IV 33
a *missing* 39 ioement 40 de] por   V 42 te *missing*
44-45 *missing* 46 de] en

E   Spanke *Lied*, 69-71, 367.

N   This song becomes a love-song only in the envoy
(st. 5), the preceding stanzas all constituting an attack on
love. Neither in Spanke nor in Boogaard is this considered
to be a refrain-song (*chanson avec des refrains*). B lists
l. 40 as a refrain, however, since it occurs in stanza-final
position in another poem as well (RS 615, st. 2): "il s'agit
de deux chansons de la même structure sans refrain (!) qui
se suivent de très près dans les mss. PX; dans les quatre
premières strophes de R[S] 1900 le poète exprime la même
idée dans le vers final qui fonctionne comme une sorte de
refrain" (p. 160).
   4 Note that *amor(s)* occurs, apparently interchange-

ably, as a plural (4), feminine singular (10), and masculine
singular (16).   35 This line is surely corrupt: *L'un*, as
in ll. 32 and 33, would call for *l'autre*, which does not occur; *tormens* has no place in the rhyme scheme; *suesfre*, like
tormens, is no doubt an erroneous anticipation of l. 40; the
expected rhyme word in *-oit* would, moreover, seem to invali-
date the plural *toz les . . .-s.*   46 The reduction of [wͤe]
to [ͤe] would account for the rhyme *foi:verai:commençai.*

IX   <u>46</u>

RS 1983, MW 1253
Mss. N 165v-166r, K 341-342, P 175v-176r, X 223r-v. Music
    in all mss.

<pre>
    I   Se j'ai du monde la flor
           Bien servie a sa devise,
           Dame de pris, de valor,
           Por qui Amors me justise,
           Je m'en aime meuz et prise,   5
           S'ele a mon cuer sanz retor;
           Car cil qui sert nuit et jor
           Doit avoir joie et joïr
                 De son desir.

    II   Des l'eure que je la vi   10
           Si doucete et acesmee,
           Ne la poi metre en oubli;
           Mon cuer a et ma pensee;
           Si n'est riens qui tant m'agree
</pre>

        Con seul ce qu'ele a sesi   15
        Mon cuer; or li cri merci,
        Que j'aie prouchain secors
            De mes amors.

III   En li a biau mireor;
        Bien l'a nature portrete: 20
        Regart a plain de douçor,
        Vis riant, bele bouchete.
        Si me doi bien entremetre
        De lui servir nuit et jor;
        Or servirai fine Amor   25
        En espoir d'avoir pardon
            Con fin prison.

IV   En former son douz reclain
        A lonc tens pensé nature;
        Reclamés sui soir et main   30
        D'amer si bele faiture.
        Or serf Amor et endure
        Et, se j'en palis et taing,
        Bien et mal en bon gré praing
        Con cil qui ma dame amer   35
            Veut sanz fauser.

V   J'envoieré ma chançon
        A ma douce amie chiere,
        Qui de s'amor m'a fet don.
        Por Deu, qu'en nule maniere   40
        N'oblit ne ne mete arriere
        Je qui sui ses liges hon,
        Car ce seroit mesprison,
        Mes vers moi gart son otroi
            En bone foi!   45

<u>MN</u>   Form: A A B.

    <u>RR</u>   III   25   Or s. nuit et ior   IV   33 taig   34
prengn   36   Uuueil

    <u>V</u>   II   12   Me   P   III   24   lui] li   KPX   26
dauoir merci   X   27   fins   X   IV   28   son] si   KPX   29
Lonc t. pensa n.   X   32   amors   KPX   34   Bon   KX   36
Woil P, Uueil   X   V   38   d. dame c.   X   43   ce] se   P

    <u>E</u>   Spanke *Lied*, 111-113, 375.

N̲ 27 *prison* 'prisoner'.   42 Note that *je* is used here as a direct object.

X   <u>47</u>

RS 1749, MW 1368
Mss. K 357, N 173v, X 232v. Music in all mss.

I   Amors me semont et proie
       De chanter, si chanterai;
       Puis que la bele m'en proie,
       Ja ne l'en escondirai;   4
       Car je l'aim et amerai,
       Ne ja Deus puis ne mi voie
       Se de li departirai;
       Pour li est mes cuers en joie.   8

II   Je sui cil qui qiert sa proie
       Partout por son cors garir,
       Si me sui mis en la voie
       D'avoir plenté d'anemis   12
       Qui la mi vuelent tolir;
       Mes, par Dieu, se il savoient
       Conbien je l'aim et desir,
       Tout en pes la mi leroient.   16

III   Je cuidai celer ma joie,
       Ce qu'Amors m'avoit promis;
       Las! conment la celeroie
       Puis que j'ai cele conquis?   20
       El m'a un besier promis
       Que, douz Deus, se je l'avoie,

Tout li saint de paradis
En devroient avoir joie.

24

MN   Form: A A B B.

RR   I   7   Que   III   21   Mes el *(+1)*

    V   I   5 et ele moi NX 6 Mes ja NX 7 Que
NX; li me partirai N   II 9 quier N 10 poir N 11
a la N   III 17 cudai celai c. N; cele m. X 22
deus *missing* X   23 Tuit X

E   Spanke *Lied*, 142-143, 382; Schutz, 269-270.

N   There is a certain casualness in the rhyming:
while *a* is constant throughout, *b* changes in st. 2 and the
change is retained in st. 3; *b*, moreover, takes the form of
assonance in st. 2 but rhyme in st. 3.
    7 The change from *Que* to *Se* seems to be required by
the sense of the utterance. *Se* + future is not unknown in
OF; see, for example, Tobler-Lommatzsch, vol. 9, col. 278.
16 *la mi* may easily be read as *l'ami*, as in Spanke *Lied*. A
play on words is no doubt intended, particularly in view of
l. 13.

48   XI

RS 146, MW 104, B 1127 (five other sources)
Ms. P 146r-v. Music.

I   Amors est trop fiers chastelains,
      Car il maintient entre ses mains
      Et chevaliers et chapelains
      Et si fet cortois les vilains.

Par m'ame,
Je sent les maus d'amer por vos.

4

Et vos por moi, sentés les vos,
Ma dame?   8

II   Amors mestroie tote gent
       Et m'a damë, a son talent;
       Et quant vilains a li se prent,
       Frans et douz et cortois le rent.   12
              Par m'ame,
       [Je sent les maus d'amer por vos.
       Et vos por moi, sentés les vos,
              Ma dame]?   16

III   Amors vient bien a chief de tous,
       Car le plus fort met au desos
       Et l'orgueillous met a genous
       Et le felon fet frans et douz.   20
              Par m'ame,
       [Je sent les maus d'amer por vos.
       Et vos por moi, sentés les vos,
              Ma dame]?   24

IV   Amors a si tres cortois non,
       Si haut et de si grant renon,
       Et si donte bien un glouton
       Et fet cortois, ou vuoille ou non.   28
              Par m'ame,
       [Je sent les maus d'amer por vos.
       Et vos por moi, sentés`les vos,
              Ma dame]?   32

V   Amors mestroie clers et lais
       Et passe bien totes lor lois
       Et prent et garde bien ses drois;
       L'aver fet larges et cortois.   36
              Par m'ame,
       [Je sent les maus d'amer por vos.
       Et vos por moi, sentés les vos,
              Ma dame]?   40

MN   Form: a a b rf (ballade?).
1. In l. 1 ms. writes a bar.

RR   III   17 tous] tor   V   36 Lauel

E   Noack, 103; Jeanroy-Långfors, 37-38; Spanke *Lied*,
256-257, 410.

N   This celebration of the power of Love is included
in the Jeanroy-Långfors collection of *chansons satiriques*,
where it is characterized as being "contre l'amour". It is
hard to understand why.

In both Noack and Jeanroy-Långfors, the refrain is
altered to read, in two lines, *Je sent les maus d'amer por
vos, par m'ame,/Et vos, por moi sentés les vos, ma dame?* MW,
citing B8 C2' B8 C2' as the refrain scheme, acknowledges the
presence of four lines, but retains the wrong order.

10 In Jeanroy-Långfors, *m'a damë, a* is emended to *ma
dame a a*. Not only metrically unnecessary, the change introduces an idea alien to the poem, which asserts only
Love's power over male lovers.

<u>49</u>   XII. (Chanson de femme)

RS 100, MW 2024, B 1040
Mss. K 343-344, N 166r-v, P 177r-v, X 224r-v. Music in all
mss.

I   Lasse, pour quoi refusai
        Celui qui tant m'a amee?
        Lonc tens a a moi musé
        Et n'i a merci trouvee.
        Lasse, si tres dur cuer ai!   5
            Qu'en dirai?
            Forssenee
        Fui, plus que desvee,
        Quant le refusai.
              G'en ferai   10

Droit a son plesir,
S'il m'en daigne oïr.

II   Certes, bien me doi clamer
Et lasse et maleüree
Quant cil ou n'a point d'amer,   15
Fors grant douçor et rousee,
Tant doucement me pria
      Et n'i a
      Recouvree
  Merci; forssenee   20
  Fui quant ne l'amai.
     G'en ferai
  [Droit a son plesir,
  S'il m'en daigne oïr].

III   Bien deüst avoir trouvé   25
Merci quant l'a demandee;
Certes, mal en ai ouvré
Quant je la li ai vëee;
Mult m'a mis en grant esmai.
     G'en morrai,   30
     S'acordee
  Sanz grant demoree
  A lui ne serai.
     G'en ferai
  Droit [a son plesir,   35
  S'il m'en daigne oïr].

IV   A touz ceus qui l'ont grevé
Dont Deus si fort destinee
Q'il aient les euz crevez
Et les orilles coupees!   40
Ensi ma dolor perdrai.
     Lors dirai:
     Genz desvee,
  Ma joie est doublee,
  Et se mesfet ai,   45
     G'en ferai
  [Droit a son plesir,
  S'il m'en daigne oïr].

V   Chançon, va sanz delaier
A celui qui tant m'agree.   50
Pour Dieu li pri et reqier
Viengne a moi sanz demoree.
En sa merci me metrai,

> Tost avrai
> Pes trouvee,   55
> Se il li agree,
> Car je trop mal trai.
>   *G'en ferai*
>   *[Droit a son plesir,*
>   *S'il m'en daigne oïr].*   60

<u>MN</u>   Form: A A B rf (ballade).

<u>RR</u>   III   28   ai uee

   <u>V</u>   I   8   que riens nee   P   II   13   men   X   14
Lasse et male e.   N   16   pitie et r.   P   20   forsee   N
III   25   trouuee   P   IV   39   leur eus   P   40   estoupees
X   45   meffait   X   47   droit *added in N*   V   49   ua ten
s.   P   55   P. recouuree   N   56   sil   P   57   Que   NX; maus
P   59-60   droit a son plaisir sil men deigne oir *added in X*

   <u>E</u>   Jeanroy *Or*, 499-501; Noack, 40; Spanke *Lied*, 114-
116, 379-380; Gennrich *Alt Lied* 2, 37-40; Gennrich *Ex*, 34-
35; Bec 2, 7-8.

   <u>N</u>   Graphic variety and dialectal adaptation mask the
unusual fact that, with the exception of the last two lines
of the refrain, there is essentially only one rhyme in this
song: *a* is -[e] and *b* is simply its feminine equivalent
-[eə].   The *a* rhyme is represented by *-ai*, *-é*, *-er*, *-ez*, and
even *-ier*; to this list must be added *-a* (17, 18).   Indeed,
the rhyme words *pria* and *a* in st. 2 lose their anomalousness
if we but regard this text as the Francien transcription of a
Lorraine poem, in which the two verbs would have occurred
quite normally as *priait* and *ait*.
   15   *amer* 'bitterness'.   33   Note the future tense used
in an 'if'-clause.   51   Understand *que* after *requier*.

CHANSONS DE CROISADE

RS 1967, MW 1149
Mss. C 245v-246r, U 127r-127v. No music.

I Vos ki ameis de vraie amor,
  Esvelliés vos, ne dormeis pais!
  L'alüete nos trait lou jor,
  Et se nos dist en ses retrais
  Ke venus est li jors de paix   5
  Ke Deus per sa tres grant dousor
  Donrait a ceals ki por s'amor
  Panront la creux et por lor fais
  Soufferront poene nuit et jor.
  Or vairait il ses amans vrais!   10

II Cil doit bien estre forjugiés
  Ki a besoing son seignor lait;
  Si serait il, bien lou saichiés!
  Aiseis averait poene et lait
  A jor de nostre dairien plait,   15
  Quant Deus costeis, pames et piés
  Mosterrait sanglans et plaiés,
  Car cil ke plux bien avrait fait
  Serait si tres fort esmaiés
  K'il tramblerait, keil greit k'il ait. 20

III Cil ki por nos fut en creux mis
  Ne nos amait pais faintemant,
  Ains nos amait com fins amins,
  Et por nos amiablement
  La sainte crox moult doucemant 25
  Entre ses brais, davant son pis,
  Com aignials douls, simples et pis,
  Portait tant angoissousement;
  Puis i fut a trois clos clofis,
  Per mains, per piés, estroitement. 30

IV J'ai oït dire en reprochier:
  "Boens marchiés trait de borce airgent"
  Et "Cil ait moult lou cuer legier
  Ki le bien voit et lou mal prant".
  Saveis ke Deus ait en covant 35
  A ceauls ki se voront croixier?
  Si m'aïst Deus, moult biaul luier:
  Paradix permenablement!

Cil ki son prout puet porchaissier
Fols est se a demain s'atant.   40

V   Nos nen avons poent de demain,
        A certes le poons savoir.
        Teil cuide avoir lou cuer moult sain
        K'ains lou quart jor tout son avoir
        Ne prixe poent, ne son savoir: 45
        Quant voit la mort lou tient a frain
        Si k'il ne puet ne pié ne main
        A li saichier ne removoir,
        La keute lait, si prant l'estrain;
        Maix trop vient tairt a persevoir.   50

RR   I   4 ses] ces   10 ses] les   III   25 *missing* 26 ses] ces   30 main   IV   37 lueir *(em.
Bartsch-Wiese)*   39 Sil   V   keuce *(em. M. Cornu,* Romania
10 [1881], 218)

V   I   2 Anveilliez   4 refrais   7 Promet a   10
Dont v̄. il ces   II   14 A. aurait et p.   16 Ke   18 ki
plus aurait bien f.   III   24 honorablemant   26 b. an
mi s.   28 Et la straing a.   30 P. piez p. mains   IV
31 reprouier   35 ait] mat   36 ki] ke   37 Si meist il
m. b. lueir   38 P. per afaitemant   39 Car ki   40 F. e.
cil a   V   43 Teis   46 Car cant la   47 Et il ne p. ne
piez ne mains   49 keuse   50 vient] est

E   Meyer, 369; Bédier-Aubry, 19-24; Bartsch-Wiese,
166-167; Cremonesi, 69-71; Groult 1, 169-170; Bec 2, 90-92;
Schöber, 237-251.

DF   Lorraine, including *a* for *au,* as in *a* (15), *pames*
(16); *ai* for *a,* as in *pais* (2), *saichiés* (13), *aiseis* (14),
tairt (50); *e* for *a,* as in *per* (6); *ei* for tonic *e,* as in
ameis (1), *keil* (20); *amins* (23) for *amis*; *o* for *oi,* as in
crox (25); *creux* (8) for *crois*; *oen* for *ein* or *oin,* as in
poene (9), *poent* (41); *boens* (32) for *bons*; *(u)ls* for *us,* as
in *ceals* (7), *aignials* (27), *douls* (27), *ceauls* (36); final
t, as in *greit* (20), *oït* (31), *prout* (39); *panront* (8) for
prendront; metathesized *mosterrait* (17) for *mostrera*; epenthesized *averait* (14) for *avra*; 3rd-pers. sing. pret. in
-ait, as in *amait* (22, 23), *portait* (28); 3rd-pers. sing.
fut. in *-ait,* as in *donrait* (7), *vairait* (10, =verra), *se-*
rait (13); 3rd-pers. sing. pres. ind. *ait* (33, 35) for *a.*

N   This song dates either from the Third Crusade
(1189), as in Bédier-Aubry, p. 20, or from the beginning of
the Fourth, as proposed in Schöber, pp. 237-238.

1-3 Religious adaptation of elements normally associated with a kind of dawn song. Thus, Gaston Paris: "le
chant d'éveil adressé non à une femme mais à un ensemble de
personnes qui doivent sans doute célébrer une fête, a dû
être assez répandu, mais ne nous a guère laissé de monu-
ments; on a une chanson de croisade [the present song], da-
tant probablement de 1189, qui nous en offre une parodie
pieuse et nous atteste par là l'existence" (p. 585 in "Les
origines de la poésie lyrique en France" in *Mélanges de littérature française du moyen âge* [Paris, 1912], pp. 539-615,
reprinted from *Journal des Savants* [1891-1892]). See, too,
Wolf, pp. 47-48.

2 Most previous editors, no doubt desirous in part of
improving the sense of the line, have changed *pais* (*pas* U)
to *mais*. If *pa(i)s* is, however, not simply an error of two
eastern copyists but the original reading, it would point to
Lorraine as the source of the song: only there would the re-
flex of *passu-* rhyme with *retrais*, *paix*, etc.   4 *se* = adverbial *si*.   11 *forjugiés* 'condemned', feudal legal term;
see Du Cange *Glossarium*, s.v. *forisjudicare*.   18 Relative
ke serves here as subject.   32 Proverb cited in Morawski,
no. 291.   33-34 Variant of proverbs cited in Morawski,
nos. 1852-1854.   35 'Do you know what God has promised'.
46 Understand *que* before *la mort*.   49 'He gives up his
feather-bed for a bed of straw'. For another interpretation, see p. 444 in Jeanroy's review of Bédier-Aubry, *Romania* 38 (1909), 443-446.

                II. (Chanson de femme)   <u>51</u>

RS 191, MW 596
Ms. M 180r-v. No music. Attribution: Gautier d'Espinau,
    Jehan de Nueville (see note below).

I   Jherusalem, grant damage me fais,
     Qui m'as tolu ce que je pluz amoie.
     Sachiez de voir ne vos amerai maiz,
     Quar c'est la rienz dont j'ai pluz male joie;
     Et bien sovent en souspir et pantais   5
     Si qu'a bien pou que vers Deu ne m'irais,
     Qui m'a osté de grant joie ou j'estoie.

II   Biauz dous amis, com porroiz endurer
      La grant painne por moi en mer salee,
      Quant rienz qui soit ne porroit deviser   10
      La grant dolor qui m'est el cuer entree?
      Quant me remembre del douz viaire cler
      Que je soloie baisier et acoler,
      Grant merveille est que je ne sui dervee.

III   Si m'aït Deus, ne puis pas eschaper: 15
      Morir m'estuet, teus est ma destinee;
      Si sai de voir que qui muert por amer
      Trusques a Deu n'a pas c'une jornee.
      Lasse! mieuz vueil en tel jornee entrer
      Que je puisse mon douz ami trover   20
      Que je ne vueill ci remaindre esguaree.

      E   Brakelmann 1, 19-20; Jeanroy *Or*, 498-499; O.
Schultz-Gora, *Zeit. f. rom. Phil.*, 15 (1891), 237; Lindelöf-
Wallensköld, 302; Bédier-Aubry, 275-279; Bec 2, 10-11.

      N   This moving lament is best regarded as anonymous.
The ms. rubric that introduces the song attributes it to
Gautier d'Epinal, but such authorship is rejected in Lindelöf-Wallensköld, p. 230. The table of contents of ms. M
attributes it to Jehan de Nueville, but Richter, p. 15,
denies that possibility. As for the particular crusade
which inspired the song, there is no way to identify it.
The composition is no doubt a fragment. The fact that stanzas 2 and 3 show the same rhymes indicates that the song,
composed in *coblas doblas*, should contain at least four
stanzas, of which the surviving st. 1 would be either the
first or second. Normally, however, poems in *coblas doblas*
contain six stanzas; and, after st. 3 (originally st. 4),
the ms. in fact shows a blank space large enough for two
more stanzas.
      12-13 Both Lindelöf-Wallensköld and Bédier-Aubry un-
necessarily eliminate the *césures épiques* in these lines by
changing l. 12 *remembre* to *membre* and l. 13 *je soloie* to *soloie* alone.   18 It is not clear whether *n'a pas c'une* is
to be understood, as in Bédier-Aubry, in its modern sense,
'does not have only one', or in the earlier sense, 'has only
one'.   20 *Que* 'so that'.   21 *Que* 'than that' (with l. 19
mieuz) with non-negative *ne*.

SOTTES CHANSONS

RS 537, MW 1835
Ms. I 6:1. No music.

I   Chans de singe ne poire mal pellee
     Ne me font pas a chanteir revenir,
     Mais ma dame qui est trop mal büee
     Me fait chanteir d'Adangier lou martir.
          Sor piez ne me puis tenir   5
          Cant elle vers moi coloie,
          Dont ait mes cuers si grant joie
          C'a poc tient je ne m'oci
             Por l'amour de li.

II   Moult est plaixans, bien samble forcenee, 10
     Sovant me fait presant d'un teil sopir
     Ke bien varroit une reupe et demee
     Ki au chainge la vandroit par loixir.
          Et Deus li voille merir
          Toz les biens k'elle m'anvoie,   15
          Car se je mualz estoie,
          Ce diroie ju ensi:
           "Dame, grant merci."

III   Dame d'onor, blanche con poix chafee,
     A vos loeir ne doi je pas mantir.   20
     La faice aveis brune, noire et ridee;
     C'a main vos voit lou soir devroit morir.
          Ceu me fait resovenir,
          De vos forment m'esferoie
          Se a vos servir failloie,   25
          Car vos m'aveis enrichi
            D'estre bien chaiti.

IV   Vint ans cinc mois avant ke fuxiés nee,
     Vostre biauteit se vint an moi flaitir
     Si aprement, j'an ai la pance anflee.   30
     Nes an sonjant ne me puet sovenir
          De vous, si fort vos desir
          Ke, se les fievres avoie,
          Dame, je les vos donroie
          Volantiers de cuer joli.   35
           N'est ce dons d'ami?

I   Encor vos don, dame hallegoutee,
         De mes jualz, ne.s voil plus retenir,
         Boutons mal keus et prunelle xadee,
         Tot ceu en boins a vostre eus por tucir.   40
              Can vos voi ver moi venir,
              A poc ke Deu ne renoie,
              Car plus volantiers vairoie
              Venir un louf dever mi.
                   Amors en graci.   45

RR   II   13   chainges

E   Arnaud, 70-71; Långfors *Sot*, 40-42.

DF   Lorraine, including *a* for *au*, as in *varroit* (12),
chafee (19); *ai* for *a*, as in *chainge* (13), *faice* (21); *ei*
for tonic *e*, as in *chanteir* (2), *teil* (11); preservation of
final *t*, as in *biauteit* (29); *x* for *s(s)*, as in *plaixans*
(10), *poix* (19), *fuxiés* (28); *lou* (4) for *le*; *ceu* (23) for
ce; *ju* (17) for *je*; 3rd-pers. sing. pres. ind. *ait* (7) for
a.

N   For discussion of certain parodic devices in this
poem, see Hoffman, pp. 120-121 et passim.   4 Långfors *Sot*,
pp. 13-15, identifies *Adangier* with Audigier, a hero of
epic parody who was widely known for his crassness.   22 *C'*
= relative *que* used as a nominative.   37 Arnaud reads *hal-
legoitree*, which he glosses as 'begemmed'.   39 *xadee* = *es-
chaudee*.   40 This line is obscure.   43 *vairoie* = *ver-
roie*.

53   II

RS 1113, MW 1844
Ms. I 6:7. No music.

I   Quant j'oi la quaile chausie
               Entre deus fosseis chanter
               Et cieus qui tient par maistrie
               La fait devant lui tumer,
               Adont voil un chant trover   5
               D'amors et de sa poissance,
               Dont j'ai si plainne la pance
         Ke jai mes vantres n'an serait alaissiez
         S'ansois ne suix des deus fesces sainniés.

II   Por ceu vos proi, douce amie,   10
            Ke vos me voillez prester
            Vos douce boiste une fie
            Por mes fesces vantouser,
            Et je vos vanrai fiever
            De mi, belle, douce, franche;   15
            Ke se je mur, mescheance
        Vos eskerrait, car de vos·suix aidiés
        Si largement ke mal greis en aiés.

III   De vos vient, dame prisie,
            Ceu ke je puix recovrer   20
            De bien si tres grant partie
            C'on me devroit cousiner
            Cant onkes osai ameir
            Dame de si grant vaillance,
            Ke de veoir vos samblance   25
        Est cuers d'amant d'amer toz desvoiez
        Por la biauteit dont vos cors est torchiés.

IV   Se j'ai misse m'estudie
            Toute en ma dame löer,
            On ne lou doit a sotie   30
            Tenir, c'amans barbeteir
            Ne poroit ne deviser
            De sa dame l'onorance;
            Et ju qui ai remanbrance
        De la belle dont je suix covoitiés   35
        Fait ke li biens ke j'en di est pechiés.

V   Dame, ki j'ai a moitie
            Mon cuer donnei sans roster,
            Flors estes de cortoisie
            Et de cens, a droit border.   40
            Cant me fait abeüter
            Bone Amors vos contenance,
            Vos dous regars tant m'avance
        Ke, cant il m'est dou cuers de vos lanciés,
        En tout lou jor ne puis estre haitiez.   45

    RR   I 1 chausiee 3 maistree 4 Lou   II 12
foie (+1)   17 eskerrai

    E   Arnaud, 76-77; Långfors Sot, 57-59.

    DF   Lorraine, including ai for a, as in jai (8); ei
for tonic e, as in fosseis (2), ameir (23), donnei (38); u

for *ui*, as in *mur* (16); *ss* for *s*, as in *alaissiez* (8), *misse*
(28); preservation of final *t*, as in *biauteit* (27); *lou* (30)
for *le*; *ceu* (10) for *ce*; *ju* (34) for *je*; 3rd-pers. sing.
fut. in *-ait*, as in *serait* (8), *eskerrait* (17).

Certain rhymes may bespeak the Picard origin, not of
the ms., but of the composition, e.g., *chausie* (1), rather
than *chauchiee*, rhyming with *maistrie* (3); *franche* (15)
rhyming with *mescheance* (16). Note, too, *k* for *ch* in *eskerrait*.

N̲   3-4 Långfors *Sot* takes *qui* as a spelling variant
of *cui* and translates: "'et que [= quand] celui qu'elle
maîtrise la fait danser devant lui'" but adds that "tout
cela n'est pas bien clair." Noël Dupire (*Romania* 69 [1946],
266), retaining the ms. reading *Lou fait*, translates "'et
que celui qui tient [un autre] sous son autorité le fait
danser devant lui'." If the first is not very clear, the
second is syntactically disputable and fails to recognize
that all four initial lines present the same image of mat-
ing. Understand, then: 'et que celui qui maîtrise [la
caille] la fait tomber devant lui'.
10-13 The lady is here presented as a physician, capable of curing the poet's love-illness with her "box" of
remedies. Any sexual overtone is surely intended.   14-15
'And I shall come to bestow upon you the fief which is myself'.   27 *torchiés* is perhaps, as suggested in Långfors
Sot, a variant of *troussés* (= *torsés*) 'laden'.   34-36 Syntax and meaning are unclear. ('And the fact that I remember
. . . Means that the good that I say . . .'?)   37 *ki = cui*
'to whom'.   40 *cens = sens*.

54̲   III

RS 1630, MW 1748
Ms. I 6:4. No music.

I   Chanteir m'estuet jusc'a jor dou juïse
      En toz les leus ke je porrai troveir,
      Car ma dame lou me mist en devise
      Premierement cant el me fist amer
            De joli cuer sans fauseir,   5
            Ma douce dame esmeree,
            En cui biauteit est doublee
      En tant de plois ke nuns hons deviseir
      Ne lou saroit, tant seüst pres viser.

II   Bien ait esteit trente deus ans juïse,   10
        Mais pour m'amour se fist crestïeneir;
        Si en mersi Amors cant covoitise
        Li vint de li de sa loi bestorner,
                Car on ne poroit parleir
                El mont de si belle nee,   15
                Ne nuns a une alenee
        N'aroit pooir, tant seüst barbeteir,
        De sa biauteit dire sans mesconter.

III   Je croi k'il n'ait dame duskes en Frisse
        Ke saiche mués amant doreloter   20
        K'elle seit moi, car, cant m'art et atisse
        Li jolis malz qui me fait regiber,
                Lors li comance a conter
                Ma chaitive destinee;
                Dont jete jus sa fuzee,   25
        Si la me fait par amors releveir.
        Ne doit on ceu don de joie apeller?

IV   Se ma pansee ai et m'entente mise
        En ma dame saverouse löer,
        On ne la doit pas tenir a faintise   30
        Ne mi laissier por ceu a coroner;
                Car s'on me dovoit tueir,
                S'an dirai je ma testee:
                De sa bouchete fresee
        Baixier asseis, sentir et langueter   35
        Se devroit on de joie deskirer.

V   Dame vaillans, vermeille con serisse,
        Saige en dormant sans mavais vent geter,
        Noire ens on vis, brune soz la chemise,
        Vos ne daigniés les traïson porter.   40
                Cant eürs me vuelt doner
                La desirouse jornee
                Qu'estes de moi regardee,
        Vos grans biauteis me vient si esclistrer
        Ke per force m'estuet esternüer.   45

VI   Ceste chanson presanter
                Voil Mehalet l'Escardee,
                Qui mon cuer de mes coree
        Fist departir par force et desevrer
        Lués ke premiers l'alai abeüter.   50

RR   I   4 elle me *(+1)*   9   deuiser *(+1)*   II   10
ans iuiue   11 se] ce   III   26 Cil la   V   39 soz]
sus

E   Arnaud, 73-74; Lǻngfors *Sot*, 47-51; Henry *Chrest*
1, 236-238; 2, 70.

DF   Lorraine, including *a* for *au*, as in *a* (1), *mavais*
(38); *ai* for *a*, as in *saiche* (20), *saige* (38); *ei* for tonic
e, as in *chanteir* (1), *esteit* (10), *asseis* (35); *nuns* (8,
16) for *nus*; *s* for *c* and *c* for *s*, as in *mersi* (12), *serisse*
(37) and Rej. Read.; intervocalic *s* and *ss* used interchange-
ably, as in *-is(s)e* rhymes; preservation of final *t*, as in
biauteit (7), *esteit* (10); *ceu* (27, 31) for *ce*; *lou* (3, 9)
for *le*; *les* (40) for *la*; *mes* (48) for *ma*; 3rd-pers. sing.
pres. ind. *ait* (10) for *a*.   Certain forms show Picard origin
of composition, e.g., *saroit* (9) for *savroit*; *aroit* (17) for
avroit; *deskirer* (36) for *deschirer*; *ens on* (39) for *en* or
au.

N   3 'For my lady so instructed me'.   7-8 The poet
is playing upon the meanings of *doublee*: 'doubled' and
'folded over'.   13 Understand *de li (= se) bestorner de sa
loi* 'to convert from her religion'.   16 Lǻngfors *Sot*, unlike Arnaud or Henry *Chrest*, emends *a une alenee* to *a une
leuee* and understands 'à une lieue à la ronde'. There is no
need for such a change; the phrase means 'in one breath'.
30 Arnaud emends *la* to *lou*, presumably referring to the
infinitive phrase in l. 29. This is unnecessary, as *la* is
quite satisfactory in reference to either l. 28 *pansee* or
entente.   31 'Nor, for that reason, fail to crown me'.
The reference is to winning the prize in one of the literary
contests of the *puys* of Picardy.   47 The sobriquet *l'Es-
cardee* is tentatively glossed in Lǻngfors *Sot* as 'écaillée'.
In the collaborative review of that work (*Romania* 69,
[1946], 257-270), A. Henry maintains, p. 261, that, "sans
aucun doute possible," the term means 'édentée, brèche-dent'
('toothless, gap-toothed').

55   IV

RS 564, MW 1830
Ms. I 6:19. No music.

I   Ce fut tot droit lou jor de lai Chandoile,
     Ke menestrei sounent lor estrumens;

Mainte chaitive a teil jor s'apaireille
D'aleir baler en ses acesmemens.
  Une en choisi en cinc cens   5
  Que moult estoit delitouse,
  Mais clope estoit et boistouse;
Et ceu me fist son gent cors covoitier
K'elle ne seit fors ploreir et tensier.

II Je l'ain et serf, dont aucun se mervoille; 10
Mais on cude ke soie hors dou sens,
Car ma dame n'ait ke la destre oreille:
L'autre perdit ens on merchiet a Lens;
  Et si recordent les gens
  De la tres douce amerouse   15
  K'el monde n'ait si visouce
De tot embler et de bources soier,
Et por ceu l'ain: je bee a gaaingnier.

III Car uns hons suis qui par ces boules veille,
S'i per sovent trestous mes wernemens, 20
Si n'ai mestier de dame qui soumeille,
Et ceste seit embler et serchier rens:
  Tost gaaingne mon despens.
  Ainmi! douce sīentousse,
  Ce sont li gent envīouse   25
Qui me vuellent de vous descompaignier,
Mais ce n'iert jai tant c'aiez un denier.

IV Se vos veeis con tres bien s'aparaille
Cant aleir doit embler dame Hersens!
Son molekin sor son chief entorteille, 30
K'il n'est nuns hons, ne Picars ne Flamens,
  Ke l'esrajaist mie as dens,
  Car ma dame dolerouse
  Est partout soupesenouse;
Por ceu l'estraint c'on ne.l puist arajeir, 35
C'on vairoit ceu k'il faut desous l'uilier.

V Par la dame c'on requiert a la treille,
Je la vorrai espouser an Valens.
S'anfant an ai, en une viés corbeille
Serait porteis a saint Jehans leans. 40
  E, Deus! con c'iert biaus presens
  De la tres douce c'arousse,
  S'elle ne fust si roignouse!
Il n'est dedus fors de li ambraisier.
Et ne fait bien teil dame a covoitier? 45

<u>RR</u>   I   3 sapairelle   4 ces   III   25 Se   27
se   <u>V</u>   37 trelle   43 Celle, ci

<u>E</u>   Arnaud, 82-83; Långfors *Sot*, 81-84.

<u>DF</u>   Lorraine, including *ai* for *a*, as in *lai* (1), *jai*
(27), *ambraisier* (44); *ei* for tonic *e*, as in *teil* (3), *aleir*
(4), *porteis* (40); *er* for *ar*, as in *merchiet* (13), *wernemens*
(20); *oil(l)e* for *eille*, as in *Chandoile* (1), *mervoille*
(10); *u* for *ui*, as in *cude* (11), *dedus* (44); *nuns* (31) for
nus; *s* for *c* and *c* for *s*, as in *visouce* (16), *serchier* (22)
and Rej. Read.; *ss* for *s* and *s* for *ss*, as in *arousse* (42),
ambraisier (44); preservation of final *t*, as in *merchiet*
(13); *lou* (1) for *le*; *ceu* (8) for *ce*; 3rd-pers. sing. pres.
ind. *ait* (12, 16) for *a*; 3rd-pers. sing. fut. in *-ait*, as in
serait (40). Note that *-oil(l)e*, *-eille*, and *-aille* all
rhyme.

<u>N</u>   1 The reference is probably to Candlemas Day.
20 *per* 'I lose'.   21-23 Långfors *Sot*, p. 9, translates:
"'Une bonne femme endormie ne fait pas mon affaire, mais
celle-là, elle sait voler et rapporter. Elle me gagne ce
que je dépense'."   24 *sïentousse* 'wise, knowledgeable'.
Arnaud reads *Ainmi, douce, si en tousse!*   28 The subject
of *s'aparaille* is l. 29 *dame Hersens*, the name of the speaker's "lady". Note that Hersent, in the *Roman de Renart*, is
a she-wolf, the wife of Isengrin.   32 *esrajaist = arra-
chast*.   35 *arajeir = arracher*.   36 *vairoit = verroit*.
   37 Långfors *Sot* offers the comment that the *dame* might
be a saint venerated at a place called La Treille or, more
likely, given the meaning of *treille* 'vinestock', the woman
who runs the tavern frequented by the poet, in which case l.
40 *saint Jehans leans* would be her husband. However, Noël
Dupire, reviewing Långfors *Sot* (*Romania* 69 [1946], 257-270),
provides grounds for believing that *treille* is to be understood as 'iron grating' and that the reference here is to a
statue of the Virgin in Lille, known as Notre Dame de la
Treille. We may add that it is entirely probable that l. 37
is to be read with both the second and third interpretations
in mind.
   42 Like Arnaud, we interpret *c'arousse* 'to whom I
drink'. Långfors *Sot* understands an adjective *carousse*, as
do both A. Henry and N. Dupire in the collaborative review
cited above; each of the three offers his own speculation on
the meaning and origin of the word.

CHANSONS SATIRIQUES

I. (Chanson historique)

RS 2127, MW 488, B 1887
Ms. T 198r-v. No music.

I

Arras, ki ja fus
Dame sans refus
   Del païs,
Tu es confondus,
Traïs et vendus   5
   Et haïs,
N'en toi n'a desfense
Se cil ne te tense
Ki en crois fu mis.
Ti vilain ouvrage   10
T'ont mis en servage;
Por c' en dirai: *gnif!*

II

E! Arras li biaus,
T'es vile roiaus
   Des cités;   15
Se tes apoiaus
Fust vrais et loiaus,
   Faussetés
N'i eüst poissance.
Il n'a vile en France,
De ci dusk'a Miaus,   21
Qui fust plus cortoise.
Te male despoise
Me fait dire: *gnauf!*

III

Je me sui perçus   25
Frekins as Sorçus
   Est tous mas.
Ausi m'aït Dieus,
Teus en fist ses jus
   Et ses gas   30
Par devant la face
Li parra tel trace

Quant poins en venra.
Qui d'autrui pesance
Veut faire beubance,   35
On en dira: *gnaf!*

IV

Ore est aparans
Li maus de lonc tans
   Porcaciés:
Il a bien trente ans   40
Que li premiers pans
   Fu tailliés
De le trequerie
Dont li bourghesie
Gist ore entrepiés.   45
J'en ai grant engaigne;
Leur mauvaise ouvraigne
Me fait dire: *gnief!*

V

Li gros grains dekiet;
Je di, qui k'il griet,   50
   Oiant tous:
Quant a l'un meskiet,
A l'autre bien siet;
   Tous jalous
Est cascuns d'esbatre   55
Le verghe a lui batre;
Nus n'est paourous
De honte entreprendre.
Je.s en voel reprendre
Et s'en dirai: *gnouf!*   60

VI

Certes je mespris:
L'ome qui est pris
   Par mal los

Quant de sen païs
Ne veut estre oïs   65
    De ses tors,
C'est mout laide cose
Quant voukier ne s'ose
Dont il fu nouris
Ne droit n'ose atendre.
S'on le maine pendre, 71
Jou en dirai: *gnif!*

VII

C'est grans estrelois
C'on fausse les drois
    Vrais escris;   75
Mesire li rois
Doit prendre conrois
    De teus cris.
Point ne m'esmervelle
Se li quens travelle   80
Hardrés n'Aloris,
Qui font le servage;
De leur grant damage
Doit on dire: *gnif!*

VIII

Li rois qui ne ment   85
Prendra vengement
    De leur cors:
En mout grief tourment
Ierent longement,
    N'est pas tors;   90
Langhe aront muiele;
Passion novele

Par devant leur mors
Leur sera voisine.
Goute palasine   95
Leur fra dire: *gnof!*

IX

Ne tieng mie a fol
Guion de Saint Pol
    N'a estout:
Premiers baissa col   100
Quant il vit sen vol
    Por le tout;
Lors devint peskieres;
En sekes gaskieres,
U eve ne court,   105
Prist un pisson rike;
Dusk'en Salenike
En dist cascuns: *gnouf!*

X

Cil de Givenci,
Sour borgne ronci   110
    Dur trotant,
Les rens i fendi.
Une rois tendi
    Maintenant;
Ce fu voirs sans faille,
C'ainques n'i prist   116
                    [quaille
N'aloe cantant,
Ains prist tel verdiere
Ainc ne vi si kiere.
Por c' en dirai: *gnauf!* 120

RR   I   12 ce en *(+1)*   X   120 ce en *(+1)*

E   Jubinal *Nouv Rec*, 382-386; Meyer, 373; Jeanroy-
Guy, 36-39.

DF   Picard, including *iaus* for *eaus*, as in *biaus*
(13), *Miaus* (21); *c* or *k* or *qu* for *ch*, as in *cascuns* (55),
trequerie (43), *dekiet* (49); *gh* for *g*, as in *bourghesie*
(44), *verghe* (56); *l(l)* for *il(l)*, as in *voel* (59), *travelle*
(80); *le* (43, 56) for *la*; possessive *te* (23) for *ta*;

possessive *sen* (64) for *son*; *jou* (72) for *je*; *fra* (96) for
fera; *aront* (91) for *avront*.

N   The poet's moral sense is outraged by a scandalous
case of tax fraud implicating a number of rich bourgeois and
fiscal administrators of Arras; the composition apparently
dates from 1269. For details, see Jeanroy-Guy, pp. 10 and
24-26.
      26 Understand *que* before *Frekins*. *Frekins as Sorçus*
(= *aux sourcils*?) was one of a family of that name that, to
judge by several of the poems in Jeanroy-Guy, played an important rôle in the affairs of Arras. The name is not, however, found in the archives of the city.   32 Understand
que before *Li*.   40-45 'It has been thirty years since the
first action was undertaken (lit., first piece of cloth was
cut) in the fraud which has now brought the burghers low'.
50 *qui* = *cui*.   81 In Jeanroy-Guy, *Hardrés* is identified
as a "nom symbolique désignant le peuple" and *Aloris*, similarly, as a "nom imaginaire symbolisant le menu peuple". We
find it more appropriate, in the present context, to think
of the well-known traitors that bear these names in a number
of *chansons de geste*; see Ernest Langlois, *Table des Noms
propres de toute nature compris dans les chansons de geste*
(Paris, 1904), pp. 22 and 325.
      98 According to Jeanroy-Guy, *Guion de Saint Paul* may
have been "un magistrat qui avait poursuivi et saisi quel-
ques-uns des bourgeois coupables de fausses déclarations.
C'est ainsi, du moins,--mais peut-être à tort,--que nous
comprenons le passage où on le compare (v. 103) à un *peskieres* qui prend un poisson riche (v. 106) dans un endroit
où il n'y a point d'eau (v. 104-105)."   109 According to
Jeanroy-Guy, *cil de Givenci*, in this rather obscure stanza,
seems to have been a magistrate who caught in his "net"
(*rois*, 1. 113) not just any bird, but a *verdiere* 'green-
finch' (1. 118)--with a pun on the name, Verdiere, of one of
Arras' most prominent families.   119 Understand *que* before
Ainc.

                              II   57

Not in RS.   MW 2505
Ms. London, BL, Cotton, Caligula A XVIII, 22v.   No music.

      I   J'ay veu l'eure qe par servise
           Conquist hom riche garisoun.
           Ore est li tens si a devise,

Qi mieuz sert meins ad geredon.
Çoe font mauveyse gent felon 5
Qe sunt [si] plein de coveitise,
  Par nule gise
Ne dorront çoe q'avront promise
A ceus qe bien servi les ount.

II Li grant seignur par lour cointise 10
Si beau promettent lour sergans;
Çoe dïent par fause feintise:
"Amis, mult estes bien servant;
Servez moy a mon talent.
Joe vous dorray, par sein Denise, 15
  De manantise
Taunt qe, kant avrez eu la prise,
Riches serrez e manant."

III Cil s'en joïst en esperaunce
De la premesse sun seignur, 20
[Ne] ne quide aver defailaunce
Dunt ja n'avra bien ne honur.
Mes qant vendra a chef de tour,
Pur une petite d'estaunce,
Par le mentir d'un escusour, 25
Si avra il perdu d'enfaunce
Sun servisë e sun labour.

IV Deu qe fra la haute justise,
Dreiturel [et] plein de vertu,
Kant vendra au jour de juïse 30
Qe touz mesfés serront rendus,
En enfern serrunt [il] ressuz
[Et] la tendrunt lour manantise.
Coveitise lour ad dessu.
Par lour fole mauveise enprise 35
Le joi du ciel avront perdu.

RR I 4 gerdon *(-1)* 6 *-1* 8 Ne d. coe qe il aueront p. *(+3)* II 12 C dient 14 *-1* 16 De ma manantise *(+1)* 17 T. qe k. vous auerez eu la p. *(+1)* 18 *-1* III 21 *-1* 22 ne auera *(+2)* 24 de estaunce *(+1)* 25 de un *(+1)* 26 auera, de enf. *(+2)* IV 29 *-1* 32 *-1* 33 *-1* 34 desseu 36 La ioie du c. aueront p. *(+2)*

E Michel *Documents*, 113-114; Aspin, 169-173.

<u>DF</u>   Anglo-Norman, including *aun* for *an*, as in *taunt*
(17), *esperaunce* (19); *(o)un* for *on*, as in *garisoun* (2),
ount (9), *sunt* (6), *sun* (20), *Dunt* (22); *(o)ur* for *eur*, as
in *seignur* (10), *labour* (27); *g* for *gu* or *j*, as in *geredon*
(4), *gise* (7), *sergans* (11); *çoe* (5) for *ce*; *joe* (15) for
je; *dorront* (8) and *dorray* (15) for *don(e)ront, don(e)rai*.

<u>N</u>   This song on the ingratitude of overlords probably
dates from about 1300. It is accompanied in the ms. by an
English version. The intended meter seems to be 8 8 8 8 8 8
4/8 8 8. Of the numerous irregularities, some have been
eliminated in the edited text through rather evident conjecture; the others, less readily corrected, have been retained
and will be commented on below.
     3 *si a devise* 'so fashioned [that]'.   6 *Qe* serves
here as subject; similarly, l. 9.   7 Understand *que* before
Par, coordinated with l. 6 *si*; cf. ll. 3-4.   8 Error in
gender, as in *promise*, is not uncommon in Anglo-Norman of
this period.   14 Perhaps, with eight syllables, a protasis
for l. 15: *Se me servez a mon talent.*   17 *la prise* 'deliv-
ery [of what I shall give you]'.   18 Perhaps, with eight
syllables: *Vous serrez riches e manant.*   20 Absolute genitive; understand *de* before *sun*.   23 'But when it comes to
the final reckoning'.   24 'On weak grounds'.   26-27
d'enfance . . . 'the service and labor [he has provided]
since childhood'.   28-29 Aspin comments, p. 173: "The syntax of these lines is problematic, in that there is no principal sentence of which *Deu* can be the subject, unless one
were to supply *est* at the beginning of line 29." We understand the verses as constituting a vocative, 'Dieu qui feras
. . .', with *et* as an obvious correction of l. 29.   31
'When all misdeeds will be paid off'.

                         III   58

RS 318a, MW 695
Ms. i 31v-32r. No music.

I   Ma douleur veil alegier en chantant;
     Or me doint Dieus grace de bien chanter.
     Il m'est avis que un chascuns s'entent:
     Hui est le jour de chascun enchanter;
     En baretant, decevant et mentant,   5
     Vieut li freres le frere soupplanter;
     Verités faut, que nul ne la defent.

II   Nostre prelat sont bien enparenté:
      Leur cousine est chascune qui enfante;
      Tantost leur sont li enffant presenté,   10
      Et li plus pres si prent la meilleur rente.
      Ainsi sont hui li lignage planté,
      Quar en ce met clergié toute s'entente;
      De tele plante avons trop grant planté.

III   La malice des clers mettre en françois   15
      Non audeo pre verecondia:
      Pour gaagnier vont au moustier, ainçois
      Ludunt, bibunt et edunt pinguia.
      D'abandonner leur cors sont trop cortois,
      Ut perpetrent opera turpia;   20
      De mal faire n'ont mesure ne pois.

IV   Son non retient a tort religion:
      Omnes vivunt jam seculariter;
      Oroison, pleurs, leçon, devocion,
      Pais, amor sont *ejecta turpiter.*   25
      Nouveles sevent de toute region:
      In hoc agunt omnes non segniter.
      D'office avoir est la contencion.

V   Tuit se painnent de deniers enmasser;
      Clerc et lai sont de ce baton feru,   30
      L'un pour gaster, l'autre pour entasser,
      Ne ja n'en iert as povres secouru.
      Les chevaliers ne veil pas trespasser:
      Bobans a si tout par mi eus couru
      Que tretuit sont plungié en cestui ru.   35

      RR   I   7 defent] soutient   IV   28 Des offices
a. *(+2)*

      E   Långfors *Not*, 531; Jeanroy-Långfors, 12-13.

      N   7 We have accepted Jeanroy-Långfors' suggestion,
p. 92, that *soutient*, surprising in rhyme position, may be
due to scribal error and have accordingly emended to *defent*.
16 'I do not dare out of shame'.   18 'They play, drink,
and eat rich foods'.   20 'So that they may commit shameful
deeds'.   23 'All now live in a secular way'.   25 'shame-
fully rejected'.   27 'In this regard none of them behaves
sluggishly'.   29-31 In Jeanroy-Långfors, *enmasser/(Clerc
et lai sont de ce baton feru),/L'un*; this punctuation may
assume that l. 30 *baton* refers, metaphorically, to the

present poetic attack. We regard *baton* as signifying the
compulsion to amass wealth (l. 29).

IV   59

RS 1153, MW 1298
Ms. C 68r-v. No music.

I   Envie, orguels, malvestiés, felonnie
        Ont le siecle si tout a lour voloir
        Ke loiaulteis, valors, joie et franchise
        Et tuit li bien sont mis en nonchaloir,
        Ne il n'est nuls c'om puisse apercevoir   5
        C'a guilleir n'ait toute s'entente mise
        Ou soulement a amaisseir avoir.

II   Felonnie est semee et bien reprise;
        Chascuns travaille a amaisseir avoir,
        N'el siecle n'ait home ki rien se prise   10
        Se il n'en puet raisine ou branche avoir;
        Car ki muels seit traïr et decevoir
        Et a mesdire ait muels s'entente mise
        Muels est prixiés et plux cuide valoir.

III   Biaus sires Deus! com est amor perie   15
        Et [tuit] li bien k'en soloient venir:
        Humiliteis, lergesse et cortoisie!
        Tout le siecle voi si avelenir
        Ke, s'il est nuls ki baie a bien servir
        Ou a bien faire por amor de s'amie,   20
        On en mesdist et gaibe a departir.

IV   Tant ont regneit mesdires et envie
        Ke li uns n'ose maix l'autre conjoïr,
        Et les dames perdent lor drüerie,
        Ne pueent maix les servixes merir;   25
        Cil les gaitent, cui Deus puist maleïr,
        Ke riens n'i ont fors soulement envie.
        Tous les amans font a joie faillir.

V   Loials, amans et sens mesure amee,
        Dame d'amor, belle et bone sens peir,   30
        Saige et cortoise et tous jors desiree,
        Je n'ose a vos ne venir ne aleir,
        Ne je ne puis un jor sens vos dureir,

Maix tant redout ke n'en soiés blaimee
Souls m'en covient dedens mon cuer ameir.   35

VI   Deus, keil dolour quant ceu c'ai plux amee
      Me covandrait por felons eschiveir!
      Ne.1 ferai voir, dame, s'il vos agree.
      Lor malvestiés ne nos puet riens greveir,
      Ne bone amor ne doit por eaus fauceir,   40
      Car ki voroit atendre lor cellee
      En fol espoir poroit son tens useir.

      RR   III   16 -1   IV   24   drueries   VI   38   fe-
rait

      E   Jeanroy-Långfors, 8-9.

      DF   Lorraine, including *ai* for *a*, as in *raisine* (11)
for *racine*, *amaisseir* (7), *gaibe* (21); *ei* for tonic *e*, as in
loiaulteis (3), *guillier* (6), *keil* (36); *muels* (12) for
mieus; *s* for *c* and *c* for *s*, as in *raisine* (11), *fauceir*
(40); *x* for *s*, as in *prixiés* (14), *plux* (14); preservation
of final *t*, as in *regneit* (22); *ceu* for *ce* (36); 3rd-pers. sing.
pres. ind. *ait* (6) for *a*; 3rd-pers. sing. fut. in *-ait*, as
in *covandrait* (37); relative *ke* or *k'* or *c'* as nominative
(6, 16, 27).

      N   16 In Jeanroy-Långfors, the problem of the miss-
ing syllable is resolved by changing *k'en* to *ki en*, which
fails to respect the 4 + 6 decasyllable typical of this
poem. Note that nominative *que* is hardly foreign to the
text (see DF, above) and indeed occurs commonly throughout
ms. C.

60   V. (Ballette)

RS 144, MW 377, B 1889
Mss. U 111r; London, BL, Add. 16559, 220r. No music.

      He! trikedondene, trikedondaine!

I   De lors ke j'acointai amors,
          Les ai servit et nut et jor;
          Onkes n'an oi fors ke dolour
                Et poinne.   5
      He! trikedondenne, trikedondene!

II   Et moi c'an chat? tan seus jolis:
            J'ains la millour de son païs,
            C'onke tant nen amait Paris
                        Helainne.   10
        He! trikedondene, [trikedondene]!

III   Ses chavols me sanblent fil d'or;
            Elle ait lou col et blanc et gros,
            I nen i peirt fronce nen os
                        Ne voine.   15
        He! trikedondene, [trikedondene]!

IV   Or veil a ma dame proier
            K'elle me gest de cest dongier;
            Elle m'avrait tost aligiet
                        Ma poinne.   20
        He! trikedondainne, trikedondene!

    <u>RR</u>   III   12   Ceu   IV   17   proeir

    <u>V</u>   Add. 16559 presents the following Anglo-Norman
version:
                Quant primes me quintey de amors
                A luy me donay a tuz jors,
                Mes unkes n'oy se dolur non   *ms.* non] noyn
                        E peyne.
                Va ester ke dundens va, etc.

                Je em la plus bele du pays;
                Kaunt je m'ene pens, si sui jolifs;
                Je l'em plus ke ne fit Paris
                        Heleyne.
                Ester, etc.

                Les chevoyz li lusent cumme fil de or;
                Ele a le col lung et gros,
                Si ne y pirt frunce ne os
                        Ne veyne.

                Elle ad les oyz vers et rianz,
                Les denz menu rengé devant,
                Buche vermayle fete cume teynt
                        En greyne.

                Ele ad beu braz pur acoler,
                Ele ad duz cors pur deporter;

Un mort purra resuciter
                Sa alayne.

Kaunt ele git entre mes braz
Et je le acole par grant solaz,
Lor vint le jor ke nus depart
                A payne.

Ore voil ma dame reprover
Ke ele me dedeyne amer.
Plus est gente ke un espervir
                K'en reclayme.

Ma dame, a Deu vus kemaund.
Seez tuz jors leal amaunt;
Nul ne pout estre vaylaunt
                S'i n'eyme.
Ester ke dundele, etc.

E   Meyer "Mélanges", 104-105; Gennrich *Ron* 1, 289; 2,
228; Jeanroy-Långfors, 33-34; Chaytor, 155-156; Bec 2, 109-
110.

DF   Lorraine, including *a* for *au*, as in *chat* (7); *ei*
for *e*, as in *peirt* (14); *oi* for *ei*, as in *poinne* (5), *voine*
(15); *u* for *ui*, as in *nut* (3); preservation of final *t*, as
in *servit* (3), *aligiet* (19); *lou* (13) for *le*; *seus* (7) for
sui; 3rd-pers. sing. pres. ind. *ait* (13) for *a*; 3rd-pers.
sing. pret. in *-ait*, as in *amait* (9); 3rd-pers. sing. fut.
in *-ait*, as in *avrait* (19).

N   14 *I = il*.   18 *gest*, 3rd-pers. sing. pres.
subj. of *geter*.

61   VI

RS 615, MW 1396
Stanza II: B 758 (one other source)
Mss. X 212v-213r, P 144r-v-145r. Music in both mss.

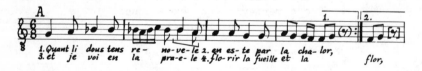

1. *Quant li dous tens re- no-ve-le* 2. *en es-te par la cha-lor,*
3. *et je voi en la   pra-e-le* 4. *flo-rir la fueille et la   flor,*

5. lors mi se- mont bone a- mor   6. que ser- vir doi- e la be- le

7. dont ma paine et ma do- lor   8. chas-cun jor me re- no- ve- le

9. sanz re- tor.

10. Deus li doint en- cor ta- lent qu'el m'aint par a- mor!

I   Quant li dous tens renovele
      En esté par la chalor,
      Et je voi en la praele
      Florir la fueille et la flor,
      Lors mi semont bone amor   5
      Que servir doie la bele
      Dont ma paine et ma dolor
      Chascun jor me renovele
            Sanz retor.   9
Deus li doint encor talent qu'el m'aint par amor!

II   Amors m'a bien deceü,
      Je le sai certainement;
      Bien m'en sui aparceü
      Quant la bele o le cors gent,
      Que j'amoie loiaument,   15
      N'a de moi merci eü.
      El m'a mis en grant torment
      Et si l'a el bien seü.
            Or m'en repent.   19
Fous est qui por fausse amor se met en torment.

III   El fait a touz biau senblant,
      Cele a qui m'iere promis:
      S'il en i venoit un cent,
      Seroient il touz amis.
      Je l'ai amee touz dis.   25
      Trop fait amer folement
      Dame qui tant a amis;
      Je le sai certainement,

                              Bien pert raison.   29
De retraire moi de li ai bele achaison.

        IV   Quant je soloie esgarder
              Ses biaus euz et son cors gent,
              Je m'i soloie mirer:
              Plus estoient clers q'argent.
              Mes or mi semblent noient,   35
              Quant el ne mi veut aidier;
              Plus sont noirs que arrement,
              Ce mi semble, [sanz] fausser;
                    Et son cors gent   39
Mi senble gros et enflé [et] tout plain de vent.

        V   Sa bele bouche tendrete
              Que je soloie baisier,
              Qui plus estoit vermeillete
              Que la rose d'un rosier,
              Söef con flor d'esglentier   45
              Getoit une savorete;
              Mes quant el ne m'a mestier,
              Trop me semble mes fadete,
                    Et son cler vis   49
Mi semble descolorés et frois et paliz.

        MN   Form: A A B.
1. Here ms. P writes a natural which was probably intended
to apply to the *b* in l. 6. 2. Ms. repeats this note, not
eliding *bone*. 3. Ms. repeats this note, not eliding *paine*.

        RR   I   10 amors   III   21 Ele *(+1)*   IV   36
Q. ele mi   38 *-1*   40 *-1*

        V   I   10 amors   II   20 a. entre en t.   III
21 Ele   30 li a bone a.   IV 34 P. erent c. que argent   36 aidier *missing*   38 sanz *missing*   40 Mi sen-
blent; e. et plain de v.   V   45 Souf a f. d.   49 cler
missing   50 descolore; froit

        E   Jeanroy-Långfors, 68-69; Spanke *Lied*, 73-75, 368.

        N   The eighth and ninth lines of each stanza form a
metric unit composed of eleven syllables. Since l. 8 *renovele* ends in feminine *-e* and l. 9 begins with a consonant,
it is, then, proper that l. 9 should contain only three syllables: the *-e* of l. 8 counts, and there is no need for such
an emendation as Spanke's *Sanz [nul] retor*.

26 Spanke *Lied*, p. 368, glosses *fait amer* as 'aime',
thinking no doubt of apparent factitives such as *fist lancier* 'lança' in RS 407 and *font aboier* 'aboient' in RS 324,
and it is surely true that a lady who has as many *amis* as
our poet states may be said to 'love madly'. It is at least
as likely, however, that we face a real factitive here, with
madness or foolishness characterizing the hopeless love of
the poet, and l. 29 *pert* can as readily be a first-person as
a third-person form. (For non-causative *faire* + infinitive
in Old French, see A. Tobler, *Mélanges de grammaire française* [Paris, 1905], 25-29.)

VII   62

RS 2070, MW 1312
Ms. C 88v. No music.

I   Ge chanterai, ke m'amie ai perdue;
      Plux bellement ne me sai conforteir.
      Mes compans l'ait a son eus retenue,
      Ki de pair moi soloit a li pairleir.
      On ne se doit en nul home fieir.   5
      Celle amor soit honie et confondue
      Ou il covient per anpairleir aleir.

II   M'amie estoit, or est ma gerroiere,
      Si m'aïst Deus, s'en ai lou cuer irei.
      Fauls losengier si m'en ont mis ariere   10
      Et envie, ke ne se puet celleir.
      Povres hons seux, se n'ai maix ke doneir,
      Et povreteis m'ait mis del tout ariere;
      Por ceu ne doit nuls povres hons ameir.

III   Honis soit il ki en femme se fie   15
      Por bel semblant ne por simple resgairt!
      La riens el mont ke plux aimme et desire
      Donroit elle por un denier sa pairt?
      Honis soit il ki jamaix amerait!
      Ma loiaulteis m'ait del tout mis ariere,   20
      Maix teils se cuide eschaufeir ke s'i airt.

IV   Je ne di pais k'elle soit m'anemie,
      Maix m'amie, ke raixon i entant.
      Ses amins seux et si ne m'aimme mie,
      Se m'aïst Deus, s'en ai le cuer dolent.   25

Grant bien m'ait fait; moult grant mercit
                                                l'en rant.
Et Deus li doinst eincor en sa baillie
Ceu k'elle ait tant desireit longuement.

V   De Damedeu soit elle maleïe,
        Ki s'amour lait por pior acoentieir,   30
        S'elle ne trueve en l'ome tricherie
        Ou teil chose ke ne li ait mestier.
        De moi laissier ne li fust il mestiers,
        Car m'amors est de si grant signorie,
        Se m'aïst Deus, s'en ai malvaix lueir.   35

        RR   II   10 si] ki *(em. Jeanroy-Långfors)*   V   31
Celle

        E   Jeanroy-Långfors, 64-65.

        DF   Lorraine, including *ai* for *a*, as in *pair* (4),
pairleir (4), *airt* (21), *pais* (22); *ei* for tonic *e*, as in
conforteir (2), *irei* (9), *povreteis* (13), *teils* (21); *amins*
(24) for *amis*; preservation of final *t*, as in *mercit* (26),
desireit (28); *x* for *s*, as in *plux* (2), *raixon* (23); *se* (12)
for *si*; *ceu* (14) for *ce*; *lou* (9) for *le*; *seux* (12) for *sui*;
3rd-pers. sing. pres. ind. *ait* (3) for *a*; relative *ke* (21,
32) for nominative.

        N   The repetition of *ariere* in ll. 10 and 13, like
that of *mestier(s)* in ll. 32-33, is questionable. The oc-
curence of *ariere* in l. 20 is surely erroneous, for it does
not assonate with l. 15 *fie* and l. 17 *desire*.
        17-18 These lines are presented in Jeanroy-Långfors
with a period at the end and evoke the comment: "La phrase
ne se construit pas; faut-il suppléer *En d.*, ce qui donne-
rait une césure épique?"

CHANSONS PIEUSES

RS 866, MW 360, B 1799 (one other source).
Mss. X 260v-261r, P 196r-v. Music in both mss.

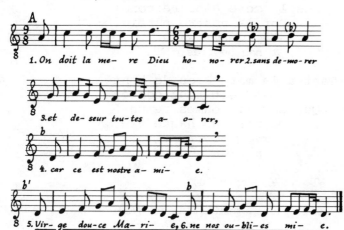

1. On doit la me- re Dieu ho- no- rer 2. sans de-mo-rer

3. et de- seur tou- tes a- o- rer,

4. car ce est nostre a- mi-   e.

5. Vir- ge dou-ce Ma- ri- e, 6. ne nos ou-bli-es mi-   e.

I On doit la mere Dieu honorer
      Sans demorer
    Et deseur toutes aorer,
      Car ce est nostre amie.
      Virge douce Marie,   5
      Ne nos oublïés mie.

II Il n'est nus, tant ait fait de pechiés,
      Tant soit bleciés,
    Qui ne soit bien tost redreciés
      Se de fin cuer la prie.   10
      Virge [douce Marie,
      Ne nos oublïés mie].

III Par li avons tuit joie et honor,
      Grant et menor,
    Car ele porta le Seignor   15
      Qui tot a en baillie.
      Virge [douce Marie,
      Ne nos oublïés mie].

IV Certes, quant Eve ot fait le forfait
      Et le mal trait   20
    Par quoi tuit estiom mort fait,

Ele nos fist aïe.
Virge [douce Marie,
Ne nos oublïés mie].

V   Eve trestout le mont confondi,   25
Je le vos di,
Mes la mere Dieu respondi
Por la nostre partie.
Virge [douce Marie,
Ne nos oublïés mie].   30

VI   Tant a la mere Dieu de bonté,
C'est tout conté,
Que par li soumes remonté
De mort en haute vie.
Virge [douce Marie,   35
Ne nos oublïés mie].

MN   Form: A b rf(b^1+b).

RR   II   7   a. mesfait de p. *(+1)*

V   I   4 Char ele e.   II   9   Que il ne   10   Se
il de bon c.   III   13   auon   IV   23   douce *added*
In stanzas V and VI, P is entirely distinct from X:
Tuit estion a Dieu descordé
Et mal cordé,
Tuit fusmes par li racordé
Et en grant seignorie.
Virge [douce Marie,
Ne nos oublïez mie].   30

Bien nos devon a li tuit corder
Et racorder,
Puis qu'ele nos veut descorder
De tote vilanie.
Virge douce [Marie,   35
Ne nos oublïez mie].

E   Noack, 122; Järnström-Långfors 2, 121-123; Gennrich *Cant*, 8.

N   Melody and poetic form of the *chansons pieuses*
were often borrowed from *chansons d'amour*; see P. Meyer,
"Types de quelques chansons de Gautier de Coinci," *Romania*
17 (1888), 429-437; Järnström 1, pp. 13-14; P. Meyer, "Mo-
dèles profanes de chansons pieuses," *Romania* 40 (1911), 84-

86; Gennrich *Bib*, pp. 329-338; and Hans Spanke, "Das öftere
Auftreten von Strophenformen und Melodien in der altfranzösischen Lyrik," *Zeit. für franz. Sprache und Lit.* 51
(1928), 73-117. The model for the present song was a composition by Richart de Semilli, RS 868.

    1 Absolute genitive: *la mere [de] Dieu.*

                              II   64

RS 1609, MW 1155
Mss. V 149r, C 140r-v. No music (see note below).

    I   L'autrier m'iere rendormiz
           Par un matin en esté;
           Adonques me fu avis
           Que la douce mere Dé
           M'avoit dit et commandé   5
           Que seur un chant qui jadis
           Soloit estre mout joïs
           Chantasse de sa bonté,
           Et je tantost l'ai empris.
           Dieus doint qu'il li viegne en gré. 10

    II   "Quant li rossinoil jolis
           Chante seur la flour d'esté"
           C'est li chans seur quoi j'ai mis

Le dit que je ai trouvé
De celi qui recouvré
Nos a le saint paradis,
De quoi nos fusmes jadis
Par Evain desherité.
Ceste dame nos a mis
De tenebres en clarté.

III A la chaste flour de lis,
Reprise en humilité,
Fu li sains anges tramis
De Dieu, qui humanité
Prist en sa virginité
Pour rachater ses amis.
En li fu noz rachaz pris
Dou saint sanc de son costé;
Mout doit estre de haut pris
Li hons qui tant a costé.

IV Se roches et quaillous bis
Erent frait et destrempé
Dou ru dou Rosne et dou Lis,
Et d'arrement attempré,
En parchemin conreé
Fussent ciel et terre mis,
Et chascun fust ententis
D'escrire la verité,
Ja si bien par ces escriz
Ne seroient recordé.

V Glorïeuse empereriz,
Chambre de la deïté,
Ja ne sera desconfiz
Qui vos sert sanz fauseté.
Aiez dou monde pité,
Qui s'en va de mal en pis;
Et moi, qui vos aim et pris
D'enterine volenté,
En vostre riche païs
Conduisiez a sauveté!

<u>MN</u> Form: A A^1 B+A^2.
1. Ms. writes *B* natural. 2. Ms. writes *a*; emended according to ll. 1 and 8. 3. This note is illegible in ms.

<u>RR</u> I 3 A donc *(-1)* 10 li *missing* III 22 Repris 33 *second* dou *missing* 36 ciel *missing*

V   I   7 m. ois   II   11   r. ioli   12   Chantent
14 ien ai   III   30 hom   IV   31 caillo   37 chascuns   39 si] sui   V   46 Kil   47 Et moi ki uos *repeated*; pri

E   Järnström 1, 26-28.

N   While many *chansons pieuses* are clearly contrafacta of secular songs, it is extraordinary to find one that
incorporates an acknowledgment of its model. The song referred to in st. 2 is known and in fact occurs in both codices containing RS 1609, as well as in other sources. It
is RS 1559, composed by either the Châtelain de Couci or
Raoul de Ferrières; the melody that accompanies it in ms. V
is the one we present here.
   30 *qui = cui*, dative object of impersonal *a costé*.
33 The Lys is a tributary of the Escaut, in northern France
and Belgium. Hardly so well known outside its own region as
the Rhone, its presence in this text, as observed in Järnström 1, suggests the locus of the poet's activity.

                      III   65

RS 519, MW 1483
Mss. V 151r-v, C 216r-v. No music.

        I   Rose cui nois ne gelee
               Ne fraint ne mue colour,
               Dedenz haute mer salee
               Fontenele de douçour,
                   Clere en tenebrour,   5
                   Joiouse en tristour,
                   En flamme rousee!

        II   Flour de biauté esmeree
               Et de triie coulour,
               Chastiaus dont onc deffermee   10
               Ne fu la porte nul jour,
                   Santez en langour,
                   Repos en labour,
                   Et pais en meslee!

        III   Fine esmeraude esprouvee   15
               De graciouse vigour,
               Diamanz, jaspe alosee,
               Saphirs d'Ynde la maiour,

Rubiz de valour,
Panthere d'odour   20
Plus qu'embausemmee!

IV   Ne seroit assez löee
Ceste monjoie d'onnour,
Se toute humaine pensee
Ne servoit d'autre labor.   25
Tigre en mireour,
En ire et en plour
Solaz et risee!

V   Empareriz coronnee
De la main au Creatour,   30
A la crueuse jornee,
Quant li ange avront paour,
Prie au Sauveour
Que ton chanteour
Maint en sa contree.   35

RR   II   8   de bonte   9   triaie   12   languour   V
32 li *repeated*

V   I   1   iallee   3   cellee   IV   28   rousee   32
li aingele a.

E   Järnström 1, 44-47; Bec 2, 79-80.

N   8 Ms. V *bonté* was rejected in favor of ms. C
biaulteit (= *biauté*) as being out of keeping with *flour* and
with *esmeree*, which customarily modifies a physical entity
or quality.   20-21 Both the Virgin and Christ are symbol-
ized in medieval writings by the panther, which was reputed
to have a sweet smell that would attract other animals (=
souls). See Järnström 1, pp. 45-46, for further detail.
24 *Se* 'even if'.   26 The image of the tigress contemplat-
ing herself in a mirror would ordinarily symbolize thought-
less and dangerous absorption in one's own beauty. As
pointed out in Järnström 1, pp. 46-47, it is no doubt to be
understood in the present context as no more than an allusion to Mary's extraordinary beauty.

66   IV

RS 1179, MW 1360
Ms. X 268v. Music.

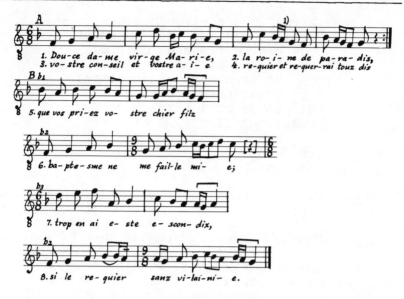

I   Douce dame virge Marie,
      La roïne de paradis,
      Vostre conseil et vostre aïe
      Requier et requerrai touz dis   4
      Que vos prïez vostre chier filz
      Baptesme ne me faille mie;
      Trop en ai esté escondix,
      Si le requier sanz vilainie.   8

II   Douce dame, j'ai grant fiance
      En cil qui en crois fu penés.
      Qui en celui n'a sa creance,
      Certes, por droit noient est nez;   12
      Son esperit [si] ert dampnez
      Ens el puis d'enfer sanz faillance.
      Cil qui ert crestïens clamez,
      Il n'a d'enfer nule doutance.   16

III   Hé las, je l'ai tant desiree,
      Et si ne la puis pas avoir.
      Toute est m'entente et ma pensee
      En crestïenté recevoir;   20
      Feme, or et argent ne avoir
      Ne nule riens tant ne m'agree
      Con fait crestïenté, por voir,
      Si ne me veut estre donee.   24

IV   A vos, douce virge honoree,
      Proi et requier mout bonement
      Que vostre fiz sanz demoree
      Proiés por moi prochainement   28
      Que de ceus m'achat vengement
      Qui crestīenté m'ont veee,
      Si con je croi veraiement
      Celui qui fist ciel et rosee.   32

<u>MN</u>   Form: A A B.
1. In 1. 2 ms. writes what looks like *g*.

<u>RR</u>   II   13 *-1*   15 Et *(+1)*   III   23 p. auoir
(+1)   IV   27 Qui   30 uee   31 Ensi *(+1)*

<u>E</u>   Järnström-Långfors 2, 149-150; Gennrich *Cant*, 26.

<u>N</u>   This *chanson pieuse* is unusual not only for its
obviously personal nature, but also because it leaves unex-
plained why an ardent would-be convert to Christianity
should have been refused baptism.
      6 Understand *que* before *Baptesme*.   15 Instead of de-
leting *Et*, Järnström-Långfors 2 would read the normally tri-
syllabic *crestiens* as dissyllabic.   23 Järnström-Långfors
2 accepts the ms. reading *Con fait crestienté por avoir*,
despite the unusual trisyllable (cf. 11. 20 and 30) and awkward syntax; it is suggested, however, that *por* might be
deleted.

<u>67</u>   V

RS 1780, MW 2485
Ms. V 154r. No music.

I   De l'estoile, mere au soleil
      Dont parmenable sont li rai,
      Toute ma vie chanterai,
        Et raisons le me conseille   4
        Que de sa valour veraie
        Aucune chose retraie,
      Que nus ne la sert bonnement
        Que gent guerredon n'en traie.   8

II   Mere sanz acointier pareil,
      Mieudre que je dire ne sai,
      Qui portastes li roi verai

A cui riens ne s'apareille,   12
Dame, por noient s'esmaie
Cil qui en vostre manaie
Se rent, car, qui a vos s'atent,
Vostre secours ne li delaie.   16

III   Palais a l'ange de conseil,
De cui sont mi chant et mi lai,
A vos servir tieng et me trai
Cuer et cors, oeil et oreille.   20
Dame, or vuilliez que si m'aie
Qu'a son acort ne me traie
Cil qui dou mont traire en torment
Adés s'eforce et essaie.   24

RR   I   1 soloil   2 Donc   II   9 paroil   III
22 atort

E   Järnström 1, 69-70.

N   The intricate rhyme scheme of this poem, quite exceptional in Old French, probably owes its inspiration to
troubadour versification. Note that a, c, and e rhyme only
from stanza to stanza, but that a and c differ from each
other only in rhyme gender, as do b and d.
    9 'Mother with no knowledge of anything similar [to
you]'.   17 'Palace of the angel of counsel'; in this metaphor for Mary, the designation of the Holy Spirit is derived
from Latin *spiritus consilii*.

VI   68

RS 1136, MW 2340
Ms. X 269v-270r. Music.

1. Por ce que ve- ri- te di- e, 2. vueil ma chan-çon co- men- cier,
3. por de- duire et so- la- cier 4. ceus qui sont en bo- ne vi- e;
5. et ceus qui sont en fo- li- e, 6. en guille et en tri-che- ri- e

7. vueill bla-smer et   lei-den-gier 8. et mo-strer leur ma-la-di-   e.

I   Por ce que verité die,
       Vueil ma chançon comencier,
       Por deduire et solacier
       Ceus qui sont en bone vie;   4
       Et ceus qui sont en folie,
       En guille et en tricherie
       Vueill blasmer et leidengier
       Et mostrer leur maladie.   8

II   Quant n'apert la maladie,
       Nus mires n'en puet aidier
       Ne bien a droit conseillier;
       Ensit est d'ypocrisie,   12
       Qui le cors a plain d'envie
       Ne par dehors ne pert mie,
       Ainz sont tel fois au mostier
       Que leur cuers est en folie.   16

III   Deus nos a mostré par vie,
       Par sarmons, par preechier,
       Coment nos devons laissier
       Tout pechié, toute folie,   20
       Tout mal, toute tricherie,
       Tout orgueill et toute envie,
       Et nos prie d'esloignier
       Doublesse d'ypocresie.   24

IV   Honi soit lor conpaignie,
       Que on n'en fait qu'enpirier;
       Bien la devons esloignier,
       Saint Gregoires nos en prie.   28
       Bien puis conparer leur vie
       A fausse pome porrie
       Qu'en met en tas estoier
       Et ses conpaignes conchie.   32

V   E! dame sainte Marie,
       Bien devés a ceus aidier
       Qui de bon cuer et d'entier
       Vos servent sanz tricherie,   36
       Qui ne font par symonie
       Ne par fausse ypocrissie

Les biens, mes por gaaignier
Joie qui ne faudra mie.   40

MN   Form: through-composed.
1. Ms. repeats this note.

RR   I   8 leu m.   IV   26 Quon *(-1)*

E   Järnström-Långfors 2, 152-154; Gennrich *Cant*, 29.

N   This song is unusual among the *chansons pieuses* in
that it is at least as much a diatribe against hypocrites as
it is an expression of piety or a celebration of the Virgin.
     16 Understand *ceux* as the antecedent of *Que*.   31-32
'which one stores in a pile and [which] spoils its compan-
ions (= the other apples)'. Note that l. 31 *Qu'* serves in
the first clause as direct object of the verb and in the
second as subject.

                         VII   69

RS 1957a, MW 620
Ms. Paris, Arsenal 3517, f. 147r. Music.

I   Chanter voel par grant amour
        Une chansonnete humaine,
        Si chanterai en l'ounour
        De Marie Magdalaine,
        A qui nostre salveour   5
        Delaissa par sa douchour
        Les pechiés dont estoit plaine.

II   Le dame dont je vous [di]
        Pecca mout ens en s'enfanche,

Mais ele s'en repenti,   10
Si en fist sa penitanche
Et si aama cheli
Ki puis ot de li merchi,
Car tous ses amis avanche.

III   Jhesus mout s'umilia   15
Adont vers les pecheours,
Quant ele ses piés lava
Et de lermes et de plours;
De ses crins les essuia
Et douchement les baisa;   20
Mieus l'en sera a tous jours.

IV   Mout deverions estre liés,
Nous qui sommes pecheours,
Car Dieus est apparelliés
A nous rechevoir tous jours   25
Pour que nous soions purgiés
De nos maus, de nos pechiés;
Mout en est liés et joious.

V   Or ne nous desesperons,
Car che seroit grans folie;   30
Mais de pechié nous jetons,
Si entrons en mellour vie,
Et Jhesu Crist en proions
Que li Rois qui tant est dous
Nous doinst pardurable vie.   35

<u>MN</u>   Form: A A B.

<u>RR</u>   II   8 *-1*

<u>E</u>   Järnström-Långfors 2, 99-100.

<u>DF</u>   Picard, including *ch* for *c*, as in *douchour* (6),
enfanche (9), *cheli* (12), *che* (30); *c* for *ch*, as in *pecca*
(9); *-1(1)* for *-il(1)*, as in *voel* (1), *apparelliés* (24),
mellour (32); epenthesized *deverions* (22) for *devrions*; *le*
(8) for *la*.

<u>N</u>   For some discussion of this song in the context of
Latin poems concerning Mary Magdalen, see Wiltrud aus der
Fünten, *Maria Magdalena in der Lyrik des Mittelalters* (Düs-
seldorf, 1966), pp. 192-193. Note that *-our*, *-ours*, *-ous*,
and *-ons* all belong to the same homophonic group in this

poem.   2 *humaine* 'concerning a human being'. That the
poet should mention this point explicitly is not surprising,
for his subject, Mary Magdalen, is indeed unique in the corpus of *chansons pieuses*.   21 'It will forever be to her
advantage'.

VIII   70

Not in RS.   MW 438.
Ms. London, Guildhall, *Liber de antiquis legibus*, ff. 160v-
    161r-v.   Music.

IV. 27. Fous est ke se a- fi- e 28. en ce-ste mor-teu vi- e,
29. ke tant nus contr-a- li- e 30. et u n'ad fors boy- di- e
31. Ore est hoem en le- es- se 32. et ore est 'en tri- ste-sce;
33. or le ga- rist, or ble- sce 34. for-tu-ne ke le qui- e.
V. 35. Virqne et mere au so- ve- rein 36. ke nus je- ta de la mayn
40. re- que-rez i- cel sei- gnur 41. ke il par sa grant dul-çur
37. al mau-fe, ki par E- vayn 38. nus out tres-tuz en sun heim
42. nus get de ce- ste do- lur 43. u nus su- mus nuyt et jor
39. a grant do- lur [et] pei- ne,
48. et doint joy- e cer- tey- ne.

I   Eyns ne soy ke pleynte fu,
        Ore pleyn d'angusse tressu.
        Trop ai mal et contreyre,
        Sanz decerte en prisun sui.
        Car m'aydez, tres puissanz Jhesu,   5
        Duz Deus et deboneyre!

II   Jhesu Crist, veirs Deu, veirs hom,
        Prenge vus de mei pité!
        Jetez mei de la prisun
        U je sui a tort geté!   10
        Jo e mi autre compaignun,
        Deus en set la verité,
        Tut pur autri mesprisun
        Sumes a hunte liveré.

III   Sire Deus,   15
        Ky as mortels
        Es de pardun veine,
        Sucurez,

```
            Deliverez
            Nus de ceste peine.                              20
            Pardonez
            Et assoylez
            Icels, gentil sire,
            Si te plest,
            Par ki forfet                                    25
            Nus suffrum tel martire.


     IV     Fous est ke se afie
            En ceste morteu vie,
            Ke tant nus contralie
            Et u n'ad fors boydie.                           30
            Ore est hoem en leesse
            Et ore est en tristesce;
            Or le garist, or blesce
            Fortune ke le guie.


     V      Virgne et mere au soverein                       35
            Ke nus jeta de la mayn
            Al maufé, ki par Evayn
            Nus out trestuz en sun heim
            A grant dolur [et] peine,
            Requerez icel seignur                            40
            Ke il par sa grant dulçur
            Nus get de ceste dolur
            U nus sumus nuyt et jor
            Et doint joye certeyne.
```

MN   Form: AA BB CC¹ DD¹ EE (lai). The melody, unique
to the Guildhall ms., is derived from sections 1, 2, 3, 7,
and 8 of the sequence *Planctus ante nescia* by Godefroy of
St. Victor (fl. 1170-90); see DobHar, pp. 83-86.
1. In l. 4 ms. repeats this note. 2. Ms. writes two notes
but no plica; emendation. 3. The remainder of the music is
missing in the ms.

     RR   I   5 puis ihesu *(-1)*   IV   33 Ore, ore *(+2)*
V   39 *-1*

     E   Delpit, 28-29; Ellis, 423-439; Gennrich "Melo-
dien", 346-348; Brown, 10-13; Reese, 204; Aspin, 1-11;
DobHar, 110-111, 229-240.

     DF   Anglo-Norman, including *ei* for *oi*, as in *veirs*
(7), *mei* (8, 9); *ui* with falling stress (thus, l. 4 *sui*
rhymes with *fu* and *Jhesu*); *u* not only for Central *u* [ü], but

also for *ou* [u], as in *vus* (8), *dulçur* (41), and for *o* before nasal, as in *sumes* (14), *prisun* (9); subjunctive in
-ge, as in *prenge* (8) for *prenne*; first-person plural in
-um, as in *suffrum* (26).

N̲   Nothing is known of the writer of this song of
captivity or the circumstances of its composition, but it
was probably composed in the mid-thirteenth century and
surely reflects a true experience. It is accompanied in the
ms. by an English version. The English song appears as No.
7 in Christopher Page, "A Catalogue and Bibliography of English Song from its Beginnings to c. 1300," *Royal Musical
Association Research Chronicle* 13 (1976), 67-83. For enten-
sive commentary, see DobHar, pp. 83-86, 112-120, 296-297;
note that a number of points, especially regarding textual
interpretation and emendation, are disputable.
    Irregularities in meter have been corrected only in
those cases where emendation has seemed to us dictated by
meaning and/or music. Thus, 1. 5 has been lengthened to
correspond to 1. 2 (just as 1. 4 corresponds to 1. 1 with
seven syllables and 1. 6 corresponds to 1. 3 with six syllables) because the music indicates two notes for monosyllabic *puis* and because the interpretation of *tres puis* as
adverbial 'very soon', as in Aspin, appears quite unlikely.
Similarly, 1. 33 has been reduced to a hexasyllable (like
all the other verses of st. 4) because the music accords
only one note to each occurrence of the word *ore*. Finally,
1. 39 has been lengthened to six syllables (and now corresponds to 1. 44, just as the heptasyllabic 11. 35-38 correspond to 11. 40-43) because the sense demands the conjunction *et* and because the music provides an extra note in the
appropriate place.
    This minimal emendation leaves the following metrical
irregularities, all borne out by the music: In st. 2, the
heptasyllabic 1. 7 corresponds to the octosyllabic 1. 11;
likewise, 1. 10 contains seven syllables while its corre-
sponding verse, 1. 14, contains eight. In st. 3, 1. 26 has
six syllables while there are five in 1. 20 (and in 11. 17
and 23).
    1 Understand *ce* before *ke*.   13 'All because of some-
one else's mistake'.   25 *ki* = *cui* 'whose'.   27 Relative
ke serves here as subject; likewise, 11. 34 and 36.

RONDEAUX

B rond. 114, refr. 631
MW 151, Gennrich *Ron* 114
Ms. I 247v. No music.

> *D'une fine amour sans fauceir*
> *Amerai je sans vilonie.*
> Au Dieu d'amor m'irai clameir
> *--D'une fine amour sans fauceir--* 4
> Des mesdixans qui sont ameir;
> Se il li plait, qu'il les ocie.
> *D'une fine amour sans fauceir*
> *Amerai je sans vilonie.* 8

E   Gennrich *Ron* 1, 88; 2, 98-99; B, 66.

II

72

B rond. 116, refr. 903
MW 780, Gennrich *Ron* 116.
Ms. I 247v. No music.

> *J'ai ameit bien sans fauceir*
> *Damoiselle de valour,*
> *Qui me welt congié doneir,*
> *Dont je n'ai a cuer poour;* 4
> Si n'an puis mon cuer osteir
> De li servir neut et jor.
> *J'ai ameit bien sans fauceir*
> *Damoiselle de valour,* 8
> Qui me fait mon cuer trembleir
> Cant je pance a sai dousour;
> Si an suis desconforteis
> Quant ne puis avoir s'amour. 12
> *J'ai ameit bien sans faceir*
> *[Damoiselle de valour,*
> *Qui me welt congié doneir,*
> *Dont je n'ai a cuer poour].* 16

RR   2 and 8 D. de grant v. *(+1)*

E   Gennrich *Ron* 1, 89; 2, 99; B, 67.

DF   Lorraine, including *a* for *au*, as in *faceir* (13);
ei for tonic *e*, as in *ameit* (1), *fauceir* (1); *sai* (10) for
sa; *welt* (3) for *vueut*; *neut* (6) for *nuit*; *ameit* (1) for
amé.

73   III

B rond. 125, refr. 1793
MW 122, Gennrich *Ron* 125
Ms. I 248r. No music.

> *Tout mon vivant servirai*
> *Loialment Amors,*
> *Car de li vient ma joie,*
> Ne jamais ne meterai   4
> Ma pancee aillors.
> *Tout mon vivant servirai*
> *Loialment Amors.*
> Un dous espoir maintanrai   8
> Bonement toz jors;
> Partir ne m'an poroie.
> *Tot mon vivant servirai*
> *Loialment Amors,*
> *Car de li vient ma joie.*   12

E   Gennrich *Ron* 1, 92; 2, 100; B, 69.

N   Both B and Gennrich *Ron* interpret the *-ai* rhyme as
internal, printing ll. 1 and 2, 4 and 5, 8 and 9, 11 and 12
as single lines.

74   IV

B rond. 126, refr. 953
MW 184, Gennrich *Ron* 126
Ms. I 248r. No music.

> *[J']ain la brunette sans orguel*
> *Ki est doucette.*
> Dieus, com ont bien choixi mi oil!
> *J'ain la brunette sans orguel.*
> N'est nuns ke m'an ostest mon veul
> De lai tousette.
> *J'ain lai brunette sans orguel*
> *Qui est doucette.*

<u>RR</u>   1   *initial letter omitted*

<u>E</u>   Gennrich *Ron* 1, 93; 2, 100; B, 69-70.

<u>N</u>   5-6   'There is no one who, with my consent, would take me away from the maiden'. *ostest* and *lai*, Lorraine forms for *ostast* and *la*.

V   <u>75</u>

B rond. 129, refr. 404
MW 784, Gennrich *Ron* 129
Ms. I 248v. No music.

> *Dame debonaire,*
> *Je me rans a vos;*
> *De cuer sanz mesfaire*
> *Je suis vostres tous.*   4
> Ne soiez contraire
> De vostre amin dous.
> *Dame debonaire,*
> *Je me rans a vos.*   8
> Bonteit qui repaire
> An cuer amerous
> Me dont examplaire
> D'ameir par amors.   12
> *Dame debonaire,*
> *Je me rans a vos;*
> *De cuer sans retraire*
> *Je suis vostre toz.*   16

<u>E</u>   Gennrich *Ron* 1, 94; 2, 101; B, 70-71.

<u>N</u>   6   *amin*, Lorraine for *ami*.

VI   <u>76</u>

B rond. 140, refr. 1758
MW 718, Gennrich *Ron* 138
Ms. I 249r. No music.

> *"Tant con je fu dezirouze,*
> *Je n'o point d'amin;*
> *Or l'ai, s'an suis dedaignouze."*
> "Belle et bone et graciouze,   4

                              Ne m'oblieiz mi."
                      "Tant com je fu dezirouse,
                          Je n'o point d'amin."
                      "Se ver moi n'estes pitouze,   8
                          Je dirai: 'Enmi!
                      J'ai perdu vie amerouse.'"
                      "Tant con je fu dezirouze,
                          Je n'o point d'amin;   12
                          Or l'ai, s'an suis dedaignouze."

      E   Gennrich *Ron* 1, 97; 2, 102; B, 74.

      N   This rondeau is exceptional in taking the form of
a dialogue.

<u>77</u>   VII

B rond. 143, refr. 905
MW 115, Gennrich *Ron* 141
Ms. I 249v. No music.

                      J'ai ameit et amerai
                      Trestout les jours de ma vie
                      Et plus jolive an serai.
                      J'ai bel amin, cointe et gai.   4
                      J'ai ameit et amerai.
                      Il m'aimme, de fi lou sai;
                      Il ait droit: je suis s'amie
                      Et loialtei li ferai.   8
                      J'ai ameit et amerai
                      Trestout les jors de ma vie
                      Et plus jolive en serai.

      E   Gennrich *Ron* 1, 98; 2, 102; B, 75.

      N   6 *lou,* Lorraine for *le.*   7 *ait,* Lorraine for
indicative *a.*

<u>78</u>   VIII

B rond. 145, refr. 1796
MW 130, Gennrich *Ron* 143
Ms. I 249v. No music.

Tres douce dame, aiez de moi merci,
Car an chantant mes fins cuers vos an proie,
Et je serai vostre loialz amins.
Tres douce dame, aiez de moi mercit.   4
De vos me vient un dous espoir [joli]
Qui me soustient, si an vivrai a joie.
Tres douce dame, aiez de moi mercit,
Car an chantant mes fins cuers vos an proie.   8

RR   5   *-2 (em. Gennrich)*

E   Gennrich *Ron* 1, 99; 2, 102; B, 76.

N   3   *amins,* Lorraine for *amis.*   4   *mercit,* Lorraine
for *merci.*

RS 1147, MW 1446
Ms. K 366-367. Music.

79   I. Chanson historique

I   Gent de France, mult estes esbahie!
Je di a touz ceus qui sont nez des fiez:
Si m'aīt Deus, franc n'estes vous mes mie;
Mult vous a l'en de franchise esloigniez,

Car vous estes par enqueste jugiez.   5
Quant desfensse ne vos puet fere aïe,
Trop i estes crüelment engingniez.
   A touz pri:
Douce France n'apiaut l'en plus ensi,
Ançois ait non le païs aus sougiez,   10
  Une terre acuvertie,
  Le raigne as desconseilliez,
  Qui en maint cas sont forciez.

II Je sai de voir que de Dieu ne vient mie
Tel servage, tout soit il esploitié.   15
Hé! loiauté, povre chose esbahie,
Vous ne trouvez qui de vous ait pitié;
Vous eüssiez force et povoir et pié,
Car vos estes a nostre roi amie,
Mes li vostre sont trop a cler rengié   20
   Entor lui.
Je n'en conois qu'un autre seul o lui,
Et icelui est si pris du clergié
  Q'il ne vous puet fere aïe;
  Tout ont ensenble broié   25
  Et l'aumosne et le pechié.

III Ce ne cuit nus que je pour mal le die
De mon seigneur, se Deus me face lié!
Mes j'ai poor que s'ame en fust perie,
Et si aim bien saisine de mon fié.   30
Quant ce savra, tost l'avra adrecié;
Son gentil cuer ne le sousfreroit mie.
Pour ce me plest qu'il en soit acointié
   Et garni,
Si que par ci n'ait nul povoir seur lui   35
Deable anemi, qui l'avoit aguetié.
  G'eüsse ma foi mentie
  Se g'eüsse ensi lessié
  Mon seigneur desconseillié.

<u>MN</u> Form: A A B B¹.

<u>RR</u> III 32 le] ne

<u>E</u> Leroux de Lincy, 215-220; Spanke *Lied*, 159, 386-387; Gennrich *Alt Lied* 1, 21-23; Gennrich *Ex*, 7-8.

<u>N</u> The lifelong efforts of Louis IX to extend the administrative and juridical authority of the monarchy at the

expense of baronial autonomy culminated in a series of or-
dinances which, inter alia, outlawed judicial combats (1260)
and established the power of the royal bailiffs to settle
feudal disputes through peaceful *enquêtes* (1270). It is
this aspect of the King's program of reform, specifically
the latter measure (see 1. 5), that the anonymous composer
of RS 1147, himself a feudal lord (see 1. 30), deplores.
The poet presents himself as a disappointed loyalist, fear-
ful lest Louis have unwittingly placed himself in the hands
of the Devil.

    4 *l'en* = *on*, as in 1. 9.   9 *ensi* plays on the simi-
larity of *France* and *franche*.   12 *desconseilliez* 'bewildered, discouraged'; cf. 1. 39, where the word is to be
understood as 'without (good) counsel'.   14 The argument
that not God, but the Devil, is responsible for Louis' measures is obviously calculated to appeal to the King's well-
known piety. It will be developed in the third stanza.   18
pié here means 'support'.   22 As noted in Leroux de Lincy
1 and in Spanke *Lied*, Louis' unnamed friend is no doubt his
chaplain, Robert de Sorbon, who founded the Sorbonne.   25-
26 Spanke *Lied* interprets these lines as a taunting allusion to the system of indulgences.

<u>80</u>   II. Chanson pastorale

RS 439a (= 1979), MW 548
Ms. X 216r-v. Music.

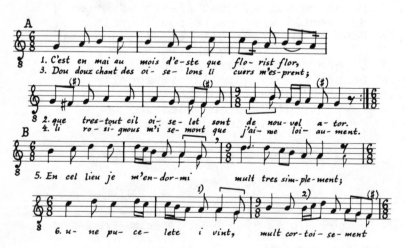

1. C'est en mai au   mois d'e-ste que flo-rist flor,
3. Dou douz chant des oi- se- lons li cuers m'es-prent;

2. que   tres-tout cil oi- se- let sont de nou-vel a- tor.
4. li ro- si- gnous m'i se-mont que j'ai- me loi- au-ment.

5. En cel lieu je m'en-dor-mi   mult tres sim-ple-ment;

6. u- ne pu- ce- lete i vint,   mult cor-toi- se-ment

7. m'es-gar-da sanz mau- ta- lent.

I

C'est en mai au mois d'esté que florist flor,
Que trestout cil oiselet sont de nouvel ator.
Dou douz chant des oiselons li cuers m'esprent;
Li rosignous m'i semont que j'aime loiaument.
En cel lieu je m'endormi mult tres simplement;   5
Une pucelete i vint, mult cortoisement
          M'esgarda sanz mautalent.

II

Je la pris, si l'enbraçai demaintenant,
L'acolai et la baisai sanz nul demorement;
Le gieu d'amors li vueil faire sanz arestement.   10
"Sire, que volés vos faire?" dist la pucelote;
"Vos m'avrois ançois doné ou sorcot ou cote,
          Et puis si avrois dou nostre."

III

Ele avoit les euz si vairs come faucon
Et si avoit bele bochë et bele façon;   15
Ele avoit les euz rians, le nes traitis,
Sa facete vermeillete com rosier floris.
Nul charbon bien alumé n'est si espris
Come je sui por celi en qui je sui assis;
          Plus l'aim que touz mes amis.   20

IV

Certes que quant la regart, il m'est avis
El me semble mult bien faite et de cors et de vis;
Ele resenble a touz ceus de paradis,
Et por ce la conois je et en fes et en dis.   24
El me fait touz jours trenbler [sanz doner confort]
Et sospirer et fremir a si grant tort;
          Mes cuers en est a la mort.

V

Chançonete, tu iras en mon païs
Et si me diras a cele qui m'a [si] traïs
Que j'amoie loiaument et de bon cuer.   30
Di li que l'amoie plus que frere ne que suer,
Et ele ne m'amoit pas ne de moi n'ot pitié,
Et s'el mi vousist amer, mult en fusse lié,
            Mes maus me fust alegié.

MN   Form: A A B.
1. Ms. repeats this note, as though *pucelete* were unelided.
2. Ms. writes ♫♪ .

RR   II *one verse apparently missing somewhere in
this stanza*   10 s. nul a *(+1)*   III   17 come *(+1)*   IV
25 *-5*   V   29 me di a *(-1 before caesura; em. Bartsch)*,
-1 after caesura

E   Bartsch, 54-55; Spanke *Lied*, 84-85, 369-370.

N   The meter of this poem is highly irregular, each
line but the last of every stanza consisting of a series of
seven syllables followed by a series of four, five, six, or
seven which may or may not begin with an atonic final *-e*.
This may be an example of one of the "free" meters studied
in, for example, Burger, where l. 10 is in fact mentioned
explicitly (p. 62), and such metrical freedom would certainly accord well with the remarkable irregularity in rhyme
scheme that the song displays. However, the metrical incon-
sistency may be due instead to scribal ignorance or inatten-
tiveness, and it is not difficult to "reconstruct" a regular
version of the text, such as is given in MW or such, slight-
ly better perhaps, as: 7 + 4, 7 + 6, 7 + 4, 7 + 6, 7 + 5, 7
+ 5, 7. It is also possible, assuming the correctness of
free meter in this poem, that certain of the irregularities
are nevertheless erroneous. This, indeed, is what the ac-
companying melody suggests, and we have accordingly regular-
ized the meter to the extent of compatibility with the music; further intervention would suppose the demonstrable
invalidity of the principle of free meter in this text (and
perhaps elsewhere as well). See Rejected Readings for the
changes made, as well as l. 15 *bochë* with unelided *-e*.
    The rhyme scheme of the poem is no less irregular
than its meter; we have made no attempt to "correct" it. It
is perhaps of no small interest that the content of the song
is similarly resistant to normal classification, combining

elements of the *pastourelle*, *reverdie*, and *chanson d'amour*.
24   In Spanke *Lied*, *por ce* is emended to *nonporquant*, but
no reason is provided. Metrically, there is no material
change, since *je* may readily be treated either as a seventh
syllable or as an uncounted syllable forming a *césure
épique*. From the point of view of meaning, it is not at all
clear that the line requires an adversative; nor, indeed, is
it certain that *por ce* is not itself an adversative in this
utterance.   25 Bartsch offers no addition to the ms. version; Spanke *Lied* supplies *sanz nul confort*.   29-30 *me* is
to be understood as a dative of interest; the clause beginning with *Que* is the direct object of *diras*; and *amoie* is
used in absolute construction (cf. l. 4).

III. Plainte funèbre   81

RS 358, MW 1227
Mss. K 311-312, N 148r-v, P 162v-163r-v, X 197r-v. Music in
    all mss.

I   Li chastelains de Couci ama tant
      Qu'ainz por amor nus n'en ot dolor graindre;

Por ce ferai ma conplainte en son chant
Que ne cuit pas que la moie soit maindre.   4
La mort m'i fet regreter et conplaindre
Vostre cler vis, bele, et vostre cors gent;
Morte vos ont frere et mere et parent
Par un tres fol desevrement mauvés.   8

II   Por qui ferai mes ne chançon ne chant,
        Quant je ne bé a nule amor ataindre?
        Ne jamés jor ne qier en mon vivant
        M'ire et mon duel ne ma dolor refraindre.   12
        Car venist or la mort por moi destraindre
        Si que morir m'esteüst maintenant!
        C'onques mes hom n'ot un mal si tres grant
        Ne de dolor au cuer si pesant fais.   16

III   Mult ai veü et mult ai esprouvé,
        Mainte merveille eüe et enduree,
        Mes ceste m'a le cors si aterré
        Que je ne puis avoir longue duree.   20
        Or maudirai ma male destinee
        Quant j'ai perdu le gent cors acesmé,
        Ou tant avoit de sens et de bonté,
        Qui valoit melz que li roiaumes d'Ais.   24

IV   Je departi de li outre mon gré;
        C'estoit la riens dont je plus me doloie.
        Ore a la mort le depart confermé;
        A touz jorz mes, c'est ce qui me tout joie. 28
        Nule dolor ne se prent a la moie,
        Car je sai bien jamés ne la verré.
        Hé las, chetis, ou iré, que feré?
        S'or ne me muir, je vivrai touz jorz mais.   32

V   Par Dieu, Amors, je ne vos pris noient,
        Car morte est cele pour qui je vous prisoie.
        Je ne pris riens, ne biauté ne jouvent,
        Or ne argent ne chose que je voie.   36
        Pour quoi? Pour ce que la mort tout
                                        [maistroie.
        Je quit amors et a Dieu les conmant.
        Jamés ne cuit vivre fors en torment;
        Joie et deduit tout outreement lais.   40

MN   Form: A A B.

RR   V   38 cuit

V   I   4 Ne ne c.   X   5 et plaindre X   6 gent
cors X   7 Mortel X   8 un *missing* X   II   11 en] a
X   III   24 li reaume de france X   IV   25 De parti
de li X   28 me toust j.   N   V   33 ne *missing* N   38
cuit N, qui X   39 cuit] quier P   40 deduis X

E   La Borde *Es*, 306; Michel, 101-102; Spanke *Lied*,
20-21, 356-357; Groult 1, 191-192.

N   As the composer states in 11. 1-3, this song is
modeled on one by the Châtelain de Couci (RS 679), which expresses the poet's sorrow at losing his lady not through
death but because he is departing on a crusade.
    7-8 It is unusual to find an OF poet blaming his
lady's family for the failure of their love, and is no doubt
reflective of true circumstances.   For two other instances,
see RS 351 (Jacques d'Autun) and RS 1645 (anon.).   30 Understand *que* after *bien*.

                IV. Chanson à contraste   82

RS 919, MW 1117:1
Ms. H 229v-230r.   No music.

        I   Oëz com je sui bestornez
             Por joie d'amors que je n'ai:
             Entre sages sui fous [clamez]
             Et entre les fous assez sai.   4

        II   Onques ne fis que faire dui;
             Qant plus m'aïre, plus m'apais.
             Je sui menanz et riens ne puis
             Avoir; mauvés sui et cortois.   8

        III Je sui müez por bien parler
             Et sorz por clerement oïr,
             Contraiz en lit por tost aler
             Et coliers por toz tens gesir.   12

        IV   Je muir de faim qant sui saous
             Et de noient faire sui las;
             De ma prode feme sui cous
             Et en gastant lo mien amas.   16

        V   Qant je chevalz, lais mon cheval;
             De mon aler faz mon venir;

Je n'ai ne maison ne ostal,
Si i porroit uns rois gesir.   20

VI   Aigue m'enivre plus que vins;
       Miel me fait boivre plus que seus;
       Prodom sui et lechierres fins
       Et si vos dirai briément queus: 24
       Alemanz sui et Poitevins,
       Ne l'un ne l'autre, ce set Dieus.

VII   La rotroange finera,
       Qui maintes foiz sera chantee;   28
       A la pucele s'en ira
       Par cui Amors m'ont bestorné.

VIII   Se li plaist, si la chantera
       Por moi qui la fis en esté.   32
       Et Dieus! se ja se sentira
       Mes cors de la soe bonté!

RR   I   3 *-2 (em. Meyer)*   4 a. iai *(em. Meyer)*
II 6̄ mapai   7 menaz   III   10 sozz   V   17 j.
cheual lez *(em. reported by Meyer as having been suggested
by G. Paris)*   VII   27 Ia r. finerai *(em. Meyer)*   28
chatee

E   Meyer "Mélanges", 102-106; Camus, 244; Voretzsch,
74; Gennrich *Rot*, 33-34; PetDyg "Moniot", 170-173; Spaziani
Ant, 57-59; Henry *Chrest* 1, 229-230; 2, 68; Bec 2, 114-116.

N   The poem occurs in the ms. divided as follows: I
1-6, II 7-12, III 13-16, IV 17-20, V 21-26, VI 27-34. This
irregularity has led to considerable corrective variation in
the several editions of the text. PetDyg "Moniot" presents
a partial survey of the editorial views, and Henry *Chrest*
provides some more recent information. The present edition,
assuming, unlike PetDyg "Moniot", the correctness of stanzaic and metrical consistency, leaves only one problem un-
solved: the exceptional length of st. 6. No pair of lines
in that stanza is obviously out of place or a spurious addition, and any deletion would therefore be unacceptably arbitrary.
      We have resolved the question of the even-line rhymes
in ll. 1-8, and with it the question of stanza division, by
emending *m'apai* (6) to *m'apais*, which rhymes with *cortois*
-[ţes]. The rhyme *dui:puis* remains somewhat problematic,
however. Cf. the more drastic emendation in Voretzsch:

. . . *m'apai;/mananz sui, riens avoir ne pui;/mauvés sui et cortoisie ai.*

The rhyme *chantee:bestorné* in st. 7 is very unusual, but acceptable without change in view of the fact that the feminine *-e* may be readily elided before *A* in l. 29. Cf. the emendation in Voretzsch: *que maintes foiz ai ja chanté*, with non-agreement of the past participle. It is possible that st. 8 is apocryphal: it is the only stanaa to repeat the rhymes of a preceding stanza and, perhaps more signifi-cant, it seems quite superfluous after st. 7, which an-nounces the end of the song (27) and concludes with a return (*bestorné*, 30) to the very first line of the text.

27 The song's self-identification, *rotroange*, is taken seriously by some, and the poem in fact appears in Gennrich *Rot*, even though it is rhymed *abab* and has no refrain. A different view is expressed in PetDyg "Moniot": "cette qua-lification ne doit être regardée, ainsi que tous les autres propos dans le poème, que comme une plaisanterie, ayant pour but d'évoquer l'hilarité des auditeurs qui savaient bien qu'une rotrouenge était une chanson à refrains" (p. 171). 30 *Par cui* 'through whom, by means of whom'.

V. Tenson   83

RS 925, MW 996
Mss. P 179r-v, X 215r. Music in both mss.

I   "Trop sui d'amors enganez
     Quant cele ne m'aime mie
     A qui je me sui donez;
     Si fet trop grant musardie   4
     Cuer qui en fame se fie
     S'il n'en a grant seürtez,

            Quar tost est müez
            Cuer de fame et tost tornés."   8

    II   "Conpaign, ne vos esmaiez!
            Lessiez ester la folie,
            Car s'el ne vos veut amer,
            Tost avrés plus bele amie;   12
            Et s'el s'est de vos partie,
            D'autretel gieu li jouez;
                Si vos en partez,
            Car bien voi ja n'en jorés."   16

    III   "Mauvés conseil me donés
            De lessier si bele amie;
            Mon cuer a enprisoné,
            Ravoir ne.l pouroie mie.   20
            Ainz vaintra sa felonie
            Ma grant debonereté
                Et ma loiauté,
            Si serai amant clamé."   24

    IV   "Conpains, se tant atendez,
            Dont vos est joie faillie.
            Que de li soiez amez!
            Il est bien honis qui prie,   28
            Et si muert a grant haschie
            Qui pent; autretel ferez,
                Se tant atendez
            Que de li soiez amez."   32

    V   "Conpains, vos me ranponez,
            Si fetes grant vilanie,
            Quant departir me voulez
            De ma douce conpaignie;   36
            C'est la riens ou plus me fie.
            Je cuit que vos i baez,
                Si me sui pensez
            Que departir m'en voulés."   40

    MN   Form: A A B.
1. In 1. 3 ms. writes no rest.

    RR   I   8 et] est   II   9 Conpaig   14 gouez
III   21 sa folie (-1)

    V   I   7 missing X   II   12 bele mie   13 cest
III   24 ami   IV   25 Conpaing   V   33 Conpaign

E   Jeanroy *Or*, 470-471; Spanke *Lied*, 79-80, 369.

N   16 Understand *que* after *voi*.   27 The exclamation is derisive, implying that the interlocutor will never win the love of his lady.

VI. Débat 84

RS 2014, MW 451
Mss. C 40v-41r, U 119r. No music.

I Consilliés moi, signor,
   D'un jeu perti d'amors
   A keil je me tanrai.
   Sovant sospir et plour
   Por celle cui j'aiour   5
   Et grief martyre en ai;
   Maix une autre en proiai
   (Ne sai se fix folour)
   Ke m'otriat s'amor
   Sens poene et sens delai.   10

II Se jai celle m'atour,
   Je ferai traïtour
   De mon fin cuer verai.
   Losengier jangleour
   Voldroient ke des lour   15
   Fuxe, maix ne.l serai.
   A celi me tanrai
   Por cui seux en errour:
   Se tenrai a gringnor
   Ma joie, se je l'ai.   20

III Or ai je trop mal dit,
   Quant celi ke m'ocist
   Veul ameir et proier,
   Et celi ki ait dit
   Ke m'aime sens respit   25
   Veul guerpir et laissier.
   La poene et li doingier
   M'avrait mort et traï;
   Nonporcant, Deus aïst
   Celi cui j'ai plux chier!   30

IV K'est ceu, Deus! c'ai je dit?
   Por ceu se m'escondist,

Je ne la doi laissier:
Siens seux sens contredit,
De si fin cuer eslit   35
Ke pertir ne m'en quier.
Nuls ne doit avancier
Ke son signor renist,
Maix celle ke m'ocist
Ain plux ke riens sous ciel.   40

V   Andous sont avenans,
        Maix l'une est plux pouxans
        De ma joie doneir;
        Trop serai mescheans
        S'a celi seux faillans   45
        Ne l'autre lais aleir;
        Celle veul aquiteir
        As felons medixans,
        Car l'autre est plux vaillans.
        Se me doignoit ameir!   50

RR   Stanza V precedes IV in ms.

V   Stanzas IV and V not included in U.
I   3 man t.   6 m. an tras   7 A u. a. an parla   II
11   celi macor   14 Medisans j.   15 Dient ke cest dolor
16   Mais certes non serait   18 Cuj ieu emme et aour   19
Satandra a g.   III   21 Qest ceu deus ke iai d. *(= 1. 31)*
24   Et celle ke me dist   29 Et por tant d.   30 Celle ke

E   Schutz, 98-100.

DF   Lorraine, including *ai* for *a*, as in *aiour* (5),
jai (11); *er* for *ar*, as in *perti* (2); *ei* for tonic *e*, as in
keil (3), *ameir* (23); *doingier* (27) for *dongier*; *poene* (10)
for *peine*; *x* for *s(s)*, as in *fix* (8), *fuxe* (16), *pouxans*
(42); preservation of final *t*, as in *otriat* (9), *eslit* (35);
seux (18) for *sui*; 3rd-pers. sing. fut. in *-ait*, as in *avrait* (28); relative *ke* (22, 38, 39) for nominative.

N   Both a ms. rubric and l. 2 identify this composition as a *jeu parti*, which it is not: the debate is univoc-
al. A Provençal version of the first two stanzas appears in
Raimon Vidal de Bezaudan's *nouvelle, So fol el tems c'om era
jays* (ed. Max Cornicelius, diss. Berlin, 1888; p. 30).
32   *se m'escondist* 'even if she rejects me'.

VII. Jeu-parti   85

RS 365, MW 2354
Mss. C 2v-3r, I 3:27a, O 13v. Music in O.

1. A- mis, ki est li muelz vail- lans:
2. ou cil qui gist tou- te la nuit
3. a- veuc s'a- mie a grant des- duit
4. et sans fai- re tot son ta- lent,
5. ou cil qui tost vient et tost prent
6. et quant il ait fait, si s'en fuit,
7. ne ju- e pais a re- me- nant,
8. ains keut la flor et lait le fruit?

I   Amis, ki est li muelz vaillans:
       Ou cil ki gist toute la nuit
       Aveuc s'amie a grant desduit
       Et sans faire tot son talent,   4
       Ou cil ki tost vient et tost prent
       Et quant il ait fait, si s'en fuit,
       Ne jue pais a remenant,
       Ains keut la flor et lait le fruit?   8

II   --Dame, ceu ke mes cuers en sent
        Vos dirai, maix ne vos anuit:
        Del faire viennent li desduit
        Et ki lou fait tan soulement   12
        Partir s'en puet ligierement;
        Car tuit li autre fait sont vuit
        S'on ne.l fait aprés ou davant;
        Dont valt muelz li faires, je cuit.   16

III   --Amis, muelz valt li acoleirs
        Et li jüers et li joïrs,
        Li desduires et li sentirs,
        Li proiers et li esgardeirs   20
        Que li faires et puis aleirs,
        S'a faire n'est li grans loixirs;
        Car trop est doulz li demorers
        Et trop est griés li departirs.   24

IV   --Dame, moult est boens li jueirs
        Et li baixiers et li gesirs,
        Li desduires et li sentirs,
        Li proiers et li esgardeirs;   28
        Sans lou faire c'est li tueirs,
        C'est la racine des sospirs
        Et ceu k'en amors est ameirs;
        Dont valt muelz faire et li foïrs.   32

V   --Amis, ne tieng pais a amor
        Lou tost faire ne tost aleir:
        Teille amor ne fait a amer,
        Car elle n'ait poent de savor.   36
        Maix cil n'ait pais moult grant dolor
        Ke puet a loisir acolleir,
        Et baissier ait joie grignor.
        En teil amor fait sen entreir.   40

VI   --Dame, onc ne vi guerir nul jor,
        Por soi deleis s'amie esteir,
        Nullui ki fust navreis d'ameir,
        S'on ne li fist aucun boen tor.   44
        Teil amor semble feu en for
        Ke ne s'en ait par ou aleir,
        Mais enclos ait si grant chalor
        C'on ne le puet desalumeir.   48

VII   --Amis, or öeis ke je di:
        Quant la bouche et li eul se paist

```
          De la chose c'a cuer li plaist,
          Dont n'en ist li feus par ici?              52
          --Dame, je ne di pais ensi,
          Maix quant li eulz plux se refait,
          Dont trait Amors a cuer son vis
          Ke par loial cuer son dairt trait.          56

VIII      --Dame, por Deu, or escouteis:
          Li jeus et li gais et li ris
          Averont maint home mal mis
          Ke li faires ait repaisseis;                60
          Dont valt muelz li faires aisseis,
          Tesmoing de Gautier de Pontis,
          C'an amor s'an est acordeis.
          Or finons la kerelle ci.                    64
```

MN   Form: through-composed.

RR   I   6   si] et   8   flor] foille   II   14   s.
ueut   III   21   *missing (reading based on O, as in Långfors)*   IV   30   r. de son pis   31   c. ke amors   V   40
f. son sen e. *(+1)*   VI   41-43   Dame on kes ne vi guerir.
nulluj ki damors fust naureis. por deleis samie seir. Ne por
deleis samie esteir *(em. Långfors)*   VIII   62-64   *missing
(reading from I)*

V   Stanzas IV-VIII not included in O.
I   1   ki] quelx O   4   touz ses talanz O   5   c. ke, et
tot I   7   Et naime p. au r. I, Ne bee p. au r. O   8
flor] foille I   II   9   Amie ce q. m. c. sent O, D.
sonkes m. c. ot san I   11   De f. uienne I; li geu tuit O
12   Et quil ont f. I; Car cil qui tost vient et tost prent
O   14   autres I; fait] geu O; son veut I   15   Sil O
16   faire IO; ce c. O   III   17   li deporters O   18
Et li iuer I; Et li ueoirs et li sentirs O   19   Li bai-
siers et li acolers O   20   esgarder I; Et li parlers et
li tenirs O   21   *missing I*; Que li tost faire et p. aler
O   22   Sans I, Sau O   23   est] iert I, *missing* ɔ   24
est] iert I   IV   26   baisier   29   *missing*   31   Et ceu
camors iert li meris   32   foir   V   33   ting, amors   34
ne] lou   37   M. cilz en ait moult grant dosour   38   Qui p.
a l. escoler   40   fait sans antrer   VI   41-43   Dame
onkes ne vi garir. nelui qui damor fut naurez. ne por deleis
samie oster   44   f. an aucun t.   45   Teile   46   Ki   47
en si] anci   48   Qui   VII   50   b. o les eus s.   53   di
mies e.   54   li oil   55   amor an c.   56   Qui, soudart t.
VIII   61   dasseis

E   Långfors *Rec* 2, 202-206.

DF   Lorraine, including *a* (7, 51) for *au*; *ai* for *a*, as in *pais* (7), *dairt* (56), *gais* (58); *ei* for tonic *e*, as in *acoleirs* (17), *aleir* (34), *teille* (35), *deleis* (42); *poent* (36) for *point*; *boen* (44) for *bon*; *ceu* (9) for *ce*; *lou* (12) for *le*; 3rd-pers. sing. pres. ind. *ait* (6) for *a*. Epenthesized future *averont* (59) suggests Picard origin of composition.

N   The lady poses the question: is it better for a man to spend the whole night with his mistress and not make love, or to make love at once and leave her immediately thereafter? The respondent chooses the second alternative. Gautier de Pontis is asked to judge the debate. Stanzas 1-6 form a pattern of *coblas doblas*, broken by st. 7 and 8; one or both of these may be apocryphal.
    21 As in Långfors *Rec*, the ms. O reading *li tost faire* is here emended to preserve the text's consistent use of nominative *-s* and because *tost* expresses an awkward anticipation of the next verse.   35 'Such love is not worth loving'.   37 Långfors *Rec* substitutes without explanation the reading of ms. I, whose only advantage seems to be a lack of coyness.   38 *Ke* functions here as nominative; cf. *c'* in ll. 51 and 63.   40 *fait sen* 'it makes sense'.   41-44 This passage is corrupt in both mss. We have adopted Långfors' reconstruction.   55-56 These lines are no doubt corrupt.

86   VIII. Chanson de jongleur

RS 436, MW 236
Ms. I 4:14. No music.

        I   A definement d'esteit
             Lairai ma jolïeteit;
             Yvers vient tous apresteis,
                Froidure repaire;
             J'ai trop en folie esteit.   5
                Si m'an voil retraire.

        II   Retraire ne m'an puis mais,
             Car je suis dou tout a bais;
             Jeus des deis m'ont mis a baix
                Par ma ribaudie;   10

Or ai perdut tous mes drais
Fors ke ma chemixe.

III   Ma chemixe voirement
Si est povre garnement;
S'or vaxist ne tant ne cant,   15
    A geu l'euxe mize,
S'alaixe legierement
    Encontre la bixe.

IV   La bixe et li autres vans
Mi guerroie mout sovent;   20
Per darrier et per devant
    Me pert la chair nue.
Or mi soit Deus en aidant:
    Ma joie ai perdue.

V   Ma joie et tous mes amins   25
Ai je perdut, lais, chaitis!
Or n'iroie an mon païs
    Por perdre la vie
Tant con je serai soupris
    De la ribaudie.   30

VI   Rebaudie m'ait costeit
Et geteit de mon osteil;
Les femes m'ont asoteit
    Ou je me fioie:
Cent livres m'ont bien costeit   35
    De bone monoie.

VII   Chascun jour me covanroit
Plain un sestier de doniers;
Se j'eüxe menoier
    Ke forgest monoie,   40
Il n'an savroit tant forgier
    Con j'an despandroie.

VIII   J'ai plus despendut d'avoir
An folie c'an savoir;
Ceu que me deüst valoir   45
    Et mettre an chivance,
Ceu ai mis en nonchaloir:
    Teille est ma jugance.

RR   I   5 esteit en folie   III   14 Si ait   18
Contre *(-1)*   V   26 lai   VII   39 menoie   42 despan-
deroie *(+1)*

E   Jeanroy *Or*, 507-509; Mary 1, 316-319.

DF   Lorraine, including *ai* for *a*, as in *bais* (8),
alaixe (17), *lais* (26); *a* for *au*, as in *vaxist* (15); *ei* for
tonic *e*, as in *esteit* (1), *deis* (9), *osteil* (32), *teille*
(48); *amins* (25) for *amis*; preservation of final *t*, as in
esteit (1), *perdut* (11), *costeit* (31); *x* for *s(s)*, as in
baix (9), *chemixe* (12), *euxe* (16), *alaixe* (17); *ceu* (45,
47) for *ce*; 3rd-pers. sing. pres. ind. *ait* (31) for *a*; 3rd-
pers. sing. impf. subj. in *-est*, as in *forgest* (40).

N   This song is among the compositions identified in
ms. I as "pastorelles". The poem shows the type of stanzaic
linking known as *coblas capfinidas*, in which the last word
or phrase of each stanza is repeated, sometimes with a
slight change, at the beginning of the following stanza.
The device seems to be treated here with some casualness,
which may be due to negligent transmission rather than any
lack of artistry on the part of the poet. Indeed, just as
the copyist's rhymeless l. 5, *J'ai trop esteit en folie*, is
readily corrected to *J'ai trop en folie esteit*, it may be
justified to attempt a correction of ll. 25, 37, and 43. We
propose, then, the following emended readings: ll. 25-26)
Perdus ai tous mes amins/Et ma joie, lais, chaitis; l. 37)
De monoie covanroit; l. 43) *Despandut ai plus d'avoir.*
    40 *Ke = qui.*

Ascribed

Songs

87   Chanson

RS 121, MW 1370
Mss. U 35r-v, C 18r-v. No music. Attribution in C.

I   Amors tençon et bataille
        Vers son champion a prise,
        Que por li tant se travaille
        Q'a desrainier sa franchise
        A tote s'entente mise;   5
        S'est droiz q'a merci li vaille,
        Mais ele tant ne lo prise
        Que de s'aïe li chaille.

II   Qui que por Amors m'asaille,
        Senz loier et sanz faintise   10
        Prez sui q'a l'estor m'en aille,
        Que bien ai la peine aprise;
        Mais je criem q'a mon servise
        Guerre et aiue li faille.
        Ne quier estre en nule guise   15
        Si frans q'en moi n'ait sa taille.

III   Nuns, s'il n'est cortois et sages,
        Ne puet d'Amors riens aprendre;
        Mais tels en est li usages,
        Dont nus ne se seit desfendre,   20
        Q'ele vuet l'entree vandre:
        Et quels en est li passages?
        Raison li covient despandre
        Et mettre mesure en gages.

IV   Fols cuers legiers ne volages   25
        Ne puet rien d'Amors aprendre.
        Tels n'est pas li miens corages,
        Qui sert senz merci atendre.
        Ainz que m'i cudasse prendre,
        Fu vers li durs et salvages;   30
        Or me plaist, senz raison rendre,
        K'en son prou soit mes damages.

V   Molt m'a chier Amors vendue
        S'onor et sa seignorie,
        K'a l'entreie ai despendue   35
        Mesure et raison guerpie.

> Lor consalz ne lor aiue
> Ne me soit jamais rendue:
> Je lor fail de compaignie,
> N'i aient nule atendue.							40

VI   D'amors ne sai nule issue,
> Ne ja nus ne la m'en die.
> Müer puet en ceste mue
> Ma plume tote ma vie,
> Mes cuers n'i müerat mie;							45
> S'ai g' en celi m'atendue
> Que je dout que ne m'ocie,
> Ne por ceu cuers ne remue.

VII   Se merciz ne m'en aiue
> Et pitiez, qui est perdue,							50
> Tart iert la guerre fenie
> Que j'ai lonc tens maintenue.

RR   IV   28 Ainz   V   33 chier] bien   34   Samor
VI   47   qui

V   6 Nest drois ca sa mercit faille   II   9 amor
11 s. ken   13 c. ken   15 Ne ueul   III   18 riens damors
21 v. a lautre   24 gaige   IV   25 ne] et   26 riens   32
Ke cest prous   V   33 amor   VI   42 men me   43 en cest m.
45 *missing*   46 Sai en   47 j. crien   VII   51 Tant

E   Brakelmann 1, 44-46; Crescini, 628; Foerster, 205-209; Voretzsch, 108-110; Cremonesi, 76-78; Toja, 185-188; Zai, 57-74.

DF   Lorraine: *lo* (7) for *le*; *cudasse* (29) for *cuidasse*; *-eie* (35) for *-ee*; *ceu* (48) for *ce*; *-t* in *müerat* (45).

N   4 'to defend his freedom'.   6 Zai substitutes (re-spelled) ms. C reading, *N'est drois qu'a sa merci faille*, claiming the series of rhyme repetitions *faille* (6, 14), *aprendre* (18, 26), *atendue* (40, 46), which reflects division into *coblas doblas*, is more consonant with "cette recherche formelle . . . essentielle dans la poésie lyrique." 16 'so free that [Love] would not have sovereignty over me'.   Lit., *taille* designates a kind of tax due an overlord. 22 *passages* 'toll'.   31 *senz raison rendre* 'though I cannot give a reason for it'.   34 *onor* 'fief'.   40 'let them have no expectation of my return'.   43 *mue* 'cage for a molting bird', whence 'prison'.   48 *por* 'despite'.

88   Chanson

RS 110, MW 2050
Mss. M 138v, C 46r-v, T 88r, U 134v-135r and 171r-v, Z 10v-
11r, a 88r-v. Music in MTZa. Attribution in MTa;
attributed to Guiot de Dijon in C.

     I   Cuer desirrous apaie
                Douçours et confors,
            Et jou d'amours veraie
                Sui en baisant mors.
        S'encor ne m'est autres dounez,   5
      Mar fui onques de li privez.
                A morir sui livrez
                Se trop le me delaie.

     II   Privez baisiers est plaie
                D'amours dedenz cors;   10
            Mout m'angoisse et esmaie,
                Si ne pert dehors.
      Ha, las! pour quoi m'en sui vantez,
     Quant ne m'en puet venir santez
                Se ce dont sui navrez   15
                Ma bouche ne rassaie?

    III   Amours, vous me feïstes
                Mon fin cuer trichier,
            Qui tel savour meïstes
                En son douz baisier.   20

A morir li avez apris
Se pluz n'i prent qu'il i a pris,
   Dont m'est il [bien] avis
   Qu'en baisant me trahistes.

IV   Certes, mout m'atraisistes   25
     Juene a cel mestier,
   N'ainc nului n'i vousistes
     Fors moi engignier.
Je sui li plus loiauz amis
Cui onques fust nus biens pramis.   30
     Hé las! tant ai je pis!
   Amours, mar me nourristes.

V   Se je Dieu tant amaisse
     Com je fais celi
   Qui si me painne et lasse,   35
     J'eüsse merci;
Qu'ainc amis de meilleur voloir
Ne la servi pour joie avoir
     Com je fais tout pour voir
     Sanz merite et sanz grasse.   40

VI   Se de faus cuer proiaisse
     (Dont je ne la pri),
   Espoir je recouvraisse,
     Mainz n'est mie einsi;
Ne ja Dieus ne me doint voloir   45
De li deçoivre sanz doloir.
     Ce me tient en espoir:
     Qu'Amours blece et respasse.

MN   Ms. Z has a second melody; ms. a has a third.
Form: A A^1 B.
1. Ms M writes this figure a 3rd lower.

RR   I 3 jou] *ms. correction of* joie 6 li] lui
II 12 Et si *(+1)*   III 23 *-1*   VI 42 Donc
48 trespasse

V   Stanzas: TZ I II III IV V VI
                a   I II III IV V
              U^1 II I IV
              U^2 II I III IV V VI
I 1 Cuers TZaCU^1; desires Z, desirans U^2; rapaiet U^1,
rapaie U^2 2 Docour a, Douso(u)r CU^{1}U^2; confort U^{1}U^2

3 Par ioie CU^{1}U^2; damo(u)rs TaC; vraie TaCU^{1}U^2
5 autre a   6 M. f. de li onques p. a   7 Ca la mort
U^1, Kar lamor U^2 8 Se] Que a; le *missing in C*; Celle
trop mi d. U^{1}U^2
II   9 Premiers aCU^1, Primiers U^2; b. et p. a
10 Amors C; D. d. le (mon a) c. Za   11 M. angoixe la
plaie C; amaie U^2 12 Et si TZC; ne] ni U^{1}U^2
13 p. que me s. a   14 Ja ne puet il uenirs s. a; Jai
(Ja U^1) ne me (mi U^1) CU^{1}U^2; peust U^1, puist U^2
15 ce] je TZ; s. vanteis C   16 me r. C; b. nairasaie
U^2
III   17-20 *occur as 25-28 in C*   17 Amor U^2 19 Quant
C, Kant U^2 20 son] cel U^2 21-28 *missing in U^2*
21 m. laues ap. Z; li] mi C   22 pran ke ieu ai pris
C; i] ni TZa   23 D. il mest b. a.   TZ   24 Que a
IV   25-28 *occur as 17-20 in C*   25 Amors uos (trop U^1)
mapreistes CU^1 26 Jonet a; a tel TZ   27 Nains a;
Ains nelui ne v. C; Onkes ne lo feistes U^1 28 F. ke
(por U^1) m. ZU^1 29 s. uostre l. U^1 30 Ki T, Qui
aU^2; bien U^2; meris a; Ki jai de vous nan kier partir
U^1 31 A tort maues guerpit U^1 32 Amor U^2
V   33-36 *occur as 41-44 in C*   33 Se ie a tant deus a.
U^2 34 Comme j. a   35 Ke C; si] tant Z; Por cui
poinne et trauaille U^2 36-43 *missing in U^2*   36 Ie
(Ieu C) eusse m. ZC   37 Kains aC; ami Z, nuls hons
C; de gringnor v. C   38 pour] sens C   39 C. iai fait
t. p. v. a, C. ieu ai fait p. v. C
VI   41-44 *occur as 33-36 in C*   47 E. ke j. r. T, E. ke
r. Z   49 Amors trop me (mi U^2) faites doloir CU^2
50 deceuoir Z; Et se uos ser sens deceuoir C, Et si vos
cers san ioie auoir U^2 51 Si U^2 52 blece] ne(i)ure
CU^2

E   Keller, 293-294; Mätzner, 51-52, 239-242; Tarbé
Blondel, 23; Brakelmann 1, 151-153; Wiese, 150-152; Bartsch-
Wiese, 162-163; Nissen, 11-12; Spaziani *Canz*, 104-107; Van
dW *Trouv*, 35-39, 560.

DF   Picard: *jou* (3) for *je*; first-person singular
imperfect subjunctive in -*aisse* (33, 41, 43).

N   1 The (double) subject of *apaie* 'appeases, calms'
is in l. 2.   5 *autres*, i.e., another kiss.   6 *privez*
'intimate'; similarly in l. 9. Antecedentless *li* designates
the lady.   12 'Yet it does not show.' Spaziani *Canz*
somehow understands the opposite: "'e ciò appare anche dal

mio aspetto'."   13 *en* refers to the kiss.   18 *Mon fin
cuer* is the object of *trichier*.   20 *son* 'her', i.e., the
lady's.   21 *li* refers to 1. 18 *cuer*.   22 *qu'* = *ce qu'*.

Chanson   <u>89</u>

RS 742, MW 633
Mss. M 143v, K 119, N45v, P 45r-v, T 92v, U 38v-39r, V 72r-v,
    X 83v-84r. Music in all mss. except U. Attribution in
    all mss. except UV.

I   Se savoient mon tourment
        Et auques de mon afaire
        Cil qui demandent conment
        Je puis tant de chançons faire,
        Il diroient vraiement   5
        Que nus a chanter n'entent
        Qui mieuz s'en deüst retraire;
        Maiz pour ce chant seulement
        Que je muir pluz doucement.

II   Trop par me grieve forment   10
        Que cele est si debonaire
        Qui tant de dolour me rent
        Ce qu'a tout le mont doit plaire;
        Maiz ne me grevast nïent,
        Se la tres bele au cors gent   15
        Me feïst touz ces maus traire.
        Maiz ce m'ocit vraiement
        Qu'el ne set que pour li sent.

    III   Se seüst certeinnement
            Mon martire et mon contraire   20
            Cele por qui je consent
            Que l'amour me tient et maire,
            Je croi bien qu'alegement
            M'envoiast procheinnement;
            Quar par droit le deüst faire,   25
            Se reguars a escīent
            De ses biaux ieus ne me ment.

    IV   Chançons, va isnelement
            A la bele au cler viaire,
            Si li di tant seulement: 30
            Qui de bons est, souëf flaire.
            Ne l'os prīer autrement,
            Quar trop pensai hautement,
            Si n'en puis mon cuer retraire.
            Et se pitiez ne l'en prent,   35
            Blondiaus muert, que pluz n'atent.

        MN   Mss. KNPX have a second melody; ms V has a third
one.   Form: A A B.
1. In l. 4 ms. repeats this note.
2. This note and part of the word are torn off in ms.

        RR   Mutiliation of the folio is responsible for those
of the following forms that appear with dashes; all readings
were readily recoverable from the other manuscripts.
I   8 M. ---r; voirement   9 Q. -- m.   II   --e c.
12   t. -- d.   13 le -ont   14 me ---uast   15 c. --nt
16   m. --aire   18 -uel ne   IV   32 penser a.

        V   Stanzas II, III, and IV are replaced by others in
U; see below.
I   1 De K;   m. corage P   3 Ceus V   4 p. tante
chanson f. U   5 Bien U; voirement KNPXVU   7 se d.   T
8 *missing in U*; voirement T   9 *missing in U*; Q. gen
KNPXV   II   10 T. me grieue malement V   11 Quele est
si po d. V   12 me tent T   14 men g.   T   16 ses m.   X
17 uoirement KNPXV   18 Ke T   III   19 Cel V, Sil
T   20 M. anui et V   22 Kamors me T, Q. la mort me
KNPXV   24 Mon voiast T   26 regart P   27 Et sa biaute
ne me r. P   IV   28 Chancon KNPX, Chanson V   29 A la
plesant debonnaire V   30 di tant] *left blank in T*
31 Ke T; des X   32 penser a. T   33 *missing in P*
35 pitie P   36 muer P

II'   Bien me revient ausiment   10
        Quant de chanter me puis traire,
        Que celi pitiez n'en prent
        Qui tel dolor me fait traire;
        Mais qank'a l'amor apant
        M'estuet faire bonement.   15
        D'un dolz regart debonaire
        M'aguise si mon talent,
        Per que je muir si sovent.

III'   Qant tuit li bien sont en li,
        De tant li ferai proiere: 20
        Qu'ele regart son ami
        Et qu'ele soit droituriere;
        Mais trop sont nostre enemi
        De granz mençonges garni
        Et de gaber par derriere;   25
        Por ce cuide avoir failli
        Guioz, qui tant a servi.

IV'   Bien la revoil esgarder
        Cui chaut se j'en muir d'envie;
        Et quant j'oi de li parler   30
        Neis la ou ele n'est mie,
        Je ne querroie finer
        De respondre ou d'escouter.
        Beauté, sens et cortoisie
        Ne sot unques Deus ovrer   35
        C'on ne puisse en li trover.

22 droitureire   34 Beate

    E   Tarbé *Blondel*, 59; Brakelmann 1, 182-185; Wiese,
141-143; Cremonesi, 101-103; Toja, 219-221; Van dW *Trouv*,
106-107, 564.

    N   8-9 *pour ce . . . Que* 'because' rather than 'so
that', which would be followed by the subjunctive.
12-13 'who turns into so much pain for me that which (i.e.,
herself) should please everyone'.   18 *que = ce que*.
31 Cited in Morawski, no. 1886. The sense here is that,
if--or since--the lady is a good person, she will surely be
good (receptive) to the suppliant. For other occurrences
and interpretations, see Wiese, pp. 188-189.

90   Chanson

RS 1618, MW 757
Mss. M 140r, T 89r-v. Music in both mss. Attribution in
  both mss.

1.En tous tans que   ven-te bi- se, 2.pour ce- le dont sui sou-pris,

3.qui n'est pas de   moi sou-pri- se, 4.de-vient mes cuers noirs et bis.

5.De fine a-mour l'ai re-qui- se, 6.qui cuer et cors m'a es-pris,

7.et, s'e- le n'en est es-pri- se, 8.pour mon grant mal la re-   quis.

I   En tous tans que vente bise,
        Pour cele dont sui soupris,
        Qui n'est pas de moi souprise,
        Devient mes cuers noirs et bis.
        De fine amour l'ai requise,   5
        Qui cuer et cors m'a espris,
        Et, s'ele n'en est esprise,
        Pour mon grant mal la requis.

II   Mais la doleurs me devise
        Qu'a la meilleur me sui pris   10
        Qui ainc fust en cest mont prise,
        Se j'estoie a son devis.
        Tort a mon cuer qui s'en prise,
        Quar ne sui pas si eslis.
        S'ele eslit, qu'ele m'eslise!   15
        Trop seroie de haut pris.

III   Et nequedent destinee
        Doune a la gent maint pensé:
        Tost i metra sa pensee
        S'amours li a destiné.   20
        Je vi ja tel dame amee
        D'ome de bas parenté

Qui mieuz ert emparentee,
Et si l'avoit bien amé.

IV   Pour c' est drois, s'Amours m'agree,   25
      Que mon cuer li ai douné.
      Se s'amour ne m'a dounee,
      Tant la servirai a gré,
      S'il plaist a la desirree,
      Que un baisier a celé   30
      Avrai de li a celee,
      Que tant ai desirré.

MN   Form: A A^1 B B^1.

RR   I   4 Deuers   IV   30 celee   31 cele

V   I   2 celj   II 13 Cort a mes cuers
III   17 non por quant   IV   29 Si li p. a la d.
30   Cun dolc b.   31-32 *missing*

E   Tarbé *Blondel*, 31; Brakelmann 1, 159-160; Wiese,
153-154; Toja, 225-226; Van dW *Trouv*, 106-107, 564.

N   The most notable trait of this poem is its use of
grammatical rhymes. The procedure is not particularly rare
in Old French lyric poetry, as indicated by MW's enumeration
of 86 instances of it (card 65).   19-20 The subject of
metra is the lady; l. 19 *i* and the understood direct object
le in l. 20 refer to the choice mentioned in l. 15.
30-31 *a celé* and *a celee* both mean 'in private'; the
redundancy is clearly due to the requirements of the
rhyme-scheme.

CONON DE BETHUNE

91   Chanson de croisade

RS 1125, MW 1347
Mss. M 46v–47r, C 1v–2r, H 227r–v, K 93–94, N 39r–v, O 90v–
     91r, P 29v–30r–v, R 40r–v, T 100r–v, V 74r–v, X 67v–
     68r, a 23v–24r, za 14. Also in x: Stuttgart fragment,
     now lost, published by F.–J. Mone in *Anzeiger für Kunde
     der teutschen Vorzeit* 7 (1838), 411, and in y: Rome,
     Bibl. Vaticana, lat. 3208, f. 54r. Music in all mss.
     except CHzaxy. Attribution in CMRTax; attributed to
     the Châtelain de Couci in KNPX.

I   Ahi, Amours! com dure departie
      Me convendra faire de la meillour
      Qui onques fust amee ne servie!
      Deus me ramaint a li par sa douçour   4
      Si voirement que m'en part a dolour.
      Las! qu'ai je dit? Ja ne m'en part je mie!
      Se li cors vait servir nostre Seignour,
      Li cuers remaint du tout en sa baillie.   8

II   Pour li m'en vois souspirant en Surie,
      Quar je ne doi faillir mon Creatour.
      Qui li faudra a cest besoing d'aïe,
      Sachiez que il li faudra a greignour;   12
      Et sachent bien li grant et li menour
      Que la doit on faire chevalerie

U on conquiert paradis et honour
Et pris et los et l'amour de s'amie.   16

III   Qui ci ne veut avoir vie anuieuse
      Si voist pour Dieu morir liez et joieus,
      Que cele mors est douce et savereuse
      Dont on conquiert le regne precïeus;   20
      Ne ja de mort nen i morra uns seus,
      Ainz naistront tuit en vie glorïeuse;
      Et sachiez bien: qui ne fust amereus,
      Mout fust la voie et bone et deliteuse.   24

IV   Deus! tant avom esté preu par huiseuse!
      Or i parra qui a certes iert preus;
      S'irom vengier la honte dolereuse
      Dont chascuns doit estre iriez et honteus, 28
      Quar a no tanz est perduz li sains lieus
      U Dieus soufri pour nous mort angoisseuse;
      S'or i laissom nos anemis morteus,
      A tous jours maiz iert no vie honteuse.   32

V   Dieus est assis en son saint hiretage;
      Or i parra com cil le secourront
      Cui il jeta de la prison ombrage
      Quant il fu mors en la crois que Turc ont. 36
      Sachiez, cil sunt trop honi qui n'iront,
      S'il n'ont poverte u vieillece u malage;
      Et cil qui sain et joene et riche sunt
      Ne pueënt pas demorer sanz hontage.   40

VI   Touz li clergiez et li home d'aage
      Qui en aumosne et en bienfais manront
      Partiront tuit a cest pelerinage--
      Et les dames qui chastement vivront   44
      Et loiauté portent ceus qui iront;
      Et s'eles font par mal conseill folage,
      A lasches gens mauvaises le feront,
      Quar tuit li bon iront en cest voiage.   48

VII   Las! je m'en vois plorant des euz du front
      La ou Deus veut amender mon corage,
      Et sachiez bien qu'a la meillour du mont
      Penserai plus que ne faz au voiage.   52

MN   The melody in ms. O is written a 4th higher, has
a partially meaningless, partially meaningful mensural notation, and differs significantly, particularly in the

B-section; mss. KNPX have a second melody; ms. R has a third
one; ms. V has a fourth; ms. a has a fifth. Form: A A B B;
the envoy is sung to ll. 5-8.
1. In ll. 2, 5, 6 ms. writes no rest.

<u>RR</u>   Stanzas: I II V VI III IV
II <u>ll</u> besoig III   20 Donc   22 A. naisteront en v.
g.   23 Qui reuendra mout sera eureus   24 A touz iours
maiz en iert honors sespeuse   IV   29 Qua nostre t.   30
mort glorieuse   V   34 com] se   VI   42 en b. morront
45 *missing*   47 A recreanz et mauvais le feront   VI (ms.
C)   49 Lais ie m. uoix p. d. eulz del f.   50 Lai ou d.
ueult amendeir m. coraige   51 Et saichies b. ca la millor
dou m.   52 P. plux ke ne fais a uoiaige

    <u>V</u>   Stanzas: T   I II   V   VI III IV
                             Ra   I II   V   VI III
                           Hyza   I II   V
                              C   I II IV III VI V VII
                              O   I II IV III VI V
                              x   I II IV III VI
                          KNPVX   I II III   V   VI
I   1 *missing in y*; He R, Oimi Ox; com] si Ox   2 *missing in y*; Moi Haza; couient C; faire] sofrir Hza; de]
po(u)r HKNPVXza, apardre C   3 *missing in y*   4 *missing
in y*; ramaine T; lui Vza; por za   5 Si vraiement RVXa;
v. com (con, cum) ien (gen, em x) COKNPVXHxyza; vait a.d.
x   6 D(i)eus q. CKNOPVXx; q(u)aie d. Hza, que ai je R,
ka je T; ja] che Hy, ie Oza; depart mie Hyza   7 li]
mos (mes za) Hyza; va ORTaza, uai H; Ainz ua mes cors s.
n. s. KNPVX   8 Li] Mes HKNPVXy, Mi za; Tous (Touz O)
li miens cuers remaint en sa b. COx
II   9 lui Rza, lei H; en su ensulie R   10 Que COPx;
nu(l)s ne doit f. son c. COKNPVXax   11 Ke C, Quant V; a
missing in V; ce R; Quar (Car) q(u)i li (le) en (e) ses b.
(besoignes H); un dia H, saia y, oblie za   12 S. de
voir q(u)il faudra a g. KNPVX, Sa(i)che de voir faurait
(faudra O) li a g. COx, B(i)en croi (cre Hy) q(u)e
d(i)eus (cades y) li faldreit (fraudra za)al (a za)g.Hyza
13 Et sa(i)chiez (-s) KNOPX   15 Con en c. COx, Con i c.
KNPVX; on *missing in R*   16 los (laus) et pris (-z) CHVax
yza; de sa vie x
III   17 ci] or Cx; v. mener honteuse uie N; vie honteuse
KPVX; Q or v. a. honte et v. a. O   18 Si v. morir lies
(-z) et baus et j. COx, Saille morir po(u)r dieu l. et j.
KNPVX; ioianz OV   19 Car CKNOPVXx; ceste KNPVX, tel(l)e
Ra; mort RV; est bon(n)e et glorieuse KNPVX   20 *missing*

in P; Con (Quen K) i (en X) c. le (la K) r. glorieus KN
VX, Ou conquis (-kis) est paradis et honor (honors O) COx
21 *missing in* V; des mors C; i aurait C; un KX; soul C
22 naisteront (nesteron R) en RTa, uiuront tuit en COx;
v. precieuse N   23 *missing in* a; Ie ni sai plus q. KNP
VX; ke ne C; Qui (Ki) reuenra mult sera (par ert R) eureus
RT   24 *missing in* a; Trop f. KNPVX; v. bele et delitouse
O; A tos (touz) io(u)rs mais en iert honors (a honneur R)
sespeuse RT; *followed in* V *by supernumerary line* pour dieu
vengier le pere precieus
IV   25 Lonc tens a. COx; prex p. T; p. por Cx   26 Or
verra on ki T   27 Quil (Kil) voist v. Cx, Uescu auons a
h. d. O   28 D. (donc O) tous (-z O, tout x) li mons
(-z) est i. et h. COx   29 Quant a (en x) nos (-z) t.
COx   30 Ou d. por nos s. COx; engoisse C, et engoisse
x, glorieuse T   31 Or ne nos (vos x) doit retenir
nul(1)e honors COx   32 Dale(i)r vengier ceste perde h.
COx
V   33 son haut O, droit V, gran y; s. s. jraie a   34
i *missing in* HO; p. bien c. O; coment za, se Ta; cil
missing in Hy, il a; li Hyza; secorreront Hy   35 Qui
Pa, Que KNRVX; iete T, gete a; A ceus quil trais d. H,
Iceu qel trais d. y, Cels qil lai trait d. za; p. de o.
Hy   36 Dont Hyza; mors] mis CHKNOPVXyza; q. tuit o. COV
za   37 Certes tuit cil sont h. q. ni uont CO, Bien sont
honi (-s X) (Aunit siont H, Hon siot y, Oni soient za)
tuit cil(1) q(u)i rema(i)n(d)ront HKNPVXyza   38 Si a; ou
mellee ou maillege C; Se nes retient pouretez (-s, pourete
V) ou m. KNPVX, Si (se za) veill (uieuz za) non es (nes-
toit y, nest o za) paubretes (poure za) e (o y, por za)
m. Hyza   39 E tuit c. q. j. za; q. j. et s. O; et r. et
j. R: F (Mais y) tut li rics que sans e j. s. Hy; Et c.
(cil *missing in* V) q. riche (-s V) et sain et fort (f. et
s. V) seront KNPVX   40 Ni KNPVX; por(r)ont CO; p. re-
maner (remanoir za) Hyza
VI   41 Tout a, Tuit CKNOPVX; clergie KNOPVX   42 au-
mo(s)nes KPVa; biens Ta; fait RX, fet KNP; mo(u)rront
RT, mauront a; Qui (Ki) de bien (-s O) fais (-z) et da(u)-
mo(s)nes viuront COx   43 to(u)t Ta, touz R; en c. C;
ce RV   44 d. ke C; chastes se tendront O, chastee
ten(d)ront KNPVX   45 *missing in* RTVa; loialteis porte C;
Se l. font a ceus qui i uont KNPX   46 Se V; cel(1)es CP
RX, eles V   47 As T, Aus V; g. et mauuais Ta, g. et a
mauez R; Ha les que(1)x gens (-z) mauuese le (mauuaises les
O) f. Ox, Elais keilz gens menasces lor f. C   48 to(u)t
RTa; b. sen vont KNPX; ce RV, cel C; voi voiage P

E   La Borde *Es* 2, 302; Michel, 85-88; P. Paris, 93; Leroux de Lincy, 113-115; Dinaux 3, 397-398; Keller, 254-256; Mätzner, 7-10, 86-93; Brakelmann 1, 75-78; Scheler 1, 1-5; Wallensköld *Conon* 1, 224-228; Sudre, 140; Oulmont, 286-288; Bartsch-Wiese, 160-161; Bédier-Aubry 27-37; Voretzsch, 116-117; Wallensköld *Conon* 2, 6-7; Brittain, 134-136; Pauphilet, 865-866; Spaziani *Ant*, 27-28; Cremonesi, 93-95; Woledge *Peng*, 108-111; Lerond, 187-192; Toja, 204-207; Mary 1, 214-217; Van dW *Trouv*, 285-292, 576-577; Bec 2, 94-96; Schöber 106-126; Frank 1, 29-33; 2, 35-42.

N   To judge by the scope and complexity of the manu-script tradition, this work was one of the most popular of the crusade songs. It was surely composed by Conon rather than the Châtelain de Couci and dates from 1188; see Bédier-Aubry, pp. 28-29, and Wallensköld *Conon* 2, pp. x-xii, xviii, and 21.

In view of the number and nature of the problems posed by the various versions of the song, for which see Bédier-Aubry et al., we have thought it not inappropriate to make several changes in the reading of ms. M beyond those strict-ly necessary; the result is a text perhaps closer to an auctorial version than that of any of the existing mss. Most notably, we have re-ordered the stanzas and have added to the six of ms. M the seventh, the envoy, that occurs in ms. C alone; see details under Rejected Readings and Vari-ants. The present arrangement of stanzas stems from the following considerations: 1) The mss. all agree on the placement of st. 1 and 2. 2) The pattern of stanzaic link-age is that of *coblas doblas*, which means that st. 3 and 4 are inseparable, that st. 5 and 6 are equally inseparable, and that st. 5 and 6, whose rhymes are repeated in the en-voy, must immediately precede the latter. 3) St. 2, 3, and 4 form a meaningful progression, in that st. 3 develops the idea of reward first expressed at the end of st. 2, and st. 4 takes l. 24 as its point of departure for a shift of focus to the crusading enterprise. 4) St. 5 follows from st. 4, in that it further develops the ideas, expressed in st. 4, of besieged Jerusalem and of the shame of those who will not join the crusade; the stanzas are linked, moreover, by the openings of their first two verses: *D(i)eus* and *Or i parra*. 5) St. 6 continues the enumeration of types of men who will or will not participate; it then shifts to the women left behind, which both relates it to the envoy and represents a return to the theme that opened the poem. For different in-terpretations, see Lerond and Schöber editions; Wentzlaff-Eggebert, pp. 152-155; J.-M. d'Heur, "Traces d'une version

occitanisée d'une chanson de croisade du trouvère Conon de
Béthune," *Cultura Neolatina* 23 (1963), 73-89; H.-H. S.
Räkel, "Drei Lieder zum dritten Kreuzzug," *Deutsche Vierteljahrsschrift für Literaturwissenschaft und Geistesgeschichte*
47 (1973), 508-550. See, too, Payen, pp. 271-274.

    12 *il* designates l. 10 *Creatour*; *li* l. 11 *Qui* 'who-
ever'.   23 *qui ne fust amereus* 'if one were not in love'.
29 *no*, Picard form for *nostre*; also in l. 32.   36 The
Saracens captured Jerusalem in 1187.   42 *manront* 'will
persevere'.   43 *Partiront* 'will share', sc., even without
leaving.   44 *Et les dames* 'and [so will] the ladies'.   47
A 'with'.

Chanson   <u>92</u>

RS 629, MW 1666
Mss. T 10lr-v, R 10r-v, e no. 8. Music in TR. Attribution
    in TR.

I   Chançon legiere a entendre
        Ferai, que bien m'est mestiers
        Ke chascuns le puist aprendre
        Et c'on le chant volentiers;
        Ne par autres messaigiers   5
        N'iert ja ma dolors mostree
        A la millor ki soit nee.

II   Tant est sa valors doblee
        C'orgeus et hardemans fiers
        Seroit se ja ma pensee   10
        Li descovroie premiers;
        Mais besoins et desiriers
        Et çou c'on ne puet atendre
        Fait maint hardement emprendre.

III   Tant ai celé mon martire   15
        Tos jors a tote la gent
        Ke bien le devroie dire
        A ma dame solement,
        K'Amors ne li dist noient;
        Neporquant s'ele m'oblie,   20
        Ne l'oublīerai je mie.

IV   Por quant, se je n'ai aīe
        De li et retenement,
        Bien fera et cortoisie
        S'aucune pitiés l'em prent.   25
        Au descovrir mon talent
        Se gart bien de l'escondire,
        S'ele ne me velt ochirre.

V   Fols sui, ki ne li ai dite
        Ma dolors ki est si grans.   30
        Bien deüst estre petite
        Par droit, tant sui fins amans;
        Mais je sui si meschaans
        Ke quanques drois m'i avance,
        Me retaut ma mescheance.   35

VI   Tous i morrai en soffrance,
        Mais sa beautés m'est garans,
        De ma dame, et la samblance
        Ki tos mes maus fait plaisans,
        Si ke je muir tous joians,   40
        Ke tant desir sa merite
        Ke ceste mors me delite.

VII   Noblet, je sui fins amans,
        Si ai la millor eslite
        Dont onques cançons fu dite.   45

    MN   Ms. R has a second melody. Form: A A B; the en-
voy is sung to ll. 5-7.
1. In l. 3 ms. writes a bar. 2. In l. 4 ms. writes no
rest.

    RR   V   35 Ne   VI   42 ceste amors

    V   I   2 F. car Re; il m. m. R   3 la p. R   5
Car e; autre Re; messagier e   6 doulour R   II   8
ualour R; montee e   9 Que orguelz et R, Orgiex et e;
hardement R   10 ja] ie e   12 besoing R   III   19

dit R   20 Et non p. q. ce m.   R   21 Nemoublirai R
IV   22 se *missing in R*   23 et] ne e; recouurement R
25 Se aucune partie R   V   29 Faus R; fui quant ne e
30 do(u)lo(u)r Re; grant R   32 fin e   34   quanque
droit R   VI   36 Tout R   37 la e; biaute R   38
et] a R   41 ma R   42 mort R   VII   43 Robers R
44 Si ainc e   45 chancon R; fust Re

E   P. Paris, 81; Dinaux 3, 385-387; Brakelmann 1, 71-
72; Scheler 1, 15-16; Wallensköld *Conon* 1, 218-220; Wallensköld *Conon* 2, 1-3; Cremonesi, 91-92; Maillard *Anth*, 39-40;
Van dW *Trouv*, 283-284, 576.

DF   Picard: *le* (3, 4) for *la*; *millor* (7) for *meilleur*; *çou* (13) for *ce*; *ochirre* (28) for *ocirre*; *retaut* (35)
for *retout*; *cançons* (45) for *chançons*.

N   PetDyg *Gace*, p. 52, shows that this song was written before 1201, when Conon left France for the Fourth Crusade, and claims that it was probably composed around 1185.
For a discussion of the poem, see Frappier, pp. 126-127.
13 'And the fact of not being able to wait', i.e.,
impatience.   19 Understand *le* (=*mon martire*) as direct
object and *noient* as a negative adverb.   26-27 'If I reveal my desire, let her take care not to reject it'.   34-35
'That whatever advantage fairness gives me is taken away by
my ill luck'.   38 *De ma dame* = 1. 37 *sa*.   41 *sa merite*
is more likely the 'reward' that it is in the lady's power
to give than a metonymic reference to the lady herself.   43
According to PetDyg *Gace*, pp. 45-53, *Noblet* designates Guillaume de Garlande V, friend to Conon de Béthune as well as
Gace Brulé and Pierre de Molins, and recipient of songs composed by each of them.

Débat   93

RS 1574, MW 626
Mss. K 226, C 98r-v, H 229r-v, I 1:14, M 45r, N 109v-110r, O
    74v-75r, P 152r-v, T 98v-99r, U 136v-137r. Music in KM
    NOPT. Attribution in CMT; attributed to Richart de
    Fournival in KN.

M

K

1. Ce fut l'au-trier en un au-tre pa-is
3. Tant com la da-me fu en son bon pris,

2. q'uns che-va-liers et [1] u-ne dame a-me-e.
4. li a s'a-mor e-scon-dite et ve-e-e,

5. jus-qu'a un jor qu'e-le li dist: "A-mis,

6. me-ne vous ai par pa-ro-le mains dis;

7. ore est l'a-mor co-ne-ue et do-ne-e:

8. Des or mes sui tout a vo-stre de-vis."

I Ce fut l'autrier en un autre païs
 Q'uns chevaliers ot une dame amee.
 Tant com la dame fu en son bon pris,
 Li a s'amor escondite et veee,   4
 Jusqu'a un jor qu'ele li dist: "Amis,
 Mené vous ai par parole mains dis;
 Ore est l'amor coneüe et donee:
 Des or mes sui tout a vostre devis."   8

II Li chevaliers la regarda el vis,
 Si la vit mult pale et descoloree.
 "Par Dieu, dame, mort sui et entrepris
 Quant des l'autrier ne soi ceste pensee. 12
 Li vostre vis, qui senbloit flor de lis,
 M'est si torné du tout de mal en pis
 Ce m'est avis que me soiez enblee.
 A tart avez, dame, cest conseil pris."   16

III Quant la dame s'oï si ramponer,
 Grant duel en ot, si dist par felonnie:
 "Danz chevaliers, on vous doit bien gaber.
 Cuidiez vous donc qu'a certes le vous die? 20
 Nenil, certes, onc ne l'oi en penser!
 Voulez vous donc dame de pris amer?
 Nenil, certes, ainz avrïez envie
 D'un biau vallet besier et acoler."   24

IV "Dame," fet il, j'ai bien oï parler
 De vostre pris, mes ce n'est ore mie;
 Et de Troie ai je oï conter
 Qu'ele fu ja de mult grant seignorie: 28
 Or n'i puet on fors les places trouver.
 Par tel reson vous lo a escuser
 Que cil soient reté de l'yresie
 Qui des or mes ne vous voudront amer." 32

V "Danz chevaliers, mar i avez gardé
 Quant vous avez reprouvé mon aage.
 Se j'avoie tout mon jouvent usé,
 Si sui je tant bele et de haut parage 36
 Qu'on m'ameroit a mult pou de biauté,
 Qu'oncor n'a pas, ce cuit, un mois passé
 Que li Marchis m'envoia son mesage
 Et li Barrois a pour m'amor ploré."   40

VI "Dame," fait il, "ce vous a molt grevé
 Que vous fïez en vostre seignorage;

Mes tel set ont ja pour vouz sospiré,
Se vous estiés fille au roi de Cartage,   44
Qui ja mes jour n'en aront volenté.
On n'aimme paz dame pour parenté,
Maiz quant ele est bele et cortoise et sage.
Vouz en savroiz par tanz la verité."   48

MN   The melody of ms. K also occurs in N and P; ms. M
has a second melody; ms. O has a third one; ms. T has a
fourth.   Form (K and M): A A B.
1. In ms. M the next two words are repeated without music.

RR   I   4 uee   6 M. mauez p.   41-48 *missing;*
reading from M

V   Stanza VI not included in NOP.
I   1 Lautrier (Lautre ier M, Latrier U) auint HIMOTU,
Il auint iai C; un] cel CHIMOTU   3 Et la (lai I) dame
toz (tous I) jors e. s. b. p. IOU   4 Li out H; escondit
U; vee CHNP   5 Tant ka C, Puis fu HMT; uns io(u)rs
HMT; Kant (Qu- O, C- U) uint apres ce (si O, se U) li
ait (a O) dit a IOU   6 Menez M, Ame O; parol(l)es CH;
main N, maint HO; Par parolles uos ai meneit tous iors
(tot dis U) IU   7 lamo(u)rs HOTU; conneuee N, conue
IU; esprouee IU, prouee CHO, mostree M, gree T   8 Tres
P; Des ore (or U) mais (maix C) suis (seux C, seus U) a
(an U) uostre plaisir (soiez li miens amis H) CHIU; Si
ferai mais dou tout uostre deuis O; Dore en auant serai a
vo deuis MT
II   9 ch. le T; lesgardait ens el v. C   10 Se CU,
Mout O; v. paule tainte et O, v. mult tainte et T, v.
tinte pale et U   11 Par dieu dame fait il mal sui bailliz
H; Dame fait il certes mal sui baillis MT; Dame fait (dit
O) il mort mauez (bien sui morz O) et trait (trahiz O) CI
OU   12 Que (Ke T, Quant O) neustes pieca (piecha T,
lautrier O) c. p. HMOT; Q. des lautre an nostes c. p. C;
Cant (K- U) de lautre (latre U) an ne sai (soi U) vostre
p. IU   13 uostres N; Vostre (-s CT) cler (-s M, biaus
C) v. CHMOT; Ke uostre uis (viz U) me s. f. (flors U) de
l. IU   14 tornez OP, torneis C; Est si alez (-s T)
dame de m. en p. HMT; Qui (Ki U) or est si (ci U) aleis
de m. an p. IU   15 Q(u)il HMO, Kil CT; av. uos IU; que
uos mestes e. H   16 Ad N; a. uers (a M) moi cest (ce
O) HMO; c. quis H
III 17 d. si soi T   18 G. honte en o(u)t si di(s)t par
sa folie (p. felonie H) HMT; Vergoi(n)gne an (en C) ot a
(au I) cuer lan (len C) prist ire CIU; Honte en ot grant

si respondi marrie O   19 Par d(i)eu vassal (-s CIOU)
CIMOTU; on (lan I, an U) vos doit bien ameir CIU; iel (ge
H) di(s) por vos (vous dis pour M) gaber HMT, ie uos sai
bien g. O   20 Ne cuidiez pas H; C. v. d. (donkes U) ca
certes (serte U) lou deisse CIU   21 N. (Onques O) par
deu CIOU, Onques (Conques H) nul io(u)r HMT; ainz n. O,
on n. P; ne me vint en p. CHIMTU   22 Savriez (Saries T)
vos HMOT; dont MT, *missing in HO*; Conkes (Conques I) nul
(nuns I) io(u)r ie uos d(o)igna(i)sse am. CIU   23 N. par
dieu HM; a. vo(u)s prendroit e. MT, plus auez grant e. H;
Ke uos aveis (auez U) par deu (souent C) gri(n)gno(u)r e.
CIU   24 Du NP; garcon HO; escoleir I
IV   25 Certes dame O, Per (Par I) deu dame CIU; conter
H   26 De uo (-s I, -z U) bia(u)(l)tei(t) CIU; ores mies
I, o. miez U   27 troies T, troiez U; rai MOT; roi ie
ia H; oir U   28 Que fu iadis O; grant *missing in N*   29
p. lon H, len M; fors] que I, ke U; la(i) pla(i)ce CIOU
30 Ensi dame O; Et si vous lo ensi a e. MT; Si uos lo
bien par tant a e. H; Por ceu vos lo (loz I, loi U) dame
a (ai U) e. CIU   31 Ke tuit c. I, Kil c. U; repris
HO, arresteit I, aratteit U; dazerie I, deresie U, de
lerisie HN, liresie M, leresie O, larecie P, iresie T,
tricherie C   32 Ke CIU; ne uoldroient H
V   33 Par (Per CU) d(i)eu vassal (-s CHIOU) CHIMOTU;
mout auez fol pense M, trop aues fol penser T, mar uos
uint en (an U) pense(i)r (pencer I, pense H, pensey O)
CHIOU   34 Ke CIU, Que HO; maue(i)z CIHMOTU   35 Se
ie(u) auoie CI, Car se iauoie H, Se ieusse O; mon
io(u)uent to(u)t MT, ia tout mon tens O   36 j. tant riche
et O, si riche et H, riche et de CIMTU; si grant p. MT,
mout haut (halt U) p. CIU   37 On CU, Lon I; a petit de
b. CHIMTU; m. p. dauantage O   38 un *missing in N*; Certes
(Ne il O) n. p. encor (ancor n. p. CU) deus (un O) mois
p. CIOU; Enco(i)r n. p. (Na pas ancor H) un mois entier
(entir T) p. CMT; passeis C, passeiz I, passeit U   39
Qui   40 bretons C, boriois I, bauiers O, baruois P;
alait por moi C, ait por moi mult U; io(u)ste HIMT, ios-
teir C
VI   41 Certes dame H, Par (Per C) deu dame CIU; ce(u)
uos puet bien (mult U) greue(i)r CIU   42 Q. uos ga(i)r-
de(i)s (fiez H) tous (toz HU) iors en (a IU) s. CHIU
43-48 *occur in CIU in the order of 46-48, 43-45*   43 M. t.
quatorze ont p. v. s. H; On (Ont U) naime(t) pa(i)s dame
por parenteit (signoraige C) CIU   44 Sor estiez f. H;
Ainz (-s C, An U) lai(m)me(t) (l)on (lom C) cant (qu- C)
elle est prous (belle C) et sa(i)ge CIU   45 Vos an sau-
re(i)z (en saueis C) par tans la ueriteit (tenson la

verteit C) CIU   46 Len H; Car teil (teilz I, teis   U)
cent (sant I) ont por vostre amor ploreit (iosteit C) CIU
47 est cortoise et prox et sage H; Ke cesties (sestieiz
I, sastiez U) fille a roi de karta(i)ge (c- C) CIU   48
Nan auront (nauront U) il (Nen aueroient C) iama(i)s
lo(u)r (la C) uolenteit (uolanteit I) CIU

E   La Borde Es 2, 194; P. Paris, 107; Leroux de Lincy, 36-39; Dinaux 3, 394-395; Bartsch, 76-77; Brakelmann 1,
84-86; Scheler 1, 20-25, 276-277; Wallensköld Conon 1, 239-
243, 250; Wallensköld Conon 2, 17-18, 31-33; Pauphilet, 866-
868; Spaziani Ant, 31-32; Chastel, 416-421; Woledge Peng,
106-108; Groult 1, 172-173; Toja, 212-214; Mary 1, 216-219;
Van dW Trouv, 306-309, 578.

DF   Picard: aront (45) for avront.

N   See Frappier, pp. 137-139, for an analysis of this
remarkable "petite comédie de moeurs," in which Conon satir-
ically reveals a later stage of courtly love. Despite the
attribution to Richart de Fournival in mss. K and N, the
authorship of this composition has never been in serious
doubt; see Wallensköld Conon 2, p. x.
    3 en son bon pris, i.e., in possession of all her
beauty. 15 Understand que before Ce.   30-32 'For that
reason, I advise you to refrain from accusing of heresy
those who . . .'. The "heresy" in question is homosexual-
ity; see the lady's accusation in ll. 23-24.   35 Se 'even
if'; likewise, l. 44.   39-40 The two men are apparently
historical figures, identified in Wallensköld Conon 2, p.
xii, and elsewhere as the Marquis Boniface II of Montferrat
(d. 1207), one of the heroes of the Fourth Crusade, and
Guillaume des Barres, a knight renowned for his physical
strength and his victory over Richard Coeur de Lion in single combat in 1188.   43 tel set (with l. 45 Qui) 'quite a
few', literally, 'seven'.   44 Carthage is meant to exem-
plify the highest nobility.

RS 1891, MW 42, B 1928
Mss. O 62v-63r, C 103v-104r, K 392-393, N 180r-v, U 104v-
    105r, X 252r-v, za I. Music in KNOX. Attribution in
    C.

I   Ja nus hons pris ne dira sa raison
     Adroitement, se dolantement non;
     Mais par effort puet il faire chançon.
     Mout ai amis, mais povre sont li don;
     Honte i avront se por ma reançon   5
          Sui ça deus yvers *pris.*

II   Ce sevent bien mi home et mi baron--
     Ynglois, Normant, Poitevin et Gascon--
     Que je n'ai nul si povre compaignon
     Que je lessaisse por avoir en prison;   10
     Je nou di mie por nule retraçon,
          Mais encor sui [je] *pris.*

III Or sai je bien de voir certeinnement
     Que morz ne pris n'a ami ne parent,
     Quant on me faut por or ne por argent.   15
     Mout m'est de moi, mes plus m'est de ma gent,
     Qu'aprés ma mort avront reprochement
          Se longuement sui *pris.*

IV   N'est pas mervoille se j'ai le cuer dolant,
      Quant mes sires met ma terre en torment.   20
      S'il li membrast de nostre soirement
      Que nos feïsmes andui communement,
      Je sai de voir que ja trop longuement
            Ne seroie ça *pris*.

V   Ce sevent bien Angevin et Torain--   25
      Cil bacheler qui or sont riche et sain--
      Qu'encombrez sui loing d'aus en autre main.
      Forment m'amoient, mais or ne m'ainment
                                          [grain.
      De beles armes sont ore vuit li plain,
            Por ce que je sui *pris*.   30

VI   Mes compaignons que j'amoie et que j'ain--
      Ces de Cahen et ces de Percherain--
      Di lor, chançon, qu'il ne sunt pas certain,
      C'onques vers aus ne oi faus cuer ne vain;
      S'il me guerroient, il feront que vilain   35
            Tant con je serai *pris*.

VII   Contesse suer, vostre pris soverain
      Vos saut et gart cil a cui je m'en clain
            Et por cui je sui *pris*.

VIII Je ne di mie a cele de Chartain,   40
            La mere Loëÿs.

      MN   Three Provençal manuscripts have a second but re-
lated melody. Form: A A B; envoy 1 is sung to ll. 4-6, envoy 2 to ll. 5-6.
1. In l. 1 ms. writes a brevis. 2. In l. 4 ms. writes a
brevis. 3. Ms. writes a longa.

      RR   II   8 normanz   III   12 Car   14 Q. ie ne
p. ne a. ne p.   17 lor m. aurai   IV   20 met] mest   V
28 F. maidessent m. il nen oient g.   29 li] et   VI   32
de chaeu   VII   39 Et p. ce sui ie p.

      V   Stanzas: C   I II III IV V VI VII VIII
                       Uza   I II III IV VI V VII VIII
                        NX   I II III IV V VII VIII
                         K   I II III IV V
I   1 hon N   2 A. sensi (sansi U) com dolans n. (nons
U)   CU, A. si com hom dolanz n. za   3 esfors KNX, con-
fort CUza   4 Pro a za; dami(n)s CUza; p. en s. KNX;

son le d. za   5 i] en CU   6 S. ces .ii. CU, candeus
za
II   7 Se C; Bien lo seuent mi   za   9 n'ai *missing in X*;
Q. j. nauoie si CUza   10 Cui U; par za   11 mie *missing in za*, pa(i)s CNU; par za   12 Car KNX
III   14 morz] ie KNX; priset U; ne KNUX; amins U   15
mi za; faut] lait CU; ne] et X   16 por ma g. za   17
ma] lor KN, la X; nauront za; reproche (reprochier U)
grant CU   18 Car tant ai este pris za
IV   19 Ne me merueil seo hai le cor d. za   20 Q. mi
za; met met X, tient CU; en] a U   21 Sor CU, Se za;
menbroit CU; de nostre de nostre X   22 fesismes X; am-
deus za   23 Bien CU, *first word illegible in za*; s. ie
bien q. za; q. seans (ceu ans U) l. CU; trop] plus za
24 ça] pa(i)s CU, çi za
V   25 Se C, Or U; Bien le seuent a. za   26 Li za;
q. sont deliure e s. za; riche] fort U   27 Quenconbre
N; autrui CUza; mains CU   28 Bien za; maida(i)ssent m.
il (meil N) ne (ni U, na za) uoient (uoien N) g. KNUX
za; maimme g. C   29 belle U; ores CU, or s za; li] et
KNX, cil U   30 ce] tant CU
VI   31 Mi compagnon za; cui CU; ie amoie za; cui CU
32 Cealz C, Cil za; dou U; caheu C, cahiul U, chaieu
za; ceaulz C, cil za; dou U   33 Me di ch. CU, Chanzon
di lor za; qui U   34 Nonkes C; Que ie eusse uers els f.
za; nan oi (no le C) cuer fau(l)s CU   35 Cil U, Sor mi
za; il] trop za; il font moult q. CU; qi v. za   36 Por
tant ke ie seux p. C; soie p. za
VII   38 gar N; sil U, celle za; a] por za; cu U, qui
NX; je *missing in za*; me CNX, mi za   39 Por ce que je s.
p. N; per CU   40 nou U, nel za; di pa(i)s CU; a] de
C, por za; celi CU

E   Leroux de Lincy, 50-59; Tarbé *Blon*, 114-117;
Brakelmann 1, 222-224; Paris-Langlois, 283-286; Bartsch-
Wiese, 161-162; Gennrich *Rot*, 20-22; Spanke *Lied*, 201-203,
396-397; Pauphilet, 841-842; Spaziani *Ant*, 36-38; Gennrich
Alt Lied 1, 12-15; Gennrich *Ex*, 6-7; Mary 1, 232-233; Archi-
bald, 149-158; Bec 2, 124-125.

N   This *rotrouenge* was composed during King Richard's
captivity (1192-94), before he had received word that the
immense ransom demanded by the German emperor, Henry VI,
would indeed be paid. There is also a Provençal version;
see RS for the mss. sources. Note that the normal verse-
long refrain of a *rotrouenge* is here replaced by a single
word, the thematic and emotionally charged *pris*. The

versification includes, rather unusually, instances of both
césure lyrique (1. 20) and *césure épique* (11. 10, 11, etc.).
For some remarks on this text, see Zumthor *Lang*, pp. 197-
198, and Dronke, pp. 212-213.

10   'Whom, for monetary reasons, I would leave in prison'.   11 *nou = ne le*.   14 *pris* 'prisoner'.   16 'It concerns me much, but it concerns my people more'.   20-22 *mes
sires* is the Emperor.   The *soirement* is evidently the ransom
agreement that Richard and he had come to before the disrup-
tive intervention of King Philip Augustus of France, which
left Richard and England woefully uncertain (*en tourment*) of
the outcome.   See Amy Kelly, *Eleanor of Aquitaine and the
Four Kings* (New York: Vintage Books, 1950), pp. 389-392.
33 *certain* 'reliable'.   35 *il feront que vilain* 'their
behavior will be contemptible'.   37 *Contesse suer* designates Richard's dear half-sister Marie, Countess of Champagne, clearly not to be confused--see 11. 40-41--with his
other half-sister, Alix, Countess of Chartres and mother of
Louis, whom he disliked.   Line 37 *pris soverain* 'sovereign
worth' is the direct object of 1. 38 *saut et gart*.

RS 679, MW 1228

Mss. M 52v-53r, A 153r-v, C 17v-18r, K 107-108, O 4v-5r, P
39r-v-40r, R 119r-v, T 155r, U 19v-20r, V 80r, X 76v-
77r.   Also in *Roman du Castelain de Couci et de la
Dame de Fayel*, ed. M. Delbouille (Paris, 1936), p. 238.
Stanza III also in Gerbert de Montreuil, *Roman de la
Violette, ou de Gerart de Nevers*, ed. D. L. Buffum
(Paris, 1928), p. 184; and in *La Chastelaine de Vergi*,
ed. G. Raynaud-L. Foulet (Paris, 1921), p. 10; ed. F.
Whitehead (Manchester, 1944), p. 8. Music in all mss.
except C. Attribution in all mss. except M (because of
ms. mutilation) and AORUV.

I   A vous, amant, plus qu'a nulle autre gent,
     Est bien raisons que ma doleur conplaigne,
     Quar il m'estuet partir outreement
     Et dessevrer de ma loial conpaigne;   4
     Et quant li pert, n'est rienz qui me
                                       [remaigne.

Et sachiez bien, Amours, seürement,
S'ainc nuls morut pour avoir cuer dolent,
Donc n'iert par moi maiz meüs vers ne laiz. 8

II   Biauz sire Dieus, qu'iert il dont, et
                                    [conment?
        Convenra m' il qu'en la fin congié praigne?
        Oïl, par Dieu, ne puet estre autrement:
        Sanz li m'estuet aler en terre estraigne. 12
        Or ne cuit maiz que granz mauz me soufraigne,
        Quant de li n'ai confort n'alegement
        Ne de nule autre amour joie n'atent
        Fors que de li--ne sai se c'iert jamaiz. 16

III   Biauz sire Dieus, qu'iert il du consirrer
        Du grant soulaz et de la conpaignie
        Et de l'amour que me soloit moustrer
        Cele qui m'ert dame, conpaigne, amie? 20
        Et quant recort sa simple courtoisie
        El les douz moz que seut a moi parler,
        Conment me puet li cuers u cors durer?
        Quant ne s'en part, certes il est mauvaiz. 24

IV   Ne me vout pas Dieus pour neiant doner
        Touz les soulaz qu'ai eüs en ma vie,
        Ainz les me fet chierement conparer;
        S'ai grant poour cist loiers ne m'ocie. 28
        Merci, Amours! S'ainc Dieus fist vilenie,
        Con vilainz fait bone amour dessevrer;
        Ne je ne puiz l'amour de moi oster,
        Et si m'estuet que je ma dame lais. 32

V   Or seront lié li faus losengeour,
        Qui tant pesoit des biens qu'avoir soloie;
        Maiz ja de ce n'iere pelerins jour
        Que ja vers iauz bone volenté aie. 36
        Pour tant porrai perdre toute ma voie,
        Quar tant m'ont fait de mal li trahitour,
        Se Dieus voloit qu'il eüssent m'amour,
        Ne me porroit chargier pluz pesant faiz. 40

VI   Je m'en voiz, dame. A Dieu le creatour
        Conmant vo cors, en quel lieu que je soie.
        Ne sai se ja verroiz maiz mon retour;
        Aventure est que jamaiz vous revoie. 44
        Pour Dieu vos pri, quel part que li cors
                                    [traie,

> Que nos convens tenez, vieigne u demour,
> Et je pri Dieu qu'ensi me doint honour
> Con je vous ai esté amis verais.   48

<u>MN</u>   The mss., particularly K and U, show many vari-
ants in the melody. Form: A A B.
1. Because of ms. mutilation, the music for measures 1-6 is
supplied from measures 9-14. 2. In l. 4 ms. writes no
flat. 3. In l. 4 ms. writes no rest. 4. Ms. writes c;
emended according to mss. TV (and mss. KOPUX, all written a
2nd higher); the c also occurs in l. 8 in ms. A.

<u>RR</u>   I   1-2 *first verse and first two syllables of*
second verse missing because of mutilation of manuscript;
reading from A   III   19/22 *transposed*   19 Et des douz
mauz dont seut a moi parler   21 sa douce conpaignie   22
Et les soulaz quel me soloit moustrer   24 Quil   VI   45
en quel lieu que ie soie

<u>V</u>   Stanzas: AT   I II III IV V VI
                       U   I II III IV V VI VII
                                               (see below)
                       C   I III II IV V VI
                       O   I II III IV VI V
                       KPRVX I II III IV VI
I   1 amanz K, amans PX, amo(u)rs OUV; ains ka nul T
2 Et (Est P) il PR; raixon C, reson KPV, raison X   3
Quant CKOPVX; p. or autrement A   4   ma loyalz R, douche
A, douce C, dolce U   5 Et se (quant O) la KOPRVX; perz
U; nai C, naim U; rien CU   6 Si TO; saiche C; cher-
tainement A, certeinement O, uraiement K, ueraiement PX,
tout uraiement RV   7 Sains A, Sainz OUV, Se CKPX; ni
C; morixe C, moront U   8 Dont TA; p. m. esmeus sons ne
l. A; Iames (Iaimaix C, Iamais RU) par (por C) m. niert
(nert R) leuz (leus PRX, meus C, chantez U) v. n. l.
CKOPRUVX
II   9 Biau A, Beau O, Douce dame C, Ahi (Iai P, Haî
R, Por deu U) amo(u)rs KPRUVX; ceu ke iert et C, quen
iert d. O, q. ce d. U; donc KORUX; ne c. A   10 C. il
TAKPRVX, moi C, Iert tex la fins O; qua KPX; ke ia li c.
p. A, a (en U) la f. c. p(r)an(d)re CU, quil mestuet c.
prendre O   11 O. certes n. KRVX   12 Morir m. V; Aler
(Por uos CU) m. (men vois CU) morir en CKPRUX   13 *miss-*
ing in R; quic T; nus A, nuns O; q. g. deus (duelx O)
AO; Ne cuidiez (-s C) pas (malz C) ke g. duels (cautres
malus C) m. s. CU, Et si ne cuit q. dolo(u)r m. s. KPVX
14 *except for* Car, *missing in C*; Que UR; ie nen ai U; c.

ne garison O; Q. (Que R) de cest (dicest R, ces V) mal
(maus V) nen ai al. KPRVX   15 Ne *missing in C*; nul A;
a. auoir AOU; Ne de nul(l)ui guer(r)edon nen at(t)ent KPR
VX   16 Forques R, Plus que O; de uos C; se cest C
III   17 Biau A, Beau O; Douce dame C; q. il des con-
sires A, que iert du desirrer O; Par dieu amo(u)rs grief
mest (miert U) a consirrer (consieurrer K, consierrier P,
consiurer X) KPRUVX   18 Des CU, Le KPRX; dou(l)z (dous
A, dolz U) s. ACOUV; et la grant c. KPRX   19 Et des
dols maus dont seut a moi parler T; Dou bel samblant C, Et
le samblanz U, Et le de(s)duit (deduiz V) KPRVX; quel KP
20 Quant uos mesties C, Quant ele mestoit U; mest AO; d.
et loiaus a. A, et compa(i)gne et a. ORU, douce dame et a.
V, et ma dame et mamie KPX   21 recorz U; la C; douc(h)e
compaignie TA   22 Et le soulas ke me soloit mostrer T;
dont s. AO; qua moi soloit paller V; sueil (soil P) a li
p. KPRX   23 le (li O) cuer KOPRX   24 Kil A, Ke C,
Que O; il ne p. V, ne me p. AKOPRX; il] mout AKOPRUX,
trop CV
IV   25 Ne me v. p. d. en perdon d. U, Ne me uuet dex pas
p. n. trouer O, Ne (De P) ma dont d(i)ex par (por V)
droit n. don(n)e KPRVX, Or uoi ie bien kil mestuet compa-
reir C   26 T. l. deduis (-z U) ACU, Tre(s)touz (Tres-
tos P, Trestous R) les (lez R) biens (bien K) KOPRVX;
eu AKPR; a ma X   27 le A; meffait T, ma f. KR, mestuet X; Deus ne mi uolt en pardon rien doneir C   28 p.
ses AO; Ansois crien molt c. C; Et se dot molt que samors
ne m. U; Quant il mestuet (mesteut V) departir de mamie
KPRVX   29 M. a. ke d. heit v. C, M. a. fut ainz tels v.
U, Si fera il sains (-z O) d. f. v. AO, M. li cri (pri R)
quainz (-c R) ne fis v. KPRVX   30 Ke AC, Que OU, Car
KPVX, Quar R; uilain CPRV; font C, faiz O; f. de la mort
A; amors T   31 Et O; Et ie ni poi A; Et j. n. p. mon
cuer de li o. C; p. de li mon cuer o. U; Ne de mon cuer ne
puis samor o. KPRVX   32 Si (Se C) me co(u)uient CKPRVX;
j. mamie l. KPVX
V   33 Or seuent bien A; li felon traitor U   34 Cui
TO; de b. T; Cauoient (K- U) duel d. CU   35 perins T;
Iai palerins ne serait a nul j. C, M. pelerins ne serai ia
lo j. U   36 Q. ie O; bien v. A; Por ceu ka els (caous
C) en bone pais me soie (paix resoie C) CU   37 t. peux
(puis U) bien p. CU; Si en porai toute perdre A, Sen porrai bien tote perdre O   38 Que O, Ke A; traietour A;
Et sa(i)chent bien li felon menteor (fals losengeor U) CU
39 uolsist kil raussent C   40 poroient A; doner U; c.
nul O; grigno(u)r AO
VI   41 Se P   42 Ki soit a uos C, Qui soit o uos U, C.

uos c. P, Vous conmant ie KRV; quel (que P) que l. q. j.
s. KPX, quel que part q. j. s. V, quelle part q. j. s. R;
Uos lais qui soit a vos ou q. j. s. O 43 Ne s. se mais
en uenres m. r. A, Ne s. se ia uerrai mais lo r. U, Et
saichies bien nians iert dou r. C, Car (Quar R) is men
uois cor(r)o(u)ciez (courrouchies R, coroucies X) et dolanz (-enz K, -ens X, -ent R) KPRVX 44 Et si ne cuit
KPRVX; se j. A 45 Mon cuer avez (aves X) en la uostre
manoie (menaie R, menoie V); en quel lieu que ie soie T,
ken keil leu ke ie soie C, ou que tengne ma uoie U 46
Q. mes CU; Q. uo(u)s penses (-z O) au cuer v. ou d. AO,
Fere (Faire RX) en po(u)ez (poes X) du (del P, dou X)
to(u)t uostre conmant (talent P) KPRVX 47 Ie si ferai
se dieus me d. h. AO, Ma douce dame a ihesu vo(u)s co(n)-
mant KPRVX 48 Que O, Ke A; urais A; Ie nen puis mes
(mais R) certes se ie uo(u)s les (lais RX) KPRVX
    Of the manuscripts collated, only *U* presents an envoy.
It is offered here with necessary emendations from *Ch[1]* (*Roman du Castelain de Couci et de la Dame de Fayel*), as cited
in Bédier-Aubry and Lerond:
       De moie part di, chançons, (si t'en croie!)
       Que je m'en vois servir Nostre Seignor;
       Et bien sachiez, dame de grant valor,
       Se je revieng, que por vous servir vois.
2 Q. sols m. v. que nai altre s. 4 s. nais

<u>E</u>   La Borde *Es* 2, 300; Michel, 79-84; Brakelmann 1,
103-105; Fath, 36; Paris-Langlois, 287-290; Bédier-Aubry,
99-106; Woledge *Peng*, 101-103; Lerond, 57-62; Maillard *Anth*,
28-30; Mary 1, 206-209; Van dW *Trouv*, 224-231, 572; Bec 2,
96-97; Schöber, 205-222; Aspland, 154-156.

<u>N</u>   The crusade to which this song refers is either
the Third (1189) or the Fourth (1202). For the problem of
dating, see Lerond, pp. 16-20, and Schöber, p. 207. For a
brief literary analysis of the text, see Dronke, pp. 127-
128. The ms. transmission of the text being unusually
marked by accidents, instances of contamination and the like
(see Schwan, pp. 137 and 165, Bédier-Aubry, pp. 99-100, and
Lerond, p. 61), we have felt justified in adopting some variant readings which were not, strictly speaking, necessary,
but which seemed to be in keeping with the poem's generally
high level of compositional art. See st. 3 in particular.
    17 *consirrer* 'separation, deprivation' more likely
than 'thought, consideration'. 23-24 Lerond places the
question mark at the caesura in l. 24 and retains the ms.
reading *Qu'il*; but one would then expect the subjunctive

parte. 28 Understand *que* after *poour.* 29-30 The accusation that God has cruelly separated two faithful lovers is not unknown in other crusade songs. See, for example, RS 21 and RS 191 or the 13th-century Italian poem by Rinaldo d'Aquino, *Già mai non mi confortto,* p. 115 in E. Monaci, ed., *Crestomazia italiana dei primi secoli,* 9th ed. (Rome, 1955). 34 *Qui = cui,* dative object of impersonal *pesoit.* 35-36 'But I will never be pilgrim enough to wish them (the *losengeour*) well'. As noted by Bédier-Aubry, p. 106, and others, the vow taken by departing crusaders ("pilgrims") included a promise to forgive all the offenses of their enemies. 37 'For that reason I may lose [the spiritual benefit of] my whole voyage'. 39 Understand *que* before *Si.* 45 *traie* rhymes with *soie, revoie,* etc. 46 *vieigne ou demour* 'whether I come [back] or stay [away]'.

<u>96</u>   Chanson

RS 985 (= 986), MW 1507
Mss. M 53v-54r, A 155r, C 125v-126r, K 95-96, L 62v-63r, O
    73v-74r, P 30v-31r, R 129v-130v, T 155v-156r, U 38r-v,
    V 75r-v, X 69r-v, a 13v-14r. Stanza I also in *Roman du
    Castelain de Couci et de la Dame de Fayel,* ed. M. Del-
    bouille (Paris, 1936), p. 227; and in Jean Renart, *Ro-
    man de la Rose, ou de Guillaume de Dole,* ed. G. Servois
    (Paris, 1893), p. 29; ed. R. Lejeune (Paris, 1936), p.
    22; ed. F. Lecoy (Paris, 1962), p. 29. Music in all
    mss. except C; incomplete in U. Attribution in MAKPT
    Xa; attributed to Muse en Borse in C.

7. *tieigne u- ne foiz en- tre mes braz nu- e- te*

8. *ainz que j'aille ou- tre- mer.*

I   Li nouviauz tanz et mais et violete
         Et lousseignolz me semont de chanter,
         Et mes fins cuers me fait d'une amourete
         Si douz present que ne l'os refuser.   4
         Or me lait Dieus en tele honeur monter
         Que cele u j'ai mon cuer et mon penser
         Tieigne une foiz entre mes braz nüete
              Ainz que j'aille outremer.   8

II   Au conmencier la trouvai si doucete,
         Ja ne quidai pour li mal endurer;
         Mes ses douz vis et sa bele bouchete
         Et si vair oeill bel et riant et cler   12
         M'orent ainz pris que m'osaisse doner;
         Se ne me veut retenir ou cuiter,
         Mieuz aim a li faillir, si me pramete,
              Qu'a une autre achiever.   16

III   Las! pour coi l'ai de mes ieuz reguardee,
         La douce rienz qui Fausse Amie a non,
         Quant de moi rit et je l'ai tant plouree?
         Si doucement ne fu trahis nus hom.   20
         Tant com fui mienz, ne me fist se bien non;
         Mes or sui suenz, si m'ocit sans raison,
          Et c'est pour ce que de cuer l'ai amee!
              N'i set autre ochoison.   24

IV   De mil souspirs que je li doi par dete,
         Ne m'en veut pas un seul cuite clamer;
         Ne Fausse Amours ne lait que s'entremete,
         Ne ne me lait dormir ne reposer.   28
         S'ele m'ocit, mainz avra a guarder;
         Je ne m'en sai vengier fors au plourer;
         Quar qui Amours destruit et desirete
              Ne s'en set ou clamer.   32

V   Sour toute joie est cele courounee
         Que j'ai d'Amours. Dieus! i faudrai je dont?
         Oïl, par Dieu, teus est ma destinee,

Et tel destin m'ont doné li felon.   36
Si sevent bien qu'il font grant mesprison,
Quar qui ce tolt dont ne puet faire don,
Il en conquiert anemis et mellee:
    N'i fait se perdre non.   40

VI   Si coiement ai ma doleur celee
    Qu'a mon samblant ne la coneüst on;
    Se ne fussent la gent maleüree,
    N'eüsse pas souspiré en pardon: 44
    Amours m'eüst doné son guerredon.
    Maiz en cel point que dui avoir mon don,
    Lor fu l'amour descouverte et moustree.
      Ja n'aient il pardon!   48

__MN__   Mss. KLX have a second melody for the B-section,
and ms. P joins them in ll. 7-8; ms. O has a third melody
for the B-section; ms. R has a second melody; ms. V has a
third one. Form: A A B.
1. Ms., like ms. U, is written a 5th lower than the other
mss. that contain this melody; its version is here transposed a 5th up. 2. In l. 1 ms. writes a B-flat. 3. In l.
1 ms. writes a bar. 4. In l. 2 ms. writes a binary ligature *e'-d'*.

__RR__   I   8 Aincoiz quaille o.   II   14 Maiz sor me
v. r. et c.   III   19 tant amee   IV   32 Ne len doit
on blasmer   V   34 Que jaim damours d. f. i ie d.   35
Nenil   VI   41 Si c. est ma doleurs cele   42 la recou-
noist on

    __V__   Stanzas: ORTa   I II III IV V VI
                      A   I II III IV V
                      KLPVX   I II IV V III
                      CU   I II IV III
I   1 nouuiau KP; Li tens deste (desteit U) et CU   2
Li ros. KLPVX; rasignol P; mi ARa; semoignent O, semo-
nent U; s. damer OU   3 me] mi LR, ma KPVX, mait C   4
Un KPVX, Dun L; p. nel doit nus O; q. ie nos (noz X) KL
PVX, q. ne doi CU   5 mi R; laist ACRTa, dont KP, doint
LUVX; en] a U; tel LOPTUX, teil C, cele A, chele a   7
Soit OR; foiz] nuit CU   8 A. ken T; aille T, voise AK
RXa, men voise L, ie uoise U; A. q. men doie aler   P
II   9 la] le Aa; A. c. fu (fu fu C) si franche et d.
CO; simplette U   10 Ja *missing in C*, Ie O, Que U,
Quainc R, Quains LP, Quonc KVX; li] lui L; maus KOPVX,
malz R   11 Et L; son LOV; cler (-s KPX) v. KLOPRVX;

Ces (ses U) simples v. CU; sa] se a; bele] douce O,
dolce U, simple C, fresche KLPVX   12 si] sui C, sei
U; bel o. ACKLPTVX; o. vair CLTVX, ver P, uert K, qui
sont r. Aa   13 Mont si sorpris (seurpris LV) que KLPVX;
que mi soie O, mi peusse A, mi puisse a, ne mi soi CKLPU
VX; donez O, garder KLPVX   14 Sel L, Si U, Or C; mi
KLORTVX; Mais (Mez R) sor m. veut (vient T) AORTa; ou] et
AORTa; r. a son per R, naquite(i)r CU, ou cuidier L   15
Iam (Jaim a) mieus Aa; M. uuel U; lui L; li seruir O;
faillir a li (lui V) CV; si prometrey O   16 Ka nulle a.
C; eschiue(i)r CL

III   17 Deus si mar fut (fu U) d. CU; esga(i)rdee CLOV
18 La france r. R; rien L; que O, ke C; amo(u)r ALa
19 El(l)e me rit (rist ACa, mocit V) ACKPVUXa, Sele me
het L; et iai li t. U; t. amee LV   20 fut C; f. naures
R; hons P   21 c. ie f. L; fut C; miex T; ne mi R; m.
fuit C, vint R   22 Et Aa; Or sui ie R; sui] seux C;
siens (-z) ACKLOPRTUVXa; mocist ACLOV, moc(c)hist RTa
23 Et (Seul KLVX, Sol P) po(u)r itant q. ACKLPUVXa   24
Ni sai C, truiz V, trueue KLPX

IV   25 De cent KLPVX; s. kelle ait a de moy C; q. le ior
d. O; par dete] de rente KLPVX   26 Ne me CKOPRUVX, mi
Aa; uoeil R; pas] el(l)e CKLPUVX; p. dun to(u)t seul (soul
O) aquiter (acuitier R) AORTa   27 Nen P, Sa C; fole
KLPVX; amo(u)r KLPRTVX; laist ARTa, uuet OU, ueult C; ne
doit met(t)re sentente KLPVX   28 Ne ne mi laist Aa, Ne
me laisse R, Ne mi laist pas T, De moi (moy C) la(i)ssier
COU, A li (lui LV) fere (faire) KLPVX; ne] et O   29
Cel(l)e CX; mocist ACL, moc(c)hist RTa; moc. saura (sau-
rait C) moins a CU   30 Si ne AORa; f. a ACLa, qal U,
quau P   31 *only* doit et deserte *in* L; Car cui CU, Qui
fole KPVX; amo(u)r KVX; ocit KPVX, destraint C; et desire T, des(h)erite CKOPVX   32 Ne se P; Len ne O; Ne
len doit on bla(s)mer ATa

V   33 Pour T; to(u)tes AORVa; ioies OR, choses Aa,
riens (-z) KLPV, rien X   34 Cui iaim d. T, Qui da-
mo(u)rs vit (uient Aa) AKLPVXa; d. faurai i ie d. T   35
Nennil R, Naie T; tel L, tele V   36 Que O, quar R,
car Ta, kar A; ce d. KVX, cel P; me (mi RT) do(u)nent
(doiuent R) AORTa   37 Qui mont tolu de mamie le don (mon
bon K) KLPVX   38 Et KLPVX; dont] il KLPVX   39 Auoir
i (en K) puet a. KLPVX

VI   41 Si que ie ment R; ai] est RTa; dolo(u)rs Ta; d.
menee O   42 ne le Oa; recon(n)oist Ta, recongnoist R;
lon R   43 Si feissent la g. apensee R   45 Rendu m.
amors mon g. O, Ainz mot amours rendu le g. R   46 ce O,
tel a; lieu a; q. deubs R, puis a   47 lamors T,

mamour a, mamors O, ma mort R; descouverte] ense(i)gnie
ORTa 48 *missing in R*

E   La Borde *Es* 2, 270; Michel, 33-35; Brakelmann 1,
114-116; Fath, 54; Bédier-Aubry, 89-96; Bartsch-Wiese, 164-
165; Brittain, 140-142; Pauphilet, 873-874; Spaziani *Ant*,
33-35; Cremonesi, 107-110; Lerond, 76-81; Toja, 229-232; Van
dW *Trouv*, 243-250, 573.

N   With the exception of Lerond, previous editors
have regarded this poem as an example of *coblas ternas*: a
group of three stanzas repeating one set of rhymes (AAA),
followed by a second group of three repeating a different
set of rhymes (BBB). Our arrangement of the stanzas, AAB
ABB, makes the poem emerge as unique in the corpus of trouvère songs (cf. Dragonetti, p. 446ff) and may thereby appear
suspect. Innovation was not unknown among the trouvères,
however, and it is indisputable that the five mss. of RS 985
that present all six stanzas present them in the sequence we
have adopted. Moreover, the text seems thus to show a progressive development of ideas that would be impaired otherwise. See Lerond, p. 80, for further comment.
    It is apparently because of l. 8 alone, *Ainz que
j'aille outremer*, that this song has been considered a *chanson de croisade* and is included in Bédier-Aubry. The reason
strikes us as insufficient to warrant that generic designation, although the reference is no doubt to a crusade,
either the Third (1189) or the Fourth (1202). For the problem of dating, see Lerond, pp. 16-20.
    For comment on the text, see L. Vaina-Pusca, "La fonc-
tionnalité des pronoms dans un texte poétique médiéval'" *Revue Roumaine de Linguistique* 19 (1974), pp. 133-137; and P.
Zumthor and L. Vaina-Pusca, "Le 'je' de la chanson . . .,"
Canadian Review of Comparative Literature 1 (1974), pp. 9-
21.
    14-16 'If she does not want either to retain me [as her
"vassal"] or free (*cuiter* = *quiter*) me [from the bond of
vassalage], I would rather fail with her, provided she promise me [love], than succeed with someone else'.   26 *cuite*
= *quite*.   31 *desirete* 'disinherits'.   35 Instead of substituting *Oïl*, Lerond retains the ms. reading *Nenil* and ex-
plains: "la négation *nenil* ne répond pas à la question du v.
34 (*Diex, faudrai i je dont?*), mais reprend plutôt le sens
négatif du verbe *faudrai*; le poète veut dire: 'Non, je n'ob-
tiendrai pas la joie d'amour: telle est ma destinee'."   44
en pardon 'in vain'.

Chanson   97

RS 40, MW 1051

Mss. K 69-70, A 154v, C 135r-v, F 108v-110r, M 54v-55r, O
74v, P 33v-34r, T 157r-v, V 76v-77r, X 71v-72r, a 13r-
v. Also in *Roman du Castelain de Couci et de la Dame
de Fayel*, ed. M. Delbouille (Paris, 1936), pp. 29-30.
Music in all mss. except C. Attribution in all mss.
except OV.

I   La douce voiz du rosignol sauvage
      Qu'oi nuit et jor cointoier et tentir
      Me radoucist mon cuer et rassouage;
      Lors ai talent que chant pour esbaudir.   4
      Bien doi chanter puis qu'il vient a plesir
      Cele qui j'ai de cuer fet lige honmage;
      Si doi avoir grant joie en mon corage,
      S'ele me veut a son oés retenir.   8

II   Onques vers li n'oi faus cuer ne volage,
      Si me deüst por ce melz avenir;
      Ainz l'aim et serf et aor par usage,

Si ne li os mon penser descouvrir.   12
Car sa biauté me fet si esbahir
Que je ne sai devant li nul langage;
Ne regarder n'os son simple visage,
Tant en redout mes euz a departir.   16

III   Tant ai en li ferm assis mon corage
      Qu'ailleurs ne pens, et Deus m'en dont joïr,
      C'onques Tristans, cil qui but le buvrage,
      Si coriaument n'ama sanz repentir.   20
      Car g'i met tot: cuer et cors et desir,
      Sens et savoir--ne sai se faz folage,
      Ançois me dout qu'en trestout mon aage
      Ne puisse li ne s'amor deservir.   24

IV   Je ne di pas que je face folage,
      Nes se pour li me devoie morir,
      Qu'el mont ne truis si bele ne si sage
      Ne nule riens n'est tant a mon plesir.   28
      Mult aim mes euz qui me firent choisir:
      Lués que la vi, li lessai en ostage
      Mon cuer qui puis i a fet lonc estage,
      Ne jamés jor ne l'en quier departir.   32

V   Chançon, va t'en pour fere mon mesage
      La ou je n'os trestorner ne guenchir,
      Que tant redout la male gent honbrage
      Qui devinent, ainz que puist avenir,   36
      Le bien d'amors. Deus les puist maleïr,
      Qu'a maint amant ont fet ire et outrage;
      Mes j'ai de ce touz jorz mal avantage
      Q'il les m'estuet seur mon cuer obeïr.   40

     MN   Mss. AOa have related but different last lines,
all differing; ms. T has a different B-section; ms. V has a
second different B-section and is written a 4th higher; ms.
F has a second melody. Form: A A B.

     RR   I   3 c. et mon corage   5 doit   8 Sele meut
a   V   39 M. de ce ai je t. *(+1)*

     V   Stanzas: ACFMTVXa   I II III IV V
                     O   I V   II
                     P   I II
I 1 Ma A 3 Madoucist si   MT, Madouc(h)i(s)t to(u)t Oa;
le c. VMTOa; et mon (le V) corage PVX   4 Quor M, Cor
oi T; re(s)baudir CFO; Que ne me puis de chanter plus

tenir V 5 Si chanterai p. F; ch. quant il v. O 6 A
cele q. X, Celi q. ACFOTa; j. fait de cuer l. MT; de mon
cuer fait h. O 7 Sen F, Bien O; doie C 8 Cel(1)e
CX; mi v. V; me digne F, doigne O; s. euls C, vues F
II 9 n'oi] no C, neuch F, neu M; fait c. O; ne corage
V 10 Si men ACFMOTa; deuroit CMOTa, deueroit A; ce]
tant CMT; c. bien a. O 11 A. aing O; ser CO, serch F
12 Se A, Mais MT; Li cui ie nos m. O; pense M; Mais mon
penser ne li os d. F 13 Que O; biautes AFa, -z M,
beautes T, -z O; si] tant M 15 Nis AMTa; nose s.
douch v. F; s. s. uiaire A, visage *missing in T* 16 re-
douch F; au d. FPT
III 17 en] ens T, uers F; li aissis mon fin c. C; mon
corage *missing in X* 18 dont] doin(s)t FVX, doenst C,
lai(s)t AMTa 19 Onques V, Vnques F; C. t. qui but le
beuerage M; de b. F 20 Plus MT; loiaument MT, loialment F 21 *occurs as 1. 29 in F*; Que VXa, Ke AC, Quat
M; mat C; t. cors et quer et F 22 *occurs as 1. 30 in F*;
Sen C, Force M, Forche T; et pooir FMT; fas X, fach F,
fai A, faic Ta, fais C, faiz M 23 *occurs as 1. 31 in
F*; Aincor C, Encoir T, Encor AMa; Et si ne quit q. F
24 *occurs as 1. 32 in F*; Ne *missing in F*; p. asses (-z M,
aisseis C) li et (ne F) samo(u)r (amor F) seruir ACFMTa
IV 25 *followed in T by redundant* encoir me dout ke trestot mon eaige ne puisse asses li et samor seruir Ie ne di
pas ke iou faice folaige 26 Ne FV, Nis ACMTa; li men
couenoit a. F; me deuoie *repeated in T* 27 Q. monde na si
F; si] tant CMT; bele] simple V 28 Ne rienz el mont n.
V; rien CF; r. tant soit a F; mon desir MT 29 *occurs
as 1. 21 in F*; quel m. V; q. mi AFTa 30 *occurs as 1. 22
in F*; Lors FM; li] si X; ostages F 31 *occurs as 1. 23
in F*; ke p. Aa 32 *occurs as 1. 24 in F*; Ne ia nul j. FM
V 33 Canchons F, Chancons X 34 trestorner] ne aler
F, ne parler O; guenchir] uenir F, tentir O 35 Car FT
VX, Quar M; male] fole MT, pute F; g. sauuage FO 36
Ke F; deuienent Aa, deuient F; quil p. FMVX 37 Les
biens (b. *missing in A*) ACFMTVa; De noz amors d. lor doint
male entente O 38 A FMT; tant a. FO; amanz O; on F,
ire] honte V; et dama(i)ge FMT, domage O 39 M. de ce
ai je t. VX, M. de cai (sai C, chai Fa) j. ACFa; jorz]
diz V; male A; M. iai de ce (cou T) mout (molt T) cruel
a. MT; Por ce dit bien guioz quen son aage O 40 Si T;
la V, le Aa; sus Aa, sos T; cuer] pois MT, gre Aa,
greit C; Que sor mon ceur les mestuet o. F; Ne porroit
bien eurs amors seruir O

E   La Borde *Es* 2, 294-295; La Borde *Mém* 2, 68-71;
Michel, 69-72; Brakelmann 1, 112-114; Fath, 49-51; Bartsch-
Wiese, 165-166; Pauphilet, 875-876; Cremonesi, 110-112;
Gennrich *Ex*, 16-17; Chastel, 422-425; Woledge *Peng*, 95-97;
Groult 1, 176-177; Lerond, 68-71; Toja, 232-234; Henry
Chrest 1, 221-222; 2, 66; Zumthor *Es*, 194-195; Van dW *Trouv*,
186-193, 590.

N   For a detailed textual analysis, see Zumthor *Es*,
pp. 194-204 and 240-241.   6 *qui* = *cui*, indirect object.

Chanson

RS 1579, MW 586
Mss. C 131v, K 69-70, L 53r-v, M 23r, N 24r-v, P 11r-v, R
120v-121r, T 158v-159r, U 34r-v, V 34v, X 53r. Music
in all mss. except CU. Attribution in KMNPTX; attributed to Guiot de Provins in C.

I   Les oxelés de mon païx
        Ai oïs en Bretaigne.
    A lors chans m'est il bien avis
      K'en la douce Champaigne
        Les oï jadis,
        Se n'i ai mespris.
    Il m'ont en si douls penseir mis
    K'a chanson faire m'en seux pris

5

               Tant que je perataigne
          Ceu k'Amors m'ait lonc tens promis.   10

II   En longue atente me languis
               Sens ceu ke trop m'en plaigne;
          Ceu me tolt mon jeu et mon ris,
               Ke nuls c'Amors destraigne
                    N'est d'el ententis.   15
                    Mon cors et mon vis
          Truis si mainte foix entrepris
          Ke fol semblant en ai enpris.
                    Ki k'en Amors mespraigne,
          Je seux cil k'ains riens n'i forfix.   20

III   En baixant, mon cuer me ravi
               Ma douce dame gente;
          Moult fut fols quant il me guerpi
               Por li ke me tormente.
                    Lais! ains ne.l senti   25
                    Quant de moy parti;
          Tant doulcement lou me toli
          K'en sospirant le traist a li;
                    Mon fol cuer atalente,
          Maix jai n'avrait de moy merci.   30

IV   Del baixier me remenbre, si,
               Ke je fix, k'en m'entente
          Il n'est hore--ceu m'ait traï--
               K'a mes leivres ne.l sente.
                    Quant elle sousfri   35
                    Ceu ke je la vi,
          De ma mort ke ne me gueri!
          K'elle seit bien ke je m'oci
               En ceste longue atente,
          Dont j'ai lou vis taint et pailli.   40

V   Pués ke me tolt rire et jueir
               Et fait morir d'envie,
          Trop sovant me fait compaireir
               Amors sa compaignie。
                    Lais! n'i ous aleir   45
                    Car por fol sembleir
          Me font cil fauls proiant dameir.
          Mors seux quant je.s i voi pairleir,
               Ke poent de tricherie
          Ne puet nulz d'eaus en li troveir.   50

<u>MN</u>   Melody from ms. M. Ms. R has a second melody;
ms. V has a third one. Form: A A B+A¹
1. In l. 1 this note is torn out in ms. 2. In l. 1 ms.
writes a bar. 3. Ms. may intend two long note heads. Although mss. KLMNPX all close with this figure, it seems
probable that it should be sung a 3rd higher, since the entire song revolves around *f*.

<u>RR</u>   I   6 Se gi ai m.   II   11 languis] seux mis
14 desdaigne   15 Niert iai atentis   17 T. si per oures
e.   III   23 q. de moy parti   IV   32 f. en manfance
33 Kil   34 l. ne s.   37 ne mot g.

<u>V</u>   Stanzas III, IV and V are not included in KLMNPRT
VX.
I   1 Des U; ois(s)e(i)llons KMNPRTVX, oisiaus L, oiselez U   2 oïs] oi RT, ueuz U   3 lor MRTUV, leur KLN
PX; chant KLNPRUVX   4 conpai(n)gne KLNPRX   5 L. ai oiz
j. L, Ie fui j. R   6 n'i ai] gi ai KNPUVX, iai L, ie y
ai R   8 me s. KLMNPRTUX   9 Si U   10 mont l. K; m.
toz iors p. U
II   11 De KLNPRTVX; longe LTU; a. mesbahis (-z) KLMNPRT
VX   12 trop] ie KLMNPRTVX   13 le j. et le r. KLMNPRTVX
14 (Que PUX) Nus (nuns U, *missing in R*) qui (cui MT, q
U) amo(u)rs KLMNPRTUVX; enprai(n)gne KNPX, enpreigne L,
emprai(n)gne RV   15 Niert ententis U, N. delessier ten-
tiz V   16 M. cuer KLNPRVX   17 T. mainte foiz si K, T.
si par eures e. U; maintez R   18 Un KLNPRVX, Cun M,
Quun U, Oun T; foiz K; en] i KLMNPTVX, y R; ai *missing
in LV*; apris KLMNPTVX, pris R, empris U   19 amer MT
20 Ainz (-s R, -c MT, Onc L) certes plus ne (ni L) li
(*missing in LR*) mesfis (-z V, meffis X, mesprins L)
III   21 me toli U   23 Trop fu U   24 qui U   25 L.
a. ne lo s. U
IV   31 Dun b. dont me me membre si U   32 Mest auis en
mentente U   36 Deus ce que ie di U   37 me garni U
38 Ele U   39 longe U
V   41 Por coi me U   46 Que U   48 M. sui U
    After stanzas I and II, mss. LMRT show a different,
evidently inauthentic, continuation of the text, consisting
of two stanzas (except in ms. L, which has only the first).
Following is the version of ms. T.
        III'   Ainc vers Amors riens ne forfis;
                Ja de moi ne se plaigne,
            Ains sui por li servir nasquis,
                Coment ke me destraigne.
                Par un tres douc ris   25

>   Sui de joie espris,
>   Ke, se iere rois de Paris
>   Ou sires d'Alemaigne,
>   N'aroie tant de mes delis
>   K'Amors me fait cuidier tos dis.   30
>
> IV'   Bien doit estre liez et jolis
>   Cui Amors tant adaigne
>   Ke il se truist loiaus amis
>   Et k'a amer l'apraigne.
>   Ne doit estre eschis   35
>   Mais adés sosgis
>   A celi qui proie mercis;
>   Puis ke son cuer a ens li mis,
>   Sans partir s'i ataigne
>   Por estre de joie plus fis.   40

V   III' 21 Ains v. ma dame ne mesprins L; mesfis R
22 Riens dom elle s. L   23 Aincois p. lui s. L   24
que mi R, que li plaiz praigne L   25 un seul d. L   27
ce L; giere M   30 mi LR; font L   IV'   31 Ien doi
e. R   32 Qui R   33 Quelle secort l. R   34 Ce M
37 celui R; cui M   38 lui m. R

E   La Borde *Es* 2, 196; Tarbé *Chans*, 43; Huet *Gace*,
40-43; Brittain, 148-150; PetDyg *Gace*, 189-193; Spaziani
Ant, 51-53; Cremonesi, 114-116; Gennrich *Ex*, 15-16; Groult
1, 174-175; Toja, 245-248; Maillard *Anth*, 45-47; Mary 1,
238-239; Van dW *Trouv*, 503-597, 592.

DF   Lorraine, including *ai* for *a*, as in *lais* (25),
jai (30), *pailli* (40), *compaireir* (43); *ei* for tonic *e*, as
in *penseir* (7), *leivres* (34), *jueir* (41); *pués* (41) for
puis; *poent* (49) for *point*; *x* for *s*, as in *oxelés* (1), *païx*
(1), *baixant* (21); *ceu* (10) for *ce*; *lou* (27) for *le*; *seux*
(8) for *sui*, 3rd pers. sing. pres. ind. *ait* (10, 33) for *a*;
3rd pers. sing. fut. in *-ait*, as in *avrait* (30); nominative
relative *ke* (24) for *qui*.

N   This is no doubt the best known of the songs of
Gace Brulé. Dragonetti, discussing the structure of the
first stanza, calls it, p. 403, "un exemple très caractéris-
tique des raffinements formels dont les trouvères se
montrent capables." For an examination of its poetic qualities and historical background, see Frappier, p. 142ff.
See, too, Peter Bürger, "Zur ästhetischen Wertung mittelalterlicher Dichtung. 'Les oiseillons de mon pais' von Gace
Brulé," *Deutsche Vierteljahrsschrift für Literaturwissen-*

schaft und Geistesgeschichte 45 (1971), 24-34.

2-4 Gace, who was a native of Champagne and belonged
to the literary circle of Marie de Champagne, refers here to
a period spent in Brittany at the court of her brother,
Geoffroi Plantagenêt. PetDyg *Gace*, p. 36, takes this as an
indication that RS 1579 was composed between 1181, when
Geoffroi moved to Brittany, and 1186, the year of his death.
18 *fol semblant* 'the appearance of a madman'. 19-20 The
sense is: though others may misbehave toward Love, Gace has
never done so. 20 *ains* 'never'. 21 *En baixant* 'with a
kiss'. 25 *ains* 'never, i.e., not at all' or perhaps
'but'. 27 The subject of *toli*, as of the remaining verbs
of this stanza, is the lady. 31-33 'So [well] do I remember the kiss I gave that in my mind there is no moment . . .'.
37 'Why did she not save me from death!'. 45 *n'i ous
aleir* 'I dare not go to her'. 46-47 'For the false sup-
pliants (i.e., false lovers) cause me to be condemned (i.e.,
rejected) [by my lady] because of my mad appearance'. 48
i designates the lady, as in l. 45.

Chanson   99

RS 1102, MW 2052
Mss. Full version: O 41r-v, C 58r-v-59r, H 226r, L 56v, U
    10r-v, za II. Short version: M 31r-v, F 103v-104r, K
    79-80, N 29r-v, R 84v-85r, T 167r, V 37r-v, X 58v-59r,
    a 20v. Music in all mss. except CHTza. Attribution in
    CFKMNTXa.

1. De bone a- mour et de le- aul a- mi- e
3. si que ja- mais a nul jour de ma vi- e

2. me vient so- vant pi- tiez et re- mem- bran- ce,
4. n'ou- bli- e- rai son vis ne sa sem- blan- ce;

5. por ce, s'A- mors ne se vuet plus sos- frir

6. qu'e- le de touz ne face a son plai- sir

7. et de tou- tes,   mais ne puet   a- ve- nir

8. que de la   moie ai- e   bone   e- spe- ran-   ce.

I   De bone amour et de lëaul amie
        Me vient sovant pitiez et remembrance,
        Si que jamais a nul jor de ma vie
        N'oblïerai son vis ne sa semblance;   4
        Por ce, s'Amors ne se vuet plus sosfrir
        Qu'ele de touz ne face son plaisir
        Et de toutes, mais ne puet avenir
        Que de la moie aie bone esperance.   8

II   Coment porroie avoir bone esperance
        A bone amor et a leal amie,
        Ne a biaus yeuz n'a la douce semblance
        Que ne verrai jamés jor de ma vie?   12
        Amer m'estuet, ne m'en puis plus sosfrir,
        Celi cui ja ne vanra a plaisir;
        Siens sui, coment qu'il m'en doie avenir,
        Et si n'i voi ne confort ne ahie.   16

III   Coment avrai je confort ne ahie
        Encontre Amour, vers cui nus n'a puissance?
        Amer me fait ce qui ne m'ainme mie,
        Donc ja n'avrai fors ennui et pesance;   20
        Ne ja nul jor ne l'oserai gehir
        Celi qui tant de maus me fait sentir;
        Mais de tel mort sui jugiez a morir
        Dont ja ne quier veoir ma delivrance.   24

IV   Je ne vois pas querant tel delivrance
        Par quoi amors soit de moi departie,
        Ne ja n'en quier nul jor avoir poissance;
        Ainz vuil amer ce qui ne m'ainme mie.   28
        N'il n'est pas droiz je li doie gehir
        Por nul destroit que me face sentir;
        N'avrai confort, n'i voi que dou morir,
        Puis que je voi que ne m'ameroit mie.   32

V   Ne m'ameroit? Ice ne sai je mie,
        Que fins amis doit par bone atendance
        Et par soffrir conquerre haute amie;

Mes je n'i puis avoir nulle fiance,   36
Que cele est teus, por cui plaing et sopir,
Que ma dolor ne doigneroit oïr;
Si me vaut mieuz garder mon bon taisir
Que dire riens qui li tort a grevance.   40

VI   Ne vos doit pas trop torner a grevance
      Se je vos aing, dame, plus que ma vie,
      Que c'est la riens ou j'ai greignor fiance,
      Que par moi seul vos oi nonmer amie.   44
      Et por ce fais maint doloros sopir
      Qu'assez vos puis et veoir et oïr,
      Mais quant vos voi, n'i a que dou taisir,
      Que si sui pris que ne sai que je die.   48

VII   Mes biaus conforz ne m'en porra garir;
      De vos amer ne me porrai partir,
      N'a vos parler, ne ne m'en puis taisir
      Que mon maltrait en chantant ne vos die.   52

VIII Par Deu, Hüet, ne m'en puis [plus] soffrir,
      Qu'en Bertree est et ma morz et ma vie.

MN   Melody from ms. M. Mss. FKLNX are written a 5th
lower; ms. O is written a 2nd lower and mensurally. Form: A
A B; envoy 1 is sung to ll. 5-8, envoy 2 to ll. 7-8.
1. Here ms. O writes a c#' (b♮), followed in the next measure by c' (b♭). 2. In l. 3 ms. M writes a bar. 3. Here
ms. O writes f#' (e♮'), followed in the same measure by f'
(e♭'). 4. Ms. M writes the music for the next syllables as

follows: ; emended according to ms. a.

RR   I   5 vuet] puet   V   33 nameroit   35
haute] tel   36 nulle] bone   VII   49 m'en] len   53 -1
      Between stanza VI and the first envoy, the ms. shows
the following interpolation:
            Hé, Clemendoz, que ferai je d'amie
            Quant je avrai trespassee m'enfance
            Et ma dame que si iert envoisie
            Avra dou tout lessié l'aler en dance?
            Lors dira l'en: "Soffriz, sire, soffriz!"
            Lors mal a tens me vient au repentir.
            Cil soffre trop qui laisse autrui joïr
            De ce dont a traite la penitance.

V   Stanza VII, or the first envoy, is not included in
CUHLza; stanza VIII, the second envoy, is not included in HL
za.
I   2 Mi L; souient p. U; pitie H; rebrance za; r. *followed by* par ues samors *(see 1. 5) in H*   4 N. ces ieuls
C, ses oels H, son cors L, ses euz za   5 Per ues s. H,
P. tant s.   za, Et puis kamors U; se] sen CU, me H   6
tout L; f. a son CHLU
II   9 por(r)ai CU   10 En CL, De Hza; dolor a. H,
douce a. za; et] ne CLUza, ni H; a] en CL, de Hza   11
Nen U; aus b. L, en (a U, au za) uairs CUza; nen la C,
de la za; douz za   12 uerra L; Q(u)e si mar ui ie
(quant H) en (ien H) perdrai la vie Hza   13 plus] mais
HUza; tenir Hza   14 Cele LU; qui L; nen v. H; Celle de
cui naurai ia nuil p. za   15 c. que L; et si (se C) ne
sai coment puist (puisse U) a. CHUza   16 Et *missing in*
L; se n. L; Ke (Que U) de li aie ne seco(u)rs ne (nen U)
a. CU, Qaie (Q ia za) de li ne (ni H) conse(i)l n. a.
Hza
III 17 a. ne (ni H) conse(i)l Hza; por(r)ai auoir secors naie CU 18 Uers fine CU, De fine Hza, En uerz L;
amours L; verz qui L, la(i) ou CU; ie nai p. C 19 Amor H,
Cameir C, Kamer U; c. ke C, c. que H; q. e. mame mie za
20 D. ie L; e possance H   21 Ne a nelui ne l. L; Ne ne
li os mon cora(i)ge g. CU   22 Celui L; t. ma fait (me
fet L) de mal (maus L) HLza; C. cui ia(i) ne uenra (uan-
rait C) a plaisir CU   23 Q(u)ar Hza, Ke C, Que U; de
cel molt H, de ce mal za   24 Et CU, Que L; ja] ie
Lza, io H, se CU; quier] puis CHLUza
IV   25 Sjo n. H; ne uoi Lza   26 Pour L, De Hza; amor
za; a. se soit L; partie Lza   27 N. j. nul io(u)r nen
quier CLU; N. je ne q. auoir nul(l)e fiance Hza   28 A.
amerai CHUza; c. ke C, c. que HU   29 Ne H, Se C, Ce
U, E za; dr. ke ie C, qe ie za, que io H, que iel U
30 d. quel L, com C   31 Nauroit L; Et se ni a(it) confort q. CU; Car quant iel (Qar qant la za) uoi ni a che
(fors za) del m. Hza   32 voi] sai CLU; quele n. L; Qar
(Que H) ie sai bien q. Hza
V   33 ice] tot ce Hza; sai] di Hza; mie *followed by*
itele amie *(see 1. 34) in L*   34 Mais (-x) CHUza; amans
(-z) puet p. CU; b. (e)sperance Hza   35 E por za; itele
amie L   36 n'i] ne CHza; p. ueoir CU; bone atendance
CU   37 Qar H, Car za; e. teille C; c. pleure L   39
Por ce aim ie m. za, Per co aim m. H; mon] me H   40 Ke
die C; rien CHUza; r. ke C; a pesance L
VI   41 Ne me d. L; d. pa(i)s atorne(i)r a CU, d. p. dont
tourner L, d. dame pas torner za; a pesance L   42 a.

plus dame q. za   43 Car Hza; plus grant f. U   44
Q(u)ant CHLza; oi] os CHLUza   45 Et de ceu trais moult
d. CU; sospirs C   46 Qu *missing in Hza*; Que (Ke C) ne
uos p. ne v. ne o. CU   47 Et CHUza   48 Que si soupirs
L, Si sui so(r)pris Hza, Si sui (seux C) destroiz (-s)
CU; q. ie ne H
VIII   53 Huet] compa(i)ns CU; ne uos os pl. gehir (iehir
C) CU   54 Que (Ke C) ma dame est CU; mort C
     In U, l. 54 is followed immediately, in a different
hand, by a variant of the second half of the interpolated
stanza of O:

          Et chascuns dist: "Sofris, sofris, sofris!"
          Aseis sofret ki voit atru merir
          Sou dont il ait traite la penitance.

I   De bone amour et de loial amie
      Me vient souvent pitiez et remembrance,
      Si que jamaiz a nul jour de ma vie
      N'oublierai son vis ne sa samblance;   4
      Por quant, s'Amours ne me veut pluz soufrir
      Qu'ele de touz ne face a son pleisir
      Et de toutes, mais ne puet avenir
      Que de la moie aie bone esperance.   8

II   Conment porroie avoir bone esperance
      De bone amour et de loial amie
      As ieuz, au vis, a la douce samblance?
      Ja n'avendra a nul jour de ma vie.   12
      Amer m'estuet, car ne m'en puis tenir,
      Cele qui ja ne vendra a pleisir
      Et de tel mort m'a jugié a morir
      Dont ja ne puiz veoir ma delivrance.   16

III   Je ne voiz pas querant tel delivrance
      Par coi amours soit de moi departie,
      Ne ja nul jour n'en quier avoir puissance,
      Ainz amerai ce qui ne m'aime mie;   20
      Car cele est tieux, pour cui plaing et
                                       [souspir,
      Que ma doleur ne deigneroit oïr;
      S'aim assez mieuz garder mon bon taisir
      Que dire rienz qui li tourt a grevance.   24

IV   Ne vous devroit pas tourner a grevance
      Se je vous aim, dame, plus que ma vie,
      Car c'est la rienz u j'ai greigneur fiance
      Quant par moi seul vous os nomer amie.   28

Et pour ce faiz maint dolereus souspir,
Quant ne vous puis ne veoir ne oïr;
Et quant vous voi, n'i a fors du taisir,
Car si sui pris que ne sai que je die.   32

   RR   I   7 Et des   III   21 plaig   23 garder]
celer

   V   Stanzas: KNPRX   I II III IV
                      Ta   I III IV
                      F   I II III
                      V   I II III IV V (see below)
I   1 Bone a. de l. amie X   2 Mi R; pitie RV   4 vis]
sens F   5 Pour oec T, Et puis (puis *missing in X*) qua-
mo(u)rs FKNRVXa; ne mi RTVa, ne se F; uuel(l)ent s. KN
RX, veut sentir V; tenir F   6 Que ie KNVX; du KNRV,
dou X, del Ta; to(u)t FKNRTVXa; ne] li V; a *missing in
FKNRX*; mon p. R   7 Et de tantes F; Ne des autres ne
uueil mes (N. d. a. mais ne mi veut R) consentir KNRVX   8
Q. de lamor F
II   9 porai F, porroit RV   10 et] ne FR   12 Ce ne
seroit a FKNRVX   13 car] que FKRVX   14 Celi F; ne
fera mon p. FKNRVX   15 Et puis quamo(u)rs mont FKNRVX
16 Et ie nen R; puiz] q(u)ier FKNRVX; veoir] auoir KNRVX
III   17 Ie ne q(u)ier p. auoir FKRV   18 de m. eslongie
F   19 Ainz (-s) seruirai to(u)z (-s) io(u)rz (-s) en es-
perance FKNRVX   20 Si KNVX, Et FR; ki naime mie T   21
q. plour et a; Cest ma dame que (qui VX) iaim (iainc R,
jaing V) tant (tant ainc F) et desir FKNRVX   22 dolours
T; Qui ne uo(u)droit (vaudroit F) ma (a F) grant (ma F)
do(u)lo(u)r oir (oir *missing in R*, partir F) FKNRVX   23
S. m. a. FKNRVX, Samaisse m. T; garder] celer FKNRVX   24
Q. d. r. contre sa bien voillance T; pesance a
IV   25 De T; vous doit pas trop Ta, deuez pas trop KN
RX, me deuez pas V; tourner] tenir KNX; pesance a   27
j. grandre K, plus grant Ta   28 os] oi R   29 ce]
uo(u)s KNRVX; faic T, fais Ra, fas X, faz KNV   30 Que
Ta; Car ades cuit que ie doie morir (morir *missing in R*)
31 *missing in R*; Quant uo(u)s regart KNVX; que d. KNVX;
que d. KNVX; de t. T   32 Que a; Tel poor (pauour R,
paor VX) ai q. KNRVX; q. ie ne sai ke d. TV; *followed by*
tant a en uouz bonte sens et vaillance *in R*
       V adds the following stanza:
          Merci, merci, bele tres douce amie!
          Por vous trai je si tres grief penitance,
          Ne ne vous os veoir que il ne dient,
          Li mesdisant, qu'en vous aie fiance.

De vous me vient li maux dont crieng morir
Et la dolour dont je ne puis guerir.
. . . .
Se de vo cors ne m'en vient alejance.

<u>E</u>   Huet *Gace*, 16-19; PetDyg *Gace*, 272-279; Pauphilet,
878; Woledge *Peng*, 92-95; Van dW *Trouv*, 447-454, 587-588;
Frank 1, 57-61; 2, 65-71.

<u>N</u>   This poem, in its complete version, is a masterly
achievement in the complexity of its versification, bringing
into play the various patterns of stanzaic linking known as
coblas capcaudadas, *capfinidas*, *retrogradadas*, and *retronchadas*. For detailed examination, see PetDyg *Gace*, pp. 272-
273, and Dragonetti, pp. 454-457. The short version is evidently the work of a *remanieur* incapable of reproducing the
ingenious structure of the full text.
    FULL VERSION: 7 *mais ne* 'never'. 14 *vanra* =
v(i)endra. 22 *Celi* is the indirect object of l. 21 *gehir*.
29 Understand *que* after *droiz*. Understand *le*, direct object of *gehir*, referring to the message of the preceding
lines. 39 'Thus it is better for me to keep a wise si-
lence'. 43-44 'For it is the thing in which I have the
greatest confidence: that I hear you called *amie* by me a-
lone'. 45-48 'And [yet] I utter many a sad sigh, because
I can often see and hear you but, when I see you, I can only
remain silent, for I am so overcome that I do not know what
to say'. 49 *Mes = mais*. 53-54 *Huet* and *Bertree* are unknown persons.
    SHORT VERSION: 13 *qui = cui*. 27-28 PetDyg *Gace*
glosses: "'Que je serai le seul qui puisse vous nommer son
amie, c'est la chose sur laquelle je compte le plus'." The
translation in Woledge *Peng* reads: "for it is the one comfort I rely upon to dare, when speaking to myself alone, to
call you my love."

Chanson   <u>100</u>

RS 838, MW 619
Mss. M 25v, K 80, L 56v-57r, N 29v-30r, O 112r, P 22r-23v, T
    161r-v, U 133v-134r, X 59r-v. Music in all mss. except
    PU. Attribution in all mss. except LOU.

I   Quant voi le tans bel et cler
        Ainz que soit nois ne gelee,
        Chant pour moi reconforter,
        Car trop ai joie oubliee.
        Merveill moi com puis durer   5
        Quant adés me veut grever
        Du monde la mieuz amee.

II   Bien set ne m'en puis torner;
        Pour ce criem que ne me hee.
        Maiz n'en faiz mie a blasmer,   10
        Car teus est ma destinee:
        Je fui faiz pour li amer.
        Ja Deus ne m'i laist fausser,
        Nis s'ele a ma mort juree.

III   Mout me plaist a reguarder   15
        Li païs et la contree
        U je n'os sovent aler
        Pour la gent mal apensee;
        Maiz si ne savront guarder,
        S'el me veut joie doner,   20
        Que bien ne lor soit emblee.

IV   Quant oi en parole entrer
    Chascun de sa desirree
    Et lor mençonge aconter
    Dont il font tel assamblee,   25
    Ce me fait m'ire doubler;
    Si me font grief souspirer
    Quant chascuns son trichier nee.

V   Amours, bien vous doit membrer
    S'il est a aise qui pree.   30
    Quant pluz cuit merci trover,
    Et pluz est m'ire doublee;
    Ce me fait mout trespenser
    Que n'os maiz a li parler
    De rienz, s'il ne li agree.   35

VI   Bien me deüst amender
    Sanz ce qu'ele en fust grevee;
    Maiz, pour Dieu, li vueill mander,
    Quant n'i ai merci trovee,
    Qu'autre n'i vueille escouter,   40
    Car mout li devroit peser
    S'ert de faus amanz gabee.

VII   Ma chançon vueill definer.
    Gui, ne vous puis oublïer;
    Pour vous ai la mort blasmee.   45

MN   Melody from ms. N.   Ms. M has unique variants;
ms. O has a different line 1 and near the end is in part
mensurally notated.   Forms (M and N): A A B; the envoy is
sung to ll. 5-7.
1. In l. 4 ms. M writes ; in l. 2 possibly a simple
note *g* is intended.

RR   IV   28   vee

V   Stanzas: OT   I II III IV V VI VII
                      KLNPX I II III IV VI
                      U   I II II' III (see below)
I   2 Ke napeirt U; noif KLOU   4 Que O, Ke U; mult ai
KLNPX   5 Merveille (-voille O) est KLNOPUX; cant U; p.
chanter KLNPX   6 Car KLNX, Quades (Cades U) bee a moi
g. OU; me] mi KT
II   8 B. sai que KNOP; nen (ne P) p. KLNOPX; passer O;
De li ne me peus osteir U   9 P. c. croi N, douz U; quel
ne L, quele m. KNOPX; ne men T   10 fait O; f. pas a

KLNOPTX; Se ne man doit on b.   U   11   Que OX, Ke U   12
J. sui KLNO; nes p.   X; lui L   13   ne men O; doint
(donst U) f.   LOU   14 N. sil K, cel(l)e LPUX
III   15 M. mi TU, M. mest bel a KLNPX; esgarder KNOPX,
remireir U   16 Le KNOPX, Mon T   17 Ou nols venir nen
aleir U   18 la grant L; maleuree KLNOPUX   19 Tant ne
mi s. g.   U; ne] nou O   20 Celle U; mi LTU
IV   23 Aucun K, Aucuns X, Chascuns N   24 Et les O;
menconges OX; conter O   25 il ont KNOPX, i a L; tele
T, mainte KLNOPX   27 Et L; Si men estuet s.   O   28
chascun PTX; t. nie LP, niee N
V   29 A. b. doit remembrer O   30 q. bee O, prie T
31 Q. mieuz O   32 PLus est ma poinne d.   O   35 De rien
qui ne O
VI   36 B. mj T; peust KOP, pouisse L, poist NX   37
Sauf O; en *missing in LO*   38 li] le PT   39 Q. nen aj
T, Q. ie nai KLNOPX   40 Q. ne KLNOPX; encontrer O   41
li] mi X   42 Sest O; amant KN
      Between stanzas II and III, U has the following stanza:
                  Moult m'avroit Deus honoreit
                  Se s'amours m'ieret donee.
                  Onkes ci tres grans biateiz   (ci = si)
                  Ne vi an nule rien nee:
                  Cors ait gent, viz coloreit;
                  Tut li bien sont asanbleit
                  An la tres bien eüree.

      E   Brandin, 252-253; Huet *Gace*, 69-71; PetDyg *Gace*,
216-219; Van dW *Trouv*, 425-428, 586.

      N   For a rhetorical analysis of this poem, see Zum-
thor *Es*, pp. 236-239.   8 Understand *que* after *set*.   25
'For which purpose they gather'.   28 'When each denies his
deceitful behavior'.   The form *nee*, like l. 30 *pree*, is unusual; one would expect *nie* (*prie*) or even *neie* (*preie*) or
noie (*proie*), none of them, of course, occurring as a proper
rhyme-word here.   29-35 We might well question the authenticity of this stanza, which is present only in mss. MOT.
It breaks the thematic continuity of stanzas 4 and 6, both
concerned, at least in part, with false lovers.   Line 30
anticipates l. 39 to an extent unusual in this poem, just as
ll. 32-33 seems a rather suspect reworking of l. 26.   It is
exceptional, moreover, to find a poem by Gace both composed
in *coblas unissonans* and containing more than five stanzas
(exclusive of an envoy); an examination of the 69 songs
attributed with certainty to Gace in PetDyg *Gace* reveals 26
composed in *coblas unissonans*, only three of which exceed

five stanzas: no. 21, RS 1119 = 1751; no. 39, RS 233; no.
67, RS 948. Of these, the first, with six stanzas, contains
one that may well be inauthentic (as noted in PetDyg *Gace*,
p. 261); the second, with seven, includes two that appear so
(p. 319); and the third, with six, is a *jeu-parti*, in which
that number of stanzas is normal.   44 *Gui* designates Gui
de Ponceaux, to whom Gace addresses no fewer than five
songs. The implication of ll. 44-45 is that Gui has recently died. In a lengthy examination of his identity,
PetDyg *Gace*, pp. 74-84, concludes that Gui was quite possibly the same person as the celebrated trouvère known as
the Châtelain de Couci; in any case, it appears that RS 838
dates from about 1200.

Chanson   <u>101</u>

RS 1006, MW 885
Mss. O 15v-16r, C 175v-176r, M 25v-26r, P 22v-23r, T 161v-
      161r. Music in MO. Attribution in MPT and in text.

I   Biaus m'est estez, quant retentist la bruille
       Que li oisel chantent per le boschage

    Et l'erbe vert de la rosee muille
    Qui resplandir la fait lez le rivage.   4
    De bone Amour vuil que mes cuers se duille,
    Que nuns fors moi m'a vers li fin corage;
    Et nonpourquant trop est de haut parage
    Cele cui j'ain; n'est pas droiz qu'el me
                                        [vuille. 8

II   Fins amanz sui, coment qu'Amors m'acuille
     Car je n'ain pas con hon de mon aage,
     Qu'il n'est amis qui aint ne amer suille
     Que plus de moi ne truit amors sauvage.   12
     Ha, las! chaitis! ma dame qui s'orguille
     Vers son ami, cui dolors n'assoage!
     Merci, Amors, s'ele garde a parage: 15
     Donc sui je mors! mais pansés que me vuille.

III De bien amer Amors grant sen me baille,
     Si m'a trahi s'a ma dame n'agree.
     La voluntez pri Deu que ne me faille,
     Car mout m'est bon quant ou cuer m'est
                                    [entree; 20
     Tuit mi panser sunt a li, ou que j'aille,
     Ne riens fors li ne me puet estre mee
     De la dolor dont sopir a celee.
     A mort me rent, ainz que longues m'asaille. 24

IV   Mes bien amers ne cuit que riens me vaille,
     Quant pitiez est et merciz obliee
     Envers celi que si grief me travaille
     Que jeus et ris et joie m'est veee.   28
     Hé, las! chaitis! si dure dessevraille!
     De joie part, et la dolors m'agree,
     Dont je sopir coiement, a celee;
     Si me rest bien, coment qu'Amors m'asaille. 32

V   En mon fin cuer me vient a grant mervoille,
     Qui de moi est et si me vuet ocire,
     Qu'a essïent en si haut lieu tessoille
     Dont ma dolor ne savroie pas dire.   36
     Ensinc sui morz, s'Amours ne mi consoille,
     Car onques n'oi per li fors poinne et ire;
     Mais mes sire est, si ne l'os escondire:
     Amer m'estuet, puis qu'il s'i aparoille.   40

VI   A mie nuit une dolors m'esvoille,
     Que l'endemain me tolt jöer et rire,

Qu'a droit consoil m'a dit dedanz l'oroille
Que j'ain celi pour cui muir a martire.   44
Si fais je voir, mes el n'est pas feoille
Vers son ami, qui de s'amour consire.
De li amer ne me doi escondire;
Nou puis noier, mes cuers s'i aparoille.   48

VII   Gui de Pontiaux, Gasçoz ne set que dire:
      Li deus d'amors malement nos consoille.

MN   Ms. M has a second melody. Form: A A B; the envoy is sung to ll. 7-8.
1. In l. 1 ms. writes a bar.

RR   I   3 de rosee se moille   5 c. sesuoille   6
fin] son   7 paraige   II   10 hons   11 amis ne hons
qui a. s.   13 d. a cui   16 D. ie sui m. m. p. quele v.
III   18 Si me trahit   21 s. en li ou quele aille   22
rien; estre amee   IV   25 Vers b. amer ie cuit riens ne
mi v.   28 m. uaee   32 messaille   V   34 est] uient
35 Fiers est li cuers quen si h. l. trauaille   36 Donc
VI   41 tolc

V   Stanzas: C   I   II   III   IV   V   VI   VII
                 P   I   II   III   IV   V   VII
                 MT   I   II   III   IV   VI (only 47-48)
                                                         VII
I   1 Biau P; Or uient e. C; ke (que M) r. CMT   2 li]
cil C   3 vers T   4 Ke C; le f. T   5 m. cors P;
cesuelle C   6 Car MT; ferm c. MT   8 C. que P; droiz
missing in C; ke (que M) CMT; moi v. C
II   9 c. kelle m. C, c. chascuns m. T   10 Mais MT
11 Ki est T; mest auis C; kil C; a. et P; ne kamors s.
C; veuille M, voille T   12 Qui M, Ki T; ne *missing in*
C; truisse CP, truist MT; amo(u)r MT   13 d. a cui C, a
qui P   14 qui P; dolor C, dolour M, doleur P; nasous-
haige T   15 s. esga(i)rde p. CMT   16 pensers MT; qel
me P; vaille MT
III   17 grant] quant T; sens MPT   19 volente MPT; ne
men P   20 Ains mest mult C; bel CMT   21 Tout MT;
pense MP   22 mee] ree MT, mire P   24 mort] li C; a.
que que l. m. P
IV   25 biens CT; amer P; ne croi C   26 Quar M, Car
T   27 Senuers P; cele qui MP, celuj ki T; si sì g. T
28 Ke ris et ieus C   29 ch. com d. deseureie C   30
dolours T   32 bien] bon P
V   33 De CP   35 A e. et forment me trauaille P   36

Ma grant doleur P; noseroie p. d. C   37 Enfin C, Issi
P; me c. CP   38 o. no C; por CP   39 M. mi P; contre-
dire C   40 q. i P
VI 41 dolor C   42 lou demain C   45 mais elle nest
pais fole C   46 a. ke por s. C   47 De bien a. C; me
puis e. MT   48 Nen (Nem T) p. muer MT
VII 49 Guis C; ponciauls C, ponciaus M, pontiaus P,
ponceaus T; iacos C, gacez P; p. ne sai de ce q. (cou ke
T) d. MT   50 Le dieu P

    E   Huet *Gace*, 4-6; PetDyg *Gace*, 219-222; Chastel,
408-413; Van dW *Trouv*, 438-439, 587.

    DF   Burgundian, including *uil(le)* for *ueil(le)*, as in
bruille (1), *vuil* (5); *oille* for *eille*, as in *mervoille*
(33); *poinne* (38) for *pein(n)e*; *nuns* (6) for *nus*.

    N   The rhyming of this poem is noteworthy, both for
the finely nuanced series *-uille/-aille/-oille* and for the
repetition of *parage, vuille/celee, m'asaille/escondire,
aparoille* (*coblas retronchadas*). For discussion of the poetic
persona, see Xenja von Ertzdorff, "Das Ich in der höfischen
Liebeslyrik des 12. Jahrhunderts," *Archiv für das Studium
der neueren Sprachen* 197 (1960-61), 1-13. For formulaic
language, see E. Vance, "Notes on the Development of Formulaic Language in Romanesque Poetry," *Mélanges Crozet*
(Poitiers, 1966), 1:427-434.
    12 The relative *Que* serves here as a nominative.   13
Exclamation with no main verb: 'my lady who is haughty toward her lover, whose grief she does not alleviate!' Huet
Gace has a question of doubtful interpretation: *ma dame a
cui s'orgueille/Vers son ami, cui dolor n'assoage?* PetDyg
Gace sees instead both a question and an answer in these
lines: *ma dame a cui s'orgueille?/--Vers son ami, cui dolour
n'assouage*, in which *a* and *vers* are apparently interchange-
able in function.   15 '[Have] mercy, Love, if she takes
rank into consideration'.   16 *pansés que me vuille* 'try to
make her want me'.   19 Understand: *[je] pri Deu que la vo-
luntez [de bien amer] ne me faille*. Cf. the construction of
1. 25.   32 *rest = re + est*.   33-34 The subject of *vient*
and antecedent of *Qui* is 1. 32 *Amors*.   45 *feoille* 'faithful'.   48 *Nou puis noier* 'I can not deny it'.   49 For
Gui de Pontiaux, see RS 838, note.

Chanson   102

RS 1465, MW 611
Mss. O 89v-90r, C 170r-v, K 92, L 61r-v, M 26v-27r, N 36v, P
      27v-28r, T 162v-163r, V 73r, X 66v-67r. Music in all
      mss. except CP. Attribution in KMNPTX and in text.

I   Oëz por quoi plaing et sopir,
       Seignor, n'en fais pas a blasmer.
       Touz jors m'estuet ma mort servir--
       Amors! n'en puis mon cuer oster;
       Mais honor ai d'ensinc morir,   5
       Si en vuil bien les maus souffrir
       Tant qu'a plus en puisse monter.

II   S'Amors me fait ses maus sentir,
       Il ne m'en doit mie peser,
       Qu'autres nou puet mais soustenir   10
       Une hore sanz soi reposer,
       Mais je sui amis sanz mentir.
       Ja Deus ne m'en lait repentir,
       Car en amant vuil bien finer.

III   Amors, tele hore fu jadis   15
       Qu'estre me laissïez en pes;
       Mais or sui je verais amis,

N'autre riens ne m'agree mes.
Serai je donc de vos ocis?
Nenil! Trop avrīez mespris,   20
Quant je tout por vos servir les.

IV   Cuers, qu'en puis mes se sui pensis,
      Quant tu m'as chargié si grief fes?
      "Ha! cors, de neant t'esbahis:
      Ja n'ama onques hom mauvais.   25
      Ser tant que tu aies conquis
      Ce que plus desirres toz dis."
      Voire, cuers, mes la morz m'est pres.

V   Gui de Pontiaus, en fort prison
      Nos a mis Amors, sanz confort   30
      Vers celes qui sanz achoison
      Nos ocirront. Dont n'est ce tort?
      Oīl, car léaument amon;
      Ja ne nos en repentiron:
      Bon amer fait jusqu'a la mort.   35

VI   Gaçot define sa chançon.
      Ha! fins Pyramus, que feron?
      Vers Amors ne somes jor fort.

MN   Mss. KLNX are written a 5th higher; ms. T has a
second melody; ms. V has a third one. Form: A A B; the envoy is sung to ll. 5-7.
1. In ll. 3-4 ms. writes a bar. 2. In l. 2 ms. writes no
flat. 3. Ms. writes F-sharp.

RR   I   5 M. en cuer ai d'e. amer   7 Iusqua   II
10 p. mie soffrir   11 hore missing   12 Et   III   16
Que uos me l. estre en p.   18 Naurai rien qui m. m.   IV
23 tu me charges   24 de] se   25 hom] cuers   26 maies
28 est p.   V   32 N. o. nen ont il t.   33 amons   34
repentirons   VI   36 Guiz d. (-1)   37 ferons

V   Stanzas: CL   I   II   III   IV   V   VI
                  KNPX   I   II   III   IV   V
                     V   I   II   IV   V
                    MT   I   II   III   IV
I   1 Sauez M, Saues T   2 Seigneurs KNPVX   3 servir]
hair V   4 Amor C, Amer L, Damo(u)rs MT; ne MT   5 M.
anor KX, amor P, honeurs (-ors T) mest d. MT; dausi P
6 v. mieus ma mort s. MT   7 qu'a missing in P, que KLN
VX, ke C; monstrer L, montrer V

II   8 Amo(u)rs KLNPX; f. cest mal C; sou(s)frir KL,
so(s)frir NVX   9 Si n. L, Ne men doit il m. p. KMNPTX
10 Quamors V; nen C, nes M, mi L, ne KNPTVX; peust
sostenir L   11 soi deporter K   13 n. me M, mj T;
doinst r. CT   14 en riant V; fine P
III   15 tel LM; fut C, fui L, vi M, vic T   16 Ques-
ter KNPX, Que ne L, Que vous M, Ke vous T; lessisiez P;
le pais T   17 j. urais L, loiaus MT   18 Cautre M,
Kautre T; rien LP; ne me grieue m. CMT   19 de] par MT
20 aueries CT   21 Car C   22-23 *missing in MT*
IV   22 mes] ie C   23 si grant PVX; fes *missing in P*
24 Ha cuers MT; n. esbahiz L   25 Ie namai LP; hons
CKNX, cuer m. L   26 Fors que tant t. a. c. L   27 C. q.
as desirre V   28 cuer KNPX, cors MT; mort KLNPVX
V   29 Guis C, Quens L; pontials C, ponciax KN, ponciaus PX, pontieu L, bouci V   30 Vos CLV   31 cel(l)e
CL; ke C, que P   32 Vo(u)s CV; occirait C, ocirra L;
d. elle ait t. C; torz L   33 O. quant C, pour V; amons
C, amours L, amer V   34 Ja damors ne vous partiront V;
repentirons C, departiron KNX, departironz L
VI   36 Iaicos C   37 piramus C, paramus L; ferons C,
feronz L   38 V. a. nan serons ia fors L

E   Huet *Gace*, 50-52; PetDyg *Gace*, 230-233; Van dW
Trouv, 474-477, 590.

N   3-4 *ma mort servir--/Amors!* 'serve death--[that
is,] Love!' The identification of *mort* with *Amors* is surely
intended.   10 *nou = ne + le*; the pronoun designates the
phrase *sentir ses maus*.   29 For *Gui de Pontiaus*, see RS
838, note.   31 *Vers* 'against, in the face of', as in l.
38.   37 *Pyramus*, the lover of Thisbe, often occurs in OF
literature as an exemplar of the perfect lover. PetDyg
Gace, p. 78, sees the name here as a *senhal* for Gui de Ponceaux.

Chanson   103

RS 1578, MW 891
Mss. M 38r, H 223v-224r. Music in M. Attribution in M.

1.Li con-   sir-rers de mon pa- is
3.qu'en es-   tran-ges ter- res lan-guis,

2. si lon- gue- ment me trait a   mort,
4. las, sanz de- duit et sanz con-   fort;

B 5. et   si dout mout mes a- ne-   mis

6. qui de moi mes-di- ent a   tort,

7. maiz tant sent mon cuer vrai et fort

8. que, se Dieu plaist, ne   m'en iert pis.

I   Li consirrers de mon païs
         Si longuement me trait a mort,
         Qu'en estranges terres languis,
         Las, sanz deduit et sanz confort;   4
         Et si dout mout mes anemis
         Qui de moi mesdïent a tort,
         Maiz tant sent mon cuer vrai et fort
         Que, se Dieu plaist, ne m'en iert pis.   8

II   Ma douce dame, ne creez
         Touz ceus qui de moi mesdiront.
         Quant vous veoir ne me pöez
         De vos biauz ieus qui soupris m'ont,   12
         De vostre franc cuer me veez;
         Maiz ne sai s'il vous en semont,
         Quar tant ne dout rienz en cest mont
         Comme ce que vous m'oublïez.   16

III   Par cuer legier de feme avient
         Que li amant doutent souvent,
         Maiz ma loiautez me soustient,
         Dont fusse je mors autrement.   20
         Et sachiez, de fine amour vient
         Qu'il se doutent si durement,
         Car nus n'aime seürement
         Et fainte est amours qui ne crient.   24

IV   Mes cuers m'a guari et destruit,
      Maiz de ce va bien qu'a li pens,
      Et ce que je perdre la quit
      Me fait doubler mes pensemens.   28
      Ensi me vient soulaz et fuit
      Et nonpourquant, selonc mon sens,
      Penser a ma dame touz tens
      Tieng je, ce sachiez, a deduit.   32

V   Chançon, a ma dame t'envoi
      Ançoiz que nus en ait chanté,
      Et si li dites de par moi
      (Guardez que ne li soit celé):   36
      Se trecherie n'a en foi
      Et trahison en loiauté,
      Donc avrai bien ce qu'avoir doi,
      Quar de loial cuer ai amé.   40

MN   The melody is seemingly written in mensural notation. Form: A A B.
1. In ll. 1-2 ms. writes a note without stem. 2. In ll.
3-4 ms. writes a note without stem. 3. Ms. writes a note
without   stem. 4. Ms. writes a longa.

RR   III   23 *missing*   24 F. e. a. que on n. c.
IV 32 Tieg   39 Dont

V   Stanzas III and IV are reversed in H.
I 1 Le   3 En   4 deport   8 Ja s.   II   10 Tot
cals 11 E qant v.   12 b. cels   13 fin c.   15 Car
ren tant ne dot en c. m.   16 Cum ce q. v. ne m.   III
20 Donc   21 bone a.   22 Je me dot si d.   23 segure-
ment   24 E false est amors qui ne c.   IV   25 me garist
26 De ce me v.   27 p. le   30 mos s.   32 Tien io par
droit a grant d.   V   33 Chancos   35 li di bien de p.
mei   36 Garde qil n.   38 e l.   39-40 *reversed*   39 D.
a. io c.

E   Jeanroy "Modène", 262-263; PetDyg *Gace*, 332-335;
Woledge *Peng*, 90-92; Toja, 245-248; Henry *Chrest* 1, 222-223;
2, 66-67; Van dW *Trouv*, 502, 592.

N   16 In both PetDyg *Gace* and Henry *Chrest*, the ms.
H reading is substituted: *Con ce que vous ne m'oubliez.* But,
as the very presence of the construction in M attests, *ne* is
not inevitable following a verb of fearing in OF, and the
emendation is unnecessary. See Moignet, p. 215   29 *quit* =

cuit.   37-38 'If there is no treachery in faith and no
treason in loyalty'.

104   Chanson

RS 1893, MW 1277
Mss. N 35r-v, C 22r, K 89-90, L 60r-v, O 4r-v, P 27r-v, V
    41v-42r, X 65r-v. Music in all mss. except CP. Attri-
    bution in KNPX.

I   A la douçor de la bele seson,
         Que toute riens se resplent en verdor,
         Que sont biau pré et vergier et buisson
         Et li oisel chantent deseur la flor,
         Lors sui joianz quant tuit lessent amor,   5
         Qu'ami loial n'i voi mes se moi non.
         Seus vueil amer et seus vueil cest honor.

II   Mult m'ont grevé li tricheor felon,
       Mes il ont droit, c'onques ne.s amai jor.
       Leur deviner et leur fausse acheson   10
       Fist ja cuidier que je fusse des lor;
       Joie en perdi, si en crut ma dolor,
       Car ne m'i soi garder de traïson;
       Oncore en dout felon et menteor.

III   Entor tel gent ne me sai maintenir   15
       Qui tout honor lessent a leur pouoir;
       Tant com je m'aim, les me couvient haïr
       Ou je faudrai a ma grant joie avoir.
       C'est granz ennuis que d'aus amentevoir,
       Mes tant les hé que ne m'en puis tenir;   20
       Ja leur mestier ne leront decheoir.

IV   Or me dont Deus ma dame si servir
       Q'il aient duel de ma joie veoir.
       Bien me devroit vers li grant lieu tenir
       Ma loiauté, qui ne puet remanoir;   25
       Mes je ne puis oncore apercevoir
       Qu'ele des biens me vuelle nus merir
       Dont j'ai sousfert les maus en bon espoir.

V   Je n'en puis mes se ma dame consent
       En ceste amour son honme a engingnier,   30
       Car j'ai apris a amer loiaument,
       Ne ja nul jour repentir ne m'en qier;
       Si me devroit a son pouoir aidier
       Ce que je l'aim si amoureusement,
       N'autre ne puis ne amer ne proier.   35

VI   Li quens Jofroiz, qui me doit consoillier,
       Dist qu'il n'est pas amis entierement
       Qui nule foiz pense a amour laissier.

    MN   Ms. O has a second melody; ms. V has a third one.
Form: A A¹ B; the envoy is sung to ll. 5-7.

    RR   I 5 amors   III   21 decheir   IV   23
uoir _(-1)_   36-38 _missing_

    V   Stanzas: LOP I II III IV V VI
                       KV   I II III IV V
                        X   I II III IV VI
                        C   I II
I 1 douce s. L 2 r. se reprent CLV, r. resplandist

O; uerdure CL   3   Q. pre sont bel   V   4 li] cil   V; ch.
ensom   O   5   L. ueul ameir   C; que t.   O; amo(u)rs CKLPVX
6 l. ne CO   7 Se v. a. et si v.   O; ceste CLOPV   II
8 M. me grieuent   V; licheor f.   C, traitor f.   K, felon
tricheour   V   9 Et   C; a. nul ior   X   10 Car leur donner
et V; deuineirs   C; et *missing in P*   13 Cains ne mi sou
C   14 dous f.   C; mendiours   L, traitours   CO   III   15
Entre   O; contenir   O   16 to(u)te LOPV   17 j. laing   V,
j. laime le m.   L   19 grant ennui KX; q. tels a.   P   20-
23 *missing in O*   21 ne seront   P; decheir   KP, dechair
VX, deceu   L   IV   22 si] tant LPVX   23 uoir KX   24
d. enuers li l.   V; loi t.   O   25 loiautez   L, leautez   O;
que LOP; puis   L   26 Que j.   L   27 v. nul   L; donner   V
V   31 ap. leaument a amer   O   32 Ne iai   O   34 Se L;
j. aim   P   VI   36 geuffroiz   L, giefrois PX; me dut
LPX   37 Dit PX; que li (li *missing in P*) hons (hom   L)
nest pas e.   LPX   38 f. bee LX; amo(u)rs LPX

   E   Huet *Gace*, 85-86; PetDyg *Gace*, 366-368; Pauphilet,
881-882; Van dW *Trouv*, 538-540, 594.

   N   For comment on this poem, see Payen, pp. 256-258.
27 Understand: *Qu'ele me vuelle merir nus des biens*.   34
Ce que 'the fact that'.   36 PetDyg *Gace*, pp. 27-37, identifies *li quens Jofroiz* as Geoffroi Plantagenêt, son of
Henry II of England and Eleanor of Aquitaine, and count of
Brittany from 1181 until his death in 1186. He is named in
several of the songs of Gace Brulé.

105   Chanson

RS 1690, MW 764
Ms. O 123v-124r. Music. Anonymous (see note below).

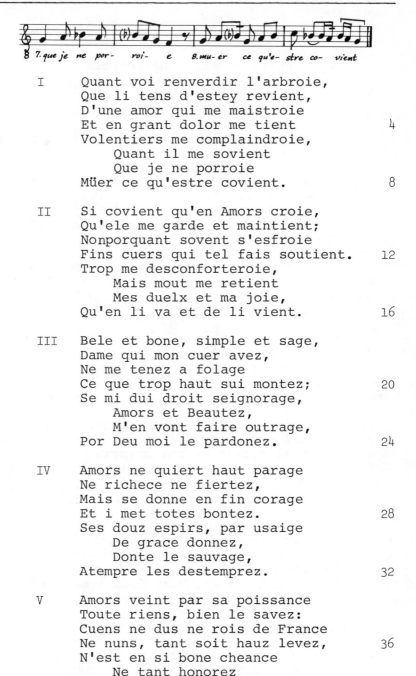

7. que je ne por- roi- e 8. mu- er ce qu'e- stre co- vient

I   Quant voi renverdir l'arbroie,
        Que li tens d'estey revient,
        D'une amor qui me maistroie
        Et en grant dolor me tient   4
        Volentiers me complaindroie,
           Quant il me sovient
           Que je ne porroie
        Müer ce qu'estre covient.   8

II   Si covient qu'en Amors croie,
        Qu'ele me garde et maintient;
        Nonporquant sovent s'esfroie
        Fins cuers qui tel fais soutient.   12
        Trop me desconforteroie,
           Mais mout me retient
           Mes duelx et ma joie,
        Qu'en li va et de li vient.   16

III   Bele et bone, simple et sage,
        Dame qui mon cuer avez,
        Ne me tenez a folage
        Ce que trop haut sui montez;   20
        Se mi dui droit seignorage,
           Amors et Beautez,
           M'en vont faire outrage,
        Por Deu moi le pardonez.   24

IV   Amors ne quiert haut parage
        Ne richece ne fiertez,
        Mais se donne en fin corage
        Et i met totes bontez.   28
        Ses douz espirs, par usaige
           De grace donnez,
           Donte le sauvage,
        Atempre les destemprez.   32

V   Amors veint par sa poissance
        Toute riens, bien le savez:
        Cuens ne dus ne rois de France
        Ne nuns, tant soit hauz levez,   36
        N'est en si bone cheance
           Ne tant honorez

                              Com cil, sanz dotance,
                         Qui bien aimme et est amez.   40

         VI   Douce amors, douce esperance,
                         Douce volentez,
                     En vostre creance
                 Croi que je serai sauvez.   44

         MN   Ms. is mensurally notated. Form: A A B; the en-
voy is sung to ll. 5-8.

         E   Jeanroy-Långfors "Chansons", 20-21; PetDyg *Gace*,
393-395; Van dW *Trouv*, 516, 592.

         DF   Burgundian: *estey* (2) for *esté*; *usaige* (29) for
usage; *nuns* (36) for *nus*.

         N   For attribution to Gace Brulé, see PetDyg *Gace*, p.
149.   21 'If my two true masters'.   29 'Its (Love's)
sweet spirit, granted, as is normal, by grace'.   43 'As
your vassal'.

106   Aube, Chanson de femme

RS 1481, MW 369, B 1453
Ms. C 44v-45r. No music. Attribution (see note below).

         I   Cant voi l'aube dou jor venir,
                 Nulle rien ne doit tant haïr,
                 K'elle fait de moi departir
                 Mon amin, cui j'ain per amors.
                 Or ne hais riens tant com le jour,
                 Amins, ke me depairt de vos.

         II   Je ne vos puis de jor veoir,
                 Car trop redout l'apercevoir,
                 Et se vos di trestout por voir
                 K'en agait sont li enuious.
                 Or ne hais riens [tant com le jour,
                 Amins, ke me depairt de vos].

         III   Quant je me gix dedens mon lit
                 Et je resgairde encoste mi,
                 Je n'i truis poent de mon amin,
                 Se m'en plaing a fins amerous.

> Or ne hais riens [tant com le jour,
> Amins, ke me depairt de vos].

IV   Biaus dous amis, vos en ireis;
A Deu soit vos cors comandeis.   20
Por Deu vos pri, ne m'oblieis!
Je n'ain nulle rien tant com vos.
> Or ne hais riens [tant com le jour,
> Amins, ke me depairt de vos].

V   Or pri a tous les vrais amans   25
Ceste chanson voixent chantant
Ens en despit des mesdixans
Et des mavais maris jalous.
> Or ne hais riens tant com lou jor,
> Amins, ke me depairt de vos.   30

RR   III   15 *followed by supernumerary line* medixant men ont fait partir

E   Tarbé *Chans*, 134; Bartsch-Wiese, 190; PetDyg *Gace*, 441-442; Pauphilet, 878-879; Woledge *Peng*, 89-90; Woledge *Eos*, 371-372, 387-388; Toja, 181-182; Bec 2, 26-27.

DF   Lorraine, including -ai- for -a-, as in *depairt* (6); *poent* (15) for *point*; *amin* (4) for *ami*; adverbial *se* (9, 16) for *si*; *lou* (29) for *le*.

N   There is no certainty that this poem was composed by Gace. As stated in PetDyg *Gace*, p. 156, "cette attribution, vu le peu d'exactitude des rubriques de *C* en général, ne constitue pas une garantie suffisante."
    6 *ke* may be understood as a causal conjunction or as a nominative relative pronoun.   10 The ms. reading *enuious* is ambiguous. The form may be understood, as here and in PetDyg *Gace*, to represent *ennuyeux* (in the medieval sense of 'wrong-doers, those who harm') or, as in Bartsch-Wiese, Woledge *Eos*, and Woledge *Peng*, *envieux*.   25 Understand *que* after *amins*.

Pastourelle

107

RS 367, MW 463, B 1408
Mss. M 99r, T 85v-86r. Music in both mss. Attribution in M.

I   [Les un pin verdoiant
Trovai l'autrier chantant
Pastore et som pastor.
Cele va lui baisant
Et cil li acolant   5
Par joie et par amor.
Tornai m' en un destor:
De veoir lor doçor
Oi faim et grant] talant.
Mout grant piece de jor   10
Fui iluec a sejor
Por veoir lor samblant.

Cele disoit: *"O! a! é! o!"*
Et Robins disoit: "Dorenlot!"

II   Grant piece fui ensi,   15
            Car forment m'abeli
            Lor gieus a esguarder,
            Tant que je departi
            Vi de li son ami
            Et ens el bois entrer.   20
            Lors eu talent d'aler
            A li por salüer;
            Si m'assis delez li,
            Pris a li a parler,
            S'amor a demander,   25
            Maiz mot ne respondi.
        Ançois disoit: *"O! a! é! o!"*
        Et Robins el bois: "Dorenlot!"

III   "Touse, je vos requier,
            Donez moi un baisier;   30
            Se ce non, je morrai.
            Bien me pöez laissier
            Morir sanz recovrier
            Se je le baisier n'ai.
            Sor sains vos jurerai: 35
            Ja mal ne vos querrai
            Ne forceur destorbier."
            "Vassal, et je.l ferai;
            Trois fois vos baiserai
            Por vos rassoagier."   40
        Ele redit: *"O! a! é! o!"*
        Et Robins el bois: "Dorenlot!"

IV   A cest mot, pluz ne dis;
            Entre mes bras la pris,
            Baisai l' estroitement;   45
            Maiz an conter mespris,
            Por les trois en pris sis.
            Ele dit en riant:
            "Vassal, a vo creant
            Ai je fait largement   50
            Pluz que ne vos pramis;
            Or vos proi bonement
            Que me tenez covent,
            Si ne me querez pis."
        Cele redit: *"O! a! é! o!"*   55
        Et Robins el bois: "Dorenlot!"

V   Li baisier par amor
         Me doublerent l'ardor
         Et pluz en fui destrois.
         Par desous moi la tour,   60
         Et la touse ot paor
         Si s'escria trois fois.
         Robins oï la vois,
         Gautelos et Guifrois
         Et cist autre pastor;   65
         Corant issent du bois
         Et je, gabez, m'en vois,
         Car la force en fu lor.
     Puis n'i ot dit "o" n'"a, é, o";
     Robins ne dit puis "dorenlot".   70

MN   Beginning lost in ms. M; melody from ms. T.   Form:
A A B+B rf (ballade). 1. In l. 6 ms. writes a bar.

RR   I 1-9 *from T, since this passage, on f. 98v,
has been excised from M* 5 li] lji-   III   42 Et R. est
el b. d.   IV   45 le estroitement

V   I   11 asseior   II   24 Pus le a aparler   27
Ancors   III   41 Ele dist   IV   44 le   45 le estroitement   48 En riant ele dist   55 redist   V   57
amors   59 en *missing*   69 Puis nj ot o a ne o

E   Monmerqué-Michel, 37-38; Bartsch, 288-290; Maillard *Anth*, 57-60.

N   For a detailed examination of this poem, together
with the other pastourelles of Jehan Bodel, see Foulon, pp.
143-242.   37 *forceur*, comparative of *fort*, modifies substantivized inf. *destorbier*.

Chanson de toile   108

RS 1616, MW 397, B 712
Mss. M 148r-v, T 57r-v, C 33r-v. Music in MT. Attribution
     in all mss.

I   Bele Ysabiauz, pucele bien aprise,
        Ama Gerart et il li en tel guise
        C'ainc de folour par lui ne fu requise,
             Ainz l'ama de si bone amour
             Que mieuz de li guarda s'ounour.   5
                  Et joie atent Gerars.

II   Quant pluz se fu bone amours entr'eus mise,
        Par loiauté afermee et reprise,
        En cele amour la damoisele ont prise
             Si parent et douné seignour,   10
             Outre son gré, un vavassour.
                  Et joie atent [Gerars].

III   Quant sot Gerars, cui fine amour justice,
        Que la bele fu a seigneur tramise,
        Grains et mariz fist tant par sa maistrise 15
             Que a sa dame en un destour
             A fait sa plainte et sa clamor.
                  Et joie atent [Gerars].

IV   "Amis Gerart, n'aiez ja couvoitise
      De ce voloir dont ainc ne fui requise.   20
      Puis que je ai seigneur qui m'aimme et prise,
         Bien doi estre de tel valour
         Que je ne doi penser folour."
           Et joie [atent Gerars].

V   "Amis Gerart, faites ma conmandise: 25
      Ralez vous ent, si feroiz grant franchise.
      Morte m'avriez s'od vous estoie prise.
         Maiz metez vous tost u retour;
         Je vous conmant au Creatour."
           Et joie [atent Gerars].   30

VI   "Dame, l'amour qu'ailleurs avez assise
      Deüsse avoir par loiauté conquise;
      Maiz pluz vous truis dure que pierre bise,
         S'en ai au cuer si grant dolour
         Qu'a biau samblant souspir et plour."   35
           Et joie [atent Gerars].

VII "Dame, pour Dieu," fait Gerars sanz faintise,
      "Aiez de moi pitié par vo franchise.
      La vostre amour me destraint et atise,
         Et pour vous sui en tel errour   40
         Que nus ne puet estre en greignour."
           Et joie [atent Gerars].

VIII Quant voit Gerars, qui fine amours justise,
      Que sa dolour de noient n'apetise,
      Lors se croisa de duel et d'ire esprise,   45
         Et pourquiert einsi son atour
         Que il puist movoir a brief jour.
           Et joie [atent Gerars].

IX   Tost muet Gerars, tost a sa voie quise;
      Avant tramet son esquïer Denise   50
      A sa dame parler par sa franchise.
         La dame ert ja pour la verdour
         En un vergier cueillir la flour.
           Et joie [atent Gerars].

X   Vestue fu la dame par cointise;   55
      Mout ert bele, grasse, gente et alise;
      Le vis avoit vermeill come cerise.
         "Dame," dit il, "que tres bon jour

Vous doint cil qui j'aim et aour!"
Et joie [atent Gerars].   60

XI   "Dame, pour Deu," fait Gerars sanz faintise,
      "D'outre mer ai pour vous la voie emprise."
      La dame l'ot, mieus vousist estre ocise.
          Si s'entrebaisent par douçour
          Qu'andui cheïrent en l'erbour.   65
      Et joie [atent Gerars].

XII   Ses maris voit la folour entreprise;
      Pour voir cuide la dame morte gise
      Les son ami. Tant se het et desprise
          Qu'il pert sa force et sa vigour   70
          Et muert de duel en tel errour.
      Et joie [atent Gerars].

XIII De pasmoisons lievent par tel devise
      Qu'il firent faire au mort tout son servise.
      Li deus remaint. Gerars par sainte eglise 75
          A fait de sa dame s'oissour.
          Ce tesmoignent li ancissour.
      Or a joie Gerars.

MN   Ms. T has another melody for the B-section.
Form: a a B rf (ballade).

RR   VIII 43 iustice   44 napetice   XIII 78 Et
ioie atent Gerars (*reading from* C)

V   Stanza VI not included in C.
I   2 A. G. par amors en t. g. T   3 Kains de f. ne fut
per luj r. C   II   7   amor C; entre aus T, entre eaus
C   10 Sai T   12 G. *added in* T, gir^S. *added in* C
III   13 amors T   15 tant *missing in* C   18 atent *not
given in* T   IV   20 c. uos loj d. ains C   22 doie C
24 atant gir^S. *added in* C   V   28 Meteis uos tost en
cel r. C   30 atant. *added in* C   VI   36 at. G.
added in T   VII   37 f. Gierarars T   38 m. mercit C
39 amors T   41 en *missing in* T   42 atent gir^S.
added in C   VIII   43 amor C   44 dolors T
45 croise T; L. sen retorne de d. et d. espris C
48 atant gir^S. *added in* C   IX   50 Devant T, Dauant
C   54 atant gir^S. *added in* C   X   56 b. grail(l)e et
gra(i)sse et a. TC   58 fait il C   60 atent gir^S.
added in C   XI   66 atant gir^S. *added in* C

XI 66 atant gir^s. *added in C*   XII   68 cuidait C   69
mesprise TC   71 tele e. T   72 *missing in T*; atant
gir^s. *added in C*   XIII   73 pamison T, pamexon C; par
tel *missing in C*   74 Que (Et C) il font f. TC   77 tesmoigne C   78 Et ioie atent gierars T, Or ait ioie Gi-
rairs C

E   P. Paris, 5; Leroux de Lincy, 94-100; Bartsch, 57-
59; Brakelmann 2, 107-109; Cullmann, 99-101, 135-137;
Bartsch-Wiese, 156-157; Brittain, 177-179; Spaziani *Ant*, 77-
80; Cremonesi, 180-183; Gennrich *Alt Lied* 1, 41-45; Saba,
92-97; Toja, 340-344; Bec 2, 39-41.

N   For the differences between Audefroi's *chansons de
toile*, of which there are five, and the anonymous ones, see
Jeanroy *Or*, p. 121 ff., Cullmann, and Zink *Chans*, pp. 25-37.
31-35 For the suggestion, based partly on the absence of
this stanza from ms. C but mainly on its content, that st. 6
is inauthentic, see Brakelmann 2, p. 107, and Cullmann, p.
67.   43 *qui* (= *cui*) serves as direct object of *justise*;
cf. l. 59.   50 In Brakelmann 2, Cullmann, et al., *Avant* is
replaced by *Devant* (as in mss. T and C), which is understood
as 'ahead'. The emendation is unnecessary on either of two
counts: first, *avant* may convey the same spatial meaning;
second, the preceding statement *tost a sa voie quise* supports the temporal 'beforehand' no less well.   51 *A sa
dame* is no doubt governed by *tramet* rather than *parler*. The
phrase *par sa franchise* means 'by his [G.'s] authority'; cf.
l. 38, where the same phrase must be understood as 'out of
noble generosity'.   68 Understand *que* after *cuide*.   75
'Their suffering comes to an end'.

RICHART DE SEMILLI

Pastourelle

RS 1583, MW 27

Stanza I: B 537, st. II: B 620 (two other sources), st. III:
B 1900, st. IV: B 1282, st. V: B 462.

Mss. N 81r-v, K 170bis-ter, P 185v-186r-v, V 45r-v, X 121v-
122r. Music in all mss. Attribution in KN.

1. L'au-trier che-vau-choi-   e de- lez Pa- ris,
3. de- scen- di a ter- re, lez li m'as- sis

2. trou-vai pa- sto- re- le gar- dant bre-biz;
4. et ses a- mo-re- tes je li re- quis.

5. El me dist:"Biau si- re, par Saint De- nis,
7. Ja, tant conme il soit me sains ne vis,

6. j'aim plus biau de vos et mult meuz a- pris.
8. au- tre n'a- me- re, je le vos ple- vis,

9. Car il est et biaus et cor- tois et se- nez."

10. Deus, je sui jo- nete et sa- dete et s'aim tes
11. qui joen-nes est, sa- des et   sa-ges as- sez.

II. 20. ja- mes vif ne me trou-ve- rez.

21. Tres dou-ce da-moi- se- le, vos m'o-cir- rez, 22. se vos vo- lez!

III 31. Ce- ste pa-sto- re- le: 32. Va-li du-re- aus li du- re- aus lair- re- le!

IV 41. por ce les mau- di." 42. Ma-le honte ait il qui A- mors par- ti

I   L'autrier chevauchoie delez Paris,
     Trouvai pastorele gardant berbiz;
     Descendi a terre, lez li m'assis
     Et ses amoretes je li requis.
     El me dist: "Biau sire, par saint Denis,   5
     J'aim plus biau de vos et mult meuz apris.
     Ja, tant conme il soit ne sains ne vis,
     Autre n'ameré, je le vos plevis,
   Car il est et biaus et cortois et senez."
     Deus, je sui jonete et sadete et s'aim tes   10
     Qui joennes est, sades et sages assez!

II   Robin l'atendoit en un valet,
     Par ennui s'asist lez un buissonet,
     Qu'il estoit levez trop matinet
     Por cueillir la rose et le muguet,   15
     S'ot ja a s'amie fet chapelet
     Et a soi un autre tout nouvelet,
     Et dist: "Je me muir, bele" en son sonet,
     "Se plus demorez un seul petitet,
         Jamés vif ne me trouverez."   20
     Tres douce damoisele, vos m'ocirrez
             Se vos volez!

III Quant ele l'oï si desconforter,
     Tantost vint a li sanz demorer.
     Qui lors les veïst joie demener,   25
     Robin debruisier et Marot baler!
     Lez un buissonet s'alerent jöer,
     Ne sai qu'il i firent, n'en quier parler,
     Mes n'i voudrent pas granment demorer,
     Ainz se releverent por meuz noter   30
             Ceste pastorele:
     Va li durëaus li durëaus lairrele!

IV   Je m'arestai donc illec endroit
     Et vi la grant joie que cil fesoit
     Et le grant solaz que il demenoit   35

Qui onques Amors servies n'avoit,
Et dis: "Je maudi Amors orendroit,
Qui tant m'ont tenu lonc tens a destroit;
Je.s ai plus servies qu'onme qui soit   39
N'onques n'en oi bien, si n'est ce pas droit;
        Por ce les maudi."
Male honte ait il qui Amors parti
    Quant g'i ai failli!

V   De si loing conme li bergiers me vit,
    S'escria mult haut et si me dist: 45
    "Alez vostre voie, por Jhesu Crist,
    Ne vos tolez pas nostre deduit!
    J'ai mult plus de joie et de delit
    Que li rois de France n'en a, ce cuit;
    S'il a sa richece, je la li cuit   50
    Et j'ai m'amīete et jor et nuit,
        Ne ja ne departiron."
    Danciez, bele Marion!
    Ja n'aim je riens se vos non.

    MN   Ms. X is written in a modern hand; ms. V has a
second melody. Form: A A A^1 b vrf (b+b).
1. In l. 11, ms. writes *f.* 2. None of the manuscripts gives
music for refrains 2-5, which is here conjecturally derived
from that of refrain 1. 3. Lines 10-11 also occur in RS 824
and 979 with another melody which, however, does not fit
rhythmically into the context here.

    RR   I   11 joenne est et s.   II   16 ia ia asamie
17 unt   21 morcirrez   III   23 el *(-1)*   IV   34 vit
35 granz   V   48 mult *missing*   49 cuiit

    V   Lines 1-27 and beginning of l. 28 missing in X in
their original form; the present folio 121, of 18th-century
origin, offers a copy of these lines as they appear in N.
Stanza V not included in PV.
I   3 delez V   4 Et et s. P   5 Il K, Ele m. V   6
et et P   7 com il V; ne mors ne v. V   8 namerai KPV
11 Q. iones (iennes V) e. KPV   II   12 matendoit K
14 sestoit K   15 rousee et V   16 fet un ch. V   20
ne mi KPV; verrez V   21 Tres] He V; besselete P   III
23 ele l. P, cele l. V   24 lui P   28 que il f. V
29 longuement d. V   32 lairrele] la durele X   IV   35
quil d. X   36 seruie V   37 di PV   38 mont tant P
39 que honme q. V   40 b. ce nest une droiz V   42 cil

q. a. pert V   V   44 con li KX   49 ce] se X   50
quit X

E   La Borde *Es*, 214; Monmerqué-Michel, 32-33;
Bartsch, 242-243; Steffens "Richart", 354-356; Gennrich *Rot*,
35-37.

N   The metric structure of the decasyllabic lines is
variable, as is sometimes the case in pastourelles and similar compositions; cf. RS 1984. For a discussion of the
question, with specific reference to this song, see Burger,
pp. 44-46. For the view that these lines are not meant to
be variable, that they require emendation so as to conform
either to a 9- or to a 10-syllable pattern, "qu'il faut
opter entre les deux systèmes," see p. 443 in A. Jeanroy's
review of Steffens "Richart" in *Romania* 31 (1902), 440-443.
     25-26 'You should have seen them . . ./ If only you
had seen them . . .!'   42 *qui = cui*, i.e., 'whom Love has
favored'.   50 *cuit*, 1st-pers. pres. ind. of *quiter* 'con-
cede'.

110   Pastourelle

RS 527, MW 536, B 1299
Mss. P 97r-v, K 174-175, N 83v-84r, V 47r-v, X 124v-125r.
     Music in all mss. Attribution in all mss. except V.

I   Je chevauchai l'autrier la matinee;
     Delez un bois, assez pres de l'entree,
          Gentil pastore truis.
          Mes ne vi onques puis
          [Ne] si plaine de deduis   5
          Ne qui si bien m'agree.

Ma tres doucete suer,
Vos avez tot mon cuer,
Ne vos leroie a nul fuer;
M'amor vos ai donee.   10

II   Vers li me tres, si descendi a terre
     Por li vöer et por s'amor requerre.
             Tot maintenant li dis:
             "Mon cuer ai en vos mis,
         Si m'a vostre amor sorpris;   15
             Plus vos aim que riens nee."
         Ma tres [doucete suer,
         Vos avez tot mon cuer,
         Ne vos leroie a nul fuer;
         M'amor vos ai donee].   20

III Ele me dist: "Sire, alez vostre voie!
     Vez ci venir Robin qui j'atendoie,
             Qui est et bel et genz.
             S'il venoit, sanz contens
         N'en irīez pas, ce pens,   25
             Tost avrīez meslee."
         Ma tres doucete [suer,
         Vos avez tot mon cuer,
         Ne vos leroie a nul fuer;
         M'amor vos ai donee].   30

IV   "Il ne vendra, bele suer, oncor mie,
     Il est dela le bois ou il chevrie."
             Dejoste li m'assis,
             Mes braz au col li mis;
         Ele me geta un ris   35
             Et dit qu'ele ert tuee.
         Ma [tres doucete suer,
         Vos avez tot mon cuer,
         Ne vos leroie a nul fuer;
         M'amor vos ai donee].   40

V   Quant j'oi tot fet de li quanq'il m'agree,
     Je la besai, a Dieu l'ai conmandee.
             Puis dit, q'on l'ot mult haut,
             Robin qui l'en assaut:
         "Dehez ait hui qui en chaut!   45
             Ç'a fet ta demoree."
         [Ma tres doucete suer,
         Vos avez tot mon cuer,

Ne vos leroie a nul fuer;
M'amor vos ai donee.]   50

    <u>MN</u>   Ms. V has a second melody. Form: a a B rf (vire-
lai).
1. In l. 2 ms. writes a bar. 2. In l. 5 ms. writes *e*;
emended according to mss. KNX; all mss. omit *ne*, and mss.
KNPX compensate by ligating the last two notes in this measure.

    <u>RR</u>   I 5 *-1 (em. Jeanroy)*

    <u>V</u>   I 1 cheuauchoie V 3 p. i truis N 4 Mes]
Si N 7 douce V 7-8 suer uos suer Vos N II 12
veoir XV 16 vos *missing in X* 17 douce seur *added in V*
III 21 ma dit V 22 robin que je ci atendoie V 23
biaux V 25 Ne mariez pas V (=*m'avriez?*) 26 T. a. m.
KNX, T. a. la m. V 27 Ma tres *alone in KNX*, douce seur
V IV 31 encor XV 35 el N; ma KN; gete KNXV; un
douz ris X 36 dist V 37 tres *added in KX*, douce V
V 41 Quant ioi de li fet tot q. m. N; quant quil X 43
dist KXV; quen K; P. d. quen len assaut X 44 Robin son
ami en haut X 45 hui *missing in NV* 47 Ma tres NXV,
doucete suer K

    <u>E</u>   Monmerqué-Michel, 33; Bartsch, 243-245; Schläger,
xxiii; Steffens "Richart", 336-339; Gennrich *Rot*, 54-56.

    <u>N</u>   12 For Steffens "Richart," *vöer* is a reflex of
votare, preceded by dative *li*; the phrase would mean 'to
make avowals [of love] to her'. Jeanroy, in his review
(*Romania* 31 [1902], 440-443), would derive *vöer* from *vedere*,
consider *li* to be accusative, and understand 'to see her'.
The reading *veoir* in mss. X and V lends support to the latter interpretation. 22 *qui = cui*; similarly in l. 45.
32 *chevrie* 'guards goats' or 'plays the chevrie (a kind of
bagpipe)'. 44 *Robin* is the indirect object of l. 43 *dit*.

<u>111</u>   Chanson

RS 1860, MW 1237, B 417
Mss. K 171-172, N 82r-v, P 101r-v-102r, V 46r-v, X 122v-
   123r. Music in all mss. Attribution in KNPX.

1. Par a- mors fe- rai chan-çon 2. pour la tres be- le lo- er;
3. tout me sui mis a ban- don 4. en li ser- vir et a- mer;
5. mult m'a fet maus en- du- rer, 6. si.n a- tent le guer- re- don,
7. n'on-ques n'en oi se mal non. 8. He las! si l'ai je tant a- me- e!
9. Dame, il fust mes bien se-son 10. que vostre a- mor me fust do- ne- e.

I Par amors ferai chançon
  Pour la tres bele löer;
  Tout me sui mis a bandon
  En li servir et amer;
  Mult m'a fet maus endurer,   5
  Si.n atent le guerredon,
  N'onques n'en oi se mal non.
 Hé las! si l'ai je tant amee!
  Dame, il fust mes bien seson
Que vostre amor me fust donee.   10

II Onques riens mes cuers m'ama
  Fors la bele pour qui chant,
  Ne jamés riens n'amera,
  Ce sai je bien, autretant.
  Ma douce dame vaillant,   15
  Bien sai, quant il vos plera,
  En pou d'eure me sera
 Ma grant paine guerredonnee.
  Dame qui je aim pieç'a,
Et quant m'iert vostre amor donee?   20

III Dame ou touz biens sont assis,
  Une riens dire vos vueil:
  Se vous estes de haut pris,
  Pour Dieu, gardez vous d'orgueil
  Et soiez de bel acueil   25
  Et aus granz et aus petiz;
  Vos ne serez pas touz dis
 Ensi requise et demandee.

Dame ou j'ai tout mon cuer mis,
Et quant m'iert vostre amor donee?   30

IV   Se vous vivez longuement,
        Dame, il ert oncore un tens
        Ou viellece vous atent.
        Lors diroiz a toutes genz:
        "Lasse, je fui de mal sens,   35
        Que n'amai en mon jouvent,
        Ou requise iere souvent;
    Or sui de chascun refusee."
        Dame que j'aim loiaument,
      Et quant m'iert vostre amor donee?   40

V   Chançon, va tost sanz delai
        A la tres bele au vis cler
        Et si li di de par moi
        Que je muir por bien amer,
        Car je ne puis plus durer   45
        A la dolor que je trai;
        Ne ja respas n'en avrai,
    Puis que ma mort tant li agree.
        Dame que j'aim de cuer vrai,
      Et quant m'iert vostre amor donee?   50

    MN   Ms. V has a second melody. Form: A A B rf (vire-
lai). 1. Ms. writes *d'*. 2. In the refrain ms. writes an
extra note *f'*. 3. In l. 8 ms. writes no flat.

    RR   III   26 as p.   V   47 arrai

    V   I   6 Si en a. P, Ien a.   V   9 f. bien mes s.
N   II   12 F. la la b. p. q. ie c. N   13 namerai X
14 Ce sachiez b. V   19-20 *not given in V* 19 que iaim
grant piecea X   20 m'iert *missing in P*   III   26 au p.
N, a p. X   28 et] ne V   29-30 D. il fust etc. V   30
Et q. etc. N   IV   32 vns t. V   35 mas s. N   36 ma
j. P   37 fui s. V   39-40 D. il fust etc. V   40 Et
q. etc. N; doner X   V   41 v. tent V, ten X   42
cler vis V   47 respons N   48 li gree V   49-50 D.
etc. V   49 c. uerai NX   50 done N

    E   Noack, 141-142; Steffens "Richart", 360-362.

    N   19 *qui = cui*, dir. obj.   31-38 This motif, well
known later, cf. Ronsard's "Quand vous serez bien vieille,
au soir, à la chandelle," is most unusual in OF lyric.

GAUTIER DE DARGIES

Descort

RS 539, MW 689, 60
Mss. M 90v-91r, C 137r-v, T 147v-148r-v. Music in MT.
Attribution in MT.

VII. 41. La ou Deus a   as- sam- ble   43. t'en va, des-cors, sanz plus di-   re
42. pris et va- leur et   bon- te   45. c'on puet bien par toi es- li-   re

44. fors i-tant, pour l'a-   mour De,
46. que je ne chant fors   pour   le,   47. dont Deus me doint estre a-   me.

I   La douce pensee
  Qui me vient d'amour
  M'est u cuer entree
  A touz jours sanz retour;
  Tant l'ai desirree,   5
  La douce dolour,
  Que rienz qui soit nee
  Ne m'a tel savour.

II   Douce damë, ainc ne vous dis nul jour
Ma grant dolor, ainz l'ai touz jours celee. 10
Mort m'ont mi oeill, qui m'ont mis en errour,
Dont la painne n'iert ja jour achevee;
Je lor pardoinz, quar tant m'ont fait d'onour
Que la meilleur du mont ai enamee.

III   Qui voit sa crigne bloie,   15
  Que samble qu'el soit d'or,
  Et son col qui blanchoie
  Desouz le biau chief sor,
  C'est ma dame et ma joie
  Et mon riche tresor;   20
  Certes, je ne voudroie
  Sanz li valoir Hector.

IV   De si belle dame amer
  Ne se porroit nus desfendre;
  Puiz qu'amours m'i fait penser,   25
  El mi devroit bien aprendre
  Conment porroie achever,
  Puiz qu'ailleurs ne puis entendre.

V   Se je li disoie
  Que s'amours fust moie,   30
  Grant orgueill feroie,
  Neïs se.1 pensoie.

V   Ainz souferrai mon martyre!
Ja ne savra mon penser,
Se par pitié ne remire   35
Les maus que me fait porter;
Car tant redout l'escondire
De sa tres grant volenté,
Tel chose porroie dire
Dont el me savroit mal gré.   40

VI   La ou Deus a assamblé
Pris et valeur et bonté
T'en va, descors, sanz pluz dire
Fors itant, pour l'amour Dé,
C'on puet bien par toi eslire   45
Que je ne chant fors pour lé,
Dont Deus me doint estre amé.

MN   Form: AA BBB CCCC DDD EE FFFF ggHH[1] (lai).
1. Ms. first writes a ternary ligature *d'-c'-b*, then half
erases the last two notes.   2. In l. 3 ms. writes a simple
note *e'*, then repeats it but half erases this.   3. In ll.
11, 19, 45 ms. writes a bar.   4. In l. 9 ms. writes no
rest.   5. In l. 10 ms. first writes this note (figure)
earlier, then half erases this.   6. The fanciful melody to
the first three syllables is replaced in ms. T by 🎵 .
7. In l. 16 ms. first writes this figure a 2nd lower, then
half erases this.   8. In l. 25 ms. writes a descending
plica.   9. In l. 26 ms. writes a binary ligature. 10 In ll.
26, 31 ms. writes no bar.   11. In l. 38 ms. first writes *a*,
c' for the next two words, then erases this.

RR   VII   46 lé] se

V   I   2 damors TC   II   10 La gr. amor C   11
ke mont mis en teil e. C   12 n. iamaix eschiuee C   13
kil mont fait teile honor C   14 del m. en ai amee T
III   16 Ki T; ke TC   18 Deseur som b. T; Per desous
son ch. C   19 et *not in TC*   20 Cest mes riches tressors
C   21 Tant lain ke ne v. C   IV   23 damei C   24 Ne
me douroit nuls blaimeir C   26 El mi T; Elle me d. a. C
27 eschiueir C   28 Quant aillors C   V   30 samor C
32 Nis se le T, Ne se iel C   VI   34 pense T   36
Les m. *followed by a blank space with four musical notes,*
followed by le T; Les m. ke iai endureit C   37 Ke C
38 De ma haute v. C   40 D. iauroie son m. g. C   VII
42 Sen et v. et bialteit C   43 Chanson uai ten s. p. d.
C   44 lamor dex T; F. i. porais bien conteir C   45 p.

tout e.   C   46 Con ne trueue en nul leu sapeir   C   47
Deus lait fait por esgairdeir   C

E   Jeanroy *Lais*, 5-6; Huet *Gautier*, 61-63; Spaziani
Ant, 42-44; Cremonesi, 164-166; Toja, 319-322.

N   For comments on the structure of this piece, see
Maillard *Lai*, p. 141.   4 Despite its six syllables, this
verse is only apparently hypermetric: the final e of l. 3
entree is elided before A, which thus does not appear in the
syllable-count of l. 4.   12 *n'iert ja jour* 'will never
be'.   39 Understand *que* before *Tel*.

113   Chanson

RS 418, MW 2396
Mss. K 127-128, C 104r-v, M 88v-89r, N 75r-v, P 53r-v-54r, T
    144r-v, U 61v, X 88v-89r, a 17r-v. Music in all mss.
    except C. Attribution in all mss. except U.

I   Desque ci ai touz jorz chanté
De mult bon cuer fin et loial entier,
      N'ainc de changier
     N'oi dedenz mon cuer volenté,   4
Ne ma paine ne m'i ot onc mestier.
Bien m'a Amors a son oés esprouvé;
Detenu m'a; ja ne la qier lessier,
Et s'en voit on les pluseurs mes targier. 8

II   Ne sont cil fol maleüré
Dont il est trop por Amors guerroier?
      Par lor pledier
    Avront maint amant destorbé,   12
Ne ja nul d'aus n'i verrez gaaingnier.
De ce deüssent estre porpensé:
Que tels puet nuire qui ne puet aidier;
Mes envïeus ne se puet chastïer.   16

III   Tele gent ont petit amé
Qui se painent de nos contralïer.
      Ce n'a mestier,
    Car ja tant n'avront devisé   20
Que nus doie pour els amors lessier.
Non fera il, s'en li n'a fausseté.
Deus! qui n'aime, de quoi se set aidier?
Voist soi rendre, qu'au siecle n'a mestier.24

IV   Je me tieng mult a honoré
De ce qu'onc jor n'oi talent de trichier
      Ne de boissier;
    Ainz me truis tous tens alumé   28
Si freschement com fui au conmencier,
Oncore m'ait guerredons demoré.
Je me confort en ce qui puet aidier:
En loiauté vueil perdre ou gaaignier.   32

V   L'en m'en a mainte foiz blasmé
De ce que trop me sui mis en dangier,
      Mes foloier
    Voi touz ceus qui le m'ont moustré; 36
Car nus ne puet melz sa poine enploier:
Tost a Amors le plus haut don doné.
Si ne s'en doit nus hons trop merveillier:
Pour sa joie se doit on traveillier.   40

VI   A vous le di, compains Gasse Brullé:

> Pensés d'Amors, de son non essaucier,
> Que mesdisant le veulent abaissier.

MN   Mss. MTUa have a related tune. Form: through-
composed; the envoy is sung to ll. 6-8.
1. Ms. first writes a clef a line too high, then erases it.

RR   Envoy not included in K; reading above from T and
a.   II   11 Pour   12 Ont a maint f. *(-2)*   13 nul] nus
14 e. bien p. *(+1)*   III   24 Deusse s. *(+2)*   IV   26
De ce que onc noi ior t. de t. *(+1)*

V   I   1 Dusques M, Duska T, Iusca C, Jvsqa U
2 De m. (mon T) fin c. bon (boin T) MT   3 Nains Xa,
Nais C, Ne U; faus(s)er MT, chanter a   5 la p. CU; mi
eust m. MTaCU   6 o. retenu P, ato(u)rne MT   7 Retenu
MTaU, Retenut C; m. iamais (-z M) nel (nen a) q. MTa, m.
ne ia (iai C) nel q. CU   8 Et si a; voi ie (iou Ta,
ieu C) MTaCU; p. esloignier CU
II   9 Ce MT, Che a, Se C, Ceu U; font c. C, folit c.
U; li f. MTa   10 *occurs as 1. 18 in CU*; par X; amo(u)r
aC   11 Po(u)r PXa   12 Ont a maint d. NPX, Ont m. a. d.
M, Ont a m. a. d. Ta   13 nus NP, un MTaC; uenres a; v.
ieu g. C   14 deuroient MTaCU; e. bien p. N   15 *occurs
as 1. 23 in CU*; tel NX; Teis (Tels U) p. n. ke (que U) il
ne p. a. CU   16 *occurs as 1. 24 in CU*; ne puet on (nus
T) ch. MT
III   17 Cele MTa, Ceste CU; gens T, genz U   18
occurs as 1. 10 in CU; poene C; dautrui c. MT   19 Se nai
C   20 Car *missing in X*, Que PaU, Ke TC; j. nauront tant
d. CU   21 nus] on MT, len a, ie C, jeu U; els] ce M,
cou T, che a, ceu CU; lame(i)r l. CU   22 N. fait nus
voir M, fait il voir T, fait nul uoir a, fait uoir nu(l)s
CU; li] lui XMTaU   23 *occurs as 1. 15 in CU*; D. ke C
24 *occurs as 1. 16 in CU*; Deust NPX, Voi a; se MTCU; r.
au T
IV   25 Molt CU; t. a bon (boin T, boen U, bone a, bien
C) eure (eureit C) MTaCU   26 que ainc noi ior tal. N,
que noi onc ior tal. X, quainz j. n. t. P, conques n. t.
MT, qainques n. t. a, cains j. n. t. C, kainz j. n. t. U
28 tr. damo(u)rs (damour a) a. MTaCU   29 franchement c.
fut C; conmencement P   30 Encores X, Aincores C; guerredon NX; demore *missing in N*   31 J. m. soulas (-laz M)
MTa, Me solais ieu C, Me solaz ie U; c. ke aC, que U
V   33 On P; maintes X; Par (Per C) maintes (-te CU) f.
ma (mait C) on (lon CU) b. MTaCU   34 q. tant MT   36
mont blasme U   37 Que (Ke T) MTa; ie ne puis m. ma p.

e. MTaCU   38 p. grant CU   39 hom t. esmaier MTaCU
40 *missing in N*; sa] tel MTaU, teil C; on] len M
VI   41 compaigne g. et b. a; gaices brulleis C, gazes
brullez U   42 de s. n. enforcier M, de s. non hauchier
a, sonor a es. C, de sonor es. U   43 *not included in MT*;
Car (Que U) li pluxor (plusor U) se poenent (peinent U)
dabaissier CU

E   Dinaux 3, 188-189; Huet *Gautier*, 8-10.

N   See Dragonetti, pp. 299-303, for a study of the
rhetorical development of this poem.   23 *qui* 'whoever'.
30 'Even though my reward has not come'.   41 To the well-
known trouvère Gace Brulé, the poet addresses another song
as well, RS 1223.

Chanson   114

RS 1565, MW 2359
Mss. T 145r-v, A 157r-v, K 130, M 94v-95r, N 76v, P 55v-56r,
    X 90v, a 16r-v. Music in all mss. Attribution in all
    mss.

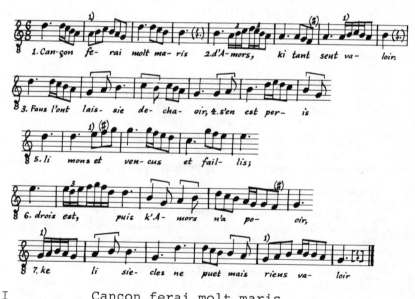

I   Cançon ferai molt maris
            D'Amors, ki tant seut valoir.
            Faus l'ont laissié dechaoir,
                S'en est peris

Li mons et vencus et faillis;   5
Drois est, puis k'Amors n'a pooir,
Ke li siecles ne puet mais riens valoir.

II   Molt nos ont a noient mis
          Amors, ki donoit savoir
          Dames, barons et valoir;   10
              Honors et pris
          En est durement amatis,
          Si ke vous savés tot de voir
Largesce et biens se fait mais peu paroir.

III   Soulas, depors, gieus et ris,   15
          Cortoisie et dire voir
          Voit on mais bien remanoir;
              Bien est traïs
          Chil, cele ki s'en fait eschis,
          Car nus ne puet grant joie avoir   20
K'il ne conviegne en douce amor manoir.

IV   Molt par est faus et chaitis
          Ki n'en set le mieus veoir;
          Ce est legier a savoir,
              Et j'ai apris   25
          A estre a boine Amor sosgis.
          Ki ke le mece en nonkaloir,
Ses liges sui, o li voil remanoir.

V   Amors m'a loié et pris;
          Tos jors serf a mon pooir   30
          Celi ki me fait doloir;
              Molt m'esjoïs
          En çou ke je sui fins amis.
          Se loiautés i doit valoir,
Pas ne faurrai a guerredon avoir.   35

VI   Molt sui garis,
          Quant je sui et serai tos dis
          La ou suel; quoi k'en doie avoir,
Sa volenté voil en gré recevoir.

MN   Mss. KNPX have many common variants, particularly
in ll. 4-5; ms. A has a second melody; ms. M has a third
one. Form: through-composed; the envoy is sung to ll. 4-7.
1. Ms. a writes a *c.o.p.* stem.

RR   II   14 biens] pris   III 19 C. et celes ki
sen font e. *(+1)*   IV   24 Cil est legiers   28 sui *missing*

V   Stanzas: M I II III IV V VI
                 Aa I II III IV V
              KNPX I II III V
I   3 laissee X   5 et] *missing in M*, est P; Li m. peris
et uaincus et f. X   6 na na p.   X   7 siecle N; puist
aA   II   8 Bien n. a a n. m.   KNPX   9 soloit M, done
KNPX; valoir M, auoir aA   10 D. et barons v. KNPX;
sauoir MaA   11 Honor KNPX   12 e. mult forment a. KNPX
13 Et bien sachiez (-s X) uo(u)s to(u)z de v. KNPX   14
bien KNPX; font MKNPX   III 14 S. et ris et doucours
aA, S. gieu et ris KNPX   16 Et c. aAN   17 on] len
KNX; bien] mout M, mult KNPX, *missing in aA*   19 Chascuns
qui M; C. et celes A; cheles a; qui chen font et chis a,
ki ce font et kaitis A   20 nus *missing in KNPX*; ni P
21 c. de d. a. mouuoir M; Ne li c. en fine a. morir KNPX
IV   22 e. folz et M   24 Cil (Chil a) est legiers aA
25 Et *missing in aA*   28 Suens l. s. et li M   V   29
A. mont MKNPX; laschie (lasssie X) et p. KNPX   30 Et si
s. KNPX   31 Cele X; se f. aA   32 Si KNPX   33 En
tant con (que K) sui f. a. KNPX   34 loiaute KNPX; me
puet v. MKNPX   35 Ne puis faillir KNPX; P. ne fausserai
au g. a. aA   VI   38 La u ie sueill que que ien d. a. M

E   La Borde *Es* 2, 155; Dinaux 3, 190-191; Huet *Gautier*, 6-8; Van d W *Trouv*, 155-158, 568.

DF   Picard, including *c* or *k* for *ch*, as in *cançon*
(1), *nonkaloir* (27); *chil* (19) for *cil*; *boine* (26) for *bone*;
çou (33) for *ce*; *le* (27) for *la*; third-person singular present subjunctive *mece* (27) for *mete*; *faurrai* (35) for *faudrai*.

N   3 *Faus* 'false ones' rather than a Picardism for
fous; all mss., including those showing no trace of Picard
scripta, offer the same reading.   6-7 'It is right [that
it should be so], since Love has no power--so that the world
can no longer have any worth'.   Mss. A and a, with subjunctive *puist* for *puet*, would present a perhaps more satisfactory reading: 'It is right, since Love has no power, that
the world should no longer be capable of having any worth'.
9-10 Understand *Ki donoit savoir et valoir [aux] dames [et
aux] barons*.   Huet adopts the reading of KNPX, which would
be understood as *savoir [aux] dames et valoir [aux] barons*,

but in view of the occurrence of a similar asyndetic construction in l. 19, there seems to be no need for an emendation.   17 *remanoir* 'cease, come to an end'; cf. l. 28,
where the word must be understood as 'remain'.   18-19 Huet
Gautier, p. 66, glosses: "'[cependant] ceux qui s'efforcent
de se soustraire à ces vertus se trouvent dupes'."   22
faus, Picardism for *fous* (ms. M *folz*), rather than 'false';
cf. l. 3.   38 The apparent hypermetry that Huet *Gautier*,
p. 66, finds here is due to a misreading of ms. T: there is
no *que* between *suel* and *quoi*.

115   Chanson

RS 684, MW 452
Mss. M 95v-96r, C 93v, K 128-129, N 75v-76r, P 54r-v, X 89r-
    v. Music in all mss. except C. Attribution in all
    mss. except C.

I   Hé, Dieus! tant sunt maiz de vilainnes gens
                Qui en si pou de tens
                Ont de moi dit folie,
          Qu'il cuidoient que teus fust mes talenz

                   Que Joies et Jouvens   5
                   Et Amours fust guerpie
Touz jours par moi, maiz einsi n'est il mie:
Ainz sui et iere a ses conmandemens;
Et lor parlers, vous di que c'est noienz,
Qu'envers Amour ne fis jour trecherie   10
Ne ne ferai a nul jour de ma vie.

II   Ahi, felon plain de grant mautalent,
               A pou d'afaitement,
               Sanz point de courtoisie!
De fauseté estes conmencement,   15
            De mal esmouvement
            Et de grant felenie.
Mout vaut petit chascun sa vilanie:
De mesdire n'est nus profitemens,   19
Si n'est nus preus, ce sachiez, ne nus sens;
Ainz eschivent tuit cil lor conpaignie
Ou il a sens, soulaz et vaillandie.

III   Trestuit cil sunt de mout fol enscïent
            Qui pour lor janglement
            Jöent de repentie;   25
Quar la painne, li travauz, li tourmens
            Est drois avancemens
            D'avoir joie furnie,
Car autrement n'a nus loial amie;
Et qui la quiert par ses losengemens,   30
C'est li cochés qui guenchist a touz vens:
Or amera et puis tantost oublie;
N'est pas sage qui en celui se fie.

IV   Douce dame, li vostres biaus cors gens,
            Vostre vis rouvelens   35
            Conme rose espanie,
Bele bouche vermeille et blans les dens
            Pluz que lis ne argens,
            Gorge blanche et polie:
De grant biauté portez la seignourie.   40
N'est merveille se je a celi pens,
C'une douçours me vient au cuer dedenz
Qui m'aliege mon mal et ma haschie,
Et je sui cil qui del tout l'en mercie.

   MN   Mss. KNPX have a different l. 10.   Form: A A B.
l. In l. 1 ms. writes a bar.

RR   II   18 sa felenie   19 afaitemens   III   30
qu. a ses auancemens   IV   37 les *missing*   43 et mon
martire

V   Stanzas: KNPX   I II IV
                C   I II III
I   1 A KNPX, Hauls C; maiz *missing in P*; vilaine gent
KNXC   3 dit de moi KNX   4 Qui KNPX   5 ioie et (et
missing in X) KNPXC   6 faillie KNPXC   7 j. por C; m.
e. ne est il m.   X   8 sui] fui KNP; son co(n)mandement
KNPXC   9 Et de (del C) parler (parlers P, pairleir C)
v. di q(u)il (kil C) est noient (niant C) KNPXC   10
Kains uers C; jour] onc KNPX
II   15 De f. est uo comencemens C   16 De maluestie *(-2)*
C   18 chascun petit sa felonie P   19 De m. sachiez (-s
X, saichies C) ce (se C) nest pas (pais C) sens KNPXC
20 nul p. P; ne nus (nul P) profitemens (-z K) KNPX,
ne nuls auancemens C   21 to(u)z ceus KNPX   22 sens ho-
nor et vaillantisse C
III   25 Loent C   26 li trauail li torment C   29 Et
C   31 C. la chose C   33 saiges C
IV   34 uostre biau KPX; gent KNPX   35 rouuelent KNPX,
rouellent C   36 esbanie N   37-39 *between* vermeille et
and polie *missing in X*   41 a li pens X   42 douco(u)r
KNPX   43 Q. malegre X   44 del] de KNPX; l'en] la P

E   Dinaux 3, 194-195; Huet *Gautier*, 10-12; Van d W
Trouv, 144-146, 567.

N   31 The *cochet à vent* is a frequent symbol of inconstancy; cf. RS 1078, 11. 79-80, and Tobler-Lommatzsch,
s.v. *cochet*.

116   Chanson

RS 1969, MW 651
Mss. M 92v-93r, A 156r-v, C 202r-v, I 1:19, K 254-255, N
     124v-125r, P 113v-114r-v, R 121r-v, T 143v, U 123v, V
     96v-97r, X 171v-172r. Music in all mss. except CIU. Attri-
     bution in MACT; attributed to Sauvage d'Arras in KNPX.

1. *Quant li tans pert sa cha- lour,*
3. *cil oi- zel pour la froi- dour*

2. que la flours blanche est pa- li- e,
4. nus n'en chan- te ne ne cri- e

5. des- que ce vient en Pa- scour; 6. lors chan-tent et nuit et jour!

7. He las! chai- tis, ein-sinc ne m'est il mi- e:

8. Touz jours ai duel, ainc n'eu joie en ma vi- e.

I   Quant li tans pert sa chalour,
                      Que la flours blanche est palie,
                      Cil oizel pour la froidour
                      Nus n'en chante ne ne crie   4
                      Desque ce vient en Pascour;
                      Lors chantent et nuit et jour!
       Hé las! chaitis, einsinc ne m'est il mie: 7
       Touz jours ai duel, ainc n'eu joie en ma vie.

II   Se je vif en grant poour,
                      Ne vous en merveilliez mie,
                      Puis que li faus trahitour
                      Ont tout le mont en baillie.   12
                      Largece, pris et hounour
                      Et sour toute rienz valour
       Nous ont einsi du tout apeticie
       Et ont tant fait que merciz est faillie.   16

III   Mout ai au cuer grant dolour,
                      Qu'Amours pert sa seignorie,
                      Qui ja ot pris et valour
                      Et joie en sa guarantie.   20
                      Or l'unt leissié li plusour,
                      Li losengier menteour,
       Ou il par a itant de villonie
       Et trahison, orguel et felenie.   24

IV   Mout souvent souspir et plour,
                      Ne sai que face ne die;
                      Et si travaill et labour
                      Tout adés par jalousie   28
                      Que j'ai u cuer a sejour;

            Si me dout de ceste amour:
        Chascuns m'i nuist, ele ne m'i veut mie,
        Einsi puis je bien faillir a amie.   32

V   Adés pens a la meillour,
            Maugré suen: pas ne m'en prie!
            Et s'il me tourne a folour,
            Autrui n'en blasmerai mie,   36
            Fors mes ieus et son atour
            Et sa tres fresche coulour
        Et sa bouche qui tant me contralie;
        Maiz ne li vaut: ja par moi n'iert guerpie. 40

VI   Par Dieu le haut creatour,
            Mout dout ceste gent haïe
            Ou il n'a point de douçour
            Ne pitié ne courtoisie.   44
            Il m'ont mis en grant tristor;
            Maiz toutes voies aour
        Droit cele part u je sai m'anemie,
        Si coiement qu'ele ne m'i set mie.   48

VII   Adés gieu de mon poiour,
        Quar ce que j'aim de la mort me desfie,
        Ne nule autre ne me puet faire aïe.

    MN   Mss. KNPX differ in ll. 5-7 and part of l. 8; ms.
R is written a 5th lower and has a different but related
melody in the B-section; ms. V is written a 2nd lower in the
A-section. Form: A A B; the envoy is sung to ll. 6-8.

    RR   II   13-14 Sour toute rienz et valour/ Largece
pris et hounour *(em. Huet)*   III   20 en *missing*   23 Ou
il par a tant enuie *(-3)*   24 Trahison et felenie *(-3)*
IV   29 Q. ia u

    V   Stanzas: T   I II III IV V   VI VII
                     A   I II III V   IV
                     KNPXR I II V   IV
                     CI   I II IV   V   VI
                     U   I II
                     V   I followed by three unique stan-
                            zas (see below)
I   1 choulour A   2 Quant X; flo(u)r AKNPXRCI   3
Cist A, Ozelet p. U   4 Ne I, Il U; ni T, ne A; noise
V, chantent IU; crient IU   5 Troske T, Tant ke (que V)
AVCIU, Tresque (-s X) KNPX, Jusques R; uient el (a I)

tens p. CI, se v. a la p. U   6 *first* et *missing in X*   8
ains ACIU, ainz V, onc KNPXR
II   9 do(u)lo(u)r KNPXRCIU   10 v. esmeruellies T, em-
meruilies A   11 treceour A, tricheor KNPX, trecheour
R; Car il felon traito(u)r CI, car li fals losangeour U
12 0. si l. U; ont *repeated after* mont *in X*   13 So(u)r
to(u)te riens la valo(u)r TA, Foi (Foy R) et larg. et hon.
KNPXR, Proesse cens et ualour U   14 toutes I; rien C;
amors I; Larg. pris et hon. TAU, Sens et pro(u)e(s)ce et
valo(u)r KNPXR   15 einsi] il si T, isi A, ici U, amors
KPXR, amor N, il pres C, si pres I; aniantie CIU   16
Mais A; tant ont f. AKNPXRU; f. camors si C, merci NPX,
mercit I, pitiez U
III   17 Tant A   19 pr. et honor T, bien et ricour A
21 Or sont remes li p. A   22 treceour A   23 U il a
tant de mal et uilounie A
IV   25 To(u)t ades (adiez R) sousp. KNPXR   26 Ke ne
mesfaice ou mesdie CI   27 Et sen C, san I   28 *missing
up to* sie *in T*; Dire et de j. AKNPXRI, Et dire et de j. C
29 u] au TI, al C, el AKNPXR   30 Mult A, Trop CI; Si
me tient et nuit et ior KNPX, Et si mi tient nuit et iour
R   31 *only* ne le me v. m. *in T*; Chascun NP; me KNPXI; n.
nel(l)e ne me v. m. AKNPXRCI   32 E. p. bien tost f. CI
V   33 Ie me tieng (taing I) TAKNPXRCI   34 pas] point
KNPXR   35 sil ne men t. T; Et se ie (ge P) faz (fas XR)
grant f. KNPXR   36 *missing in T*; Nului A, Nulluj C, Nelui I; Nu(l)s ne men doit blasmer m. KNPXR   37 F. seul
m. *(+1)* KNPXR, F. mon sens A   39 sa] la KNPXR; qui]
dont TKNPXRCI; tant *missing in C*, si I   40 par] pour A;
n'iert *missing in T*
VI   41-42 *blank between* P *and* dot c. *in T*   42 Moi dont
I; cel(l)e TCI   43 ualour CI   44 Pitie ne de c. T,
Maix orguel et felonnie C, Mais orgoil et vilonie I   45
Mis mont il T; Se mont greueit li pluxor C, Si mont greuei
li plusor I   46 toute v. a iour I   47 p. la ou ie sai
mamie I   48 kil ne le seuent m. T, ke nuls (nuns I) nel
persoit (par- I) m. CI
VII   50 Quant T   51 mj p. T
    After stanza I, ms. V presents the following:
    II'   Je me tieng a la meillour
        (Maugré sien: point ne m'en prie!)   10
        Qui soit u mont, et l'aour.
        En li a tant cortoisie,
        Bonté plaine de douçour,
        Senz avoeques grant valour,
        Tous biens en li monteplie.   15

          Bien me seroit avenu
          Se ele m'estoit amie.

III'   Je plaing souvent et si plour
          Et si n'en ai nule aïe
          Et si travail et labour   20
          Et d'ire et de jalousie,
          Puis que li faus tricheour
          Ont toute joie abessie,
          Senz, cortoisie et honour,
          Prouece, largece, valour;   25
     Nous ont amours du tout apetisie
     Et tant ont fet que merci est faillie.

IV'   Se je n'ai de li secours,
          Mis m'avra a grant haschie.
          Mors sui, n'i voi autre tour,   30
          Se ele ne m'est amie.
          Ce est ma greignour paour,
          Mes en ce me resvigour
              Qu'ele est si garnie
          Que tost m'avra donné santé   35
          Par sa bonne volenté,
          S'orgueil ne la contralie.

     <u>E</u>   Huet *Gautier*, 22-25; Van d W *Trouv*, 175-182, 569.

     <u>N</u>   Sauvage d'Arras, to whom several mss. ascribe this
song, is otherwise unknown.   29   *u = en le*; *a sejour* 'per-
manently'.   34   The subject of *prie* is 1. 33 *la meillour*.
35   *il* 'it, that', i.e., the situation just mentioned.   45
Il evidently refers to 1. 42 *ceste gent haïe*.   48   Since
the stanza is chiefly concerned with the lover's reaction to
the *gent haïe*, it would be poetically more satisfying to
adopt the reading of ms. T: *Si coiement k'il* [= *gent*] *ne le
sevent mie*; cf. corroborative variants in mss. C and I.   49
gieu = jo; *poiour = peiour*; 'I play a losing game; I am an
unlucky player'.

THIBAUT DE BLAISON

Pastourelle

RS 293, MW 1492
Mss. M 18v, K 122-123, N 72v-73r, P 61v-62r, T 108r, V 50r,
X 85v-86r, a 109v-110r. Music in all mss. Attribution
in all mss. except Va.

I   Hui main par un ajournant
      Chevauchai les un buisson;
      Les l'oriere d'un pendant
      Guardoit bestes Robeçon.
      Quant le vi, mis l' a raison: 5
      "Bregier, se Dieus bien te dont,
      Eüs ainc en ton vivant
      Pour amour ton cuer dolant?
      Quar je n'en ai se mal non."

II   "Chevalier, en mon vivant   10
      Ainc n'amai fors Marion,
      La courtoise, la plaisant,
      Qui m'a doné riche don,
      Panetiere de cordon,
      Et prist mon fermaill de plom.   15
      Or s'en vait apercevant
      Sa mere qui li deffant,
      Si l'en a mise a raison."

III   A pou ne se vait pasmant
        Li bregiers pour Marion.   20
        Quant le vi, pitiez m'en prent,
        Si li dis en ma raison:
        "Ne t'esmaie, bregeron;
        Ja si ne l'enserreront
        Qu'ele lait pour nul tourment   25
        Qu'ele ne t'aint loiaument,
        Se fine Amours l'en semont."

IV   "Sire, je sui trop dolens
        Quant je voi mes compaignons
        Qui vont joie demenant;   30
        Chascuns chante sa chançon
        Et je sui seus environ;
        Affuble mon chaperon,
        Si remir la joie grant
        Qu'il vont entour moi faisant.   35
        Confors n'i vaut un bouton."

V   "Bregier, qui la joie atent
        D'amours fait grant mesprison,
        Se les maus en gré n'en prent
        Touz sanz ire et sanz tençon: 40
        En mout petit de saison
        Rent amours grant guerredon,
        S'en sunt li mal plus plaisant
        Que on a soufert devant
        Dont on atent guarison."   45

VI   "Chevalier, pour rienz vivant
        N'os parler a Marion
        Et si n'ai par cui li mant
        Que je muir en sa prison
        Pour les mesdisans felons   50
        Qui ne dïent se mal non;
        Ainz vont trestout racontant
        Que j'aim la niece Coustant,
        La fillastre dant Buevon."

MN   Mss. K, N, P, T, X, a are written a 5th higher;
mss. K̄, N, P, X have a different l. 9, ending on f (=c');
ms. V has a second melody. Form: A A B.
l. In l. 3 ms. writes a bar.

RR   I   5 m. le a r. *(+1)*   6 te doint   II   17 Sa
m. par mesdisanz

V   Stanzas: NTa   I II III IV V VI
                 P   I II III IV VI
                 KVX   I II III IV V

I   1 Au m. KNPX, Ier m. T; Hui matin p. i iornant V   2
Chevauchoie l. V   4 Bestes (Beste PT) gardoit KNPTVXa
5 mis le a Va   6 te doinst Ta   7 onc en KNPVX   8
Par amors T; dolant] joiant KNPTVX   9 Car ien as se T
II   10 Chevaliers PV; ens m. T   11 Ains a; Namai-onc
f. KNPVX   12 Le c. et le T; plaisant] vaillant KPTVX,
uailant N   15 print a; plonc V, plont a   16 Or len
N; va V   17 Sa m. qui lamoit tant KNPVX   18 mis   TV;
en prison KNPV
III   19 A poi KNPTa, po V; va KNPVXa   21 le *missing
in N*, la   a; pitie KNPVX   22 Se li d. ens •T   23 tes-
maier KNVX, tesmoier P   24 ne la (nel te V) celeront
(seleront P) KNPVX, ne le sara on T, ne len serreron a
25 Quel ne l. V   27 fine] bonne V; amo(u)r KNPVXa
IV   28 trop] mult T; dolent KNPX, dolant a   29 mi
(maint T) conpaignon KNTX   31 Chascun NPa; chante] note
T   33 Af(f)ublez NV, Aflubes P, Affubles X, Embronchies
T   35 Qui v. a   36 Confort KNPV, Confor X
V   37 Bergiers K; atens KXa, atenz NV   38 fez K, fes
NV, fais TXa; granz KNVa   39 Se] To(u)z KNVX, To(u)s
Ta; em boin gre preg T, gre enpren (enprenz V) KNVX, gre
lenprent a   40 Touz] Tout KNVXa, Et T   41 Ens T   42
Renc T; a. le guerredon K   44 Que on] Q(u)on en KX, Con
en Va, Quen en N, Com on T   45 on] len KNVX; a. guer-
redon X
VI   46 p. nul torment NP   48 cui] qui NPT   49 muir]
sui NP, muire a   50 les] li N; mesdisant NT; felon
NPT   51 non *missing in T*   53 niece] fille NP   54 La]
Le T; Ou la f. b. NP

E   Monmerqué-Michel, 34-35; Tarbé *Chans*, 18; Bartsch,
227-228; Brakelmann 2, 77-78; Faral "Pastourelle", 216-217;
Pinguet, 42-46; Newcombe *Thib*, 86-90.

N   This is a most unusual pastourelle, substituting
shepherd for shepherdess and a discussion of love for the
poet-knight's quest of love. Note, esp. in ll. 48-51, the
perhaps intentionally comic intrusion even into the shepherd's speech of language belonging to the courtly register.
     24-26 'They will never lock her up so [securely] that
she would, whatever her torment, desist from loving you loy-
ally'.   48-49 'And indeed I have no one with whom to send
her the message that . . .'.   53 *la niece Coustant*, absolute genitive; also in l. 54.

118   Chanson

RS 1402, MW 1095
Mss. K 123-124, C 14v-15r, N 73r, O 6r-v, P 62r-v, T 107r,
     U 167v-168r, V 80v, X 86r-v, a 30v-31r. Music in all
     mss. except CU. Attribution in KNPTX.

I   Amors, que porra devenir
        Li vostres frans hons naturiaus,
        Quant cele ne me veut guerir
        Qui je sui fins amis loiaus?   4
            Hé, Deus! pour quoi fui je tiaus
            Que li osai descouvrir
            Les maus qu'el m'a fet sentir?
            Et touz jorz la truis cruaus.   8

II   Enquerant va chascuns vassaus
        Qui cele est pour qui je souspir.
        Et qu'en tient il a desloiaus?
        Mes lessent moi vivre ou morir!   12
            Bien me devroit Deus haïr,
            Se g'iere si conmunaus
            Que g'eüsse dit entre aus
            Dont mal li deüst venir.   16

III   Ançois me leroie partir
        Les menbres et trere a chevaus
        Qu'osasse dire ne gehir
        Qu'amasse nule riens charnaus;   20
            Que li siecles est si faus

Que l'uns veut l'autre traïr.
Ançois diront, sanz mentir,
De quoi servi li graaus.   24

IV   Assez plus cointes et plus biaus
Avendroit il a li servir
Que je ne sui, ne cent itaus;
Et si sui cil qui plus desir   28
A fere tout son plesir,
Car sui ses amis coriaus
Et sai bien celer mes maus
Et en gré prendre et sousfrir.   32

V   Mult par se set bien contenir,
Et mult li siet bien ses mantiaus.
Avis m'est, quant je la remir,
Que soit angres esperitaus   36
Que li rois celestïaus
Ait fet de lassus venir
Pour moi la vie tolir;
Et si sui je ses fëaus.   40

VI   Ma douce dame coraux,
Qui senblés, aprés dormir,
La rose qui doit florir,
Alegiés moi mes douz maux!   44

MN   Ms. V has a second melody. Form: A A B B; the
envoy is sung to ll. 5-8.

RR   III   24   De q. ueut seruir li garauz *(+1)*   IV
30 Et si sui *(+1)*   V   33 set] sout   34 siet] sist   VI
41-44 *envoy missing; reading from N*

V   Stanzas: N   I   II   III   IV   V   VI
                  P   I   II   III   IV   VI
                  X   I   II   III   IV   V
                  V   I   II   III   V
                  Ta   I   II   III   V   IV   VI
                  O   I   IV   V   II   III   VI
                  C   I   V   IV   II   III
                  U   I   IV   III
I   1 ki C; porrai a   2 Si U; vostre PCU; hom VTa,
et U; naturais C   3 elle C; ne mi PVCU; let P, lait
OaCU; oir T   4 Cui VOTC; a cuj s. U; fuj T; fin a;
amans C; coraus O   5 He *missing in X*; He las O, lais
C; fu OU; onc O, ains C, elle U; caus T, itals U   6

Q. ie li V, Cant ne li U   7 que NPXa, quele V; me PO
Ta, mi V; L. m. ke ie sant por li CU   8 la] le Ta, les
U; t. si c. V, t. plus greuals U; Dont t. j. mest plus c.
O, Ades me sont plux c. C
II   10 p. cui OaC; j. languis V   11 Et *missing in N*;
q. monte T; il as (aus V) PXVT; Alor quen tient les d.
O, Ken t. il a sous d. C   12 Lessent moi ou v. V; laisse
C   13 mi a; doueroit C   14 Sestoie s. OT   15 Q. ie
eusse d. P, Q. deisse riens e. C; Q. riens deisse entor a.
O   16 maus Oa, max T, malz C; me O; peust C
III   17 Ainz me VO, Miels me U; l. departir OCU   18
Mes C; Menbre a menbre t. U; m. detraire O; m. et detraire C   19 Que osasse d. V; ne ioir T; Que puissent
enquerre noir O, Ke iai per moi pust on oir C, Ke iosaise
descourir U   20 Que iainme r. O; A uos vn home ch. U;
rien OC; charna(u)l OCU   21 Car NPXU, Et C; mondes O;
si] tant Ta; mals C   22 Q. lum N, lun P, li uns VTa;
Li uns bee a l. t. U   23 Mais ainz (or U) sauront OU,
Ains sauroient C   24 seruoit O; D. q. ueut seruir li
garaux (-aus P, -ans X) NPX, Que ie serf conme home
loiaus V, D. coi seruent si deloial U
IV   25 Dasses p. cointe et a; Mout plus uaillant et leaux
O, Moult plus veillans et moult plus biaz U   26 Couen-
droit O, A(s)ferroit TaC; il] *missing in Ta*, bien CU   27
s. et c. O; Mais ne sui pais de san i. C, Ke ie ne soie en
nul cental U   28 Mais ie s. OU; Ains sui cil ki plux la
d. C   29 Et C; tous ces plaisirs U   30 Et si sui NP
XT; Et sui se samis c. a, Et qui plus uers li sui feaus O,
Car ces amins seux feauls C, Et ke plus li seus feals U
31 Si TaC; Et si s. b. N, Et sa b. X, Et miels sai c.
U; mieuz c. O   32 et sousfrir *missing in O*; Et panre an
greit et santir U
V   33 se so(u)t NXV; bel c. V; M. p. li s. b. son courir
O, M. p. (Deus com C) se(i)t bien son cors cointir TaC
34 li sist NXV; li m. O; Et com li s. b. ces bliaus C
35 A. met a; Il mest uis C   36 Se C   37 cestiaux N
38 A O; f. entre nos v. C; de ses ciels v. O   39 P. a
m. O   40 je s. f. *missing in T*; Qui li sui amis leaus O,
Ki seux ces amis loiauls C
VI   41 leaus O, loiaus Ta   43 q. uuet f. O; Cors con
doie enseuelir a   44 Car nous dounes les coutiaus a

E   Brakelmann 2, 73-74; Pinguet, 2-7.

DF   Poitevin: retention of Lat. free tonic *a* before *l*
makes it possible for such forms as *charnaus* (20), *t(i)aus*

(5), *itaus* (27) to rhyme with *vassaus* (9), *chevaus* (18), etc.

N   4 *Qui* = *cui*.   11 *qu'en tient il* 'what does it matter'.   16 Understand *rien* or the like as antecedent of *Dont*: 'anything from which'.   23-24 To illustrate how far his contemporaries are willing to go in their treachery, the poet maintains that they would even reveal the function of the Grail. (For the tradition of secrecy about the Grail, see Wm. A. Nitze et al., *Le Haut Livre du Graal: Perlesvaus*, II [Chicago, 1937; rpt. New York: Phaeton, 1972], pp. 325-326.) The readings in Brakelmann 2 and Pinguet--*Ainc* ('never') *sauroient*, etc., and *Mais* ('never') *sauroient*, etc., resp., neither of which is wholly authentic (see Variants) --express an uncertain grasp of the sense of the stanza. 27 *itaus* = *tels*.

Chanson de rencontre   119

RS 584, MW 2072
Stanza I: B 189 (one other source), st. II: B 1277 (one
    other source), st. III: B 1782, st. IV: B 1137, st. V:
    B 65 (five other sources), st. VI: B 347, st. VII: B
    1061 (one other source).
Mss. U 72r-v-73r, C 117r-v, H 228v-229r. No music. Anony-
    mous (see note below).

I   Quant se resjoïssent oisel
      Au tens que je voi renverdir,
      Vi deus dames soz un chastel
      Floretes en un pré coillir.   4
      La plus jone se gaimentoit,
      A l'ainneie se li disoit:
      "Dame, conseil vos quier et pri
      De mon mari qui me mescroit,   8
      Et se n'i a encor nul droit,
      C'onques d'amors n'oi fors lo cri."
          A tort sui d'amors blasmeie,
          Lasse! si n'ai point d'ami.   12

II   "Conseil vos donrai boen et bel,
      Por lui faire de duel morir,
      Ke vos faites ami novel,
      Que d'amer ne se doit tenir   16
      Nule dame qui jone soit,
      Ainz face ami cointe et adroit;

Et vos avez cors seignori,
Graille et grasset et lonc et droit.   20
S'uns chevaliers de vostre endroit
Vos prie, s'en aiez merci."
    Mal ait qui por mari
    Lait son leial ami.   24

III   "Mout m'avez bien selonc mon cuer
Conseillie, se Deus me saut.
Or ne m'en tenroie a nul fuer,
Car qui n'aime mout petit vaut,   28
Si com li monz tesmoigne et croit,
Que por mari lassier ne doit
Joune dame ne face ami.
Uns beals cheveliers m'en prioit;   32
Or lo desir, or lo covoit,
Or li outroi m'amor desci."
Toz li monz ne me garderoit
    De faire ami.   36

IV   "Mout m'anuie, ma bele suer,
Quant li jalous ou lit m'asaut;
Adonc en voldroie estre fuer
En prez ou en bois ou en gaut   40
Avoc celui qui me soloit
Proier et qui de cuer m'amoit;
Car li jalous m'anuie si,
De Deu maldi, et j'ai bien droit,   44
Qui lo me dona, qui qu'il soit,
C'onques si tres malvais ne vi."
Je fui mal mise al marïer,
Si me vuel amander d'ami.   48

V   Quachiez m'iere soz un ramier
Pres d'eles por lo meuz oïr.
Atant ai veu un chevelier
A cheval par lo pré venir,   52
Qui mout biaus et jones estoit.
Tantost com la dame aperçoit,
Del cheval a pié dessendi,
Envers eles lo cors aloit;   56
Et qant la tres bele lo voit,
Andeus ses biaus braz li tendi.
    Ansi va bele dame
    A son ami.   60

VI   S'onques li fist mal ne dongier,
       La dame bien li sot merir
       De bel parler et d'acointier
       Et de faire tot son plaisir.   64
       Celle qui toz les biens savoit
       Petit et petit s'esloignoit
       . . . .
       Et quanques cil adés baisoit,   68
       K'es biaus braz s'amie gisoit,
       El chante et note et dit ensi:
       Chescuns [me] dist: "Bele, amez moi."
       Deus! et j'ai si leial ami!   72

VII   Li chevaliers est retornez
       Quant il ot fait tot son plaisir.
       L'autre, qui trestous les biens seit,
       Est revenue vers celi;   76
       Et cele un pou se hontioit,
       Et la dame li demandoit:
       "Ai vos je boen conseil doné?"
       "Oïl, mais petit m'a duré,   80
       Que trop tost sumes desevré,
       Car je l'aim plus que mon mari."
       Je li ai tot mon cuer doné,
       Si n'en ai point avueques mi.   84

         RR   IV   46 m. felon ne ui *(+2)*   VI   62   soit
65 Con cil q.   67 *verse missing*   71 *-1*   VII   75   L.
q. seit de bien assez   84   auuec *(-1)*

         V   Stanzas IV and VII not included in H.
I   2 radoucir C; Au doz tens qil uoient uenir H   3
soz] en C   4 En un pre fl. c. H   5 La p. ioenete se
plaingnoit H   6 Et a lautre souent d. C, A sa compaigne
d. H   9 e. de quoi H   12 He dex H; ie n. C
II   14 P. le ialos faire m. H   15 faciez H   16 Donc
dame n. H   17 Dame nulle ke C   18 Por son mari laissier ne doit *(= 1. 30) followed by* Por riens qele ne face
ami *(= 1. 31)* H   20 Graillet et grais et C, Et gras et
graisle et H   21 bachelers H   22 prioit H
III   25 M. m. or bien consillie C, Or m. b. consel done
H   26 Selonc mon cuer s. CH   27 ne me CH   29 *missing
in H*   30-31 *occur as 11. 18-19 in H*   31 d. ke nait a. C
32 Suns C; bacheliers H; me CH   35 mi g. H
IV   37 douce s. C   38 lit me sent C   40 preit ou en
broil C   43 Maix C   44 Ie lou m. et sai C   45 d.
keils C   47 J. seux C   49-50 *missing in H*

V   49 m'iere] me fui   50 P. diluec C 51 A. ez uos   C
52 Maintenant p. les prez v. *followed by* Sor un palefroi
cheuauchoit et si uenoit de grant air H   53 Q. ioenes et
mout biaus e. H   54 Qant andos les dames connoist H   55
A p. do ch. d. H   56 Deuers C; Et cele qui samie estoit
H   57 De tant loing com ele le v. H   59 A. doit en aler
H   60 *followed by* Et plus mignotement que ie ne di H
VI 61 m. et H; anuit C   62 La bel(1)e CH   63 Et de
baisier et dacoler H   64 De solacier de conioir H   66
P. a p. C; saloignoit C, lesloignoit H   67 *missing in*
CH 68 com ke sil cades C; Et cil auoit quanquil uoloit
H   69 Ken C; Qentre les braz samie estoit H   70-72
missing in H   70 Elle ch. C   72 si tres bel a. C
VII 76 Cest C   77 Celle un petit s. h. C   78 d.
bien li dissoit C   84 Se ne lai pais C

    E   Bartsch, 31-33; Brakelmann 2, 84-85; Pinguet, 98-
107; Newcombe *Thib*, 91-104.

    DF   Lorraine, including *a* for *ai*, as in *lassier* (30);
ei for tonic *e*, as in *ainneie* (6), *blasmeie* (11); final *ie*
for *iee*, as in *conseillie* (26); *boen* (13) for *bon*; *se* (6, 9)
for adverbial *si*; *lo* (10, 33) for *le*.

    N   There is a Provençal version of this song, pub-
lished in Bartsch, pp. 343-344, and Newcombe *Thib*, pp. 98-
104; the ms. attributes it to Thibaut de Blaison.   30-31
'For a young lady, just because [she has] a husband, must
not refrain from taking a lover'.   43 *si* 'so much [that]'.
45 *Qui*, direct object of l. 44 *maldi*.   56 *lo cors* 'at a
run'.   69 Understand *de* before *s'amie*.   79-81 Following
the rhyme scheme of the other stanzas, these verses should
end in -*i*, -*oit*, -*oit*. Bartsch, p. 343, suggests: . . .
conseil forni?/ . . . *petit me duroit,/* . . . *tost de mi*
desevroit. Note, however, that this final stanza shows
other unique rhyming irregularities as well: l. 73 *retornez*
is paired with l. 75 *seit*, l. 74 *plaisir* with l. 76 *celi*,
and the final word of the refrain is *mi* rather that *ami* as
in all the earlier refrains.

GONTIER DE SOIGNIES

Chanson satirique

RS 723, MW 823, B 340
Ms. C 137v-138r. No music. Attribution.

I Li xours comence xordement:
   Xors est li siecles devenus
   Et xort en sont toute la gent.
   Xors est li siecles et perdus:
   Ki de l'autrui veult maix noient,   5
   Moult xordement est respondus;
   Et malvestiés le mont porprent,
   Ke les barons fait xors et mus.
   Chanteis, vos ki veneis de cort,
   La xorderie por lou xort!   10

II Duel ai del clergiet tout avant
    Ki nos devroient chaistoier,
    Ki en lor sen se fïent tant
    Ke il veullent Deu engingnier;
    Prendre veullent et mentir tant   15
    . . . .
    . . . .
    Et adés avoir faus lueir.
    Chanteiz, [vos ki veneis de cort,
    La xorderie por lou xort]!   20

III Duel ai des dames ki mesfont
     Et a tort laissent lors maris,
     Ke signors boens et loiaulz ont
     Et sor ceaus aimment les faillis.
     Lais! ces dolentes, ke feront   25
     Quant vanrait a jor del juïs,
     Ke li martir i trambleront?
     Lors les consaut sains Esperis!
     Chanteis, vos ki veneis de cort,
     [La xorderie por lou xort]!   30

IV Duel ai des povres cheveliers
    Dont si haus suet estre li nons,
    Car on les soloit tenir chiers
    Et faire signors des barons.
    Or est grans chose li maingiers   35
    Et en tout l'an uns petis dons,
    Et, s'un pouc monte li dongiers,

Aincor en est li respis lons.
Chanteis, vos [ki veneis de cort,
La xorderie por lou xort]!   40

V   Amors soloit faire jaidis
      Plux de miraicles ke li saint,
      Maix or est tous perdus ses pris
      Et li bruis des tornois remaint.
      Je ne sai dix en nul païx   45
      Dont nulz de bien faire se poent.
      Gontiers deproie ses amis
      Et lors lowe ke chascuns aint.
      Chanteis, vos ki veneis de cort,
      La xorderie por lou xort!   50

RR   I   3 toutes les gens   7 porprent] porsaint
(em. Scheler)   II   16-17 *missing*   III   24 sors   V
42 mriaicle   43 ses] ces   47 ses] ces

E   Scheler 2, 39-41; Jeanroy-Långfors, 3-4;
Cremonesi, 142-144; Toja, 282-284.

DF   Lorraine, including *ai* for *a*, as in *chaistoier*
(12), *lais* (25), *maingiers* (35), *aincor* (38, = *encor*), *mi-*
raicles (42); *e* for pretonic *a*, as in *cheveliers* (31), *ei*
for tonic *e*, as in *chanteis* (9), *lueir* (18); *lueir* for
loier; *boens* (23) for *bons*; *poent* (46) for *point* (rhyming
with *aint*); final *s* for *z*, as in *devenus* (2), *chanteis* (9),
sains (28); *x* for *s*, as in *xours* (1), *maix* (5); *lou* (10) for
le; third-person singular future in *-ait*, as in *vanrait* (26).

N   This *serventois*, directed against unfaithful wives
and hypocritical clergy but above all against an indifferent
and ungenerous aristocracy, has been thought by some to
include mockery of the Spanish accent that Blanche de Castille (1188-1252) presumably brought with her to the royal
court of France. Thus, for example, does Dinaux 4, p. 278,
explain initial   in the first stanza: it would represent
"le son guttural du *jota* espagnol." This is mere fancy,
however; one of the many graphic peculiarities of ms. C, the
only source of the poem, is its frequent use of *x* where *s*
(or *ss*) would normally be expected; see Schutz, p. 24.
      5 'Anyone who now desires anything belonging to some-
one else, i.e., who asks for material help', dative object
of 1. 6 impersonal passive *est respondus*.   8 *Ke* = *qui*,
referring to 1. 7 *malvestiés*.   9-10 Jeanroy-Långfors notes,
p. x: "Le sens de ce refrain nous paraît être: 'Chantez,

vous qui venez des cours, pour les sourds dont elles sont
peuplées, cette *sourderie*', c'est-à-dire cette pièce, qui
raille leur surdité." This seems preferable to Scheler 2,
p. 304: "'Chantez, réjouissez-vous, vous qui venez de la
cour, mais laissez l'humeur sombre (*sorderie*) à celui qui
est triste'." 12 *devroient*, plural verb with collective
subject 1. 11 *clergiet*; cf. l. 3 *sont* with *la gent*.
24 *sor* 'more than'. 25 *vanrait*, impersonal, 'when it
comes to judgment day'. 27 *li martir* '[even] the mar-
tyrs', rather than 'les misérables' (Scheler 2), which
would apparently refer to the *dames* and their *faillis*.
32 *suet*, though in the present tense, clearly has the same
temporal value as l. 33 *soloit*; cf. Tobler-Lommatzsch, s.v.
soloir. 35 *est* 'is considered to be'. 37 Scheler 2,
p. 305, glosses: "'et si ce don est quelque peu considé-
rable','" observing that "*dongier*, dans l'esprit de l'au-
teur, paraît offrir un rapport de parenté avec *doner*."
According to Jeanroy-Langfors, p. 136, *dongier* would be
"'faste mondaine, luxe coûteux (peut-être par extension du
sens de "puissance, domination")'." Neither interpretation
seems to be borne out by other attestations of the word;
see Tobler-Lommatzsch, s.v. *dangier*. We suggest, instead,
that *dongiers* may be a scribal error for the substantivized
infinitive *doigniers* 'act of consenting, deigning, granting'; various occurrences of the verb appear in ms. C with
the spelling *doign-* instead of the more usual *daign-*, as
noted in Schutz, p. 319. 38 Probably 'still, the wait is
long', as in Scheler 2, rather than 'still respect [for the
povres cheveliers] is far', as in Cremonesi. 44 *remaint*
'has come to an end'. 46 *poent*, third-person singular
present subjunctive of *poindre*. 47 Gontier frequently
names himself in his songs; see, for example, RS 2031.
48 *lowe* (= *loe*) 'counsels'.

Rotrouenge   <u>121</u>

RS 636, MW 178, B 1926
Ms. T 115r. Music. Attribution.

1. Chan-ter m'e-stuet de re-co-mens 2.quant l'ore est doche et clers li tens,
3. et non-pour-quant si sui do-lens.

I   Chanter m'estuet de recomens
       Quant l'ore est doche et clers li tens,
       Et nonpourquant si sui dolens.
              Oiés pour quoi:
       Quant cele a qui sui atendens   5
       Ne velt avoir merchi de moi.

II   Molt aim ma dame et voil et pri,
       Mais d'une cose m'a traï:
       Quant li paroill, si m'entrobli.
              Oiés pour quoi: 10
       Tant par desir l'amor de li
       Ke tous sui faus quant je la voi.

III   Ne puis mon coraige covrir.
       De ço ke plus voil et desir,
       Bien m'en devroie repentir.   15
              Oiés pour quoi:
       Car molt voi a noient venir
       Çou dont on fait plus grant desroi.

IV   Se ma dame seüst le voir
       Com je sui siens a mon pooir,   20
       De moi aroit merci, espoir.
              Oiés pour quoi:
       Car ne me puis de li movoir;
       Som plaisir faice, je l'otroi.

V   Iceste amors me fait soulas   25
       Sol del penser, quant plus n'en fas,
       Et si resui dolans et mas.
              Oiés pour quoi:
       Quant je me gis, si m'en porchas;
       Por el ne.l di ne m'i anoi.   30

VI   Ma rotruenge finera;
       Bien puet savoir ki amé a
       Se bien ou malement m'esta.

Oiés pour quoi:
Car je sui chil ki l'amera,   35
Si n'en fera plus grant effroi.

<u>MN</u>   Form: a a¹ a² B.   1. Ms. writes ♪♫ .

<u>RR</u>   I   2 li vens *(em. suggested by Scheler)*
II 9 li] i   V   26 Soll

<u>E</u>   Scheler 2, 11-12, 291; Gennrich *Rot*, 15-17; Bec 2,
120-121.

<u>DF</u>   Picard, including *ai* for *a*, as in *coraige* (13),
faice (24); *au* for *ou*, as in *faus* (12); *c* for *ch*, as in
cose (8); *ch* for *c*, as in *doche* (2), *merchi* (6); *aroit* (21)
for *avroit*.

<u>N</u>   As noted in Gennrich *Rotrouenge*, pp. 12-17, this is
one of only seven OF songs self-identified as *rotrouenges*
(see 1. 31).   Together with the rest of its form, its unique
placement of the refrain—within the stanza rather than at
the end—appears to imitate Marcabru's Provençal composition, "Dirai vos senes doptansa" (no. 18 in the *Poésies
complètes*, ed. J.M.L. Dejeanne [Toulouse, 1909]).
   1 *de recomens* 'once again'.   9 *Tant par desir* 'so
very much do I desire'.   18 'What one is most excited
about'.   Scheler 2 misreads *desroi* as *desir* and "corrects"
to *effroi*; the erroneous emendation is repeated in Gennrich
Rotrouenge and thence in Bec 2.   21 *espoir* 'perhaps'.
27 *Et si resui* 'and yet I am'.   29 *si m'en porchas* 'and
I worry'.   36 'Yet will make no more noise about it'.

                    Rotrouenge   <u>122</u>

RS 1505a (= 768), MW 41, B 306
Ms. T 116r-v.   No music.   Attribution.

I   Je n'em puis mon cuer blasmer quant il
                                          [sospire,
     Car je vif a grant dolor et a martire;
     Grans dolors est de penser, ki n'ose dire,
     Et plus grief [est] de proier pour escondire.
     De legier me puet la belle desconfire,   5
     Quant li pains de som païs me samble chire;
          Car mieus aim de li songier
              Belle mençoigne

K'avoc une autre couchier
De jor sans soigne.   10

II   Je tenroie volentiers s'obedïense,
     K'il n'a nule si vaillant dusk'en Provence;
     Certes, jou aim mieus assés k'ele me mence
     C'une autre me desist voir ki mains m'agence.
     Bien fust m'ame em paradis tot em presence   15
     Se je sosfrisse por Dieu tel penitence.
            Car [mieus aim de li songier
                  Belle mençoigne
             K'avoc une autre couchier
                  De jor sans soigne].   20

III Je ne puis entroblïer mon grant damaige,
     Dont je sospir nuit et jor ens mon coraige;
     Mais tant ai de reconfort ki m'asouage
     Ke ne li sui riens forfais par men folage.
     Ses hom serai a tos jors, ja n'ier salvage.   25
     Bien venroie d'outremer par son message,
            Car [mieus aim de li songier
                  Belle mençoigne
             K'avoc une autre couchier
                  De jor sans soigne].   30

IV   A mon cuer n'avroit pas [fait] si grant
                                    [outraige,
     Tant par est mieudre de moi, sans signoraige;
     Ne portant si humelie mon coraige,
     C'ainc n'oï k'amors vausist gaigier paraige.
     Bien saice pour li irai en hermitaige,   35
     Et se li ferai conter par mon messaige;
            Car [mieus aim de li songier
                  Belle mençoigne
             K'avoc une autre couchier
                  De jor sans soigne].   40

V   Se jou l'aim de tot mon cuer, drois est ke.l
                                         [faice,
     Car molt doit grant joie avoir qui ele
                                      [embraice.
     Ele me fist l'autre soir une manaice,
     Pour qui il m'estuet canter; si m'en solace.
     Las! se çou avient jamais k'ele me bace,   45
     Pis arai ke forsenés ki porte mace;
            Car [mieus aim de li songier
                  Belle mençoigne

> *K'avoc une autre couchier*
> *De jor sans soigne].*   50

VI   Mes chanters n'est pas soshais, quoi que on
>   [die,
>   Mais si voil mon duel mener ke on en rie.
>   Bien vous di, et puis jurer, tel cortoisie,
>   K'amors se velt bien garder sans villonie;
>   En tel lieu velt asambler sa compaignie   55
>   Ki ne li consent a faire villonie.
> > *Car [mieus aim de li songier*
> > *Belle mençoigne*
> > *K'avoc une autre couchier*
> > *De jor sans soigne].*   60

VII Rotruenge, je t'envoi droit em Borgoigne
>   Au conte ke jou molt aim, k'il te despoigne;
>   Car ne sai trover som per dusqu'en Gascoigne.
>   A lui voill plaindre mon duel et ma besoigne;
>   Par amors li voil proier c'un don me doigne: 65
>   Qu'en chantant le laist savoir et le
> >   [tiesmoigne.
> > *Car [mieus aim de li songier*
> > *Belle mençoigne*
> > *K'avoc une autre couchier*
> > *De jor sans soigne].*   70

RR   I   4 *-1* 10 songe   III   25 n'ier] niert
IV   31 nauoit; *-1 (em. Scheler)*   V   41 ke.l] ke
46 mache   44-46 *repeated as follows:* P. q. il m. chanter
si m. solasse L. se c. a. j. k. me bache P. a. que f. ki p.
mache   VI   51 q. con d. *(-1)*   VII   62 desponge

E   Scheler 2, 21-25, 296-298; Gennrich *Rot*, 24-25.

DF   Picard, including *ai* for *a*, as in *damaige* (21),
coraige (22), *gaigier* (34), *saice* (35), *faice* (41); *au* for
ou, as in *vausist* (34); *c* for *ch*, as in *saice* (35), *canter*
(44); *ch* for *c*, as in *chire* (6); *çou* (45) for *ce*; *jou* (13)
for *je*; *men* (24) for *mon*; *venroie* (26) for *vendroie*; *arai*
(46) for *avrai*; subjunctive in *-ce*, as in *mence* (13) for
mente, *bace* (45) for *bate*.

N   This is one of the seven OF songs which, as
pointed out in Gennrich *Rotrouenge*, p. 12ff., identify themselves as *rotrouenges* (see 1. 61). The verses of eleven
syllables are divided 7 + 4 + e, with the exception of

11. 5, 33, and 56, divided 7 + e + 3 + e.   3 *ki n'ose dire*
'for anyone who dares not speak'.   4 *pour escondire* 'only
to be rejected'.   6 Scheler 2, p. 297, finds the meaning
of this metaphor elusive and wonders, "*cire* doit-il expri-
mer la dureté?" Tobler-Lommatzsch, s.v. *cire*, offers the
gloss, 'das Geringere was von ihr kommt, ist mir so wert wie
Besseres von anderswo', which has the virtue of leading
directly into the refrain; the final word of the refrain,
soigne, means both 'dream' and 'candle'.   10 *De jor* is
inexplicably omitted from the refrain in Scheler 2 and
therefore in Gennrich *Rotrouenge* as well; this falsifies the
meter presented in RS and MW.   15 *tot em presence* 'even
now'.   24 *riens forfais* 'in no way guilty'.   25 *ja n'ier
salvage* 'I shall never be alienated [from her]'.   31-32
'She would not have so overwhelmed my heart—so much better
is she than I am—if not for her nobility'.   34 *vausist
gaigier paraige* 'was willing to risk a loss of standing'.
35 *Bien saice* 'let her be assured [that]'.   36 *se li = si
le li*; 'And I will indeed have my messenger tell her so'.
44 The antecedent of *qui* is l. 43 *Ele.*   46 'I will be
worse off than a club-bearing madman'; the club, or mace,
was a conventional mark of madness.   51 *soshais* 'a thing
done with pleasure'.   53 *tel cortoisie* 'this fact of
courtliness'.   56 Scheler 2, p. 297, is no doubt right to
suspect the authenticity of *villonie,* which repeats the
rhyme-word of l. 54.   62 Petersen Dyggve "Onom", p. 57,
reports that the patron in question here is believed to have
been the count of Upper Burgundy between 1190 and 1200.

<u>123</u>   Rotrouenge

RS 2031, MW 79, B 312
Ms. T 113r-v.   Music.   Attribution.

6. ten- roit uns au- tres a grant bien.

I   Li tans nouveaus et la douçors
    Ki nous retrait herbes et flors
    Me fait estre pensieu d'amors
    Et renovelle mes dolors.
      Ce dont me plaing sor tote rien   5
      Tenroit uns autres a grant bien.

II Vers une dame de haut pris
    Avoie mon coraige mis;
    Trop legierement le conquis,
    Autrui fust boin et moi est pis.   10
      Ce dont [me plaing sor tote rien
      Tenroit uns autres a grant bien].

III Savés por quoi je m'en deshait?
    Ele estoit molt de riche fait;
    Or croi ke mains de bien i ait,   15
    Quant jou si tost i trovai plait.
      Ce dont [me plaing sor tote rien
      Tenroit uns autres a grant bien].

IV Un grant termine li celai
    C'onques jehir ne li osai;   20
    Et tantost ke jou li proiai,
    Tout quanques je quis i trovai.
      Ce dont [me plaing sor tote rien
      Tenroit uns autres a grant bien].

V   Molt li seüsse millor gré   25
    S'un petit m'eüst refusé
    Ou tart ou a envis doné
    Çou ke jou avoie rové.
      Ce dont [me plaing sor tote rien
      Tenroit uns autres a grant bien].   30

VI Or proi Gontier ke chant en haut
    Et si li die ke poi vaut
    Chasteaus c'om prent par un assaut;
    K'il se tiene, ou autrui n'en chaut!
      Ce dont [me plaing sor tote rien   35
      Tenroit uns autres a grant bien].

<u>MN</u>   Form: A A rf (B).

<u>RR</u>   I   5   plaig   VI   34   Ki se tient ou il a. n.
ch. *(+1)*

<u>E</u>   Dinaux 4, 273-274; Scheler 2, 43-44, 306.

<u>DF</u>   Picard: *coraige* (8) for *corage*; *millor* (25) for
meill-; *pensieu* (3) for *pensif*; *boin* (10) for *bon*; *tenroit*
(6) for *tendroit*; *jou* (16) for *je*; *çou* (28) for *ce*; *le* (9)
for *la*.

<u>N</u>   The message of this love song is an unusual one:
the poet complains of the disappointment produced by an
easy conquest. 2 *retrait* 'brings back'. 16 *trovai
plait* 'found satisfaction'. 20 Understand *ce* before *C'*
(= *que*). 31 Scheler 2, like Dinaux 4, changes *Gontier* to
Gauthier; he identifies the latter, p. 306, simply as the
intermediary between the poet and his lady, dismissing as
"par trop subtil" the idea that the two G. may in fact be
the same person. We, however, see this as very likely; it
is a playful device that the poet allows himself in at
least two other songs as well (RS 1411 and RS 1914).
33 *un* 'a single'. 34 Dinaux 4 has *Et se tient vers cil
cui n'en chaut* and Scheler 2 *Ki se rent où autrui n'en
chaut*, neither of which is satisfactory. We read, with
minimal emendation, 'Let it hold out, or no one cares about
it', i.e., without resistance, the castle (the lady) has no
attractiveness.

GUIOT DE DIJON

Chanson de croisade, chanson de femme, rotrouenge

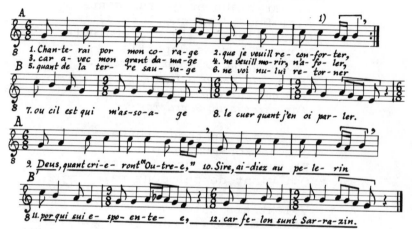

RS 21, MW 861, B 552

Mss. M 174v, C 86v-87r, K 385-386, O 28r, T 128v-129r, X
248r-248v. Music in all mss. except C. Attribution in
M; attributed to the Dame du Fayel (fictitious heroine
of the *Roman du Chastelain de Couci*) in C.

I   Chanterai por mon corage
Que je vueill reconforter,
Car avec mon grant damage
Ne vueill morir n'afoler,
Quant de la terre sauvage   5
Ne voi nului retorner
Ou cil est qui m'assoage
Le cuer quant j'en oi parler.
Deus, quant crïeront "Outree",
Sire, aidiez au pelerin   10
Por qui sui espöentee,
Car felon sunt Sarrazin.

II   Souffrerai en tel estage
Tant que.l voie rapasser.
Il est en pelerinage,   15
Dont Deus le lait retorner.
Et maugré tot mon lignage
Ne quier ochoison trover
D'autre face mariage;

Folz est qui j'en oi parler.   20
Deus, [quant crïeront "Outree",
Sire, aidiez au pelerin
Por qui sui espöentee,
Car felon sunt Sarrazin].

III   De ce sui au cuer dolente   25
       Que cil n'est en cest païs
       Qui si sovent me tormente;
       Je n'en ai ne gieu ne ris.
       Il est biaus et je sui gente.
       Sire Deus, por que.l feïs?   30
       Quant l'une a l'autre atalente,
       Por coi nos as departis?
       Deus, [quant crïeront "Outree",
       Sire, aidiez au pelerin
       Por qui sui espöentee,   35
       Car felon sunt Sarrazin].

IV   De ce sui en bone atente
       Que je son homage pris;
       Et quant la douce ore vente
       Qui vient de cel douz païs   40
       Ou cil est qui m'atalente,
       Volentiers i tor mon vis;
       Adont m'est vis que je.l sente
       Par desoz mon mantel gris.
       Deus, [quant crïeront "Outree",   45
       Sire, aidiez au pelerin
       Por qui sui espöentee,
       Car felon sunt Sarrazin].

V   De ce fui mout deceüe
       Que ne fui au convoier.   50
       Sa chemise qu'ot vestue
       M'envoia por embracier.
       La nuit, quant s'amor m'argüe,
       La met delez moi couchier,
       Toute nuit a ma char nue,   55
       Por mes malz assoagier.
       Deus, [quant crïeront "Outree",
       Sire, aidiez au pelerin
       Por qui sui espöentee,
       Car felon sunt Sarrazin].   60

MN   Mss. KOX have a related melody. Form: A A A B rf
(A+B[1]). 1. In l. 2 ms. omits this note. 2. Ms. writes *c'*,

but the *b* is confirmed by ll. 1, 3, and 5.

RR   II   13-14 Ie souferrai mon damage/ Tant que lan
verrai passer   V   49 deceüe] engignie   50 Quant

V   Stanzas: TC   I II   III IV   V
                 XKO   I III II   V IV
I   1 Ge ch. C   2 resconforteir   C   3 Quauecques   XKO
4 vueill] quier XKO; ne foler   X   6 nului] mes nul XKO
7 rassoage XKO   8 Le cuer] Mes maus   XKO; ai   K   9
crierons XKO; entree O   10 apalerin   C   11 qui *missing
in X*; enpoentee   C   II   13 Ie sofferrai mon damaige
(outraige   C)   TC   14 Tant qou uoie repasser   O, Tant ke
lans iert trespasses TC   16 laist TC; Mult atent son retorner XKO   17 Et] Ne   C; Car autre (augre O) de mon l.
XKO   19 Dautrui XO, Autrui K; faites   C   20 oi] os   C;
Mult est fox qui en ueut parler XKO   21 quant crieront
outree *added in C*   III 25 ceu seux a cuer   C   26 Q. c. n.
en biau uoisin XKO   27 En qui iai (cui ia   O) mise mentente XKO   28 Je] Or   XKO, Ke ie nai   C   29 Il] Sil
XKO   30 S. por quoi le f.   XKO; Sires   C; (coi   C) fesis
TC   31 lun O   32 que O; as] en XKO   33 quant *added
in O*; quant crieront outree *added in C*   IV   37 fui O,
seux C; entente XKO   38 Quant XO   39 Quant lalaine
douce uente XKO   40 Ke   C; de cel] dou (du K) tres   XKO
43 Adont m. v.] dex m. v.   K, et lors mestuet   O, *missing
in X*; je.l] ie le   XK, ie la   O, ie   T   45 quant crierons
added in O; quant crieront outree *added in C*   V   49 sui
T, seux C; mout] ie O; deceüe] engignie TC   50 Quant
XO; au] a C   53 samors OT   54 delez] auec XKO   55
Toute n.] mult estroit XKO   56 rassouaigier TC   57
quant *added in T*

E   Michel, 95-98; Leroux de Lincy, 105-108; Meyer,
368; Crépet, 188-191; Bédier-Aubry, 107-117; Gennrich *Rot*,
44-45; Spanke *Lied*, 188-190; Nissen, 1-3; Pauphilet, 905-
906; Woledge *Peng*, 111-113; Henry *Chrest* 1, 227-228; 2, 67-
68; Mary 1, 226-229; Bec 2, 92-94.

N   For doubts about attribution to Guiot, see H.
Spanke's review of Nissen, *Zeit. für franz. Sprache und
Literatur* 53 (1930), 357-363. For identification as a rotrouenge, see not only Gennrich *Rot*, but also Bec 1, p. 188.
For a brief analysis of the text, see Wentzlaff-Eggebert,
pp. 156-157.
    9 *Outree* 'Forward!' Gaston Paris identifies this as
the refrain of a pilgrims' song and cites several attesta-

tions; the word is found not only with the verb *crier*, but with *chanter* as well. See pp. 44-45 in "La chanson du Pèlerinage de Charlemagne," *Romania* 9 (1880), 1-50.   13-14 Following Bédier-Aubry, we have substituted the reading of mss. KXO for that of ms. M, which seems markedly incorrect and which, moreover, receives little support from T and C, the other members of its ms. family. In the first verse, initial *Je* destroys a clearly deliberate compositional pattern (*Chanterai-Souffrerai* / *De ce-De ce-De ce*). In the second verse, *passer* has none of the logical sense of *rapasser*. The emendation in l. 50 is similarly motivated.
14 The enclisis *que.l*, also in l. 30, served as Bédier's principal justification for linking this song to the crusade of 1189 (Bédier-Aubry, pp. 111, 116). First, he was unaware of the period of Guiot's career, which Nissen, in her Introduction, was later able to place in the first half of the 13th century. Second, and more to the point, Bédier believed that the linguistic feature in question did not survive the 12th century; see Ph. Ménard, *Syntaxe de l'ancien français* [Vol. I of Y. Lefèvre, *Manuel du français du moyen âge*], 2nd ed. (Bordeaux, 1973), p. 65, for the well-grounded observation that such enclitics did not disappear for at least another hundred years.
18 Understand *que* after *trover*.   39 See J.-M. d'Heur, "Le motif du vent venu du pays de l'être aimé. . .," *Zeitschrift für romanische Philologie* 88 (1972), 69-104. 50-51 Bédier-Aubry notes, p. 117: "La *chemise* est une tunique qui recouvrait les autres vêtements. Les croisés s'équipaient en pèlerins . . . et partaient, accompagnés jusqu'à une prochaine étape par leurs parents et amis, d'ordinaire 'dechauz, a pié et en langes'. C'était 'le convoier'. A l'étape, cette sorte de cérémonie prenait fin; le croisé se rechaussait et reprenait ses vêtements ordinaires. Ce que notre pèlerin a ici envoyé à sa dame, c'est sans doute la *chemise*, portée sur ses autres vêtements, qui avait symbolisé au départ son voeu de pèlerin." In his review of Bédier-Aubry (*Romania* 38 [1909], 443-446), Jeanroy maintains: "il doit y avoir là une réminiscence du passage de *Cligès* (1640 ss.), où Alexandre, la nuit, 'embrasse' la chemise, présent de Soredamors, où ont été cousus des cheveux de celle-ci."

125   Chanson

RS 589, MW 1322
Mss. C 40r-v, I 5:74. No music. Attribution in C.

I   Chanteir m'estuet por la plux belle
       Ke soit ou monde vivant,
    Car s'amor m'est tous dis novelle,
       S'en ai le cuer plux joiant.
          Biaus tres dous Deux, quant   5
       Iere je de sa bouchete
       Appelleis loiauls amans?

II   Cuer et cors li doing come celle
       Ke en ferait son talent,
    Et li proi ke de ma destresce   10
       Me faicë aligement,
          Car a li me rant
       Sens faintixe et sens peresce
       M'otroi a son biaul cors gent.

III   Plux est ke rose vermillete   15
       Celle por cui je vos chans,
    Si est simple et jone et tandrete
       Et grailete per les flans;
          De tous biens ait tant
       C'onkes ne vi sa pareille   20
       Ne de biaulteit ne de sen.

RR   I   4 Si en *(+1)*   7 1. amis   II   8 com
(-1)   9 ke bien en *(+1)*   III   17 Cest *(-1)*

V   I   2 on m.   3 dis *missing*   4 Si an ai   6
I. ie par sa bouche   II   10 pris   11 faicet   14
biaus   III   17 Cest s.   21 Ne *missing*; sant

E   Nissen, 21–22.

DF   Lorraine, including *ai* for *a*, as in *faice* (11);
ei for tonic *e*, as in *chanteir* (1), *appelleis* (7); *loiauls*
(7) for *loiaus* and *biaul* (14) for *beau*; preservation of
final *t*, as in *biaulteit* (21); *x* for *s*, as in *plux* (1),
faintixe (13); 3rd-pers. sing. pres. ind. *ait* (19) for *a*;
3rd-pers. sing. fut. in -*ait*, as in *ferait* (9); nominative
ke (2, 9) for *qui*.

N   The versification of this poem, esp. the somewhat
approximate rhyming, is sufficiently inconsistent with the
usual practice of Guiot de Dijon for Nissen to remark, p.
48, that the work can be attributed to him only with reser-
vations.

126   Chanson (de femme)

RS 810 (=796), MW 1469
B 1555 (two other sources).
Mss. M 118v-119r, T 118r-v, a 44r-v. Stanza I also in *Roman de la Violette*, ed. D. L. Buffum, p. 20. Music
only in M but, because of mutilation, incomplete and
hence not presented here. Attribution in all mss.

I   Amors mi fait renvoisier et chanter
      Et me semont ke plus jolie soie,
      Et mi doune talent de mieuz amer
      C'onques ne fis. Pour c' est fous qui m'en
                                  [proie,
      Quar j'ai ami, n'en nul fuer ne voudroie   5
      De bone amor mon voloir trestourner,
      Ains amerai et serai bien amee.
      Quant pluz me bat et destraint li jalous,
      Tant ai je pluz en amours ma pensee.

II   Mon cuer voudrai metre en amor guarder,   10
      Quar sanz amour ne puet nus avoir joie
      Et d'amours doit bele dame amender;
      Pour c' est fole qui son tanz n'i emploie.
      Quant li jalouz me bat pluz et chastoie,
      Lors me fait pluz esprendre et alumer,   15
      Qu'amours n'iert ja pour jalous oublïee.
      Quant pluz [me bat et destraint li jalous,
      Tant ai je pluz en amours ma pensee].

III   Quant je mi doi dormir et reposer,
      Lors me semont amours qui me maistroie   20
      Et si me fait et veillier et penser
      A mon ami en cui braz je voudroie
      Estre touz jours; et quant a moi dosnoie
      Et il me veut baisier et acoler,
      Lors est ma joie enforcie et doublee.   25
      Quant [pluz me bat et destraint li jalous,
      Tant ai je pluz en amours ma pensee].

IV   Biau m'est quant puiz ochoison controuver
      Par quoi g'i puisse aler, c'on ne mi voie,
      A mon ami conseillier et parler.   30
      Et quant g'i sui, partir ne m'en voudroie,
      Et quant n'i puis aler, si i envoie

Mon cuer au mainz; ce ne puet trestourner
Qu'il ne voist la u j'ai m'amour dounee.
Quant [pluz me bat et destraint li jalous,   35
Tant ai je pluz en amours ma pensee].

V   Nus ne me doit reprendre ne blasmer
      Se j'ai ami, car plevir vous porroie
      C'on ne porroit en mon mari trouver
      Nule teche dont on amer le doie.   40
      Il me gaite, maiz son tans pis emploie
      Que cil qui veut sour gravele semer,
      Quar il iert cous, ja n'iere si guardee.
      Quant [pluz me bat et destraint li jalous
      Tant ai je pluz en amours ma pensee].   45

VI   Trestuit li bien c'on porroit deviser
      Sont en celui a cui del tout m'otroie;
      Bien set son cuer envers autrui celer
      Et envers moi volentiers le desploie.
      Non pluz c'on puet Tristan n'Yseut la bloie 50
      De lor amour partir ne dessevrer,
      N'iert ja l'amours de nous deus dessevree.
      Quant [pluz me bat et destraint li jalous,
      Tant ai je pluz en amours ma pensee].

RR   I   1-4 *Mutilation has left only* doune talent
de mieuz ame/ ques ne fis. pour ce est fous q/ men proie;
reading from T   4   p. ce est f. *(+1)*   8   Que   III   21
followed by supernumerary line quant li soulaz de mon mari
manoie   VI   50   tristan dyseut

     V   I   1   et] de a   4   fist p. ce est f. a; me T
5 na nul f. nen v. a   7   A. ame et T; siere b. Ta   9
T. aie T; miex (mieus a) en amo(u)r Ta   II   12   damor
T   14   mi destraint et ch. a   17-18   me bat *added in a*
III   20   Adont me fait a. a   21   Toute la nuit et v. a;
verse followed by supernumerary line q(u)ant li so(u)las de
mon mari manoie *in Ta*   23   Estre tostans et q. T, Toutans
estre car q. a; dannoie a   25   Dont a   26-27   plus
added in Ta   IV   28   p. amour c. a   32   p. parler lor
j. a   33   ne] nen a   35-36   *added in Ta*   V   39   en]
ens T; m. ami t. a   43   si nere g. Ta   44-45   plus
added in T   VI   46   Tresto(u)t Ta; le T   50   Nient
Ta; pot a; dyseut T, dyselt a   53-54   plus *added in T*;
refrain complete in a

E   Jeanroy *Or*, 496-498; PetDyg "Moniot", 83-86; Spaziani *Ant*, 54-56; Cremonesi, 169-171; Toja, 326-328; Bec 2,
18-20.

DF   Picard: *enforcie* (25) for *enforciee*.

N   As PetDyg "Moniot" points out, pp. 30-33, this
song must have been composed before 1227-1229, for its first
stanza is quoted in Gerbert de Montreuil's *Roman de la Violette*, written during those years.

127   Chanson de rencontre

RS 94, MW 477
Mss. N 79r-v, H 218r, K 135-136, P 59r-v, V 82v-83r, X 93v-
     94r. Music in all mss. except H. Attribution in KNPX.

I   Ce fu en mai
           Au douz tens gai,
       Que la seson est bele;
           Main me levai,
           Jöer m'alai
       Lez une fontenele.   4
           En un vergier
           Clos d'esglentier
       Oï une vïele;   8
           La vi dancier
           Un chevalier
       Et une damoisele.   12

II   Cors orent gent
         Et avenant,
   Et Deus! tant biau dançoient!
         En acolant   16
         Et en besant,
    Mult biau se deduisoient.
         En un destour,
         Au chief du tor,   20
    Dui et dui s'en aloient;
         Desor la flor,
         Le gieu d'amor
   A lor plesir fesoient.   24

III   J'alai avant,
         Trop redoutant
   Que nus d'aus ne me voie,
         Maz et pensant   28
         Et desirant
   D'avoir autretel joie.
         Lors vi lever
         Un de lor per,   32
   De si loign con g'estoie,
         A apeler,
         A demander
   Qui sui et que queroie.   36

IV   J'alai vers aus,
         Dis lor mes maus:
   Que une dame amoie
         A qui loiaus,   40
         Sanz estre faus,
    Tout mon vivant seroie,
         Por qui plus trai
         Paine et esmai   44
   Que dire ne porroie.
         Las, or morrai,
         Car bien le sai,
   S'ele ne mi ravoie.   48

V   Cortoisement
         Et gentement
   Chascun d'aus me ravoie
         Et dïent tant   52
         Que Deus briément
   M'envoit de cele joie
         Por qui je sent
         Grant marrement;   56

> Et je lor en rendoie
> Merciz mult grant
> Et, en plorant,
> A Deu les conmandoie.   60

MN   Ms. V has a second melody. Form: A A¹ B B¹.

RR   II   20 dun t.   III   28 Maiz   IV   43 pl.
sent 44   et torment   V   55 q. iatent   57 redoie

V   I   1 Lautrier en m.   H   3 saisons HX, sesons
K   6 A H   9 pucele X   10 dancior H, dancer K   12
u. dam H   II   13 genz V   14 auenanz V   15 Et molt
tres b. (bien H) HK   18 deduioient H   19-20 *transposed in H*   20 de t. H   22-23 *transposed in H*   22 Sor
l. f. X   23 damors PX   III   26 Molt H   27 nul P,
no H; hom V   28 Laz V; pensanz KV, pensans X   29
desirranz KV, desirrans X   30 ausi grant H, autele V
34 Por H, Et V   35 Et HV   36 s. ni H   IV   38 Di
KX   39 Et cune H   40 cui H   43 cui HV; tant V;
sent KPVX   44 et *missing in H*; torment KPVX   45 qui
missing in H; iatent KPVX   46 Tel V; Paine et torment H
48 Merci HP

E   La Borde *Es*, 205; Dinaux 3, 331-332; Bartsch, 78-
79; PetDyg "Moniot", 118-121; Gennrich *Ex*, 27-29.

N   For some doubt about the attribution to Moniot
d'Arras, see PetDyg "Moniot", p. 26.   20 'At the end of
the dance'.   28-29 Ms. N here sacrifices grammatical correctness (-*anz*) to regularity in rhyming.   54 Understand:
joie de cele.

128   Chanson

RS 503, MW 315
Stanza I: B 197, st. II: B 1102, st. III: B 321 (one other
    source), st. IV: B 405 (two other sources), st. V: B
    392.
Mss. T 120r-v, M 120v-121r. Music in both mss. Attribution
    in both mss.

> 1. Dame, ains ke je voise en ma con- tre-   e,
> 2. vous 'iert ma can- çons dite et chan- te-   e.

3. S'e- le vous a- gre- e, 4. tost vous ert a- pri- se, 5. car mes fins cuers tant vous pri- se

6. k'ail- lors n'a pen- se- e, 7. bien le puis tes- moi- gnier.

8. Au- tre- ment n'os a vous par- ler 9. fors qu'en chan- tant: mer- chi vous quier.

II. 15. joi- e ne tro- ve- e 16. k'au- tre ke vous ne voil a- mer.

17. Je ne sai si loins a- ler 18. ke vous puisse en- trou- bli- er.

III. 25. lors ert ma do- lors ga- ri- e.

26. Ce m'o- chist ke je ne vous voi 27. plus so- vent, douce a- mi- e.

IV. 34. vous ai en- si.

35. Da- me de fin cuer a- me- e, 36. mer- chi!

V. 43. sai- chies ke pour vous mor- roi- e.

44. Da- me, a- mer ne por- roi- e 45. nu- le au- tre que je voi- e.

I   Dame, ains ke je voise en ma contree,
        Vous iert ma cançons dite et chantee.
                S'ele vous agree,
                Tost vous ert aprise,

Car mes fins cuers tant vous prise   5
K'aillors n'a pensee,
Bien le puis tesmoignier.
Autrement n'os a vous parler
Fors qu'en chantant: merchi vous quier.

II   Dame, en chantant vous iert demandee   10
Vostre amors, ke j'ai tant desiree.
S'or ne m'est donee
Ou au mains pramise,
Jamais n'ert ens mon cuer mise
Joie ne trovee,   15
K'autre ke vous ne voil amer.
Je ne sai si loins aler
Ke vous puisse entroublïer.

III   Dame, lonc tans vos avrai celee
Ceste amor, mais or vos ert mostree.   20
Dieus, ki vous fist nee,
Mete en vous franchise,
Si ke l'amors ki m'atise
Soit ens vos doblee;
Lors ert ma dolors garie.   25
Ce m'ochist ke je ne vous voi
Plus sovent, douce amie.

IV   Dame, proi vos ne soiés iree
De çou k'amie vos ai clamee,
Car la renomee   30
De vo vaillandise,
Ke Dieus en vous a asise,
M'a fait que nomee
Vous ai ensi.
Dame de fin cuer amee,   35
Merchi!

V   Dame, a droit porriés estre blasmee
Se ne vous n'estoit merchi trovee.
Ore iert esprovee
Vostre gentelise,
Car, se l'amors ke j'ai quise   40
M'aviés refusee,
Saichiés ke pour vous morroie.
Dame, amer ne porroie
Nule autre ke je voie.

<u>MN</u>   Form: a a B vrf
1. Ms. T includes the melody of refrains 1-3 and ms. M that
of refrains 1 (different from ms. T) and 4 (a 5th lower than
here transcribed); no music for refrain 5 is extant.

<u>RR</u>   II   11 tant *missing*   IV   29   ke amie *(+1)*

<u>V</u>   I   2   chancon   II   14   en   18   Que ie v. p.
e.   III   23   lamour   24   en   25   doleur   IV   29   que
amie   V   38   mercis   41   lamour

<u>E</u>   PetDyg "Moniot", 101-103.

<u>DF</u>   Picard, including *c* for *ch*, as in *cançons* (2); *ch*
for *c*, as in *merchi* (9), *ochist* (26); *çou* (29) for *ce*; *ens*
(14) for *en*; *vo* (31) for *vostre*.

<u>N</u>   Rita Lejeune, "Moniot d'Arras et Moniot de Paris,"
Neuphilologische Mitteilungen 42 (1941), 1-14, suggests, p.
14, that this song was composed between 1229 and 1239.   28
Understand *que* between *proi* and *vos*.

Chanson   129

RS 1231, MW 2350
Mss. P 57r-v-58r, K 134b-135, N 79r, V 82r-v, X 93r-v. Mu-
    sic in all mss. Attribution in KNPX; attributed to
    Perron in text.

9. ju-giez, A-mors, main-te-nant: 10. Doit ele e-stre fors-ba-ni-   e?

I   Amors, s'onques en ma vie
           Fis riens a vostre talent,
           Vostre vengance demant
           De cele qui j'ai servie,
           Qui de moi s'est esloignie   5
           Et vet autres acointant.
           De deus ne me plaing je mie,
           Mes se le tiers la renvie,
           Jugiez, Amors, maintenant:
           Doit ele estre forsbanie?   10

II   A pucele n'afiert mie,
           Estrete de bone gent,
           Qu'ele face a escīent
           Chose dont chascun se rie;
           Por ce ne sai que je die   15
           De cele qui longuement
           M'a fet grant senblant d'amie.
           Bien se desfent de risie
           Quant si debonerement
           Fet ce que chascun li prie!   20

III   Par le filz sainte Marie
           Qui en la crois fu penez,
           Je sueil estre melz amez
           De nus de ma conpaignie;
           Or sui remez en la lie.   25
           Ne sui je bien reculez?
           J'en sui hors de la baillie,
           Car trop la m'ont enchierie
           Trois bachelers touz jurez,
           Qui vont chaçant grant folie.   30

IV   A ma dame, que qu'en die,
           Envoi toute ma chançon,
           Je c'on apele Perron,
           Qui merci li quiert et prie.
           Se j'é dit par ma folie   35
           De li riens se tot bien non,
           Ce fet la grant seignorie,
           Deus! de s'amor, qui me lie
           Si durement que reson
           Est en moi tote perie.   40

__MN__   Ms. V has a second melody. Form: through-composed.

__RR__   III   29   bacheler tuit iure   IV   37   Se

__V__   I   4   qui *missing in X*, que   N   5   cest   X   8
le] lī   KVX; la ramaine V   9   amort   X   10   f. blamee V
II   12   Estre de haute gent   V   13   encient   K   14   chascuns KV   16   q. par enuie   V   18   dyrisie N, de resie V
20   F. quanque K, quant que X; chascuns KNVX   III   21
fil N   24   Que KNVX   30   v. chantant V, querrant X
IV   31   quon d. N   33   quen VX   24   q(u)ier KN   35
j'é] iai KNVX   39   raisons X   40   E. toute en moi p.   X

__E__   PetDyg "Moniot", 121-123.

__DF__   Picárd: *esloignie* (5) for *esloigniee*, *risie* (18)
for *risee*.

__N__   Because of l. 33 *Perron* and for a formal reason,
PetDyg "Moniot" doubts that this song was composed by Moniot
d'Arras; see pp. 25-26 for detailed argument and counterargu-
ment. For Rita Lejeune, "Moniot d'Arras et Moniot de Paris," *Neuphilologische Mitteilungen* 42 (1941), 1-14, "Dans
cette pièce où le poète demande vengeance parce que sa dame
l'a abandonné et écoute trop complaisamment les propos de
trois bacheliers, il y a une ironie contenue complètement
étrangère à Moniot" (p. 8).
4   *qui = cui*.   23   For pres. *sueil* instead of the expected imperfect, see Elwert, pp. 76-78.   24   *De* 'than'.
29   The grammatical forms are wrong for the clearly nominative function of this noun phrase. We have nevertheless
adopted them in the place of the grammatically correct reading of ms. P out of respect for proper rhyming; note that
all the other mss. differ here from ms. P.

130   Chanson

RS 69, MW 1187
Mss. M 41r-v, T 137v-138r. Music in both mss. Attribution
   in both mss.

I   Iriez, pensis, chanterai
        Com cil qui maint en estour.
        Onques merci ne trouvai
        En mon vivant en amour,
        Ainz sui tous tanz en irour.   5
        Ce me tient en grant esmai
        Que nes un confort n'en ai,
        Dont j'ai souvent grant dolour,
        S'en souspir et des eus plour.

II   Mescheans sui, bien le sai;   10
        Prouvé l'ai, ja a maint jour;
        Quant pluz l'aim, et pluz mal trai,
        Le bele od fresche coulour
        Dont je fis trop grant folour
        Quant mon cuer metre i osai;   15
        Maiz quant en li remirai,
        Cors gent et plaisant atour
        Mon cuer ot sanz nul destour.

III   Ne sai se secours avrai,
Quar li felon trahitour   20
Me font touz les maus que j'ai;
Ne sai u faire clamour.
Nuisi m'ont a la meillour
C'ainc vi ne jamaiz verrai;
Maiz pour Dieu li proierai   25
Que ne croie trecheour
Pour li ne pour sa valour.

IV   Deus! ne sai que je ferai,
Quar je n'ai tant de vigour;
Dire ne li oserai   30
Mon tourment ne ma tristour,
S'ele n'i guarde s'onnour.
Bien sai que pour li morrai:
Ne set pas les maus que j'ai,
La bele a cui je aour.   35
Rienz fors li ne m'a savour.

V   A li merci proierai,
Maiz trop avrai grant paour:
Ne sai se ja ataindrai
La tres bele sanz folour.   40
Maiz tant a en li douçour,
Pitié, raison, bien le sai,
Ne m'i desconforterai;
En gré prendrai ma langour
Pour avoir joie greignour.   45

VI   Touz sui suens, sanz nul retour.
Andrius sui, qui l'amerai.
Hors du païs m'en irai;
Pour li ai fait lonc sejour,
Ce sachent bien li plusour.   50

VII   Arraz, plainne de baudour,
A vous congié prenderai;
Ne sai quant je revendrai;
Deus vous maintieigne en hounour!
Des citez estes la flour.   55

MN   Form: A A[1] B; both envoys are sung to ll. 5-9.
1. Ms. here writes the following half measure, then half
erases this but does not correct.

RR   I   8 Donc   9 s. des ex et p.   II   14 Donc

V   I   2   C. chis   II   11 ja] molt   12 aim et
III ‾24 ne fors li v.   IV   35 belle cui
V   39 atendrai   42 raisons

E   Schmidt, 42-43.

DF   Picard: epenthetic *e* in future *prenderai* (52).

N   47 Andrieu identifies himself within the text of
no fewer than eleven of the eighteen songs that Schmidt
attributes to him.

131   Lai, plainte funèbre

RS 81, MW 14,1
Ms. T 75v-76r-v.   No music. Attribution.

I   De belle Yzabel ferai
      Un lai ke je vos dirai.
      Sa grant valor retrairai
         Et s'en chanterai.
         Ne l'oublïerai.   5
      Je l'amai de cuer verai.
      Morte est. Ja ne.l chelerai,
      Ja mais aillors n'amerai
         Ne n'i penserai;
         Siens sui et serai.   10
      Ne mais autre amor n'arai;
      Tel dame ne trouverai.
      Ja vers li ne fauserai
         Ne n'i mesferai;
         Bien m'en garderai.   15
         Ensi languirai
         Tant com [je] vivrai.

II   Mors, ti mal sont descendu
      Sor moi anvïeusement.
      Ton mal talent as vendu   20
      Ma dame et moi cruelment;
      Grant mal m'as por bien rendu
      Sans nis un desfiement.
      Ce ke j'avoie atendu
      M'as tolu hasteement.   25

III   Mout tost briefment
M'estuet del mont partir;
     Prochainement
Me doit li cuers partir.

IV   J'ai perdu kankes j'avoie,   30
Si me fait Dieus correchier.
[Tres]tos mes cuers se desvoie,
Si ne me puis leechier.
Dieus [me mete] en itel voie
Ke tant me puist avanchier   35
D'amor servir tote voie
Loialment et sans trichier.
Saichiés bien, se jou savoie
Ma mort tost adevancier,
Volentiers, se Dieus me voie,   40
Le vauroie porchaschier.

V   Ce afichier
Puis jou et mout bien dire
     Et fianchier;
Nus ne m'en puet desdire.   45

VI   Ma doce amie avenans,
     Ke porrai je faire?
Jouene et gente et bien venans,
     Sans nului mesfaire,
Ainc ne fustes destornans   50
     Grans honors a faire.
     Je sui en contraire,
     Je doi bien retraire.

VII   Ahi! belle doce amie,
Ke porrai jo devenir?   55
Ne me fustes anemie:
De vos me doit sosvenir.
Je muir; n'ai mestier de mie,
J'en voil bien a chief venir.
Li cuers me part et esmie,   60
La dolor m'estuet sosfrir
     Por sostenir
Tes biens sans villonie.

VIII Felon, or pöés chanter:
Chaüs sui en grant torment.   65
Maufés vos puist deschanter!

RR   I   17 *-1 (em. Jeanroy)*   II   18 ti mal
repeated   IV   32 *-1 (em. Schmidt)*   34 *-2 (em.*
Jeanroy)   VIII   65   en repeated

E   Jeanroy *Lais,* 22-23; Schmidt, 44-45.

DF   Picard, including ch for c, as in *chelerai* (7),
correchier (31), *leechier* (33); *arai* (11) for *avrai*;
vauroie (41) for *voudroie; jou* (38) for *je; le* (41) for *la.*

N   Of the five extant OF *plaintes funèbres*, this is
the only one in the form of a *lai*. Editions and commentary
show some variation in the poem's stanzaic division, partly
because of the placement of ornamental letters in the mss.:
ll. 1, 18, 26, 34, 38, 42, 54, 62. The present arrangement
is determined by the changes in the rhyme scheme.
6 In Jeanroy *Lais,* *verai* is emended, without comment, to
vrai and the line is divided into two (rhyming) tri-
syllables. Hans Spanke, p. 66 in "Sequenz und Lai," *Studi
Medievali* n.s. 11 (1938), 12-68, implicitly accepts this
apparently gratuitous change.   19   *anvieusement* could as
easily be *anuieusement* (= *ennuieusement*).   58   *mie*
'physician'. Jeanroy *Lais* emends to *vie*.   63   *Tes = tels.*
The ms. is not quite clear; Jeanroy *Lais* has *ces.*
      62-66   Jeanroy *Lais* places ll. 62-63 at the beginning
of the following stanza and, understanding a lacuna, arranges
them as follows: *Por sostenir/ Ces biens . . ./ Sans
villonie.* Commenting on the entire stanza thus constituted,
he states: "Le sens du dernier couplet est peu satisfaisant
(à qui s'adresse le vocatif du v. [64]?): la construction
rythmique en est aussi bien singulière; ces vers font
l'effet d'une interpolation." Schmidt, who keeps ll. 62-63
where we do, says of the final stanza, p. 74: "Es ist höchst
wahrscheinlich, dass wir in den letzten 3 Versen nur ein
Bruchstück einer längeren Strophe haben." Spanke, p. 67 in
the article cited above, believes that ll. 62-63 belong to
the final stanza, where they form a quotation from an
otherwise undocumented song and serve as the direct object
of l. 64 *chanter*. We find no need to separate ll. 62-63
from st. 7, where their rhymes are perfectly normal and
their syntax and meaning (perhaps with an ironic interpretation of *biens*) entirely congruent with what precedes; nor
does *chanter* require a direct object to be intelligible.
In light of the widespread occurrence of unnamed lovers'
enemies in OF lyric poetry, l. 64 *Felon* needs no elaboration. The only element of st. 8 that is truly problematic
is l. 65 *torment*, which is the poem's sole rhyme-word

without a partner; Schmidt may be right in considering the
stanza fragmentary, although l. 66 does have a ring of
finality.

66 Of the meaning of *deschanter* Jeanroy *Lais* says
nothing; Schmidt, p. 74, finds it "dunkel" but understands
the line in general to mean "'que le diable vous emporte!'."
A. Guesnon, p. 387 in his review of Schmidt (*Le Moyen Age,*
ser. 2, 7 [1903], 385-391, notes: ". . . l'on comprend
'Maufés vos puist *faire deschanter*', antithèse encore
aujourd'hui dans l'usage. 'Déchanter' après avoir 'chanté',
c'est tomber du triomphe dans l'humiliation, de l'espérance
dans la désillusion, etc." Surely, Spanke, p. 67 in the
article cited above, offers the most appropriate gloss: 'to
sing the accompaniment' (*die Begleitung singen*). One might
at the same time understand a second, punning sense: 'to
"unsing", to undo/disavow by singing', as is suggested in
Tobler-Lommatzsch, s.v. *deschanter*.

Reverdie

132

RS 1039, MW 453
Mss. M 110v-111r, T 30v-31r. Music in both mss. Attribution in both mss.

I Mout a mon cuer esjoï
 Li louseignolz qu'ai oï,
   Qui chantant
 Dit: "Fier, fier, oci, oci
 Ceus par cui sunt esbahi   5
   Fin amant.
 Trahitour et mesdisant,
 Se la fussiez consuï,
 De faus janglois amuï
 Fussiez, dont avez dit tant   10
   En mentant."

II   Li dous chans tant m'abeli,
      Jus de mon cheval sailli
            Maintenant.
      La ou le louseignol vi   15
      Me trais, c'ainc ne s'esbati,
            Ainz dist tant
      U language de son chant:
      "Touz loiaus amans grassi
      Et loiauz dames ausi,   20
      Qui les confortent souvant
            En baisant."

III   A cest mot plus n'atendi;
      Le louseignol respondi
            Simplement: 25
      "Louseignol, pour Dieu, ne.l di!
      Trop ai baisier enhaï:
            Oste l'ent,
      Quar baisiers que cuers ne sent
      Est Judas, qui Dieu trahi.   30
      Faintis baisiers a honi
      Maint amant a grant torment,
            Coiement.

MN   Ms. T has a different but related melody in ll.
9-10. Form: through-composed.
1. From here on ms. T is written mostly a 5th higher. 2.
Here ms. changes from a C clef to an F clef, which lowers
the remainder by a 5th, ending the melody on a modally impossible *f*; the F clef has therefore been emended to be read
as a C clef, more or less parallel to the passage in ms. T
(see preceding note).

V   I 1 resioi   5 qui

E   Bartsch, 83-84; Ménard, 137-139; Bec 2, 62.

DF   Picard: *ent* (28) for *en*.

N   There are only about ten *reverdies* in the corpus
of OF lyric poetry. For a recent discussion of the genre
and bibliography, see Bec 1, pp. 136-141. 4 This perhaps
surprisingly bloody cry of the nightingale is not unusual in
OF literature. It occurs first in Chrétien de Troyes' *Phi-
lomena* (l. 1467), where, typically, it is directed against
les mauvés. For other attestations, see Tobler-Lommatzsch,
s.v. *oci.*

133   Pastourelle

RS 1350, MW 63, B 1565
Mss. K 257-258, H 219v, I 4:11, N 126r-v, X 173v-174r.
    Music in KNX. Attribution in KNX.

I   Quant ces moissons sont cueillies,
            Que pastoriaus font rosties,
            Baisseletes sont vesties,
            Rabardiaus font rabardies,
                Maint musart i va.   5
            Cil de Feuchiere et d'Aties
            Ont prises espringueries
            Et mult granz renvoiseries
            De sons, de notes d'estives
                Contre ceus de la.   10
                Mes vous orroiz ja
        Que Guiot i vint qui turuluruta:

Valuru valuru valuraine
Valuru va.

II   Cil d'Avaines les parties   15
           Vinrent a granz genz rengies.
           En loges et en fueillies
           Et en mult granz praeries
             Chascuns s'envoisa.
           Li ami et les amies   20
           Orent ganz et souquanies
           Et coteles haubergies
           Et coifes a denz pincies.
             Chascuns s'escria
             Ci et ça et la,   25
    Mes Guiot i vint qui turuluruta:
     [*Valuru valuru valuraine*
         Valuru va].

III   Li filz au prestre d'Oignies,
           Qui tant en a barcheignies   30
           Que cinc en a fiancies,
           Dont les trois sont engroissies,
             Mult se merveilla
           De Guionet: granz envies
           Li prist; lors fist deablies,   35
           Qu'il vet saillant a poignies
           Entor un chapiau d'orties.
             Mult se debruisa,
             Mes touz les passa
   Guion; pour ce tant biau turuluruta: 40
     [*Valuru valuru valuraine*
         Valuru va].

IV   A deus touses renvoisies,
           Cointement apareillies,
           Vint Poissonet et Helies,   45
           Quant Fouques de Sapignies
             Vers aus s'avança:
           Des mains leur a enrachies.
           Celes n'en sont mie lies,
           Ainz en sont si esmaries   50
           Et s'en sont si corocies
             Que l'une en plora.
             Tost la rapaia
   Guion; por ce tant biau turuluruta:
     [*Valuru valuru valuraine*   55
         Valuru va].

V   Antoines et Acaries
           Et Pinçonnez et Helies
           Jurent les saintes hachies
           Que Fouques ses glotonnies   60
              Encor conperra.
           Quant Guiot vit les folies,
           Lors conmença melodies,
           Notes et espringueries,
           Si que leur melencolies   65
              Tost leur rapaia.
           Le pris enporta
        Guion, que touz tant biau turuluruta:
           Valuru [valuru valuraine
              Valuru va].   70

    MN   Form: A A B rf (ballade).
1. In 1. 7 ms. omits this note; so do mss. NX. 2. In 1. 3
ms. writes f.

    RR   I   9 de note et destiues   II   16 Virent les
gr. III   31 Qui tant   35 Li fist   37 chapiau   40
G. et p. (+1)   IV   54 G. et p. (+1)   V   67 Tant biau
turuluruta   68 Guion que touz le pris enporta

    V   I   1 ces] les H; faillies HI   2 rostiees N;
Q. cil uallet f. amies H   3-4 transposed in I   3 Et
baiseles H; Baisseles (Baicelles I) s. reuesties NXI   4
Rabardiau H   5 Mains muzars I   6 Ciz I; feugi H   7
O. prise lour ballerie I   8 E tres H; Et ont fait grant
aaitie I   9 de note (notes N) et destiues (destrues H)
NXH; Ke muez uadrait lour partie I   10 Que celle deilai
I   11 Mais tous les passait I   12 Q. guiot (guioz H)
NXH; i missing in N; Guiones qui uint qui lour ture lor tura
13-14 Vadeure vadeure vadeure deine vadeure vadeure ua H,
Vallereu vallereu valereu delle vallereu va I
II   15 C. de baruain l. p. H, Aubris et cilz des p. I
16 Virent les NX; grant H; rengiees NX, rangiees I
17-18 transposed in HI   17 second en missing in N   18
Entre beles praeries H, An une grant praierie I   19
Chascun NH; querola H, kerolait I   20 Li amins I   21
ganz] ceinz H, gens I; et missing in X   22 Et coteletes
hauies H   23 c. dedenz N; au dans parties I   24 sati-
fa H, satrica I   25 Fi H   26 M. guiot NX; Qant gioz
i uint qui biau tu relicta H, Guiones i uint ke ture lour
turait I   27-28 Vadeure va. H, Val. I
III   29 fil N; au mere dangres H; danties I   30 Que
t. amait bergeries I   31 Q. dis I   32 D. le fui s. H;

cinc I; engroissees X, angroissiees I   33 Grant bruit
demena H 34 guionez N; grant X; De guion li prist
anuie I   35 Li fist N, Li uint X; Lors fist il grant
dyablie I   36 Il HI; dance et balle a H; poigneis X
37 En son chief ch. doities H; durtries I   38 Toz H;
debrusa N   40 Buionetz li preuz tant biau turelicta H,
Guionet ki vint ki lour turait I   41-42 Va. H, Valer. I
IV 43 O H; renuoisiees H   44 *missing in I*; apareil-
liee H   45 Tint I; poissonez N, poinconet H, poincenes
I   46 f. cil de poingnies H   47 Si deuant lour vait I
48 D. poinz (-s I) HI; errachies N, esrachies X, arra-
chies H, arachiees I   49-50 *transposed in I*   49 Eles
H; mies liees HI   50 en *missing in X*; en sont *missing in
N*; si] mult NH; esbaiadies H; Con ce fut or batenie I
51 Ains an s. mout correciees I   53 Mais tout r. I   54
Guionez li proz tant biau turelicta H, Guiones ki vint ke
lour ture lour tura I   55-56 Vadeure. H, Valer. I
V   57 et caries I   58 poisconez N; Cosins poinconet
daties H, Poincenet et vint deliez I   60 f. cil de
poignees H   61 Encoparra N   62 Q. guiat et l. foiles
H, Cant guions ot lour f. I   63 conmcent H; melodie I
65 Et ait samie acoillie I   66 Totes r. H, Le pris an-
portait I   67 Tant biau turuluruta (turelicta H) NXH
68 Guionet de t. H; t. le pris enporta NXH; Guiones ki
uint ke lour ture lour turait I   69-70 Vadeure vaudeure
vaudeure deine Vaudeure uaudeure ua H; Valer. valer. valer.
de le aller. I

    E   Dinaux 3, 226-227; Bartsch, 273-274; Ménard, 223-
230.

    DF   Picard: *ie* for *iee*, as in *rengies* (16), *fueillies*
(17), *fiancies* (31); *iau(s)* for *eau(s)*, as in *pastoriaus*
(2), *chapiau* (37). Note that the rhymes in *-ie*, some equivalent to *-iee* and others to *-ie* in other dialect areas, reflect rather clearly the Picard origin of the composition.

    N   There are two peasant dances mentioned in this
harvest celebration, l. 4 *rabardies* and l. 7 *espringueries*.
The first, described in Spanke *Lied*, pp. 363-364, included
pantomime and song, and the second, as suggested by the Germanic etymon of the name, involved jumping or leaping.
    6 Ménard, p. 229, identifies *Feuchiere* as Fouquières-
lès-Lens and *Aties* as a small village near Arras.   11 *ceus
de la* designates an opposing group in the dances, who have
come from another town. This group will be named in l. 15.
12 *turuluruta* is no doubt a playful variant of *turlüeter*

'to play the bagpipe', based on *turelurete* 'small bagpipe'.
The following refrain would then represent the sounds of the
instrument.   15-16 Ménard identifies *Avaines* as Avesnes-
lès-Bapaume, near Arras, and is probably correct in glossing
"'Ceux d'Avesnes vinrent en force participer au concours',"
though the prepositionless *les parties* seems somewhat awkward. It may be, however, that *les parties* is a geographi-
cal reference (see the variant in ms. I).   21 Gloves,
rather than mittens, and *souquanies* (q.v. Tobler-Lommatzsch
under *soscanie*) are items of attire reflecting the holiday
setting of the poem.   23 'And pleated headdress'.   36
saillant a poignies 'doing somersaults'.   59 The "holy
sufferings" by which they swear are those of Christ.

134
Jeu-parti (partner: Thibaut de Champagne)

RS 1185, MW 1159
Mss. O 127v-128r, A 137r-v, K 41, M 71r-v, N 9r, T 20r, V
   21r-v, X 40v-41r, a 134v-135r, b 139v. Music in AKMO
   VX. Attribution in KTX.

I   Sire, ne me celez mie
       Li quelx vos iert plus a gré:
       S'il avient que vostre amie
       Vos ait parlement mandé
       Nu a nu lez son costey   5
       Par nuit, que n'an verroiz mie,
       Ou de jor vos bait et rie

```
                    En un beau pré
                    Et enbraz, mais ne di mie
                    Qu'il i ait de plus parlé?                    10

        II          --Guillaume, c'est grant folie
                    Quant ensi avez chanté;
                    Li bergiers d'une abbaïe
                    Eüst assez mieuz parlé.
                    Quant j'avrai lez mon costé            15
                    Mon cuer, ma dame, m'amie,
                    Que j'avrai toute ma vie
                            Desirré,
                    Lors vos quit la drüerie
                    Et le parlement dou pré.                 20

        III         --Sire, je di qu'en s'enfance
                    Doit on aprendre d'amors;
                    Mais mout faites mal semblance
                    Que vos sentez les dolors:
                    Pou prisiez esté ne flors,            25
                    Gent cors ne douce acointance,
                    Beaus resgarz ne contenance
                            Ne colors;
                    En vos n'a point d'astenance;
                    Ce deüst prendre uns priors.           30

        IV          --Guillaume, qui ce comance
                    Bien le demoinne folors,
                    Et mout a pou conoissance
                    Qui n'en va au lit le cors,
                    Que desoz beaus covertors             35
                    Prent on tele seürtance
                    Dont l'on s'oste de doutance
                            Et de freors;
                    Tant comme soie en balance,
                    N'iert ja mes cuers sanz paors.        40

        V           --Sire, por rien ne voudroie
                    Que nuns m'eüst a ce mis.
                    Quant celi cui j'ameroie
                    Et qui tout m'avroit conquis
                    Puis veoir en mi le vis               45
                    Et baisier a si grant joie
                    Et embracier toute voie
                            A mon devis,
                    Saichiez, se l'autre prenoie,
                    Ne seroie pas amis.                    50
```

        VI   --Guillaume, se Deus me voie,
                Folie avez entrepris,
                Que, se nue la tenoie,
                N'en prendroie paradis.
                Ja por esgarder son vis   55
                A paiez ne m'en tendroie
                S'autre chose n'en avoie.
                        J'ai mieuz pris,
                Qu'au partir se vos convoie,
                N'en porteroiz c'un faus ris.   60

        VII   --Sire, Amors m'a si sopris
                Que siens sui, ou que je soie,
                Et sor Gilon m'en metroie
                        A son devis,
                Li quelx va plus droite voie   65
                Ne li quelx maintient le pis.

        VIII   --Guillaume, fous et pensis
                I remaindroiz tote voie,
                Et cil qui ensi donoie
                        Est mout chaitis.   70
                Bien vuil que Gilon en croie,
                Et sor Jehan m'en sui mis.

     MN   Ms. A has a second melody; ms. V has a third one;
ms. O is mensurally notated, ms. A mostly so, ms. V only
through l. 5.   Form: A A B; both envoys are sung to ll. 5-
10.
1. Ms. seems to write ♪♫ for all three-note figures.   2.
Ms. writes a longa.   3. In l. 4 ms. writes no rest.

     RR   II   17 Quant laurai   IV   31 ce demande   35
Q. soz *(-1)*   40 paor

     V   Lines 1-15 missing from N through loss of folio.
Stanzas: A(N)Tab   I II III IV V   VI   VII VIII
            M   I II III VI VII VIII
            VX   I II III IV V   VIII
            K   I II III IV V
I   1 nel m. Kb   2 Le quel b; est V, vient b; plus]
mieus ATab, melz K   4 p. done M   6 q. ne V, nel b;
venres a   7 de] par Aa; iors TX, iorz KV; baut V   9
enbrast V; dis Aa
II   11 Vuillaumes Aa; grans Aa   13 Uns A, Un a   15
N begins with coste   16 ma da A; d. et mamie ANVXa   17

Quant (Tant K) laurai KMNTVX   18 desirree VX   19 Dont
b 20 le p. d. p. *missing in A*
III   21 quen enfance b   23 M. poi en f. s. b   24 Q.
en Aa, nen MT; ses d. M; Q. vous en s. d. b   25 entes
n. b   26 d. samblance Tb, samblanche Aa   27 Bel Aab,
Biau KMX; regart Aa   30 un N; prious AÑa
IV   31 ce demande AKNTVXa   32 Moult b   34 Kil a; ne
KNVb   35 Quar de son b. b; couvretour Aa, couuertos N
36 Prent on *missing in V*; P. icele b; on il t. A, on
jtele a; sustanche Aa, asseurance b   37 D. on AKNTVX-
ab; oste V   38 Et *missing in N*   39 Quar b; com (-n) ie
s. AKNTVXa, tant com s. b; sui V
V   41 riens (-z V) AKNTVXa   43 cele ANXb; ki A, qui
NTa, que KVXb; q. ie a. X   44 q. tant T   50 pas] mie
KNVXb
VI   53 Quar b; trouuoie Aab   55 Ne b; resgarder AMa,
regarder Tb   56 paie Aa, paiet Tb; me t. ab   58 J.
le m. p. Aa, A mon devis b   59 sel v. ATa; Quar sau
partir me c. b   60 porterai b
VII   63 sus b; m. tenroie b   64 Et sus ses dis b   66
Et le quel soustient le p. b
VIII   67 fol Aa   68 remaurai Aa, remaindroit T; uoies
Aa   69 qui *missing in a*   70 mout] bien AMNTXab; E. tout
pen ch. V   72 Mais (Mes M) AMTab; sus Mb; me s. Mb

E   La Ravallière, 110; Tarbé *Thib*, 107-109; Wallensköld *Thib,* 139-144; Långfors *Rec* 1, 19-23; Toja, 406-409;
Ménard, 193-199.

DF   Burgundian: *costey* (5) for *costé*; *nuns* (42) for
nus; *saichiez* (49) for *sachiez*.

N   It is not entirely certain that the Guillaume of
this poem is Guillaume le Vinier. See Wallensköld *Thib*, p.
143, and Ménard p. 9. Lines 7 and 8 of each stanza form a
single metric unit of eleven syllables: 7 + -*e* + 3 (beginning with a consonant) or 4 (beginning with a vowel, in
which case -*e* is elided). Guillaume poses the question:
would you rather make love at night in total darkness, or
enjoy the company of your mistress in daylight without making love? Thibaut chooses the first alternative. Gilon and
Jehan are asked to judge the debate.
9-10 'but I do not say that there is talk of anything
else', i.e., there is no love-making.   30 'A prior should
make such a choice'.   34 'who does not go straight to
bed'.   52-54 'You have spoken foolishly [in maintaining]
that, if . . .'.   59 The subject of *convoie* is the lady.

135   Chanson

RS 1086, MW 1752
Mss. M 108r, A 129v, T 28v, a 33v-34r. Music in all mss.
   Attribution in all mss.

I   S'onques chanters m'eüst aidié,
         Trop me sui de chanter teüs;
         Nonpourquant tant m'a avancié
         Qu'en loiauté m'est loz creüs.
         Par cel löer sui deceüs,   5
         Si com cil c'on loe au jöer,
         Cui tant plaist ce qu'il s'ot löer
         Ne set mot s'a ses dras perdus;
         Einsinc sui de sens deceüs.

II   S'Amours ot ainc en soi pitié,   10
         Puis que sui pour loial tenus,
         Trouver doi loial amistié,
         Car lonc tans m'i sui atendus.
         Avoir la doi, se ainc l'ot nus!
         Mais onques, ce me fait douter,   15
         Cordoaniers n'ot bon soller,
         N'ainc drapiers ne fut bien vestus,
         N'ainc n'ot amie loiauz drus.

III   De tant m'a Amours alegié,
        Quant g'i vois, que bien sui venuz.   20
        Maiz s'i truis noient d'amistié:
        Lors que m'en part, m'est retoluz.
        Si sui li povres durfeüs
        C'on fait l'or fouir et quester;
        Se.l guaite on si pres qu'enporter   25
        N'en puet rienz, tant l'ait bien repus;
        Si s'en depart povres et nus.

IV   Et quant si me sent atirié,
        Ne me feroit bon traire ensus
        Ainz que plus m'ait adamagié?   30
        Or ai je dit que recreüs,
        Si fais com l'enfes desseüs.
        Quant s'est ars par trop pres chaufer,
        En l'iaue court son doit bouter
        Pour alegier; lors se cuist pluz: 35
        Char que fus blece sane fus.

MN   Ms. A has many variants and is written partly a
2nd lower; ms. T is written a 5th higher; ms. a is written
partly a 4th, partly a 2nd higher. Form: A A¹ B.
1. In l. 1 ms. writes *c'*. 2. Ms. writes an extra note *c'*.

RR   II   13 *missing, reading from a*   III   25 p.
que porter

V   I   2 tenus Aa   4 loiautes A; mes Aa   5
P. tel Aa   7 Ki Aa   8 Kil ne set sa s. Aa   II   11
loiaus Aa   12 T. li d. l. a. T   13 *missing in T*; t.
men s. A   14 d. sainq(u)es l. Aa   17 Ne d. Aa; ventus
a   18 Ne n. Aa   III   21 M. ni t. a; noient] samblant
Aa;   22 Lues TAa   25 p. que p. T   27 Ains TAa   IV
28 Qant ensi me A, Qant jssi me a   29 Dont me Aa; b.
retraire e. T   31 Dit (Doute a) ai com falis r. Aa   33
Q. est T   34 A Aa; s. bras a   36 *final* fus *missing in*
T

E   Ulrix, 802-804; Ménard, 86-88.

DF   Picard: *iaue* (34) for *eaue*; *fus* (36) for *feus*.

N   This poem is quite unusual for the degree to which
it incorporates images and proverbial expressions of a non-
courtly stamp: gambling, shoemaking, mining, etc.   7-8

'Who is so pleased to hear himself praised [that] he does
not know if he has lost his shirt'.   9 *de sens* 'cleverly';
deceüs, here as in l. 5, may be either 'fallen, brought low'
(from *dec(h)eoir*) or 'tricked, deceived' (from *decevoir*).
20 *bien sui venuz* 'I am welcome(d)'.   26 *tant l'ait bien
repus* 'however well he may have hidden it'.   29 *traire en-
sus* 'to go away, take my leave'.   31 *dit que* 'spoken like
a'.   32 *desseüs = deceüs*, past participle of *decevoir*.

136   Chanson

RS 169, MW 2371, B 1567
Mss. M 110r, R 99v-100r, T 30r. Music in all mss. Attribu-
     tion in MT.

1. Bien doit chan- ter   la qui chan- çon set   plai-   re

2. en   ma-nie- re   d'a-mour et   de bon- te.

3. Je.1 di pour moi   qui tel fois   ai chan- te

4. que   au- si   bien   u mieuz me   ve- nist tai- re.

5. Maiz qui sert   sanz   son ser- vi-   ce par- fai-   re,

6. vis m'est qu'en fo-   lour ait   son   tanz u- se.

7. Pour   ce, et   pluz pour ma grant   vo- len- te,

8. ser- vi- rai tant que je   sa-   vrai par- ti-   e

8 9. quel joie est d'a- voir a- mi-   e.

I   Bien doit chanter la qui chançon set plaire
        En maniere d'amour et de bonté.
        Je.l di pour moi qui tel fois ai chanté
        Que ausi bien u mieuz me venist taire.
        Maiz qui sert sanz son service parfaire,   5
        Vis m'est qu'en folour ait son tanz usé.
        Pour ce, et pluz pour ma grant volenté,
        Servirai tant que je savrai partie
                Quel joie est d'avoir amie.

II   De bien amer avrai joie u contraire,   10
        Qu'ensi l'ai pieç'a pramis et vöé,
        Si com firent nostre ancissour ainsné
        En qui cuers ot fine Amors son repaire.
        Or voi chascun l'amourous contrefaire
        Sanz cuer de desirrier entalenté,   15
        Dont trop se tendroient pour engané,
        S'il avoient seü une foïe
                Quel joie [est d'avoir amie].

III   La vïele et Amours par essamplaire
        Doivent estre d'un samblant comparé,   20
        Car la vïele et Amours sunt paré
        De joie et de soulaz qui l'en set traire.
        Mais cil qui ne set vïeler fait raire
        La vïele, si li tolt sa bonté;
        Ausi fait l'en Amours par fausseté: 25
        A soi la tolt ne ne set, que qu'il die,
                Quel joie [est d'avoir amie].

IV   Li rubis a tesmoins del lapidaire
        Est des pierres sires en dignité,
        Et Amours dame de joliveté,   30
        Resjoïssanz en fin cuer debonaire.
        Mes cuers en li s'esjoïst et resclaire.
        Pieç'a l'a de moi parti et sevré,
        Et s'il li plaist qu'ait le cors de bonté
        Pour savourer cuer et cors sanz partie--   35
                Quel joie [est d'avoir amie]!

V   Com de celui qui l'or de son aumaire
        A si maumis, despendu et gasté
        Qu'i ne parose savoir la purté

A comfait chief li remanans puet traire   40
Est il de moi, quant voi cors et viaire
Furni de sens, de valour, de bonté.
La n'os savoir ma mort ne ma santé,
Quar, qui bon espoir pert, il ne set mie
    Quel joie [est d'avoir amie].   45

VI Sire freres, trop vous voi demoré,
    Si cuit qu'aiez seü et savouré
       Quel joie est d'avoir amie.

   MN   Form: through-composed + rf; the envoy is sung to
11. 6-7 + rf.
1. In ms. this note seems to be erased or washed out. 2.
Ms. has *b*; emended according to ms. T.

   RR   III   20 D. e. ensamble andui c.   21 s. assene
(+1)   IV   29 dignitez   30 ioliuetez   33 et desseure
(+1)   V   38 si *missing*

   V   Stanzas: R I II III IV V
                      T I II III
I   1 B. doi R; cui chancons T   3 teus f. T; a ch. R
4 Causi b. v m. me couenist t. T   6 ait] a R   7 Et p.
ce p. par ma g. v. R   9 Quex T
II   11 Car ainsi lai et p. et v. R   13 Enques c. ot
bone amour s. r. R   14 chascuns R   16 sentendroient
R; pour] a RT 17 fie R 18 Quex. T; est et cetera
added in R
III   21 parel T   22 s. qui en R, s. kis en T   23 Et
R; M. ciex T; f. braire R   24 Sa R; li *missing in T*
25 Et cil qui fait a. R, Ausi qui faint a. T; p. folete
R   26 le t. nil ne RT; quel con d. R, quel kil d. T
27 Queus T; et c. *added in R*, est dauoir *added in T*
IV   28 et t. R   30 Et a. et dame en j. R   32 Mon R;
cuers *missing in R*   33 l'a *missing in R* ·34 Si li p.
prengne le c. de b. R   35 P. sauoir c. de c. s. p. R
36 et c. *added in R*
V   37 Di quil est de celi qui son afaire R   38 despendi
R   39 purete R 40 le remanant puist R   41 voi vo
cler v. R   42 biauté R   43 Dont vos s. R   45 est
dauoir amie *added in R*

   E   Noack, 105-106; Ménard, 124-128.

   N   The poem shows a number of varied exceptions to
the normal 4 + 6 decasyllabic meter; see, for example,

11. 5, 6, and 15.   1 *la qui* (= *cui*) *chançon* 'whose song';
the antecedent of the relative, and subject of *doit*, is an
understood *cil*.   4   *Que*, correlative of 1. 3 *tel*, 'when'.
5-6 Cf. the proverb *Qui sert et ne parsert son loier pert*,
cited in Morawski, no. 2138.   8 *partie = en partie.*   13
qui = cui 'whose'.   20 *d'un samblant* 'in one respect'.
22 *qui* 'for anyone who'.   28 Of the ruby, which occurs in
a number of *chansons*, Dragonetti, p. 268, states: "Les au-
teurs de *Lapidaires* attribuent [au rubis] des propriétés
merveilleuses ou mystiques vraiment souveraines . . .; [se-
lon] Marbode de Rennes: 'Li rubis . . . est principaus sor
totes pieres . . .'."   34 *de bonté* 'out of [Love's] good-
ness'.   35 *sanz partie* 'exclusively'.   39-40 'That he (*i*
= *il*) dares not determine in pure truth how much the balance
amounts to'.   46 'I see that you are very quiet'. The reference may be to Gilles le Vinier, Guillaume's brother, who
apparently composed very few love songs.

SIMON D'AUTHIE

<u>137</u>   Pastourelle

RS 1381 (= 1385), MW 2288, B 1882 (four other sources)
Mss. M 123r, T 37v-38v, U 62v-63r. Music in all mss. Attribution in MT.

        I   Quant li dous estez define
              Et li frois yvers revient,
              Que flors et fueille decline
              Et ces oisiaus n'en soviant
              De chanter en bois n'en brueill,   5
              En chantant si com je sueill
              Toz seus mon chemin erroie;
              Si oï pres de ma voie
              Chanter la bele Emmelot:
              "*Deurenleu!* j'aim bien Guiot,   10
              Toz mes cuers a lui s'otroie."

        II   Grant joie fait la meschine
              Quant de Guiot li souvient;
              Je li dis: "Amie fine,

Cil vous saut qui tot maintient!   15
Vostre amor desir et vueill,
A vous servir toz m'acueill.
Se volez que vostres soie,
Robe vous donrai de soie,
Si laissiez cel vilain sot,   20
Deurenleu! c'ainc ne vous sot
Bien amer ne faire joie."

III   "Or parlez vous de folie,
        Sire, foi que je doi vous,
        Ja, se Dieu plaist, de s'amie   25
        Ne sera mes amis cous.
        Tournez vous! fuiés de ci!
        Ja ne lairai mon ami
        Pour nul home que je voie;
        Ne m'a pas dit que je.l doie   30
        Pour autrui entrelaissier.
        Deurenleu! pour un baisier
        M'a doné gans et corroie."

IV   "Hé, douce rienz envoisie,
        Cuers debonaires et douz,   35
        Recevez par cortoisie
        Mon cuer qui se rent a vous,
        En qui je del tout m'afi;
        Mains jointes merci vous cri,
        Mes que vostre amour soit moie   40
        Qui mon cuer destraint et loie
        Si que ne l'en puis sachier.
        Deurenleu! pour embracier
        Mes cuers au vostre se loie."

V   "Bien m'avez ore assaïe,   45
        Mes pou i avez conquis.
        Mainte autre en avez proïe:
        Ne l'avez pas ci apris,
        N'encore ci ne.l lairoiz.
        N'est pas li cuers si destrois   50
        Com il pert a la parole;
        Teus baise feme et acole
        Qui ne l'aime tant ne quant.
        Deurenleu! alez avant!
        Ja ne mi troveroiz fole."   55

MN   Ms. U has many variants. Form: A A¹ B B¹.

RR   II   15   qui vous m.   22   Bien bien a. *(+1)*
III   31   autrui] nul home

V   Stanzas III and IV not included in U.
I   1 Q. la douce saisons fine   U   2   Que li fel yuer r.
U   4   Que ces oiselez ne tient   U; souien   T   7   esroie   T
8   p. dune noie   U   9   b. aielot   U   10   Dorenlot   U   11
lui] li   T; cuers *missing in U*   II   15   ki vos m.   T   18
Se dangniez q.   U   19   reube   T, ceyntur   U   21   Dorenlot
cainz   U   III   27   T. fuies vos de ci   T   IV   39   vos
cri merci   T   40   amors   T   44   M. c. a lautre se l.   T
V   45   Sire or mauez essaie   U   47   maint   T   48   Ci ne
lauez pas apris   U   49   Nencor ci ne le l.   T, Nen ici ne
lo l.   U   53   Kil   T   54   Dorenlot   U   55   troueres   T,
trouerez   U

E   Dinaux 3, 451-452; Bartsch, 137-138; Bartsch-
Wiese, 217; Gennrich "Simon", 84-87; Cremonesi, 62-63; Zink
Past, 139-140.

DF   Picard: *ie* for *iee*, as in *envoisie* (34), *assaïe*
(45).

N   Gennrich "Simon," pp. 62-64, sees this pastourelle
of the early 13th century, the only one known to have been
composed by Simon d'Authie, as one of the first in French
depicting honest and forthright, and successful, resistance
to the knight's advances. Indeed, he considers it symbolic
of the decline of aristocratic song and the ascent of Northern bourgeois lyric, noting that the very setting in which
the knight's unsuccessful venture takes place, ll. 1-5, is,
exceptionally, autumnal. Note the unusual inclusion of the
refrain *Deurenleu* within the body of each stanza. See Gennrich "Simon," p. 75.

Chanson historique   <u>138</u>

RS 699, MW 1820
Mss. M 97r-v, T 149v-150r. Music in both mss. Attribution
in both mss.

I   Je chantaisse volentiers liement
       Se je trouvaisse en mon cuer l'ochoison,
       Et deïssë et l'estre et l'errement,
       Se j'osaisse metre m'entention,
       De la grant court de France au douz renom,   5
             Ou toute valour se baigne;
       Des preudomes me lo, qui que s'en plaigne,
       Dont tant i a que bien porrons veoir,
       Ce quit, par tans lor sens et lor savoir.

II   De ma dame vous di je vraiement   10
       Qu'ele aime tant son petit enfançon

Qu'el ne veut pas qu'il se travaut souvent
En departir l'avoir de sa maison,
Maiz ele en doune et depart a fuison;
    Mout en envoie en Espaigne   15
Et mout en met en esforcier Champaigne,
S'en fait fermer chastiaux pour mieuz valoir.
De tant sunt ja par li creü si hoir.

III   Se ma dame fust nee de Paris,
Et ele fust roïne par raison;   20
S'a ele assez fier cuer, ce m'est avis,
Pour faire honte a un bien haut baron
Et d'alever un trahiteur felon.
    Deus en cest point le maintaigne
Et guart son fius que ja feme ne praigne,   25
Quar par home ne puis je pas veoir
Qu'ele perde jamaiz son grant pooir.

IV   Preudome sunt et sage et de haut pris,
S'en doivent bien avoir bon guerredon
Cil qui li ont enseignié et apris   30
A eslongier ceus de ci environ;
Et ele a bien fermee sa leçon,
    Quar touz les het et desdaigne.
Bien i parut l'autre jour a Compaigne,
Quant li baron ne porent droit avoir   35
Ne ne.s deigna esguarder ne veoir.

V   Que vont querant cil fol baron bregier
Qu'i ne viennent a ma dame servir,
Qui mieuz savroit tout le mont justicier
Qu'entr'eus trestouz d'un povre bourc joïr? 40
Et del tresor, s'ele en fait son plaisir,
    Ne voi qu'a eus en ataigne.
Conquise en a la justice roumaigne,
Si qu'ele fait les bons pour maus tenir
Et les pluseurs en une hore saintir.   45

VI   Deus! li las de la Bretaigne
Trouvera il jamaiz ou il remaigne?
S'ensi li veut toute terre tolir,
Dont ne sai je qu'il puisse devenir.

MN   Ms. T is written a 4th higher and from line 6 on
has a different melody. Form: A A B; the envoy is sung to
ll. 6-9.
1. Ms. writes a clef a line too high, so that the notes to

the next nine syllables seem to be a 3rd lower; emended according to ms. T and the many manuscripts that carry the
contrafactum RS 700, all of which, despite major variants,
carry this line, except ms. V. 2. Ms. first writes a ligature starting with *g'-f'*, then half erases this and corrects. 3. Ms. may have intended an ascending plica.

RR   I   4 Se iosaisse mention *(-3)*   8 porront
III 19 ne *(-1)*   46 la *missing*

V   I   3 desisse   6 valors   8 ki b. porront   9 Par
tans ie quic   II 12 Ke ne v. p. ki se   16 enforchier
compaigne   III   25 s. fill   V   38 Kil

E   P. Paris, 182; Leroux de Lincy, 165-168; Tarbé,
Thib, 182; Gennrich *Alt Lied* 1, 15-17.

DF   Picard: first-person sing. imp. subj. in *-aisse*,
as in *chantaisse* (1); *le* (24) for *la*; *fius* (25) for *fiz*.

N   This work is a contrafactum of the Châtelain de
Couci's love song RS 700, with which it shares not only melody, rhyme scheme, and rhymes, but also the two opening
verses. The historical event inspiring Hue's *serventois* was
the revolt (1226-30) of a group of feudal lords, including
the poet, against Blanche of Castille, who, upon the death
of her husband, King Louis VIII of France, and because of
the minority of Louis IX, assumed the powers of regent. Hue
attacks her character, accusing her of diversion of royal
funds, alluding to her apparent liaison with the powerful
Count of Champagne, the trouvère Thibaut, and alleging brib-
ery of the Church. For greater detail, see Régine Pernoud,
La reine Blanche (Paris: Albin Michel, 1972), pp. 150-159.
    4 Parenthetical statement: 'if I dared give [it] my
attention'.   9 *quit = cuit* 'I believe'.   17 'And she is
having castles reinforced in order to resist better'.   18
'To this extent, [the fortunes of] her heirs are increased'.
20 'She would then rightfully be queen'. *Et* is not a conjunction here, but an intensifier; see Tobler-Lommatzsch,
s.v. *et*, col. 1510f.   21 *S'* = adverbial *si*.   25 The nominative form *fius* would be correctly replaced here by *fil*.
32 'And she has learned her lesson well'.   35 *droit avoir*
'make their cause prevail'.   37 The *fol baron bregier* in
this heavily ironic passage are, of course, Hue and his fel-
low rebels.   38 *i = il*.   39-40 *Qu'entr'eus trestouz*
'than all of them [would know]'.   43 *roumaigne* 'Roman'.
46-47 The "tired wretch" who will perhaps never find rest

is Pierre Mauclerc, Count of Brittany, particular enemy of
the Queen.   49 *dont = donc*; understand *ce* before *qu'il*.

<u>139</u>   Chanson historique

RS 1129, MW 1414
Mss. T 150r-v, M 97v. Music in both mss. Attribution in
  both mss.

I   En talent ai ke je die
       Çou dont me sui apensés.
       Cil ki tient Campaigne et Brie
       N'est mie drois avöés,   4
       Car puis ke fu trespassés
       Cuens Tiebaus a mort de vie,
       Saichiés, fu il engenrés.
       Or gardés s'il est bien nés!   8

II   Deüst tenir signorie
       Teus hom, chasteaus ne cités,
       Tresdont k'il failli d'aïe
       Au roi ou il fu alés?   12
       Saichiés, s'il fust retornés,

Ne l'em portast garantie
Hom ki fust de mere nés
K'il n'en fust desiretés.   16

III   Par le fill sainte Marie,
      Ki ens le crois fu penés,
      Tel cose a faite en sa vie
      Dont deüst estre apellés.   20
      Sire Dieus, bien le savés,
      Il ne se deffendist mie,
      Car il se sent encopés.
      Signeur baron, k'atendés?   24

IV   Cuens Tiébaus, dorés d'envie,
      De felonie fretés,
      De faire chevallerie
      N'estes vous mie alosés;   28
      Ançois estes mieus maullés
      A savoir de sirurgie.
      Vieus et ors et bosofflés:
      Totes ces teches avés.   32

V   Bien est France abastardie
      (Signeur baron, entendés!)
      Quant feme l'a em baillie,
      Et tele com bien savés.   36
      Il et ele, les a les,
      Le tiegnent par compaignie.
      Cil n'en est fors rois clamés
      Ki piech'a est coronés.   40

MN   The melodies in mss. M and T are unique but related. Form (M and T): A A B.
1. In l. 2 ms. M writes no rest.

RR   I   7 engerres   II   13 recornes

V   I   7 engendrez   8 Reguardez   III   17 fix
22 sen   IV-V   29-40 *text following* estes *is cut out of*
folio

E   P. Paris, 186; Leroux de Lincy, 169-171; Tarbé
Thib, 178; Gennrich *Alt Lied* 1, 17-19; Van d W *Trouv*, 553-
554, 595.

DF   Picard, including *au* for *ou*, as in *maullés* (29);
signorie (19) and *signeur* (24) for *seign-*; *c* for *ch*, as in

Campaigne (3), *cose* (19); *ch* for ç, as in *piech'a* (40); final *s* for *z*, as in *apensés* (2), *gardés* (8); *ens* (18) for *en*;
çou (2) for *ce*; *le* (18, 38) for *la*.

N̲   For the historical background of this *serventois*,
see notes to RS 699; see, too, Leroux de Lincy, pp. 153-159.
The present poem is chiefly aimed at Thibaut de Champagne.
4 *drois avöés* 'true lord'.   5 *puis ke* 'after'.   6 The
reference here is to Thibaut *père*.   9-16 These verses repeat the widespread rumor that Thibaut, having gone to the
aid of King Louis VIII at Montpensier, was responsible for
his death there.   Line 13 *il* designates the king; l. 14 *l'*
(= *li*) and l. 16 *il* designate Thibaut.   17 Absolute genitive: 'the son of Mary'.   29-30 The ironic statement that
Thibaut is more skilled in medicine than in knighthood al-
ludes to Louis' death by poisoning.   39 'He, i.e., Louis
IX, is king in name only'.

THIBAUT DE CHAMPAGNE

Chanson

RS 2075, MW 2437
Mss. X 26v-27r, A 152r, B 1r, C 9r-v, F 131r-v-132r, K 29,
   M 75v-76r, O 1r, R 38v-39r, S 230v, T 13v, U 125v-126r,
   V 15r-v, Z 2r-v, a 7v-8r. Music in KMORVXZa. Attribu-
   tion in KRTXa; attributed to Pierre de Gand in C.

I   Ausi conme unicorne sui
        Qui s'esbahit en regardant
        Quant la pucele va mirant.
        Tant est liee de son ennui,
        Pasmee chiet en son giron;   5
        Lors l'ocit on en traïson.
        Et moi ont mort d'autel senblant
        Amors et ma dame, por voir;
        Mon cuer ont, n'en puis point ravoir.

II   Dame, quant je devant vos fui   10
        Et je vos vi premierement,
        Mes cuers aloit si tresaillant
        Qu'il vos remest quant je m'en mui.

Lors fu menés sanz raençon
En la douce chartre en prison,   15
Dont li piler sont de talent
Et li huis sont de biau veoir
Et li anel de bon espoir.

III   De la chartre a la clef Amors,
Et si i a mis trois portiers: 20
Biau Semblant a non li premiers,
Et Biautez ceus en fait seignors;
Dangier a mis a l'uis devant,
Un ort felon, vilain puant,
Qui mult est maus et pautoniers.   25
Cist troi sont et viste et hardi;
Mult ont tost un home saisi.

IV   Qui porroit soufrir la tristors
Et les assaus de ces huissiers?
Onques Rollans ne Oliviers   30
Ne vainquirent si fors estors;
Il vainquirent en conbatant,
Mais ceus vaint on humiliant.
Soufrirs en est gonfanoniers;
En cest estor dont je vos di,   35
N'a nul secors que de merci.

V   Dame, je ne dout mes riens plus
Fors tant que faille a vos amer.
Tant ai apris a endurer
Que je sui vostres tout par us;   40
Et se il vos en pesoit bien,
Ne m'en puis je partir por rien
Que je n'aie le remenbrer
Et que mes cuers ne soit adés
En la prison et de moi pres.   45

VI   Dame, quant je ne sai guiler,
Merciz seroit de saison mes
De soustenir si grevain fes.

MN   In lines 1, 2, and 8 several mss. deviate.
Form: through-composed; the envoy is sung to ll. 7-9.
1. Ms. writes a diamond-shaped note.

RR   I   9 ont *missing*; p. auoir   II   13 vos
missing; m'en] me   18 de] dou   III   22 biaute   26 et
missing   IV   29 de ses   V   40 je *missing*

V   Ms. A, because of loss of a folio, lacks stanzas
I, II and most of III, beginning with l. 24 *puant*. B, for
the same reason, lacks st. I and most of st. II, beginning
with l. 18 *espoir*. F, because of erasure, lacks st. I and
the first four words of II. St. VI is not included in ACKR
SU.
I 1 Einsi M, Ainsi R; com (cum O) lunicorne (li u. U)
CORSU; seus U   2 Ke C; esgardant R   4 liee *missing C*;
ennui] mirer M, ami R   6 La RZa; on] lan S; Et la lo-
cit ent. T   7 mort] fait S; par tel R, de tel S, ditel
Za   9 ont] a   a; ne le puis r. R, nel puis pas r. Za;
auoir CKV
II   10 Douce dame quant ie uos vi (cant uos conu U) CU
11 Et uos conu p. C; premierent Z   12 Li CU; malait
CU, maloit R   13 Q. se FMT, Q. i S, Que il K, Can uos
C, vos *missing V*; je mesmui R; m. mux C, meus U   15 la]
vo R   17 sont *missing M*, est FRZa   18 annes R, anials
U; dun dous e. R
III   19 a] ont CU; le FZ, les CRSUa; cel B, clez M,
cle(i)s CRSUa; damours V   20 a] ont CU; tr. uxiers U
21 Beaus T, Biaus Z; sanblans B, samblans FTZa   22
biaute AKV; ceut B, ceaus F, ces MOT, ciaus Z, chieus
a, cil R; ont f. seigneur R; Et de bonteit ont f. signor
CU, Et biaute a non li secons S   23 Dangiers B; a] est
B, ont CRST, on U; m. el front d. Ra   24 ors U; vilain
felon RSVZa, vilain ser(f) et p. CU   25 Ke CU; mult
missing Z, tant CU, est ARa; mauues et R, et maus et Aa;
maus] fel BCU, faus T, mais Z; et *missing BC*; pautonier
R, posteis C, poestis U   26 Ci K, Cil FMORSTZ, Chil
Aa; et *missing MR*, fort FS, molt T; Atraians et v. B, Li
dui en (an U) sont CU; viste] uistes B, ruiste R, prou
CO, prout U; hardiz B
IV   28 les essaulz C, assaus S, tormans U   29 Et
missing V, Ne B; les tormens C, destroiz S; des trois
CU; portiers CR   30 ni Aa, nen U   31 Ne soufrirent
B; fort BSU, grans (-z) AFMRTZa, grant C; esto(u)r CSU
32 Qui S; vancoient C, uenquoient F, uankoient U   33
Amors uoint (vaint U) CU; ces FOT, cez M, ses B, cil
RSZ, chil Aa; on] en ABCSa   34 Sousfrir R, Soffrir S;
Des .iij. ont fait g. C, De cortois font g. U   35 Mais
en c(h)estui ARZa, Sil (Cil U) est ensi CU, En cest as-
saut S; com j. CU, que (ke) j. FMS   36 Ni at pitie C,
Ni valt pitiet U; confort S; que] fors ABCFMORSTUZa; ke
CTU
V   37 je ne ne d. M, nen R; mes *missing V*; rien M; plus
missing M; D. je ne redout (-c A, -s U) ARSUZa; mais plus
ARa, mais riens Z, tant rien U; Douce dame ne dout tant

rien C   38 F. t. ne B, F. que ne S, Que (Ke) t. q. MT,
Ke tans me F, Ke ie ne CU, Mes t. q. V, Puis que (ke)
tant ARZa; fail ARZa   39 ai *missing* M; empris BTZa; a]
et CU; endureit C, endure V   40 uostre sui M; uostre
FS; toz uostres C, tous uostre U; tous ARa   41 poise
B; Et se (sil S) uos en p. or bien CS, Et cil ne man fail-
loit de riens U   42 Ne m'en] Nan R; riens RU   43
missing U; je *missing* B, ien T; la remembrance R   45 la]
vo ARZa, sa B; Dedans la cha(i)rtre CU; et moi apres R;
moi] uos CFMSU
VI   46 je *missing* V   47 Merci BFMTV, Merchi a; s. bien
de s. m. Z   48 A F; greueus BFMT, greuous O, grief Z,
tres grant a

 E La Ravallière, p. 70; Dinaux 2, 343-344; Tarbé
Thib, 4-6; Scheler 1, 144-146; Voretsch, 172-173; Wallen-
sköld *Thib*, 111-116; Spaziani *Ant*, 87-92; Cremonesi, 194-197;
Spaziani *Canz*, 51-54; Chastel, 474-479; Toja, 403-406;
Maillard *Anth*, 71-73; Mary 1, 354-357; Goldin, 466-469.

 N Wallensköld *Thib* notes, p. lxxxvii, that, toward
the end of the 13th century or beginning of the 14th, the
musicographer Jean de Grouchy cites this composition as a
cantus coronatus (crowned, or prize, song). Pierre de Gand,
to whom ms. C attributes it, is unknown. For a brief analysis of the allegory, see Dragonetti, pp. 246-247. See, too,
J. M. Butler, "The Lover and the Unicorn'" *Studies in Medieval Culture* 11 (1977), 95-102.
 1-6 It was a widespread belief that the only way to
capture a unicorn was to expose it to a virgin; the animal
would be irresistibly drawn to her and swoon in her lap; see
Réau 1, pp. 89-92. For the best-known OF presentation of
the legend, with allegorical interpretation, see the *Bestiaire* of Philippe de Thaün, ll. 393-460, in the critical
edition by E. Walberg (Paris-Lund, 1900), pp. 15-18, or in
Bartsch-Wiese, pp. 66-67. 3 *la pucele* is the direct object of *mirant*. 9 *en = de mon cuer*, complement not of *ra-
voir* but of *point*, itself construed as dir. obj. of verb.
15 *en prison* 'as a prisoner'. 18 *li anel* are the iron
rings used to chain the prisoner. 22 'And it (*ceus*, for
l. 19 *Amors*) makes Beauty their chief'. The plurality of
seignors, confirmed by the rhyme, must stem from agreement
with a plural *Biautez* rather than the ms. form, *Biaute*. The
form *ceus* is grammatically curious, and Wallensköld, Voretsch, and others replace it with *cele*; since *cele* occurs in
none of the fifteen mss., however, we choose to retain *ceus*.
33 'But those (l. 29 *huissiers*) one defeats by humbling

oneself'.   34 No doubt 'Suffering is one's standard-bearer' rather than 'their standard-bearer'.   41 *Et se* 'even
if'.   45 *et de moi pres* 'even though with me'.   47-48
Probably 'Mercy would now be opportune [as a reward] for
[my] bearing such a heavy burden', i.e., the poet asks that
his lady relieve him of his torment by granting him her mercy (= love).   Cf. the varying success in capturing the syntax or sense of these lines in the following glosses: 'il
conviendrait plutôt d'avoir pitié de moi qui porte un si
pesant fardeau' (Picot), 'sarebbe certo più vantaggioso per
me ottenere la ricompensa piuttosto che sopportare un sì
grave peso' (Spaziani *Canz*), 'mercy now would be seasonably
given, to help me bear so grave a burden' (Goldin), 'il serait à propos de m'octroyer la grâce de soutenir si lourd
fardeau' (Mary), 'sarebbe grande atto di mercè di sostenere
così gravoso fardello' (Cremonesi).

Chanson   <u>141</u>

RS 1479, MW 1468
Mss. X 25r-v, B 4r-v, K 26-27, M 75r-v, O 133r-v, R 73v-74v
    (=R¹), R 170v-171v (=R²), S 314v, T 12v-13r, U 142v-
    143r, V 14r-v. Music in all mss. except STU. Attribu-
    tion in KX.

8 2 da-me; si fas grant vi- gor   10.de chan-ter quant de cuer plor.

I   Tout autresi con l'ente fait venir
     Li arrosers de l'eve qui chiet jus,
     Fait bone amor nestre et croistre et florir
     Li remenbrers par costume et par us.
     D'amors loial n'iert ja nus au dessus,   5
     Ainz li covient au desouz maintenir.
              Por c' est ma doce dolor
              Plaine de si grant paor,
              Dame, si fas grant vigor
              De chanter quant de cuer plor.   10

II   Pleüst a Dieu, por ma dolor garir,
     Qu'el fust Tisbé, car je sui Piramus;
     Mais je voi bien ce ne peut avenir;
     Ensi morrai que ja n'en avrai plus.
     Ahi, bele! tant sui por vos confus!   15
     Que d'un quarrel me venistes ferir,
              Espris d'ardant feu d'amor,
              Quant vos vi le premier jor;
              Li ars ne fu pas d'aubor
              Qui se traist par grant douçor.   20

III Dame, se je servise Dieu autant
     Et priasse de verai cuer entier
     Con je fas vos, je sai certainement
     Qu'en paradis n'eüst autel loier;
     Mais je ne puis ne servir ne proier   25
     Nului fors vos, a qui mes cuers s'atent;
              Si ne puis aparcevoir
              Que ja joie en doie avoir,
              Ne je ne vos puis veoir
              Fors d'euz clos et de cuer noir.   30

IV   La prophete dit voir, qui pas me ment,
     Que en la fin faudront li droiturier;
     Et la fins est venue voirement,
     Que cruautés vaint merci et prier,
     Ne servises ne peut avoir mestier,   35
     Ne bone amor n'atendre longuement;
              Ainz a plus orgueils, pooir
              Et beubanz que douz voloir,
              N'encontre amor n'a savoir
              Qu'atendue sans espoir.   40

V   Aygles, sans vos ne puis merci trover.
      Bien sai et voi qu'a toz biens ai failli
      Se vos ensi me volés eschiver
      Que vos n'aiés de moi quelque merci.
      Ja n'avrez mais nul si loial ami,   45
      Ne ne porrois a nul jor recovrer,
        Et je me morrai chaitis.
        Ma vie sera mais pis
        Loing de vostre biau cler vis,
        Ou naist la rose et li lis.   50

VI   Aygles, j'ai touz jors apris
         A estre loiaus amis,
         Si me vaudroit melz un ris
         De vos qu'estre en paradis.

MN   Ms. R^1 has a second melody. Form: A A B; the envoy is sung to ll. 7-10.
1. Ms. writes a diamond-shaped note.

RR   I   3 n. ne c.   II   17   damors   III   23
ueraiement   24 n. tel l. *(-1)*   IV   32 Car

V   Stanzas: BMOSTV   I II III IV V VI
                    KR^1 I II III IV V
                    R^2 I II III IV
                    U   I IV II III
I   1 con] que R^2 2 aroser R^1, arrouseir U; de lente
q. R^2; sus R^{2}S 3 F. bien U; amo(u)rs MOR^{2}U;
cro(i)stre et na(i)stre OU, naistre croistre R^2 4 remenbrer R^1, remanbreir U 5 Damo(u)r BOST; liaus M,
loiaus R^{1}R^2, loals U; ia mis au T 6 li] le BOR^{2}T, les
R^1, la SU 7 P ce est BMV, P. quoi S; ma dame S, ma
tres grans U; dolo(u)rs R^{2}T 8 si *missing in T*, tres S;
g. doucour(s) R^{1}R^2 9 Dame *missing in S*; li f. S 10
d. tuer p. T
II 11 p. me R^2; mes dolors OSV 12 Q. f. *missing B*;
Que O, Quele S, Kelle U; fu R^2; que j. BM 13 ce] se
B 14 Jci R^1; m. car K; ie BS; ne uiurai p. B; q. nen
aurai ia p. V; Ke ia nul ior nan vandra a desus U 15
bele] dame R^{1}R^2, amors U; tant com (-n) BOR^{1}R^{2}STU 16
Quant OR^{1}R^{2}S, Cant U; ferir *missing S* 17 ardant B, de
gent V; damo(u)rs BKMR^{2}STUV 18 *occurs as l. 19 in R^2*;
Q. ie v. v. V; Mult per lains de tres grant deucour U 19
occurs as l. 18 in R^2; daubours R^2 20 *occurs as l. 19 in*
R^2; Ke U; Q. tr. p. si g. R^1; par] de SU; g. vigo(u)r
R^{2}UV

III   21 se le O; j. priaisse R^2, amase U; amesse *added*
between deu *and* au. *in* O; autant *missing* V   22 Et seruice
d. R^2; vrai c. et ent. (dantier B) BR^2T, fin c. et dentie
R^1, vrai c. ent. SU   23 v. bien s. STU; s. a escient
R^1, a essiant R^2, a esciant U   24 p. nauroit V; autre
V, nul(1)(s) te(i)l MR^{1}R^{2}U; Q. ie en p. en eusse l. S   26
Nule U, Cainc R^2; a cui BMOSTUV; mon c. R^1; sentent M
27 Se BTU   28 Co(m)ment joie R^{1}R^2; Q. ma j. V; joie]
bien S; doie] puisse R^2V   29 Ne *missing* S, Et R^{1}R^{2}TU;
vos *missing* O
IV   31 Li BR^2UV; prophetes BR^2U, prophecie R^1; dist R^2
TUV; qui] ne R^2 32 Car BKOR^{1}STV, Ki U; foi f. B   33
Et li R^2; fin R^1; nouuiaument R^1, maintenant R^2, droite-
ment S   34 Quant R^{1}R^{2}S; cruaute O   35 Et R^1; biau
seruir R^1, faus seruis R^2, nul seruise S; ni BR^2ST; Ke
bone amors ni auroit mais mestier U   36 Ne biau R^1,
biau(u)z R^2U; amors M, parler R^1, parlers R^2, seruir U;
atendre S; bonemant U   37 orgueil KR^1, beubans R^2,
ourdeanz S; o. et p. V; ponees S   38 beuban(t) KT, bo-
bant M, orguex R^2; uoloirs B   39 Contre O, Quencontre
R^1; orgueil R^2; na saunon O, pouoir R^{1}R^2, auoir S   40
Quat. *missing* S, Catendroie B, Quatendre MOR^{1}V, Quatente
R^2, Fors catandre an bone e. U; desespoir R^{1}R^{2}S
V   41 Aygle MR^{1}T, Plaisans S; sen BR^1, en S; uont B;
ni BT   43 v. issi R^1; vo(u)s v. R^{1}S; achieuer B, esso-
rer R^{1}S   44 de moi naiez (neussiez B, naies T) BKMOSTV:
quelque] dame S   45 James n. nul R^1; nauriez B; m. un
si S   46 Ne p. V, Ne nou M, Ne nel S; Ne iames iour ne
pourrez r. R^1; a nul jor *missing* S   47 me *missing* BOS,
men M; chaitis *missing* R   48 *occurs after* 1. 50 *in* R^1;
sera *missing* O; seroit miex plus S   49 L. dou S; b. cl.
vis *missing* S   50 Or V; est R^1; la flours B; et le l.
R^1
VI   51 Aygle MOTV; jai *missing* T, ia B; ie O; j. cor-
roux a. O   51-52 *occur in* S *as* Ia touz iors loiaus amis
53 Si ne O; vns r. S   54 vos] li S; quautre par. M,
kautres par. T, quautre en par. O

     E   La Ravallière, 67; Tarbé *Thib*, 68-70; Wallensköld
Thib, 68-72; Cremonesi, 188-190; Toja, 398-401.

     N   5-6 'No man will ever control loyal love; one
must, rather, remain under its control'.   12 For the story
of Pyramus and Thisbe, see Ovid's *Metaphoses*, Bk. IV. For
OF versions, see Bossuat *Man*, items 1082, 1083, and *Sec.*
Suppl., item 7293.   13 Understand *que* before *ce*.   28
Wallensköld understands *en* 'de vous'. The particle may as

easily, however, refer to the infinitives *servir* and *proier* in l. 25. 31-32 See I Timothy 4:1. 41 *Aygles* is a *senhal*, or code-name intended to conceal the identity of the poet's lady. 46 *porrois = porrez.*

Chanson   <u>142</u>

RS 407, MW 1007
Mss. M^t 68v-69r, B 2v-3r, C 50r-v, I 1:35, K 49-50, M 12r-v, N 13v-14r, O 38r-v, P 50v-51r, R 43v-44r-v, T 17r, U 122r-v, V 25r-v, X 32r-v, Z 7v-8r, a 6r-v, e III. Music in all mss. except CIUe. Attribution in CKMNPRT Xa.

I   De fine amor vient seance et bonté,
     Et amors vient de ces deus autressi.
     Tuit troi sont un, qui bien i a pensé;
     Ja ne seront a nul jor departi.   4
     Par un conseil ont ensemble establi
     Lor correors, qui sont avant alé.
     De moi ont fet tout lor chemin ferré;
     Tant l'ont usé, ja n'en seront parti.   8

II   Li correor sunt de nuit en clarté
      Et de jor sont por la gent obscurci:
      Li douz regart plaisant et savoré,
      La grant biauté et li bien que g'i vi.   12
      N'est merveille se ce m'a esbahi:
      De li a Deus le siecle enluminé,
      Car qui avroit le plus biau jor d'esté,
      Les li seroit obscurs de plain midi.   16

III   En amor a paor et hardement;
      Cil dui sont troi et dou tierz sont li dui,
      Et grant valor est a aus apendant,
      Ou tuit li bien ont retrait et refui.   20
      Por c' est amors li hospitaus d'autrui
      Que nus n'i faut selonc son avenant.
      J'i ai failli, dame qui valez tant,
      A vostre ostel, si ne sai ou je sui.   24

IV   Or n'i voi plus mes qu'a lui me conmant,
      Que toz pensers ai laissiez por cestui:
      Ma bele joie ou ma mort i atent,
      Ne sai le quel, des que devant li fui.   28
      Ne me firent lors si oeil point d'anui,
      Ainz me vindrent ferir si doucement
      Dedens le cuer d'un amoreus talent
      Qu'encor i est le cous que j'en reçui.   32

V   Li cous fu granz, il ne fet qu'enpirier;
      Ne nus mires ne m'en porroit saner
      Se cele non qui le dart fist lancier,
      Se de sa main i voloit adeser.   36
      Bien en porroit le cop mortel oster
      A tot le fust, dont j'ai tel desirrier;
      Mes la pointe du fer n'en puet sachier,
      Qu'ele brisa dedenz au cop douner.   40

VI   Dame, vers vos n'ai autre messagier
      Par cui vos os mon corage anvoier
      Fors ma chançon, se la volez chanter.

      MN   Ms. O is mensurally notated; ms. T is written a
5th higher. Form: A A B; the envoy is sung to ll. 6-8.
1. In l. 1 ms. writes no rest. 2. This word, but not its
music, is repeated in the ms.

      RR   I   1 et biautez   3 que b. i ai p.   5 o.
tuit troi e.   6 avant *repeated*   II   10 Et de iors s.

p. la g. obscur *(-1)*   11 Et d. r. et li mot s.   14 le]
cest   15 Quant nos aurons le   III   18 t. son li   19
Et granz ualors sest a aus apendanz   21 P. ce est *(+1)*
23 Mes iai   24 En   IV   25 Ie; mes a l.   26 penserz
28 des ques   29 si] mi   V   34 mirez   36 i] me   40
dendenz

       <u>V</u>   Stanzas: OTZe   I II III IV V VI
                            BIKMNPRUVXa   I II III IV V
                                     C   I II   IV V
I   1 fine] bone BCIKMNOPUXe, ienne V; bonte(i)s CUe,
biaute KNPVX, biautez BM, beautes (-z) OT   2 Et de c.
d. v. bone amour a. B; (au)tressi *illegible in e*   3 T. t.
s. *illegible in e*; Tout TZa, Tous R, Li BKMNPVX; trois
R; vns R, dun CU; que BKNOPVX, ke CIU; ie bien iai p.
B; i ai p. CIO; b. i a garde e, b. lai espro(u)ue KNPVX
4 Ja nen Z; Ia a BKNPVX, Ia maiz M, Ne ia(i) CIUe; nul
(nuns I, un e) io(u)r nen (ne IUe) s. d. BCIKMNPUVXe   5
Por CTZ; conseil *illeg in e*; sont R, sunt M, cont BCI;
ensemble] touz trois R, tout troi (.iij.) TZa, antre ous
U, entreus e   6 Li BCIKMNOPUVXe; co(u)r(r)eo(u)r BCKMNO
PRUVXZae; qui] ke I, en O; ont Ra; auant sunt a. e,
deuant sont (sunt) BCIMU   7 o. fai R, o. font T; De mon
cuer o.f.l.ch.f. BCIKMNPUVXe   8 usé] mene e; ja] mais
IU; ne e; Ia a nul iour nen seront departi B
II   9 de] la BIKMNPVXe; nuis T   10 Et *illeg in e*; dou
T, le BKMNPVXe, lou IU; lors C; les gens CU; g. en obs-
cur O; oscureit I, occursir U   11 rega(i)rs BIRU;
plaisans BI; Li d. r. et li (le R) mot (r. li mot douc e)
s. ORTUZae; sauoreis I, sauoureus R   12 Et la C, Et li
IU; grans (-z) MTZae; biautes (-z) MZae, bia(u)(l)teis
CIU; et] o P; le BR, les P; biens MPTUZa, sans B; q. ie
PRZ; ivi RZ; Et les granz biens quen ma dame choisi KNVX
13 N'est *illeg in e*; N. pas meruelle I, Ne men merueill
M; merueilles BPV; ce se ma R, si ie men BKMNPUVXe, se de
ce O, sel resgairt C, san regairt I; mesbahi CIO, esbahiz V   14 Ainsi a d. R; le mont e. e   15 avroit] vairoit CIU, ver(r)oit Ma, venroit R; Quant no(u)s a(u)rons
le OTZ; plus biau *missing Z*; biaus I; jor *missing C*, jours
a   16 Vers (-z) BCIMU; lui B; oscur KNPVXa, ocur B; en
BKMNX, am I, an U; a miedi e, endroit meidi C; L. li si
seroit oscur a miedi Z
III   17 a] ai I; pro(u)ece KNPV, pro(u)esse BX, pooir
O; Sans et ualor sont ai vn acordant U   18 Li BIKMNPUVX;
troi Ra; font I; dui R, doi a, un X; et entier s. R
19 Mult R; grans a, granz (-s) valo(u)rs MOTZ, valors
e, bone amour B, bone amors U; out R, ont a; en O, ai

U; ceus BKNPVX, ciauz M, lor O, ioie e; apendanz (-s)
MOTUZ, atendans e; San uient a aulz grant ualour espandant
I 20 Out R; tout RTZae, tous U; biens U, bon e; sont
R, est l U; Ou amo(u)rs a et BKMNPVX; recet KNPVX, reget
B, recoi M, repos U; et refus U, raui R; Et lai biauteit
i recest et desduit I 21 P. ce est a. MVZ; amor I; si
R; (l)i hos(pitaus) *illeg in e* 22 f. contre s. I 23
Et BKMNPVX, Mais U, Je Re; iai BKMNOPUX; failli ai V;
(da)me qui v(ale)z ta(nt) *illeg in e* 24 A mon KNPVX;
amor I; se U; ne soi O; s. qui M; ou le U; fui O, seus
U
IV 25 Ie ORTZae; voi] a BKMNPVX, ait CU, ai I; plus]
mais U; mes] fors BCIKMNPUVX; a ORTZae; li CIKMNOPUVX,
di(e)u PTZa; (d)ieu me (com)mant *illeg in e* 26 Car CIK
MNPVXe; t. biens (bien et B) fez (fais, fes) BCIKMNPVX,
consaus e; lessie KNPRV, laissie(t) IZ, laixiet U; celui
IKNPX, celi V 27 Ma douce I; joie] vie BKMNPVX, mort
CU; mort] ioie .CU; i] an U; (m)a mort i at(ainc ?) *illeg
in e* 28 Ne s. que cest CP; des] mes BKNPV, mais (-z)
MRXa; quant BKMNPRVX; lui BR; fu I; (m)ais q(uant)
d(eu)ant li *illeg in e* 29 Lors ne me f. s. C, Dont ne mi
f. s. U; me] mi O; fissent Z; lors *missing B*, onc KNPV,
ont X, si MRa; si] mi OTZe, vair MRa; s. biaul eul p. d.
C; danut U 30 Il M; me] men O, mont MU; vir(r)ent
Ta, naure M, naureit U; ferir] parmi M, si tres U; de
(tout C) maintenant BCKNPVX, ou (le M) cuer dedens IM,
doucetemant U, dun douc (dous R) talent (-ant a, t. *missing R*) RZa; (m)e vindrent ferir si douceme(nt) *illeg in e*
31 *missing Za; all but* talent *missing R*; Par mi (mei CU)
BCIKNPUVX; 1. cors BIKNOPUVX, giex *(?)* e; dun dairt damors
tranchans I; tal(ent) *illeg in e*, senblant (sem-, san-)
BCKNPVX; Dun douz reguart si amourousement M 32 Que R,
missing BCIKMNPUVXe; li c. BIMOTUZae; co(u)p CKNPRVX; q. ie
IKNOPRVX, jou a, gi B; res(s)u CI; co(ls) que j'en r(e-
ceu) *illeg in e*
V 33 cop R; grant PR; il] se C, si O; fist C; g. ne
fait fors empirier e 34 m'en] me e, le M, lou U;
(por)roit saner *illeg in e*; Il nest nuns mires ki lou peust
senneir I 35 Se c(ele) *illeg in e*; Ce c. R; Fors ke
celee q. I; non *missing X*; dart fist lanci(er) *illeg in e*
36 sa *missing K*; sa main *illeg in e*; i] mi BO; da(i)gnoit
(dei-) BKMNPVXe, degnast U; adeser *illeg in e*; Se de samour i deignoit aseneir C, Ce de ces eulz me dignoit regardeir I 37 Bien *illeg in e*, Tost BCKMNPVX; mortel cop
R; (m)ortel (os)ter *illeg in e* 38 O BKNPX, Ou V; A
to(ut) *illeg in e*; fust] fer R; tel] grant BCIKMNPRUVX;
(desir)rier *illeg in e*; Ke ia fut fais per si grant d. U

39 du] de B; puet] puis RV; p. nen (nan) por(r)oit nu(l)s
(fors 0) s. COU; Mes la (po)inte (del) fer n'en (p)uet *illeg in e* 40 Que elle donna R; brisa *illeg in e*; (don)er
illeg in e, ferir C
VI 41 (D)ame vers vos n(ai a.) messagier *illeg in e* 42
mon messaige noncier O 43 se la volez chanter *illeg in e*

E   La Ravallière, 13; Tarbé *Thib*, 18-20; Wallensköld
Thib, 16-22; Spaziani *Ant*, 85-87; Cremonesi, 185-187; Spaziani *Canz*, 80-83; Goldin, 454-457.

N   For a brief discussion of the development of the
allegory in this well-known song, see Dragonetti, pp. 245-
246.
    1 Wallensköld *Thib* glosses *seance* as 'sagesse, sa-
voir'; it is no doubt on that authority that Cremonesi
translates 'senno' and Goldin gives 'wisdom'. While that
gloss is surely justifiable in the context of the poem, it
appears to be unsupported by any external evidence. Other
attestations, like etymology, argue for some such interpretation as 'propriety, fitting conduct, grace, charm', and a
term designating a social quality is indeed at least as de-
fensible in this passage as one denoting mental or intellectual strength. That the meaning of Thibaut's first verse
was less than certain even in the Middle Ages emerges from
the form in which Dante quotes it in *De vulgari eloquentia*
(I: 9:3, II 5:4): *De fin amor si vient sen et bonté.* The
authenticity of *bonté* rather than ms. M^t *biautez* is suggested by the evident contextual demand for a moral quality
instead of a physical one; it is ensured by the identification of *biauté* in l. 12 as one of the *correors* of the original three entities, for beauty could hardly occur in both
rôles.
    3 *qui* 'to anyone who'.   7 *chemin ferré* 'highway'.
10 *por* 'because of'.   11 The ms. M^t reading, *et li mot*,
adding a fourth member to the group of *correors*, needs to be
rejected for that reason alone: the context requires only
three "scouts"; moreover, "words" is poetically inappropriate in a group treated throughout the stanza as a visible
phenomenon.   15-16 'For, if anyone considered the most
beautiful summer day, in comparison with her it would be
dark at high noon'.   19 *aus = eus*.   20 *retrait et refui*
'refuge and shelter'.   28 *le quel*, neuter reference to l.
27 *joie* and *mort*.   35 *fist lancier = lança.* 38 *A tot le
fust* 'together with the shaft'.   40 *Qu'ele brisa* 'for it
broke'.

143   Chanson

RS 1596, MW 2062
Stanza I: B 1127 (five other sources), st. II: B 1225, st.
   III: B 583, st. IV: B 1217 (one other source), st. V:
   B 1692 (two other sources), st. VI: B 530.
Mss. N 7r-v-8r, K 12-13, M 61v-62r, O 21v-22r, R 175r-176v,
   S 315r, T 5r-v, V 6v-7r, X 15v-16r, za 16. Music in
   KMNORVX. Attribution in KNTX.

I   Chançon ferai, car talent m'en est pris,
     De la meillor qui soit en tout le mont.
     De la meillor? Je cuit que j'ai mespris.
     S'ele fust tels--se Deus joie me dont--

De moi li fust aucune pitiez prise,   5
Qui sui touz siens et sui a sa devise.
Pitiez de cuer, Deus! que ne s'est assise
En sa biauté? Dame, qui merci proi,
    Je sent les maus d'amer pour vous,
        Sentez les vous pour moi?   10

II   Douce dame, sanz amour fui jadis,
     Quant je choisi vostre gente façon;
     Et quant je vi vostre tres biau cler vis,
     Si me raprist mes cuers autre reson:
     De vous amer me semont et justise,   15
     A vos en est a vostre conmandise.
     Li cors remaint, qui sent felon juïse,
     Se n'en avez merci de vostre gré.
         Li douz mal dont j'atent joie
             M'ont si grevé,   20
         Mors sui s'ele mi delaie.

III Mult a Amours grant force et grant pouoir,
     Qui sanz reson fet choisir a son gré.
     Sanz reson? Deus! je ne di pas savoir,
     Car a mes euz en set mes cuers bon gré,   25
     Qui choisirent si tres bele senblance
     Dont jamés jor ne ferai desevrance;
     Ainz sousfrerai por li grief penitance
     Tant que pitiez et mercis l'en prendra.
         Dirai vous qui mon cuer enblé m'a?   30
         Li douz ris et li bel oeil qu'ele a!

IV   Douce dame, s'il vous plesoit un soir,
     M'avrïez vous plus de joie doné
     C'onques Tristans, qui en fist son pouoir,
     N'en pout avoir nul jor de son aé.   35
     La moie joie est tornee a pesance.
     Hé, cors sanz cuer! de vous fet grant
                                        [venjance
     Cele qui m'a navré sanz defiance,
     Et neporquant je ne la lerai ja.
         L'en doit bien bele dame amer   40
         Et s'amor garder, qui l'a.

V   Dame, pour vous vueil aler foloiant,
     Que je en aim mes maus et ma dolor;
     Qu'aprés les maus ma grant joie en atent
     Que g'en avrai, se Dieu plest, a brief jor. 45
     Amors, merci! ne soiez oubliee!

S'or me failliez, s'iert traïson doublee,
Que mes granz maus por vos si fort m'agree.
Ne me metez longuement en oubli!
Se le bele n'a de moi merci,   50
Je ne vivrai mie longuement ensi.

VI   Sa grant biautez, qui m'esprent et agree,
      Qui seur toutes est la plus desirree,
      M'a si lacié mon cuer en sa prison.
          Deus! je ne pens s'a li non.   55
      A moi que ne pense ele donc?

      MN   Ms. O is mensurally notated. Form: A A B vrf;
the envoy is sung to ll. 6-8.
1. In l. 3, ms. writes no rest.   2. No music is extant for
refrains 2-6; however (a) refrain 4 reappears in a motet of
ms. Montpellier H 196 (No. 27), but the melody there used
does not fit rhythmically into the context here; and (b) refrain
5 is partially present in a motet of ms. Wolfenbüttel 1206
(W₂), f. 232v-233; see also RS 575, refrain 2.

      RR   IV   41   qui laura

      V   Stanzas V and VI not included in R.
I   1 car] que MOSTVza; talenz M, -anz O, -ens RSV,
-ans T   2 Por S   3 le m. R; je *missing in za*; cuit]
croi S   4 Cele X; S. le fust se R   5 De mi R; pitie
K, pite R   6 a] en S; se d. R   7 Pitie SV; Deus] las
S; quel X, qi za; cest X; ne soit esprise S   8 De S;
En uo b. R; cui MOTza, que RS; pri V   9 m. damors za;
pour vous *missing T*   10 moi *missing M*
II   11 amors MOT; fu za   12 j. uous ui et uo g. V;
gente] douce K, clere R   13 biau] bel TV, bien R   14
Et si ni prist V; reprist za   16 An R; en *missing M*; A
v. san ua an v. S; a] et T   17 Li cuer za   18 Sen
naues m. T; n'en] riens S; gré *missing R*   19 maus KMOR
STXza, maux V; dou S; iaten M, iatenc T   20 Ma R, Me
S; si *missing S*   21 *missing R*; *only* se mi d. *in S*; Mort
KX; cele X, sil za; me Mza
III   22 grant *missing M*, granz za   23 f. chair V   24
je nel puis p. V   25 sot OSTV; mon KX, li MST; cuer
KXza, cors T; C. ce fu fait tout par ma volente R   26
Quant ie choisi R; sa RS   28 p. lui M, le T; A. s.
toudis em p. R   29 m. et p. S; pitie SV; merci MRSV
za; m. li en p. za   30 Dont v. V; Je uos dirai qi m.
za; q. tot m. c. K, q. m. fin c. X; c. auez et e. ma V,
c. e. a RT   31 d. vis R; bel] douc R, uair *crossed out*

in V; o. que elle a R
IV   32   dame *missing S*; si   M   33   Maueries RT, Mauroiez
za; vous *missing OS*; pl. de j. *missing R*; dou(n)ee OSVza
34   trist(r)an MRX   35   Ne S; a. en trestot s. ae M, a.
tant comme il ot duree S   36   Se ma j. M; joie *missing O*;
t. a pensee M; Se nest ma j. t. a grant pesance RT; Ma j.
mest a pesance tornee S   37   Ne za; cuer s. cors V; v.
prent g. V, v. ai fait v. R; uenlance za   39   la *missing*
Rza, li V; aura ia V   40   On doit belle d. a. RT   41
s'amor *missing V*; g. cil q. KMX; quil M; q. laura OV,
lauera za
V   43   e. ai O; mes dolors MS   44   Que par l. O; mes m.
SVza; la g. MST; aten T   45   Q. ie MS; aura za; sa d.
za, sil uous p. V; p. aucun j. O   47   S. mi V; ciert
KO, cert TVza, cest S; tra(h)isons MOT; prouee S   49
me *missing X*, men O; m. tenes l. T   50   n'a] ne a O, nen
a za   51   mie] pas za; lonc temps O; l. en fui S
V   52   La MOSTV; granz OSza, -s T; biaute MV; et magree
Mza   53   e. belle e la pl. d. za   55   je] ia T; pense
MS; p. ie s. ST   56   pens S

<u>E</u>   La Ravallière, 6; Tarbé *Thib*, 10-11; Wallensköld
Thib, 76-82; Pauphilet, 890-891; Henry *Chrest* 1, 223-225; 2,
67; Goldin, 460-463.

<u>N</u>   It is unusual to find variable refrains, generally
borrowed from popular sources, in the aristocratic *chanson
d'amour*. Zumthor *Es* comments, p. 248: "De manière très sub-
tile, le poète souligne cette discordance, en intervertis-
sant les formes de discours: quand la strophe parle de la
dame à la troisième personne, le refrain emploie le *vous* (I
et III), ou l'inverse (II, IV, V)."
9 *qui = cui*.   10 *raprist* 'taught, for its (i.e., my
heart's) part'.   21 Understand *que* before *Mors*. The cor-
respondence *joie : delaie*, considered an imperfect rhyme, no
doubt stems from a dialectal reduction of [we] to [e] in
joie.   24 *savoir* 'a sensible statement'.   26-27 *si . . .
dont = si . . . que . . . en*.   34 Tristan was widely regarded as the perfect lover.   38 *defiance* 'formal chal-
lenge'.   40 *L'en = on*.   41 *qui l'a* 'if one has it'.   46
oubliee 'forgetful'.   55 *s'a li non* 'of anyone but her'.

Chanson historique, chanson pieuse   <u>144</u>

RS 273, MW 2458
Mss. X 29v-30r-v, B 3v-4r, K 34-35, M 67v-68r, O 37r-v-38r,

S 317r-v-318r, T 16r-v, V 17v-18r, za 21. Music in KM
OVX. Attribution in KTX.

I   Deus est ensi conme li pellicans,
      Qui fait son ni el plus haut arbre sus;
      Et li mauvais oisiaus, qui vient de jus,
      Ses oisellons ocit, tant est puanz;
      Li peres vient destrois et angoisseus,   5

Dou bec s'ocit; de son sanc dolereus
Vivre refait tantost ses oisellons.
Deus fist autel quant fu sa passions;
De son douz sanc racheta ses enfans
Dou deable, qui mult estoit puissanz.   10

II   Li guerredons en est mauvais et lens,
       Que biens ne drois ne pitiés n'a mes nus;
       Ainz est orgueils et baraz au dessus,
       Felonie, traïsons et beubans.
       Mult par est or nostre estat perillous,   15
       Et se ne fust li essamples de ceus
       Qui tant aiment et noises et tençons--
       Ce est des clers qui ont laissié sarmons
       Por guerroier et por tüer les gens--
       Jamés en Dieu ne fust nus hons creans.   20

III   Nostre chief fait touz noz menbres doloir,
       Por c' est bien drois qu'a Dieu nos en
                                        [plaignons,
       Et grant corpe ra mult seur les barons,
       Qui il poise quant aucuns veut valoir;
       Et entre gent en font mult a blamer   25
       Qui tant sevent et mentir et guiller.
       Le mal en font deseur els revenir;
       Et qui mal quiert, mal ne li doit faillir.
       Qui petit mal porchasse a son pooir,
       Li grans ne doit en son cuer remanoir.   30

IV   Bien devrions en l'estoire veoir
       La bataille qui fu des deus dragons,
       Si com l'en trove el livre des Bretons,
       Dont il covint les chastiaus jus cheoir:
       C'est cist siecles, qui il covient verser,   35
       Se Deus ne fet la bataille finer.
       Le sens Mellin en covint fors issir
       Por deviner qu'estoit a avenir;
       Mes Antecriz vient, ce pöez savoir,
       As maçues qu'Anemis fait mouvoir.   40

V   Savez qui sont li vil oisel puant
       Qui tüent Dieu et ses enfençonez?
       Li papelart, dont li mont n'est pas nez.
       Cil sont puant, ort et vil et mauvais;
       Il ocïent toute la sinple gent   45
       Par lor faus moz, qui sont li Dieu enfant.
       Papelart font le siecle chanceler;

Par saint Pierre, mal les fait encontrer!
Il ont tolu joie et solas et pais;
Cil porteront en enfer le grief fais.   50

VI   Or nos doint Deus lui servir et amer
      Et la dame c'on ne doit oublïer,
      Qui nos vueille garder a touz jors mais
      Des puz oiseaus qui ont venin es bes.

    MN   Ms. O is mensurally notated and in mode 3; ms. V
has a second melody and in l. 7 supports mode 3.   Form:
through-composed.

    RR   II   15   ore *(+1)*   IV   35   couint   V   42
enfeconez   47   chancelier   48   Et p. s. pere *(+1)*

      V   Stanza VI not included in K or S.
I   1 cum li   za   3   vient] est   S   4   ocist   BMOSTVza
5   angoises   za   6   socist   BMOSTV, se fiert   za; son *missing T*   7   Fait reuiure   S, Reuiure fet   V   8   ful sus   B,
vint   T; passion   BS   10   mult] trop   MT, tant   OS; par est
p.   S, est or p.   V; puanz   K
II   12   Qui   Bza; bien ne (et   T) droit ne (et   T) pitie
BKMOSTVza; nen na nus   B, nan a nus   S   14   F. tencons   M,
traison   SV   15   ore   BKMOSTV; vostre   MV; estas (-z) BOSTV
18   Or e.   O; de c.   Mza; laissies (-z)   MO   19   guerroie
M   20   J. nus hon ne f. en deu c.   za; hon (-m)   BMTV;
creant   B
III   21   Nostres   OT, Vostre   S; ciez   B, chiez   M, chies
S; t. les m.   T   22   P. ce est b.   BMSVza   23   grans (-z)
MO; corpes   MO, co(u)pes   BT; c. ramaint s.   B; sus   Oza
24   Cui   MOST, Qil p.   za; a. puet auoir   S; vo(u)loir   KV,
ualoit   M   25   Et entendre g.   B; genz   Oza; mult a b.
missing za; desus   S   26   *missing za*; Quant   B; guilir   M
27   Le m. en f.   *missing za*; desus   S   28   q. quiert mal m.
S; maus ne   MST, malz ne   O   30   doit] puet
IV   31   deuron mes en   B; uooir   K   32   De la b.   T; qui
fu *missing za*   33   es liures   K   34   cou(u)ient   MO; le
chastel   S   35   Ce est c.   O; C. cil   B, ce   za, li   S; qu
S, que   Bza, cui   MOT; i couuint   K   36   fait] uuet   S   37
Le sanc   MS, Les iauz   O; couient   BSTza   38   P deliurer
qui estoit a uenir   B; a *missing za*   40   A   B, Es   O, Au
malices   S
V   41   li oiselet   S; punais   M, pugnais   T   42   et ses
missing za   43   papelars   O; dou   S; le   za; mont   Xza,
nons   MT; pas nest   za   44   Ains   B; C. ort p.   O; s. bien
o.   MST; vil] puant   MT; et mauueis et puant   S   45   la

bone g. S 46 Pour B; mot qil za; son M 48 Et p.
BKV; s. pere KOV 49 tolue B, toloit O; *first* et *missing* Vza 50 Sen p. S; les g. BTza; gries B, grans T, granz za, grant MOS
VI 51 doinst T; li O 53 Quel n. V 54 De O; puz] maus MOTV; q. si ont bes mauuais B; venins T

E̱ La Ravallière, 158; Tarbé *Thib*, 119-121; Wallensköld *Thib,* 194-199; Järnström-Långfors 2, 41-43; Cremonesi, 202-204; Gennrich *Ex*, 32-34; Toja, 417-420; Van dW *Chans*, 121-125.

N̲ This *serventois* is unique among the works of Thibaut in its combination of religious sentiment, political concerns, and moral indignation. It is not clear whether its frame of reference is Thibaut's involvement in the Albigensian crusade (1226) or in the troubled preparations for the prolongation of the Sixth Crusade to the Holy Land (1236-39). In the first instance, the two battling dragons (st. 4) would represent either the Church and the Albigensian heresy or Simon de Montfort and the Count of Toulouse. In the second, they would symbolize Pope Gregory IX and Emperor Frederick II of Germany, and the *chief* of l. 21 would be the Pope. For further detail, see Järnström-Långfors 2, pp. 5-8.
1 For the allegorical use of the pelican as Christ, explained in ll. 8-10, see Réau 1, pp. 94-96 or Schiller 2, pp. 136-137. 12 Grammatical correctness would require the oblique forms *bien, droit, pitié*; similarly, l. 15 *estat* and l. 28 *mal*, both nominative in function, should be *estas* and *maus*. 16-20 This statement is to be understood as ironic. 23-24 'And there is great guilt, too, among the barons, who are grieved when anyone attempts to show valor'. *Qui* = *cui*. 27 'They [unwittingly] bring their evil back upon themselves'.
29-30 Wallensköld *Thib* provides the gloss, "'Celui qui se prépare à combattre un petit mal (le pouvoir musulman en Palestine) ne doit pas garder dans son propre coeur un grand mal (l'hypocrisie)'," and others. e.g., Cremonesi and Van der Werf, have accepted it. This interpretation, however, seems somewhat unrelated to the preceding lines; moreover, it quite surprisingly attributes to Thibaut the view that the Moslem evil was not, relatively speaking, a serious matter. We propose, taking *porchasse* 'pursue' in its usual sense of 'seek to effect, engage, in' rather than 'combat' and *doit* as expressing an inevitable future rather than an injunction: 'Whoever indulges wholeheartedly in petty evil

is bound to forget the great evil [which threatens him]',
i.e., by pursuing their fights among themselves, the barons
are losing sight of their common enemy (the Albigensians?
the Saracens? Satan?).

31-34 The "historical" allusion is to a castle whose
construction was rendered impossible by the underground
struggles of two dragons; according to the legend, reported
in Geoffrey of Monmouth's *Historia regum Brittaniae* and
Wace's French adaptation, the *Roman de Brut*, it was the
Arthurian magician Merlin (1. 37), who revealed the cause of
the problem.   34 'As a result of which the castle(s) in-
evitably kept falling down'.   35 'It is [representative
of] this world, which must fall'. *qui* = *cui*, accusative object of impersonal *il covient*; cf. the same construction in
1. 34.   37 *Le sens Mellin*, absolute genitive, 'the wisdom
of Merlin'.   40 'With the clubs that Satan causes to be
wielded'.   43 'The hypocrites, of whom the world is not
free (cleansed)'.   46 The antecedent of *qui* is 1. 45 *la
sinple gent. li Dieu enfant*, absolute genitive, 'the child-
ren of God'.   48 *mal les fait encontrer* 'it is bad to meet
them'.   52 *la dame* is the Virgin Mary.

<u>145</u>   Chanson de croisade

RS 6, MW 1980
Mss. M 13v, K 1-2, N 1v-2r, O 127r-v, S 316r-v, T 2v, V 1v,
    X 8v-9r. Music in all mss. except ST. Attribution in
    KNX.

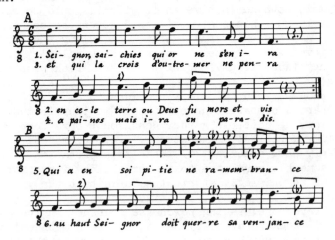

7. et de-li- vrer sa terre et son pa- is.

I   Seignor, saichiés qui or ne s'en ira
En cele terre ou Deus fu mors et vis
Et qui la crois d'outremer ne penra
A paines mais ira en paradis.
Qui a en soi pitié ne ramembrance   5
Au haut Seignor doit querre sa venjance
Et delivrer sa terre et son païs.

II   Tuit li mauvés demorront par deça,
Qui n'aiment Dieu, bien ne honor ne pris;
Et chascuns dit: "Ma fame que fera?   10
Je ne lairoie a nul fuer mes amis."
Cil sont cheoit en trop fole atendance,
Qu'il n'est amis fors que cil, sanz doutance,
Qui por nos fu en la vraie crois mis.

III   Or s'en iront cil vaillant bacheler   15
Qui aiment Dieu et l'eunor de cest mont,
Qui sagement vuelent a Dieu aler;
Et li morveux, li cendreux demorront:
Avugle sunt, de ce ne dout je mie.
Qui un secors ne fait Dieu en sa vie   20
Et por si pou pert la gloire dou mont.

IV   Dieus se lessa en crois por nos pener
Et nos dira au jor que tuit vendront:
"Vos qui ma crois m'aidastes a porter,
Vos en irez la ou mi angle sont;   25
La me verrez et ma mere Marie.
Et vos par cui je n'oi onques aïe
Descendrés tuit en enfer le parfont."

V   Chascuns cuide demorer toz haitiez
Et que jamés ne doie mal avoir;   30
Ainsi les tient Anemis et pechiez
Que il n'ont sen, hardement ne pooir.
Biaus sire Dieus, ostés leur tel pensee
Et nos metez en la vostre contree
Si saintement que vos puissons veoir!   35

VI   Douce dame, roïne coronee,
Proiez por nos, virge bien aüree!
Et puis aprés ne nos puet mescheoir.

<u>MN</u>   Ms. O is mensurally notated. Form: A A B; the
envoy is sung to ll. 5-7.
1. In l. 2 ms. repeats this note, as though *terre* were not
elided. 2. Ms. writes *a*, but the *g* is confirmed by l. 7 and
by mss. KNOX.   3. Ms. adds a ligature *b-a*, as though *terre*
were not elided. 4. This figure seems to indicate a ritar-
dando.

<u>V</u>   I   1 Seigneurs K   3 c. por dieu or ne p.   S
5 en soi a KNVX; et r.   TX   II   8 Tout T, Quant S
9 honor] amor KNVX   12   cheet K, assis en S; male a.   X
14 fu po(u)r no(u)s KNVX   III   15 cil] li V; v.
cheualier K   18 Et li anuieus del mont S   19   s. tout
ce S, s. ice T   20   Qui dieu ne font un secours en sa uie
V; font d. en lor uie S   21 gloire] ioie TV; du KNTV,
del S   IV   22 Bien se S; po(u)r nos en croiz (-s TX)
KNOSTX   23 que] ou KNOSTVX   24 ma crois *missing* S   25
la ou] ou tuit KNVX; li T; angre KNVX, ange O, angele T
27 p. qui KNTVX   28 Descendes T, -z V   V   29 tout
h. K   30 doie] quide T   31 Ensinc le O; A. le tien-
nent ennemi en pechie S   32 sens KNTX, senz V, sus S
33 Biau K, Beau X; penser S   34 menez en la douce c.
S   35 Si faitement que nos puissons auoir de noz pechiez
pardon S *(+6)*; puisse T; uoir K   VI   37 bieneuree O,
beneuree VX, boneuree K, bone euree ST   38 Que p. S;
puist SV

<u>E</u>   La Ravallière, 132; Leroux de Lincy, 125-127;
Tarbé *Thib*, 124-125; Meyer, 370; Noack, 119-120; Bédier-
Aubry, 167-174; Wallensköld *Thib*, 183-186; Wagner, 80-82;
Pauphilet, 896-897; Cremonesi, 200-202; Gennrich *Alt Lied* 1,
9-12; Toja, 415-417; Mary 1, 360-363; Goldin, 476-481.

<u>N</u>   This song was composed sometime between 1235, when
Thibaut began crusade preparations, and 1239, when he departed for the Holy Land; see Bédier-Aubry, p. 170. For
comment on the poem, see Payen, pp. 274-275.
    1 Understand *que* after *saichiés*.   20 *Dieu*, ind. obj.
of *fait*.   21 *Et*, intensifier here rather than conjunction,
'even'.   38 *ne nos puet mescheoir*, impersonal, 'evil cannot befall us'.

<u>146</u>   Pastourelle

RS 342, MW 847
Mss. K 2-3, M 13v-59r, N 2r-v, O 57v-58r, S 375v, T 2v-3r,

V 1v-2r, X 9r-v. Music in KMNOVX. Attribution in MOS
TV.

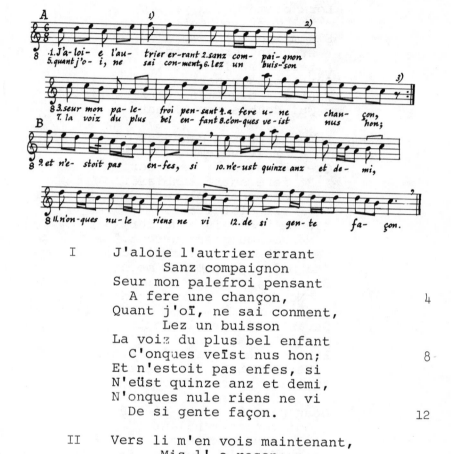

I   J'aloie l'autrier errant
                  Sanz compaignon
        Seur mon palefroi pensant
            A fere une chançon,   4
        Quant j'oï, ne sai conment,
              Lez un buisson
        La voiz du plus bel enfant
            C'onques veïst nus hon;   8
        Et n'estoit pas enfes, si
        N'eüst quinze anz et demi,
        N'onques nule riens ne vi
            De si gente façon.   12

II   Vers li m'en vois maintenant,
              Mis l' a reson:
        "Bele, dites moi conment,
            Pour Dieu, vous avez non."   16
        Et ele saut tout errant
            A bon baston:
        "Se vous venez plus avant,
            Ja avroiz la tençon.   20
        Sire, fuiez vous de ci!
        N'ai cure de tel ami,
        Car j'ai mult plus biau choisi,
            Qu'en claime Robeçon."   24

III   Quant je la vi esfreer
              Si durement

Qu'el ne mi daigne esgarder
    Ne fere autre senblant,   28
Lors conmençai a penser
        Confaitement
Ele me porroit amer
    Et changier son talent.   32
A terre lez li m'assis;
Quant plus regart son cler vis,
Tant est plus mes cuers espris,
    Qui double mon talent.   36

IV   Lors li pris a demander
            Mult belement
      Que me daignast esgarder
          Et fere autre senblant.   40
      Ele conmence a plorer
          Et dist itant:
      "Je ne vos puis esgarder,
          Ne sai qu'alez querant."   44
      Vers li me trais, si li di:
      "Ma bele, pour Dieu, merci!"
      Ele rist, si respondi:
          "Nou faites pour la gent."   48

V   Devant moi lors la montai
          De maintenant
      Et trestout droit m'en alai
          Vers un bois verdoiant.   52
      Aval les prez regardai,
          S'oï criant
      Deus pastors parmi un blé
          Qui venoient huiant   56
      Et leverent un haut cri.
      Assez fis plus que ne di;
      Je la les, si m'en foï:
          N'oi cure de tel gent.   60

MN   Ms. O is mensurally notated. Form: A A B.
1. In l. 5 ms. writes g'. 2. In l. 6 ms. writes a bar.
3. In l. 4 ms. writes no rest.

RR   II   14 la a *(+1)*   V   55 Dels

V   I   1 lautre ier   T   3 pensant] anblant   NX   4
A fere *illeg in O*; A] Por   X, une *missing S*   7 dou MOTX,
dun S; enfancon T   8 hons S   9 enfent M; si] quil
SV   11 Onques O; rien T

II   13 maintenant] en riant O   14 la a NSVX, lai a MO
15 B. por deu d. m. c. O, B. d. m. por dieu c. S   16
Vos auez n. OS; vous *missing* V   17 Et *missing* X; tout er-
rant] maintenant MNOSTVX   18 son] un S   20 aurez MO
SV; la *missing* S   22 Ie nai c. O   23 Car] Que OSTV;
biau] ami, choisi *missing* T   24 Con S; Quanque iai me ro-
becon V
III   25 Lors fu esfraee S   27 Que MSV, Quele OTX; me
MNOSTVX; daigna NSX; regarder S   29 conmence a porpenser
NS   30 Conmant S   31 *illeg in* M; Mi p. a. S   33 Arriere S   34 Com p. resgar O; plus *missing* V   35 mon
cuer X
IV   37 Lor M   38 Tout b. V   39 Quele me d. regarder
S   40 autre] bel V   42 dit MO; Et d. tantost S   43
Je *missing* OX; puis] os V; puis plus e. X; escouter MT,
p. oblier escouter S   45 dis MNOSTVX   47 rit MNOSTV
48 Non NX, Ne MT, Nel V; dites pas a la g. S; Uos f.
paour la g. O
V   49 monte V   50 De *missing* X   51 Et *missing* S;
droit *missing* T   52 Lez un O   53 esgardai O   55 pas-
touriaus p. S; blef OS   56 v. criant S   57 leuoient
ST; haut grant MOST   58 plus bele q. S   60 Ne oi c.
O, Ie noi c. S; telx genz O, tex gens T

    E   La Ravallière, 89; Tarbé *Thib*, 89-91; Bartsch,
231-232; Wallensköld *Thib*, 176-179; Pauphilet, 902-903;
Spaziani *Ant*, 90-92; Bec 2, 47-48; Aspland, 163-166.

    N   This pastourelle, "qui n'est pas loin d'être un
petit chef-d'oeuvre" (Frappier, p. 189), is one of only two
known to have been composed by Thibaut; the other is RS 529.
    24 *en = on*.   36 *Qui = ce qui*.   48 *Nou = ne le*.
33-35 The tradition that allows imperfect rhymes in pastourelles and similar compositions is somewhat refined in this
poem: only in st. 3 is the *c* rhyme, which appears in all
stanzas, interpreted as *-is* rather than *-i*, and in that
stanza it is *-is* exclusively.

Pastourelle   147

RS 529, MW 1762
Mss. X 28r-v, B 7r-v, K 31, M 66v-67r, T 14v-15r, V 16r-v.
    Music in all mss. except T. Attribution in KTX.

I   L'autrier par la matinee
     Entre un bois et un vergier,
     Une pastore ai trovee
     Chantant por soi envoisier,
     Et disoit en son premier: 5
     "Ci me tient li maus d'amours."
     Tantost cele part me tor
     Que je l'oï desresnier,
     Si li dis sans delaier:
     "Bele, Deus vos doint bon jor."   10

II   Mon salu sanz demoree
     Me rendi et sanz targier;
     Mult ert fresche, coloree,
     Si mi plot a acointier.
     "Bele, vostre amor vos quier,   15
     S'avrez de moi riche ator."
     Ele respont: "Tricheor
     Sont mes trop li chevalier;
     Melz aim Perrin mon bergier
     Que riche honme menteor."   20

III "Bele, ce ne dites mie.
     Chevalier sont trop vaillant.
     Qui set donc avoir amie
     Ne servir a son talent
     Fors chevalier et tel gent?   25
     Mais l'amor d'un bergeron
     Certes ne vaut un bouton.
     Partez vos en a itant

Et m'amez; je vos creant,
De moi avrés riche don."   30

IV   "Sire, par sainte Marie,
        Vos en parlés por noient.
        Mainte dame avront trichie
        Cil chevalier soudoiant;
        Trop sont faus et mal pensant,   35
        Pis valent que Guenelon.
        Je m'en revois en maison,
        Car Perrinés qui m'atent
        M'aime de cuer loiaument.
        Abaisiés vostre raison."   40

V   G'entendi bien la bergiere,
        Qu'ele me veut eschaper;
        Mult li fis longue priere,
        Mais n'i poi riens conquester.
        Lors la pris a acoler   45
        Et ele gete un haut cri:
        "Perrinet, traï! traï!"
        Dou bois prenent a huper.
        Je la lez sans demorer,
        Seur mon cheval m'en parti.   50

VI   Quant ele m'en vit aler,
        Ele dist par ranponer:
        "Chevalier sont trop hardi."

MN   Form: A A B; the envoy is sung to ll. 8-10.
1. In l. 3 ms. omits this note. 2. In l. 2 ms. writes a
diamond-shaped note. 3. In l. 4 ms. writes no rest.

RR   I   2 bois en un   IV   35 mal et faus   V
43 Mes li f.

V   I   2 Entrai un M   5 un son MT, el son V   6
Si me B   7 men t. MT, men cours B   8 del rainier B
9 Se li MT   10 dont K, doinst T   II   11 demore M,
demorer V   12 Me tendi V   13 fresche] simple V; f.
(s.) et c. BMTV   14 Se mi MT   16 Sauroiz BKM; atort
B   18 li] sil B   20 h. gengleour B, tricheor K   III
21 Bene ce M; se ne B   25 Fois ch. B   26 lamors T
28 en vous B   30 auroiz B   IV   31 saintes T   32
en missing MT; parle or por M   33 auront] ont or B; trichiee KV   34 Sil ch. B   35 fox M, fol T   36 que]
de MT   37 r. (vois T) en (ens T) ma m. MT   38 Car]

Que M, Ke T; perrins B; qui mi a. BV V 42 Qui me
uoloit e. B; engingnier K 43 riens ni poi K; ni peuc
r. T 45 grant c. T; crit B 46 a *missing* B; huer TV
VI 51-53 *not included in K* 52 Si me d. MT; dist *missing B*; pour ramprosner T

E̲   La Ravallière, 92, 313; Tarbé *Thib*, 92-94; Wallensköld *Thib*, 180-183; Bartsch, 232-234; Chastel, 478-483;
Toja, 420-422; Goldin, 474-477.

DF̲   Picard: *trichie* (33) for *trichiee*.

N̲   This song and RS 342 are the only pastourelles
known to have been composed by Thibaut.   5 *son* 'song'.   6
This is part of a known refrain, see B, no. 534 and note.
7 *Que* 'where'.   36 Here as in numerous other medieval
works, Ganelon, the traitor of the *Song of Roland*, provides
the standard against which all treachery may be measured.
48 The subject of *prenent* is an understood indefinite plural, equivalent to modern French *on*.   53 As suggested in
Wallensköld *Thib*, this verse has the character of a refrain;
it occurs nowhere else, however, and is not listed in B.

148   Chanson pieuse

RS 1410, MW 1886
Mss. M 75v, B 4v-5r, K 27-28, O 81r-v, R 76v-77r and 183v-
    184r-v, S 375r-v, T 13r, V 14v-15r, X 25v-26r-v. Music
    in all mss. except ST. Attribution in KTX.

1. Mau-vez ar-bres ne puet flo-rir, 2. ainz se-che toz et va cro-lant;
3. et hom qui n'ai-me, sanz men-tir, 4. ne por-te fruit, ainz va mo-rant.

5. Fleur et fruit de coin-te sem-blant 6. por-te cil en qui naist a-mors.

7. En ce fruit a tant de va-lor 8. que nus ne.l por-roit es-li-gier,

9. que de toz maus puet al-le-gier.

10. *Fruit de na-tu- re l'a- pele on; 11.or vos ai de- vi- se son non.*

I Mauvez arbres ne puet florir,
  Ainz seche toz et va crolant;
  Et hom qui n'aime, sanz mentir,
  Ne porte fruit, ainz va morant.
  Fleur et fruit de cointe semblant 5
  Porte cil en qui naist amors.
  En ce fruit a tant de valors
  Que nus ne.l porroit esligier,
  Que de toz maus puet allegier.
  Fruit de nature l'apele on; 10
  Or vos ai devisé son non.

II De ce fruit ne puet nus sentir,
  Se Dieus ne le fait proprement.
  Qui a Dieu amer et servir
  Done cuer et cors et talent, 15
  Cil queut dou fruit trestot avant,
  Et Dieus l'en fait riche secors.
  Par le fruit fu li premiers plors,
  Quant Eve fist Adan pechier;
  Mes qui dou bon fruit veut mengier 20
  Dieu aint et sa mere et son non,
  Cil quiaudra le fruit de saison.

III Seignor, de l'arbre dit vos ai
  De nature, de qu'amours vient;
  Du fruit meür conté vos ai 25
  Que cil quiaut qui a Dieu se tient.
  Mes du fruit vert me resovient
  Qui ja ne moi ne meürra;
  C'est li fruiz en qu'Adans pecha.
  De ce fruit est plains mes vergiers: 30
  Des que ma dame vi premiers,
  Oi de s'amor plain cuer et cors,
  Ne ja nul jor n'en istra fors.

IV Bien cuit dou fruit ne gosteré
  Que je cueilli, ainçois m'avient 35
  Si com a l'enfant, bien le sé,
  Qui a la branche se sostient
  Et entor l'arbre va et vient
  Ne ja amont ne montera;
  Ainsi mez cuers foloiant va. 40

```
        Tant par est granz mes desirriers
        Que je en tieng mes grans maus chiers,
        Si sui afinez com li ors
        Vers li, cui est toz mes tresors.


  V     Dieus, se je pooie cueillir                45
        Du fruit meür de vos amer
        Si com vos m'avez fait sentir
        L'amor d'aval et comparer,
        Lors me porroie saouler
        Et venir a repentement.                     50
        Par vostre douz commandement
        Me donez amer la meillor:
        Ce est la precïeuse flor
        Par qui vos venistes ça jus,
        Dont li deables est confus.                 55


  VI    Mere Dieu, par vostre douçor
        Dou bon fruit me donez savor,
        Que de l'autre ai je senti plus
        C'onques, ce croi, ne senti nus.
```

MN   Ms. R[1] has a different melody in the B-section.
Form: A A B; the envoy is sung to ll. 8-11.

RR   I   7 ualor   8 nus ne p. alegier   III   25
Du f. m. uos ai conte   28 meurera   31 D. q. ui ma dame
p.   IV   38 va iuant   41 granz] tant   V   53 Cest la
(-1)   54 uenistes   55 deablez   VI   56 Pere dieu

V   Stanzas: KR[1]   I II III IV V
                 R[2]   I II III IV VI
I   1 arbre R[1], abre V; p. morir S   2 tout KR[1]; et
uait B; crolant *missing S*   3 *missing S*; hons KOR[2]X; q.
lainme B; sanz m. *missing B*   4 Ne p. f. a. v. *missing S*
5 Flors B, Fueille S, Fruis et flours R[2]; de c. s. *missing B*   6 *missing B*; Pour ce (cou T) R[1]R[2]TV; cil en] est
faux R[2]; en *missing V*; cui OR[1]S; na a. R[2]   7 En ce f.
missing B; cel f. T; tant] mult S; ualo(u)r BKOR[1]TVX,
doucours R[2]   8 ne.l] ne KS, ni R[1], nen T, nou O; alegier S   9 *missing K*; Que *missing in R[2]*, Car R[1]ST; fait
il a. S   10 Fleur R[1]; lapelon BO   11 Or ne sai deuiser s. n. R[1]
II   12 cel f. T; sentir] esmes B   13 Dieus] il S; nou
fait premierement O   14 Qui a de seruir a amer O; et
sentir R[1]   15 D. et cuer et t. S, D. c. et entendement
V   16 Cils R[2], Cis T; qui R[1], quierat B, qui en tel f.

S; du BKR^{1}R^{2}V; f. premierement BKOR^{1}VX   17 l'en] li S
18 le] ce R^1 19 Quant *missing* S; Eue i fist S;
pechier] mengier K   20 du KR^{1}R^{2}V, de BS; son f. B   21
et so son non B   22 *missing* V; Cil] Si BKOR^{1}R^{2}STX; aura
le S; du f. BKR^1, dou OX
III   23 S. dit uos ai de larbre O, S. de l. uos ai dit S
24 n. dont a. R^{1}R^2, n. de quoi a. T; n. iuqua miex sieut
S   25 *missing* S; Dou R^{1}TX, Del R^2; vous conterai R^2
26 *missing* S; c. cueillent B; Dieu] lui R^2; tienent B,
tiens R^1 27 *missing* S; dou KOTX; vers R^1 28 *missing*
S; ne meurera O, ne se tenra R^2, ne mainterra T   29
missing S; frui R^2; f. en que a. BK, f. en quoi a. T, f.
dont a. R^2; Adam R^{1}R^{2}V   30 *missing* S; tel f. BT; me v.
R^2 31 *missing* S; De q. B; ken ma T; vi] uit B, *missing*
T   32 *missing* S; Ai de B, Euc ie de R^2 33 Dont a nul
S; ia a nul T; jor *missing* O; ne sen i. B, nistera S; is-
trai K
IV   34 B. croi B, sai R^2, qui S, quio T; du BR^{2}V; del
S; goutera O, goustera SV   35 Que iai c. OS, Que c. ai
R^{2}T; samours ne vient R^2, aincois man uient S, au cors m.
V   36 c. de l. S   37 Qui en O; a la b. se s. *missing*
BKR^{1}VX; se s. *missing* O   40 folement ua S   41 grant
BR^2, mes granz d. O; desiries T   42 je *missing* X; ie
maintien S; chies R^1 43 afinez] esfraez B, esfrees X,
esfreez K, effraes R^1, effreez V   44 V. lui V; qui
BKOR^{1}R^{2}TVX, *missing* S; mes seco(u)rs BK
V   46 Dou OTX; de v. a. *missing* S   47 v. auez B   49
Bien me R^1 52 Mi d. R^1, Me d. *missing* V; daigniez B
53 Cest la B   54 Par cui BOS, quoi R^{1}V
VI   56 pour v. B   57 Du BR^{2}TV   58 Car R^{2}T; Que ce
B; je] iou T; ai et sen senc plus R^2 59 C. ie croi
R^{2}T, C. encore B, encor OX, Concor V; ne s.] sentist B,
nen senti O, ne fist S
    S adds the following envoy:
        Phelipe, laissiez vostre errour.
        Je vos vi ja bon chanteor.
        Chantez, et nos dirons desus
        Le chant Te Deum laudamus.

    E   La Ravallière, 161; Tarbé *Thib*, 122-124; Wallen-
sköld *Thib*, 203-208; Järnström-Långfors 2, 45-48.

<u>149</u>   Chanson (de femme)

RS 498, MW 666, B 1427 (see note below).
Mss. a 68v, U 137v–138r. Music in a. Attribution in a.

I   *Onques n'amai tant que jou fui amee.*
     Or m'en repenc, se ce peüst valoir,
     Q'Amours m'avoit au meillour assenee
     Pour toute hounour et toute joie avoir,
     Et au plus bel de toute la contree;   5
     Mais ore a il autrui s'amour dounee,
     Qui volentiers a soi l'a retenu.
     Lasse! pour koi fui je de mere nee!
     Par mon orguel ai mon ami perdu.

II   Si me doint Dieus d'amours longe duree,   10
     Que je l'amai de cuer sans decevoir

Qant me disoit k'iere de li amee,
Mais n'en osai ains descouvrir le voir:
Des mesdisans doutoie la noumee.
Biau sire Dieus, baisie et acolee   15
M'eüst il or et aveuc moi geü,
Mais qu'il m'eüst sans plus s'amour dounee,
Si m'eüst bien tous li siecles veü!

III   Or m'a Amours malement assenee
       Qant çou que j'aim fait a une autre avoir, 20
       Ne ne m'en laist retraire ma pensee,
       Ne si n'en puis soulas ne joie avoir.
       Lasse! l'amour que tant li ai veee
       Li sera ja otroiie et dounee--
       Mais tart l'ai dit, car je l'ai ja perdu.   25
       Or me convient amer sans estre amee,
       Car trop ai tart mon felon cuer vaincu.

MN   Form: A A B; lines 1+9 recur as a motet refrain.
1. Ms. repeats this note in l. 3 to compensate for the non-
elision of the preceding *toute*. 2. Ms. omits this note;
emended according to three motet manuscripts.

RR   II 18 li] ci   III 21 Ne le me l.   23 ai uee

V   After stanza I, U shows the first two lines of III
(19-20), immediately followed by the last seven lines of II
(12-18) and a reprise of the last two lines of I (8-9). U
then presents stanzas III and II, in that order. (Variants
stemming from the corrupt passage are identified below by
x.)
I 1 que] con   2 se ce] si me   4 P. tot desdut   5 Et
a millou de   7 Ke; l. detenut   8 L. con mar f. ains de m.
n.   II 11 Con ie de cuer lamai s. d.   12 Om (on x)
me d. ke de li (lui x) iere a.   13 Nonkes (Onkes x) nan
poi (pos x) reconoistre lou v.   14 la criee   15 Biaz
16 m. geist   18 Et bien leust t. li s. v.   III 19
m'a] mont   20 font ai atruj a.   23 vee   24 seroit   25
j. la j.   26 Si

E   Jeanroy *Or*, 501-502; Zarifopol, 43-44; Gennrich
Alt Lied 2, 40-42; Bec 2, 11-12.

DF   Picard: final *ie* for *iee*, as in *baisie* (15), *ot-
roiie* (24); *jou* (1) for *je*; *çou* (20) for *ce*; *repenc* (2) for
repent.

N̲   This chanson is apparently an elaboration of a
well-known two-line refrain, preserved as such in various
sources. In our text, the refrain occurs in split form, as
the first and last lines of st. 1. See, in addition to
Boogaard, Gennrich *Ron* 2, no. 1239. The poem occurs as a
motet in a number of sources. For details, see Gennrich
BibMot, no. 820, and the edition by Gennrich, pp. 16-20, in
"Trouvèrelieder und Motettenrepertoire," *Zeit. für Musikwis-
senschaft* 9 (1926), 8-39 and 65-85.

150   Chanson

RS 443, MW 688
Mss. T 96r-v, M 152v. Music in both mss. Attribution in
   both mss.

I   Gente m'est la saisons d'esté,
       Mais je tieng iver a plus gent,
       Car il m'a molt plus gens esté
       Et m'a assés plus gentement
       Secouru a ma volenté;   5
       Si m'en lo a tote la gent.

II   La gente m'a del puis jeté
       Ou j'ai jeü si longement,
       En qui j'ai deus coses trové
       C'om n'i trove pas molt sovent: 10
       De gentil cuer gentil pensé,
       De gent cors gent contenement.

III   Gentement a vers moi erré,
       Car gentillece li aprent;
       Si m'a plus gentement moeublé   15
       Ke s'ele m'eüst tot l'argent
       Et tot l'or d'un païs doné;
       Por çou a gent don gent gré rent.

IV   Mais jou en sai ausi mau gré
       La male ki si malement   20
       M'avoit el mal puis avalé
       Ou nus autres maus ne se prent;
       Mais j'ai tout mon mal oublïé,
       Si ke mal ne dolor ne sent.

V   Maudite soit ele de Dé   25
       Ki tant m'a fait mal et torment;
       Ke, se ele m'a mal presté,
       Je li doi mal rendre ensement.
       Mal li envoi tot de mon gré.
       Maus li viegne prochainement!   30

VI   Ki mal quiert mal a encontré
       Et ki mal chasce mal atent;
       Ke li mal sont plus tost torné
       Ke li kokés ki torne au vent;
       La dont il viegnent sont alé   35
       Ki li avoient en covent.

VII   Entre le gentil genteé
       Et le malaoit maltalent
       S'ont esté mis en champ malé
       Et combatu par jugement;   40
       Mais la gentillesce a outré
       Et li maus est vencus, si pent.

VIII   Se la gentillece a outré,
       C'est a boin droit se li maus pent.

MN   Form (M and T): through-composed; the envoy is
sung to ll. 5-6.

RR   I   2   tieg   5   Sescouru   III   18   Et p. *(+1)*
IV   22   a. mais mais ne *(+1)*   V   27   Ke sele *(-1)*   VI
32   ki male *(+1)*   VII   38   mal auoit m.   *(em. Jeanroy)*
39   mis] nus   VIII   43   De

V   II   9   cui   IV-VII   20-41   *from* qui *to* [gen]-
tillece *missing because of manuscript mutilation*   VIII
43-44   *not included*

E   Zarifopol, 15-16.

DF   Picard: *coses* (9) for *choses*; *çou* (18) for *ce*;
jou (19) for *je*; *boin* (44) for *bon*.

N   This poem is most unusual in its lexical design:
three stanzas playing upon *gent*, three upon *mal*, and a con-
clusion which not only combines the two lexemes but weaves
them into an extended metaphorical battle.
        31-32   Cf. such proverbs as *Qui mal dit mal luy vient,
Qui mal fera mal trouvera* (Morawski, nos. 1979, 1983).   34
The weather vane occurs with some frequency in Old French as
an image of inconstancy; see Tobler-Lommatzsch, s.v. *cochet*.
35-36   The sense of these lines is unclear.   "Dunkel," notes
Zarifopol, and Jeanroy, p. 426 of his review of Zarifopol
(*Romania* 33 [1904], 424-429), states: "Je ne comprends pas
ces vers plus que l'éditeur."   37-38   *Entre . . . Et* 'both
. . . and'.   37   *genteé = genteté*.

151   Chanson

RS 1080, MW 538
Mss. M 153r, T 97r, a 42v.   Music in all mss.   Attribution
    in all mss.

1. Quant chante oi- siauz tant se- ri   2. sor le gaut flo- ri,

3. lors m'est d'un sou- laz mem-bre 4. que j'ai a- des e- spe-re;

5. maiz a tart vient l'e- spe-ran-ce, 6. qu'en tot mon a- e

7. d'a- mors ne jo- i 8. fors en pen- se.

I   Quant chante oisiauz tant seri
          Sor le gaut flori,
      Lors m'est d'un soulaz membré
      Que j'ai adés esperé;   4
      Maiz a tart vient l'esperance,
          Qu'en tot mon aé
          D'amors ne joï
            Fors en pensé.   8

II   Tant m'a Amors honoré
          Et tant m'a doné,
      Por quant que j'ai desservi,
      Qu'ele m'en a fait hardi   12
      Et m'a de bone esperance
          Mon fin cuer guarni
          Et asseüré
            D'avoir merci.   16

III   Quar, se je mesfis vers li
          Et je l'en perdi,
      Je l'ai trop chier comperé,
      Se j'ai puis adés celé   20
      Mon anui, en esperance
          Qu'el ne m'ait grevé
          Fors por son ami
            Avoir prové.   24

IV   Et se pluz l'ai eschivé
          Qu'il n'i ot dehé,
      Por ce que trop la cremi,
      Ja si tart ne m'iert meri,   28
      Que bien ne quit m'esperance
          Avoir acompli,
          Car tot preing en gré
            Et l'en merci.   32

V   Chançon, va t'en, si li di
          Que quant j'entendi
      Qu'ele m'ot congié doné,
      Se ne m'eüst conforté   36
      Haute emprise et esperance,
          J'eüsse adiré

Gai cuer et joli,
Que j'ai gardé.   40

MN   Ms. T writes part of l. 3 and ll. 4-5 a 3rd higher. Form: through-composed.

RR   III   20 puis] tot   24 auoit esproue *(+1)*
IV 31 preig   V   39 Cuer ioli *(-2)*

V   I   2 foilli a   6 Que a   7 Damour a   8
F. qen a   II   14 fin] haut Ta   III   17 j. mespris
v. T, j. pri v. a   19 J. la T; ch. aconpere a   20 Si
ai a   21 M. ami T   22 Quele m. g. a   24 Auoit T;
esprouue a   IV   25 se puis a   26 Qui a   27 trop]
iou T, je a; lai a   V   33 Chancons T   39 Cuer ioli
T   40 Iai garde T

E   Zarifopol, 32-33.

N   This poem is especially noteworthy for the way in
which the stanzas are linked through rhyme. The *a* and *b*
rhymes are identical in stanzas 1, 3, and 5, and are reversed in stanzas 2 and 4 (*coblas retrogradadas*), the first
rhyme of each stanza being the same as the last of the preceding stanza (*coblas capcaudadas*). The *c* rhyme occurs only
once in each stanza (*rim estramp*), but is carried throughout
the poem by the single word *esperance*.
    29 *quit = cuit.*

152   Chanson satirique

RS 760, MW 2489
Mss. A 132v-133r, a 43r-v. Music in both mss. Attribution
    in both mss.

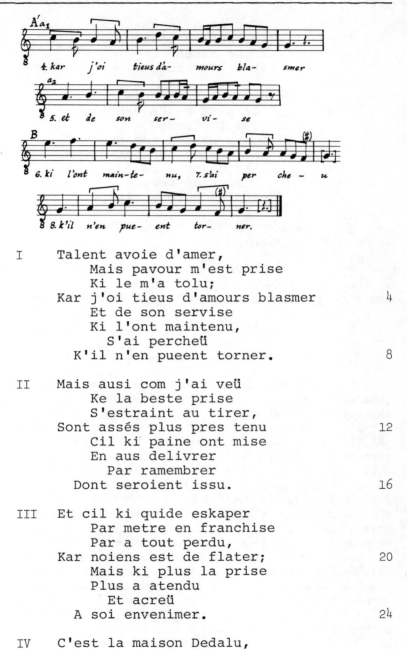

4. kar j'oi tieus d'a- mours bla- smer

5. et de son ser- vi- se

6. ki l'ont main-te- nu, 7. s'ai per che - u

8. k'il n'en pue- ent tor- ner.

I   Talent avoie d'amer,
        Mais pavour m'est prise
        Ki le m'a tolu;
     Kar j'oi tieus d'amours blasmer   4
        Et de son servise
        Ki l'ont maintenu,
        S'ai percheü
     K'il n'en puent torner.   8

II   Mais ausi com j'ai veü
        Ke la beste prise
        S'estraint au tirer,
     Sont assés plus pres tenu   12
        Cil ki paine ont mise
        En aus delivrer
        Par ramembrer
     Dont seroient issu.   16

III   Et cil ki quide eskaper
        Par metre en franchise
        Par a tout perdu,
     Kar noiens est de flater;   20
        Mais ki plus la prise
        Plus a atendu
        Et acreü
     A soi envenimer.   24

IV   C'est la maison Dedalu,
        U a se devise
        Set cascun entrer,
     Et tout i sont deceü,   28

<pre>
          Kar en nule guise
          Ne pueent trouver
          Ne assener
          Par u l'entree fu.   32

     V   Ge ne me kier ja mesler
          De plus haute emprise
          Que la Theseü,
          Q'amours sans corde nouer   36
          N'iert ja par moi prise,
          Kar mains a eü
          Plus de vertu
          Que ains ne pot finer.   40
</pre>

MN   Ms. a has a second melody. Form: A A¹ B.
1. Ms. writes a *c.o.p.* stem.

RR   I   4 cieus *(em. Jeanroy-Långfors)*   5 seruiche
6 Kil 7 perchu *(-1)*   IV   28 issont   V   33 me]
men   35 ihesu *(em. Zarifopol)*

V   IV   28 jssont detenu

E   Zarifopol, 24-25; Jeanroy-Långfors, 24-25.

N   This poem is a *canso redonda*. Rhyme-scheme of odd
stanzas is *abcabcca*; even stanzas reverse *a* and *c*: *cbacbaac*.
14 *aus* is reflexive.   18 'by accepting [Love's] authority'?   21-24 Apropos of l. 23 *acreü*, glossed as "'emprun-
té'(?)," Jeanroy-Långfors comments: "Le sens de toute la
strophe nous échappe" (p. 136). Obstacle in first half of
stanza appears to be simply l. 18; see preceding note. The
second half seems to mean that the more a man esteems Love
(or his lady?), the more he is apparently determined (*atendu*
= *entendu*) and of a mind (*acreü*, past part. of *acroire*) to
poison himself.   25 *Dedalu*, abs. gen., 'of Daedalus'. Reference is to the legendary Athenian craftsman responsible
for the Labyrinth on Crete where the Minotaur was kept.   35
la Theseü = *l'emprise de Theseüs*. Theseus was able to enter
the Labyrinth, kill the Minotaur, and find his way out again
thanks to a trail of thread he had unwound behind him.   38
mains 'many a man'.   39 *vertu* 'ability'.   40 *Que* = *qui*,
referring to l. 38 *mains*.

RAOUL DE SOISSONS

Chanson

RS 2107, MW 1499
Mss. V 118r-v, C 197v-198r, F 101r-v-102r, K 141-142, N 65v-
66r, P 85r-v-86r, R 93v-94r, S 231r, U 128r-v-129r, X
97r-v-98r, a 29r-v. Music in all mss. except CSU.
Attribution in FKPXa; attributed to Thierri de Soissons
in N, to Perrin d'Angicourt in C.

I Quant voi la glaie meüre
   Et le douz rosier fleurir
   Et par desus la verdure
   La rousee resplendir,
     Lors soupir   5
   Pour cele que tant desir,
   Que j'aing, las! outre mesure.
   Tout aussi conme l'arsure
   Fet quanqu'ele ataint bruïr,
   Fet mon vis taindre et palir   10
   Sa simple regardeüre,
   Qui me vint au cuer ferir
   Pour fere la mort sentir.

II Mout fet douce bleceüre
   Bonne amour en son venir,   15
   Mes mieus vendroit la pointure
   D'un escorpion sentir
     Et morir
   Que de ma dolour languir.

```
        E las! ma dame est si dure              20
        Que de ma joie n'a cure
        Ne de ma dolour guerir,
        Ainz me fet vivre martir.
        Tele est adés m'aventure
        C'onc dame ne poi servir               25
        Qui le mi deignast merir.


III     E las! je l'ai tant amee
        Tres dont que primes la vi
        C'onques puis d'autre rienz nee,
        Nes de mon cuer, ne joï;               30
                 Ainz sui si
        Soupriz de l'amour de li
        Que ailleurs n'est ma pensee.
        Mes se ma dame honoree
        Set qu'ele ait loial ami,              35
        Bien devroit avoir merci
        Se loiautez li agree;
        Mes souvent avient ainsi
        Que ce sont li plus haï.


IV      Bele et bonne et desirree,             40
        Onques dame ne fu si!
        Se vous m'avez refusee
        La joie dont je vous pri,
                 Enrichi
        Sont mi mortel anemi                   45
        Et leur joie avez doublee
        Et a moi la mort donnee,
        Qui ne l'ai pas deservi,
        C'onques amans ne transi
        De mort si desesperee;                 50
        Mes bien voeil estre peri
        S'a vostre amour ai failli.


V       Dame, ne me puis desfendre
        De la mort que pour vous sent,
        Ne que cil c'on mainne pendre          55
        Encontre son jugement;
                 Ainz atent
        Vostre douz conmandement.
        Si vous fas bien a entendre:
        Se vous m'ociez sanz prendre,          60
        Blame en arez de la gent,
        Car cil qui toz jorz atent
        Et qui ne se veut desfendre
```

        Doit avoir legierement
        Merci quant s'espee rent.   65

    VI Chançon, va t'en sanz atendre
        A ma dame droitement
        Et li di que sanz reprendre
        De moi face son talent,
                Car souvent   70
        Vif plus dolereusement
        Que cil que mort fet estendre.
        Mes sa douce face tendre,
        Ou toute biauté resplent,
        M'art si mon cuer et esprent   75
        Que li charbons sous la cendre
        N'art pas plus couvertement
        Que cil qui merci atent.

    MN   Ms. a melody has some deviations. With other
texts, RS 1104, 2091, 2096, 2112, and a Latin contrafactum
by Adam de la Bassée, the melody is also extant in mss. KN
RVX (twice in X) and Lille, Bibl. mun. 397. Form: A A^1 B B.
1. In ll. 3 and 9 ms. writes no flat.   2. In ll. 2 and 12
ms. writes a bar.

    RR   II   25 Conques dame ne serui   III   33   Car
IV 42 mauiez

    V   Stanzas: KNPXRa   I II IV   III VI
                   F   I II IV
                   S   I II IV   III V
                   C   I II III IV   V
                   U   I II IV   III VI V
I 1-9 *missing in F*   2   Et le (lou CU) rosier espanier
KNPXSCUa   3 Et seur (Desour U, sus N, sur R, sor a,
par S) la bel(l)e (douce S) v. KNPXRSUa   6 celi CUa;
cui SCU, qui a   7 Et aim l. a; He las (Las et R, Elais
C, Lais cui U) iaim (ie laim N, iain RC, iaig S, iains
U) o. m. KNPXRSCU   8 Car a. R, Autresi KNPX; T. aus c.
a   9 atent XU   10 m. cors a   11 douce r. a, tres-
douche esgardeure F   12 Et F, Ke CU; me vient FSU; a
c. CU; Q. au cuer me vient f. R, Q. el cors me vint f. a
13 so(u)sfrir Ca
II 15 Fine RC; amours a; au souenir S, et souenir U
16 Et KNPX; Mex me v. S; uaudroit KNPXRS, uauroit C,
uadroit U   20 Las et m. R   21 ma dolo(u)r nait c. CU
22 Ne de mes maus alegir S, Ne de mes mals amerir C, Ne
de mes griez mals santir U, Na soi ne me veut tenir a   23

mi R; a mar. FS, et languir C, et morir U; Si mocist a
son plaisir a 24 Et cest a. KNPXRU, Mais adies en F,
Lais cest tous iors C, Mais cest a. a 25 Quainz P,
Quains ma d. R, Cainc F, Maiz S, Cains C, Ca U, Kains
a; Conques (Onques N) dame ne serui KNX 26 Quel(l)e
RFS; me KNPXFSCUa; uausist a
III 27 H. dex KNPX, deus U, dieus a 28 Des primes
que ie la ui KPX, Des lors que primes la ui N, Dez lor que
primez la ui R, Des lors que premiers la ui S, Despues ke
premiers la ui C, De lors ke premiers la ui U, Des ce que
premiers la ui a 29 Onques p. autre S; Ke onkes pues de
r. C; rien XCU 30-33 *missing in S* 30 Ne KNPX; De
mon cuer ie ne j. C 31 A. ma (mait U) s. KNPXRUa 32
Lessie KN, Lessier P, Laissie Xa, Laisiet U, Blecie R,
Destrois C; l'amour de *missing in C*; amour a; lui R 33
Ke aillors nai ma p. C, Que ie naim autre riens nee KNPXa,
Ke ie ne ains atre nee U, Et se ma dame honneree R 34
Et S; M. quant a; Qui est si france et senee R 35 ait]
a a 36 B. deusse R, en doit SC 37 loiaute KNPX,
loalteit U
IV 40 He (Le X) tres douce d. KNPX, Douce (Douche F)
dame d. RFSU, Belle blonde d. C, A tres boine et d. a
41 Conques R, Konkes C, Conke U 42 mauiez (-s X)
KPX; uee KPX, deuee NF, dauee U 43 Lamor dont ie uos
pri si U 46 auront d. C; Saurez (-s X) leur (lor X)
ioie d. KPX, Saues (-z SU) lor (la R) ioie d. RFSU 48
Si KNPRSCUa; la U 49 C. (Onques N) honme (home XU)
KNPXU, C. mais hons R, C. nus hom a, Car ainc mais hons
F, Car onques hons S, Lais onkes hom C 50 tresesperee
S 51 Et KNPXSU; Bien en v. R; periz S, peris U; Iainc
mius ces maus a soufrir F 52 Puis qua (ka U) samo(u)r
ai f. KNPXRSU, Ca tel ioie auoir f. F, Pues (Puis a) ke
(que a) jai a uo(u)s f. Ca
V 53 Elais U; ie ne mos (mois U) d. SCU 54 p. li s.
U 55 Nes CU; moinent U 58 Mersit debonaremant U
59 Et si uos fais bien e. S, Et se uos ueul faire e. C,
Et ci uos fas ai e. U 60 sanz] puis U; faindre S 61
en] i CU 62 Et C; q. ne se de(s)fent (defant U) SCU
63 Et a merci (mersit U) se veult (uiaut S) randre
(rendre S) SCU 65 M. ki C
VI 66 Ma cancounete je tenuoi a 67 mamie d. RU 68
Prie li que (ke U) sanz (-s XU) mesprendre (mesprandre U)
KNPXU, Si li di que sans atendre mesprendre (*sic*) R, Se li
prie de par moi a 69 Te die to(u)t s. t. KNPXR, Me diet
tout s. t. U, Cor face tout s. t. a 72 cuj mors U, qui
mors a 73 belle RU; facon R. 74 toutes a, fine NRU;
biautes a; En qui grant b. KPX 75 le cors KPXa; Mon

cors (cuer N) alume et e.   NRU   76   seur   a; Li charbons
desoz (dedens U) NRU   77   p. si s.   KNPXU; contenement a
78 Con (Com K) fet (fait Xa) li (le P) las qui atent,
Que (Con U) ie fas quant (cant U) a la (li U) pens (pans
U) RU

    <u>E</u>   La Borde *Es*, 218; Keller, 262–264; Mätzner, 18–20,
162–168; Steffens *Per*, 282–290, 352–354; Winkler, 65–69.

    <u>N</u>   This song apparently enjoyed great popularity, as
attested not only by the number and variety of ms. sources
but also by the number of songs composed in imitation of it
(see Jeanroy "Philippe", p. 521); one of these, Philippe de
Remi's *Aussi com l'eschaufeüre* (RS 2096), is included in the
present collection. Both earlier modern editions, Steffens
Per and Winkler, take ms. K as their base and add the missing stanza from ms. V as the final one, thus presenting the
order: I II IV III VI V. The order of ms. V, followed here,
seems to us more satisfying poetically.
    6–7 'For the one whom I desire so much [and] whom I
love . . .'. The lines (without a comma after *desir*) may as
readily be understood to mean 'For the one whom I desire so
much that I love excessively'.   16 Steffens *Per* and Winkler select the variant *vaudroit*, which normal usage should
indeed require; we prefer to retain the reading of ms. V as
a poetically more interesting echo of l. 15 *venir*.   28
'Ever since I first saw her'.   30 *Nes* '(not) even'.   39
ce generalizes l. 35 *loial ami*.   48 *l'* may either refer to
l. 47 *la mort*, in which case the form *deservi* would provide
evidence of the relative freedom of participial agreement in
OF (see Foulet, p. 102; Moignet, p. 206), or else serve as a
neuter meaning 'that you should kill me'.   49–50 *transi de
mort* 'died a death'.   53–56 'I cannot defend myself a-
gainst death . . . any more than the man being led to the
gallows [can defend himself] against his sentence'. Both
Steffens *Per* and Winkler emend l. 54 *la mort*, found in all
mss., to *l'amor*. *La mort*, however, is entirely appropriate
in view of the present order of stanzas (which it helps to
justify), the comparison expressed in ll. 55–56, and the
occurrence in l. 13 of the phrase *la mort sentir*.   60 *sanz
prendre* 'instead of accepting [me as your lover]' and 'instead of taking [me prisoner]'; ll. 62–65 make it clear that
the double meaning is intended.   61 *arez = avrez*.   68
sanz reprendre 'with no reproach'.   73–78 Note that the
image of burning links the final stanza to the first (ll.
8–9).

154   Chanson

RS 778, MW 469
Mss. N 61v-62r, K 293-294, V 86v-87r. Music in all mss.
Attributed to Thierri de Soissons in KN.

I   Chançon legiere a chanter
       Et plesant a escouter
       Ferai conme chevaliers,
       Por ma grant dolor mostrer
       La ou je ne puis aler   5
       Ne dire mes desirriers.
       Si m'en sera bien mestiers
       Qu'ele soit bone et legiere,
       Por ce que de ma priere
       Me soit chascuns mesagiers   10
       Et amis et enparliers
       A ma douce dame chiere.

II   De ma douce dame amer
       Ne me sai amesurer,
       Ainz i pens si volentiers   15
       Qu'en la joie du penser
       Me fet amors oublïer
       Touz ennuiz et touz dangiers.
       Ha! tant m'est douz li veilliers
       Quant recort sa douce chiere   20

Et sa tres bele maniere:
Lors puis de deus eschequiers
Doubler les poinz touz entiers
De fine biauté entiere.

III Bien seroit de joie plains   25
Qui porroit estre certains
De s'amor par un besier.
Hé las! c'est ma plus grant fains!
Mes de sospirs et de plainz
Sont mi boivre et mi mengier,   30
N'autres delices ne quier
Tant con de li me souviengne;
Car quant plus mes maus me graigne,
Plus le truis douz et legier,
Quant amors me fet cuidier   35
Que par li santé me viengne.

IV Bele dame, droiz cors sains,
Je vos enclin jointes mains
Au lever et au couchier,
Car quant plus vos sui lointains, 40
Plus vos est mes cuers prouchains
De penser et de veillier;
Et se merci vos requier,
Ançois que mort me sorprengne,
Por Deu, pitié vos en preigne!   45
Car ne voroie changier
La joie de vos songier
A l'empire d'Alemaigne.

V Quant je voi vostre cler vis
Et je puis avoir vo ris   50
De vos biauz euz esmerez,
Sachiez que moi est avis
Que d'un rai de paradis
Soit mes cuers enluminez,
Car vostre plesant bontez,   55
Qui tant est fine et veraie,
Me fet oublïer la plaie
Dont je sui el cors navrez;
Mes n'en puis estre sanez
Sanz vostre douce manaie.   60

VI Ma dame a, ce m'est avis,
Vers euz rianz, bruns sorcis,
Cheveus plus biaus que dorez,

Biau front, nes droit bien assis,
Color de rose et de lis,   65
Bouche vermeille et souez,
Col blanc qui n'est pas hallez,
Gorge qui de blanchor raie.
Plesant, avenant et gaie
La fist nostre sire Dés,   70
Plus bele et plus sage assez
Qu'en ma chançon ne retraie.

MN   Ms. V has a second melody. Form: A A B.
1. In 1. 5 ms. writes a bar. 2. In 1. 3 ms. writes a
bar.

RR   II   21 *missing*   22 Car 1. p. de ij eschiers
III   31 Quautres   35 amors *missing*   V   53 du roi
60 manoie   VI   67 blant   68 roie   70 Dés] dex

V   Stanza VI not included in KV.
I   7 me KV; grant m. K   II   21 *missing in* V   22
Car 1. p. de d. -e. KV   23 Doubliers V   III   28 granz
V   31 Quautres V   33 mengraigne K, engreigne V   IV
44 soupraigne KV   46 esloignier V   47 La j. non pas
changier V   V   52 qua V   53 du roi V   54 cors K

E   Winkler, 41-43.

N   The ms. attribution to Thierri de Soissons is no
doubt erroneous. It is generally accepted that, in all the
lyric mss. in which it appears, that name is a mistake for
Raoul de Soissons; see Winkler, p. 20, and p. 159 in Jeanroy's review of Winkler (*Romania* 44 [1915-1917], 159-160).
    23-24 *Doubler les poinz de l'eschequier de qqch.* (or
doubler l'eschequier de qqch.) is a well-attested idiom (cf.
Tobler-Lommatzsch, s.v. *eschequier*) used to express a very
great or even infinite quantity of something, literally the
result of a geometric doubling of the sixty-four spaces of a
chessboard. For the origin of the phrase, see Charles H.
Livingston, "Old French *doubler l'eskiekier*," *Mod. Lang.
Notes* 45 (1930), 246-251. Note that in the present occurrence the immensity of 1. 24 *fine biauté* is underscored by
the poet's doubling of the chessboard itself. Jeanroy, op.
cit., would emend 1. 22 *puis* to *puet*, with the lady as subject, for *fine biauté* is of course hers rather than the
poet's. The emendation, however, for all its apparent log-
ic, would undermine the poetic message; in the context of
revery provided by 11. 19-21, it is not the lady herself but

the speaker's mental image of her that magnifies her beauty, and the first-person *puis* is indeed correct.

26 *Qui* 'he who'. 46 *voroie = voudroie.* 61-72 In
his review of Winkler (*Neuphilologische Mitteilungen* 17
[1915], 125-133), A. Wallensköld suggests, p. 131: "Tout le
couplet m'a l'air d'avoir été ajouté par un copiste (v. no-
tamment la façon dont parle le poète de sa dame à la 3e personne du sing., après l'avoir apostrophée aux couplets IV-
V)."

Chanson   155

RS 1154, MW 1239
Mss. C 64v-65r, O 12v. Music in O. Attribution in C.

I   E! coens d'Anjo, on dist per felonnie
     Ke je ne sai chanteir fors por autrui.
     Il dïent voir, je ne.s en desdi mie,
     C'onkes nul jor de moi sires ne fui;

Et s'il veullent savoir a cui je sui,   5
Je lor dirai per ma grant cortoixie:
Saichiés, Amors m'ait si en sa baillie
Ke je n'ai sen, volenteit ne raixon
Ke je sens li saiche faire chanson.

II   Sire, saichiés et si n'en douteis mie   10
Ke cheveliers n'iert jai de grant renom
Sens bone Amor ne sens sa signorie,
Ne nuls sens li ne puet estre proudom;
Car sous ses piés met le plux hault baron,
Et le povre fait meneir haute vie;   15
Prouesse, honors, solais vient de s'aïe,
Et done plus de joie a ses amis
Ke nus ne puet avoir sens paradix.

III Bien m'ait Amors esproveit en Sulie
Et en Egypte, ou je fui meneis pris,   20
C'adés i fui en poour de ma vie
Et chascun jour cuidai bien estre ocis;
N'onkes por ceu mes cuers n'en fut partis
Ne decevreis de ma douce anemie,
Ne en France per ma grant maladie,   25
Ke je cuidai de ma goute morir,
Ne se pooit mes cuers de li partir.

IV N'est mervoille se fins amans oblie
Aucune foix son amerous desir
Quant outre mer en vait sens compaignie   30
Dous ans ou trois ou plux sens revenir.
Bien me cuidai de sa prixon partir,
Maix dou cuidier fix outraige et folie,
C'Amors m'ait pris et tient si fort et lie
Ke por fuïr ne la puis oblieir,   35
Ains me covient en sa mercit torneir.

V   De l'angoixe ke j'ai por li sentie
Ne devroit nuls sens morir eschaippeir,
Et por paour demort ke me desfie
Seux je vers li venus mercit crieir;   40
Et s'en plorant ne puis mercit troveir,
Morir m'estuet sens confort d'autre amie
Et, s'elle veult, l'amor de li m'ocie!
Dur cuer avrait, felon et sens dousour,
Se me laissoit morir a teil dolor.   45

VI Hé! cuens d'Anjo, per vostre chanterie
Poriés avoir joie et prix et honor;
Maix ma joie est sens gueridon fenie
Et tuit mi chant sont retorneit a plour,
Si ke jamaix ne chanterai nul jor.   50
Por ceu vos pri, et ma chanson vos prie,
Ke la chanteis tant k'elle soit oïe
Davant celi ke paisse de bonteit
Toutes celles de la crestïenteit.

VII Si voirement com je di veriteit,   55
Se m'envoist Deus de li joie et santeit!

MN Form: A A B.
1. In 1. 3 ms. writes no rest.

RR II 14 ses] ces; les plux hauls barons 15
les poures 17 ses] ces   V 43 s'elle] celle

V Ms. O contains only stanza I.
I 1 Avcune gent ont dit p. f.   2 par a.   4 C. un j.
sires de moi ne f.   7 Quamors ma si dou tout en sa b.   9
li puisse f.

E Winkler, 46-48.

DF Lorraine, including ai for a, as in saichiés (7),
saiche (9), jai (11), paisse (53); ei for tonic e, as in
chanteir (2), douteis (10), esproveit (19), teil (45); per
(6) for par; c for s(s) and s for c, as in decevreis (24),
dousour (44), and Rejected Readings; preservation of final t,
as in volenteit (8), esproveit (19), mercit (36); x for
s(s), as in cortoixie (6), plux (14), angoixe (37); ceu (23)
for ce; seux (40) for sui; 3rd-pers. sing. pres. ind. ait
(7, 19, 34) for a and vait (30) for va; 3rd-pers. sing. fut.
in -ait, as in avrait (44); nominative relative ke (39, 53)
for qui; adverbial se (56) for si. Note that the rhyme-word
1. 5 sui is evidence of the non-Lorraine origin of the composition.

N The tight stanzaic linking of this poem is
achieved both through the retention of -ie as the a rhyme
throughout and through the change of c to b in successive
stanzas. The song is an unusually personal one, especially
in the third stanza, where Raoul evokes his tribulations as
a crusader in 1249-50. For historical background, see
Winkler, pp. 13-15 and 26.

1 The count of Anjou is Charles (1226-1285), brother
of king Louis IX, protector of several poets, and a trouvère
in his own right. See RS 138, Notes.   18 'Than anyone can
have, except for Heaven'.   19 *Sulie*, elsewhere *Surie*
'Syria', designates the Holy Land.   20 *pris* 'as a prisoner'.   34 Understand *tient et lie si fort*.

<u>156</u>   Chanson

RS 1204, MW 2363
Mss. N 63v-64r, B 8v, V 59v-60r. Music in NV. Attributed
    to Thierri de Soissons in N.

9. si que la face en ai tainte et pa- li- e.

I   Se j'ai esté lonc tens en Rommanie
    Et outre mer fait mon pelerinage,
    Sousfert i ai maint doulereus damage
    Et enduré mainte grant maladie;
    Mes or ai pis c'onques n'oi en Surie,   5
    Car bone Amor m'a doné tel malage
    Dont nule foiz la dolour n'asouage,
    Ainz croist adés et double et monteplie,
    Si que la face en ai tainte et palie.

II Car juene dame et cointe et envoisie,   10
    Douce, plesant, bele et cortoise et sage,
    M'a mis el cuer une si douce rage
    Que j'en oubli le veer et l'oïe
    Si comme cil qui dort en letardie,
    Dont nus ne puet esveillier le corage;   15
    Car quant je pens a son tres douz visage,
    De mon penser aim meuz la conpaignie
    C'onques Tristan ne fist d'Iseut s'amie.

III Bien m'a Amors feru en droite vaine
    Par un regart plain de douce esperance,   20
    Dont navré m'a la plus bele de France
    Et de biauté la rose souveraine.
    Si me merveil quant la plaie ne saine,
    Car navré m'a de si douce senblance
    Q'unc ne senti si trenchant fer de lance;   25
    Mes senblant est au chant de la seraine,
    Dont la douçour atret dolor et paine.

IV Si puisse je sentir sa douce alaine
    Et reveoir sa bele contenance,
    Com je desir s'amor et s'acointance   30
    Plus que Paris ne fist onques Elaine!
    Et s'Amors n'est envers moi trop vilaine,
    Ja sanz merci n'en feré penitance;
    Car sa biautez et sa tres grant vaillance
    Et li biaus liz ou la vi premeraine,   35
    M'ont cent sospirs le jor doné d'estraine.

V   Car sa face, qui tant est douce et bele,
    Ne m'a lessié q'une seule pensee,

Et cele m'est au cuer si enbrasee
Que je la sent plus chaude et plus isnele   40
C'onques ne fis ne brese n'estancele;
Si ne puis pas avoir longue duree
Se de pitié n'est ma dame navree,
Qu'en ma chançon li diré la nouvele
De la dolor qui por li me flaele.   45

MN   Ms. V has a second melody, related to that of ms.
N in ll. 1-4, and seems to be mensurally notated in ll. 1-2.
Form: through-composed; the envoy in ms. B is sung to ll. 7-
9.
1. In the first staff, ms. evidently writes a C clef where
an F clef was intended, so that the notes to the first eight
syllables appear a 5th higher than transcribed here.

RR   III   26 est] sont *(em. Winkler)*   IV   29
reuoieir   V   40 isnele] mellee   42 Et si *(+1)*

V   Stanzas: V   I II III
                     B   I II III IV V VI (see below)
I   1 Se ie ai e. V; lonc tans este B   3 La oi souuent
maint anui maint d. V   5 Laz or ai p. quainz noi iour de
ma vie V   6 Que BV; tel] un V   7 D. ma plaie nule
foiz n. V   8 c. touz iorz et d. et monte V   9 ma f. en
est V; toute en p. B
II   10 Geune dame plesant et e. V   11 D. et p. B;
Simple et cortoise et del mont la plus s. V   13 Dont ien
perdi la veue et l. V; et la ioie B   14 Aussi com c. V;
sil B; q. gist en V   15 son c. BV   16 Mes V   17
Dont iaime miex assez sa c. V   18 tristans B; C. nama
tristranz yseut s. V
III   19 B. mont feru amours V   20 P. le r. dune doce
semblance V   21 Que V; p. sage B   22 Onques ne vi si
cruel fer de lance V   23 Si me doint diex seruir sa douce
alaine V   24 Et reueoir sa douce contenance V   25 Conques ne ui si B; Que naure ma la plus bele de france V
26 est] *verb missing in B*; Car seurpris ma au son de la s.
V   27 doucours atant dolours B; d. me tret anui et V
IV   29 Et retenir sa simple c. B   30 Que B   32 samour n. en moi t. v. B   34 biaute B   35 liz] uis B
V   38 douce p. B   41 fis] fu B   43 p. nai ma B   44
Quant ma c. li dira B
         Ms. B adds the following lines:
             Chançon, va t'en a Archier qui vielle
             Et a Raoul de Soissons qui m'agree;
             Di leur c'amours est trop tranchant espee.

<u>E</u>   La Ravallière, 144; Tarbé *Thib*, 63-65; Winkler,
75-77.

<u>N</u>   For doubtfulness of attribution to Raoul (= Thier-
ri), see Winkler, pp. 24-25. The three additional lines
provided by ms. B, which identify Raoul de Soissons as a recipient of this song, are not necessarily authentic and cannot be regarded as proof of authorship by another poet.
    1 *Rommanie* designates the Byzantine Empire.   4 Cf.
Raoul's evocation of his illness in RS 1154, ll. 25-26.   5
Surie 'Syria' designates the Holy Land.   23 *saine* =
saigne.   33 *feré* = *ferai*; likewise, l. 44 *diré* = *dirai*.
35 For *liz* 'bed' Winkler substitutes ms. B *vis* 'face', no
doubt understanding *ou* as 'when'.
    Note that the three additional lines in ms. B do not
constitute an envoy, as Winkler assumes they do: their sequence of rhymes fails to reproduce that of the final three
verses of st. 5.   They are no doubt intended as the opening
of a sixth stanza, repeating, in the same order, the rhymes
of the fifth and thus completing a three-part chain of *coblas doblas*. In his review of Winkler (*Neuphilologische Mitteilungen* 17 [1915], 125-133), A. Wallensköld points out, p.
133, that these lines occur at the end of f. 8v, where the
fragmentary ms. B comes to a stop, and thereby suggests
that, were f. 9 still preserved, it would surely be found to
contain the rest of the stanza. It happens, however, that,
after the last verse, there is still a half-line of unused
space on f. 8v; that suggests to us that the copyist of ms.
B was unaware of any further text and, just as Winkler was
to do, interpreted the three extra verses as an envoy.

ETIENNE DE MEAUX

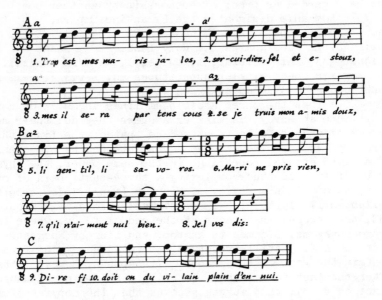

<u>157</u>   Chanson de femme

RS 2045, MW 1875, B 1062
Ms. P 131v-132r-v. Music. Attribution in text.

I   Trop est mes maris jalos,
      Sorcuidiez, fel et estouz,
      Mes il sera par tens cous
      Se je truis mon ami douz,
      Li gentil, li savoros.   5
          Mari ne pris rien,
          Q'il n'aiment nul bien.
             Je.l vos di:
             Dire fi
      Doit on du vilain plain d'ennui.   10

II   Quant a la fenestre vois,
      Il me guete trestoz jorz;
      Sachiez q'il vit seur mon pois,
      Car por lui pert mes amors.
      Il set bien que j'aime aillors;   15
          Or se puet desver,
          Car je vueil amer.
             Je.l vos di:

Dire fi
[*Doit on du vilain plain d'ennui*].   20

III   Cuidë il por son avoir
      Metre en prison cuer joli?
      Nenil voir! il n'a pouoir
      Que soie du tot a lui;
      A m'amor a il failli.   25
          Nus ne doit avoir
          Ami por avoir.
          Ce vos di:
          Dire fi
      Doit on [*du vilain plain d'ennui*].   30

IV   Hardiement li dirai:
      Fol vilain maleüros,
      Amer m'estuet sanz delai,
      Sachiez, un autre que vos;
      Or pöez estre jalos;   35
          Je vos guerpirai,
          Un autre amerai!
          Ce vos di:
          Dire fi
      Doit on [*du vilain plain d'ennui*].   40

V   Por tot l'avoir de Cisteaus
      Ne doit avoir cuer joli,
      Ce dit Estiene de Miauz,
      Jolive dame mari,
      Ançois doit avoir ami.   45
          Et je l'en crerrai
          Et ami avrai.
          Ce vos di:
          Dire fi
      Doit on du vilain plain d'ennui.   50

MN   Form: A A¹ B rf (ballade).
E   Tarbé *Chans*, 41; Spanke *Lied*, 255-256, 409-410;
Van d W *Chans*, 142-143.
N   13 *seur mon pois* 'to my regret'.   41 Reference
is to the abbey of Cîteaux, near Dijon.   42-45 Spanke
Lied, p. 409: "*ne doit le mari de jolive dame avoir cuer
joli, ançois ami le doit avoir* (oder *ançois ele doit avoir
ami?*)." We understand *cuer joli* (subject), *jolive dame* (ap-
positive), *ne doit avoir mari, ançois doit avoir ami*. Line
43 serves to name the real composer of the text while main-
taining the fiction that it is a woman's song.

JACQUES D'AUTUN

158   Chanson

RS 351 (=350), MW 1179
Mss. K 247-248, H 228r-228v, N 121r-121v, P 65v-66r, X 167v-
168r. Music in all mss. except H. Attribution in all
mss. except H.

I   Bele, sage, simple et plesant,
       De vous me couvient desevrer,
       Mes g'en ai plus le cuer dolent
       Que nus hons ne porroit penser.
       Je ne.l di pas pour vous guiler,   5
       Bien a esté aparissant:
       Cuer et cors ai mis, et argent,
       Paine de venir et d'aler,
       Pour cel sevrement destorner.

II   Bien fui herbegiez chierement   10
       La nuit que jui lez vo costel;
       Saint Juliens, qui bien puet tant,
       Ne fist a nul honme mortel
       Si douz, si bon, si noble ostel.
       Ha Deus, hé las! et je coment   15
       Touz jorz vivrai mes languissant,
       S'oncores ne l'ai autretel?
       Car nuit et jour ne pens a el.

III   Mal vos diront vostre parent
       Et felon mesdisant de moi,   20

Mes sage estes et conoissant,
Si ne.s crerrez mie, ce croi;
Car je vos aim en bone foi
Et sui vostre loial amant
Et serai trestot mon vivant.   25
Certes que bien fere le doi,
Qu'assez i a reson pour quoi.

IV   Je n'ai en rien confortement
Qu'en vostre debonaireté
Et en un biau petit enfant   30
Qu'en vostre cors ai engendré.
Graces en rent a Damledé,
Quant il de vous me lessa tant;
Car s'il puet vivre longuement,
Norrir le ferai par chierté,   35
Pour ce que de vous a esté.

V   Ma douce dame, a Dieu conmant
Vostre sens et vostre biauté
Et vostre parler simplement
Et voz euz plains de simpleté.   40
Ma conpaignie ou j'ai esté,
A qui nule autre ne se prent,
Douce dame proz et vaillant,
De cuer dolent et abosmé
Vous conmant a la Mere Dé.   45

MN   Form: A A B
1. In l. 3 ms. writes a bar. 2. In l. 4, ms. seems to have
first written *b* then corrected it.

RR   I   9 Pour la vostre amor conquester   II   11
lez uoz costez 16 longuissant   III   20 f. losengier
V   38 et v. bonte   43 He dex he las et ie conment

V   I   1 et *missing in X*; Douce dame s. et plaisanz
H   3 mon c. H   4 hon P, hom H   5 Si H   6 Car il est
bien a. H   7 Tout iai mis cors et a. H   9 P. cel cere-
ment d. P, Dou deseurement destorber H, P. la uostre amor
conquester NX
II   10 Mout H; h. hautement H, richement P   11 lez
uoz (-s) costez (-s) NPX   12 julien NPX; puet bien X;
Ainc sainz juliens qui pout t. H   14 Si biau si b. si
riche hostel H   15 Ha douz X; He las chaitis he las c.
H   16 Uiurai mais toz jorz l. H   17 Sancor nen ai un a.
H   18 Que N; n. ne j. XH

Between II and III, H presents the following unique
stanza:

Mout fist Amors a mon talent
Qant de moi fist vostre mari,
Mais joie m'eüst fait plus grant
S'ele m'eüst fait vostre ami.
Or n'i atant fors que merci.
A vos et a Amors me rent,
Et se pitiez ne vos en prent,
Par tans em plorront mi ami,
Car longues ne puis vivre ensi.

III   20   Felon et N; losengier d.   NX   21   connoissanz H
22 Si n. en croirez pas ce c.   H   23 Et H   24   Car ie
sui uostres ligement H   25   Et le serai tout m. v.   H   27
Car il i a assez de q. H
IV   28   riens PX; Dame ie nai c.   H   30   un sol p.   H
31 Q. uoz biaus costez s.   H   32   r. la mere de H   33
de ce uos l.   X; ma laissie H   34   Norrir le ferai doce-
ment H   35   Et mout bien ledefiere H   36   P. ce q. uos
lauez porte H
V   38   et v. bonte PX   39   Et v. gent cors auenant   H
41   La H   42   Qui a H   43   vaillanz H; He d(i)ex he las
et ie co(m)ment NPX   44   et de a.   X

    E   Långfors *Mél*, 339-345; Cremonesi, 211-213; Woledge
Peng, 158-160; Toja, 432-434; Rosenberg, 558-559.

    N   This poem is remarkable as the only chanson to in-
clude mention of a child born to the poet-lover and his
lady. The extra stanza found in ms. H speaks, just as
uniquely, of marriage as well. For the considerable commentary which this has occasioned, see O. Jodogne, "La person-
nalité de l'écrivain d'oïl du XIIe au XIIIe siècle," p. 101,
in A. Fourrier, ed., *L'humanisme médiéval* (Paris, 1964);
Dronke, pp. 129-131; A. Menichetti, "Tre note di filologia
francese e italiana," *Cultura Neolatina* 29 (1969), 159-163;
Zumthor *Es*, p. 208. The present edition is the first to reject the extra stanza of ms. H as inauthentic; for explanation see Rosenberg.
    42 *se prent* 'compares'.

Chanson

159

RS 1108, MW 18
Mss. X 238v-239r, K 365-366. Music in both mss. Attribution in text.

I   Amors, qui m'a en baillie, veut qu'envoissié
                             [soie;
    Je ferai chançon jolie, puis qu'ele l'otroie.
    Puis que ma dame a mon cuer, drois est qu'a
                             [li soie;
    S'el ne me veut recevoir, jamés n'avrai joie.
    Bien est fous qui contre amor par force
                          [maistroie: 5
    Amors n'ont point de seignor, je le vos
                             [otroie.

II   Amors n'ont point de seignor, dire le porroie,
    Car il n'est ne rois ne cuens qu'ele ne
                           [mestroie.
    Puis qu'ele a un home çaint desoz sa corroie,
    Il ne s'en puet pas desfendre n'aler autre
                           [voie. 10
    D'amors ne me qier partir, ne faire ne.l doie,
    Por tout l'avoir de cest mont; ainz vueil que
                          [siens soie.

III   Siens sui et serai touz dis, que que nus en
                                                    [die,
      Mais je sui ausi con cil, voir, qui ne vit
                                                    [mie.
      Puis que ma dame a m'amor toute en sa baillie,
      Ele m'aprent et enseigne toute cortoisie.   16
      As vilains dont Dieus mal jor et grant
                                        [vilainie,
      Qui mesdïent des amans, il font grant folie.

IV   Grant folie font il, voir, je le vos affie;
      Ceus qui mesdïent d'amans, Jhesus les maudie,
      Car il l'ont bien deservi par lor tricherie. 21
      Deus aime les vrais amans et het vilainie;
      As vilains dont Deus mau jor et male nuitie
      Et leur doint grant mescheance, qu'il l'ont
                                        [deservie.

V   Deservie l'ont il, voir, que nus ne les aime;
      Il n'est clerc ne chevalier nus qui ne s'en 26
                                        [plaigne.
      Ne finent ne nuit ne jor, n'onques ne se
                                        [faignent
      De nuire les fins amans, et leur font grant
                                        [paine;
      Por ce doit l'en bien garder la chose qu'en
                                        [aime.
      Ce dit Jaque de Dosti, qui par amors aime.   30

      MN   Form: A A¹ B B¹. 1. In 1. 2 ms. writes no rest.

      RR   I 4 me uoit r.   III   18 il f. uilainie
IV 24 quil ont

      V   Stanza V not included in K.   I   2 lotrie   5
amors   III   19 affie] otrie   IV   24 grant repeated

      E   Spanke Lied, 156-157.

      N   The dodecasyllabic lines of this poem are composed
of 7 syllables + an occasional uncounted e + 5 + e. The device of coblas capfinidas is interpreted somewhat casually:
1. 7 repeats the first hemistich of 1. 6 and repeats it
exactly; 1. 13 repeats the end of the second hemistich of 1.
12 but with some modification; etc.   29 l'en = l'on; en =
on.

MAHIEU LE JUIF

Chanson

160

RS 313, MW 839, B 166
Mss. M 175r-v, T 93v-94r. Music in M. Attribution in both
mss.

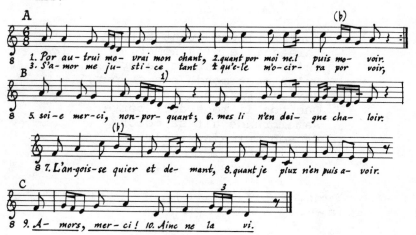

I   Por autrui movrai mon chant,
        Quant por moi ne.l puis movoir.
        S'Amor me justice tant
        Qu'ele m'ocirra por voir,
        Soie merci, nonporquant!   5
        Mes li n'en deigne chaloir.
        L'angoisse quier et demant,
        Quant je pluz n'en puis avoir.
                Amors, merci!
                Ainc ne la vi.   10

II   Je l'aim pluz que mon pooir
        Et si n'en fui ainc joïs.
        S'Amors ne li fait savoir,
        Dont sui je par li trahis.
        Mout me set bel decevoir.   15
        Sachié a mon cuer del pis
        Cele qui pluz puet valoir,
        Por cui sui si esbahiz.
                Amors, [merci!
                Ainc ne la vi].   20

III   Ja par moy n'iert maiz gehis
       Mes conseus a li nul jor,
       Tant redout les escondis
       De li ou j'atent l'amor.
       De sa biauté est delis,   25
       Et del monde est la meillor.
       Or m'en aït Jhesucris,
       Dont j'ai fet novel seignor!
            Amors, [merci!
            Ainc ne la vi].   30

IV   Mout me livre grant estor
       Cele cui je n'os nomer,
       Qu'en li a tant de valor
       Qu'en cest monde n'a sa per.
       Por li cria Deus la flor   35
       Que toz li mons doit porter.
       Ramembrance ait sa color
       Et son bel viaire cler.
            Amors, merci!
            [Ainc ne la vi].   40

    MN   Form: A A B rf (ballade).
1. Ms. may intend an ascending plica.

    RR   IV   37   ai

    V   I   3 Samors   II   16 Saichies   18 P. quj
19-20 mercj *added*   IV   32 C. quj   34 som p.   36 li]
chis   37 ai   40 ains ne la vj

    E   Noack, 109-110; Wolff, 15.

    N   3-5 'Even if Love oppresses me so much/ That it
will surely kill me,/ Let it do so (i.e., oppress me) nevertheless!' We understand *soie merci*, lit. 'by its grace', as
a polite urging of a known action. Wolff takes *soie* as *so
je*, understands *so* as pret. of *savoir*, and reads l. 5 as a
question; this supposes that l. 3 *S'amor* = 'love for her
(i.e., my lady)'.   6 *li* refers to the lady.   15 *bel* is
adverbial.   27-28 Mahieu was obviously a convert. Cf. his
statement in RS 752: *Pour vostre amour ai guerpie ma loi/ Et
croi Dieu maugré touz mes amis* (ll. 51-52).   37-38 'May
her color and her . . . face be remembered'. Both Noack and
Wolff retain ms. reading *ai*; after l. 36 *porter*, Noack has
no punctuation, Wolff a period; neither version is readily
understood.

Pastourelle   161

RS 936, MW 1761
Mss. P 90v-91r, K 242-243, N 118r-v, V 69r-v, X 164v. Music
in all mss. Attribution in all mss. except V.

I   L'autrier estoie montez
      Seur mon palefroi anblant,
      Et pris m'estoit volentez
      De trouver un nouviau chant.
            Tot esbanoiant   5
              M'en aloie;
            Truis enmi ma voie
            Pastore seant
                  Loing de gent.
                  Belement   10
                  La salu,
      Puis li dis: "Vez ci vo dru."

II   "Biau sire, trop vos hastez,"
      Dist la touse. "J'ai amant.
      Il n'est gueres loing alez,   15
      Il revendra maintenant.
            Chevauchiez avant!
              Trop m'esfroie
            Que il ne vos voie,
            Trop est mescreant;   20
                  Ne talent
                  Ne me prent

               De vo ju;
          Ailleurs ai mon cuer rendu."

     III "Damoisele, car creez   25
          Mon conseil, je vos creant;
          Jamés povre ne serez,
          Ainz avrez a vo talent
               Cote traïnant
                    Et coroie   30
               Ouvree de soie,
               Cloee d'argent."
               Bonement
               Se desfent,
               N'a valu   35
          Quanque j'ai dit un festu.

     IV   "Biau sire, car en alez,"
          Dist ele. "C'est por noient.
          Vostre parole gastez
          Que je ne pris mie un gant,   40
               Ne vostre beubant
                    N'ameroie;
               Vo don ne prendroie
               Ne si n'autrement;
                    Vostre argent,   45
                    Vo present
                    N'ai eü.
          Maint prameteus ai veü."

     V   "Damoisele, car prenez
          La çainture maintenant   50
          Et le matin si ravrez
          Trestot l'autre couvenant."
               Lors va sozriant
                    Et j'oi joie;
                    Tant fis qu'ele otroie   55
               Mon gré maintenant.
               Le don prent
               Bonement,
               S'ai sentu
          De quel maniere ele fu.   60

     MN   Ms. V has a second, but related, melody, which is
a 5th lower. Form: A A B.

     RR   II 15 loig

V   I   1   Lautri   X; mestoie   V   2   Sus   X   3   volente N   7   parmi   V   12   Et li   KNVX   II   13   Biaus
V   14   ie ai a.   X   15   guieet res l. de ci   V; ale   N
18   Que t. mefferoie   V   19   vos *missing in X*   20   mes-
cheant   V   23-24   De vous car aillours   V   24   Iai aillors
m. c. tendu   N   III   26   Mon seil   N   28   auroiz   K   31
Cloee de s.   X   32   Ouuree dargent   X   36   Quanqua dit un
seul f.   V   IV   37   Biaus   V; alerz   N   40   Ie ne uos p.
N; mie] pas   V   42   Mameroie   N   43   Vos dons   V   44
Ainsi   V   46   En p.   V, Vos   X   48   Mainz   V   V   51
aurez   V   58   Maintenant   KX

E   La Borde *Es*, 72; Dinaux 4, 112-113; Bartsch, 248-
249; Scheler 1, 46-48, 308; Henry *Hen*, 75-84.

DF   Picard: *iau* for *eau,* as in *nouviau* (4), *biau*
(13); *ju* (23) for *jeu*; *vo* (12) for *vostre.*

N   32   'decorated with silver studs'.   48   The suffix of the form *prameteus* 'men who promise much' is the popular counterpart of *-eur(s)* and the source of the now standard feminine suffix *-euse.*   52   'all the rest of what I
have promised'.

162   Chanson

RS 511, MW 2281, B 760
Mss. M 6r, F 116v-117r, a 24r-v.   Music in MF.   Attribution
    in M.

9. fors   li   10. cui j'aim si

11. que j'en ai et cuer et cors jo-   li.

I   Amors m'est u cuer entree;
         De chanter m'a esmeü,
         Si chant por la bele nee
         A cui j'ai mon cuer rendu
             Ligement;   5
           Et sachent la gent
               Mercīer
         Ne doit on de mon chanter
               Fors li
               Cui j'aim si   10
      Que j'en ai et cuer et cors joli.

II   Se j'ai dolor enduree
         Por amor et mal sentu,
         Il me plaist bien et agree.
         Quant j'ai si bien esleü,   15
             N'ai talent
           D'amer faussement;
               Amender
         Vueill et loiaument amer
               Por li   20
               Cui j'aim si
      Que j'en ai [et cuer et cors joli].

III   Amors est en moi doublee
         Pluz que onques maiz ne fu,
         Si servirai a duree.   25
         Deus doint c'on m'ait retenu
             Temprement,
           Amorousement,
               Sans fausser,
         Car je ne puis oublīer   30
               Celi
               Cui j'aim si
      Que [j'en ai et cuer et cors joli].

IV   Et s'Amors les suens avance,
         De moi li doit sovenir,   35
         Car je sui suens sanz faillance,

A toz jors sanz repentir.
         Ententis
     Serai mes touz dis
         D'avancier   40
   Amors et son nom haucier
         Por li
       Cui j'aim si
 Que [j'en ai et cuer et cors joli].

V   Adés me croist ma poissance   45
     Et volentez de servir;
     Sanz celi ou j'ai fiance,
     Ne porrai mie guarir;
         Si conquis
         M'ont si tres douz ris   50
         Sanz cuidier,
     Sai que ne puis eslongier
         De li
       Cui j'aim si
 Que [j'en ai et cuer et cors joli].   55

VI   Quens jolis
         De Flandres, amis
           Cui j'ai chier,
     Me savriez vous conseillier
         De li   60
       Cui j'aim si
 Que j'en ai et cuer et cors joli?

MN   Form: A A¹ B rf (ballade); the envoy is sung to
ll. 5-8.

V   Stanzas: a   I II III IV V VI
                F   I IV III
I 1-5 *scratched out in F, except initial* A, mon cuer ren
in l. 4, *and* ment *in l.* 5 4 qui a 7 mierchijet F
8 on] nus F 10 Qui Fa 11 cors et j. *(+1)* a   II
21 Ki a 22 et cuer et cors joli *added in a*   III 25
Si] Or F 27 Vraiement F 30 p. escaper F 32 Qui
Fa 33 Que] et c. F; jen ai et cuer et cors joli *added in
a*   IV 34 avance] auoie F 36 siens Fa 41 et sou-
nour h. F 43 C. ie ain si a 44 jen ai et cuer et
cors joli *added in a*   V 55 jen ai et cuer et cors joli
added in a   VI 58 Qui a

E   La Borde *Es*,174; Dinaux 4, 109-110; Scheler 1, 41-
43, 286-287; Henry *Hen*, 55-65.

N   3 *nee* 'creature'.   6 Understand *que* after *gent*.
25 *a duree* 'endlessly'.   51 *Sanz cuidier* 'without a
doubt, certainly'; understand *que* afterward.   56-57 According to Scheler, p. 287, and PetDyg "Onom", p. 94, the
count in question is probably Guillaume de Dampierre. Henry
Hen, p. 61, finds it more likely that he is Guillaume's
younger brother, Gui, and believes that the poem was composed between 1252 and 1261; for details, see Henry *Hen*, pp.
30-32.

PERRIN D'ANGICOURT

Chanson

RS 625, MW 2285
Mss. N 58r-v, K 170-170b, R 124r-v, V 92r-v, X 116r-v, Z
16r-v-17r. Music in all mss. Attribution in KNX.

I   Quant partiz sui de Prouvence
     Et du tens felon,
    Ai voloir que je conmence
     Nouvele chançon   4
      Jolie
     Et qu'en chantant prie
      Bone Amour
     Que tant de douçor   8
   Mete a mon chant conmencier
   Qu'ele me face cuidier
  Que ma douce dame daigne vouloir
  Que ja la puisse a son gré revooir. 12

II   Atorné m'est a enfance
     Et a mesprison

       Li desirs d'aler en France
         Que j'ai par reson.   16
             Folie
       Fet qui me chastie
            Se j'ator
         Mon cuer au retor,   20
       Quant je ne le puis lessier;
       Car tout autre desirrier
   Me fet metre du tout en nonchaloir
  Cele sanz qui riens ne me puet valoir.   24

III   De biauté et de vaillance
         A si grant foison,
       Lués que g'en oi conoissance,
         Mis en sa prison   28
            Ma vie.
       Je ne mesfaz mie
            Se j'aor
         Et aim la meillor,   32
       Car pour ce m'aim j' et tien chier
       Que je sui en son dangier.
  Deus! quant g'i pens, je ne m'ai dont doloir,
  Et mes pensers i est sanz ja mouvoir.   36

IV   Sousfrir loial penitance
         Me senble plus bon
       Que avoir par decevance
         Ne par traïson   40
            Amie.
       Fausse drüerie
           Sanz savor
         Ont li tricheor,   44
       Q'il conquierent par pledier.
       Tel joie ne m'a mestier;
  Dou porchacier n'aie je ja pouoir!
  J'aim melz languir que fausse joie avoir. 48

V   Onques n'oi cuer ne vueillance
         Ne entencion
       Que je feïsse senblance
         D'amer s'a droit non.   52
          Polie
       Langue apareillie
          A folor
         En set bien le tour;   56
       Mes ce n'i puet riens aidier,
       Qu'a la parole afetier

    Puet on choisir qui bee a decevoir;
    Et Deus en lest ma dame apercevoir!   60

VI   Fenie,
           Chançon, envoïe
           Sanz demor
           Seras a la flor   64
       Des dames a droit jugier;
       Et par pitié li reqier,
    S'eürs te fet devant li aparoir,
    Q'il li plese que je vive en espoir.   68

    MN   Ms. R has a second melody; ms. V has a third one.
Form: A A B; the envoy is sung to ll. 5-12.

    RR   III   33 ie et *(+1)*   V   59 P. len uoer q.
VI 63 *missing*

    V   Stanza VI not included in KV.
I   3 Ai ie voloir que c. V, Ai volente ke c. Z; que re-
commence R   7 Fine K   8 Qui R   10 mi R   12
reuoir KX, receuoir Z   II   15 Le desir R, Li retours
Z   15-16 Li d. que iai en f. daler p. r. V   21 Car ie
ne la p. l. V, Car kant ie nel p. l. Z   24 cui Z; mi
K; Et mez pensers y est sanz ia mouuoir R   III   26 Oi
R   27 Auez q. R, Lors q. V; q. ie en oi X; acointance
R   30 meffis V   33 ie et KRVXZ   34 je] gen K   35
Ke q. Z; q. ie i p. X; j. ne mesmai d. d. R, j. nai mal
ne dol. V   IV   38 Mi R   43 ualor X   45 Qui R, Ki
Z   47 De p. nai ie p. R; porchier X   V   49 cuer ne]
autre V   50 Nentencion R   57 ne R; doit r. Z   58
Car la p. afaitie Z   60 Amours en Z; d. perceuoir K,
percheuoir R, parceuoir X   VI   61-62 Bonne ch. e. R
62 Chancons Z; enuoiee X   66 le Z   67 Se eurs se f.
R; Seurs li a pooir Z   68 Que li p. q. ie muire en e. R

    E   Tarbé *Chans*, 7; Steffens *Per*, 214-218, 319-322;
Spaziani *Canz*, 132-135.

    DF   Picard: *envoïe* (62) for *envoiee*.

    N   In addition to authorship, the rubric in ms. X in-
dicates that this song was "crowned" (*coronee*) with a prize.
Steffens *Per*, p. 32, maintains that it was composed ca.
1250. 12 *revooir = reveoir*. 13 *enfance* 'childishness'.
15 *France* here designates the north, in contrast to l. 1
Prouvence. 18 *qui* 'whoever'. 22-24 Understand *desir-*

rier as dir. obj. and *cele* as subj. of *fet metre*. 26 Understand *que* after *foison*. 35 *je ne m'ai dont doloir* 'I have no cause for grief'. 45 *Q'il conquierent* 'for they (i.e., *li tricheor*) make their conquests'. 47 'May I never be capable of such a pursuit'. 52 *s'a droit non* 'in any but the right way'. 58-59 'For by his turn of phrase you can identify whoever is eager to deceive'. 62-65 Understand: 'you will be sent without delay to the one who, to judge correctly, is the flower of all ladies'.

164   Chanson

RS 1470, MW 635
Mss. N 54r-v, C 106v-107r, K 167, O 63v-64r, R 154r-v, S
    320v, V 90v, X 112r-v-113r, Z 15r-v, a 96r-v. Music in
    all mss. except CS. Attribution in CKNXa.

I   J'ai un jolif souvenir
        Qui en moi maint et repaire,
        Qu'Amours i a fet venir
        Pour moi conpaignie faire,
               A servir   5
        Ma dame sanz defaillir
               Et sanz mesfaire.
        Amours, qui tant puet merir,

        Li dont voloir d'amenrir
        Les maus que je vueil bien traire.   10

II   Tout adés quant je remir
        Son gent cors, son cler viaire,
        Ses euz qui a cuer sesir
        Ont senblant si debonaire,
            Sanz sentir   15
        Me done Amours de joïr
            Un essamplaire;
        Mes c'est pour moi soustenir,
        Que je ne puisse cheïr
        En volenté de retraire.   20

III   Ja Deus ne m'en doint loisir:
        Trop seroie demalaire;
        Je voudroie melz vestir
        Tout mon eage la haire
            Que guerpir   25
        Cele qui puet convertir
            Tout mon asfaire
        En joie et moi retenir,
        Et me puet plus enrichir
        Que faire roi de Cesaire.   30

IV   Bien me deüst recueillir
        Et d'aucun douz mot refaire,
        Mes el ne me veut oïr
        Ne par chanter ne par taire;
            S'en souspir   35
        Et d'amoreus cuer m'aïr
            Quant el n'esclaire
        Moi qui ne li puis guenchir,
        Ainz me fet plus maus sousfrir
        Qu'Alixandres ne fist Daire.   40

V   Dame, je sui sanz mentir
        Vostres et sanz contrefaire.
        Riens ne me porroit nuisir
        Se mes chanz vous pouoit plaire.
            A! languir   45
        Aim bien pour vous et palir
            Tant q'il i paire,
        Voire, s'il vous plest, morir.
        Ne me sousfrez a perir,
        Gentius cuers de bon afaire!   50

VI   Maintenir
        Loiauté sanz repentir
        Ne puet desplaire
      A cuer qui sert sanz traïr,
      Mes li faus s'en veut partir   55
      Lués q'un pou de mal le maire.

<u>MN</u>   Form: A A B; the envoy is sung to 11. 5-10.
1. In 1. 1 ms. writes ♫♫. In 1. 1 ms. writes no rest.

<u>RR</u>   I   2 Q en   4 En m.   II   12 uiere   13 Si
oil   III   22 de male aire   28 *missing*   29 plus puet
30 Qua   IV   34 chanter] parler   V   47 me] i

<u>V</u>   Stanza VI not included in KRSVZa.
I   2 Q. en mon cuer m. et r.   S   3 a] ont   V   6 sanz
defaillir *missing in S*; messeruir O   7 Et s. faire S   8
Amor ke C; tout p. RVZa   9 *missing in RS*; pooir V, uo-
lente X; de menrir O   10 q. vuil mout b. taire O, q.
veul b. tr. R, q. pour lui voeil tr. V, q. ien v. b. tr.
Z, q. jen v. tr. a
II   12 Sont X; son uiaire cler O   13 S. iex vairs qui
a seisir R; a] au OSV   16 amor   s; de ioie RS; Men
dounent (doignent a) am. joir Za   17 Dun Za   19 je
missing in C; puis bien c. O, puisse en c. V   20 mesfaire a
III   21 n. me O, n. mi a; lest ioir K   23 Iameroie K;
mulez C; Miex (Mieus a) ameroie (a Z) v. VZa   24 Touz
les iours du mont la h. V; le h. R   25 Ka Za   26 Celi
CKOSZa, Celui R; ke C   27 Trestot m. O; contraire CORS
VZa   28 *missing in V*; et] en Ca; reuertir C, detenir R
29 Ke Z; mi R, moi Za   30 Ken a; estre rois C
IV   31 Bien bien d. R; mi V; acueillir V   32 daucuns
d. mos (-z O) ORV; atraire V   33 el] elle C, ele SV
Za, sel O; me *missing in Za*, mi KRVX   34 po(u)r ch. n.
po(u)r t. CORV   36 Et *missing in R*; damour au c. Za; c.
air a   37 el(1)e CSVZ   38 M. ke CZ   39 Et RVZa; mi
RZa; p. de m. C; mal COSVa; sentir Xa
V   41 faillir R, fouir V   43 me *missing in R*, mi CKSV
44 mon chant v. poist p. V   45 Et O   46 Vuil O; miex
RV; m. touz diz et p. V   47 Et t. q. C, Si q. S; i] me
COS   48-50 *missing in S*   48 vous] li V   49 mi RV;
partir Z   50 Gentil KV; cuer KVa
VI   52 s. mentir X   56 Lors C

<u>E</u>   Tarbé *Chans*, 1; Steffens *Per*, 195-198, 311-313;
Spaziani *Canz*, 127-129.

DF   Picard: *gentius* (50) for *gentis*.

N   In addition to authorship, the rubrics of mss. X
and C indicate that this song was "crowned" with a prize.
In X, the word *coronee* inside a sketch of a crown; in C, the
poet's name is followed by *et si fu corenaie et arez* (= *a
Arras*?).

15 'without carnal contact'.   19 *Que* 'so that'.   27
asfaire = a(f)faire.   28 *moi retenir* 'accept me as lover'.
30 Elliptical construction meaning 'than if she made me
king of Caesarea'.   Caesarea, in the Holy Land, occurs here,
like Persia or Tarsus in other songs, as a token of power
and wealth; see Steffens *Per*, pp. 312-313.   40 The reference is to Alexander the Great's victory over Darius, king
of Persia.   45-48 'I am willing, on your account, to lan-
guish and to grow pale to the point where it would be no-
ticeable [and] even, if you like, to die'.

Chanson   165

RS 591, MW 2336
Mss. a 97r-v-98r, O 66r-v.   Music in both mss.   Attribution
  in a.

1. Il cou- vient k'en la can- deil- le 2. ait tre- ble su- stan- ce,
3. ains k'e- le soit en vail- lan ce 4. ne k'ele ait po- oir
5. ke- le fa- che son de- voir; 6. car il i doit par rai- son
7. a- voir cire et lu- mi- gnon, 8. et el cief met on le fu;
9. et dont a ver- tu 10. de fai- re l'au- trui ser- vi- ce
11. tant qu'ele est arse et re- mi- se.

I Il couvient k'en la candeille
   Ait treble sustance,
  Ains k'ele soit en vaillance
   Ne k'ele ait pooir
  K'ele fache son devoir;   5
  Car il i doit par raison
  Avoir cire et lumignon,
  Et el cief met on le fu;
   Et dont a vertu
  De faire l'autrui service   10
  Tant qu'ele est arse et remise.

II Et je sui tout en tel guise
   Et en tel samblanche:
  Espris d'un fu k'Amours lanche,
   Ke me fait ardoir   15
  Le cuers et le cors doloir
  Et fondre sans garison.
  Cis fus me vint par enson,
  Car jou m'en senti feru
   Loés que j'euc veü   20
  Çou dont li mons s'esmerveille,
  Dont j'art et souspir et veille.

III Mais cuers qui se desconseille
   Par desesperance
  Fait trop vilaine chevanche,   25
   Car, au dire voir,
  Cuers ki chiet en desespoir
  Par delai de gerredon
  Sanle le faus campion
  Sain et haitié recreü;   30
   Mais j'ai esleü
  A morir en la justice
  D'Amour, dont li fus m'atise.

IV Mais qant la candeille est mise
   Par mescounissance   35
  En liu u vens la balance
   Ne face mouvoir,
  Il couvient par estouvoir
  K'ele en ait mais de fuison.
  Et se mesdisant felon   40
  Sont, de moi grever, creü,
   Ves moi lués fondu,

> Se la bele a grant merveille
> A pité ne se conseille.

> V   Bele et boine sans pareille   45
>   U j'ai ma fiance,
>   Car daigniés metre en soufrance
>   Et en noncaloir
>   Çou c'onques ossai voloir
>   De vostre amour le haut don.   50
>   Et jou, pour la mesproison
>   Del bel tort que j'ai eü
>   Qui grans est et fu,
>   M'otroi a vostre devise
>   De merci u de juïse.   55

> VI   Dame, par vostre franchise,
>   Faites m'aleganse
>   Tele k'en vostre ligance
>   Puisse tant manoir
>   Que mercis me puist valoir,   60
>   Se jou serf sans traïson;
>   Et recevés ma cançon;
>   Si m'ert si bien avenu
>   Que tot m'ert rendu
>   65
>   Çou dont mes cuers se traveille.

MN   Melody from ms. O, which is mensurally notated.
Form: through-composed.
1. Ms. a writes ♩♩. 2. Ms. a writes ♩♩.

RR   IV 39 mains   41 greue   VI 57 F. moi a.
(+1)   58 lingance   65 *missing*

V   Stanzas IV-VI not included in O.
I 9 dont] lors   II   18 Ce   20 Lors

E   Steffens *Per*, 266-269, 343-346; Cremonesi, 246-248; Toja, 460-463.

DF   Picard, including *iu* for *ieu*, as in *liu* (36); *u* for *eu*, as in *fu* (8), *fus* (22); *c* for *ch*, as in *candeille* (1), *cief* (8), *campion* (29), *noncaloir* (48); *ch* for *c*, as in *fache* (5), *samblanche* (13); *ge* for *gue*, as in *gerredon* (18); *g* for *j*, as in *aleganse* (57), *ligance* (58); *c* or *ss* for *s*, as in *service* (10), *justice* (32), *ossai* (49); final *s* for *z*, as in *cis* (18), *vens* (36), *ves* (42), *daigniés* (47);

unepenthesized *sanle* (29) for *semble*; *boine* (45) for *bone*;
jou (19) for *je*; *çou* (21) for *ce*, lst-pers. sing. pret. *euc*
(20) for *oi*. Note, too, that the rhyme *candeille* (= *chan-
deile*) : *s'esmerveille*, etc., is a Picardism.

    <u>N</u>   For some doubt about attribution to Perrin, see
Steffens *Per*, pp. 253 and 266. As noted in Steffens *Per*, p.
343, the central image and the versification of this composition may have been inspired by Peire Raimon's song, *Al-
tressi cum la candela*; the text appears in Karl Bartsch,
Chrestomathie provençale, 6th ed. rev. by Eduard Koschwitz
(Marburg: Elwert, 1904), pp. 97-98. The versification of
the poem includes a noteworthy type of stanzaic linking.
The first rhyme in each stanza has no correspondent within
the stanza (*rim estramp*), but does repeat the rhyme of the
last two verses of the preceding stanza (*coblas capcaudadas*); this technique is combined with a stanza-by-stanza
alternation of the a and f rhymes (*coblas retrogradadas*).
    9 *dont* 'as a result'.   11 *remise* 'consumed'.   15
Ke for nominative *qui*.   18 *par enson* 'from above', i.e.,
through the eyes; see l. 20.   25 'Gains a very poor advantage'.   29-30 'Resembles the false champion [who has] sur-
rendered [while still] safe and sound'. Steffens *Per*
chooses to understand *faus* as a Picardism for 'foolish' (=
fous) rather than read it as 'false', but the respect for
morphological correctness evident elsewhere in these lines
makes us reject that possibility.   32 *en la justice* 'under
the authority, judgment'.   39 *mais de fuison* 'more melt-
ing'; cf. the poet's parallel experience in l. 42; interpretation and emendation (from ms. *mains*) proposed by A. Guesnon, p. 77, in "Publications nouvelles sur les trouvères artésiens," *Le Moyen Age*, ser. 2, 13 (1909), 65-93. Steffens
Per, accepting *mains*, understands 'less brightness,
strength'.   41 *creü* probably 'believed' rather than, as in
Steffens *Per*, p. 345, 'increased in number' (from *croistre*).
47-50 *Car* introduces imperative. 'Deign to accept and tol-
erate my daring to desire the great gift of your love'.   51
pour la mesproison 'because of my failure to acknowledge'.
63 'Then I will be so pleased'.

<u>166</u>   Chanson

RS 1390, MW 1246
Stanza I: B 1133, st. II: B 426 (one other source), st. III:
    B 1638, st. IV: B 289 (three other sources).

Mss. K 162-163, N 52r-v, O 118v-119r, V 88v, X 109v-110r.
Music in all mss. Attribution in KNX.

I   Quant je voi l'erbe amatir
        Et le felon tens entré
        Qui fet ces oisiaus tesir
        Et lessier jolieté,
        Pour ce n'ai je pas osté   5
        Mon cuer de loial desir;
        Mes pour mon us maintenir
        A cest motet me reclaim:
        Je sui jolis por ce que j'aim.

II   J'aim loiaument sanz traïr,   10
        Sanz faindre et sanz fausseté
        Cele qui me fet languir
        Sanz avoir de moi pité
        Et bien set de verité
        Que je sui siens sanz guenchir,   15
        Mes en espoir de joïr
        Li ert cest motet chantez:
        Dame, merci! vos m'ociez.

III   Vous m'ociez sanz reson,
        Dame sanz humilité.   20
        Ne pert pas a vo façon
        Qu'en vo cuer ait cruauté,
        Mes grant deboneretré;
        Pour ce sui g' en soupeçon;
        Simple vis et cuer felon   25

>   M'ont mis en grant desconfort.
>   *Sa biauté m'a mort.*

IV   Mort m'a sanz point d'acheson
          Cele en qui j'ai atorné
          Mon sens et m'entencion   30
          Pour fere sa volenté.
          S'or le daignoit prendre en gré,
          Pour tout autre guerredon
          Mis m'avroit fors de friçon,
          Si diroie sanz esmai: 35
          Bone amor que j'ai mi tient gai.

MN   Ms. O is written a 5th higher and partially in
mensural notation; ms. V has a second melody. Form: A A B
vrf.
1. In l. 1 ms. writes no rest. 2. No music is extant for
refrains 2-4, but a refrain similar to refrain 4 occurs in a
monophonic motet in ms. M f. 3v a 5th higher than here

transcribed:

Bone a- mo- re- te   me   tient gai.

V   Stanza IV not included in V.
I 2 entrer OV 3 Que V   II   11 Et s. V   16 de
merci O   17 cist motoz O, ce m. X   III   24 g'en] ie
en NOVX   27 beautez O   IV   29 cui O   30 sen O
31 ma X   33 toute N; t. mon a. g. X

E   Brandin, 262; Steffens *Per*, 241-242, 326; Toja,
467-469.

DF   Picard: *vo* (21) for *vostre.*

N   All four of these stanzas are linked not only by a
constant *b* rhyme but also through the technique of *coblas
capfinidas,* which here serves too to integrate the refrains
into the main text.   8 *motet,* here as in l. 17, refers to
the brief refrain, the 'little word', that follows rather
than the entire song.   27 Both Brandin and Steffens *Per*
find a three-syllable lacuna here, and the latter's edition
incorporates a conjecture: *Sa [tres fine] biauté m'a mort.*
But in a *chanson avec des refrains* it is unnecessary for the
refrains to be metrically identical, and we may well consider the verse to be complete as it stands.   34 'she would
[by now] have relieved me of my anxiety'.

Chanson   <u>167</u>

RS 438, MW 1892, B 722
Mss. K 165-166, N 53v, O 118r-v, V 89v-90r, X 111r-v. Music
in all mss. Attribution in KNX.

I   Quant voi en la fin d'esté
           La fueille cheoir
         Et la grant jolieté
           D'oisiaus remanoir,
         Lors ai de chanter vouloir   5
         Greigneur que je ne soloie,
         Car cele a qui je m'otroie
           Ligement
         M'en a fet conmandement,
           Si chanterai.   10
       Et quant ma dame plera, joie avrai.

II   Cuer qui n'aime ou n'a amé
           Ne puet riens valoir;
         Pour ce, j'ai le mien doné
           Sanz jamés mouvoir,   15
         Et si sai bien tout de voir
         Que par haut penser foloie.
         Conment qu'avenir m'en doie,
           Loiaument

A Amors servir me rent,   20
        Tant com vivrai.
    Et quant ma dame [plera, joie avrai].

III   Tant me plest sa grant biauté
                A ramentevoir,
        Que j'ai tout autre pensé   25
                Mis en nonchaloir,
        Las! et si ne puis savoir
        Se mon penser bien enploie,
        Car pour rien ne li diroie
                Que je sent,   30
        Fors qu'en chant si fetement
                Li gehirai.
    Et quant [ma dame plera, joie avrai].

IV   Dame, en droit loiauté
                Et sanz decevoir,   35
        En vo debonereté
                Met tout mon pouoir.
        Car me daigniez recevoir,
        Dame en qui touz biens ondoie!
        Vo grant biauté me guerroie   40
                Si griément,
        Se je n'ai alegement,
                Pour vous morrai.
    Et quant [ma dame plera, joie avrai].

V   Mesdisanz, vo mauvesté   45
                M'a mult fet doloir,
        Et s'ai mainte foiz douté
                Vostre apercevoir.
        Mau feu les puist touz ardoir
        Si voir com je le voudroie!   50
        Hé, bone Amor qui g'en proie,
                Vengiez m'en!
        Donez chascun un torment
                Tel com je ai.
    Et quant ma dame plera, joie avrai.   55

    MN   Ms. V has a second melody. Form: A A B rf (vire-
lai).

    V   I   7 cui O   II   22   et c. *added in N*; ma
dame *missing in O*; plera ioie aurai *added in VX*   III   23
granz O   29 riens NX, rienz V; li] le V   31 quant
V, que X; chantant *(+1)* O; fierement V   3 ma d. p. j.

a. *added in V*; Dame. 0; Dame etc. N   V   45 Mesdisant
OV; mauuaistiez 0   46 Mont V   47 maintes X   49 Maus
feus OV   51 cui OV, que X   52 ment VX

 E   Noack, 110-111; Steffens *Per*, 235-237, 324-325.

 DF   Picard: *vo* (36) for *vostre*.

 N   30 Understand *ce* before *Que*.   32 Understand
direct object *le* (= 1. 30 *que je sent*).   38 *Car* introduces
imperative.   47-48 *douté/Vostre aparcevoir* 'feared being
discovered by you'.   49 *Mau feu* for nominative *maus feus*.
51 *qui* = *cui*.   52 *m'en* for *m'ent*, normal in Picard and
forming a more obvious rhyme with 1. 53 *torment*.

RAOUL DE BEAUVAIS

<u>168</u>   Chanson de rencontre, débat

RS 368, MW 497
Stanza I: B 1169 (one other source), st. II: B 1839, st.
    III: B 1188 (one other source), st. IV: B 1769, st.
    V: B 362 (one other source).
Mss. K 208-209, N 100v, P 124v-125r, T 101v. Music in all
    mss. Attribution in KP; attributed to Jehan Erart in N
    and to Gilles le Vinier in T.

I   Delez un pré verdoiant
     Trouvai deus dames seant.
     "Que ferai," dist l'une a l'autre,
     "De mon ort vilain puant,
     Qui, pour mon ami le cointe,   5
     Me va tote jour batant?
     Et vous savez vraiement:
     Jolis cuers doit bien amer
     Par amors mignotement."

II   "Conpaingnete, or m'entendez   10
     Et le mien conseil creez:
     Se li vilains vous deboute,
     Onques garde n'i pernez,
     Mes soiez cointe et mignote,
     Ou jamés bon jor n'avrez,   15
     Et dites hardiement:
     Vilain jalos, il n'est joie
     Que d'amer bien par amors."

III   "Conpaignete, je ne puis:
         Il siet toute jor a l'uis.   20
         Se je vois a la fenestre,
         Tant est cismes et requis
         Que je n'i ose mes estre,
         Si felon vilain le truis.
         Mes je li faz bien a savoir: 25
          La joliveté de moi
        Fera vilain le cuer doloir."

IV   "Bele conpaigne, or vaut pis;
         Tel n'est mie mes maris.
         Il ne me fiert ne ne touche,   30
         Ainz est cointes et jolis
         Le jor q'il puet de ma bouche
         Seulement avoir un ris.
    Enondieu! tant en ai je trop meilleur mai."
   Tel mari n'avez vous mie conme j'ai,   35
   Qui me dit q'il me batra ou j'amerai.

V   "Conpaignete, or vous crerrai.
         Ja d'amer ne recrerrai;
         Et se li vilains en groce,
         Savez vous que g'en ferai?   40
         Je n'iere point vers li douce,
         Mes trop bien le baterai,
         Jamés ne mengera de pain."
     Ci le me foule, foule, foule,
     Ci le me foule le vilain.   45

MN   Ms. N has a strongly variant melody. Form: a a B
+B'   rf (ballade).
1. In l. 1 ms. T writes a bar. 2. St. 4, l. 7 may be sung
from here on. 3. No music is extant for refrains 2-5, but
refrains 2 and 3 may be sung to the melody of refrain 1.

     V   I   1   un bois   N   3   d. lun   NP   7   veraiement
N   8   cuer   N; Cuers iolis   T   II   14   et iolie   T, et
ioliue   N   15   j. ior bien n.   P   17   Vilains j. i. n. deduis   T   18   Ne solas fors ke damors   T   III   20   Il se
s. toz iorz a l.   N   21   Quant ie siec a l. f.   T   22
cismes] mauuais   T   23   Car   T; o. plus e.   T   24   Tant   T
25   Et j. l. f. b. s.   T   27   F. le v.   N; le *missing in T*
IV   28   Compaignete or va il p.   T   29   Tex   T   30   n. n.
boute   T   32   ki p.   T   34   En non dieu T; trop *missing*
in T   35   m. ke iou aj   T   36   Qui dit que il m.   P, Il
dist ki me batera   T   V   38   Ia damors ne partirai   T

39 le vilain N; gronce T   40 k. ie f. T   41 Iamais
nere v. T   42 M. si b. T   44 foule *occurs only twice
in T*

E   Bartsch, 85-86; Newcombe *Jeh*, 144-148; Newcombe
"Raoul", 326-329; Newcombe *Songs*, 25.

DF   Picard: *pernez* (13) for *prenez*; *baterai* (42) for
batrai.

N   For the question of authorship, see Newcombe
"Raoul," pp. 318-320.   5 *pour* 'because of'. To judge by
the rhyme scheme of the following stanzas, this verse should
rhyme with l. 3.   22 The adjective *cisme(s)* is unknown.
In view of the context, we suggest the possibility that
cismes is the noun for 'schism' being used adjectivally to
mean 'quarrelsome' or 'inimical' or 'perfidious'. The form
requis = *recuis* (past part. of *recuire*) 'crafty, sly'.   27
vilain, prepositionless dative.   28 *or vaut pis* 'that's a
pity'.   35-36 Bartsch ascribes these verses to the speaker
of ll. 28-34; likewise, Newcombe *Jeh*, who comments, p. 148
(= "Raoul," pp. 328-329): "Le sens de ce refrain--l'inter-
locutrice dit que son mari la battrait si elle ne lui démon-
trait pas toujours son amour--révèle que les menaces du mari
sont bien plus efficaces que ne l'est son caractère (cf. vv.
29-31)." It is more likely that the refrain coincides with
a shift back to the other speaker, the *mal mariée*, whose
unhappy lot it clearly expresses; the "voice" of the refrain
may be either that of the *mal mariée* or that of an extrinsic
commentator. The word *ou* (= *où*) means, as often in OF,
'when, if'.   40 Understand *ce* before *que*.

Plainte funèbre

RS 485, MW 1477
Ms. T 130v-131r. Music. Attribution.

I   Nus chanters mais le mien cuer ne leeche
     Des ke chil est del siecle departis
     Ki des honors iert la voie et l'adreche,
     Larges, cortois, saiges, nes de mesdis.
     Grans dolors est ke si tost est fenis;   5
     A oés tos ceaus a cui estoit amis,
     D'aus honorer et aidier n'ot perece.

II   Gherart, amis, la toie mors me blece,
     Quant me sosvient des biens ke me fesis.
     Dieus, ki en crois soffri mort et destreche 10
     Pour son pule jeter des andecris,
     Le vos rengë ensi com jou devis;
     K'il vous otroit le sien saint paradis:
     Bien avés deservi c'om vos i mece.

III Mors, villaine iés, en toi n'a gentillece, 15
     Car tu as trop villainement mespris;
     Bien deüssiés esparnier le jonece,
     Et le cortois, le large, au siecle mis.

Mais tel usaige as de piech'a apris
Ke nus n'en iert tensés ne garandis,   20
Ne haus ne bas, jonece ne viellece.

IV   N'i puet valoir ne avoirs ne richesse
Contre la mort; de çou soit chascuns fis.
Pour çou se fait boin garder c'on n'endece
L'armë en tant ke on n'i soit sospris.   25
Ki en honor et em bien faire iert pris
Et avra Dieu par ses biens fais conquis,
Il avera faite boine pröeche.

V   Mors, tolu m'as et men blé et me veche
Et mes cortieus; tos les mes as ravis.   30
Bien est raisons ke ma joie demece
Puis ke tu m'as tolu et jeu et ris.
Bien mi deüst reconforter Henris,
Robers Crespins, ou j'ai mon espoir mis:
En ceaus ne sai nule mauvaise teche.   35

VI   Des serventois va t'en tos aatis;
Signeur Pieron Wyon et Wagon dis
Ke petit truis ki me doinst ne promece.

MN   Form: A A B; the envoy is sung to ll. 5-7.

RR   I   7 no p. *(em. Gennrich)*   II   12   ensi en
com   III   17 ionete   21 iouenete ne viellete   IV
22 Si   24   garde con nendete

E   Springer, 105-106; Brandin, 237-238; Gennrich *Ex*,
37-38; Newcombe *Jeh*, 129-132; Newcombe *Songs*, 21.

DF   Picard, including *ai* or *e* for *a*, as in *saiges*
(4), *usaige* (19), *teche* (35); *aus* (7) for *eus* and *ceaus* (6)
for *ceus*; *boin* (24) for *bon*; *pule* (11) for *pueple*; *ch* for *c*,
as in *leeche* (1), *chil* (2), *piech'a* (19); final *s* for *z*, as
in *departis* (2), *grans* (5), *mors* (8), *tos* (36); *jou* (12) for
je; *çou* (23) for *ce*; *le* (17) for *la*; *men* (29) for *mon* and *me*
(29) for *ma*; epenthetic *e* in fut. *avera* (29) for *avra*; 3rd-
pers. sing. pres. subj. in *-ece* for *-ete*, as in *mece* (14),
endece (24), *demece* (31), *promece* (38).

N   Of the five lyric death-laments in OF, all concern
a beloved except Jehan Erart's composition, which mourns the
passing of his protector, a certain Gherart, and concludes
with an appeal for new sources of support.

4 *nes de* 'free of', rather than Newcombe's gloss, 'not
even'.   5 *fenis* 'dead'.   6 *A oés* 'for the benefit of'.
7 'he was not slow to honor and aid them'.   Newcombe, retaining ms. *no* 'our' and placing a comma after l. 5 *fenis*,
apparently understands 'finished . . . honoring them and
aiding our laziness'.   8 *amis* is not clear in the ms.
Most editions and Pet Dyg "Onom" read *Aniel*, which would be
the family name of Gherart; Newcombe reads *amics* (= *amis*).
11 'to deliver his people from the antichrists'.   12
rengë, 3rd-pers. sing. pres. subj. of *rendre*, here 'reward
for'.   24 There is no normal caesura; the enjambment with
l. 25 is equally unusual.   30 *mes as* = *m'as.*   33-34 Henri
and Robert Crespin are identified in Pet Dyg "Onom", p. 219,
as members of one of the richest and most powerful families
of Arras in the 13th century.   37 Pierre and Vaugon Guion
are identified in Pet Dyg "Onom", p. 203 and pp. 247-248, as
brothers in a family of financiers in Arras; Pierre died in
1268 and Vaugon in 1272 or 1273.   38 'that I have difficulty finding anyone who will give or promise me [any-
thing]'.

170　　　　　　　　　Chanson

RS 414 (= 412), MW 1218, B 1911
Mss. K 148-149, C 105r-v, N 69r-v, O 65v-66r, U 110r-v, V
　43r-v, X 101v-102r.　Music in all mss. except CU.
Attribution in KCNX.

I　　　J'ai souvent d'Amors chanté;
　　　　　　　　Oncore en chant:
　　　　Toz jorz sui et ai esté
　　　　　　　En son conmant.　　　　　　　　　　　　　　4
　　　　S'a la foiz m'a fet dolent
　　　　　　　Et desconforté,
　　　　Or m'a si bien assené
　　　　　　　Qu'a mon vivant　　　　　　　　　　　　　8
　　　　　　　　N'oi mes tant
　　　　De joie a ma volenté
　　　　　　　N'a mon devis
　　　　Con en amer *Bietriz.*　　　　　　　　　　　12

II　　Cil qui sont espoanté
　　　　　　　Et esmaiant
　　　　Par fame sont tost maté
　　　　　　　Et recreant;　　　　　　　　　　　　　16
　　　　Or ferai plus que devant

De joliveté.
Pour ce, s'on m'a marié,
 N'ai je talent,   20
  Poi ne grant,
Que je soient mi pensé
 Ailleurs assis
Qu'a la bele *Bietriz*.   24

III Toutes dames ont bonté,
   Mien encïent,
 Mes sachiez, pour verité
   Le vous creant,   28
 Que la lune tost luisant
   Soleil en esté
 Passe de fine clarté;
   N'a son senblant   32
    Ne se prent,
 N'a la tres grande biauté
   Ne au doz ris
 De la bele *Bietriz*.   36

IV Clers soleus sanz tenebror
   Enluminez
 Passe toute autre luor,
   Bien le savez;   40
 Autresi a sormontez
   Toz cuers de valor
 Cele qui de tout honor
   Est dame et clés.   44
    Ja mes grez
 N'iert que j'aie bien nul jor
   Nes paradis
 Sanz la bele *Biatriz*.   48

V Bele dame qui j'aor,
   Qui tant valez,
 Je me tieng a grant seignor
   Quant mes pensez   52
 Est en vos servir tournez;
   Et pour vostre amor
 Sui de mon cuer sanz retor
   Desheritez: 56
    Vous l'avez,
 Si que n'ai mal ne dolor,
   Tant m'esjoïs,
 Quant j'oi nonmer *Bietriz*. 60

__MN__   Ms. O has a second melody; ms. V has a third.
Form: A A B; the envoy in ms. C is sung to ll. 5-12.
1. Ms. adds a *g* for an extra word *et*.

__RR__   I   2 Et o. *(+1)*   5 Sa la fin me f. d.   12
De bien a. b.   II   22 penser   IV   46 Niert qaie b.
(-3)   V   52 pensers

__V__   Stanzas: NVX   I II III IV V
                     C   I II III IV V VI (see below)
                     O   I II III V
                     U   I III IV II
I   1 J. tous iors U   2 Et o. en c.   N, Et encor (an-
U) c. XU   3 Car touz s.   V   4 En lor c.   C; couant U
5 A la VU; Mainte f.   O; la fin me NX   7 Or seux si b.
aseneis C   8 mont C   9 Na V, No C   11 Na de delit
C   12 De bien a. b.   NX, Com de bien a. b.   VC, Com iai
dameir b. U
II   13 Acuns s. e. U   14 En N   15 Por C, De U;
fames N, femes X, dame U   17 Lors fera U   19 som ait
m. U   20 Noi X, Na U   21 Tant ne quant (kant U) OVU
22 penser NX, panser O, pensser V, penseir C, panseis
U   24 Quen O, Ken C
III   26 Mon X   27 Me N, Et U; par O, en C, de U
28 Tout uraiemant U   29 Nes ke la nuit vait l.   C, Nes
ke li rais dou l. U   30 Solaus C   31 Ne puet randre la
c. C, Puet antandre la c. U   32 Ne lou s. CU   33 si
U   34 A O; Ne a la t. grant b.   N, Nulle autre grans b.
C, Nus a la t. grant b. U   35 Nen U; a CU
IV   37 Cler X   41 Ausement C; sormonterz N, seurmonte
V, trepesseit U   42 Ces U   43 C. de qui V; toute NVCU
44 De dames est c. U   45 Mes iai g.   C, A mon greit U
46 Nert quaie b. *(-3)* NVX, N. ke iaie iai nus biens U
47 Nan U   48 S. si faite b.   C
V   49 Bone C; que O, cui C; d. de valour V   50 Ke C
51 g. valour V   52 Q. uo X; pensers O, penseirs C
53 Ai OC; en *missing in X*; v. serimi t. N   58 nai nulle
d. C   59 Si N
    Ms. C concludes with the following envoy:

            Dame d'Adenairde, oiés,
                Si senteis tristor.
            Or n'en aiés jai paor;
                Tost la perdreis,
                    S'aprendeis
            Mon chant: de si grant savor

Et de teil pris
Est li haus nom *Beatris*.

E   Scheler 1, 92-95; Waitz, 72-74.

N   The person whose name occurs as a refrain in this song is in all likelihood Béatrice de Brabant, sister of Henri II, duke of Brabant from 1248 to 1261. She was the protectress of several trouvères and is referred to in more than one poem by Gillebert. The *Dame d'Adenairde* (= *Audenarde*) of the envoy found only in ms. C (see variants) is apparently the same person. See Dragonetti, pp. 349-350. As Dragonetti points out, "les chansons de Gillebert sont un bel exemple de cet amour fictif du trouvère à l'égard de sa protectrice."

5 *a la foiz* 'sometimes'. 19 *s'on m'a marie* 'even if I have been married'. 29-36 Scheler 1, following the text of ms. C, finds, p. 299, that it is "impossible d'y découvrir un sens satisfaisant." Waitz, following the same text as here, glosses, in German, p. 111: 'I assure you that she surpasses the moon [and] the sun; nor does it (the sun) compare to her appearance or to the great beauty . . .'. Understandably dissatisfied, he then proposes replacing l. 10 *Ne* with a subject *Nus* or *Nule,* and glossing: 'I assure you that she surpasses the moon [and] the sun; [no one] has her appearance and no one compares to the great beauty . . .'. This reading strikes us as at least as doubtful as the first. It is very awkward syntactically, but, more important, it fails to make clear the complex comparative relations of the original text. We propose, then, assuming only one, readily explained, scribal error: 'I assure you that the sun (*soleil* for nominative *soleus*) surpasses the moon; and [yet] to her appearance it does not compare, neither to the great beauty nor to the sweet smile . . .'. Thus, the phases of the comparison are clear: all ladies = the shining moon; the sun is brighter than the moon; Beatrice surpasses even the sun. For the importance of acknowledging the contrast between the sun and moon, see ll. 37-40 in the following stanza, where that contrast is repeated, and in terms which admit no doubt. 45-47 'Never will it be my desire to have . . .'. The word *bien* may be interpreted as an adverbial intensifier or, with commas before and after l. 47 'even Heaven', as a direct object of *j'aie*. 49 *qui* = *cui,* direct object of *j'aor*.

171   Chanson

RS 138, MW 883
Mss. N 69v-70r, K 149-150, O 91v, R 118r-v-119r, V 43v-44r,
    X 102r-v. Music in all mss. Attribution in NKX.

I   Onques d'amors n'oi nule si grief paine
        Qui me fesist nul jor desesperer,
        Tant aim de cuer sanz pensee vilaine
        Cele del mont qui plus fet a löer.   4
        Bien m'est amors et nuit et jor prochaine
        Qu'el cuer me maint; ne me verra aver,
        Car je li doing quanque li puis doner:
        Et cuer et cors et pensee souvraine.   8

II   Onques amors ne fu de moi loingtaine
        Ne je de li, tres ce que soi amer;
        Tout a mon cuer en son lige demaine,
        Et si sai bien que ne m'en puet sevrer.   12
        Longue atente tant soit a moi grevaine,
        Tant m'a conquis qu'el me fet aorer
        Li, et la croi tant qu'el me fet senbler
        Que c'est li deus de la joie mondaine.   16

III   Cele qui j'aim est tant de bonté plaine
      Qu'il m'est avis que la doi conperer
      A l'estoile qu'on claime tremontaine,
      Dont la bonté ne puet onques fauser.   20
      Le marinier par mi la mer hautaine
      Fait ravoier et a droit port sigler,
      Et set et voit quel part il doit aler
      Par l'estoile, dont la vertuz est saine.   24

IV   Ausi vos di qui forvoie en outrage,
      En fauseté, en penser folement,
      S'il vuet en bien müer son fol usage,
      Voist esgarder le biau contenement   28
      Et la valor de la tres bone et sage:
      Ravoiez ert en bon ensaignement
      Con marinier a qui l'estoile aprent
      Par mi la mer le plus seür passage   32

V   Tant set, tant vaut, tant a loial corage
      Que touz li biens en li croist et reprent;
      Honor a pris en son cuer son ostage,
      Si ne porroit manoir plus hautement   36
      Ne ou feïst plus de son avantage;
      Ce c'onnor veut, veut ses cuers bonement.
      Por ce, me lo d'amors, qui la me rent,
      Et met mon cuer de tout a heritage.   40

VI   Cuens d'Anjou, j'ai mis mon cuer en ostage
      Que vers amors n'ouverrai fausement;
      Toz jorz serai loial en son honmage.
      Hé! filz de roi, car li fetes present   44
      De vostre cuer! Ja n'i avrez damage,
      Et s'en croistra vostre honor ensement;
      Car il n'est nus, se fine amor l'enprent,
      Ne soit adés plus cortois son aage.   48

      MN   Ms. R has a second melody; ms. V has a third.
Form: A A B.

      RR   I   7   doig   8   souueraine *(+1)*   II   9   loig-
taine   III   21   Li   VI   44   fil

      V   Stanzas: KOVX   I   II   III   IV   VI
                          R   I   II   III   IV   V
I   2   Que R; mi KRVX; un j.   V   4   La riens O
6   mi R, men V   7   Que O   8   Et c. et c. p. souueraine
R   II   10   li puis que ie s. O, li t. dont que s. R

11 a *missing in X*   12 puet] puis V   14 mi f.   R   15
Moy R; mi R   III   17 cui O; bontez R   19 qui O,
quen V; nonme K, no(m)me ORVX   20 o. cesser V   23
second et *missing in X*   24 uertu VX; Et par lestoille con
nomme tresmontainne R   IV   25 que X; se noie V   27
Si R   31 mariniers R; a cui O; apent V   V   34
biens] sens R; et se prent R   35 s. c. son cuer son estage R   38 Que toute honnour v. s. R   40 du t. en h.
R   VI   43 leaus O, loiaux V   45 cors O   46 Et
sen croistra ausiment O   47 amors O; le prent. V

E   Scheler 1, 113-115; Waitz, 71-72.

N   4 *plus fet a löer* 'is most worthy of praise'.
10 *tres ce que soi amer* 'ever since I learned to love'.
13 'However grievous a long wait may be for me'.   15 This
is striking both for the enjambed *Li* and for the displace-
ment of the caesura from the fourth syllable to the fifth.
17 *qui = cui*. In the context of this stanza, *bonté* is to
be understood as 'trueness' or 'salutary power'; likewise
in l. 20.   19 The reference is to the North Star, more
frequent as a simile or metaphor for the Virgin Mary ("Stel-
la Maris") than a mortal beloved.   21-23 *Le marinier* is
the direct object of *fait* and the subject of *set et voit*.
24 *vertuz* 'power'.   25 Understand *que* after *di*; *qui* 'whoever'.   34 *reprent* 'grows, increases'.   35 *ostage* 'dwelling'; cf. l. 41 *ostage* 'hostage'.   40 'And I confer my
heart lastingly'.   41 The syllabic division of this verse,
3 + 7, is so exceptional in OF *chansons* that it does not
even figure in the synoptic table of caesura-types in Dragonetti, p. 499. *Cuens d'Anjou* designates Charles d'Anjou (b.
1226), King of Naples and Sicily from 1265 until his death
in 1285. He was the protector of several trouvères and a
trouvère himself. For details, see Petersen Dyggve *Charles*
and Dragonetti, pp. 345-348.   48 *son aage* 'throughout his
life'.

172   Chanson

RS 1573, MW 1971, B 1733
Mss. M 160r-v, K 145-146, N 68r, P 193v-194r, R 115r-v, U
    144v-145r, X 100r-v, a 80r-v. Music in all mss. except
    U. Attribution in KNX; attributed to Robert de la
    Pierre in Ma.

I   Hé, Amors, je fui norris
             En vostre covent
         Et cuidai manoir toz dis
             En vos ligement
                 Sanz ja dessevrer;   5
             Mais je n'i porrai durer,
                 Ce m'est avis,
         Car de totes pars sui assaillis,
             Se n'i ai mort deservie;
             Mes bien vueill qu'amors m'ocie.   10

II   Ainc mais nus si entrepris
             Ne fu por noient,
         N'onques si loiaus amis
             N'ot tant de torment
                 Con j'ai por amer,   15
             Car ceus ou me doi fïer
                 Truis anemis.
         Deus m'en doint venjance a mon devis,
             Car n'i ai mort [deservie;
             Mes bien vueill qu'amors m'ocie].   20

III   Mout est mes cuers esbahiz
             Qui tant de maus sent,
         Si ne.s ai pas deservis,
             Ne ne sai conment
                 M'en puisse eschiver.   25

Hé las! por li foi porter
       Sui je trahis,
Si que des mauvés en sui haïs,
       Si n'i ai mort [deservie;
       Mes bien vueill qu'amors m'ocie].   30

IV   Et puis que sui acueilliz
              De si male gent,
          Bele, en qui j'ai mon cuer mis,
              Car aiez talent
              De moi conforter,   35
          U je ne puis eschaper
              De lor mains vis;
          Et se vos volez, je sui garis,
              Car n'i ai mort [deservie;
              Mes bien vueill qu'amors m'ocie].   40

V   Tout le pooir mout pou pris
              Et le nuisement
          De ceus dont je sui faidis,
              S'en vo biau cors gent
              Puis merci trover.   45
          Aidiez m' a resvigorer,
              Car vos porfis
          Iert, s'eschaper puis sanz estre ocis,
              Car n'i ai mort [deservie;
              Mes bien vueill qu'amors m'ocie].   50

VI   Damoisele de grant pris,
              Tasse, proiez l'ent
          Qu'a ceus par cui sui nuisis
              Prende vengement.
              Par moi rapeler,   55
          Les cuers lor feroit crever,
              De ce sui fis;
          Et je n'ai pas ces maus deservis;
              Et quant n'ai mort deservie,
              N'est pas drois qu'amors m'ocie.   60

<u>MN</u>   Form: A A B rf (ballade).

<u>RR</u>   III   28 maiues en fui   V   43 donc   46 me
a *(+1)*

<u>V</u>   Stanzas: KNPRX   I II III   IV V
                    a   I II III   IV VI
                    U   I II III[1] IV[2] (see below)

I 1 Mamors j. f. n. P; sui aNR 3 cuida U; toudis
aR 6 Bien uoi ni pora d. U 9 Si KNPRX; Ie ni a m. d.
U 10 Et KNRX; qamor mocient P
II 11 Ains a; Onques (Onke U) mes (mais U) si e.
(ebahis U,) KNPRXU 12 fui KNPRXU 13 si] mais a, nus
P, nulz R; loi a. a; Nen onkes nus fins amins U 15 C.
ioi R, ia U; amour R 16 do f. U 18 devis] plesir
N, plaisir U 19 *not in R*; Se a, Si N, Ie U; deservie
added in aKPXU 20 *given in U*; Car mieus voeil camours
mochie a
III 22 Que t. de mal s. R 23 Si ne lai p. desserui R
25 Les a, Lez R, Ges KNX, Ie P 26 par li a 28 d.
(de X) mesdisanz (me- X, -ans PRX) s. h. KNPRX 29 Se
a; deservie *added in aKNPX*, deserui R 30 Mes bien woil
&c P
IV 31 pus R; q. ie s. X; enuaiz KN, enuais PRX 33
Dame ou iai (ie ai X) to(u)t m. c. m. KNPRX 36 Car
KNPX, Quar R; ni p. RX 38 v. v. gere g. a; D(i)ex men
do(i)n(s)t ueniance (-gance RX) a mon deuis KNPRX 39
not in R; deservie *added in aKNPX* 40 *given in aP*; mocient
P
V 41 T. lor (leur K) p. mont po(u)q(u)is KNPRX 42
lor NPR, leur KX 43 Icil (Ycilz R) d. j. s. honiz
(honnis R, honis X) KNPRX 44 Mes (Mez R) sen uo (uos
P, son R) c. g. KNPRX 46 Ie (Ge N) porrai (porre N,
pourai P) bien respasser (eschaper PX) KNPRX 47 Et
KNRX; vo KPX 48 s'e. en p. P 49 a m. N; deservie
added in KNPRX
VI 50 Bien v. q. m'o. N, Et b. v. q. m'o. R 53 c.
dont je s. n. a 56 feroient a 59 Et *missing in a*
    In place of stanzas III and IV, U contains the follow-
ing:

III'   Biaz dous cuers fins et antiers,
              Por vos voil morir,
          Ne ja de vostre dongier
              Ne kier mais issir,
              Ce.l volés sosfrir.
          Mais ceu m'i fait resjoïr
              C'a mon plaisir
      Morra por celi cui tant desir.
          Je n'i ai mort deservie,
          Mais bien voil c'amors m'osie.

IV'   Or puent li medissant
              Asseis abaier,
          Car j'a de l'avoir asseis

            Et bleif an grenier
            Et bia palefroit,
        Belle dame a mon voloir
            Ke bien me siet;
    Et s'ai bien cent sols tout sans dongier,
        Mais je ne les gaingnai mies:
        J'a troveit lou nit de pie.

Stanza III[1] is rhymed somewhat differently from both the
stanzas that precede it in U and those that appear in the
other mss., but from the point of view of meaning and tone
it is consistent with the rest and may simply be regarded as
the work of a serious *remanieur*. Stanza IV[1], on the other
hand, is a jongleuresque invention entirely out of keeping
with the foregoing stanzas. Its rhyme-scheme, somewhat different from both the first two stanzas and III[1], is exactly
the same as that of the *chanson pieuse* (RS 1570; see Notes,
below) which is modeled after Gillebert's song. Stanza IV[1],
then, appears to be a jocular contrafactum of the pious imitation of RS 1573.

    E   Scheler 1, 86-89; Waitz, 66-68.

    N   This poem served as the secular model for RS 1570,
an anonymous *chanson pieuse* beginning *Mout sera cil bien
norris/ Et en bon couvent*; see Järnström-Långfors 2, pp.
115-117.   9 *Se = si* 'yet'.   37 *vis* 'alive', referring to
1. 36 *je*.   51-52 Scheler 1, p. 297, comments: "*Tasse* est
sans doute le nom du personnage auquel la demoiselle est
priée de s'adresser." Petersen Dyggve "Onom.", p. 238, on
the contrary, equates *Damoisele* and *Tasse*, and identifies the
lady as Tasse Wagon, wife of André Wagon, a rich banker of
Arras; this would be the same person as Tassain Wagoune,
mentioned in RS 1612 by Robert de la Pierre (composer of the
present song as well, according to mss. Ma). The imperative
proiez, then, would be addressed to someone not named in any
way in the poem. It seems to us at least as likely that
Tasse is a vocative designating one of the figures conven-
tionally appearing in envoys: the jongleur-messenger, who
will carry the poet's song to his lady. And it is the lady
(*Damoisele = l'*) who will be asked to "take vengeance" upon
the poet's enemies--by calling him back (1. 55 *rapeler*) to
her.

Chanson satirique   <u>173</u>

RS 1857, MW 2222, B 440
Mss. N 68r-v, I 1:48, K 146-147, P 116v-117r-v and 138v-
139r, U 92v-93r, X 100v-101r. Music in all mss. except
IU. Attribution in NKP[1]X.

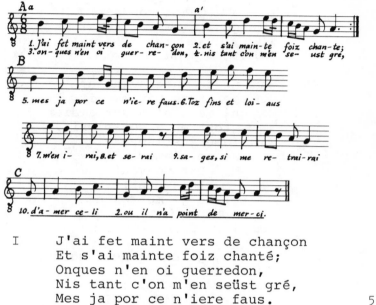

I   J'ai fet maint vers de chançon
      Et s'ai mainte foiz chanté;
      Onques n'en oi guerredon,
      Nis tant c'on m'en seüst gré,
      Mes ja por ce n'iere faus.   5
          Toz fins et loiaus
            M'en irai,
            Et serai
      Sages, si me retrerai
         D'amer celi   10
     Ou il n'a point de merci.

II   Je ne donroie un bouton
      D'Amors ne de sa fierté;
      Issuz sui de sa prison,
      Ou j'ai maint mal enduré.   15
      Amors n'est fors paine et maux,
          Tormenz et travauz;
            Joie n'ai
            Quant les ai;
      Et por ce me retrerai   20
         D'amer [celi
     Ou il n'a point de merci].

III   Se j'amasse traïsson
       Ne medit ne fauseté,
       L'on m'eüst tenu a bon   25
       Et si m'eüst on amé.
       Certes, Amors desloiaus,
           Ja n'iere de çaus,
              Ainz ferai,
                Quant voudrai,   30
       Chançon, si me retrerai
          [*D'amer celi*
       Ou il n'a point de merci].

IV   Nus ne se puet avancier
       En amer fors par mentir;   35
       Et qui meuz s'en set aidier,
       Plus tost en a son plesir.
       Qui fame justisera
          Ja ne l'amera
             Par couvent   40
             Loiaument;
       Et por ce je me repent
          D'amer [*celi*
       Ou il n'a point de merci].

V   Certes, ja celer ne.l quier: 45
       G'enpris ma dame a servir;
       Rendu m'en a tel loier
       Qu'ele me cuida traïr.
       Voirs fu, s'amor m'otroia,
          Mes el me gaba   50
             Por vil gent.
             Vengement
       M'en doint Deus! Je me repent
          D'amer celi
       [*Ou il n'a point de merci*].   55

<u>MN</u>   Form: A A B rf (ballade).

<u>RR</u> 6 loiauis   20 Et p. ce ie men r. *(+1)*   31
missing 53 men r.

   V   Stanzas II, IV, and V not included in I.
I 1 mains I 2 Sai par m. U 3 Nonkes I, Ki ains
U 4 Ne U 5 Ne I; fais I 6 Mais IU; f. a leal U
7-8 Serai et ferai I 8 A s. U 9 Biaus chans si m.
r. I; men P^2; recroirai U 10 celui P^{1}P^2, cele U 11
mercis U

II 12 J. ni U 13 Damor U 14 Issu P^2, Usus U
15 mains K; maus KP^1, mas U 16 p. a mal U 17
Anujs a trauail U 18 Loie U 19 lou sai U 20 Et
p. ce ie (si K) me retrai KP^{1}P^{2}X, Por tant si me recroirai
U 21 *not given in* P^{1}X; celi *added in* KU, celui *added in*
P^2 22 *not given in* KP^{1}X; mersis U
III 24 Maluistiet ne f. I, Mal uestie n. f. U 25 Len
KX, On IU 26 Si maust on muelz a. U 27 He a. d. I,
Ei a. de loial U 28 A nul ior niere de ciaus I 30
missing in I 31 Biaus chant si me r. I, Biau chan si me
recroiraj U 32 *not given in* P^1; celui P^2 33 *not
given in* KP^{1}P^2; ou. *given in* X; mersis U
IV 35 amors IU 36 Sil *(=cil)* ki muel U 37 en ait
ces delis U 38 chastoiera U 39 lameraj U 40-41
reversed in U 42 je] si X; Por tant mes cuers se repant
U 43 *not given in* X; celi *added in* KU, celui *added in* P^2
44 *not given in* KP^{1}P^{2}X; mersis U
V 45 C. ia nou qer noier U 46 prei U 48 Q. man U
49 Uoir P^1; est U 50 M. ele me g. X, M. ele g. U
51 Uoirement U 52 Por uil gent U 53 Por tant mes
cuers se repant U 54 celui P^2 55 *not given in* KP^{2}X;
mersis U

E La Borde *Es* 2, 166; Dinaux 2, 190-192; Scheler 1,
89-91; Waitz, 94-96.

N 28 *çaus* 'those', i.e., who love betrayal (l. 23),
etc. 36 *s'en set aidier* 'knows how to make use [of
lies]'. 38 *justisera* 'will reproach'. 48 *cuida traïr*
'almost betrayed'.

174

Jeu-Parti (partner: the Dame de Gosnai)

RS 931, MW 685
Ms. b 168r-v. No music. Attribution.

I   Dame de Gosnai, gardez
     Que soiez bien conseillie;
     A Robert Bosquet parlez
     Tant qu'il soit de vostre aïe.
     Je vous part: seignor avrez;   5
     S'a vo voloir le prenez,
     C'iert sans le gré vos amis
     --Ensi est le jeu partis--

Ou vous l'avrez par leur gré
Maugré vostre volenté.   10

II   --Gilebert, c'est grans vieutez
        A dame d'user sa vie
        Aveuc home qui amez
        N'est de lui; mes ne doi mie
        Contre tous mes foulz pensez,   15
        S'aim mieus faire pis assez
        Par leur los et par leur dis.
        A ce me tenrai tout dis,
        Ne ja ne m'iert reprouvé
        Qu'aie conseil refusé.   20

III   --Dame, retenu avez
        Le plour en vo partie.
        De joie vous departez,
        Si estes trop forvoïe.
        Des ore mais soufferrez   25
        Soulas trop malz savourez,
        S'iert vos jugemens enquis
        As vrais amans du païs
        De ce qu'avez trespassé
        Ce qu'Amours a commandé.   30

IV   --Gilebert, vous mesprenez.
        Amours veult bien et otrie
        Que joie et ses biens doublez
        Ait dame qui se marie,
        Et je croi tant mes privez   35
        Qu'a leur pooir m'iert donnez
        Autieux ou mieudres maris
        Que se je l'eüsse pris;
        S'aim bien ce que m'ont greé,
        Et s'ai grant blasme eschivé.   40

V   --Dame, bien sai que savez
        Assez sens et cortoisie;
        Tant iert vo cuers plus desvez
        S'Amours est par vous traïe.
        Pour Dieu, or vous repentez!   45
        Jamais Robert ne creez!
        Bien sai qu'il a conseil mis
        A ce que vous avez pris.
        Portez Amours loiauté,
        Si vous iert tout pardonné.   50

VI   --Gilebert, vous me tenez
      A sage et a bien norrie;
      Pour tant cuidier ne devez
      Que je face desverie,
      Ains m'est li mieudres remez   55
      . . . .
      Robert m'a bon conseil quis,
      Mes vous vous estes partis
      Du droit, s'avez mal ouvré,
      S'avrez blasme et je bonté.   60

VII   --Hue d'Arras, soustenez
      Le droit d'Amours et parlez
      Adés droit de nos estris.
      En vous m'en sui du tout mis,
      Et, s'il vous plest, si chantez   65
      Ce chant quant apris l'arez.

RR   VI   56 *missing*   VII   63   A deus drois *(em.
Långfors)*

E   Waitz, 88-90; Långfors *Rec* 2, 153-156.

DF   Picard: *-ie* for *-iee,* as in *conseillie* (2) and
forvoïe (24); *tenrai* (18) for *tendrai*; *arez* (66) for *avrez.*

N   Gillebert asks the Dame de Gosnai whether she
would prefer a husband pleasing to her but not to her family, or one pleasing to her family but not to her. She
chooses to comply with the wishes of her family. Only one
person, Hue d'Arras, is formally called upon to judge the
debate; Robert Bosquet, however, mentioned several times,
perhaps serves as the second judge.
      14 *lui* 'her'   14-15 Långfors, though misreading
first-person *doi* as third-person *doit,* is no doubt basically
correct in his interpretation of these lines: an infinitive
complement of *devoir* must be understood. The meaning is
'but I must not, in opposition to everyone else, insist on
my own foolish thoughts'.   27-30 'And true lovers will be
asked to pass judgment on you for having infringed the rules
of Love'.   47-48 In other words, Robert has advised the
lady in her choice of debating position.

175   Rotrouenge

RS 317, MW 312, B 915
Mss. M 174v, T 35r and 84v. Music in all mss. Attributed
to Guiot de Dijon in M and to Gillebert de Berneville
in T¹T².

I   De moi dolereus vos chant.
         Je fui nez en descroissant,
         N'onques n'eu en mon vivant
                  Deus bons jors.
         J'ai a nom Mescheans d'Amors.   5

II   Adés vois merci criant:
         Amors, aidiez vo servant!
         N'ainc n'i peu trover noiant
                  De secors.
         J'ai a nom [Mescheans d'Amors].   10

III   Hé! trahitor mesdisant,
         Con vos estes mal parlant!
         Tolu avez maint amant
                  Lor honors.
         J'ai a nom [Mescheans d'Amors].   15

IV   Certes, pierre d'aÿmant
         Ne desirre pas fer tant
         Con je sui d'un douz samblant
                  Covoitoz.
         J'ai a nom Mescheanz d'Amors.   20

     MN   In both T¹ and T² the melody is written a 2nd
lower. Form: a a B rf (virelai).

<u>V</u>   I   3   Onques T^1, Onque T^2 II   6 voz T^2
7 seriant T^1T^2 8 p. n. tr. T^1T^2 10 mescheans damors
added in T^1T^2 III   12 Vos estes si m. p. T^1T^2 13
Maint amant aues tolu T^1T^2 15 mescheans damors *added in*
T^1T^2 IV   17 pas] le T^1 20 mescheanz damors *missing*
in T^1T^2

<u>E</u>   Scheler 1, 74, 295; Meyer, 377; Waitz, 82; Nissen,
14-15; Gennrich *Rot*, 49-51; Mary 1, 228-229; Bec 2, 119-120.

<u>N</u>   Authorship by Gillebert is by no means certain,
and this song might almost as readily have been grouped with
those of Guiot de Dijon.   For the rhyming of such forms as
l. 4 *jors*, l. 14 *honors*, and l. 19 *covoitoz*, see Elwert, pp.
47-52.
2 *en descroissant* 'under the waning moon'.   13 *maint
amant* 'from many a lover', prepositionless dative.   16
pierre d'aÿmant 'lodestone'.

COLIN MUSET

176   Chanson de jongleur

RS 1298, MW 851
Ms. U 136-136v.   No music.   Anonymous (see note below).

I   Qant je lou tans refroidier
          Voi et geleir
      Et ces arbres despoillier
          Et iverneir,   4
      Adonc me voil et aizier
          Et sejorneir
      A boen feu leiz lou brazier
          Et a vin cleir   8
          An chade mason,
          Por lou tans fellon.
          Ja n'ait il pardon
      Ki n'amet sa garison!   12

II   Je ne voil pais chivachier
          Et feu bouteir,
      Et se haz mout garroier
          Et cris leveir   16
      Et grans proës acoillier
          Et jant robeir:
      Aseiz i et fol mestier
          A tot gasteir.   20
          A poc d'ochoson
          Se prannent baron;
          Par consoil bricon
      Muevent gerres et tanson.   24

III   Asseis valt muez tornoier
          Et behordeir
      Et grosses lances brisier
          Et bial josteir   28
      Et joie rancomansier
          Et tout doneir
      Et despandre sans dongier
          Et fors geteir.   32
          Avoirs an prison
          Ne valt un bouton.
          Kant plus ait prodon,
      Plus vient avoirs a foison.   36

IV   Qant je seus leis lou brasier
         Et j'oz vanteir
     Et je voi plain lou hastier   40
         A feu torneir
     Et lou boen vin dou sillier
         Amont porteir,
     Adonc voil boivre et maingier   44
         Et repozeir
     A feu de charbon.
     Se j'ai grais chapon,
     N'ai pas cuzanson
     D'aisaillir a un donjon.   48

V   Nen a [un] plonjon
         Tandut sus glaison:
         N'avrai gueridon
     Par ceste froide saison.   52

VI   A Saillit, Guion,
         Ki antant raison,
         Anvoi ma chanson,
     Voir se je fas bien ou non.   56

RR   I   1 Q. ie uoi l. t. r. *(+1)*   2 Et g. *(-1)*
3 ces] ses   10 lou] son   II   17 acoillir   19 mes-
teir   24 tansons   III   25 tornoer   35 prodons
IV   45 charbons   46 chapons   V   49 *(-1)*   VI   53
faillit *(em. proposed by Jeanroy-Lǎngfors)*

E   Meyer, 381-382; Jeanroy-Lǎngfors, 74-76; Bédier
Col, 25-26; Henry "Chanson", 108-115; Cremonesi, 158-160;
Woledge Peng, 163-165; Toja, 309-312; Henry Chrest 1, 242-
243; 2, 72-73; Mary 2, 42-45; Aspland, 160-163.

DF   Lorraine, including a for au, as in chade (9),
chivachier (13); ai for a as in maingier (43), grais (46),
aisaillir (48); ei for tonic e, as in geleir (2), leiz (7),
pais (13); bial (28) for beau; o for oi, as in proës (17),
ochoson (21); boen (7) for bon; preservation of final t, as
in amet (12) for aime, tandut (50); adverbial se (15) for
si; lou (2) for le; 3rd-pers. sing. pres. ind. et (19) and
ait (36) for a; seus (37) for sui.

N   The attribution of this composition to Colin
Muset, originally proposed in Jeanroy-Lǎngfors, pp. xiii-
xiv, has been generally accepted. This song has usually
been considered simply a depiction of the jongleur's hard

life in winter in contrast to the easy and pleasant life of
courtly or bourgeois society; Henry, in "La chanson R.
1298," *Romania* 75 (1954), 108-115, suggests that it has the
practical purpose of soliciting material support from Gui de
Joinville, lord of Sailly (1206-1256), who is named in l.
53.   17 'And gather herds/flocks', reference to pillage.
22 *se prannent* 'quarrel'.   33 'Money kept under lock and
key'.   35-36 Woledge's translation expresses the usual
interpretation: "'The more a worthy man has, the more freely
does wealth come to him'." Henry emends *vient* to *vieut*
'veut' and understands: "'Plus il a, plus il veut avoir'."
In neither case is the logical relation of the statement to
the preceding verses especially clear.   49-52 Following
Bédier *Col*, Woledge translates: "'Not under a stook set up
on a clod shall I find comfort in this cold season'." With
well-documented lexical arguments, Henry "Chanson", p. 114,
understands : "'Il n'y a même pas un grèbe tendu [dressé, le
cou tendu, aux aguets, pour plonger sur sa proie] sur une
motte [= l'hiver est très dur]; je n'aurai nul recours en
cette froide saison'. En un raccourci vigoureux . . . Colin
Muset évoque tout l'hiver." Banitt, p. 164, points out that
gueridon = *guerison* 'protection'. See, too, Levy, pp. 243
and 246, and Aspland, p. 322.   56 Understand *pour* before
Voir.

177   Chanson de jongleur

RS 582, MW 443, B 1897
Ms. C 6v-7r. No music. Attribution.

    I   Ancontre le tens novel
         Ai le cuer gai et inel
         A termine de Pascor;
         Lors veul faire un triboudel,   4
         Car j'ain moult tribu martel,
         Brut et bernaige et baudor;
         Et quant je suis en chaistel
         Plain de joie et de rivel,   8
         Lai veul estre et nuit et jor.
         Triboudaine et triboudel!
         Deus confonde le musel
         Ki n'aime joie et baudor!   12

    II   De toute joie m'est bel,
         Et quant j'oi lou flaihutel
         Soneir aveuc la tabor;

Damoiselles et donzel   16
Chantent et font grant rivel;
Chascuns ait chaipel de flour;
Et verdurë et brondelz
Et li douls chans des oixels   20
Me remet en grant badour.
Triboudainne, triboudel!
Plus seux liés, per saint Marcel,
Ke teils ait chaistel ou tour.   24

III   Ki bien broiche lou poutrel
      Et tient l'escut en chantel
      A comencier de l'estor
      Et met la lance en estel,   28
      Por muelz vancre lou sembel
      Vait asembleir a millour;
      Cil doit bien avoir jüel
      De belle dame et anel--   32
      Per drüerie, s'amor.
      Triboudainne, triboudel!
      Por la belle a chief blondel
      Ki ait frexe la color.   36

IV   Teilz amesce en un moncel
      Mil mairs et fait grant fardel
      Ki vit a grant deshonor;
      Jai n'en avra boen morcel,   40
      Et diauble en ont la pel,
      Cors et aime sens retor.
      Por ceu veul jeu mon mantel
      Despandre tost et inel   44
      En bone ville a sejor.
      Triboudainne, triboudel!
      K'i valt avoirs en fardel,
      S'on ne.l despent a honor?   48

V   Quant je la tieng ou praiel
      Tout entor clos d'airbrexelz
      En esteit a la verdour
      Et j'ai oies et gaistel,   52
      Pouxons, tairtes et porcel,
      Buef a la verde savor,
      Et j'ai lou vin en tonel,
      Froit et fort et friandel,   56
      Por boivre a la grant chalor,
      Muels m'i ain k'en un baitel
      En la meir en grant poour.

Triboudainne, triboudel!   60
Plux ain le jeu de praiel
Ke faire malvaix sejor.

RR̲   II   19 broudelz   V   50 draibexelz

E̲   Tarbé *Chans*, 90; Bédier *Nic*, 119; Bédier *Col*, 18-
20; Pauphilet, 912-914; Cremonesi, 156-158; Chastel, 684-
688; Toja, 304-306; Mary 1, 332-335.

DF̲   Lorraine, including *a* (3, 27, 30) for *au*; *ai* or *e*
for *a*, as in *bernaige* (6), *chaistel* (7), *lai* (9), *mairs*
(38), *jai* (40), *per* (23), *amesce* (37); *ei* for tonic *e*, as
in *soneir* (15), *teils* (24), *esteit* (51); *oi* for *o*, as in
broiche (25); *u* for *ui*, as in *brut* (6); *boen* (40) for *bon*; preservation of final *t*, as in *escut* (26), *esteit* (51); *x* for
s(s) or *ch*, as in *oixels* (20), *pouxons* (53), *plux* (61),
frexe (36); *jeu* (43) for *je*; *ceu* (43) for *ce*; *lou* (14) for
le; *seux* (23) for *sui*; 3rd-pers. sing. pres. ind. *ait* (18,
24) for *a*.

N̲   4-5 The words *triboudel* and *tribu martel* are not
attested elsewhere. The first, along with l. 10 *tribou-
daine,* seems to designate a kind of playful, exuberant song;
the sense of *tribu martel* is no doubt readily inferred from
l. 6.   13 Impersonal *m'est bel* has two complements: the
phrase *de toute joie* and the clause *quant j'oi . . ..*
24 Understand relative *qui* before *ait* (= *a*).   30 'Goes to
compete with the best man'.   33 Bédier *Col*, p. 55, wonders
whether to amend *s'amor* to *d'amor* or to *et amor*. In fact,
no correction is necessary; understand a sequence of three
direct objects of *avoir*: *jüel de belle dame et anel* [de
belle dame] [et], *per drüerie, s'amor*.   58-59 It is
doubtful whether these lines belong in the stanza, which
does not repeat the earlier pattern, *aabaabaabAab*, but shows
the unique structure, *aabaabaababAab*. Without them, the
sentence begun with three parallel subordinate clauses (ll.
49-57) would conclude--after the syntactically independent
refrain in l. 60--with ll. 61-62 *Plux ain . . .* as its main
clause.

178   Chanson de jongleur

RS 2079, MW 1552
Ms. U 103v-104r. No music. Anonymous (see note below).

I   Qant li malos brut
          Sor la flor novele
          Et li solaus luist
          Qui tout resplandelle,
Lour mi plaist la damoizelle,   5
Qui est jone et jante et belle,
Et por li suis an grant joie
Aseis plus que ne soloie.
Je suis siens et elle est moie.
Dehait ait qui ne l'otroie,   10
Que por riens n'en partiroie.

II   Joie et grant desduit
          Ai por la donselle;
          G'i pans jor et nuit,
          Et s'amor m'apelle.
Je l'oï an la praielle   15
Chanter a la fontenelle
Par desoz une codroie,
Soule, an un blïaut de soie;
Chapial d'or ot et coroie.   20
Deus! com elle s'esbanoie
Et com elle se cointoie!

III   Ki ainmet valour
          Et met sa pansee
          A lëaul amor   25
          Et il l'ait trovee,
Bien ait sa joie doblee;
N'an doit partir por riens nee.
Qui se met an avanture
D'amer, Amor l'aseüre   30
De joie et d'anvoiseüre
Et de bien et de mesure;
Toute sa vie li dure.

IV   J'ain lou grant signor
          C'an haut honor beie,   35
          Large doneour,
          Et bien fiert d'espee
Cant il vient a la melee;
Iceu me plaist et agree.
Mais des mavais n'ai ge cure,   40
C'on ne s'en poroit desduire;
Plain sont de malle faiture;
N'i ait raison ne droiture;
Fous est qui s'i aseüre.

<pre>
V   J'ain lou chevalier   45
          Qui bien met sa terre
          An bial tornoier
          Et a lous conquere.
          Ceu li doit an bien soferre:
          Puis qu'il son avoir n'anserre,   50
          Brut d'armes et drüerie
          Maintient et chevalerie
          Aveu bone compaignie,
          Lors avra bien deservie
          L'amor de sa douce amie.   55

VI   Je ne quier aler
          An poingnis de gerre,
          Mais ou froit celier;
          La me puet on querre.
          A Boin Ferreit que bien ferre,   60
          La voil mon argent offerre;
          Et se j'ai trute florie,
          Gastiaus et poille rostie,
          Bien i vodroie m'amie,
          Qui sanble rose espanie,   65
          Por faire une raverdie.
</pre>

RR   I   2 novele *added above line in a more modern
hand   II   14 nuit et ior   17 an la fontelle   18
desor   III   28 par r.   30 laraure   IV   44 aseue
VI   62 trutes flories   63 poilles rosties

E   Bartsch-Wiese, 221-222; Jeanroy-Långfors, 72-74;
Bédier *Col*, 27-29.

DF   Lorraine, including *a* for *au*, as in *mavais* (40),
a (60); *ei* for tonic *e*, as in *aseis* (8), *beie* (35), *Ferreit*
(50); *ial* for *eau*, as in *chapial* (20), *bial* (47); *u* for *ui*,
as in *brut* (1), *trute* (62); *lëaul* (25) for *le(i)al*; *boin*
(60) for *bon*; preservation of final *t*, as in *ainmet* (23),
Ferreit (50); *lou* (34) for *le*; 3rd-pers. sing. pres. ind.
ait (26,27,43) for *a*.
Note that in the language of the poet there is no pertinent distinction between *u* and *ui*; thus, l. 40 *cure* rhymes
with l. 41 *desduire*.

N   Though anonymous in its sole ms. source, there can
be little doubt of the authorship of this poem; both stylis-
tically and thematically, it clearly recalls the work of
Colin Muset. For details, see Bédier *Col*, pp. xv-xvi.

35 *C'* = *que*, relative pronoun frequently found in Lorraine
texts functioning as a subject.   44 *qui* 'whoever'.   48
lous = *los* 'renown, honor'.   49 'This should suffice in
his favor'.   57 'Into combat in war'.   60 Rather than
the name of a tavernkeeper, as in Jeanroy-Långfors, *(Au) Bon
Ferré* is no doubt, as proposed in Bédier *Col*, pp. 69-70, the
name of a tavern, *ferré* being a kind of wine (see Tobler-
Lommatzsch, s.v. *ferrer*) and the adverb 1. 61 *La* serving to
confirm its designation of a place.   *que* (for *qui*) *bien
ferre* 'which makes you good and drunk'.   65 *raverdie*
usually designates a kind of song celebrating love and the
return of spring, and that is the meaning attributed to its
present occurrence by previous editors of this poem as well
as Tobler-Lommatzsch.   In view of the context, however, and
a few attestations provided in Tobler-Lommatzsch under the
various entry-forms *raverdie*, *renverdie*, and *reverdie*, we
suggest as no less likely the sense of 'picnic', with a particularly strong overtone of amorous play.   Cf. st. 5 of
Colin's song RS 582, which evokes the delights of *le jeu de
praiel*.   One sense, of course, hardly precludes the other,
and instances are not unknown in which a reference to song
or dance acts as a transparent mask for sexual activity;
see, for example, the "teaching" of the *virelai* in stanzas 5
and 6 of RS 2084 (Bartsch, p. 293).

                        Reverdie, lai   <u>179</u>

RS 972, MW 4, 16
Mss. U 78r-v-79r-v, C 226v-227r. No music. Attribution in
    C.

    I   Sospris sui d'une amorette
          D'une jone pucelette.
          Belle est et blonde et blanchette
          Plus que n'est une erminette,
          S'a la color vermeillette   5
          Ensi com une rosette.

    II   Itels estoit la pucele,
          La fille au roi de Tudele;
          D'un drap d'or qui reflambele
          Ot robe fresche et novele;   10
          Mantel, sorcot et gonele
          Mout sist bien a la donzelle.

III   En son chief ot chapel d'or
        Ki reluist et estancele;
        Saphirs, rubiz ot encor   15
        Et mainte esmeraude bele.
        Biaus Deus, cor fusse je or
        Amis a tel damoisele!

IV   Sa ceinture fut de soie,
        D'or et de pieres ovree;   20
        Toz li cors li reflamboie,
        Ensi fut enluminee.
        Or me doinst Deus de li joie,
        K'aillors nen ai ma panseie.

V   G'esgardai son cors gai,   25
        Qui tant me plaist et agree.
          Je morrai, bien lo sai,
        Tant l'ai de cuer enameie.
          Se Deu plaist, non ferai,
        Ainçois m'iert s'amors donee.   30

VI   En un trop bel vergier
        La vi cele matinee
          Jüer et solacier;
        Ja par moi n'iert obliee,
          Car bien sai, senz cuidier,   35
        Ja si bele n'iert trovee.

VII   Lez un rosier s'est assise
        La tres bele et la sennee;
        Ele resplant a devise
        Com estoile a l'anjornee.   40
        S'amors m'esprent et atise,
        Qui enz el cuer m'est entree.

VIII   El regarder m'obliai
        Tant qu'ele s'en fu alee.
        Deus! tant mar la resgardai,   45
        Quant si tost m'est eschapee,
        Que ja mais joie n'avrai
        Se par li ne m'est donee.

IX   Tantost com l'oi regardee,
        Bien cuidai qu'ele fust fee.   50
        Ne lairoie por riens nee
        Q'encor n'aille en sa contree,

Tant que j'aie demandee
S'amor, ou mes fins cuers bee.

X   Et s'ele devient m'amie,   55
     Ma granz joie iert acomplie,
     Ne je n'en prendroie mie
     Lo roialme de Surie,
     Car trop meine bone vie
     Qui aime en tel seignorie.   60

XI   Deu pri qu'il me face aïe,
     Que d'autre nen ai envie.

<u>N</u>   The stanzaic correspondences in this poem are re-
markable, as shown by the following schema:

It is the careful balance of this structure that we believe
justifies the reduction of ll. 13, 15, and 17 from octosyl-
lables to heptasyllables (see Rejected Readings), the longer
verses being rather clearly the product of scribal misinter-
pretation; for an opposing view, see Bédier *Col*, p. 54. For
a note on *reverdies*, see RS 1039 (Guillaume le Vinier). For
a recent discussion of the *lai* and bibliography, see Bec 1,
pp. 189-208.
     8 *Tudele*, in Navarre, is often named in OF works in
association with ideas of riches and power; for appearances
in lyric poetry, see PetDyg "Onom", p. 246.   17 *cor*, used,
like *car*, to introduce a wish or an imperative.   35 *senz
cuidier* 'without illusion'.   39 *a devise* 'as much as could
be wished'.   51-52 'For no creature born would I renounce
returning to her country'.   57-58 'Nor would I trade it
for the kingdom of Syria (the Holy Land)'.

RR   I   6 Plus que nest u. r. *(em. Bédier)*   III
13 chief sor ot *(+1)*   15 rubiz i ot *(+1)*   17 deus et
cor *(+1)*   IV   23 doist   V   26 plaisst et agre

V   I   1 seux   II   7 Iteile est la damoiselle
8 Fille est a roi de t.   9 ke restancelle   12 siet
III   13 En s. ch. sor ot ch. d.   15 S. r. i ot entor
16 maintes   17 Et iu ke fui se ieu   18 A. a la d.   IV
20 oureis   22 Si com fust enlumineis   V   25 Ieu esgardai   26 Ke trop   27 Ien   29 Non ferai se deu plaist
30 samor   VI   31 un *missing*   35 sai senz *missing*
VII   37 Leis un uergier cest a.   38 belle la senee   41
Samor mamprant et a.   42 Ke   VIII   43 A li r. m.   44
fut   IX   49 lo esgardeie   51 rien   X   55 celle
56 grant; aseuie   XI   61 men

E   Tarbé *Chans*, 81; Hofmann "Anzahl", 520-522;
Bartsch, 355-357; Bédier *Nic*, 93; Jeanroy *Lais*, 9-11; Bédier
Col, 15-17; Pauphilet, 907-909; Spaziani *Ant*, 71-73; Cremonesi, 153-156; Chastel, 680-685; Pottier, 91-92; Toja, 295-
298; Bec 2, 63-65.

DF   Lorraine: *ei* for tonic *e* in *panseie* (24), *enameie*
(28); *lo* (27, 58) for *le*.

180   Descort

RS 1302, MW 902, 17
Mss. U 77r-v-78r, C 170r-v. No music. Attribution in C.

I   Quant voi lo douz tens repairier,
         Que li rosignols chante en mai,
         Et je cuiz que doie alegier
         Li mals et la dolors que j'ai,   4
         Adonc m'ocïent li delai
         D'Amors, qui les font engregnier.
         Lais! mar vi onques son cors gai
         S'a ma vie ne lo conquier.   8

II   Amors de moi ne cuide avoir pechiez
      Por ceu que sui ses hom liges sosgiez.
      Douce dame, pregne vos en pitiez!
      Qui plus s'abasse, plus est essauciez.   12

III   Et qant si grant chose empris ai
      Con de vostre amor chalengier,
      Toz tens en pardons servirai
      Se tout n'en ai altre loieir.   16
      Ma tres douce dame honoree,
       Je ne vos os nes proier:
      Cil est mout fols qui si haut bee
      Ou il nen ose aprochier.   20

IV   Mais tote voie
      Tres bien revoudroie
      Vostre amors fust moie
      Por moi ensengnier,   24
       Car a grant joie
      Vit et s'esbanoie
      Cui Amors maistroie;
      Meux s'en doit prosier.   28

V   Qui bien vuet d'amors joïr
      Si doit soffrir
      Et endurer
     Qan k'ele li vuet merir;   32
      Au repentir
      Ne doit panser,
     C'om puet bien tot a loisir
      Son boen desir   36
      A point mener.
     Endroit de moi, criem morir
      Meuz que garir
      Par bien amer.   40

VI   Se je n'ai la joie grant
      Que mes fins cuers va chacent,
      Deffenir m'estuet briément.
      Douce riens por cui je chant, 44
      En mon descort vos demant
      Un ris debonairement,
      S'en vivrai plus longemant;
      Moins en avrai de torment. 48

VII   Bele, j'ai si grant envie
      D'embracier vostre cors gent,
      S'Amors ne m'en fait aïe,
      J'en morrai coiteusement.   52
      Amors ne m'en faudrat mie,
      Car je l'ai trop bien servie
      Et ferai tote ma vie

Senz nule fause pansee.   56
Preuz de tote gent löee
Plus que nule qui soit nee,
Se vostre amors m'est donee,
Bien iert ma joie doublee.   60

VIII   Mon descort ma dame aport,
        La bone duchesse, por chanter.
          De toz biens a li m'acort,
        K'ele aime deport, rire et jüer.   64

IX   Dame, or vos voil bien mostrer
              Que je ne sai vostre per
              De bone vie mener
              Et de leialment amer.   68
              Adés vos voi enmender
              En vaillance et en doner:
              Ne.l lassiez ja por jangler,
              Que ceu ne vos puet grever.   72

    V   I   1 Or   3 cuit   4 dolour   II   9 pechiet
10 ces liges hons sougis   12 e. haities   III   13 ai
missing   15 perdon   16 Se tost   19 e. trop f.   20
Com ni o.   IV   22 T. b. uoroie   23 amor   26 senba-
noie   28 Bien se d.   V   33 A   38 cuit m.   40 Por
VI   42 Ke mes cuers desire tant   44 rien   VII   52
prochiennement   53 ne me   54 tous iors s.   57 Plux
59 amor   VIII-IX   63-65 De tous biens moustreir   69
amendeir   72 Kil ne uos puet riens g.

    E   Tarbé *Chans*, 85; Bédier *Nic*, 114; Jeanroy *Lais*,
11-13; Bartsch-Wiese, 250-251; Brittain, 189-191; Bédier
Col, 13-15; Henry *Chrest* 1, 241-242; 2, 72.

    DF   Lorraine, including *ai* for *a*, as in *lais* (7); *a*
for *ai,* as in *s'abasse* (12), *lassiez* (71); *ei* for tonic *e,*
as in *loieir* (16); *o* for *oi*, as in *prosier* (28); *boen* (36)
for *bon*; *meux* (28) and *meuz* (39) for *mieuz*; preservation of
final *t*, as in *faudrat* (53); *ceu* (10) for *ce*; *lo* (1, 8) for
le.

    N   3 *doie*, third-person singular present subjunctive
of *devoir*; subject is 1. 4 *Li mals et la dolors*. 7 *mar vi
onques* 'woe that I ever saw'. 9 'Love does not think it
has wronged me'. 15 *en pardons* 'in vain'. 22-23 Understand *que* between *revoudroie* and *Vostre*. 27 *Cui* 'whom-
ever'. 47 *S'* = *si* 'and so'. 47-48 Jeanroy *Lais*

unnecessarily transposes these lines.   61 *ma dame*, ind.
obj. of *aport*.   61-72 For Jeanroy *Lais*, "il paraît évident
que les deux dernières [strophes] doivent être transposées."
Bédier *Col*, p. 52, rejects the idea.   The *Dame* of l. 65 is
La bone duchesse of l. 62 and a different personage from l.
49 *Bele*; the ms. ordering of stanzas makes that clear.

                Tenson with Jacques d'Amiens   181

RS 1966, MW 607
Ms. C 35v-36r. No music. Attributed to Jacques d'Amiens.

I   Colins Musés, je me plaing d'une amor
            Ke longuement ai servie
        De loiaul cuer, n'ains pitiet [ne retor]
            N'i pou troveir, nen aïe;
        S'i truis je mult semblans de grant dousor, 5
        Maix ce m'est vis ke il sont traïtor,
        Ke bouche et cuers ne s'i acordent mie.

II   --Jaikes d'Amiens, laissiés ceste folor!
            Fueis fauce drüerie,
        N'en biaul semblant ne vos fieis nul jor: 10
            Cil est musairs ki s'i fie.
        Pués ke troveis son cuer amenteor,
        Se plux l'ameis, sovent duel et irour
        En avereis, et pix ke je ne die.

III   --Colin Muset, ne m'iert pais deshonor   15
            Se de li fais departie.
        Pués c'ai troveit son samblant tricheor,
            Porchaicerai moy d'amie,
        Car je li ai veü faire teil tour
        Et teil samblant et teil ensaigne aillors   20
        Per coy je hais li et sa compaignie.

IV   --Jaikes d'Amiens, il n'est duels ne irour
            Fors ke vient de jalousie.
        Povres amans sousfre mainte dolor
            Ki baie a grant signorie,   25
        Et un usaige ont borjoises tous jors:
        Jai n'amerait, tant soit de grant richour,
        Home, s'il n'ait la borce bien garnie.

V   --Colins Musés, gentils dame ait honor
            Ke a ceu ne baie mie,   30

Maix lai ou voit sen, prouesce et valour,
    Joliveteit, cortoisie.
La fauce lais por ceu, se m'en retour
A la belle, la blonde et la millor
Ki onkes fust d'amors nul jor proïe.   35

VI   --Jaikes d'Amiens, et j' arant m'en retour
          As chaippons a jance aillie
      Et as gastiauls ki sont blanc come flor
          Et a tres boen vin sor lie.
      As boens morcés ai donee m'amor   40
      Et as grans feus per mi ceste froidour:
      Faites ensi, si moinrés bone vie!

VII   --Colin Muset, kier t'aixe et ton sejor
      Et je querrai d'amors joie et baudor,
      Car consireir d'amors ne me puis mie.   45

      RR   I   1 Biaus Colins muses *(+1)*   2 Ke lons ai s.
(-2; em. Bédier)   3 *-3 (em. Gaston Paris as cited by
Bédier)*   5 semblant   IV   28 H. cil   VI   37 As
grais chaippons et a la jancellie *(+3)*

      E   Tarbé *Chans*, 94; Bédier *Nic*, 127; Simon, 47;
Bédier *Col*, 7-9; Pauphilet, 914-915.

      DF   Lorraine, including *ai* for *a*, as in *Jaikes* (8),
pais (15), *porchaicerai* (18); *lai* (31); *ei* for tonic *e*, as
in *troveir* (4), *fueis* (9), *teil* (19); *loiaul* (3) for *loial*
and *biaul* (10) for *beau*; *boen* (39) for *bon*; preservation of
final *t*, as in *pitiet* (3), *troveit* (17); *pués* (12) for *puis*;
ceu (30) for *ce*; adverbial *se* (33) for *si*; 3rd-pers. sing.
pres. ind. *ait* (28) for *a*; 3rd-pers. sing. fut. in *-ait*, as
in *amerait* (27). Picard: epenthesized future *avereis* (14);
final *ie* for *iee*, as in *proïe* (35).

      N   12 *amenteor* 'mendacious' is apparently unattested
elsewhere, and Bédier *Col* and others may be right to read *a
menteor*. The *trover* construction, however, is not normally
found with *a* before the adjective, nor is it in l. 17.   18
'I shall find myself [another] mistress'.   26-27 Shift
from plur. *ont borjoises* to sing. *n'amerait* and *soit* is
somewhat awkward, though not palpably incorrect. No emendation is necessary; see Bédier *Col*, p. 49.   30 Relative *Ke*
(= *que*) serves here as subject.   36 *j'arant* = *je errant* 'I
right away'.   37 *jance aillie* 'garlic sauce'.   39 *sor
lie* 'well decanted'.

Chanson

RS 1091, MW 2002
Ms. a 77r-v. Music. Attribution.

I   Poissans Amours a mon cuer espiié
      Qui, passé a lonc tans, n'avoit amé
      Par chou que mors m'en avoit eslongié,
      Ne mais n'avoie a amer enpensé;   4
          Se j'amai jour de ma vie
          Ma douche dame jolie,
      Dont mors et Dius ont fait lor volenté,
      Jou me cuidai avoir bien aquité.   8

II   Avoir cuidai a tous jours renonchié
      A bien amer, u j'ai tout conquesté,
      Et tant je ai le musage paiié
      Que me deüst bien avoir deporté;   12
          Mais Amours, qui tout maistrie,
          M'a remis en l'aubourdie

Et fait amer de nouvele amisté
Saje et vaillant et passant de biauté.   16

III Et puis qu'Amours m'a sus ses mains sakié,
     Dame vaillans, et a vous m'a douné,
     Je tiens mon cuer a mout bien enploié
     Se vous deigniés seulement prendre en gré   20
          Que de moi soiés servie;
          Et s'il ne vous plaisoit mie,
     S'ert il ensi, car j'ai mout bien usé
     A [vous] servir, pieche [a], et enduré.   24

IV   De chou que n'ai, lon tans a, conmenchié
     Vous a amer, me tieng a engané:
     De tant m'a trop Amors despaisiié
     Q'a vous servir m'a si tart descouplé;   28
          Nepourqant est a la fie
          Uevre bien tart conmenchie
     Mout pourfitans, car, s'on a bien ouvré,   31
     Ch'a fait li cuer, nient li lonc jour d'esté.

V   Dame, s'Amours m'a trop tart acointié
     Le bien de vous, le sens et le bonté,
     Je n'en puis mais; j'amasse le moitié
     Mieus que plus tost m'i eüst assené   36
          Si c'un grant pan de ma vie
          Vous eüsse ançois coisie;
     Mais jou ne sai u vous avés esté
     Entreus que j'ai mon tans pour nient gasté. 40

VI   Dame de valour [garnie],
          Courte orison bien furnie
     Vaut assés mieus, che dïent li sené,
     Que s'on avoit bien longement limé.   44

MN   Form: A A B; the envoy is sung to ll. 5-8.

RR   I   5 Se jamais   II 9 tout   11 jai *(-1)*
15 nouuel amistie   III   24 *-2; em. Raynaud*   IV   29
feie 30 Vueure   VI 41 *-2; em. Raynaud*

E   Raynaud, 330-331.

DF   Picard, including *ie* for *iee*, as in *fie* (29),
conmenchie (30); *iu* for *ieu*, as in *Dius* (7); *ch* for *c*, as in
douche (6), *pieche* (24), *ch'* (32), *che* (43); *k* or *c* for *ch*,

as in *sakié* (17), *coisie* (38); *chou* (3) for *ce*; *jou* (8) for
je; *le* (34, 35) for *la*.

    N̲   This song is most unusual in its concern with the
unexpected rebirth of love after the death of the poet's
first mistress.   11-12 'And so much did I pay for my idle
pleasure that it should have satisfied me'.   17 'And since
Love has taken me in hand'.   29 *a la fie* 'in the end'.
35-38 The sense is: 'I treasure the half [I now have] more
than [what I would have had if Love] had allowed me to meet
you much earlier in my life'.

                         Chanson   183

RS 1355, MW 2100
Ms. a 75v-76r.   Music.   Attribution.

1. Uns dous regars en larrechin soutieus
3. qu'ele me fist de l'un de ses dous ieus,
2. de ma dame que j'ai en remembranche,
4. retient mon cuer en jolie esperanche
5. d'avoir merchi qant li venra en gre;
6. et s'amors m'a tant de bien destine,
7. j'avrai ma joie ains que soit deservie,
8. car deservir ne le porroie mie.

I   Uns dous regars en larrechin soutieus
     De ma dame que j'ai en ramenbranche,
     Qu'ele me fist de l'un de ses dous ieus,
     Retient mon cuer en jolie esperanche   4
     D'avoir merchi qant li venra en gré;

Et s'amors m'a tant de bien destiné,
J'avrai ma joie ains que soit deservie,
Car deservir ne le porroie mie.   8

II   Se Dieus m'aït, douche dame gentieus,
        Se j'avoie le roiaume de Franche
        Et vous amasse aveuc chou cent tans mieus
        Que jou ne faic, n'aroie jou poissanche   12
        De deservir la merci u je bé;
        Mais vous avés de vostre autorité
        Forche et pooir de faire courtoisie
        A vostre ami, se vo fins cuers l'otrie.   16

III   Cors avenans, a bien faire ententieus,
        En qui jou ai ma sovraine fianche,
        Je sui adés de vos servir taskieus,
        Et com plus vif, plus ai grant abondance   20
        De desirer vo bone volenté;
        Si voie jou vo cuer entalenté
        De moi aidier, com jou vous ai servie
        En bone foi et servirai ma vie.   24

IV   Bele cui j'aim, se je sui volentieus
        De mon preu faire et j'eskieu vo grevanche
        Et je vous serf desirans et doutieus
        Et gart vo pais, ch'est bien senefianche   28
        Que jou ne kier fors droite loiauté;
        S'aferroit bien que par humulité
        Me deignisiés conforter a le fie
        Cheleement, sans blasme et sans folie.   32

V   Dame de moi, se poins venoit et lieus
        Que deignisiés a moi faire pitanche,
        Si vous proi jou d'eskiever les perieus,
        Vostres et miens, et toute perchevanche: 36
        Li biens d'amours doivent si estre emblé
        Que nus ne.s sache; et qant il sont crïé,
        Dame en queut blasme et joie en amenrie
        Et fins amis i pert sa seignorie.   40

VI   Sire Audefroi, qant dame fait bonté
        A son ami, che doit estre en secré,
        Q'amours criee est mout adamagie;
        Garder s'en doit et amis et amie.   44

/   MN   Form: A A B; the envoy is sung to ll. 5-8.
1. In l. 1 ms. writes no flat.

RR   I   3   ieus] ius   IV   31   fie] fre   V   39
en quel   VI   43   crie

E   Raynaud, 327-328.

DF   Picard, including *ie* for *iee*, as in *fie* (31),
adamagie (43); *ieu* for *if*, as in *eskieu* (26); *ieus* for *is*,
as in *soutieus* (1), *gentieus* (9), *ententieus* (17); *ch* for *c*,
as in *larrechin* (1), *ramenbranche* (2), *merchi* (5), *ch'* (28),
che (42); *chou* (11) for *ce*; *jou* (12) for *je*; *le* (8, 31) for
la; *venra* (5) for *vendra*; *aroie* (12) for *avroie*; 1st-pers.
sing. pres. ind. in -*c*, as in *faic* (12); *vo* (16) for *vostre*.

N   31   *a la fie* 'in the end'.   41   PetDyg "Onom",
pp. 42-43, identifies *Audefroi* as Audefroi Louchart, a rich
bourgeois of Arras, named in a number of poems and appearing
as a partner of Jehan Bretel in several *jeux-partis*.

Jeu-parti (partner: Adam de la Halle)   184

RS 950, MW 2464
Mss. W 26r-26v, A 150v-151r, Q 322v, a 178r-v.   Music in all
mss. except Q.   Attribution in W.

1. A-dan, a moi re-spon-des 2. con lais hom a cest af- fai- re,
3. car ne sai point de gra-mai- re, 4. et vous e-stes bien le-tres.
5. Le quel a-ries vous plus chier: 6. ou vo dame a ga-ain-gnier
7. ou-tre son gre, par droi-te tra-i-son,
8. ou li ser-vir loi- au-ment en par-don
9. tres-tou-te vo vi-e 10. et si s'en tiegne a pa-i- e?

I   Adan, a moi respondés
Con lais hom a cest affaire,
Car ne sai point de gramaire,
Et vous estes bien letrés.
Le quel ariés vous plus chier: 5
Ou vo dame a gaaingnier
Outre son gré, par droite traïson,
Ou li servir loiaument en pardon
      Trestoute vo vie
Et si s'en tiengne a païe?   10

II   --Sire, on voit les plus senés
A le fois traïson faire
Pour riqueche a eus atraire.
Que me pourfite li grés
De me dame, au droit jugier,   15
Qui m'ara fait traveillier
Tout mon vivant sans autre guerredon?
A ses autres biens voeil avoir parchon,
      Se n'i faurrai mie
Se le truis appareillie.   20

III   --Adan, jamais ne prendés
Cose ou traïson repaire,
C'a tous fins cuers doit desplaire.
Certes, che me samble assés
Quant on set tant esploitier   25
C'on set sa dame paier
Par li servir en droite entention.
En li traïr conquerre ne puet on
      Si grant singnourie,
Et si l'a on courouchie.   30

IV   --Sire, a chou que dit avés,
En vous a foivle contraire.
Comment puet li hom meffaire
Qui a parture est menés
De deus maus, s'il laist glachier   35
Le pïeur pour li aidier
Dou mains mauvais! Sans acomplir mon bon,
Ne porroie finer se par mort non.
      Mieus vient querre aïe
C'atendre si grief haschie.   40

V   --Adan, fort me trouverés
Et deffensavle adversaire,
Car au pïeur vous voi traire

       Pour chou que trop goulousés
       Chou qui ne vous a mestier.   45
       On doit savoir sans cuidier
    Que loiautés est de fine boichon
    Et traïson de trop vilain renon,
         Par coi chascuns prie
       Que traïson soit honnie.   50

VI   --Sire, chis cas est prouvés
       Que traïson ne doit plaire;
       Mais ma dame est debonnaire;
       Par coi, se je sui outrés
       Par forche de desirier,   55
       Si l'en cuit jou apaier.
    A sen besoing fait on bien mesproison
    Sour cuidance de pais et de pardon.
        Grans pais, coi c'on die,
       Gist en grant guerre a le fie.   60

VII   --Ferri, bon se fait gaitier
    De commenchier outrage ne tenchon
    Sour l'espoir de venir a raenchon.
       Li faus se cointie
       Dont li sages se castie.   65

VIII   --Grieviler, ne doi cachier
    Vers ma dame simpleche ne raison,
    Car volentiers tient femme a compaignon,
        Tant l'ai assaïe,
       Chelui qui bien le manie.   70

    <u>MN</u> Ms. A has a second melody; ms. a has a third.
Form: through-composed; both envoys are sung to ll. 6-10.

    <u>RR</u>   I   7 son] uo   III   23 Car   26 C. s. de d.
apaier   28 traïr] seruir   IV   31 a] en   VI   58
cuidante

    <u>V</u>   I   5 q. aues AQa   8 seruirs a   II   14 Ki
a   <u>15</u> De celi au d. j. AQa   16 trauuillier A   18 g.
par cou Aa   19 Si Aa   20 li Aa   III   22 traisons
Q   25 set] puet AQa   26 set] puet Q   IV   32 f.
corage A   35 s'il laist *missing in Q*, si l. Aa   36 Que
Q   38 mort] moi Aa   V   42 auersaile A   44 Par AQa
45 Conq(u)este (-s A) qui (ki A) na m. AQa   48 traisons Q   50 traisons AQ   VI   52 traisons Q   56 Si

missing in Q; j. bien pai(i)er (apaiier   Q)   AQa   59   Grant
Aa; condoie   A   VII   61   garder   A   64   cointoie   A

E   Coussemaker, 152-156; Nicod, 68-72; Långfors *Rec*
2, 51-54; Wilkins, 33-34.

DF   Picard, including final *ie* for *iee*, as in *païe*
(10), *appareillie* (20); *ch* for *c* or *ç*, as in *parchon* (18),
che (24), *courouchie* (30), *tenchon* (62); *qu* or *c* for *ch*, as
in *riqueche* (13), *cose* (22), *castie* (65); *vle* for *ble*, as in
foivle (32), *deffensavle* (42); *ariés* (5) and *ara* (16) for
avriez, *avra*; article *le* (12, 60) for *la*; pronoun *le* (20)
for *la*; *me* (15) for *ma*; *sen* (57) for *son*; *jou* (56) for *je*;
chou (31) for *ce*; *chis* (51) for *cil*; *vo* (6) for *vostre*.

N   Jehan Bretel poses the question: which is preferable, to win one's lady against her will or to serve her
selflessly with the sole reward of seeing her pleased?   Adam
chooses the first alternative.   Ferri and Grieviler are
called on to judge the debate.   2 *Con lais hom*, 'as a lay-
man, unschooled man, i.e., in terms I will understand'.   13
eus, reflexive; likewise, l. 36 *li*.   19 'And so I shall
not fail [to do what I wish] if I find her accessible'.   47
The meaning of *boichon* is not clear.   Nicod risks no guess
at all.   Långfors 2 suggests 'arrow', with reference to
Tobler-Lommatzsch, s.v. *bouzon*, which, however, is not of
the same gender.   Nevertheless, the form is apparently a
regular Picard equivalent of Central *boiçon*, and the idea of
linking loyalty with a drink can hardly be improbable in a
society that easily granted brews and potions the power to
produce various emotions and virtues.   Or else, the link is
moral and socio-esthetic, the "courtoisie" of loyalty and
good wine standing opposed to all that is *vilain* (l. 48).
59-60 Variant of proverbs cited in Morawski, nos. 110 and
501.   65 *Dont* 'de ce dont'.

185   Jeu-parti (partner: Jehan de Grieviler)

RS 693, MW 2250
Mss. a 154r-v, b 159v-160r.   Music in a.   Attribution in b.

B
5. que sa feme aint et qu'e-le soit a- me- e,

6. mais n'en set nient, se çou n'est pas pen- se- e,

7. u cil ki set que sa feme a a- me

8. et que ses a- mis a sa vo- len- te

9. l'eut main-tes fois, mais four-ju-re- e l'a,

10. et se- urs est que ja- mais n'a-ven- ra?

I   Grieviler, un jugement
           Me faites de deus maris:
           Li qels a plus de tourmens,
           U chieus ki cuide toudis
Que sa feme aint et qu'ele soit amee,   5
Mais n'en set nient, se çou n'est pas pensee,
U cil ki set que sa feme a amé
Et que ses amis a sa volenté
L'eut maintes fois mais fourjuree l'a,
Et seürs est que jamais n'avenra?   10

II   --Sire Bretel, erroment
           Vous en sera li voirs dis.
           Cil a cuer dolent souvent
           Qui de sa feme est tous fis
K'ele a esté par autrui violee,   15
Mais sa dolours est aukes trespassee;
Je di que chil a trop plus de griété
Ki adés a en cuer et en pensé
Ke sa feme aint: ja dolour ne morra
En cuer jalous tant coum' il le savra.   20

III   --Grieviler, mauvaisement
             Savés jugier, ce m'est vis.
             Voirs est que grant dolour sent
             Cuers jalous, mais cent tans pis
A cil ki set k'il a honte prouvee;   25
La vergoune est adés renouvelee
De viés pecié; cil qui n'a riens prouvé
Se repent bien qant il a tant dasé
En sa folie, et sa dolours tresva;
Mais cil qui set ne l'oublīera ja.   30

IV   --Sire, sachiés vraiement
             Que jou n'ai de riens mespris;
             Bien dirai raison coument
             Li jalous est plus maris.
Jalous n'a pais ne soir ne matinee;   35
D'ire a toustans la cervele escaufee;
Il n'a en lui nul point de fermeté;
Toutans cuid' il c'on li ait tout emblé.
Tel mal n'a pas li wihos qui piecha
Fu et bien set que mais n'i enkerra.   40

V   --Jehan, trop plus cruelment
             Est tourmentés et hounis
             Cil qui tout certainement
             Set k'il fu wihos jadis;
A tous jours mais en harra s'espousee;   45
En haant ert sa dolour demenee.
Mais li jalous mescroit par amisté;
Jalousie vient de fine chierté;
Ja amoureus tourment ne grevera
Tant con cil qui de haīne venra.   50

VI   --Bretel, nus maus ne se prent
             A jalous; bien est traīs
             Li hom ki teus maus souprent.
             Toustans a le cuer espris
D'ire et d'anui et de paour dervee.   55
Li jalous boit par an mainte orde euwee,
Mais li wihos a le mal pas passé
Puis qu'il voit bien et est en seürté
Que sa feme mais autrui n'amera.
Par tant di jou que li jalous pis a.   60

VII   --Robert amis, çou c'on set est outré,
      Mais en cuidier n'a fors que vanité.

Li viés ferus plus se gramĭera
Que li nouviaus manechiés ne fera.

VIII --Jaket, on doit mieus tenir a navré   65
Le jalous cuer que le wiot sané:
Maus trespassés ja tant ne se daurra
Coume chil fait qui tout adés tenra.

<u>MN</u>   Form: A A B.
1. In l. 1 ms. writes no rest.

<u>RR</u>   III   25 set] seut   IV   36 le ceruel escaufe
V   46 Et   47 amistie

<u>V</u>   Stanzas VII and VIII not included in b.
I   3 Le quel, torment   4 cui c. t.   6 nient] riens   8
son ami   9 Lot mainte   10 namera   II   12 uoir d.
16 doleur a a.   17 pl. grant gr.   20 t. que il   III
22 S. choisir   24 Cuer   25 ot h.   27 pechiez   29
first sa *missing*, doleur   IV   36 a tous iours   V   43
C. q. set c.   44 Que il f. w. j.   47 M. le 49 tormens
50 T. com celui q. de h. v.   VI   51 Sire n.   52 Au
53 tel mal   54 Tous temps est son c. emplis   56 Le   58
b. quil en a s.   59 Et que sa f. iamais iour n.   60
Pour, le j.

<u>E</u>   Långfors *Rec* 1, 140-143.

<u>DF</u>   Picard: -au- for -ou- and no epenthesis in *daurra*
(67) for *doudra*; unepenthesized futures *avenra* (10), *venra*
(50), *tenra* (68); *chieus* (4) for *cilz*, *manechiés* (64) for
menaciés, *piecha* (39) for *pieça*; *pecié* (27) for *pechié*; *escaufee* (36) for *eschaufee*; *çou* (6) for *ce* and *jou* (60) for
je.

<u>N</u>   Jehan Bretel poses the question: is there greater
unhappiness in always suspecting one's wife of infidelity
and never knowing the truth, or in knowing of a past infidelity and being sure there will be no recurrence? Grieviler finds greater unhappiness in constant suspicion.
Robert and Jaket are asked to judge the exchange.
20 Långfors substitutes *sera* (ms. b) for *savra* and
glosses "'tant qu'il sera jaloux'," adding that the rejected
reading could "à la rigueur" mean "'aussi longtemps qu'il
aura la certitude de son malheur'." The emendation is hardly necessary, for *tant coum'* may just as readily mean 'until'; thus, 'never will pain die in a jealous heart until he

knows so' [*le* = *ke sa feme aime*]. This reading is supported
by Bretel's contradiction in 1. 30, *cil qui set ne l'oublie-
ra ja*, and by the repeated insistence on "knowing" in 1. 40
and throughout.   26-27 Cf. Morawski, no. 574: *De viez
pechié novele vergoigne.*   34   *maris* 'tormented'.   63-64
'The man hurt in the past will feel more pain than the one
who has just been threatened'.

<u>186</u>   Jeu-parti (partner: Jehan de Grieviler)

RS 1346, MW 1964
Mss. a 155v-156r, c 1v. Music in a. Attribution in text.

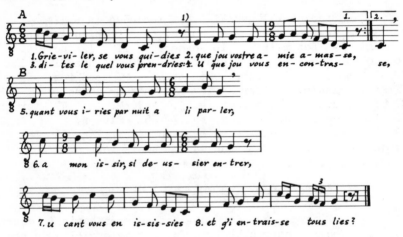

I   Grieviler, se vous quidiés
             Que jou vostre amie amasse,
             Dites le quel vous prendriés:
             U que jou vous encontrasse,   4
         Qant vous iriés par nuit a li parler,
         A mon issir, si deüssiés entrer,
             U cant vous en ississiés
             Et g'i entraisse tous liés?   8

II   --Sire Jehan, che sachiés:
             Se courechier vous ossaise,
             Ja respondus n'en fuisiés,
             Car ne voi bonté ne grasse   12
         En nul des deus; mais pour vous hounerer
         Responc: je vous aim mieus a encontrer
             Qant vous entrer i devriés
             Et j'en istroie paiiés.   16

III   --Grieviler, vous kieusisiés
             Le pïeur, qar trop se quaise
             Qui d'amie est eslongiés
             Et son anemi i laisse.   20
        Cent tans de duel ariés a recorder
        Les biens que je porroie en li trouver
             Que se parti m'en saviés
             Et vous i demouriciés.   24

IV   --Bretel, bien voi les meschiés.
             Ja a çou ne m'acordaisse,
             Mais li trouvers est trop griés.
             Sachiés que chil trop s'abaisse   28
        Qui avant veut le bien [autrui] douner
        Dont il languist et muert par desirer;
             Chil qui avant est baigniés
             N'est mie plus cunquïés.   32

V   --Grieviler, vous vous aidiés
             De çou dont point ne m'aidasse.
             Cil est assés mains quaisiés
             Qui englot chou c'on li maske.   36
        Li premiers n'a fait fors eskapeler;
        Li deerains qui fait l'uevre asoumer
             Clot l'uis, s'est li mieus logiés
             Li daerains aaisiés.   40

VI   --Sire, del pïeur plaidiés;
             Envers vous bien le prouvaise
             S'entendre me vausisiés.
             Trop vilainement se quaisse   44
        Qui d'amie se veut tant consirer
        K'autres i puist devant lui abiter.
             J'aim [mieus] a prendre haitiés
             Mon deduit que courechiés.   48

VII   --Simon Pouchin, cil qui veut sormonter
       Son anemi el camp doit demourer
             Daerrains: cil est plaisiés
             Ki premiers en est cachiés.   52

VIII   --Jaket, Triamodés seut bien parler
       Premierement, che li fist conquester
             Maintes teres et mains fiés.
             Mieus vaut li nués que li viés.   56

MN   Form: A A B; both envoys are sung to ll. 5-8.
1. In l. 1 ms. writes no rest.

RR   I   3 prendes 7 issies *(-1)*   II   15 deue-
ries *(+1)*   16 jsteroie *(+1)*   III   21 Cent ans   22 je
missing   IV   29 *-2 (em. Långfors)*   30 desirier   V
39 cest   VI   47 *-1 (em. Långfors)*

V   Stanzas IV through VIII not included in c.
I 2 je *missing*   6 si] et   II   11 respondu   12 Que
ny   14 Responc je *missing*; a *missing*   15 entrer i *missing*; venriez   III   18 · Le p. que t. se irasse   20 Et
sen aucun i l.   21 Car temps   23 men samee   24 *ms. mutilation leaves only* vous *and* demouriez

E   Långfors *Rec* 1, 133-136.

DF   Picard, including free variation of *-s-*, *-ss-*,
and *-c-*, as in *quaise* (18), *quaisse* (44), *grasse* (12), *de-
mouriciés* (24); *maske* (36) for *masche*; imp. subj. in *-aisse*,
as in *entraisse* (8), *acordaisse* (26); *ch-* for c- [s], as in
courechier (10), *chil* (28); *c-* [k] for *ch-*, as well as the
preceding feature, in *cachiés* (52) for *chaciez* and *k-* for
ch-, as in *eskapeler* (37); *jou* (4) for *je* and *çou* (26) or
chou (36) for *ce*; 1st-pers. *responc* (14) for *respont*; *ariés*
(21) for *avriez*; *deerains* (38) for *derniers*. The rhymes
show that in the dialect of the poets themselves the equiva-
lents of Francien *amasse*, *grace*, etc., and *laisse*, *s'a-
baisse*, etc., all contain the same vowel phoneme.

N   Jehan Bretel poses the question: supposing I love
your mistress, would you prefer to see me leaving her house
when you arrive, or arriving when you leave? Grieviler
chooses the second alternative. The judges of the debate
will be Simon Pouchin and Jaket.
    21-23 'You would have a hundred times the grief . . .
that [you would have] if . . .'.   27 The thought is that
finding the right position to take in a debate on this issue
is very difficult.   53 The allusion to Triamodet, whether
the character in *Aspremont* or another figure, is unclear.

187   Jeu-parti (partner: Jehan de Grieviler)

RS 668, MW 2191
Mss. a 144v-145r, A 144v-145r, G no. 4, Z 41v-42r, b 163r.
    Music in AZa.   Attribution in b.

I   Grieviler, vostre ensīent
        Me dites d'un ju parti:
        Se vous amés loiaument
        Et on vous aime autresi,
        Li qieus sera mieus vos grés,   5
        U chele qui vous amés
        Sera bele par raison
        Et sage a tres grant fuison,
        U sage raisnaulement
        Et tres bele outreement?   10

II   --Sire Jehan, bel present
        M'offrés et j'ai bien coisi.
        Pour plus vivre longuement
        Sans estre jalous de li,
        Veil que ses cuers soit fondés   15
        En sens, puis que bele assés
        Est; sens est sans soupechon.
        Biautés a plus cuer felon:
        Orgeus i maint, qui souvent
        Muet grant joie en grant tourment.   20

III   --Grieviler, biautés n'entent
        Ne n'ot ne voit, je vous di,
        Ne n'a nul apensement
        De griété faire a ami;
        Mais tres grant sens est fondés   25
        De felounie et retés
        D'orguel et de traïson,
        Et par si fait cas pert on;

Et biautés doune talent
Toutans d'amer asprement.   30

IV   --Sire, sachiés vraiement
        Grant biautés enorgeilli
        Lucifer, qui trop vilment
        Dedens infer en kaï;
        Par grant sens n'est pas dampnés.   35
        Par sens est deduis menés.
        Puis que ma dame a le non
        Que bele est par grant raison,
        Del sens ait abondamment
        Pour mieus amer fermement.   40

V   --Grieviler, mauvaisement
        Respondés, je vous afi.
        Li rois u Navare apent
        Le tres grant sens desfendi
        Qu'en aucun point est sieunés,   45
        Mais tres grant fine biautés
        Est tout adés en saison.
        Pour tres grant biauté aim' on
        Plus ferm et plus taillaument
        Que pour grant sens contre un cent.   50

VI   --Sire, si sauvagement
        Ains mais parler ne vous vi.
        S'uns rois parla folement
        Volés vous faire autresi?
        Bons sens n'ert ja refusés   55
        Se çou n'est de faus dervés.
        Amours vous done tel don
        K'adés bele amie a on
        Puis c'on aime corelment.
        Al grant sens pour çou m'asent.   60

VII   --Dragon, vous nous jugerés.
        Je di, et s'est verités,
        Que pour le sens Salemon
        N'aime on pas tant Marion
        C'on fait pour son bel jouvent,   65
        C'on n'aime pas sagement.

VIII   --Demisele Oede, entendés.
        Je di qu'il est faus prouvés
        Qui a tele entencion.
        Bons sens dure duq'en son,   70

Mais n'est, a droit jugement,
Biautés c'un trespas de vent.

<u>MN</u>   Ms. A has a second melody; ms. Z has a third.
Form: A A B; both envoys are sung to ll. 5-10.

<u>RR</u>   II   16 plus q.   17 E. sans soupechon *(-2)*
20 Met *(em. Långfors)*   III   28 si biaus c.   29 talens
V   45 Quaucun *(-1)*   VI   55 Bon   VII   64 marison

    <u>V</u>   I   1 escient Gb   5 Le quel seroit m. uo g.   b
6 Ou‾ce G; cui G, ke Z, que b   10 entierement G
II   11 tel p. b   12 Moustrez b   13 P. vivre plus G
14 de lie G   15 q. son sens s. b   16 plus q.   A   17
E. sans soupechon A; Quar b   18 Biaute Z   19 Orgueil
b   20 Met AGZb   III   22 je] ce Gb, iel Z   25 trop
b; grans Z; e. doutez (-s) GZb   26 et] est b; routes Z
28 fait] fais Zb, biaus A   IV   32 Grans Z   36 deduit b   38 e. sans (-z) mesproison (mesprison G) GZb
40 mieus] plus G   V   41 Cuuelier Z   42 je] iel Z
45 Et en tel p. e. cis nez b   46 grans Z   47-48 *missing up to* ai(m)me on *in GZ*   49 et *missing in G*   VI   52
Ainc Z, Onc b   53 Sun roi b   54 V. fere tout ausi b
55 Bon A   57 A. nous Z   58 a] ai Gb; non A   59 P.
que on a. G   VII   62 Je di que cest v. G   65 bele G
66 Quar nulz naime s. b   VIII   67 Sire audefroi e.
GZb   68 di cil G   70 Bon b; d. iusque en s. b   71
a] au Gb, al Z   72 cuns t. GZ

    <u>E</u>   Långfors *Rec* 1, 98-102; Cremonesi, 224-227, Genn-
rich *Alt Lied* 2, 64-69; Spaziani *Canz*, 273-277; Toja, 351-
354.

    <u>DF</u>   Picard: *faus* (56, 68) for *fous*; *ju* (2) for *gieu*;
raisnaulement (9) for *raisnablement*; *çou* (56) for *ce*; *ch* for
c, as in *chele* (6); *c-* or *k-* for *ch-*, as in *coisi* (12) and
kaï (34).

    <u>N</u>   Jehan Bretel poses the question: would you prefer
ordinary beauty and great intelligence in your mistress, or
ordinary intelligence and great beauty? Grieviler chooses
the first combination. Dragon and Demoiselle Oede are
called upon to judge the exchange.
    6 *qui = cui*.   25 *fondés* 'skilled (in), grounded
(in)' is replaced by the variant *doutés* 'feared (for)' in
Långfors, Gennrich *Alt Lied,* Cremonesi, Spaziani *Canz*, etc.,
partly, no doubt, because of the belief that a rhyme word is

not supposed to be repeated (see l. 15) and partly, perhaps,
because *doutés* appears to be associated more closely with l.
26 *retés* 'accused'. We find these reasons for emendation
insufficiently persuasive, particularly in view of the adversative power of the repetition of *fondés*.   31   Understand *que* after this clause.

43-44   These lines, referring to Thibaut de Champagne,
himself a participant in a number of jeux-partis, have been
interpreted in various ways, largely because both *grant sens*
and *desfendi* are ambiguous terms.   The verb may mean either
'defended' or 'rejected', and the noun may either have the
same reference as it has had in the poem until this point or
mean the 'intelligent, reasonable opinion', i.e., that beauty is more to be prized than intelligence.   Two recent Italian translations illustrate the difficulty: Thibaut "ha di-
feso il gran senno" (Cremonesi), "si dichiarò contrario alla
grande intelligenza" (Spaziani *Canz*).   It is true, in any
case, that the single surviving jeu-parti in which Thibaut
confronts this issue (or, rather, one that is very similar)
shows him defending the case of beauty (RS 294).   For more
detail of this controversy, see note in Långfors.   It should
be observed, finally, that, in his reply to these verses,
Jehan Bretel, ll. 53-54, obviously takes them to mean that
Thibaut preferred beauty.

45   'which at times is rejected'.   57-58   The thought
is that, in the eyes of a true lover, his mistress is always
beautiful.

Rondeau

B rond. 73, refr. 12 (one other source)
MW 919, Gennrich *Ron* 70
Ms. W 33r. Music. Attribution.

A Dieu commant amouretes,
        Car je m'en vois
Souspirant en terre estraigne.
Dolans lairai les douchetes,   4
        Et mout destrois.
A Dieu commant [amouretes,
        Car je m'en vois].   8
J'en feroie roïnetes
        S'estoie roys;
Comment que la chose empraigne,
A Dieu commant amouretes,   12
        Car je m'en vois
[Soupirant en terre estraigne].

RR   3 estrange

E   Gennrich *Ron* 1, 60-61; 2, 79; Gennrich *AltRon*, 84; Wilkins, 60-61, B 52-53.

189   Rondeau

B rond. 78, refr. 80 (two other sources)
MW 260, Gennrich *Ron* 75
Ms. W 33v-34r. Music. Attribution.

A jointes mains vous proi,
Douche dame, merchi.
Liés sui quant je vous voi;
A jointes mains vous proi: 4
Aiiés merchi de moi,
Dame, je vous em pri.
A jointes mains vous proi,
Douche dame, merchi.   8

E   Gennrich *Ron* 1, 65; 2, 82-83; Zumthor *Lang*, 134; Wilkins, 56; B, 54-55.

190   Rondeau

B rond. 79, refr. 823 (three other sources)
MW 282, Gennrich *Ron* 76
Ms. W 34r. Music. Attribution.

Hé, Dieus, quant verrai
Cheli que j'aim?
Certes, je ne sai,
Hé, Dieus, quant verrai.   4
De vir son cors gai,
Muir tout de faim.
Hé, Dieus, quant verrai
Cheli que j'aim?   8

1.4.7. He, Dieus, quant ver- rai 2.8. che-   li   que j'aim?
3. Cer-   tes, je   ne   sai,
5. de   vir   son cors gai; 6. muir   tout   de faim.

E   Gennrich *Rond* 1, 65; 2, 83; Wilkins, 56; B, 55.

N   5 *vir*, Picard for *veoir*.

Rondeau   191

B rond. 83, refr. 1759
MW 271, Gennrich *Ron* 80
Ms. W 34r. Music. Attribution.

1.4.7. Tant con   je   vi-   vrai,
3. Ja   n'en   par- ti-   rai
5. ains vous   ser- vi-   rai;

2.8. n'a- me-   rai   au-   trui   que   vous.
loi- au-   ment   mis   m'i   sui   tous.

> *Tant con je vivrai,*
> *N'amerai autrui que vous.*
>   Ja n'en partirai
>   *Tant con je vivrai,*   4
>   Ains vous servirai;
>   Loiaument mis m'i sui tous.
>   *Tant con je vivrai,*
>   *N'amerai autrui que vous.*   8

E   Gennrich *Ron* 1, 68; 2, 84-85; Wilkins, 58, B, 56.

<u>192</u>   Jeu-parti (partner: Rogier)

RS 359, MW 2087
Mss. W 30r-v, Q 320v-321r.   Music in W.   Attribution (*Adan*)
     in W.

I   Adan, si soit que me feme amés tant
       C'on puet amer, et jou le vostre aussi;
       Andoi sommes de goie desirrant;
       Amés n'estes, aussi est il de mi.   4
       Et pour itant demanch se vous vaurriés

Que je fuisse de le vostre acointiés
Si tres avant c'on en puet avoir goie,
Et s'eüssiés tout autel de la moie.   8

II   --Rogier, metés vo coc en plache avant;
Adont sarai se j'ai le jeu parti.
Se vo feme cuidasse aussi vaillant
Con le moie, j'eüsse tost choisi.   12
Se pour vo feme ensi le moie aviés,
Encontre dis un tout seul meteriés,
Et cat en sac a vous acateroie
Se sans assai tel escange prendoie.   16

III   --Adan, vers moi alés debat cachant.
A deus dames sommes andoi ami,
Et vous m'alés de coc aatissant.
Vous ne savés quant je vo feme vi.   20
Je vous demant le voie dont issiés,
Et par orgueil d'une autre m'arainiés;
Et pour vous di c'amans trop se desroie
Qui ne s'assent a che c'Amours envoie.   24

IV   --Rogier, d'Amours ne savés tant ne quant.
Se j'aim vo feme, il n'affiert point pour li
Que vous aiés le moie en vo commant,
Ne point Amours ne le commande ensi,   28
Et qui le fait mout en est avilliés.
Je ne sui pas, sans che faire, esmaiés,
Se l'aim et serf de cuer, que je ne doie
Avoir merchi; mais vo cuers faut et ploie. 32

V   --Adan, non fait, ains vous va cuers faillant
Quant refusés le deduit de merchi
Pour vo feme, que vous alés doutant,
A vo sanlant, sans amour; pour che di   36
Que vous estes de sens amenuisiés.
S'en me vie m'escaoit tes marchiés
Que vous gagiés, certes trop faus seroie
Se mon desir pour mon anui laissoie.   40

VI   --Rogier, chil sont musart et nonsachant
Qui pour un seul goïr sont si hardi
Qu'il emprendent honte et damage grant.
Prendés che bon marcié, car j'en di fi.   44
Mieus ameroie adés estre entre piés
Qu'estre en amour par tel cose essauchiés

Et contre Amour de vo feme gorroie,
Car che seroit marchiés que je feroie.   48

VII   --Adan, pourfit de damage cuidiés.
Li espreviers est trop mal affaitiés
Qui refuse, quant il a fain, se proie.
Tesmoingniés le, sires de le Tieuloie.   52

VIII   --Ferri, amours d'amie est courte et briés,
Mais sen baron sert feme en tous meschiés;
Seroie je dont faus se je laissoie
Me feme a che que tost reperderoie!   56

MN   Form: A A B; both envoys are sung to ll. 5-8.

      RR   I   3   desirrans   6   acointise   III   22   dun
a.   VIII   53   dame

      V   I   1   A. sil   4   A. n. autel di iou de mi   6
de uo feme a.   7   con hon p.   8   Et sussies autretel   II
11   cuidies a. plaisant   III   23   Et plus v. di que cil
t.   IV   25   damour   26   point] pas   27   a. me feme a vo
c.   29   Car q. le f. il en   31   Se l. de cuer et sers q.
ie ne ne d.   32   uos c.   V   36   che di *missing*   VI
41   et pau sacant   46   ensauchies   VII   51   il] plus
52   le] ment   55   se ie cangoie

      E   Coussemaker, 184-188; Nicod, 102-105; Långfors
Rec 2, 69-72.

      DF   Picard, including *au* for *ou*, as in *vaurriés* (5)
and *faus* (39, 55); fem. determiners in *e*, as in *me* (1), *le*
(2), *se* (51); *sen* (54) for *son*; *vo* (9) for *vostre*; *jou* (2)
for *je*; *g* for *j* and *c* for *ch*, as in *goie* (3), *cat* (15), *aca-*
teroie (15); *ch* for *c*, as in *plache* (9), *che* (24); 1st-pers.
sing. pres. ind. *demanch* (5) for *demant*; *sarai* (10) for
savrai; epenthesized *meteriés* (14) for *metriez* and *reperde-*
roie (56) for *reperdroie*; *sanlant* (36) for *semblant*.

      N   Rogier poses the question: supposing each of us
loved the other's wife and were not loved by his own, would
you agree to let me be your wife's lover while you became
the lover of mine?   Adam begins by declining to answer, not
knowing Rogier's wife.   The Sire de la Tieuloie and Ferri
are asked to judge the debate.
      7 Given ms. Q *con hon*, Långfors, unlike Nicod, prefers
the reading *con en* (*en* = *hon*).   9 "Image empruntée au

marché à la volaille. Adam veut dire qu'on ne peut se pro-
noncer sur la valeur d'une femme tant qu'on ne la connaît
pas bien." (Långfors *Rec* 2, p. 72)   15 Cf. the modern expressions Fr. 'acheter chat en poche' and Eng. 'to buy a pig
in a poke'.   45 *estre entre piés* 'to be unhappy'.   55
Långfors adopts the no doubt clearer reading of ms. Q, *se je
cangoie.*

Chanson   193

RS 888, MW 1718
Mss. P 214v-215r-v, Q 313r-v, R 101r-v-102r, T 228r, W 5v-6r
      and 12v-13r. Music in all mss. except T. Attribution
      in PTW[1]W[2].

I   Jou senc en moy l'amor renouveler,
      Ki autre fois m'a fait le doc mal traire
      Dont je soloie en desirant chanter,
      Par koy mes chans renouviele et repaire.   4
            C'est bons maus ki cuer esclaire,
      Mais Amors m'a le ju trop mal parti,

        Car j'espoir et pens par li
        Trop haut, s'est drois k'il i paire.   8

II   Et nepourquant bien fait a pardouner,
    Car quant dame est noble et de haut afaire
    Et biele et boine et gent set honorer,
    Tant desiert mius c'on l'aint par essem-
                        [plaire; 12
        Et doit estre deboinaire
  Enviers povre home en otriant merchi,
      Sauve s'ounor, car jou di:
      Ki de boins est, souëf flaire.   16

III Et par mi chou le m'estuet comparer:
    Mes cuers me laist, ma dame m'est contraire,
    Et vous, Amors, ki de ma dame amer
    Dounés talent autrui por moi mal faire.   20
        Les gens ne se poeënt taire,
    Et nis pitiés s'est repunse pour mi;
      Asés de meschiés a chi,
      Ains c'on en puist joie estraire.   24

IV   Dame, vo oeil me font joie esperer,
    Mais vo bouce se paine de retraire
    Le largeche k'il font en resgarder;
    Par leur douçour vienc en espoir de plaire, 28
        Car il sont en un viaire
    Si amoureus, si doc et si poli
      C'onkes courous n'en issi
      Fors ris et samblans d'atraire.   32

V   Pour si dous ieus doit on bien lonc aler
    Et moult i a pressïeus saintuaire;
    Mais on n'i laist baisier ni adeser,
    Ne on ne doit penser si haut salaire.   36
        Drois est c'on se fraingne et maire
    Viers tel joiel et c'on soit bien nouri,
      Sans faire le fol hardi
      De parole u de pres traire.   40

    MN   Ms. R has many variants. Form: A A B.
1. In 1. 1 ms. R writes a *c.o.p.* stem. 2. In 1. 2 ms. Q
writes a *B*-flat. 3. In 1. 2 ms. Q writes a *c.o.p.* stem.
4. Mss. Q and W¹ write a *c.o.p.* stem.

    RR   I 8 i] me   IV 26 vo] vostre *(+1)*   28
vient *(em. Berger)*   30 pol *(-1)*   40 de ris taire

V   I   1 lamour en moi Q   2 autres T   4 mon
chant R   5 bon mal R   6 trop] si Q   7 C. espoir R;
pour lui T   8 cest RT; h. drois est W², qui li RT;
plaire T   II   10 C. q. plus e dame de h. a. Q; haut]
grant RW²   11 Et *missing in RTW²*; et digne dounerer Q
16 des b. TW²   III   18 Mon cuer R   19 amour Q   20
mal] pis Q   22 pitie R; reposte R   23 meschief R
IV   25 vo] vostre QRW²   26 M. vostre W¹; bonte RW²;
se p.] ne cesse TW²; dou TW¹   27 La RT; en] a R; esgarder W¹, rauarder W²   28 vient QRTW¹W²; en] on R
32 samblanc R, semblant T; d'atraire *missing in Q*   V
33 on] len R; loins a. RW¹   35 1. ne besier nadeser T;
b. ne a. QW¹   36 Non ne doit pas p. Q; on] len R, nus
W²   37 c'on] quence R   38 t. oiel R   40 de pis faire
R, de ris taire W¹

E   Coussemaker, 31-35; Berger, 135-150; Cremonesi,
265-266; Toja, 371-373; Wilkins, 8; Marshall, 51-53, 116.

DF   Picard, including *ie* for *e*, as in *renouviele* (4),
biele (11), *desiert* (12), *viers* (38); *(i)u* for *(i)eu*, as in
ju (6), *mius* (12); *boine* (11) for *bone* and *boins* (16) for
bons; *ch* for *c*, as in *merchi* (14), *chi* (23), *largeche* (27);
doc (2) for *douz*; *chou* (17) for *ce*; *jou* (1) for *je*; *le* (27)
for *la*; *vo* (25) for *vostre*; 1st-pers. sing. pres. ind. in
-c, as in *senc* (1), *vienc* (28).

N   6 Understand word-play here: *ju* as in *jeu d'amour*
and as in *jeu-parti*.   8 'and it is right that it should be
apparent'.   9 *fait a pardouner* 'it is forgivable, [what I
am doing]'.   For the view that *fait* is an error for first-
person *faic* and that the meaning is then 'I am to be for-
given', see Berger, pp. 141-142.   16 Cited in Morawski,
no. 1886. The same proverb occurs in Blondel de Nesle, RS
742. See, too, Berger, pp. 143-145.   17 'And nevertheless
I must pay'.   22 'And even pity has hidden from me'.   28
Marshall, p. 116, prefers to retain the ms. reading *vient*,
claiming that the third-person form "makes sense if one
takes the subject of the verb to be *joie* (25)." It is hard
to see, however, how joy could be both the goal of the lover
(1. 25) and a metonymic designation of him (1. 28).   32
'But only smiles and attractive looks'.   34 *saintuaire*
'relic' or 'reliquary'.   37 'It is appropriate to restrain
and control oneself before such a jewel and to behave pro-
perly'.

194   Chanson

RS 1599, MW 2164
Mss. P 226v-227r, I 1:1a, W 9v. Music in P. Attribution in
    PW.

1. On-kes nus hom ne fu pris 2. d'a-mours qui n'en vau-sist mieus
3. et qui n'en fust plus jo-lis 4. et mieus ve-nus en tous   lius,

5. car bone a-   mours li fait plai- re. 6. Si est bien drois qu'il i pai- re,

7. car toute hou-nours de li vient; 8. faus est ki ne   le main-tient.

I   Onkes nus hom ne fu pris
        D'amours qui n'en vausist mieus
        Et qui n'en fust plus jolis
        Et mieus venus en tous lius,   4
        Car bone amours li fait plaire;
        Si est bien drois qu'il i paire,
        Car toute hounours de li vient;
        Faus est ki ne le maintient.   8

II   Et puis ke jou m'i sui mis,
        Grant bonté m'en a fait Dieus:
        De la millour sui espris
        Ki ains fust veüe d'ius.   12
        Ne m'i sont mie contraire
        Mi penser quant son viaire
        Remir, car teus maus me tient
        Ki en goie me sostient.   16

III   Car si vair oel de dous ris
        Et ses gens cors signouriux
        Et ses dous cuers bien apris,
        Ki de nature est gentius,   20
        Dounent cuer et essamplaire
        De toute honour dire et faire;
        N'il n'aime point ki ne crient
        Et ki de mal ne s'astient.   24

        IV   Dame, se de paradis
                Et de vous estoie a kieus,
                Pres me seroit vos dous vis,
                Ki a tort m'est ore eskieus;   28
                G'i aroie mon repaire,
                Se c'estoit sans vous desplaire,
                Ne ja ne m'amissiés nient,
                Tant bien estre vous avient.   32

        V   Car a vous et a vos dis
                Seroie si ententieus
                Ke li mal dont jou languis
                Seroient plus douc ke mieus.   36
                Las! et or ne sai u traire,
                Ne jou ne m'en puis retraire,
                Car mes cors si las devient
                Que percevoir s'en couvient.   40

<u>MN</u>   Form: A A B.
1. In 1. 2 ms. writes no rest.

   <u>RR</u>   II   9-16 *missing*; *reading from W*   III   20
e. ap g.

   <u>V</u>   Stanzas: I   I II (see below)
                             W   II
I   1 hons I   2 ke n. I   5 amor lou f. faire I   6
Bien est raisons q. I   7 Puez ke tous li biens en v.   I
8 Folz I   II   10 f. duez I   12 Conkes f. I   13
Elle ne mest pas c. I   14 Son gent cors son cleir v.   I
15 R. cant cilz m. I   16 Sa grant biateit me souïent I
   Ms. I closes with the following stanza:
                    Onkes mais nuns fins amis
                    Ne fut d'amors si eschieus
                    Con suis et serai tous dis,
                    Car mes eürs en est tieus.   4
                    Douce dame debonaire,
                    Coment me poroie taire,
                    Kant cilz jolis mal me tient
                    Et si ne vos an sovient?   8
1 f. amans   2 eschiueis   3 t. tens   8 Et ci

   <u>E</u>   Guy, 582-583; Berger, 477-486; Marshall, 107-108;
128-129.

   <u>DF</u>   Picard, including *ius* for *ieus*, as in *lius* (4),
ius (12); *ius* or *iux* also for *i(l)s*, as in *signouriux* (18),

gentius (20); *ieus* (= *ius*) for *i(f)s*, as in *eskieus* (28),
ententieus (34); *kieus* (26) for *chois*; *au* for *ou*, as in *faus*
(8); *millour* (15) for *meill-* and *signouriux* (18) for *seign-*;
g for *j*, as in *goie* (16); *k* for *ch*, as in *eskieus* (28); *jou*
(9) for *je*; *le* (8) for *la*; *aroie* (29) for *avroie*.

Note that in this text *-ieus* and *-ius* have the same
phonetic value and that such rhymes as *mieus : lius : gentius : eskieus* are peculiar to Picard.

N̲   5 *li fait plaire* 'makes him pleasing, attractive'.   6 'And it is right that it should so appear'.   7-
8 The pronouns *li* and *le* both refer to fem. *amours*.   25-26
'if I had the choice between . . .'.   31 'Or even if you
did not love me at all'.   32 'So much does [a feeling of]
well-being suit you', i.e., the lady's qualities are such
that in her presence the lover naturally has a sense of
well-being.   40 'That it must be obvious'.

195   Chanson

RS 1383, MW 2397
Mss. W 18v-19r, P 223v-224r, R 104r-v-105r, T 230v-231r, a
    50v-51r. Music in PRW. Attribution in PTWa.

1. Da-me, vos hom vous e- stri-ne 2. d'u-ne nou-ve- le can- chon.

3. Or ven-rai a   vo-stre don   4. se cour-toi-sie   i est fi-   ne?

5. Je   vous aim sans tra-i-son: 6. A tort m'en por-tes cue- ri- ne,

7. car con plus a- ves fui- son   8. de biau-te sans mes-pri- son,

9. plus fort cuers s'i   en- ra- chi-   ne.

      I   Dame, vos hom vous estrine
            D'une nouvele canchon.
            Or venrai a vostre don

Se courtoisie i est fine?
Je vous aim sans traïson: 5
A tort m'en portés cuerine,
Car con plus avés fuison
De biauté sans mesprison,
Plus fort cuers s'i enrachine.

II   Tel fait doit une roïne   10
Pardonner a un garchon,
Qu'en cuer n'a point de raison
Ou Amours met se saisine.
Ja si tost n'ameroit on
Une caitive meschine   15
Maigre et de male boichon
C'une de clere fachon,
Blanche, riant et rosine.

III   En vous ai mis de ravine
Cuer et cors, vie et renon,   20
Coi que soit de guerredon;
Je n'ai mais qui pour moi fine.
Tout ai mis en abandon,
Et s'estes aillours encline;
Car je truis samblant felon   25
Et oevre de Guennelon:
Autres got dont j'ai famine.

IV   Hé! las, j'ai a bonne estrine
Le cunquiiet dou baston,
Quant je vous di a bandon   30
De mon cuer tout le couvine
Pour venir a garison.
Vo bouche a dire ne fine
Que ja n'arai se mal non
Et que tout perc mon sermon: 35
Bien sanlés estre devine.

V   Vous faites capel d'espine,
S'ostés le vermeil bouton
Qui mieus vaut, esgardés mon,
Comme chieus qui l'or afine   40
Laist l'ort et retient le bon.
Je ne.l di pas pour haïne
Ne pour nule soupechon,
Mais gaitiés vous dou sourgon
Que vous n'i quaés souvine.   45

VI   Jalousie est me voisine,
        Par coi en vostre occoison
        Me fait dire desraison,
        Si m'en donnés decepline.

<u>MN</u>   Ms. R has many variants and a different melody in part of l. 3 and 11. 4-5. Form: through-composed; the envoy is sung to 11. 6-9.

<u>RR</u>   I   3   uerrai   8   s. traison   9   fors   V   41
L. lor et r. le plonc

<u>V</u>   Stanza VI not included in R.
I   l   hons R; estrainne R, estreinne T   3   vendra R
4   Se courtoise estes et f.   a   7   fuison *missing in R*   8
mesproison Ra   9   fort *missing in R*; cuer   R   II   10
T. don doune u. r.   P; d. done r.   T   12   Quant au cuer n.
R   14   Ausi t.   T   15   meskix P   16   M. *missing in T*,
Male P   18   B. et r.   a   III   20   Cuers a   21   Quel
qui s.   R   22   mais] nus *expunged in T*   23   Tant   T   24
Et si estes P; acline   a   25   Et si t.   R   IV   28   Be
P; b. amour estrainne R; estreinne   T   33   Vo biaute d.   R
34   Car R   V   37   despines P   40   C. cil PRa, cils   T
41   Laist l'ort *missing in R*, L. lor   T; le plon RT   42
ne T   44   v. dun   a; fourcon *expunged and* sourion *added in
margin in T*   VI   47   sen v. auencon a   48   Ma   a

<u>E</u>   Coussemaker, 88-92; Berger, 368-415; Wilkins, 23;
Marshall, 92-94, 124.

<u>DF</u>   Picard, including *c* for *ch*, as in *canchon* (2),
capel (37); *ch* for *c* [s], as in *canchon* (2), *enrachine* (9),
boichon (16); *g* for *j*, as in *got* (27, =*joït*), *sourgon* (44);
final *s* for *z*, as in *portés* (6), *avés* (7); unepenthesized
sanlés (36) for *samblez*; *se* (13) for *sa*; *me* (46) for *ma*; *vos*
(1) and *vo* (33) for *vostre*; *chieus* (40) for *cil*; 1st-pers.
sing. pres. ind. in -*c*, as in *perc* (35); *arai* (34) for *avrai*.

<u>N</u>   2 The song may well be *nouvele* not only in the
sense of 'newly composed' but also in that of 'belonging to
a new or different type'. As a musical composition, it has
the distinction of being Adam's only refrainless *chanson*
that is through-composed, i.e., with a tune showing no repetition of melodic phrases. As a text, it is much more a
personal reprimand than a conventional expression of love.
3 *venrai a* 'reach, be awarded'.   7-9 'For the greater

your abundance of blameless beauty, the more firmly does
[my] heart take root in it'.   12-13 'For there is no reason in a heart which Love takes into its possession'.   16
de male boichon 'of bad temperament' or 'of poor stock'.
17 *fachon* 'face'.   19 *de ravine* 'impetuously'.   21 'Re-
gardless of the possible reward'.   22 *qui* 'anyone who';
fine 'pays' (cf. 1. 33 *fine* 'stops').   24 *Et s'* 'and yet'.
25 'And Ganelon-like behavior'. The reference is to the
archetypal traitor in the *Chanson de Roland*.   27 'Another
enjoys what I hunger for'.   28 *bonne* is to be understood
ironically.   29 'The dirty end of the stick'; see Dragonetti, p. 106.   30 *a bandon* 'freely'.

37-41 The comparison is somewhat confusing, for the
parallel between the lady's selection of thorns rather than
the rosebud and the smelter's selection of *le bon* rather
than dross is limited to the act of selection alone; the
objects of selection, on the other hand, are contrastive.
(The garland of thorns, of course, is intended for the luck-
less lover.) The 1. 41 reading of mss. RTW, substituting
l'or for *l'ort* and *plon* 'lead' for *bon*, reveals a scribal
effort to simplify the comparison by extending it beyond the
act of selection to the objects selected; this interpretation, accepted by Berger and Wilkins, is rejected here because of the factual, rather than hypothetical, nature of
the clause in 11. 40-41.

39 *esgardés mon* 'consider [this] well'.   44 As suggested by Marshall, p. 124, *sourgon* is better understood as
'sucker, runner (of a bush or tree)' than as 'spring, foun-
tain' (as in Berger). In that sense, it fills in the pic-
ture of rose-gathering that opens the stanza.   47 *en
vostre occoison* 'concerning you'.

Chanson

196

RS 612, MW 2389, B 1444
Mss. P 216r-v, Q 319r, R 159v-160r, T 228r, W 6v-7r and 13v.
     Music in PQRW¹W² (but incomplete in Q). Attribution in
     PTW¹W².

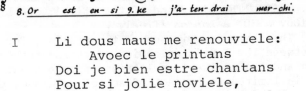

I   Li dous maus me renouviele:
           Avoec le printans
      Doi je bien estre chantans
      Pour si jolie noviele,
      C'onkes mie pour plus biele   5
      Ne plus sage ne millor
      Ne senti mal ne dolor.
           Or est ensi
        Ke j'atendrai merchi.

II   Au desus de ma querelle   10
           Ai esté deus ans
      Sans estre en dangier manans
      De dame u de damoisiele;
      Mais vair oeil, clere maissiele
      Rians et vermeille entor   15
      M'ont cangiet cuer et coulor.
           Or est ensi
        Ke j'atendrai merchi.

III   Tant grate kievre en graviele
           K'ele est mal gisans;   20
      Si est il d'aucuns amans:
      Tant jue on bien et reviele
      Ke d'une seule estincele
      Esprent en ardant amor.
      Jou sui espris par cel tor.   25
           Or est ensi
        Que j'atendrai merchi.

IV   Dous vis, maintiens de pucele,
           Gens cors avenans,
      Viers cui cuers durs c'ahymans   30
      De joie oeuvre et esquartele,
      Mar fui a la fonteniele

U jou vos vi l'autre jor,
Car sans cuer fui u retor.
    Or est ensi   35
    Que j'atendrai merchi.

MN   Form: through-composed + rf.
1. Ms. writes 𝄞♪♪ . 2. Ms. seems to write a descending
plica.

RR   III   21 mol   IV   34 sui

V   I   1 mi RT   5 Car onq. nus p. plus (si   Q) b.
QR, Conques mais nus (nuz   T) p. si (plus   T) b.   TW^2 9
Que ie a. m.   R   II   12   dangiers R   14   vairs R;
clere] blance QR, blan que   T, blanche W^2 16   Ment R;
coulor] uigour RTW^2 18   Et c.   R   III   20   mol Q   22
T. iuue en b.   R   24   en] er   Q, on   W^1 25   fui   TW^2;
cel] cest   Q, ce   R, tel   TW^2 26   est *missing in R*; ain-
sint T   27   Et cetera R, Et c.   W^2; Que ie a. m.   T   IV
28   maintien R   29   Gent RT   30   qui RT   31   j. en
eure et e.   T   32   Mal QT   34   Quant W^1; sui Q   36   Et
c. W^2

E   Coussemaker, 39-42; Berger, 161-174; Chastel, 754-
757; Toja, 371-373; Wilkins, 10; Marshall, 55-56, 117.

DF   Picard, including *ie* for *e*, as in *renouviele* (1),
biele (5), *viers* (30); *ch* for *c*, as in *merchi* (9); *c* or *k*
for *ch*, as in *cangiet* (16); *kievre* (19); preservation of
final *t* in *cangiet* (25); *jou* (25) for *je*.

N   This *chanson*, popular rather than courtly, is the
only one by Adam to include a refrain.   10 'Master of my
own affairs'.   10-13 Berger, pp. 167-168, understands the
two-year-long respite from love as referring to a period of
monkhood early in Adam's life.   19 Cited in Morawski, no.
2297. For other occurrences of this proverb, see Berger,
pp. 168-169.   30 'Before whom a heart hard as diamond
splits open with joy and breaks into pieces'.

197   Chanson historique

RS 1522, MW 603
Mss. M 5r, U 144r-v.   Music in M.   Attribution in M.

I   De nos seigneurs que vos est il avis,
       Compains Erart? Dites vostre samblance:
       A nos parens et a toz nos amis
       Avom i nos nule bone esperance
       Par coi soions hors du thyois païs,   5
       U nos n'avom joie, soulaz ne ris?
       Ou conte Othon ai mout grant atendance.

II   Dux de Brasbant, je fui ja vostre amis
       Tant con je fui en delivre poissance;
       Se vos fussiez de rienz nule entrepris,   10
       Vos eüssiez en moi mout grant fiance:
       Por Dieu vos proi, ne me soiez eschis.
       Fortune fait maint prince et mainte marchis
       Meillor de moi avenir mescheance.

III   Bele merë, ainc rienz ne vos mesfis   15
       Par qu'eüsse vostre male vueillance;
       Des celui jor que vostre fille pris,
       Vos ai servi loiaument, des m'enfance!

Or sui por vos ici loiez et pris
Entre les mainz mes morteus anemis.   20
S'avez bon cuer, bien en prendrez venjance.

IV   Bons cuens d'Alos, se par vos sui hors mis
De la prison ou je sui en doutance,
Ou chascun jor me vient de mal en pis--
Toz jors i sui de la mort en baance--   25
Sachiez por voir, se vos m'estes aidis,
Vostres serai de bon cuer a toz dis,
Et mes pooirs, sanz nulle retenance.

V   Chançon, va, di mon frere le marchis
Et mes homes ne me facent faillance;   30
Et si diras a ceus de mon païs
Que loiautez mainz preudomes avance.
Or verrai je qui sera mes amis
Et connoistrai trestoz mes anemis;
Encor avrai, se Dieu plaist, recovrance.   35

MN   Form: A A b+A'.
1. In ll. 1 and 3 ms. omits this figure; emended according
to l. 6. 2. In l. 4 ms. writes a bar.

RR   I   1   seigneur   4   atendance   V   31   Et si
di tas

V   Stanza IV not included in U.
I   1 n. barons   2   erairs   3   An n. p. ni an t.   4
Auez i uos   5   P. c. fusiens   7   ai ieu mout grant fiance
II   9 Cant ieu estoie an d. p.   10   Sadons f., rien   11
An moi puisiez auoir m. g. f.   13   m. merchit   14   Millors
III   15   B. m. onkes uers uos ne fis   16   P. coi euse   17
Tres icel j.   18   Vostre uoloir ai ie fait tres mafance
19   s. formant por uos l.   20   m. de mes mals enemins   21
Sauiez   V   29   Chansons   30   Kil a mes omes ne faicet f.
31   Et me d. toz ceaz   32   loalteit et p. auansent   33   Or
uara, seront mi amin   34   conostra toz mes mals enemins
35   Deus mar uaront la moie delivrance

E   La Borde Es, 161; Dinaux 2, 38-39; Leroux de
Lincy, 45-49; Tarbé Chans, 17; PetDyg "Garnier", 150-153.

N   The ms. rubric for this song of captivity does not
include the name Thibaut II. This identification, along
with that of the persons mentioned in the text, is provided
in PetDyg "Onom" and PetDyg "Garnier". Captured in the

Flemish wars in 1253, Thibaut was imprisoned in Germany for over a year. 2 The reference is to Erart de Valery, well-known crusader under King Louis IX, d. 1277. 7 *Othon* is Otto III, Count of Guelders from 1229 to 1271. 8 The reference is to Henry III, Duke of Brabant from 1248 to 1261. 13 *prince* and *marchis* serve as prepositionless dative object of 1. 14 *avenir*; similarly, 11. 29-30 *frere* and *homes*. 15 *Bele mere* designates Thibaut's mother-in-law, Marguerite, Countess of Flanders and Hainaut. 20 Understand *les mainz* [de] *mes . . ..* 22 *Alos* is the county of Loss, in the province of Limburg; the count is Arnoul IV. 29 The *frere* is Thibaut's brother-in-law, Henry III, Count of Luxemburg from 1226 to 1281 and Marquis of Arlon.

DUCHESSE DE LORRAINE

Plainte funèbre

RS 1640, MW 2344
Mss. U 97r-v, C 182r-v. No music. Attribution in C.

I   Par maintes fois avrai esteit requise
C'ains ne chantai ansi con je soloie;
Car je suix si aloingnie de joie
Que j'en devroie estre plus antreprise,
Et a mien voil moroie an iteil guise   5
Con celle fist cui je sanbler voroie:
Didol, qui fut por Eneas ocise.

II   Ahi, amins! tout a vostre devise
Que ne fis jeu tant con je vos veoie?
Jant vilainne cui je tant redotoie   10
M'ont si greveit et si ariere mise
C'ains ne vos pou merir vostre servise.
S'estre poioit, plus m'an repantiroie
C'Adans ne fist de la pome c'ot prise.

III   Ains por Forcon ne fist tant Afelisse   15
Con je por vos, amins, s'or vos ravoie;
Mais ce n'iert jai, se premiers ne moroie.
Mais je [ne] puis morir an iteil guise,
C'ancor me rait Amors joie promise.
Si vuel doloir an leu de mener joie: 20
Poinne et travail, ceu est ma rante assise.

IV   Par Deu, amins, en grant dolour m'a mise
Mors vilainne, qui tout lou mont gerroie.
Vos m'at tolut, la riens que tant amoie!
Or seu Fenis, lasse, soule et eschise,   25
Dont il n'est c'uns, si con an le devise.
Mais a poinnes m'en reconfortiroie
Se por ceu non, c'Amors m'at an justice.

     RR   III   18 -*l*   IV   25   eschiue   26   le] la
28   Ce

     V   I   2   Ke ne   3   Ke tant per seux a. de j.
4   Ke ie uodroie e. muels entr.   5   Et *missing*   6   C. fist
celle c. resembleir v.   7   Dido ke f. p. eneam o.
II   8   Biaus douls am.   9   tandis com uos auoie   10   Gens

14 Cadam ne fust   III   15-19 *occur as ll. 22-26*
15 tant ne fist anfelixe   16 s'or] se   17 se aincois ne
m.   18 Ne j.   20 Or v.   21 t. iert maix ma r. a.
IV   22-26 *occur as ll. 15-19*   22 P. d. amors   23   qui]
ke   24 Tolut maueis la r. ke plux a.   25   eschiue
27 M. a mien ueul se men repentiroie   28 Se p. tant niert
c.

E   Tarbé *Chans*, 25; Hofmann "Anzall", 516.

DF   Lorraine, including *ai* for *a* in *jai* (17); *ei* for
tonic *e*, as in *esteit* (1), *iteil* (5), *poinne* (21) for *peine*;
an for *en*, as in *antreprise* (4), *jant* (10) for *gent*, *rante*
(21); progressive nasalization in *amins* (8); *ss* or *c* for *s*,
as in *Afelisse* (15), *justice* (28); preservation of final *t*,
as in *esteit* (1), *at* (24), *tolut* (24); *jeu* (9) for *je*; *ceu*
(21) for *ce*; *lou* (21) for *le*; *seu* (25) for *sui*; third-person
singular present indicative *rait* (19) for *ra*.

N   As becomes gradually apparent, this song is a
death-lament, one of only five such OF compositions to have
survived and the only one composed by a woman.   2 *C'* 'why'
15 The reference is to Fouque and Anfelise, hero and
heroine of Herbert le Duc de Dammartin's epic poem, *Fouque
de Candie*. The characters appear as well in OF romance
literature; see Flutre, p. 14 and p. 80.   16 *ravoie = re +
avoie*; similarly, l. 19 *rait*.   18-19 'But I cannot die
that way, for Love has yet promised me joy.'   20 *Si* 'yet,
nevertheless'.   21 *ma rante assise* 'the tribute I must
pay'.   25 *Fenis*, masculine, is the phoenix; the three
feminine adjectives characterize the speaker. The feminine
form *eschise*, here substituted because of the rhyme for the
normal *eschive* which occurs in both mss., is attested in
Tobler-Lammatzsch, s.v. *eschif*.   28 'Love has me in its
power'.

RS 1671, MW 2019
Mss. Z 52r-v, E no. 2, b 156r, c 2r. Music in Z. Attribution in b.

I   Cuvelier, j'aim mieus ke moi
        Le feme a un chevalier;
        Ele m'aimme en boine foi
        Et ses sire m'a mout chier
        Et forment en moi se fie.   5
        Doi je, se Dieus vous benie,
        Pour lui la dame eslongier,
        U j'en doi le dosnoiier
        Prendre s'ele le m'otrie?

II   -Gamart, se par son otroi   10
        En pöés vo desirier
        Avoir, n'aiés pas effroi
        Ne doutance d'embrachier
        S'amour et sa compaignie,
        Coi ke ses maris en die.   15
        S'ele vous veut otroier
        Son deduit par bel proiier,
        Dont ne le refusés mie.

III   -Cuvelier, mon grant anoi
        Me löés a pourchacier.   20
        Se de li preng le dosnoi,

        J'en perdrai sans recouvrier
        Mon ami par ma folie,
        Et s'ert la dame laidie
        De lui pour moi courecier;   25
        Lors porai vis esragier,
        Et s'ert cele maubaillie.

IV   -Gamart, a çou ke vous voi,
        N'amés pas de cuer entier.
        Vous ne devriés pour un roi   30
        La vostre amie laissier;
        Trop est peu de vous prisie
        Quant si tost l'arés guerpie
        Pour un homme compaignier;
        S'ele vous aimme et tient chier,   35
        C'est bontés mal emploïe.

V   -Par le foi ke je vous doi,
        Sire Jehan Cuvelier,
        De traïson vous mescroi,
        Ki me volés consillier   40
        Ke face tel vilonnie
        Ke prenge la drüerie
        De celi ki est mouillier
        A celui ki sans trechier
        M'aimme autant comme sa vie.   45

VI   -Gamart, ses maris, je croi,
        Vous aimme sans losengier;
        Mais mieus le vous vient un poi
        Destourber et courechier
        Ke perdre tel signourie   50
        Com l'amour de vostre amie,
        Se vous l'amés sans boisier.
        Faisons ent le droit jugier
        A tel ki le voir en die.

VII   -Cuvelier, de ma partie   55
        Je preng la dame jolie
        De Fouencamp sans targier;
        S'en voelle le droit jugier,
        S'ert no tençons apaisie.

VIII   -Gamart, se Dieus me benie,   60
        Gillart preng, de quel maisnie
        Vous estes, se li requier

K'il voelle la dame aidier;
S'ert no chose mieus jugie.

<u>MN</u>   Form: A A B; both envoys are sung to ll. 5-9.
l. Ms. inserts a note *f* before and an *a* after this note.

<u>RR</u>   I   4   se s.   II   10 Sire se p. mon o.
VI   52   s. boisdie

<u>V</u>   Stanzas: b   I II III IV V VI VII VIII
                     E   I II III IV V VI VII
                     c   I II III
I   1 C. jaime m. de m.   c   3 E. moi en   b   4 Et *missing in c*; sires Ec   8 le deuoir   c   II   10 Sire Ec;
se bien par o. E; mon o.   b   11 desir   c   13 De samour
a embrachier b   17 Le d. p. le p.   b   18 Ce ne r. m.   c
III   20   a *missing in c*   21 Se de luj le preng je croy   c
24 siert l. E, si est l.   c   26 Dont   b; vif enragier   c
27 c. blastengie b   IV   28 vous] je   b   29 Naves p.
le c. e. E   30 Vous *missing in b*   33 laries E   34
acompaignie E   V   40 Que E   43 cele b   VI   46
je] che E, bien b   50 la s.   b   51 O E, De b   52
s. boisdie b   54 t. que E   VII   57 foulenchamp b
58 d. trier b   VIII   61 de cui b   64 Si ert no ch.
iugie b

<u>E</u>   Långfors *Rec* 2, 29-32; Spaziani *Canz*, 333-336.

<u>DF</u>   Picard, including -*ie* for -*iee*, as in *maubaillie*
(27), *prisie* (32), *apaisie* (59), *ch*- for *c*-, as in *embrachier* (13), *courechier* (49); *boine* (3) for *bone*; *poi* (48)
for *pou* or *peu*; non-etymological *s* before consonant, as in
dosnoiier (8); *cou* (28) for *ce*; *le* (2, 37) for *la*; *vo* (11)
and *no* (59) for *vostre*, *nostre*; *arés* (33) for *avrez*; subjunctive in -*ge*, as in *prenge* (42).

<u>N</u>   Gamart de Vilers asks whether he should take as
his mistress a woman who loves him but is the wife of his
friend. Cuvelier says yes. The Dame de Fouencamp and
Gillart will judge.   10 We have adopted Långfors' judgment
that, given Gamart's social status (ll. 61-62), the vocative
Sire of ms. Z (and Ec) needs to be corrected to *Gamart*,
which appears in ms. b. The emended form, moreover, is in
keeping with the pattern of vocative throughout the poem.
62 *se* = *si* 'and'.

SAINTE DES PRES AND THE DAME DE LA CHAUSSEE

<u>200</u>   Jeu-parti

RS 1112, MW 1986
Ms. b 167r. No music. Attribution.

I   Que ferai je, dame de la Chaucie,
      S'il est ensi c'on me requiert m'amour?
      Conseilliez moi, par vostre courtoisie,
      El quel des deus j'avrai plus grant honnour:
      Ou ce que je lesse a celui tout dire   5
      Sa volenté, ou ançois l'escondire?
      Par fine amour, löez m'ent le meillour.

II   --Damoisele, de la moie partie
      Vous loe bien et pour vostre valor   9
      Que vous vueilliez souffrir que cil vous die
      Sa volenté, sans lui metre en errour;
      Qu'en lui oiant porrez vous bien eslire
      Se il vous plaist l'otroi ou le desdire,
      Et si savrez s'il dist sens ou folour.

III   --Dame, c'est voirs, mes fame ne doit mie   15
      Home escouter, ains doit avoir paour
      Qu'ele ne soit a l'oïr engignie,
      Quar home sont trop grant losengeour
      Et leur raisons sevent tant bel descrire
      Qu'en eulz oiant puet a cele souffire   20
      Chose dont tost cherroit en deshonour.

IV   --Damoisele, poi est de sens garnie
      Fame qui chiet pour parole en freour
      D'omme, s'il n'est cheüz en frenesie.
      Bien escouter donne sens et vigour   25
      De bel parler, ci a bel maestire.
      Ja pour oïr homme n'iert fame pire
      S'el ne se veult obeïr a folour.

V   --Dame, bien voi tost seriez otroïe
      A home oïr, se veniez a ce tour;   30
      Mes, se Dieu plest, je n'iere ja moquie
      D'omme vivant, ne de nuit ne de jour,
      Quar de bien fait sevent il tost mesdire;
      Pour ce, les vueil au premier desconfire,
      Si que nulz n'ost a moi fere retour.   35

<u>RR</u>   IV   26   bele mestrie

<u>E</u>   Fiset, 534-535; Schultz-Gora, 500-501; Långfors
Rec 2, 169-170.

<u>DF</u>   Picard: *-ie* for *-iee*, as in *Chaucie* (1) and *en-gignie* (17).

<u>N</u>   Sainte des Prés asks whether it is more honorable
to let a man go ahead and request her love, or to prevent
him from speaking. The Dame de la Chaussée believes he
should be allowed to express himself. No judge is named.
    23-24 Långfors' interpretation, *Fame qui chiet en
freour pour parole d'omme*, is not only syntactically aber-
rant but also unnecessary, as *freour d'omme* makes good sense
here. 29 Understand *que* after *voi*.   34 *au premier*
'right away'.

201 Chanson

RS 1987, MW 2487
Mss. M 15r-v, K 219-220, N 48r-v, P 155v, V 70r-v. Music in
  all mss. Attribution in MK; attributed to Perrin d'Angicourt in N.

1. Con-tre la froi-dor 2. m'est ta-lent re- pris
4. por tres bone a- mor, 5. qui si m'a sou- pris

3. de chan- ter jo- li- e- ment
6. que je sai a e- sci- ent

7. que ja n'en ie- re par- tis 8. nul jor tant con soi-e vis,

9. ainz ser- vi- rai loi- au- ment, 10. li- ge- ment,

11. bone A- mor a son de- vis.

        I   Contre la froidor
                    M'est talent repris
                De chanter joliement
                    Por tres bone amor,
                    Qui si m'a soupris   5
                Que je sai a escïent
                Que ja n'en iere partis
                Nul jor tant con soie vis,
                Ainz servirai loiaument,
                        Ligement,   10
                Bone Amor a son devis.

        II   Ja n'iere a nul jor
                    Louseignolz faillis
                Qui a femele se prent,
                    Qui pert sa baudor,   15
                    Sa joie et ses cris,
                Quant vivre doit liement.
                Se mes chanters m'est meris,
                N'en doi estre mains jolis,
                Maiz pluz envoisiement   20
                        Et souvent
                Doi chanter, ce m'est avis.

        III   Dame de valor
                    Qui maintient bon pris
                Tient fin ami en jouvent;   25
                    S'en bee a honor
                    Cuers qui est assis
                En tel lieu veraiement,
                Se guerredons en est pris.
                Cil n'est mie fins amis   30
                Qui n'en a amendement,
                        Quant il prent
                Don de si bon lieu tramis.

MN   The melody of ms. K is also extant in mss. N and
P; the melody of ms. M is unique; ms. V has a third melody;
ms. M is mensurally notated. Form: M: A A B, K: A A B+A'.
1. Ms. M writes a longa followed by a brevis rest at all
phrase endings.

V   I   3 joliuement V   4 De KNPV   5 sorpris
N, seurpriz V, conquis KP   6 Q. siens (-z V) sui a
KNPV   7 Ne KNPV   8 j. que ie s. KNPV   10 Et souuent
KNP, Bonnement V   II   12 niert KNPV; a n. j. *missing
in V*   13 Rosignol (Roussignol V) iolis (-z V) KNPV

15 Q(u)il KP, Il N, Et V   16 et *missing in KNPV*   17
Q. doit viure loiaument KNPV   18 chanteres m. m. P; nest
m. V   20 renuoisiement KNP 21 *missing in V*   III
25 Qui a fin (-s NP) ami (-s NP) en (de V) j. KNPV   27
Cuer KNP   28 En t. (tele N) amor vraiement KNP, En cele
a amour le ramaine V   29 guer(r)edon KP   31 Q. tent a
V; alegement P   33 si haut l. KNPV

     E̲   Scheler 2, 72-73; Steffens *Per*, 275-277, 349-350;
Hoepffner, 95-96.

     N̲   For the question of attribution, see Hoepffner,
pp. 73-74. Steffens *Per*, although including this song, rejects Perrin's authorship (p. 274). Steffens *Per*, pp. 349-
350, on doubtful formal grounds, finds the poem fragmentary.
Hoepffner, p. 96, maintains the opposite, rather surprisingly seeing it as related to three-stanza *ballettes*. In the
absence of objective evidence for one side or the other, it
appears judicious simply to observe that the composition
shows a high degree of poetic integrity and ends with a
sense of completeness.
     1 *Contre* is interpreted in Steffins *Per*, p. 349, as
'despite'; 'at the approach of' is more likely, as noted by
Hoepffner; see not only Tobler-Lommatzsch, s.v. *contre* with
nouns of time, but also Jacques de Cysoing himself: *Quant
l'aube espine florist/Contre la douce seson* (RS 1647;
Hoepffner, p. 85).   23-25 *en jouvent* refers not to the
state of the *dame* but to that of the *fin ami*.

Chanson de rencontre   202

RS 1255, MW 934, B 961 (two other sources)
Mss. P 171v-172r, K 192-193, N 92r-v. Music in all mss.
Attribution in KN.

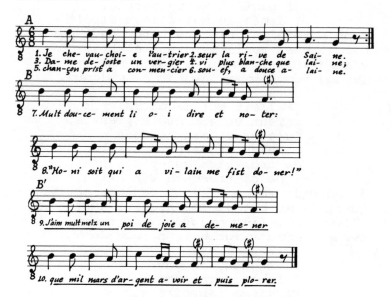

I   Je chevauchoie l'autrier
              Seur la rive de Saine.
          Dame dejoste un vergier
              Vi plus blanche que laine;
          Chançon prist a conmencier   5
              Souëf, a douce alaine.
      Mult doucement li oï dire et noter:
      "Honi soit qui a vilain me fist doner!"
      J'aim mult melz un poi de joie a demener
      Que mil mars d'argent avoir et puis plorer.   10

II   Hautement la saluai
              De Dieu le filz Marie.
          El respondi sanz delai:
              "Jhesu vos beneïe!"
          Mult doucement li proié   15
              Q'el devenist m'amie.
      Tot errant me conmençoit a raconter
      Conme ses maris la bat por bien amer.

J'aim [mult melz un poi de joie a demener
Que mil mars d'argent avoir et puis plorer].   20

III   "Dame, estes vos de Paris?"
                       "Oïl, certes, biau sire;
                      Seur Grant-Pont maint mes maris,
                       Des mauvés tot le pire.
                      Or puet il estre marris: 25
                       Jamés de moi n'iert sire!
              Trop est fel et rioteus, trop puet parler,
              Car je m'en vueil avec vos aler jöer."
              J'aim [mult melz un poi de joie a demener
              Que mil mars d'argent avoir et puis plorer].   30

IV   "Mal ait qui me maria!
                       Tant en ait or le prestre,
                      Qu'a un vilain me dona
                       Felon et de put estre.
                      Je croi bien que poior n'a   35
                       De ci tresqu'a Vincestre.
              Je ne pris tot son avoir pas mon souler,
              Quant il me bat et ledenge por amer."
              [J'aim mult melz un poi de joie a demener
              Que mil mars d'argent avoir et puis plorer.]   40

V   "Enondieu, je amerai
                       Et si serai amee,
                      Et si me renvoiserai
                       El bois soz la ramee,
                      Et mon mari maudirai   45
                       Et soir et matinee."
              "Dame de Paris, amez, lessiez ester
              Vostre mari, si venez o moi jöer!"
              J'aim [mult melz un poi de joie a demener
              Que mil mars d'argent avoir et puis plorer].   50

     MN   Form: A A A B rf (virelai); only ms. N repeats
the melody of the B-section almost exactly for the refrain.

     RR   III   26 m. miert   28 a. oer   V   48 Uos
maris et s.   49 J. trop etc.

     V   I 8 Honiz K   II   12 fil N   14 Ihesus
KN 15 priai   17-18 me sonmencoiter Con.   N   18 Conment KN; la batoit po(u)r amer KN   19-20 mult *added in N*
III   21 de] a N   24 touz li pires K   26 sires K
28 C. me v. a. v. aleioer N   29-30 J'aim *not given in K*

IV   32 li p.   K   33   A KN   35 b. q(u)il na poior
(peior N) KN   36   c. iusqua K, iusca N   37 par m.   N
38 p. amor N   39-40 J'aim *given in N*   V   43-44 *occur*
after 45-46 in KN   47 Dames KN   48 Uoz maris (-z N) et
s. KN; o] a K   49-50 mult *added in N*

   E   Bartsch, 87-88; Gennrich *Rot*, 67-69; PetDyg "Moniot", 197-200; Spaziani *Ant*, 101-103.

   N   15 *proié* = *proiai*.   36 The allusion to Win-
chester, in England, is to be taken as simply indicating a
great distance.   47-48 The evidence of the mss. (*Dames*
KN, *Vos maris* KNP) is largely in favor of an exhortation by
the woman--or by the knight--to all the ladies of Paris, and
previous editors have in fact so interpreted these lines,
attributing them to the woman. Such generalization of the
woman's sentiments, however, seems unjustified in the context of the entire poem; moreover, the phrase *venez o moi
jöer* appears intended as a reply by the knight to the lady's
phrase, l. 28, *avec vos aler jöer*.

Chanson   <u>203</u>

RS 969, MW 591
Mss. K 198, N 94v-95r, P 184r-v. Music in all mss. Attribution in KN and in text.

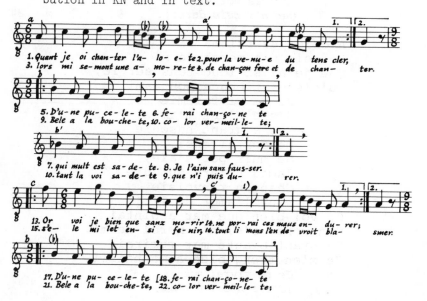

1. Quant je oi chan-ter l'a- lo- e- te 2. pour la ve-nu-e du tens cler,
3. lors mi se-mont une a- mo-re-te 4. de chan-çon fere et de chan— ter.

5. D'u-ne pu-ce-le-te 6. fe- rai chan-ço-ne te
9. Bele a la bou-che-te, 10. co- lor ver-meil-le- te;

7. qui mult est sa-de- te. 8. Je l'aim sanz faus-ser.
10. tant la voi sa-de- te 9. que n'i puis du-   rer.

13. Or   voi je bien que sanz mo-rir 14. me por-rai ces maus en- du- rer;
15. s'e— le mi let en- si fe-nir, 16. tout li mons l'en de- vroit bla-   smer.

17. D'u-ne pu- ce-le- te [18. fe- rai chan-ço-ne- te
21. Bele a la bou-che-te, 22. co- lor ver- meil-le- te;

19. qui mult est sa- de- te. 20. Je l'aim sanz faus-ser.
23. tant la voi sa- de- te 24. que n'i puis du- rer.]

I   Quant je oi chanter l'alöete
    Pour la venue du tens cler,
    Lors mi semont une amorete
    De chançon fere et de chanter.   4
        D'une pucelete
        Ferai chançonete
        Qui mult est sadete.
        Je l'aim sanz fausser.   8
        Bele a la bouchete,
        Color vermeillete;
        Tant la voi sadete
        Que n'i puis durer.   12
    Or voi je bien que sanz morir
    Ne porrai ces maus endurer;
    S'ele mi let ensi fenir,
    Tout li mons l'en devroit blasmer.   16
        D'une pucelete
        [Ferai chançonete
        Qui mult est sadete.
        Je l'aim sanz fausser.   20
        Bele a la bouchete,
        Color vermeillete;
        Tant la voi sadete
        Que n'i puis durer].   24

II A dolor userai ma vie
    Se cele n'a merci de mi
    Que je ai si lonc tens servie,
    Qu'ele mi tiengne pour ami.   28
        Je ne vivrai mie
        S'ele n'est m'amie,
        Mes a grant haschie
        Me morrai ensi.   32
        Se muir por s'aïe,
        Jamés n'iert qui die
        Chançon renvoisie
        Pour l'amor de li.   36
    Or voi bien que mar acointai
    Son cors, s'el n'a merci de mi.
    Sa grant biauté mar remirai;
    Je m'en tieng bien a maubailli.   40
        Je ne vivrai mie
        [S'ele n'est m'amie,

> *Mes a grant haschie*
> *Me morrai ensi.*
> *Se muir por s'aïe,*
> *Jamés n'iert qui die*
> *Chançon renvoisie*
> *Pour l'amor de li].*   44

                                                           48

III   Oncor tenir ne mi porroie
        De chanter com loiaus amis.
        Je chant et plorer deveroie
        Conme dolenz et esbahiz.   52
> *Se cele n'est moie*
> *Laou mes cuers s'otroie,*
> *Faillie est ma joie*
> *Et touz mes deliz;*   56
> *Et Deus, qui g'en proie,*
> *Dont qu'ele soit moie*
> *Si c'oncore en soie*
> *Joianz et jolis.*   60
        Jehan Moniot dit ensi
        Q'il a en tel lieu son cuer mis
        Laou il a bien du tout failli.
        Gardez que ne faciez ausi!   64
> *Se cele n'est moie*
> *Laou [mes cuers s'otroie,*
> *Faillie est ma joie*
> *Et touz mes deliz;*   68
> *Et Deus, qui g'en proie,*
> *Dont qu'ele soit moie*
> *Si c'oncore en soie*
> *Joianz et jolis].*   72

MN   Form: A A B B C C B B (lai?).
1. In 1. 14 ms. writes ♪♫♪ for the next 2 notes.

RR   III   50   comme *(+1)*

V   I   7 Car m. P   14 Ni P   II   26 Ce sele
P   27 Que iai si longuement s. N   31 Mes *missing in N*
37 mal a. N   38 meci N; na de moi merci P   41 *only*
je ne viure *in N*   III   50 comme NP   51 deuroie NP
61 Cil qui cest vers fist d. e. P   65-66 *only* S. c. n.
in P, only S. c. n. m. *in N*

E   Raynaud, 340; Spanke *Bez*, 92; PetDyg "Moniot",
211-214.

<u>DF</u>   Picard, including *renvoisie* (35) for *renvoisiee*;
mi (38) for *moi*; *deveroie* (51) for *devroie*.

<u>N</u>   The form of this song, in which the middle section
of each stanza is repeated as a refrain at the end of the
stanza, is unique in the corpus of OF lyrics and may have
been inspired by contemporary Latin poetry; see Spanke *Bez*,
p. 94, and PetDyg "Moniot", p. 186.   54 *Laou*, contraction
of *la ou*, is syntactically equivalent to *ou* alone and is
also monosyllabic; likewise, l. 63.   57 *qui = cui*.

<u>204</u>   Chanson

RS 1424, MW 1265, B 545
Mss. P 100v-101r, K 195-196, N 93v-94r, R 90r-v. Music in
    all mss. Attribution in KNP.

I   Qui veut amors maintenir
         Tiengne soi jolivement,
         Car nus ne doit avenir
         A fine amor autrement.
         Cil qui aime loiaument   5
         Se doit netement tenir
         Et belement contenir,
       Si avra de s'amie joie.
         Deus me lest anuit venir
         En tel lieu que m'amie voie!   10

II   Amors se veut detenir
         Par chascun bien cointement:

Beau chaucier et beau vestir
Et aler mignotement
Et contenir sagement.   15
Qui veut amors retenir
De parler se doit tenir
Vilainement, se Deus me voie.
[*Deus me lest anuit venir*
En tel lieu que m'amie voie!]   20

III   Braz estroitement laciez
Doit li fins amanz avoir,
Blans ganz, piez estroit chauciez,
Netes mains; si doit savoir
Que, s'il a petit d'avoir,   25
Soit cortois et renvoisiez.
Lors ert d'amors essauciez
Et s'avra de s'amie joie.
[*Deus me lest anuit venir*
En tel lieu que m'amie voie!]   30

IV   Net chief, cheveus bien pigniez
Doit li fins amis vouloir;
Beaus sorciz, denz afetiez
Ne doit metre en nonchaloir;
Riens ne li puet tant valoir   35
Les ungles nez et deugiez,
Le nez souvent espinciez.
Lors avra de s'amie joie.
[*Deus me lest anuit venir*
En tel lieu que m'amie voie!]   40

V   Soit cortois et enseigniez
Fins amis vers tote gent;
Euz nez, blans dras et nez piez
Et de bel acointement,
Et parot cortoisement;   45
Si en sera melz prisiez.
Ja nus hons n'ert d'amors liez
Qui vilainement se cointoie.
[*Deus me lest anuit venir*
En tel lieu que m'amie voie!]   50

MN   Ms. R has a second melody. Form: A A^1 B rf
(virelai).
1. In l. 8 ms. writes no flat.

<u>RR</u>   II   17-18   De p. vilainement se doit tenir se
dex me uoie   III   22   amant

<u>V</u>   Stanzas IV and V not included in R.
I   1 amor N   2 ioliement R   5 Car q.   R   6 Si doit
amours maintenir R   9 lest] doinst R   II   12 P. ch.
iour contenir R   13 beau chaucier *missing in R*   16 *missing in R*   17-18 De p. vilain(n)ement se doit tenir se
d(i)ex me uoie KNR   III   22 f. amis K   26 enuoisiez
R   IV   32 f. amanz K, amant N   37 Li KN   V   49
Dex *given in N*

<u>E</u>   Raynaud, 338; Langlois 2, 314; PetDyg "Moniot",
205-208; Cremonesi, 234-236; Toja, 450-452; Mary 2, 30-33.

<u>N</u>   The claim made by Langlois 2, p. 314, that this
song on the proper dress and behavior of the good lover was
inspired by a passage in Guillaume de Lorris' *Roman de la
Rose* (ll. 2131-2176) is refuted by PetDyg "Moniot", pp. 188-
190, on the grounds that the resemblance between the two
works is rather general and that the rules they give were
medieval commonplaces.
21 Sartorial elegance required sleeves laced tightly
down to the wrists, cf. RS 1371, l. 4   45 *parot*, 3rd-pers.
sing. subj. of *parler*.

Rondeau

205

B rond. 85, refr. 993
MW 65, Gennrich *Ron* 42
Ms. a 117v-118r. Music. Attribution.

Jamais ne serai saous
D'eswarder les vairs ieus dous
Qui m'ont ocis.
Onques mais si au desous
--*Jamais ne serai saous*--   5
Ne fu nus cuers amourous,
Ne ja n'erc a tans rescous
Quant muir tous vis.
Jamais ne serai saous
D'eswarder les vairs ieus dous   10
Qi m'ont ocis.

E̲   Bartsch-Wiese, 224-225; Gennrich *Ron* 1, 31-32; 2,
172; B̲, 57.

N̲   2 *eswarder*, Picard for *esgarder*.   7 *erc*, Picard
for *er(e)* 'I shall be'.

Rondeau

206

B rond. 87, refr. 1717 (two other sources)
MW 274, Gennrich *Ron* 44
Ms. a 118r. Music. Attribution.

Ses tres dous regars
M'a mon cuer emblé.
Ce n'est mie a gas,

Ses tres dous rewars.   4
Ele m'ocirra
Se li viegne a gré;
Ses tres dous rewars
M'a men cuer emble.   8

E   Gennrich *Ron* 1, 33; 2, 172-173; B, 57-58.

N   8 *men,* Picard for *mon.*

207   Rondeau

B rond. 90, refr. 477 (three other sources)
MW 272, Gennrich *Ron* 47
Ms. a 119r. Music. Attribution.

De ma dame vient
La grant joie que j'ai.
De li me souvient,
--De ma dame vient--   4
N'en partirai nient,
Mais tous jours l'amerai.
De ma dame vient
La grant joie que j'ai.   8

E   Gennrich *Ron* 1, 36; 2, 173; B, 58-59.

JACQUEMIN DE LA VENTE

Chanson satirique

RS 1171, MW 781, B 740
Mss. C 151v-152r, K 364-365, X 238r-v. Music in KX. Attribution in C.

I   <u>M</u>a chanson n'est pais jolie
        Ke vos vuel retraire;
     Trop ai museit a folie,
        Ne m'en puis plus taire.   4
     Je cuidai avoir amie
        Saige et debonaire,
     Maix je la truis anemie
        Et vers moi contraire.   8
     Fauce feme soit honie
        Et de fol afaire,
     Ke de chascun ki la prie
        Veult son amin faire.   12

II   <u>A</u>utant aimme velonnie
        Entor li atraire

Com elle fait cortoissie:
    Bien fait a desplaire.   16
Pués k'elle s'est aploïe
    Del tout a mal faire,
Guerpir doi sa compaignie
    Et arriere traire.   20
Fauce femme soit honie
    Et [de fol afaire,
Ke de chascun ki la prie
    Veult son amin faire].   24

III   Retenir vuel de m'amie
        Un teil examplaire:
Chascuns ki a li s'otrie
    En fait tout son plaire.   28
Teille amor est tost perie
    Ke croist en teile aire;
Longuement ne la puet mie
    Moneir k'il n'i paire.   32
Fauce femme soit ho[nie
    Et de fol afaire,
Ke de chascun ki la prie
    Veult son amin faire].   36

IV   Grant riote ait enchairgie
        Cui teil femme maire,
Car il est de jalousie
    Et prevos et maire;   40
Et s'est cous, je n'en dout mie,
    C'on ne puet defaire;
Jamaix n'avrait bone vie,
    Si ait mult grief haire.   44
Fauce femme soit honnie
    [Et de fol afaire,
Ke de chascun ki la prie
    Veult son amin faire].   48

V   Or vos dirai k'elle endure
        Per son grant folaige:
Elle ait sovent batteüre--
    Tant ait d'aventaige!   52
En vilteit et en ordure
    Ait mis son usaige.
Ce li fait honte et laidure;
    C'est per son outraige.   56
Fauce femme [soit honie
    Et de fol afaire,

> *Ke de chascun ki la prie*
>   *Veult son amin faire].*   60

VI   Se jamaix ai de li cure
         En tout mon ëaige,
      Deus me doinst male aventure
            Per mei mon visaige!   64
      Fauce femme soit honie,
         Ki ait cuer volaige,
      Ki a chascun ki la prie
            Done son coraige.   68

MN   Melody from ms. K. Form: A A^1 rf; both envoys are
sung to ll. 5-8+rf.
1. Ms. writes *c'*. 2. Ms. writes this figure a 2nd higher.

RR   I   4 Se m. ueul retraire   II   17 cest
III   25 ueult de masnie   26 Et done e.   28 Et ueult a
tous p.   31 Car l. ne p. m.   IV   41 Et cest   V   55
Se

V   Stanza VI not included in KX. Ms. X concludes
with the first four lines of stanza V, immediately followed
by the opening phrase of the refrain.
I   3 ai pense KX   5 cuidoie KX   6 Douce KX   10
fol] put KX   11 Qui KX   II   16 Ce K   17 P. que
ele s.   X   18 *missing in X*   21 Fausse fame (feme) KX
III   27 Chascun X   29 T. a. ne pris ie mie KX   30
Qui set a touz plaire KX   33 Fausse K; *refrain entirely
omitted in X*   IV   37 enchargiee X   38 Qui KX   41
Icele (Icelui X) ne pris ie mie KX   42 Qui est de tel
afaire KX   43 Ne ia n. KX   44 Q(u)il a trop g. KX
45 Fausse K; *refrain entirely omitted in X*   V   52 Cest
tout d. KX; *followed by* fausse feme *in X*   55 Sen K   57
Fausse fame soit honie K

E   Jeanroy-Långfors, 50-52; Gennrich *Rot*, 28-30;
Spanke *Lied*, 154-156, 384-385; Chastel, 544-549.

DF   Lorraine, including *ai* for *a*, as in *pais* (1), *enchairgie* (37), *folaige* (50); *per* (50) for *par*; *ei* for tonic
e, as in *museit* (2), *teil* (26), *moneir* (32); *mei* (63) for
mi; final *ie* for *iee*, as in *aploïe* (17), *enchairgie* (37);
amin (12) for *ami*; *pués* (17) for *puis*; *c* for *s* and *s* for *c*,
as in *fauce* (9) and Rejected Readings; preservation of final
t, as in *museit* (2), *vilteit* (53); 3rd-pers. sing. pres.
ind. *ait* (37, 44, 51, 54) for *a*; 3rd-pers. sing. fut. in

-ait, as in *avrait* (43). Note that final *ie* for *iee* is at
least as characteristic of Picard as of Lorraine; its occurrence in rhyme position bespeaks an authorial intention.

N   The woman who is the object of the poet's attack
is identified by an acrostic, MARGOS. For the rarity of
acrostics in OF songs, see Spanke *Lied*, p. 385.   11 *Ke*
serves here, as often happens in Lorraine texts, as a nominative; similarly in l. 30.   15 *fait* 'does', i.e., *aimme
atraire.*   31-32 'Not for long can she indulge in it (= l.
29 *teille amor*) without its becoming apparent'.   37-40
'The man whom such a woman controls has assumed a great burden, for he is overcome by jealousy'.   41 *s'* = adv. *si.*
49 Understand *ce* before *k'.*   52 Unlike its other occurrences (see Dialectal Features), *ait* functions here as a
subjunctive.

RS 514, MW 1834
Ms. C 216v-217r. No music (see note below). Attribution.

I   Remambrance que m'est ou cuer entreie
    De Jhesucrist, qui por nous vout morir,
    Mi fait laixier et guerpir lai contreie,
    Si m'en irai mon droi signor servir.
            Lou monde m'estuet guerpir,   5
            Car trop duremant m'anoie,
            Et pour ceu je lou renoie;
            Sor mai chairoigne di fi,
                Car trop l'ai norri.

II Cant je recors la vie c'ai meneie,   10
    Li cuers ou cors me commance a fremir;
    J'ai droit, c'an dit, an fais et an panceie
    M'ai maintenut com folz, n'an doi mantir.
            Lais! que puix je devenir?
            Que, se je mil ans vivoie,   15
            Empenir je ne poroie
            Les maulx que j'ai fait en mi,
                S'en pri Deu merci.

III [Hé!] jone gens, a cui jonesse aigreie,
    Vous ne savreis vos cors si bien polir   20
    Que Mors, que fiert grans colz et sens espeie,
    Ne vous faicë en lai terre porrir:
        Bien vous en doit souvenir!
        Li mondes adés tornoie,
        Pouc dure solés et joie;   25
        Pensons au vray crucifi,
        Qui en creux pendi.

IV Je di a tous, et c'est choze prouveie,
    Tout ceu que nest, il lou couvient morir:
    Biauteis, bonteis, orguelz, haulte panceie, 30
    Tout ceu couvient a niant revenir;
        Mais cil qui vuet Deu servir
        Son tens en boin us emploie.
        AÏ foi! je ke diroie
        De sa meire? Mar vesquit   35
        Qui sert l'ainemin.

V   Meire Deu, franche dame honoreie,
    Per vos pitié me voiliés consantir
    M'airme ne soit perie ne dampneie
    Cant Deus vorrait son jugement tenir.   40
        Frans estandairs sens faillir,
        Com pechieres que je soie,
        M'airme vous don et otroie.
        Dame, aieis pitié de mi,
        De cuer lou vous pri.   45

    MN   Melody from ms. W, f. 15r. Form: A A B.
1. In ll. 3-4 ms. writes a bar.
2. In l. 2 ms. writes no rest.

    RR   II   10 meneit   12 cau d. au f. et aus
penceirs   15 se] ce   III   19 -1   V   38 me] ne

    E   Dinaux 4, 49-50; Järnström 1, 97-98.

    DF   Lorraine, including *ai* for *a*, as in *lai* (3), *mai*
(8), *chairoigne* (19), *aigreie* (19), *ainemin* (36), *ei* for
tonic *e*, as in *entreie* (1), *savreis* (20), *biauteis* (30),
meire (35), *creux* (27) for *crois*; *boin* (33) for *bon*; *ainemin*
(36) for *anemi*, preservation of final *t*, as in *maintenut*
(13); *c* for *s*, as in *panceie* (12), *x* for *s(s)*, as in
laixier (3), *puix* (14), *creux* (27); *lou* (5, 7) for *le*;

third-person singular future in *-ait*, as in *vorrait* (40).
The forms *mi* (3, 17) for *me*, *moi* and *vos* (38) for *vostre* are
more characteristic of Picardy, where this song no doubt
originated.

<u>N</u>   This composition is in form an imitation of a
chanson d'amour by Adam de la Halle (RS 500); the meter, the
rhyme scheme, and even the rhymes being the same, we are
presenting RS 514 with the music of RS 500.   1   *que = qui.*
25 *solés = solaz*; the usual Lorraine spelling would be
solais.   39 Understand *que* before *M'airme*.

PHILIPPE DE REMI

Tenson

RS 2029, MW 1494
Ms. V 56v-57r. Music. Attribution.

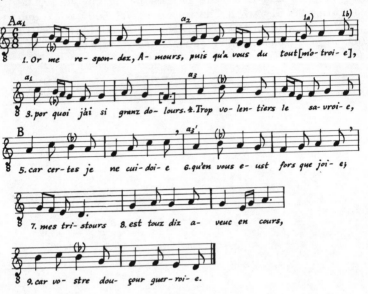

1. Or me respondez, Amours, puis qu'a vous du tout[m'o-troi-e],
3. por quoi j'ai si granz do-lours. 4. Trop vo-len-tiers le sa-vroi-e,
5. car cer-tes je ne cui-doi-e 6. qu'en vous e-ust fors que joi-e;
7. mes tri-stours 8. est touz diz a-veuc en cours,
9. car vo-stre dou-çour guer-roi-e.

I   Or me respondez, Amours,
        Puis qu'a vous du tout [m'otroie],
        Por quoi j'ai si granz dolours.
        Trop volentiers le savroie,
        Car certes je ne cuidoie   5
        Qu'en vous eüst fors que joie;
            Mes tristours
        Est touz diz aveuc en cours,
        Car vostre douçour guerroie.

II   --Ge.1 vous dirai, amis douz: 10
        Se chascun confort donnoie
        Si tost c'on fet l'amourous,
        Trop mainz prisiee en seroie;
        Por ce m'esteut qu'aspre soie
        Por oster hors de ma voie   15
            Tricheours,
        Car c'est ma plus granz paors
        Que mauvés de moi n'ait joie.

III   --De ce m'acort bien a vous,
           A tort vous en blameroie;   20
           Mes de ce sui mout irous
           Que j'esgart, quant faux cuers proie,
           Il set mieus trouver la voie
           De vous trere a sa corroie
                    Que tretouz   25
           Ceus qui se tienent a vous,
           Car qui mieus aime pis proie.

IV   --Biaus amis, c'est la dolours
           Dont mes finz mestiers s'effroie;
           Mes il i a tant priors,   30
           Por rienz touz ne.s connistroie.
           Compere fausse monnoie
           A celui qui ainsi proie,
                    Car finz mout
           Semble par fausses clamours;   35
           Par ce mon senz me desvoie.

V   --Or vous pardoing mon corrous,
           Amours, et a vous m'otroie;
           Quant vous haez traïtors,
           A tort aussi vous harroie.   40
           Mes de la simple, la coie,
           M'aidiez que ele soit moie,
                    Car si douz
           Sont si maintieng savourous
           Que sienz sui, ou que je soie.   45

MN   Form: A A¹ B.
1. a) In l. 2 both *m'otroie* and its music are omitted from
ms.; b) in ms. this note is actually placed above the first
syllable of l. 3; since the following music is exactly like
that of l. 1, it has been conjectured that the notes of l. 3
are all shifted one syllable to the right, with the last
note omitted; the missing three notes in l. 2 have been
added in conformance with l. 6.

RR   I   2 -2 *(em. Jeanroy)*   3 grant dolour   7
tristece *(em. Jeanroy)*   II   18 ne j. *(em. Jeanroy)*   IV
34   mont   V   42   quele *(-1)*

E   Jeanroy "Philippe", 535-536; Cremonesi, 260-261;
Toja, 482-484.

N   This is one of only four OF lyric dialogues with the allegorical figure of Love. The others are a *tenson* by Perrin D'Angicourt (RS 1665), a *jeu-parti* by Gillebert de Berneville (RS 1075), and an anonymous song (RS 892).

8 *en cours* 'in a race, competition'. 11 *chascun*, prepositionless dative. 13 *Trop mainz* 'too little'. 23 Understand *que* before *Il*. 32-25 'False money is like the man who thus beseeches, i.e., the man who thus beseeches is like false money, for through his false supplications he much resembles a true lover'. The approximativeness of the rhyme-word l. 34 *mout* (: -*ou(r)s*) leads us to suggest that *finz mout* may be an error for *amours*, in which case ll. 34-35 would mean 'for through false supplications it (= what he is expressing) resembles love'.

<u>211</u>   Chanson

RS 2096, MW 1498
Ms. V 54v-55r. Music. Anonymous (see note below).

I   Aussi com l'eschaufeüre
       Du fu fet l'iaue boulir,
       Me fet la douce pointure
       De fine Amour resjoïr
               Et fremir.   5
       Remenbrance, sanz mentir,

Ai touz jorz de l'aventure
Qui navra sanz perceüre
Ma car; par l'ueil assaillir
Me vint et mon cuer sesir					10
Amours, qui outre mesure
Me fet ses assaus sentir
Et atendre sanz merir.

II		Douz est li chaus de l'arsure
		Dont je me sent si benir.				15
		Bontez et bele estature,
		Granz senz et biau maintenir
				Font emplir
		Mon corage et enrichir
		D'une couvoitise pure,					20
		Qu'ausement com la nature
		Du douz tenz fet fruit florir
		Fet ma penssee espanir
		Bons espoirs, qui m'asseüre;
		Mes, encontre ce, soupir				25
		Por doutance de faillir.

III		Hé! simple regardeüre
		Qui si me fetes gemir,
		N'os dire que mespresure
		Feïssiez de moi traïr,					30
				Se servir
		Me fetes et obeïr
		A la plus bele figure
		Qui ainz vestist de vesture.
		Je ne m'en doi repentir,				35
		Que tieus biens en puet venir
		Que cil qui plus maus endure
		Ne porroit mes por morir
		Le guerredon deservir.

IV		Lis souz vermeille tainture,				40
		Ieus vairs en front d'ecremir
		Portanz en desconfiture
		Mon orgueil sanz revertir,
				Qu'esbahir
		Me font ma dame d'oïr					45
		Sa tres doce palleüre.
		Mout m'est grief la teneüre
		De tout ensemble sosfrir,
		Quant sanz plus me fet languir
		De sa bouche une ouverture				50

        Que j' en riant vi ouvrir,
        Dont l'odor me vint sesir.

V   Chançon, a cele ou ma cure
        Ai mise, va tost jehir
        Que, s'il li plest, mort oscure   55
        A brief tenz m'estelt sousfrir;
            Son plesir
        En face, que departir
        N'en vueil por nule ledure.
        Tant me soit douce ne sure   60
        S'amour, ja n'en quier issir;
        Car, se loiauté venir
        Puet jamés a sa droiture,
        Ne me dout pas que guerir
        Ne me face et resjoïr.   65

MN   Form: A A^1 B B$^{(1)}$.
1. In l. 3 ms. repeats this note. 2. In l. 2 ms. writes a bar. 3. In l. 7 ms. writes this note somewhat low, almost like *f*. 4. In l. 7 ms. omits this note. 5. In ms. l. 9 is apparently faulty and should be replaced by l. 13; cf. RS 2107, which has the same melody.

RR   8 naure *(em. Jeanroy)*

E   Jeanroy "Philippe", 530.

DF   Picard: *fu* (2) for *feu*; *iaue* (2) for *eau(e)* and *biau* (17) for *beau*; *boulir* (2) for *bouillir*; *car* (9) for *char*.

N   For attribution, see Jeanroy "Philippe", pp. 517–521. This song, in its meter and rhymes, is an imitation of Raoul de Soissons' *Quant voi la glaie meüre* (RS 2107).
    15 Jeanroy "Philippe" notes: "*si benir* n'offre pas de sens. Corr. *abenir*, éprouver un sentiment de bien-être? cf. le prov. *abenar*." To us, on the contrary, *si benir* seems appropriate, the verse meaning 'by which I feel myself so blessed'. 38 *por morir* 'even by dying'. 41–43 *d'ecremir . . . revertir* 'by fencing, bringing my pride irreversibly to defeat'. Lines 40–43 constitute a nominal clause, in which *Portanz = portent*. 44–46 *Qu'* is resultative: 'so that they (=l. 41 *Ieus*) cause me to be stunned by my lady when I hear her sweet speech'. Jeanroy "Philippe" emends *font* to *fait*, thus making *ma dame* the subject of the

conjugated verb rather than that of the infinitive *esbahir*.
56   *estelt = estuet.*

Chanson   212

RS 450, MW 1009
Ms. V 55r-v. Music. Anonymous (see note below).

I   Quant voi venir le tres douz tenz d'esté
     Et la froidure de l'iver departir
     Et je voi l'air, qui oscur a esté
     De toutes pars reluire et esclarcir   4
     Et ces oixiaus a leur chanz revertir,
     Donques me vient une tel volenté

D'estre joliz, de chanter a plenté
De Jehanete, dont je ne quier partir.   8

II   Partir n'en quier a jour de mon aé;
        Tant com vivrai, la voudrai je servir,
        Car g'i sai tant de debonnereté
        Que nus du mont ne la porroit haïr.   12
        Bien a deus anz qu'ele deigna oïr
        Ma priere dont me servi a gré,
        Que departir fist tote la griété
        Qui en moi ert, je n'en quier ja mentir.   16

III   Mentir? non certes! Ce seroit cruauté
        Se de s'amour me vouloie partir;
        Vers li nul jor ne ferai fausseté;
        Du tout m'i vueil donner et obeïr.   20
        Si me lest Dieus en paradiz venir
        Ne de mon cors me doint bonne santé,
        Que j'ai trouvé en li tel loiauté
        Que nus du mont ne porroit tele oïr.   24

IV   Oïr? vrais Dieus! Qui verroit sa biauté
        Bien se devroit de joie resbaudir;
        Plaine est de senz et de grant loiauté,
        Que sa pareille ne porroit on veïr.   28
        A toz se fet et amer et chierir;
        Quant on l'esgarde de bonne volenté
        En ses vairs ieus qu'ele a u chief planté,
        Se puet on bien et mirer et veïr.   32

V   Veïr? vrais Dieus! Mout sui bien assené,
        Ce m'est avis, quant el volt consentir
        Qu'ele m'amast. Or ai mon chant mené
        A ce que voi que tenz est du tezir.   36
        Puis qu'ainsi est, vueille li couvenir
        De moi qui sui ses amis et serai;
        Entierement li ai trestout donné
        Mon cuer, mon cors; s'en face son desir!   40

    MN   Form: through-composed.
1. Ms. repeats this note, as though *reluire* were not elided.

    RR   II 13-15 Bien a .ij. anz que me serui a gre de
ma priere quele deigna oir dont le mien cuer fist tant fort
resioir que departir fist tote la griete *(emendation as in
Jeanroy "Philippe", except 1. 15, which Jeanroy changes to*

Si que partir *etc)*.   III   17   cruautez   IV   28   Queisa
p.   30   on] en   V   33   mont   34   velt

E   Jeanroy "Philippe", 531-532.

DF   Picard: *veïr* (28, 32) for *veoir*.

N   For attribution, see Jeanroy "Philippe", pp. 517-
520.   The *césure épique*, extremely rare in the courtly *chanson*, is well represented in this poem (ll. 2, 8, 17, 28,
30), as it is in others by Philippe; see Jeanroy "Philippe",
p. 523.   This composition also shows the stanzaic linking of
coblas capfinidas.   The song is quite exceptional in its
concern with love granted rather than love sought and in its
incorporation of personal detail (l. 8 *Jehanete*, l. 13 *Bien
a deus ans*).   This is not unknown elsewhere in the poetry of
Philippe, however; see RS 557.
     31   *u = en + le*.   32   *veïr* occurs twice in this stanza
as a rhyme-word.   The correctness of this occurrence is ensured by l. 33; in the case of l. 28, one may well suspect a
scribal error, perhaps for *choisir* 'to perceive, see'.

Chanson   213

RS 557, MW 1064
Ms. V 55v-56r.   Music.   Anonymous (see note below).

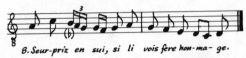

B. *Seur-priz en sui, si li vois fere hon-ma-ge.*

I   Ne finerai tant que j'avrai trouvee
     Une chançon fete de vrai courage
     Pour la plus bele qui soit de mere nee,
     Et si n'a pas quinze anz en son aage.   4
     Mout est gentilz et s'est de grant parage;
     Sa cortoisie a ele abandonnee
     A tout le mont; mout est de senz peuplee.
     Seurpriz en sui, si li vois fere honmage.   8

II   Servirai la et soir et matinee;
     A li servir metrai tout mon courage.
     Tel volenté i ai et tel pensee
     N'en puis avoir nul meilleur seignorage,   12
     Car je la voi si plesant et si sage
     Et de biauté est toute enluminee.
     Quant je la vi, mout tost li oi donnee
     M'amour; priz sui con li oisiaux en cage.   16

III Puiz que priz sui, n'i ferai demouree;
     Dire li vueil, n'i quier autre mesage.
     Or doigne Dieus qu'el soit de moi privee;
     En li vueill prendre ostel et hebergage.   20
     Bien croi que s'ele savoit le mien malage,
     Qu'ele mout tost m'aroit santé prestee;
     Mout a lonc tenz que je l'ai desirree;
     S'el m'escondist, j'en cuit morir a rage.   24

IV   Fel mesdisant, n'i puis avoir duree
     La ou je vueil detenir mon estage:
     C'est la bele que vous ai devisee.
     Encor li pri que ele m'assouage;   28
     S'ele ne.l fet, trop avra cuer volage,
     Bien porrai dire qu'amors est enversee
     A touz amanz et du tout bestournee.
     Baillier li vueil et cors et cuer en gage.   32

V   Chançon, va t'ent, car tu es achevee,
     De brief deport, n'i fai ja lonc musage;
     Di a la bele que ele est recouvree
     El tenz d'esté et el tenz yvernage,   36
     Que, s'ele vieut, je l'en menrai a nage
     En mon païz sanz fere demoree

. . . .
Si la prendrai, s'el veut, par mariage.   40

MN   Form: A A B.
1. In 1. 3 ms. writes *g*. 2. In 1. 1 ms. writes *d*. 3. For
1. 2 ms. writes:

RR   V 37 vient *(em. Jeanroy)*   39 la] le

E   Jeanroy "Philippe", 533-534.

DF   Picard: *aroit* (22) for *avroit*.

N   For attribution, see Jeanroy "Philippe", pp. 517-
522. For the *césure épique* (11. 3, 21, 30, 35), see RS 450,
Notes. This poem, exceptional in the corpus of courtly
chansons, is clearly addressed to an adolescent girl (1. 4)
and contains an offer of marriage (1. 40).
    12 Understand *que* before *N'en*.   37-38 The promise to
'take her by ship to my country' strengthens the hypothesis
that Philippe de Remi spent several years of his youth, probably 1261 to 1265, in England, where this song would have
been composed; see Jeanroy "Philippe", p. 522.   39 The
rhyme scheme suggests that a line has been omitted either
before or after 1. 38; the meaning of the final lines, which
in fact seems unimpaired by the omission, would place the
missing verse at this point.

<u>214</u>   Chanson pieuse

RS 602, MW 47
Ms. C 209r. No music (see note below). Attribution.

I   Retrowange novelle
           Dirai et bone et belle
           De la virge pucelle,
           Ke meire est et ancelle   4
       Celui ki de sa chair belle
           Nos ait raicheteit
       Et ki trestous nos apelle
           A sa grant clairteit.   8

II   Ce nos dist Isaïe
           En une profesie:
           D'une verge delgie
           De Jessé espanie,   12
       Istroit [flors] per signorie
           De tres grant biaulteit.
       Or est bien la profesie
           Torneie a verteit.   16

III   Celle verge delgie
           Est la virge Marie;
           La flor nos senefie,
           De ceu ne douteis mie,   20
       Jhesu Crist, ki la haichie
           En la croix sousfri;
       Fut por randre ceaus en vie
           Ki ierent peri.   24

<u>MN</u>   Melody from ms. K 308. Form: A A B B¹.
1. In 1. 4 ms. writes no rest.

<u>RR</u>   II   9 Se   11 Cune v. degipte *(em. Bartsch-*
Wiese)   13 *-1 (em. Bartsch-Wiese)*   III   17 v. degipte

<u>E</u>   Järnström 1, 93-94; Bartsch-Wiese, 223; Gennrich
Rot, 43; Gennrich *Ex*, 32; Bec 2, 71; Rivière *Jac*, 87-89.

<u>DF</u>   Lorraine, including *ai* for *a*, as in *raicheteit*
(6), *haichie* (21); *ei* for tonic *e*, as in *meire* (2), *raiche-*
teit (6), *torneie* (16), *douteis* (20); *s* for *c* (see Rejected
Readings); preservation of final *t*, as in *raicheteit* (6),
clairteit (8), *biaulteit* (14); intervocalic *w*, as in *retro-*
wange (1); 3rd-pers. sing. pres. ind. *ait* (6) for *a*.

<u>N</u>   This is the only *chanson pieuse* of Jacques de
Cambrai whose secular model is not specified in the ms. It
has been widely accepted, however, that the text is meant to
be sung to the melody of RS 599, whose metric pattern it
follows, and we therefore present it with that music.
    1 This is one of eight Old French songs that identify
themselves as *rotrouenges*; see Gennrich *Rot*, p. 14, and
Gennrich, "Zu den altfranzösischen Rotrouengen," *Zeit. für*
rom. Phil. 46 (1926), 335-341. The nature of the genre is
rather elusive and the form ill-defined, and the present
self-identification casts little light on the issue, for,
unlike the other compositions, RS 602 is heterometric and
lacks a refrain. For the most recent discussion of the
rotrouenge, see Bec 1, pp. 183-189; to the bibliography contained therein, we add H. Spanke, *Beziehungen zwischen ro-*
manischer und mittellateinischer Lyrik (Berlin, 1936), pp.
67-69.   5 *Celui* is an absolute genitive; understand *de* (or
a) *celui*.   10 The reference is to Isaiah 7:14 and 11:1-10.
23 In Bartsch-Wiese, Järnström 1, Gennrich *Rot*, and Rivière
Jac, *Tout* is unnecessarily substituted for the ms. reading
Fut.

GUILLAUME DE BETHUNE

<u>215</u>   Chanson pieuse

RS 1176, MW 2109
Ms. a 127r-v. Music. Attribution.

I   On me reprent d'amours qui me maistrie,
     S'est a grant tort qant aucuns m'en reprent,
     Car ensi est que jou voel de ma vie
     A bien amer metre l'entendement   4
     Et par vrai cuer canter d'ardant desir
     De la sainte vierge dont pot issir
     Une crape de cui vint l'abondance
     Del vin qui fait l'arme serve estre franke.   8

II   Cele vigne est la tres vierge Marie,
     Si fu plantee es cieus souvrainement,
     Car ele fu d'ame et de cuer ficie
     A Dieu amer et servir humlement   12
     Et par çou pot au fil Dieu avenir,
     Et il i vint conpaignie tenir,
     Si print en li cors humain et sustance
     Sans li metre de corompre en doutance.   16

III C'est li crape, de la vigne nourrie,
    Ki vin livra pour saner toute gent
    De l'enferté dont li ame est perie
    Qui n'a reçut de cel vin le present;   20
    Mais ains se vaut par meürer furnir
    Que se laissast de la vigne partir,
    U print roisins de si tres grant vaillance
    Ke d'enricir tous mendis ont poissance.   24

IV Cil douç roisin dont la crape est saisie
    Sont li menbre Jhesu Crist proprement,
    Et li crape est ses cors q'a grief hatie
    Fu traveilliés a l'estake en present;   28
    [Si] trestous nus c'on le paut desvestir,
    Fu tant batus k'il n'en remest d'entir
    Le quarte part de sa digne car blance,
    N'eüst de sanc u de plaie sanlance.   32

V   De la crape qui fu ensi froisie
    Doit cascuns cuers avoir ramenbrement,
    Et des roisins; faus est ki les oublie,
    Car mis furent en presse estroitement   36
    Entre le fer et le fust par ferir,
    Si c'onques blés k'en molin puet qaïr
    Ne fu pour maure en plus fort estraignance
    Con li car Dieu fu pour no delivrance.   40

VI El presseoir ki la crois senefie
    Fist Dieus de lui osfrande entirement,
    Si presenta a humaine lignie
    Tel vin qui fait l'oume estre sauvement.   44
    Qui il souvient de çou qu'il vaut sousfrir
    Si voelle a Dieu son cuer et s'ame osfrir;
    Ensi boit on par foi et par creance   47
    Cel vin dont Dius fait as vrais cuers pitance.

MN   Form: A A B.

RR   III   22   la uiege p.   23   V il p. *(+1)*   24
tout m.   IV   29   *-1 (em. Järnström)*   32   sans lance
VI   45   de tou   47   b. ont

E   Wallensköld *Conon* 1, 286-288; Järnström 1, 161-
164.

DF   Picard, including *au* for *ou*, as in *vaut* (21, 45),
paut (29), *faus* (35), *maure* (39 = *moudre*); *ie* for *iee*, as in

ficie (11), *froisie* (33), *lignie* (43) and *ir* for *ier*, as in
entir (30), *Dius* (48) for *Dieus*; *c* or *k* or *q* for *ch*, as in
canter (5), *franke* (8), *ficie* (11), *estake* (28), *car* (31,
40), *qaïr* (38); *voel* (3) for *vueil* and *voelle* (46) for
vueille; absence of epenthetic *b* in *humlement* (12), *sanlance*
(32); preservation of final *t*, as in past part. *reçut* (20);
çou (13) for *ce*; *jou* (3) for *je*; *no* (40) for *nostre*; fem.
nom. *li* (17, 40) and oblique *le* (31) for *la*.

    <u>N</u>   Like many *chansons pieuses*, this one is a contra-
factum of a secular poem. It borrows from RS 1175 not only
metrical structure, rhyme scheme, and rhymes, but the first
line as well. The song is unusual among *chansons pieuses* in
its elaboration of a single symbolic motif throughout its
six stanzas. As noted in Järnström 1, following the art
historian Emile Mâle, the motif is that of the mystical
winepress, a symbol often occurring in medieval religious
literature and art and originating in a rapprochement of two
passages of the Bible, Numbers 13:23 (Vulg. 24) and Isaiah
63:3.
    13 *fil Dieu*, absolute genitive for *f. de D.*; cf. l. 26
and l. 40.   16 'without making her fear corruption'.   17
C' designates l. 13 *le fil Dieu*. 19-20 *li ame . . . Qui*
'the soul of anyone who'.   21-22 'but He wished to be fully
formed through [normal] ripening before He let himself take
leave of the vine'.   23 *print roisins* 'developed, grew
grapes'.   27 The relative form *q'* functions here as a nominative.   45 *Qui* (= *cui*) *il souvient* 'whoever remembers'.

RUTEBEUF

Chanson satirique

RS 835a, MW 419, B 1470
Mss. Paris, B.N. français 837, f. 314v-315r; Paris, B.N.
français 1593, f. 67r; Paris, B.N. français 1635, f.
2r. (Not in Paris, B.N. français 24432 although so indicated in RS.) No music. Anonymous.

I Du siecle vueil chanter
 Que je voi enchanter;
 Tels vens porra venter
 Qu'il n'ira mie ainsi.
  Papelart et Beguin   5
  Ont le siecle honi.

II Tant d'ordres avons ja
 Ne sai qui les sonja;
 Ainz Dieus tels genz n'onja,
 N'il ne sont si ami.   10
  Papelart et Beguin
  [*Ont le siecle honi*].

III Frere Predicator
 Sont de mout simple ator
 Et s'ont en lor destor,   15
 Sachiez, maint parisi.
  Papelart et Beguin
  [*Ont le siecle honi*].

IV Et li Frere Menu
 Nous ont si pres tenu   20
 Que il ont retenu
 De l'avoir autressi.
  Papelart et Beguin
  [*Ont le siecle honi*].

V Qui ces deus n'obeïst   25
 Et qui ne lor gehist
 Quanqu'il onques feïst,
 Tels bougres ne nasqui.
  Papelart et Beguin
  [*Ont le siecle honi*].   30

VI Assez dïent de bien,
 Ne sai s'il en font rien;

Qui lor done du sien,
Tel preudomme ne vi.
Papelart et Beguin   35
[*Ont le siecle honi*].

VII   Cil de la Trinité
Ont grant fraternité;
Bien se sont aquité:
D'asnes ont fet ronci.   40
Papelart et Beguin
[*Ont le siecle honi*].

VIII   Et li Frere Barré
Resont cras et quarré;
Ne sont pas enserré: 45
Ja les vi mercredi.
Papelart et Beguin
[*Ont le siecle honi*].

IX   Nostre Frere Sachier
Ont luminon fet chier;   50
Chascuns samble vachier
Qui ist de son mesni.
Papelart et Beguin
[*Ont le siecle honi*].

X   Set vins filles ou plus   55
A li rois en reclus;
Onques mes quens ne dus
Tant n'en congenuï.
Papelart et Beguin
[*Ont le siecle honi*].   60

XI   Beguines avons mont
Qui larges robes ont;
Desouz lor robes font
Ce que pas ne vous di.
Papelart et Beguin   65
[*Ont le siecle honi*].

XII   L'ordre des Nonvoianz,
Tels ordre est bien noianz;
Il tastent par leanz:
"Quant venistes vous ci?"   70
Papelart et Beguin
[*Ont le siecle honi*].

     XIII   Li Frere Guillemin,
             Li autre Frere Hermin,
             M'amor lor atermin: 75
             Je.s amerai mardi.
             Papelart et Beguin
             Ont le siecle honi.

     <u>RR</u>   III   16 Mainte bon p. *(em. Faral-Bastin)*   VII
40 roncin   XI   61 mout

     <u>V</u>   Stanza IX not included in ms. 1593. Stanzas X and
XI transposed in ms. 1635.
I   4 miel] pas 1635   II   7 drodre 1593   9 Aint d.
tel gent n. 1593   10 Ne ne 1593   III   16 De maint
bon p. 1593   IV   20 N. ront 1593, 1635   V   27
Canques (Quonque 1635) il onques fist 1593, 1635   VII
40 roncins 1635   VIII   44 gros 1593   X   58 enge-
nui 1593, engenuy 1635   XI   61 a on m. 1593   63 Desor 1593; les 1635; ont 1635   XII   67 Lordres 1635
XIII   78 le] cest 1593

     <u>E</u>   Jubinal 1, 202-207; Kressner, 56; Jeanroy-Långfors,
13-16; Cremonesi, 273-275; Faral-Bastin 1, 330-333.

     <u>N</u>   The attribution of this text is ensured not only
by its subject and style but also by its ms. inclusion among
the works of Rutebeuf. In ms. 837 it bears the title *Des
ordres*; in ms. 1593, *La Chanson des ordres*; in ms. 1635, *Les
autres diz des ordres*; this last is a reference to another
poem by Rutebeuf on the same subject, *Les ordres de Paris*.
The "orders" are mendicant religious societies, particularly
numerous in the mid-thirteenth century. Faral-Bastin dates
the poem from 1263 or shortly thereafter.
     3-4 The poet may mean either that the world will per-
ish or that the orders will be disbanded.   5 The *Papelart*
do not constitute an order, but are simply all those guilty
of ostentatious and hypocritical religious zeal. The *Beguin*
'Beghards', with a distinctive form of dress, did form an
order but not one legitimized by the Church. For information on these groups, as well as the others mocked by Rutebeuf, see Faral-Bastin 1, pp. 68-82 and 318-321.
     8 Understand *que* before *Ne*.   13 *Frere Predicator*,
i.e., the Dominicans.   19 *Frere Menu*, i.e., the Francis-
cans.   40 The Trinitarians were originally forbidden to
ride on horses, but the restriction was lifted in 1263.   43
Frere Barré, i.e., the Carmelites.   44 *Resont* 'are, for
their part'.   46 Faral-Bastin suggests the possibility

that *mercredi* is intended as a pun on l. 44 *cras*. With *r* weakened or effaced before consonant, well attested in late OF, *mercredi* would recall the adjective *maigre*.   49-50 The Brethren of the Penitence of Jesus Christ, called *Sachiers* or *Sachets* because of the sackcloth they customarily wore, received the proceeds of a special tax for their lamp oil. For another interpretation of these lines, see Félix Lecoy, "Sur un passage difficile de Rutebeuf," *Romania* 85 (1964), 368-372.   55 The 140 or more Daughters of the King seem to be the order usually known as the *Filles-Dieu*.   57 *quens* = *cuens*.   61 The *Beguines* were the female counterparts of the *Beguins*; see note to l. 5. *mont* = *mout*.   67 The *Non-voianz* are the *Trois-Cents Aveugles*, commonly known as *les Quinze-Vingt*.   73 *Frere Guillemin*, i.e., the Guillelmites. 74 *Frere Hermin*, not the name of a real order, apparently refers to both Armenians and the hermitic origins of the Guillelmites.   76 According to Faral-Bastin, *mardi*, like l. 46 *mercredi*, is perhaps meant as a pun; it would call to mind the strongly negative idea of the adverb *mar*.

217   Chanson pieuse

RS 1998, MW 1968
Mss. Paris, B.N. français 1635, f. 82r; Paris, B.N. français
    1593, f. 61r. No music. Attribution.

I   Chanson m'estuet chanteir de la meilleur
       Qui onques fust ne qui jamais sera.
       Li siens douz chanz garit toute doleur;
       Bien iert gariz cui ele garira.
                 Mainte arme a garie;   5
                 Huimais ne dot mie
                 Que n'aie boen jour,
                 Car sa grant dosour
                 N'est nuns qui vous die.

II   Mout a en li cortoizie et valour;   10
       Bien et bontei et charitei i a.
       Con folz li cri merci de ma folour;
       Foloié ai s'onques nuns foloia.
                 Si pleur ma folie
                 Et ma fole vie,   15
                 Et mon fol senz plour
                 Et ma fole errour
                 Ou trop m'entroblie.

III Quant son doulz non reclainment picheour
 Et il dïent son Ave Maria,   20
 N'ont puis doute dou maufei tricheour
 Qui mout doute le bien qu'en Marie a,
    Car qui se marie
    En teile Marie,
    Boen mariage a.   25
    Marions nos la,
    Si avrons s'aïe.

IV Mout l'ama cil qui, de si haute tour
 Com li ciel sunt, descendi juque ça.
 Mere et fille porta son creatour,   30
 Qui de noiant li et autres cria.
    Qui de cuer s'escrie
    Et merci li crie
    Merci trovera;
    Jamais n'i faudra   35
    Qui de cuer la prie.

V Si com hom voit le soloil toute jor
 Qu'en la verriere entre et ist et s'en va,
 Ne l'enpire tant i fiere a sejour,
 Ausi vos di que onques n'empira   40
    La vierge Marie:
    Vierge fu norrie,
    Vierge Dieu porta,
    Vierge l'aleta,
    Vierge fu sa vie.   45

RR IV 29 ça] sa

V Stanza IV not included in ms. 1593.
I 2 fu 4 qui II 14 p. et f. V 37 envoit

E Jubinal 2, 149-151; Kressner, 200; Voretzsch, 149-150; Faral-Bastin 2, 245-246.

DF Lorraine: *ei* for tonic *e*, as in *chanteir* (1), *bontei* (11), *teile* (24); *boen* (7) for *bon*.

N The text is introduced in ms. 1635 by the phrase *C'est de Notre Dame* and in ms. 1593 by *Une chanson de nostre Dame*. 3-5 *garit*, *gariz*, etc.: for the rhetorical device of *annominatio*, see Regalado, pp. 219-221, 235. 5 *arme* 'soul'. 31 *cria* 'created'.

Appendix: The Trouvères

The sources of the data presented below are various, including Dragonetti, PetDyg "Onom", PetDyg "Trouvères", works on particular trouvères cited in the Bibliography, and R. Bezzola, *Les Origines et la formation de la littérature courtoise en Occident (500-1200)*, 3e partie: "La Société courtoise: Littérature de cour et littérature courtoise", 2 vols. (Paris: Champion, 1963). A few of the trouvères, participants in jeux-partis, appear in the Table of Contents only, or a second time, under the names of their collaborators; such occurrences are signaled below by "(S.)" and "(S. too)", resp. Abbreviations include "app." for "apparently" and "incl." for "including".

ADAM DE LA HALLE, also A. LE BOSSU. Most famous poet of Arras, b. ca. 1237 prob. in Arras, d. 1288 in Italy. Studied in Paris. Was in service of Robert, Count of Artois, with whom he went to Italy in 1283. Composed almost 100 songs, incl. many jeux-partis and rondeaux. Wrote two notable works for theater: *Jeu de Robin et Marion*, *Jeu de la feuillée*. (S. too Jehan Bretel.)

ANDRIEU CONTREDIT D'ARRAS. D. 1248. Knight and app. minstrel at court of Louis IX. 20 or more songs.

AUBERTIN D'AIRAINES. Picard, app. 2nd half of 13th c. 2 songs.

AUDEFROI LE BATARD. Prob. Picard, active 1215 on. Member of Puy of Arras. 17 songs. Notable for reworking the *chanson de toile*.

BLONDEL DE NESLE. Prob. Jean II, lord of Nesle (near Amiens), b. 12th c., d. 1241. Close ties with many poets. Married and departed for Holy Land as crusader in 1202. Participated in Albigensian crusade in 1209, again 1226. About 24 songs. See Ertzdorff, pp. 38-31.

CHATELAIN DE COUCI. Perhaps Guy de Ponceaux, friend to whom Gace Brulé dedicated several songs; b. 12th c., d. 1203. Participated in 4th Crusade. 9 or more songs. See Baum for recent discussion of identity.

CHRETIEN DE TROYES. Greatest French poet of the 12th c., active from ca. 1160; d. ca. 1183, prob. in Flanders. From Champagne, had as patrons first Marie de Champagne, then Philippe d'Alsace. 2, perhaps up to 5, songs. Works include the romances *Erec et Enide*, *Cligès*, *Lancelot*, *Yvain*, *Perceval*.

COLIN MUSET. From area straddling Champagne and Lorraine; app. active 2nd third of 13th c. Professional singer-composer. About 20 songs of non-courtly character. For recent observations on his vocabulary, see Banitt and Levy.

CONON DE BETHUNE. B. mid 12th c. into noble Artois family; d. ca. 1220. Took part in 3rd and 4th Crusades. Relative of Baudouin IX, first French emperor of Constantinople; named Seneschal, then Regent, of the Empire (1217, 1219). 12 songs. For life and poetry, see Becker, pp. 174-182; for name, Adnès, pp. 67-75; also Muraille.

DAME DE GOSNAI. 13th c. (S. Gillebert de Berneville.)

DAME DE LA CHAUSSEE. 13th c. 1 jeu-parti. (S. Sainte des Prés.)

DUCHESSE DE LORRAINE. Several identifications possible, incl. Marguerite, daughter of the trouvère Thibaut de Champagne, who married Ferri III, Duke of Lorraine, in 1255. 2 songs.

ETIENNE DE MEAUX. 13th c. 1 song, perhaps 2.

GACE BRULE. Famous poet, mentioned by various fellow-trouvères. B.

1159 or earlier into minor Champenois nobility; still alive in 1212. Almost 70 songs attributed to him with reasonable certainty, incl. the oldest jeu-parti (RS 948) and 3 songs incorporated into Jehan Renart's *Guillaume de Dole*. See Ertzdorff, pp. 24-31, and Muraille.

GAMART DE VILERS. Unknown, but must have been a contemporary of Jehan le Cuvelier (see below). 1 song.

GAUTIER DE DARGIES. B. ca. 1165 into Beauvaisis nobility; still alive in 1236. Participated in 3rd Crusade. Friend of Gace Brulé and other trouvères. About 25 songs, incl. the first descort known to have been written in French.

GILLEBERT DE BERNEVILLE. App. active 1255-1280 at court of Brabant and among Arras poets. Over 30 songs, incl. jeux-partis and many refrain songs.

GONTIER DE SOIGNIES. App. active early 13th c. as one of the first professionals among the trouvères of Artois. Took part in a crusade, perhaps the 4th. Up to 30 songs, almost all with refrains.

GUILLAUME D'AMIENS. Wrote his *Dit d'Amour* in 2nd half of 13th c. 14 songs, incl. 10 rondeaux.

GUILLAUME DE BETHUNE. Two *chansons pieuses*, both contrafacta; given the models, he probably lived in last third of 13th c.

GUILLAUME LE VINIER. D. 1245. Belonged to bourgeois family of Arras; brother Gilles was a canon, Guillaume himself in lower orders. App. in contact with numerous poets and well known. 35 songs, incl. chansons, jeux-partis, devotional.

GUIOT DE DIJON. App. active in 1st half of 13th c. 6 or more songs.

HENRI III, DUC DE BRABANT. Duke 1248-1261. Patron as well as poet, maintained close relations with Artois trouvères. 4 songs.

HUE DE LA FERTE. From western nobility (Maine), an opponent of Blanche de Castille's 1228-30 regency. 3 songs, all *serventois*.

JACQUEMIN DE LA VENTE. Prob. a wandering cleric with some ties to the Arras poets of 2nd half of 13th c. 3 songs.

JACQUES D'AMIENS. Active 1250-1280. Presumed author of Ovidian *Art d'amour* and *Remède d'amour*. 7 songs. (S. Colin Muset.)

JACQUES D'AUTUN. 13th c. 1 song.

JACQUES DE CAMBRAI. 13th c. 12 songs, incl. 7 *chansons pieuses*.

JACQUES DE CYSOING. Active 3rd quarter of 13th c. From noble family of Flanders, belonged to poetic circles of Arras and Lille. 10 songs.

JACQUES DE DOSTI. 13th c. 1 song.

JEHAN BODEL. Poet and jongleur of Arras, b. c. 1165, d. 1210 of leprosy. Aside from 5 songs, all pastourelles, wrote numerous works, incl. fabliaux, *Chanson des Saisnes*, *Jeu de saint Nicolas*, *Congés*.

JEHAN BRETEL. Bourgeois, b. ca. 1200, d. 1272. Admitted to Confrérie des jongleurs et bourgeois d'Arras in 1244. Most prolific writer of jeux-partis, co-composing no fewer than 90; a few other songs as well. (S. too Jehan de Crieviler.)

JEHAN DE GRIEVILER. D. ca. 1255. Married cleric. Admitted to Confrérie des jongleurs et bourgeois d'Arras in 1240. 34 jeux-partis, 7 chansons. (S. too Jehan Bretel.)

JEHAN ERART. App. active in 2nd quarter of 13th c., d. 1258-59. No rank or wealth. At court of Brabant at same time as Gillebert de Berneville and Perrin d'Angicourt. Ca. 25 songs, incl. many past.

JEHAN LE CUVELIER D'ARRAS. Active 3rd quarter 13th c., app. figure of importance. 7 chansons, 9 jeux-partis. (S. Gamart de Vilers.)

MAHIEU LE JUIF. 13th c. 2 songs.

MONIOT D'ARRAS. Active 1213-1239. Monk for some time. In contact with some of the most famous figures of his time. 16 or more songs.

MONIOT DE PARIS. Prob. a monk active as poet in 3rd quarter of 13th c. 9 songs of non-courtly stamp, incl. pastourelles, rotrouenges.

PERRIN D'ANGICOURT. Active mid 13th c. at court of Brabant and among poets of Arras. In contact with a number of well-known poets, incl. patron Charles, Count of Anjou. About 30 songs.

PHILLIPPE DE REMI, SIRE DE BEAUMANOIR. Born 1246-50 in Orléanais, d. 1296. Visited Britain in 1260s. Held succession of royal appointments from 1279, incl. Seneschal of Poitou, Seneschal of Saintonge; sent on mission to Rome in 1288-89. About 10 songs, but much better known for other works, incl. *Coutumes de Beauvaisis* (1283) and *La Manekine*.

RAOUL DE BEAUVAIS. Prob. active mid 13th c.; contemporary of Jehan Erart (d. 1258-59). 5 songs.

RAOUL DE SOISSONS. App. same as Thierry de Soissons. B. ca. 1210, undocumented after 1270. Became Sire de Coeuvres in 1232. Participated in crusades 1239-1244 and 1248-1253; new departure in 1270. Over 15 songs, perhaps all composed 1243-1255.

RICHARD COEUR DE LION. B. 1157 in Oxford; reigned as Richard I of England from 1189 to death in 1199. 2 songs.

RICHART DE FOURNIVAL. B. 1201 in Amiens, d. 1260. Canon, later chancellor, of Notre-Dame d'Amiens. Over 20 songs of various types, but better known for other writings, incl. Latin treatise on alchemy and, in French, *La Puissance d'Amour*, *Le Bestiaire d'Amour*, etc.

RICHART DE SEMILLI. Active perhaps end of 12th c. 11 songs, incl. pastourelles, rotrouenges, chansons.

ROGIER. Co-composer of 1 jeu-parti. (S. Adam de la Halle.)

RUTEBEUF. The first great poet of Paris, professional jongleur, b. in Champagne, active 1250-1280. Participated in the intellectual and political quarrels of his day, e.g., the discord at the University of Paris. 2 songs. Numerous other works include much non-lyric poetry, *Miracle de Théophile*, *Vie de sainte Marie l'Egyptienne*.

SAINTE DES PRES. 13th c. Prob. in Artois poetic circle. 1 jeu-parti.

SIMON D'AUTHIE. Active in ecclesiastical functions, mainly in Amiens, from 1222; still alive in 1232. About 10 songs.

THIBAUT II, COMTE DE BAR. Count from 1239 to death in 1291. Through marriage, was involved in Flemish political strife, 1247-1256. Taken captive in 1253, spent a year in German prison. 2 songs.

THIBAUT DE BLAISON. Born into Angevin nobility; Seneschal of Poitou from 1228 to death in 1229. Politically active life. Between 9 and 13 songs, mainly courtly chansons.

THIBAUT DE CHAMPAGNE. Prolific poet, patron of poets, b. 1201, d. 1253. Became Count of Champagne and Brie 1214, King of Navarre 1234. Took part in crusade 1239-1240. First adversary, then ally, of Blanche of Castille, widow of Louis VIII and Regent, in her troubled relations with feudal lords. Some 60-70 songs of various genres. For study of chansons, see Dolly-Cormier. (S. too Guillaume le Vinier.)

Index of Names

The following list is complete in that it includes all names that occur in our texts and cites all texts in which they occur; line references, however, are limited to two, the presence of other occurrences being indicated by the abbreviation *et p.* No identifications are provided here since, when not wholly obvious, they are given in the Notes to the relevant texts. The figure preceding the colon in each reference is the poem number; the figure following designates the line.

Glossary

Necessarily brief, the Glossary assumes knowledge of modern French and familiarity with OF. It omits terms glossed in Notes, made recognizable by inclusion in Dialectal Features, or readily found in A.J. Greimas, *Dictionnaire de l'ancien français* (Larousse, 1969). Line references are limited to one per meaning. Grammatical data identify only verb forms; these are listed, as needed, under infinitive or a finite form. Persons are numbered 1 to 6. Abbreviations: *C* conditional, *F* future, *I* imperative, *II* imperfect indicative, *IS* imperfect subjunctive, *o.* oneself, *PI* present indicative, *PP* past participle, *PrP* present participle, *Pret* preterit, *PS* present subjunctive, *(R)* (sometimes) pronominal, *SI* substantivized infinitive.

aatis *zealous, eager* 169:36
aatissant *PrP* aatir *compare* 192:19
abandonee *revealed* 213:6
abeüter *to watch (for)* 53:41
acointier, acoentieir *to meet* 27: 36; *SI first meeting* 45:6
adrecié *redressed* 79:31 [183:30
afferroit *C3* afferir *be fitting*
agence *PS3* agencier *please* 122:14
aidel *accomplice* 26:56
aïe, ahie, aiue *aid* 87:8
aïr(e) *PI1 R* airier *become angry*
alaissiez *relieved* 53:8 [82:6
alowe *meadowlark* 15:6
amatir *to wither* 166:1
amatis *brought low* 114:12 [37:2
ambaniant *PrP* ambanaier *enjoy o.*
ambleir *to steal, take away* 19:17
amender *to profit* 126:12; *R to do*
ancontre *see* en- [*better* 119:48
anfes *see* enfes
anfleit *insensed man* 30:20
anfruine *reluctant* 15:14
anoi *pain, torment* 199:19
anpairleir *intermediary* 62:7
anradie *anger, indignation* 4:11
antreprise *see* entrepris
anvoiseüre *see* en- [18:37
apant *PI3* apendre *be attached*
apareille *PI3 R* appareillier *be compared* 67:12
apareillies, appareilliés *apparelled* 133:44; *ready* 69:24
aparissant *evident* 158:6
apensés *concerned* 139:2
apercevoir *SI being seen* 106:8
apoiaus *support* 56:16
appellés *accused* 139:20
arme, airme *soul* 215:8

arrement *ink* 61:37
ars *burned* 135:33 [86:33
asoteit *PP* assoter *make a fool of*
asoumer *to complete* 186:38
assené *treated* 170:7
assis *besieged* 91:33 [70:22
assoylez *I5* assoyler *absolve*
ataigne *PS3* ataindre *touch* 138:42
atendance *concern, care* 145:12
atent *PI3 R* atendre *aspire* 141:26
atirié *mistreated* 135:28
ator, atour *finery* 80:2; *equipment* 108:46; *condition* 32:36
atorné *attributed* 163:13
aubor *alburnum, sapwood* 141:19
aubourdie *(unknown; refers to domain of love)* 182:14
ausement com *just as* 211:21
aventure est que *perhaps* 95:44
aveu *with* 210:53
bait *PS3* baisier *kiss* 134:7
barcheignies *wooed* 133:30
baretant *PrP* bareter *deceive*
baron *husband* 44:17 [58:5
bé *PI1* baer *desire, aspire* 81: 10; baie, bee, beie *PI3*
berguignier *to bargain* 2:4
bernaige *noble company* 177:6
bois(s)ier *to deceive* 133:27
border *to lie* 53:40
borsel *bump* 26:62
bouchet, bouset *small wood* 36:4
boules *gambling dens* 55:9
bouteir, feu b. *to set fire*
brondelz *branches* 177:19 [176:14
brueill, bruille, bruelet *wooded area* 34:3
bruïne *fog* 6:33
cercel *tambourine* 26:31

chamoi *hay-covered field* 27:3
chantel, en c. *in a defensive position* 177:26 [131:65
chaüs, cheoit *PP* cheoir *fall*
chausie *covered (by male)* 53:1
chef de tour *outcome* 57:23
choisir *to see, perceive, discern* 97:29; choisi *Pret1*
chosit *PP* choisir *perceive* 8:7
cismes *heretical(?)* 2:22
cler, a c. *sparsely* 79:20
cointise *elegance* 108:55; *cunning* 57:10
cointoier *to chirp* 97:2; cointoie, cointie *PI3 improve* 26:37; *R dress up* 204:48, *adorn o.* 26:21, *be presumptuous* 184:64
coiteusement *without delay* 180:52
compaireir, conparer *to pay for* 95:27; conperra *F3*
conperé *paid for* 151:19 [216:58
congenuï *Pret3* congenuir *engender*
consalz *counsel; support* 87:37
consaut *PS3* consievre *aid* 120:28
conseil, conseus *decision* 93:16; *secret* 160:22
consirer, consireir *(R) to be deprived* 181:45; *SI* consirrer(s) *deprivation* 95:17, *absence* 103:1
consuï *struck* 132:8
contenir *R to behave* 204:6
contenue *behaved* 45:20
contraiz *paralyzed* 82:11
coree *region of the heart* 54:48
coriaus, coraux *sincere* 118:30
cortieus *gardens* 169:30
couez *fringed* 26:17 [53:22
cousiner *to "roast", punish(?)*
couvine *disposition, state* 195:31
criem *PI1* criembre, cremir *fear* 87:13; cremi *Pret1*, crient *PI3*
cuerine *anger, hatred* 195:6
cuit, cuiz *PI1* cuidier *think, believe* 93:38; quidai *Pret1*; cudasse *IS1 (had) thought*
cuitainne *jousting practice* 8:6
cunquïés *insulted* 186:32
Dameledé *Lord God* 158:32
daurra *F3 R* doloir *be suffered* 185:67
debruisier *to bend or twist the body in dancing* 109:26
decerte *justification* 70:2

deduxans *pleasant, charming* 3:1
dehait, dehé, dehez *damnation* 151:26; d. ait *damned be* 110:45
demerrons *F4* demener *express* 20:14; demoinne *PI3 control* 134:31
deport *pleasure* 17:26; *delay*
descors *descort* 112:43 [213:34
deseure, par d. *in spite of* 31:27
desfendre *R to escape* 87:20
desherité *expelled* 64:18; desiretés *disinherited* 139:16
despoigne *PS3* despondre *interpret* 122:62
desrainier *to defend* 87:4
desresnier *to recite* 147:8
dessevrer, desever *(R) to leave* 158:2; *undo, separate* 95:30
destornans *reluctant* 131:50
destoupeit *PP* destouper *start to play* 30:10
destroit, a d. *in distress* 109:38
desvee, dervee *mad, crazy* 49:8
desvoie *PI3* desvoier *be bewildered* 131:32
deviner *gossip, stories* 104:10
devis, devise *satisfaction* 46:2
die *PS3* dire *tell* 87:42
doing *PS1* doner *give, grant* 171:7; doinst, doint, dont *PS3*; dorray *F1*, dorront *F6*
donoie, dosnoie *PI3* donoier *womanize, have relations with women* 134:69; dosnoiier *SI favors, the sexual relationship* 199:8
dont *then, indeed* 96:34
dosnoi *love affair* 199:21
dout *PI1* douter *fear* 103:5
duel(s), duelx *grief, sorrow* 104:23; *shame* 93:18
dui *Pret1* devoir *must* 82:5
el *something, anything else* 158:18
empenir *to expiate* 209:16
encontre *despite* 211:25; *toward, approaching* 177:1
encopés *guilty* 139:23
enfes *child* 135:32; *young man* 8:6
engrengnier *increase, grow* 180:6
enmender *see* amender
enpris *Pret1* enprendre *undertake*
enprise *undertaking* 57:35 [173:46
enrachies *snatched* 133:48
entente *intent, attention* 58:13
ententis, ententieus *attentive*

98:15; *eager* 162:38
entre...et *both...and* 15:1
entreus que *while* 182:40
envoisie, envoissié, anvoixie
  joyous, gay 159:1
envoixeüre *verve* 28:4
errant, tot e. *right away* 202:17
erré *behaved* 150:13
errement *situation* 138:3
erroment *right away* 185:11
ert *II3 estre be* 95:20
escondire *to deny, refuse* 101:
  39; escondist *PI3*; escondirai
  Fl R justify o. 7:19; *SI refus-
  al, denial* 112:37
escondite, excondix *refused* 66:7
esforcier *to reinforce* 138:16
eskapeler *to reduce* 186:37
eslire *discern* 112:45; eslit *PI3
  choose* 90:15, eslise *PS3*
eslis *choice, excellent* 90:14
eslite *sweetheart* 92:44
esmaiant *dismayed* 170:14
espernement *kindling, arousal*
espoir *perhaps* 88:43   [43:5
estage *sojourn* 97:31; *situation*
  124:13; *dwelling, place* 213:26
estel *pieces* 177:28
estout, estouz *foolish* 56:99
estre *condition* 138:3
estuet, esteut *PI3 estovoir be
  necessary* 89:15; esteüst *IS3*
eu *Pretl avoir have* 116:8
eus *see* oés
euwee *a drink of water* 185:56
façon *face* 80:15
faintemant *half-heartedly, false-
  faintis false* 44:28   [ly 50:22
faiture *character, nature* 178:42;
  creature 6:21
faudrai *Fl faillir fail* 96:34;
  faudra, faudrat *F3*; faudront *F6*;
  faut, fat *PI3; end, come to end*
fenis *phoenix* 41:23   [8:1
fetement, si f. *thus* 167:31
fi, fis *sure, certain* 185:14; de
  f. *as a certainty* 77:6
flaihutel *type of flute* 177:14
flaitir *R to rush* 52:29
foïrs *hasty departure* 85:32
franchise *freedom* 87:4; *noble
  act* 108:26
fremiant *shining, bright* 19:15

fresee *raw, peeled* 54:34
frot *cassock* 37:26
garison *well-being* 176:12
garnement, wernemens *garment(s)*
garni *warned* 79:34   [55:20
garrai *Fl garir be healed* 22:6
gas, gais *joke, jest* 85:58
gaskieres *arable land* 56:104
geirai *Fl gesir lie* 1:17
gent(e), jante *nobly beautiful*
gent *people* 90:18   [180:50
gerroie *PI3 guerroier attack,
  make war on* 198:23
getoit *see* jetons
geü *PP gesir lie* 149:16
gileor *deceivers* 32:26
gix *PI1 R gesir lie* 106:13
glachier *to slip away* 184:36
gorroie *Cl joïr enjoy* 192:47
goulousés *PI5 goulouser covet*
  184:44   [56:95
goute palasine *paralytic gout*
grain, ne... *not at all* 94:28
graislel, estroit g. *in a high-
  pitched voice* 26:23
gramoie *PI3 R gramoier become
  angry* 26:47
grever *to hurt* 100:6; griet *PS3*
groce *PI3 grocier grumble* 168:39
hallegoutee *tattered* 52:37
harroie *Cl haïr hate* 210:40
haschie, haichie *torment, suffering* 115:43; *Passion (of Christ)*
hatie *shame* 215:27   [214:21
haubergies *reinforced with mail*
heim *hook* 70:38   [133:22
iert *F3 estre be* 179:30
indete *purple* 31:2
irour *anguish* 181:13
issir, eissir *to leave* 186:6;
  ist *PI3*, issent *PI6*, ississiés
  IS5, istrai *Fl*, istra *F3*, is-
  troie *Cl*, istroit *C3*
ius *eyes* 194:12
jaglolai *gladiolae* 16:10
janglement *mendacity, lying* 115:
  jangler *to slander* 180:71   [24
jant(e) *see* gent(e)
jetons *I4 (R) jeter release* 69:31
jeü *see* geü   [ful 162:11
joli, -s, -z, -e, -f, -ve *cheer-
  jorés F5 joïr enjoy* 83:16
jualz, juëlz *jewels* 29:27

jugance *judgment* 86:48
jui *Pret1* gesir *lie* 158:11
juïse *judgment* 54:1
juïse *Jewish* 54:10
kamelin *a kind of woolen cloth*
keus *PP* cuire *cook* 52:39   [30:6
lassant *PrP* lacier *lace* 35:4
latin *language* 17:8
ledure *wrong, mistreatment* 211:59
lera *F3* laier *leave*; ne l. a *refrain from* 25:46
letardie *lethargy* 156:14
liement *joyfully* 138:1   [171:39
lo *PI1* soi löer de *be glad of*
löer *to praise* 111:2; löés *PI5*
  advise 199:20, löez *I5*
loie *PI3 (R)* lïer *bind* 137:41
loié *rewarded* 114:29
loier(s), loieier, luier *reward*
loiez *bound* 197:19   [173:47
lour *then, at that time* 178:5
main *morning* 46:30; *early* 35:1;
  in the morning 127:4
maintenant (de m.) *right away*
  132:14; m. que *as soon as* 27:50
maire *PI3* mairer *control* 164:56
maire *bigger, greater* 10:37
mais, maiz *henceforth* 114:17;
  (n)ever 131:1; m. que *even
  though* 5:8
malage *sickness* 91:38   [150:39
malé, champ m. *field of combat*
maleïe, malaoit, malois *cursed*
manadie *property* 31:11   [62:29
manaie *care and pity* 154:60;
  dwelling 67:14
manant, menanz *wealthy* 57:18
manoir *to dwell* 172:3; maint *PI3*;
  manans *PrP* *remaining* 196:12
mas, maz *humbled* 56:27
mee *physician* 101:22
menant *PrP* mener *express* 24:4;
  mainent *PI6*; moinrés *F5* *lead*
menour *little folk* 91:13 [181:42
merir, sanz m. *undeservedly*
mescine *medicine* 42:15   [211:13
message *messenger* 93:39
mieus *honey* 194:36
mont, mons *world* 90:11
morel *dark-colored* 26:41
müel, muiele *a mute* 30:17; *mute*
muse *bagpipe* 26:10   [56:91
musel *idler* 177:11

nes, nis *even* 97:26; *not even* 130:7
neü, nuisi *PP* nuisir, nuire *harm*
noif, nois *snow* 32:1   [14:65
noumee *gossip* 149:14
o *yes* 11:16
o, od *with* 61:14
o, oi *Pret1* avoir *have* 76:2; ot
  Pret3, orent *Pret6*
oés *avantage* 62:3; *service* 97:8
oïr *to hear* 212:13; oi, oz *PI1*;
  oï *Pret1*; oï, ot *Pret3*; oï *PP*;
  ooie *II1*; öeis *I5*; or(r)ai *F1*,
  oreis *F5*; oiant *PrP*
onja *Pret3* ongier *have contact
  with* 216:7
ort, ors, orde *filthy, repulsive*
outré *past, ended* 185:61 [168:4
païe, paiïés *satisfied* 184:10
pamee *slap with palm of hand* 4:28
panetiere *bread bag* 117:14
panie *open* 36:1
pantais *PI1* pantiser *pant* 51:5
parchon *part* 184:18
pardon, en p. *in vain* 184:8
paroill *PI1* parler *speak* 121:9
paroir *to appear* 22:2; parra *F3*,
  pert *PI3*
part *direction* 147:7   [98:9
perataigne *PS1* perataindre *attain*
pickenpot *refrain? advantage?*
pis *breast* 50:26   [26:12
pis *pious* 50:27
plaire *pleasure* 208:28
plaisiés *defeated* 186:51
plevie *bride* 25:10
poc, pou, pouc *little* 176:21;
  briefly, a short while 209:25
poise *PI3* peser *disturb* 12:22
porchaicerai *F1 R* porchacier
  provide o. 181:18
posteïs *powerful* 41:44
prent *PI3 R* prendre *compare* 185:51
preu, prou, prout *advantage* 183:26
print *Pret3* prendre *grow* 215:23
prison *prisoner* 45:7   [10:21
prist a *Pret3* prendre a *begin*
privee *mistress* 213:19
proie *flock* 29:4
prové *tested* 151:24
quaés *PS5* cheoir *fall* 195:45
quais(s)e *PI3 R* quaisier *suffer*
quidai *see* cuit   [186:18
raison, reson *utterance* 11:13;

mind 7:11; metre quelqu'un a r.
address, speak to someone 146:14

ramaint *PS3* ramener *bring back*

raponne *reproach.* 4:27   [91:4

rasouteiz *foolish* 34:40

ravoie *PI3* ravoier *comfort* 127:48

recercelé, menu r. *tightly
curled, in small curls* 7:27

recors, recort *PI1* recorder *remember* 95:21

recouvree *sheltered* 213:35

remanoir *to stop* 167:4; remain-
droiz *F5*; remaint *PI3* remain

remenant *the rest* 85:9   [91:8

remis *melted* 41:30

remue *PI3* remüer *change* 87:48

requistrent *Pret6* requerre, re-
querir *ask* 24:24

rescous *PP* rescorre *rescue* 205:7

retenement *welcome* 92:24

retraire, retrere *to relate* 22:
21; *(R) to withdraw* 131:53

retrais *speech* 50:4

rivel *revelry* 177:8

roie *stripe* 26:19   [53:38

roster *to take back, withdraw*

rousee *dew-like freshness* 49:16

rouvelens *blushing* 115:35

sachier, saichier *to pull out*
137:42; *to draw up* 50:48

sainturet, -ette *a little belt*

sainz *holy relics* 7:20   [35:31

saut *PS3* sauver *save* 135:15

sembel *joust* 177:29

semblance, samblance, sanlance,
-ans, -ant *appearance* 99:4; *o-
pinion* 197:2; *glance* 175:18; 96:
42; *manner* 140:7

semont *PI3* semondre *summon, urge*
96:2; semon *I2*; semonant *PrP*

seri(e), seriette *bright(ly)* 151:1

seus *salt* 82:22

seut, suet *PI3* soloir *be wont*
114:2; sueil, suel *PI1*; soloie
II1; soloit *II3*

sillier *cellar* 176:41

soi, soy *Pret1* savoir *know* 70:1;
soier *to steal* 55:17   [sot *Pret3*

soigne *dream? candle?* 122:10

solacier *to enjoy* o. 179:33

son, duq'en s. *forever* 187:70

son(s) *poem, song* 16:2

sor *reddish-blond* 112:18

sorcuidiez *presumptuous* 157:2

sosgis, sosgiez, sougiez *subject*
114:26; *subdued* 79:10

sotterel *fool* 26:44

so(u)ëf, -efz, -eif, -ez, -weif
sweet(ly), soft(ly) 193:16

souffire *to be appealing* 200:20

sousfrete *penury* 31:16

stinte *pale* 8:16

taillaument *strongly* 187:49

tant ne kant *however great or
small* 18:43

tant que *until* 179:53

taskieus *eager* 183:19

tenceir *to protect* 19:41

tençon(s) tanson *dispute* 87:1

tendroie *Cl (R)* tenir *refrain*
21:7; tieigne *PS1* hold* 96:7

tessoille *PI3* tessoillier *aspire*
thyois *Germanic* 197:5   [101:35

tolt, tout *PI3* tolir, toldre
take away 98:13; toli *Pret3*

traire, trere *to draw* 136:22;
trai(s), tres *PI1* endure* 111:
46; *R approach* 67:19; trait
PI3; traie *PS3* obtain* 67:8;
traites *I5 R go away* 2:9

travail, travauz *suffering* 198:21

trespas de vent *breeze* 187:72

triie *distinguished* 65:9

trouver *to compare* 161:4; truis
PI1 find 108:33; truit *PS3*

tucir *to cough* 52:40

uilier *eye-slit in a helmet* 55:36

usage, par u. *with constancy* 97:11

veche *vetch* 169:29

veine *source* 70:17

vers *in comparison with* 45:23

veul *desire* 74:5

vez, ves *behold* 165:42

vieutez *vile thing* 174:11

vis *alive* 199:26

visouce *adept* 55:16

voie, tote v. *even so* 180:21

vois, voiz *PI1* aler *go* 157:11;
voise *PS1*, voist *PS3*, voixent *PS6*

voukier *to invoke* 56:68

wernemens *see* garnement